MySocialWorkLab offers:

- A complete **Pearson eText** of the book
- A wealth of engaging **videos**
  - **Brand-new videos**—organized around the competencies and accompanied by interactive assessment—that demonstrate key concepts and practices
  - **Career Exploration videos** that contain interviews with a wide range of social workers
- Tools for **self-assessment and review**—chapter specific quizzes tied to the core competencies, many written in the same format students will find on the licensing exam
- A **Gradebook** that reports progress of students and the class as a whole
- **MySocialWorkLibrary**—a compendium of articles and case studies in social work, searchable by course, topic, author, and title
- **MySearchLab**—a collection of tools that aid students in mastering research assignments and papers
- **And much more!**

Save time and improve results!

MySocialWorkLab is a dynamic website that provides a wealth of resources geared to help students develop and master the skills articulated in CSWE's core competencies—and improve their grades in their social work courses.

MySocialWorkLab is available at no extra cost when bundled with any text in the **Connecting Core Competencies Series.** Visit **www.mysocialworklab.com** to learn more.

"I would require [MySocialWorkLab]—especially if there were a way to harvest the results for program assessment."

—Jane Peller, *Northeastern Illinois University*

In recent years, many Social Work departments have been focusing on the CSWE Educational Policy and Accreditation Standards (EPAS) to guide their accreditation process. The current standards, issued in 2008, focus on mastery of the CSWE's ten core competencies and practice behaviors. Each of the ten core competencies now contains specific knowledge, values, skills, and the resulting practice behaviors as guidance for the curriculum and assessment methods of Social Work programs.

In writing this text, we have used the CSWE core competency standards and assessment recommendations as guidelines for structuring content and integrating the pedagogy. For details on the CSWE core competencies, please see www.cswe.org.

For the core competencies highlighted in this text, see page iv.

CSWE EPAS 2008 Core Competencies

Professional Identity

2.1.1 Identify as a professional social worker and conduct oneself accordingly.

Necessary Knowledge, Values, Skills

- Social workers serve as representatives of the profession, its mission, and its core values.
- Social workers know the profession's history.
- Social workers commit themselves to the profession's enhancement and to their own professional conduct and growth.

Operational Practice Behaviors

- Social workers advocate for client access to the services of social work;
- Social workers practice personal reflection and self-correction to assure continual professional development;
- Social workers attend to professional roles and boundaries;
- Social workers demonstrate professional demeanor in behavior, appearance, and communication;
- Social workers engage in career-long learning; and
- Social workers use supervision and consultation.

Ethical Practice

2.1.2 Apply social work ethical principles to guide professional practice.

Necessary Knowledge, Values, Skills

- Social workers have an obligation to conduct themselves ethically and engage in ethical decision-making.
- Social workers are knowledgeable about the value base of the profession, its ethical standards, and relevant law.

Operational Practice Behaviors

- Social workers recognize and manage personal values in a way that allows professional values to guide practice;
- Social workers make ethical decisions by applying standards of the National Association of Social Workers Code of Ethics and, as applicable, of the International Federation of Social Workers/International Association of Schools of Social Work Ethics in Social Work, Statement of Principles;
- Social workers tolerate ambiguity in resolving ethical conflicts; and
- Social workers apply strategies of ethical reasoning to arrive at principled decisions.

Critical Thinking

2.1.3 Apply critical thinking to inform and communicate professional judgments.

Necessary Knowledge, Values, Skills

- Social workers are knowledgeable about the principles of logic, scientific inquiry, and reasoned discernment.
- They use critical thinking augmented by creativity and curiosity.
- Critical thinking also requires the synthesis and communication of relevant information.

Operational Practice Behaviors

- Social workers distinguish, appraise, and integrate multiple sources of knowledge, including research-based knowledge, and practice wisdom;
- Social workers analyze models of assessment, prevention, intervention, and evaluation; and
- Social workers demonstrate effective oral and written communication in working with individuals, families, groups, organizations, communities, and colleagues.

Diversity in Practice

2.1.4 Engage diversity and difference in practice.

Necessary Knowledge, Values, Skills

- Social workers understand how diversity characterizes and shapes the human experience and is critical to the formation of identity.
- The dimensions of diversity are understood as the intersectionality of multiple factors including age, class, color, culture, disability, ethnicity, gender, gender identity and expression, immigration status, political ideology, race, religion, sex, and sexual orientation.
- Social workers appreciate that, as a consequence of difference, a person's life experiences may include oppression, poverty, marginalization, and alienation as well as privilege, power, and acclaim.

Operational Practice Behaviors

- Social workers recognize the extent to which a culture's structures and values may oppress, marginalize, alienate, or create or enhance privilege and power;
- Social workers gain sufficient self-awareness to eliminate the influence of personal biases and values in working with diverse groups;
- Social workers recognize and communicate their understanding of the importance of difference in shaping life experiences; and
- Social workers view themselves as learners and engage those with whom they work as informants.

Human Rights & Justice

2.1.5 Advance human rights and social and economic justice.

Necessary Knowledge, Values, Skills

- Each person, regardless of position in society, has basic human rights, such as freedom, safety, privacy, an adequate standard of living, health care, and education.
- Social workers recognize the global interconnections of oppression and are knowledgeable about theories of justice and strategies to promote human and civil rights.
- Social work incorporates social justice practices in organizations, institutions, and society to ensure that these basic human rights are distributed equitably and without prejudice.

Operational Practice Behaviors

- Social workers understand the forms and mechanisms of oppression and discrimination;
- Social workers advocate for human rights and social and economic justice; and
- Social workers engage in practices that advance social and economic justice.

Research Based Practice

2.1.6 Engage in research-informed practice and practice-informed research.

Necessary Knowledge, Values, Skills

- Social workers use practice experience to inform research, employ evidence-based interventions, evaluate their own practice, and use research findings to improve practice, policy, and social service delivery.
- Social workers comprehend quantitative and qualitative research and understand scientific and ethical approaches to building knowledge.

Operational Practice Behaviors

- Social workers use practice experience to inform scientific inquiry; and
- Social workers use research evidence to inform practice.

Human Behavior

2.1.7 Apply knowledge of human behavior and the social environment.

Necessary Knowledge, Values, Skills

- Social workers are knowledgeable about human behavior across the life course; the range of social systems in which people live; and the ways social systems promote or deter people in maintaining or achieving health and well-being.
- Social workers apply theories and knowledge from the liberal arts to understand biological, social, cultural, psychological, and spiritual development.

Operational Practice Behaviors

- Social workers utilize conceptual frameworks to guide the processes of assessment, intervention, and evaluation; and
- Social workers critique and apply knowledge to understand person and environment.

Policy Practice   2.1.8 Engage in policy practice to advance social and economic well-being and to deliver effective social work services.

Necessary Knowledge, Values, Skills

- Social work practitioners understand that policy affects service delivery and they actively engage in policy practice.
- Social workers know the history and current structures of social policies and services; the role of policy in service delivery; and the role of practice in policy development.

Operational Practice Behaviors

- Social workers analyze, formulate, and advocate for policies that advance social well-being; and
- Social workers collaborate with colleagues and clients for effective policy action.

Practice Contexts

2.1.9 Respond to contexts that shape practice.

Necessary Knowledge, Values, Skills

- Social workers are informed, resourceful, and proactive in responding to evolving organizational, community, and societal contexts at all levels of practice.
- Social workers recognize that the context of practice is dynamic, and use knowledge and skill to respond proactively.

Operational Practice Behaviors

- Social workers continuously discover, appraise, and attend to changing locales, populations, scientific and technological developments, and emerging societal trends to provide relevant services; and
- Social workers provide leadership in promoting sustainable changes in service delivery and practice to improve the quality of social services.

Engage, Assess, Intervene, Evaluate   2.1.10 Engage, assess, intervene, and evaluate with individuals, families, groups, organizations, and communities.

Necessary Knowledge, Values, Skills

- Professional practice involves the dynamic and interactive processes of engagement, assessment, intervention, and evaluation at multiple levels.
- Social workers have the knowledge and skills to practice with individuals, families, groups, organizations, and communities.
- Practice knowledge includes
  - identifying, analyzing, and implementing evidence-based interventions designed to achieve client goals;
  - using research and technological advances;
  - evaluating program outcomes and practice effectiveness;
  - developing, analyzing, advocating, and providing leadership for policies and services; and
  - promoting social and economic justice.

Operational Practice Behaviors

(a) Engagement
- Social workers substantively and affectively prepare for action with individuals, families, groups, organizations, and communities;
- Social workers use empathy and other interpersonal skills; and
- Social workers develop a mutually agreed-on focus of work and desired outcomes.

(b) Assessment
- Social workers collect, organize, and interpret client data;
- Social workers assess client strengths and limitations;
- Social workers develop mutually agreed-on intervention goals and objectives; and
- Social workers select appropriate intervention strategies.

(c) Intervention
- Social workers initiate actions to achieve organizational goals;
- Social workers implement prevention interventions that enhance client capacities;
- Social workers help clients resolve problems;
- Social workers negotiate, mediate, and advocate for clients; and
- Social workers facilitate transitions and endings.

(d) Evaluation
- Social workers critically analyze, monitor, and evaluate interventions.

CONNECTING CORE COMPETENCIES **Chapter-by-Chapter Matrix**

Chapter	Professional Identity	Ethical Practice	Critical Thinking	Diversity in Practice	Human Rights & Justice	Research Based Practice	Human Behavior	Policy Practice	Practice Contexts	Engage, Assess, Intervene, Evaluate
1	✔	✔						✔		✔
2		✔						✔	✔	
3			✔	✔	✔			✔		
4				✔			✔	✔		
5	✔	✔	✔		✔					
6	✔	✔				✔				
7			✔					✔	✔	
8			✔		✔	✔		✔		
9			✔		✔	✔		✔		
10	✔				✔			✔		
11					✔	✔		✔		✔
12	✔		✔	✔	✔					
13			✔			✔		✔		✔
14	✔		✔		✔				✔	
Total Chapters	6	4	8	3	8	5	1	10	3	3

Policy Practice for Social Workers

New Strategies for a New Era

(Updated Edition)

Linda K. Cummins
Capella University

Katharine V. Byers
Indiana University

Laura Pedrick
University of Wisconsin-Milwaukee

Allyn & Bacon

Boston   Columbus   Indianapolis   New York   San Francisco   Upper Saddle River
Amsterdam   Cape Town   Dubai   London   Madrid   Milan   Munich   Paris   Montréal   Toronto
Delhi   Mexico City   São Paulo   Sydney   Hong Kong   Seoul   Singapore   Taipei   Tokyo

Editor in Chief: Dickson Musslewhite
Executive Editor: Ashley Dodge
Editorial Product Manager: Carly Czech
Executive Marketing Manager: Jeanette Koskinas
Senior Marketing Manager: Wendy Albert
Marketing Assistant: Shauna Fishweicher
Production Manager: Kathy Sleys
Cover Designer: Kristina Mose-Libon/Suzanne Duda
Creative Art Director: Jayne Conte
Cover Image: Fuse/Getty Images
Editorial Production and Composition Service: Aparna Yellai,
   PreMediaGlobal

Library of Congress Cataloging-in-Publication Data

Cummins, Linda K.
Policy practice for social workers : new strategies for a new era / Linda K. Cummins, Katharine V. Byers, Laura Pedrick.—1st ed.
p. cm.
Includes bibliographical references and index.
ISBN-13: 978-0-205-02244-1 (alk. paper)
ISBN-10: 0-205-02244-8 (alk. paper)
1. Social service—Government policy—United States.   2. Social case work—United States.
3. United States—Social policy.   I. Byers, Katharine V. II. Pedrick, Laura E.   III. Title.
HV95.C857 2011
361.6'1—dc22   2010044673

10 9 8 7 6 5 4 3 2 EB 14 13 12

Student Edition:
ISBN-10: 0-205-02244-8
ISBN-13: 978-0-205-02244-1

Instructor Edition:
ISBN-10: 0-205-02251-0
ISBN-13: 978-0-205-02251-9

a la Carte Edition:
ISBN-10: 0-205-02280-4
ISBN-13: 978-0-205-02280-9

Allyn & Bacon
is an imprint of

www.pearsonhighered.com

Contents

Preface   xv

1. Defining Policy Practice in Social Work   1

Introduction   2

About the Book   2

About the Chapter   3

Policy Practice at the Core of Social Work   3
   Experiences of Three Social Workers   3
   Person-in-Environment Perspective in Generalist Practice   5
   The Relationship of Policy Practice to Micro Practice   7

Defining Policy Practice   8
   Multiple Definitions of Policy Practice and Advocacy   9

Conceptualizing Policy Practice in Action   11
   Settings and Environmental Levels Within the Policy Practice Arena   11
   Interactivity of Environmental Levels and Settings   15
   Foundations of Policy Practice in Generalist Practice   16

The Social Work Perspective on Policy Practice   19
   Application of Generalist Practice Skills to Policy Practice   19
   Relevance of Generalist Practice Perspectives   21
   A Recommitment to Policy Practice   23

Preparing for Policy Practice Roles   23

Conclusion   24

PRACTICE TEST   25

 MySocialWorkLab   25
   Core Competency Video: Policy Practice, Judith Willison
   Health Care SCS

2. History of Policy Practice in Social Work   26

Introduction   27

Historical Roots in Social Work's Dual Focus   27
   Jane Addams at Hull House   28
   Charity Organization Societies   29

Progressive Era Reforms   31

Social Work's First Retreat from Policy Practice   34

Depression and the New Deal   35

Second Retreat from Activism by the Profession   38

Social Reforms of the 1960s   39

Social Workers Doing Policy Practice—Some Efforts of the Last Forty Years   42

Today's Social Workers in Policy Practice   45

Looking at Future Policy Practice   45

Conclusion   47

PRACTICE TEST   48

MySocialWorkLab   48

Connecting Core Competency videos on Human Rights and Justice
Housing SCS

3. The Politics of Policy Practice   49

Introduction   50

Civic and Social Responsibility   50

The Evolution of U.S. Political Parties   53

Political Ideologies and U.S. Political Parties   67

Conservatives   68

Liberals   70

Conclusion—Republican or Democrat?   73

PRACTICE TEST   75

MySocialWorkLab   75

Connecting Core Competency Practice Video: "Keeping up with
shifting contexts"
Gay Marriage SCS

4. The Forces That Move and Shape Policy   76

Defining Policy   77

Types of Public Policy   78

Policy Formation   79

Social Institutions   80

Political Economy   85

Political Forces   88

Economic Forces   93

The Social Welfare System in a Democratic-Capitalist Political Economy   98

Conclusion   99

PRACTICE TEST   100

MySocialWorkLab   100

Health Care SCS
Gay Marriage SCS

5. Ethics in Policy Practice   101

Introduction   102

Ethical Frameworks for Policy Practice   103

Boundaries of Ethical Policy Practice   109
    Boundary: The NASW Code of Ethics   109
    Boundary: NASW Standards for Advocacy and Political Action   111
    Boundary: Laws   113
    Boundary: Societal Norms and Personal Beliefs   115

Ethical Decision Making: Application   115
    Application of the Model   117

Conclusion   119

PRACTICE TEST   120

 MySocialWorkLab   120
    SCS on Health Care Reform
    Connecting Core Competency videos on Affordable Green Housing SCS

6. Entering the Policy Practice Arena   121

Introduction   122

Case Study   122

Ecology of Policy Practice Across Policy Settings   126
    Overview of Social Worker Roles in Policy Practice   126

Social Work Careers in Policy Practice   127

Executive Settings   127
    Elected Executive   127
    Appointed Executive Policymaker   128
    Role of Agency Board in Making Policy   130
    Advisor/Staff to Policymaker   130
    Agency Policymaking at the Direct Service Worker Level—The Case for
       Street-Level Bureaucrats   131

Legislative Settings   131
    Legislative Policymaker   131
    Legislative Assistant/Constituent Services   133

Judicial Settings   134
    Expert Witness   134
    Amicus Curiae Briefs   134
    Consultants in Judge Education Programs   135
    Elected Judge   135
    Advocate in Judge Appointment Processes   135

Community Settings   136
    Campaign Director or Worker on a Campaign   136
    Part-Time or Volunteer Policy Advocate   137
    Lobbyist   137
    Research/Policy Analysis Positions   137
    Policy Practitioner/Educator   138
    Grass Roots Organizer of Community Groups   140
    Policy Practice Roles for Direct Service Practitioners   140

      Informal Opportunities to be a Policy Advocate   *140*
      Policy Practice by Professional Associations   *141*

Conclusion   **141**

PRACTICE TEST   142

MySocialWorkLab   **142**
      Connecting Core Competency Series on Engage, Assess, Intervene,
         and Evaluate
      Health Care SCS

---

7. The Media and Public Opinion in Policy Practice   **143**

Introduction   144

The Basics   145
      Understanding the News Media   *145*
      Working with the News Media   *147*

Communication Strategies for Policy Campaigns   151
      Summary Model   *154*

New Media Advocacy   155
      E-mail   *157*
      Advocacy Web Sites   *158*
      Blogs   *160*
      Podcasts   *160*

Evaluating Advocacy Communication   165

Conclusion   **167**

PRACTICE TEST   168

MySocialWorkLab   **168**
      SCS on Health Care Reform
      SCS on Gay Marriage

---

8. The Stages of Policymaking: Integrating Knowledge and Action   **169**

Introduction   170

Social Workers as Policymakers   175

Approaches to Policymaking   179
      Rational Model   *180*
      Political Model   *183*
      Incremental Model   *184*

The Policymaking Process   186
      Stage One: Problem Identification and Case Finding   *189*
      Stage Two: Data Collection and Analysis   *191*
      Stage Three: Informing the Public and Identifying Stakeholders   *194*
      Stage Four: Selecting Policy Options and Developing Policy Goals   *196*
      Stage Five: Building Public Support and Developing Coalitions   *198*

   Stage Six: Program Design 201
   Stage Seven: Policy Implementation 201
   Stage Eight: Policy Evaluation 206

Conclusion 207

PRACTICE TEST 208

 **MySocialWorkLab 208**
   Health Care SCS

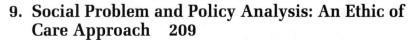

9. **Social Problem and Policy Analysis: An Ethic of Care Approach 209**

Introduction 210

Theoretical Analysis 211

Budget Analysis 212

Value Perspectives: Adequacy, Equity, and Equality 213
   Ethic of Care Values: Collaboration, Inclusion, Interdependence 219

Policy Interventions: Preventive, Alleviative, and Curative Interventions 219

Social Problem Analysis 222
   The Usefulness of Social Problem Analysis 225

Policy Analysis 228

An Ethic of Care Policy Analysis Framework 230
   Elements of Care 231
   The Framework 233
   Application of the Model 236

Conclusion 239

PRACTICE TEST 240

MySocialWorkLab 240
   Housing SCS
   Gay marriage SCS

---

10. **The Legislative Process, Interest Groups, and Lobbying 241**

Introduction 242

The Legislative Process 243
   Advocacy Roles in the Legislative Process 249

Defining Interest Groups 256
   Theoretical Approaches to Understanding Interest Groups 257
   The Recent Growth of Interest Groups 258
   Sources of Power 261

Lobbying 262
   Ethical Lobbying 263
   Social Workers as Lobbyists 266
   How to Lobby 269

Involvement of Clients in the Advocacy Effort 278

Conclusion 279

PRACTICE TEST 280

MySocialWorkLab 280

    Connecting Core Competency videos on Policy Practice
    SCS on Gay Marriage

11. Building a Coalition to Create Change 281

Introduction 282

Forming Coalitions 283

    Defining Coalitions 283

    Advantages and Drawbacks of Coalition Membership 287

    Identifying Likely Allies to Form Coalitions 288

    Have Some Problem or Broad Goals in Mind 288

    Recruitment Strategies 291

Generating the Agenda for Inclusion 293

    Finding Common Ground 294

    Continuing to Expand the Circle by Inviting Others to Attend Meetings 294

    Integrating New Members 295

Coalition Developmental Stages 296

    Build the Group's Expertise 298

    Develop an Identity 300

    Engage Participants in Action 302

    Involving Members in the Organizational Structure 303

Meeting the Challenges in Coalitions 305

    Handling Disagreements 305

    Sharing Power 307

    Staying Organized 307

    Raising Funds 308

Creating Ongoing Networks of Influence—Moving from Ad Hoc to Ongoing 308

Characteristics of Successful Coalitions 310

Importance of Coalition Leadership 315

Celebrate the Small Victories and Have Fun as Part of the Process 316

Conclusion 316

PRACTICE TEST 317

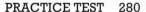

MySocialWorkLab 317

    Core Competency Series videos on Policy Practice
    Gay Marriage Amendment SCS

12. Campaigns 318

Introduction 319

Overview of Campaign Processes 320

    Resources 321

Campaign Roles for Social Workers   327

Campaign Roles for the Social Work Profession   336

Laws and Ethics of Campaigning   337
    Campaign Finance Reform   338

Conclusion   344

PRACTICE TEST   345

MySocialWorkLab   345
    SCS on Gay Marriage
    Connecting Core Competency videos on Career
      Exploration

13. Evaluating Policy Implementation and Outcomes   346

Introduction   347

The Rulemaking Process   347

Rulemaking Case Example   348

A Note About the Budget Process   349

Why Monitoring Implementation and Evaluation are Important   350

Privatizing Eligibility in Indiana: Case Study in Implementation Challenges and Need for Evaluation   351

Types of Evaluation   354

The Context of Policy and Program Evaluation   357

Welfare Reform Policy Evaluation Case Example   358

Evaluation Resources   359

Common Questions for Program/Policy Evaluation   361

Conclusion   364

PRACTICE TEST   365

MySocialWorkLab   365
    Connecting Core Competency videos on Policy
      Practice
    SCS on Housing

14. A Vision for Political Empowerment   366

Introduction   367

Opportunities   369
    A New Era   369
    New Strategies   369

Challenges   370
    Overcoming Cynicism   372

Countering the Upsurge in Hate Groups   *372*
Thinking Globally   *373*

Making a Difference in Your Corner of the World   374

PRACTICE TEST   **376**

MySocialWorkLab   **376**

Connecting Core Competency videos on Human Rights and Justice
Housing SCS

Appendix   377

Notes   382

Photo Credits   401

Index   402

Preface

Policy practice for social workers: New strategies for a new era grew out of a need for a policy macro practice text that two of the authors were in search of (for years) to facilitate the teaching of their assigned policy courses each semester. Finally, we just decided to write our own. Knowing from experience how baffled students are at the word "policy," we designed the book around actual policy case studies to bring policy to life and to help students see and understand the roles of social workers in the policymaking, implementation, and evaluation processes. Policy case studies occur throughout the book and are also included in the Simulated Case Studies (SCS) that accompany this book and are accessible through Pearson's *MySocialWorkLab* Web site. The book was written with the advanced undergraduate and the graduate social work student in mind, with the hope that it will facilitate the beginning development of policy practice skills necessary to effect policy change at the agency, community, state and federal levels.

As students explore the book and the many dimensions of policy practice, we are hopeful that they will gain an appreciation for the rich history of policy practice in social work, and take note of the importance of context and time in the moment-to-moment decisions required of policy practitioners in the field. Policy formation, analysis, implementation, and evaluation are just some of the areas that students will engage in the book within a range of conceptual and theoretical frameworks. As well, they will explore the skills and roles required to build coalitions, lobby and participate in the legislative process, and run policy and election campaigns. The critical role of the media and new technologies in the fast-paced field of policy practice is a consistent focus throughout the book. While exciting and complex, policy practice for social workers must occur within the ethics of practice set forth by the profession of social work, and in the pursuit of social justice for the individuals, families, and communities that they serve. We have attempted to keep these two important elements in the fore when discussing each area of policy practice, and we hope that the core values and mission of social work will inspire greater social worker and client involvement in policy-making toward the goal of a more just society.

LINDA K. CUMMINS
KATHARINE V. BYERS
LAURA PEDRICK

Connecting Core Competencies Series

The new edition of this text is now a part of Pearson Education's new *Connecting Core Competencies* series, which consists of foundation-level texts that make it easier than ever to ensure students' success in learning the ten core competencies as stated in 2008 by the Council on Social Worker Education. This text contains:

▶ **Core Competency Icons** throughout the chapters, directly linking the CSWE core competencies to the content of the text. **Critical thinking questions** are also included to further students' mastery of the CSWE's standards. For easy reference, page iv displays which icons are used in each chapter, in a chapter-by-chapter matrix.

▶ **An end-of-chapter Practice Test**, with multiple-choice questions that test students' knowledge of the chapter content and mastery of the competencies. These questions are constructed in a format that will help prepare students for the **ASWB Licensing exam.**

▶ **Additional questions pertaining to the videos and case studies are found on the new MySocialWorkLab** at the end of each chapter to encourage students to access the site and explore the wealth of available materials. If this text did not come with an access code for MySocialWorkLab, you can purchase an access code at: www.mysocialworklab.com.

Acknowledgments

"Thank you" seems so inadequate for the work provided by our research assistants, Sonya and Bethany. Sonya Powers worked diligently on this book and on the Simulated Case Studies for three years, providing extensive research materials, and doing just about anything asked of her, always with a smile and a positive attitude. Bethany Reed, our last-minute angel, spent the summer of 2009 securing the many permissions for materials used throughout the book, editing and formatting the final draft, and researching photos for each chapter. To both these outstanding young women we are grateful.

We also acknowledge the wonderful work of Eric Brown, creator of the patented Digital Epistolary Novel software, which was used as the platform for the Simulated Case Studies. Thanks also goes to our friend and editor of many years, Patricia Quinlin, who kept us focused on the final product and provided invaluable support, and was beyond understanding when time constraints or writers block set in to slow the development process. We thank David Estrin for his editorial assistance during the early draft phase of writing and editor Ashley Dodge and assistant editor Carly Czech for their expert technical advice and assistance as the final draft of the book was being prepared for submission. We also thank the Durham Community Land Trustees and DCLT Executive Director Selina Mack, for the use of their housing plans in the Affordable Green Housing Simulated Case study. DCLT is a nonprofit, community-based organization committed to providing permanently affordable housing for low-to-moderate income people and promoting community revitalization in the neighborhoods in which it operates.

Linda Cummins also thanks her daughter, Bethany Reed, not only for her superior work on the book but also for the many wonderful meals she cooked, and for her joyful presence during the summer of 2009 and 2010 as the final version and then revisions of the book was being written. She also thanks her daughter Sara Jo Royalty, son-in-laws Oscar Rodriguez and Akus Rodrigues, and grandsons Sol and Cuyen for their steadfast support and love over the course of the project.

Kathy Byers acknowledges the support of Jim and the rest of her family, colleagues, and friends throughout the book development process, particularly the invaluable help from her son Clark who cheerfully volunteered as a research assistant, fact-checking and finding research resources.

Laura Pedrick would like to thank David, Meg, and Carrie Allen, who endured all the "writing Saturdays" with good humor and offered encouragement along the way, making this work possible. Thanks also to Margaret Pedrick, Beatrice Allen, and friends and family near and far, for years of love, support, and understanding.

We also acknowledge our students over the years who have taught us as much as we have taught them.

Finally, we are grateful for our bonds of friendship and collegial respect that continued to grow over the course of the project, and for the mutual support and patience we afforded each other many times over. We truly count ourselves as being blessed personally and professionally in this friendship.

1

Defining Policy Practice in Social Work

CHAPTER OUTLINE

Introduction 2

About the Book 2

About the Chapter 3

Policy Practice at the Core of Social Work 3
Experiences of Three Social Workers
Person-in-Environment Perspective in Generalist Practice
The Relationship of Policy Practice to Micro Practice

Defining Policy Practice 8
Multiple Definitions of Policy Practice and Advocacy

Conceptualizing Policy Practice in Action 11
Settings and Environmental Levels Within the Policy Practice Arena
Interactivity of Environmental Levels and Settings

Foundations of Policy Practice in Generalist Practice

The Social Work Perspective on Policy Practice 19
Application of Generalist Practice Skills to Policy Practice
Relevance of Generalist Practice Perspectives
A Recommitment to Policy Practice

Preparing for Policy Practice Roles 23

Conclusion 24

Chapter Review 25

Practice Test 25

MySocialWorkLab 25
Core Competency Video: Policy Practice, Judith Willison
Health Care SCS

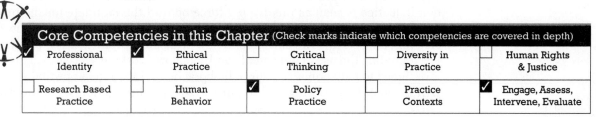

Core Competencies in this Chapter (Check marks indicate which competencies are covered in depth)				
✓ Professional Identity	✓ Ethical Practice	☐ Critical Thinking	☐ Diversity in Practice	☐ Human Rights & Justice
☐ Research Based Practice	☐ Human Behavior	✓ Policy Practice	☐ Practice Contexts	✓ Engage, Assess, Intervene, Evaluate

INTRODUCTION

> *Advocacy is the cornerstone upon which social work is built. It is so important that it is framed in three sections of our Code of Ethics. Advocacy for individuals, communities and systems is not just a suggested activity for social workers. It's not a 'do it if you have some extra time' or a 'do it if the inequity and disparity are very great' activity. It is a requisite.*
>
> NASW EXECUTIVE DIRECTOR, ELIZABETH J. CLARK.[1]

Policy practice is defined as using social work skills to propose and change policies in order to achieve the goal of social and economic justice.

The power of policy practice has been demonstrated throughout the history of the social work profession (as discussed in more detail in Chapter 2), from Julia Lathrop's early efforts to establish the juvenile court system, to social workers' recent advocacy for universal health care. Through policy practice, social workers have made a difference in the lives of millions of Americans throughout history. This textbook examines the role of policy practice within social work and helps students apply their basic social work skills to policy practice arenas so that they can become successful advocates for just social welfare policies.

Policy practice is an integral element of social work as practiced in all settings—at the local, state, and national levels, as well as within micro, mezzo, and macro levels of intervention. Including policy practice in the daily life of social work practice is an effective and powerful avenue for enhancing the profession's goals and mission of social and economic justice.

ABOUT THE BOOK

There are few things that get our attention more than a moving story about social justice, and social workers throughout history have provided us with an endless number of examples of how to affect change on behalf of vulnerable populations. Storytelling provides some of the most powerful learning experiences for those learning new skills and material. For this reason, the text uses vignettes and case studies in chapters of the book itself but also refers to the companion Web site that includes the Simulated Case Studies (SCS) of policy practice efforts by social workers in collaboration with other human service professionals, political actors, and business people. Within the SCS, both the characters and the specific situations are fictional but are based on the lived experiences of social workers who have engaged in policy practice. Some of the case studies in the textbook are real and were written with the permission and review of the social workers involved. Other fictional case studies are based on the practice experience of real social workers. In addition to the SCS, this text is different from other policy textbooks in its use of a more collective and holistic perspective for analyzing policy options and determining social work's role in the policy process. Social work's ethical commitment to social and economic justice is seen as the driving force behind the mandate for the profession's involvement in policy practice. Incorporating the experience of the 2008 election, the text reviews current and new strategies for influencing public policy, including the use of new media and social networking Web sites. This book is designed to help enhance your policy practice skills in the hope that you, too, will influence the policy-making processes in your agencies, communities, states, and nation. In doing so, you can make a tremendous difference in the lives of individuals and families living and working in unjust conditions and living on the margins of society, just as Jane Addams and many other social workers have done in the past. Social workers reclaiming the responsibility and power of policy practice today are again making important contributions to clients' lives, organizations, communities, and the nation in achieving new levels of social and economic justice.

ABOUT THE CHAPTER

To introduce you to the idea of how policy practice often infuses social work practice, this chapter begins with several fictional vignettes within a range of settings that depict social workers engaging in policy practice. The scenarios demonstrate the variety of roles that social workers can play in improving social work practice by seeking changes in policies that limit practice options for populations that social workers often encounter. These vignettes set the stage for a more in-depth look at the many dimensions of policy practice and how they play out in the practice of social work in various settings across a variety of levels of intervention. The principles and values related to policy practice are discussed, and an overview of later chapters is provided that details specific aspects of policy practice. It is worthwhile to see policy practice in several contexts and how individual social workers can make a real difference. Such experiences are demonstrated in the vignettes that follow. Try to imagine yourself in these social work roles.

POLICY PRACTICE AT THE CORE OF SOCIAL WORK

Experiences of Three Social Workers

Vignette #1
Emily was shadowing the state agency workers responsible for licensing day care facilities in the state when they made their visit to New Prospect Mission Day Care in a small town—some distance from the state capital. As a church-affiliated day care center, New Prospect Mission was not required to be licensed by the state, but one of the parents had requested the visit. Emily was appalled by the conditions they found: formula and milk in a refrigerator that did not work, roaches in the cupboard, few toys and little play equipment, and too few staff supervising children. She was incensed that nothing could be done legally to better protect the health and safety of the children attending this day care center. Several weeks later, she learned about hearings being conducted at the State House on a bill to require state licensing of all child care facilities in the state, including those operated by churches.

Ethical Practice

Critical Thinking Question

Based on the Code of Ethics, what would you do in each of these vignettes?

Vignette #2
Juan, a case manager at the local Area Agency on Aging, was working with a fiercely independent elderly gentleman, Mr. Anderson, who lived alone. All of

his children lived out of state, though they were in close touch with him by phone. On a recent home visit, Mr. Anderson appeared to have lost some weight since their last appointment, and Juan became concerned that Mr. Anderson might not be eating properly. When Juan called the local Meals on Wheels program, he found out Mr. Anderson was not eligible for services because his road was outside their service area.

Vignette #3

Jennifer, a social worker for a local homeless shelter, was working with the Rodriguez family, who recently moved to the area. Both parents worked at minimum-wage jobs at the local poultry processing plant south of town. Even with their combined wages, they could not afford the expensive health insurance offered by the company or any independent policies. Their three children were in elementary school and doing well. The family also could not find affordable housing in the community. Their older-model car was not reliable, so housing outside of town—which might have been less expensive—was not practical. The wait for Section 8 Housing (subsidized housing) was over two years and, at the time, the office was not even taking applications.

Many social workers begin their careers with a passion for helping individuals and families like the Anderson and Rodriguez families above. They have learned how to engage clients in the helping process, do comprehensive assessments, collaboratively develop intervention plans, and monitor their implementation. Even though part of the intervention may involve linking families and individuals with community resources to meet identified needs, many social workers focus on micro practice—helping specific people in need. When social workers monitor family progress, they are often able to see specific improvements in the family's situation as a result of their planned interventions.

At other times, progress is not so easily achieved. Analyzing family circumstances using systems theory, social workers can determine what factors are creating barriers to change. Sometimes the barriers are internal, such as low motivation or limited ability to cook nutritious meals, as in Mr. Anderson's situation described in vignette #2. Sometimes the barriers are external (e.g., community and societal barriers), such as Mr. Anderson living outside the service area of the Meals on Wheels program or laws that do not apply in certain situations. When social workers encounter difficulties in linking people to community resources or in making sure that the services are adequate to address the need, they are confronted with the need for policy practice, for making changes in the community and social systems within which clients live (the clients' environment) and work, so that individuals and families can achieve safe and stable lives. Sometimes the services needed are not available in a particular geographic location, as with the case of Mr. Anderson. If so, then services need to be expanded or created. Sometimes the economic structure of a community creates challenges for parents who are already working hard to care for their families, as with the Rodriguez family. To assist the Rodriguez family and others in similar circumstances, new opportunities need to be created through major policy changes, such as raising the minimum wage and building more affordable housing closer to the available jobs. These macro-practice changes will require great effort and take time before changes can take hold because the targets of change may include several environmental components (such as new laws, changes in agency policy, or additional resources). So although they represent a long-term solution, they may not offer much hope for immediate relief.

As a student, Emily learned that sometimes the law must be changed before conditions can improve. Emily testified at the hearing regarding her observations about several day care centers that were not meeting state licensing standards. During the hearing, a powerful state senator who was supported by many of the same churches that operated the day care centers in question, confronted Emily about her facts. He insisted that conditions were not as bad as she had reported, but Emily stood by her observations. That day, Emily did not yet realize that she would be setting the wheels in motion for a change in the state law. She also did not realize that her outspoken advocacy and policy practice that day would lead to a job offer to become the legislative aide for a state child welfare advocacy agency. She did not realize that she had begun to work in policy practice.

Like Emily, when social workers are faced with community (or macro) challenges, they recognize the need for policy practice—interventions in the larger systems in the client's social environment that will create the conditions conducive to growth, development, and empowerment. This recognition—of the need to effect change in larger systems to help individuals—dates back to the very beginnings of the profession, when people were understood within their environmental context, not as isolated individuals experiencing difficulties.

Person-in-Environment Perspective in Generalist Practice

When social workers use the person-in-environment perspective, they situate the person within a context. Although much of social work practice is focused on helping individual people make changes in their thinking and behavior so that they can reach their goals, this micro focus is not the whole of social work practice. Using the systems perspective, social workers recognize that people interact with an environment that may provide both opportunities and barriers to individual development and goal achievement. For most people, that environment is first encountered in interactions with families, particularly parents who first meet basic needs as children are growing and developing. But other systems, external to families, support families and enhance their abilities to carry out their nurturing, educating, and socializing functions.

Informal networks of friends and extended family members may provide both material and psychological/social support of friendship, child care, and play opportunities. For most people, this informal support network, together with families, is the first line of defense when individuals struggle to meet needs, both physical and psychological.[2] Many neighborhoods include both formal and informal networks of support for families and individuals, including neighborhood watch programs for crime prevention, garden clubs and plots, and social events that serve to meet a variety of needs. Putnam[3] highlights the importance of the needs-meeting aspects of this informal network in his discussion of the decline of civic engagement and informal group support activities that he observed. Others[4] have since repudiated Putnam's assertions, indicating that informal group support is just beginning to take different forms. Stengel and Blackman[5] assert:

> There hasn't been a disappearance of civic activism in America so much as a reinvention of it. It is not dissolving, but evolving. Yes, Little League participation has leveled off, but that's because everyone's kicking a ball not catching it. . . . Yes, fewer people are signing up for the Y, but they are joining health clubs for the StairMasters and the camaraderie. Yes, there are fewer ladies' garden clubs, but working women are meeting in evening book clubs to discuss high literature and low husbands. . . . And while people may not be going to political clubs anymore, they are discussing politics in the Internet equivalent of smoke-filled rooms.

More recent additions to the informal support systems of our technological age include online chat rooms, social networking sites such as Facebook and MySpace, and other new forms of social interaction.

Cities and communities provide a wide variety of formal social, educational, and economic supports for families, including jobs for wage earners, schools for children, stores for shopping for goods and services, and civic activities and events for social, cultural, and political participation of community members. Beyond the interactions at the local community level are the corresponding state structures that support local community efforts, including statewide organizations for many different activities and functions, state government agencies that regulate services at the local level, and state political entities that make, adjudicate, and enforce the policies set by state government. National systems of nonprofit, for-profit, and public organizations may appear to be remote from the everyday lives of people at the local community level, but they may directly affect their lives when they respond to disasters—as the Red Cross did when Hurricane Katrina hit the Louisiana and Mississippi coasts. National organizations have an impact on local communities as when a U.S. automaker decides to move the parts manufacturing operation in Kokomo, Indiana, to a border town in Mexico.

And certainly, the federal government affects individual lives when it increases the Earned Income Tax Credit for low-income workers or proposes cuts in funding for vocational education programs when there is a need to reduce the federal deficit. At the international level, organizations operate to extend education and health care to underserved countries and communities. For example, former president Bill Clinton has established the William J. Clinton Foundation to fight AIDS and other health and environmental challenges internationally. Web media and blogs make international communication among people from different countries possible. According to its Web site, the mission of the William J. Clinton Foundation is to "strengthen the capacity of people in the United States and throughout the world to meet the challenges of global interdependence."(See www.clintonfoundation.org/index.htm for information about the Foundation and its efforts worldwide.) International grassroots community organizations serve as resources to help local communities in their economic development and sustainability efforts. Multinational corporations extend employment opportunities to India's college-educated population, resulting in a growth of their middle class, while promoting an outsourcing of middle-class jobs from the United States. In the economic downturn of 2008, the mortgage and banking crisis in the United States had an impact on markets around the world as Americans bought fewer products manufactured overseas. More and more global connections are extending in ever more complicated webs of interaction. Understanding these interconnections helps social workers appreciate the complexity of the policy process as well.

The Relationship of Policy Practice to Micro Practice

The person-in-environment perspective (see Figure 1.1) helps social workers conceptualize and make sense of how individuals are enveloped by layers of environmental systems that can both facilitate and hinder their development across time. Social workers can think of the individual person being in the center, with the family in the next circle surrounding the individual, then neighborhood and community institutions coming in succession before the layers or surrounding circles of state, national, and international organizations and forces. For example, in trying to assess Mr. Anderson's situation, described at the beginning of this chapter, from a person-in-environment perspective, Juan would see Mr. Anderson at the center of this series of concentric circles. Mr. Anderson does have an emotionally close family network, but they are at some distance and are unable to provide a great deal of direct assistance. Looking beyond his family to his neighborhood, Juan would note Mr. Anderson's "fierce independence" as a potential challenge in assisting him to ask for help from the informal networks of neighbors and friends who might be willing to be of assistance. Examining the next layer of support in the community, Juan has already encountered difficulty in accessing one agency due to Mr. Anderson's location, but he could explore other community services that might be available. The policy challenge that Juan faces may take him to the state level in inquiring about

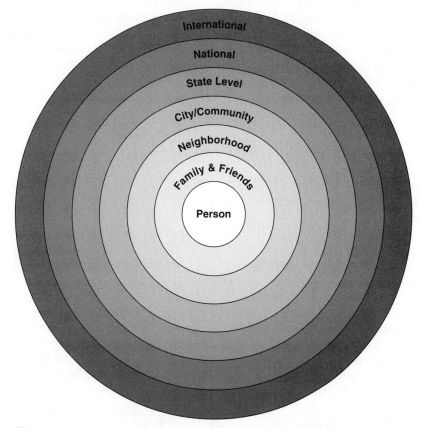

Figure 1.1
Person-in-environment perspective

how service areas are determined for different agencies and whether there is one mandated to serve Mr. Anderson's area. He may even decide to examine some of the state laws, programs, and funding mechanisms to see whether resources could be mobilized to serve Mr. Anderson and others who are outside designated service areas. These questions and inquiries may even take him to the federal level to examine authorizing legislation and mandates that the state may be required to address. In this way, Juan's person-in-environment perspective helps him look for ways to address Mr. Anderson's needs at all the different layers of potential resources that surround and may be available to Mr. Anderson. This perspective also allows Juan to identify gaps in those needs-meeting systems, some of which may need to be addressed by the policy practice activities discussed in this text.

Though Figure 1.1 appears as a static figure, what it represents is far from static. It is a dynamic reality of constant interaction and change as events unfold and take place in one layer resulting in changes or effects not only inward—toward the individual but also outward—toward broader systems. For example, when the federal law No Child Left Behind was passed, local school systems subsequently changed how they measured their annual progress toward their student achievement goals, focusing more on the use of standardized tests. Another unforeseen impact of this change has been an increase in the demand for mental health services for high school students during the week of state tests to assess their learning accomplishments.[6] The systems perspective further informs practitioners that these different levels of influence may assume different levels of prominence at different times. In recent years, for example, international events have become more influential on U.S. businesses and communities as multinational corporations make decisions about job location, outsourcing, and other restructuring changes and as concerns about possible terrorism have led to new restrictions in air travel procedures. Figure 1.1 will be revisited later to increase understanding of how policies at different levels interact with one another to create both the opportunities and the barriers that people experience firsthand in their communities.

DEFINING POLICY PRACTICE

As stated at the beginning of this chapter, policy practice is defined as using social work skills to propose and change policies in order to achieve the goal of social and economic justice. In doing policy practice, social workers apply generalist social work perspectives and skills to make changes in laws, rules, budgets, and policies and in the bodies that create those policies, whether they be local, state, or federal agencies or other decision-making bodies, in the pursuit of the social work mission of social and economic justice. The goal of policy practice in social work is to ensure social and economic justice in the social environment so that all people, regardless of their socioeconomic status, race, ethnicity, religion, or sexual orientation, have opportunities to achieve success for themselves and their families, in a sense so that all those layers in the concentric circles of Figure 1.1 will work to assist them in meeting their needs. This policy practice goal and effort has been part of the social work profession since its very beginnings. Chapter 2 traces that development and discusses how policy practice has been manifested in social work practice historically.

Policy practice speaks to the core mission of social work.

Policy practice speaks to the core mission of social work. It is reflected in the National Association of Social Workers (NASW) Code of Ethics: "To enhance human well-being and help meet the basic human needs of all people, with particular attention to the needs and empowerment of people who are vulnerable, oppressed, and living in poverty."[7] It reflects the values that the profession holds: "Service, social justice, dignity and worth of the person, importance of human relationships, integrity, and competence."[8] Effective policy practice involves learning how to apply the core generalist practice skills (engagement, goal setting, planning, implementing, and monitoring progress) to larger social systems where the outcomes are not individual client change but larger system change in both laws and social conditions that will affect the lives of millions of families and individuals.

Multiple Definitions of Policy Practice and Advocacy

Social work policy scholars have only recently identified policy practice as an important aspect of social work generalist practice, though as noted above, it has clearly been part of the profession's ethical mandate for a long time. Jansson (2005) was one of the first social policy scholars to conceptualize policy practice as a distinct aspect of social work practice. He distinguishes between policy practice and policy advocacy in the following manner:

> I define *policy practice* as efforts to change policies in legislative, agency, and community settings, whether by establishing new policies, improving existing ones, or defeating the policy initiatives of other people. People who are *skilled* in policy practice increase the odds that *their* policy preferences will be advanced. I define *policy advocacy* as policy practice that aims to help powerless groups, such as women, children, poor people, people of color, gay men and lesbians, and people with disabilities, improve their resources and opportunities.[9]

Policy advocacy work for Jansson is the aspect of policy practice that represents traditional social work advocacy on behalf of others who seek to improve their social and economic circumstances. Advocacy is part of policy practice but is not the whole of policy practice.

Barusch also makes the distinction between policy practice and advocacy and, like Jansson, indicates that policy practice is inclusive of advocacy:

> Just as "individual practice" attempts to change individuals, "policy practice" focuses on changing policy. Although the two are closely entwined, policy practice does not *always* involve advocacy. It encompasses a range of activities that, while they sometimes overlap, can be loosely categorized in four groups: assessment and analysis, coalition building, advocacy, and empowerment.[10]

Barusch's delineation of four clusters of activities further demonstrates the different aspects of policy practice that require four different clusters of skills, some of which overlap with one another, and some of which do not. For example, assessment may involve reviewing existing data to discern trends and impacts, whereas conducting a new needs assessment to document local needs may require cooperation and coalition building among stakeholding groups.

Schneider and Lester use the term *advocacy* instead of policy practice, defining it as "the exclusive and mutual representation of a client(s) or a cause in a forum, attempting to systematically influence decision making in an unjust or unresponsive system(s)."[11] Their understanding of advocacy would fit within our definition of policy practice. The term *policy practice,* used

Box 1.1 Stakeholders

Stakeholders are all those groups and individuals who have an interest in the outcomes of a policy practice initiative. For some initiatives, such as health care for those without insurance, it could be argued that many people in a community will have an interest and are, therefore, members of a stakeholding group. But some groups have particular vested interests in the development of any such new initiatives. Local physicians, nurses, social workers, and others working in health care will have particular perspectives and views that will be important to include. Others who work with people without insurance, such as emergency-room personnel, staff at a shelter for people who are homeless, and even owners of small businesses unable to offer employees insurance may

also have perspectives to share. Perhaps the most important stakeholding group is the target client population (in this example, people without insurance). This group is sometimes left out of assessment and planning processes that come from the top down. Certainly, social workers understand that the views of this stakeholding group would be essential to the successful implementation of any important policy change affecting their lives. While these stakeholders may favor changes in the current health care system, other stakeholders such as insurance companies may launch powerful opposition to any change efforts. The health care Simulated Case Study (SCS) demonstrates some of the dynamics in health care change efforts.

throughout this book, refers to the full range of activities and roles that social workers engage in while attempting to change the larger systems in communities with the long-term goal of creating a more just social environment for all people. The perspective that is taken in this text is similar to that of both Jansson and Barusch in distinguishing advocacy as one aspect of policy practice. Advocacy has long been an important and essential activity within what is now called policy practice, but advocacy is only one activity within the broader field of policy practice, as noted in Table 1.1.

Table 1.1 Policy Practice Activities

Policy Practice Activity	Definition	Examples
Policy analysis	Studying the policy to understand its goals, strategies, and potential impact	Analyzing provisions of No Child Left Behind and implications for student assessment procedures
Advocating for policy change	Interacting with policy makers in order to influence their policy decisions on particular proposals	Writing to members of Congress about changes needed in No Child Left Behind to make it more effective in meeting its goals
Building coalitions	Developing relationships with other groups to develop a coordinated advocacy message and strategy	Bringing educators, parents, and child advocate groups together to work on advocating for changes in No Child Left Behind legislation
Launching a campaign	Creating an overarching strategy and a message to influence not only policy makers but the public about an issue	Developing a coherent message for radio ads, flyers, a Web site, etc., to present arguments and rationale to support needed changes in No Child Left Behind

The term *policy practice* reflects an understanding of where this social work role fits with other roles within the profession. Policy is not just a topic social workers study and understand in order to help clients access programs and resources. The policy arena is also an arena for social work action and for social work practice, just as social workers practice with individuals, families, organizations, and communities. Social workers are advocates, to be sure, but that is not their only role in policy practice. Social workers are actively engaged in many aspects of policymaking and implementation, as discussed in Chapter 6.

The definitions of policy practice, as articulated by other social work scholars, may vary somewhat from the one presented here, but all focus on changing larger systems through internal changes in community organizations' policies, state and federal legislative and rule changes, or through increasing funding levels for social programs. Further exploration of the complexities of policy practice in action requires an understanding of the matrix of opportunities for policy practice within the broad social environment in which both social workers and clients live.

CONCEPTUALIZING POLICY PRACTICE IN ACTION

Settings and Environmental Levels Within the Policy Practice Arena

Opportunities for policy practice occur within each of the concentric circles of the environment in Figure 1.1 that surround individuals and that help them meet their basic needs. Social workers attempt to influence policymaking in four different settings within the social environment. The executive branch of government (regardless of level from the White House and president, to the governors of the states, and mayors in local communities) is responsible for implementing and enforcing the policies and actions passed by the legislative branch of government, whether that is the Congress, the state general assembly, or the city council, through their respective democratic processes. Social workers can influence policymaking in all three branches of government (executive, legislative, and judicial), but the challenges are different in each, requiring different strategies to be successful. The judicial branch of government determines whether laws have been broken and whether those laws themselves are constitutional at the state or federal level. Attempts to influence the judicial branch of government may be targeted to the Supreme Court, state supreme courts, or local family, civil, and criminal courts in both the federal and state justice systems. In judicial settings, laws and policies are both challenged and upheld as well as punishments meted out for those who violate the policies and laws as passed by the legislative branch. Strategies for influence in judicial settings differ from those in legislative settings. Sometimes social workers and their organizations are actively engaged in fighting repressive laws, such as contemporary efforts to defeat the bans on gay marriage in a number of states, and may be involved directly in filing constitutional challenges to existing laws; or social work organizations may file amicus curiae ("friend of the court") briefs (see Box 1.2) on a particular side in a court case. For example, NASW has filed amicus curiae briefs in the following court cases: *Roper v. Simmons* (U.S. Supreme Court, 2005) challenging the death penalty for 17-year-olds; in *T.B. v. L.R.M.*

Box 1.2   Amicus Curiae Brief

An amicus curiae brief is one that is filed as a "friend of the court" to support one side in a pending court decision. This legal brief provides arguments in favor of that position from the law and the evidence from practice and research.

Box 1.3   Simulated Case Study

You will see how an advocacy effort might proceed when you visit the mythical state of Factoria in the Gay Marriage Simulated Case Study. This fictional story unfolds through simulated e-mails and Web pages and chronicles the efforts of a social worker, Julia Cohen, and her colleagues to defeat a repressive amendment to the state constitution. As you work your way through this simulated case study and the two others that come with this text, you will see many of the concepts and strategies discussed in the text come to life. Watch for these inserts to help you find relevant illustrations in the simulated case studies.

(Pennsylvania Supreme Court, 2001) granting lesbian visitation rights; in *Anderson (Saenz) v. Roe* (U.S. Supreme Court, 1999) challenging California's one-year waiting period for welfare benefits for new residents; and, in *Anspach v. City of Philadelphia* (U.S. District Court, 2005),[12] upholding access of youth to family planning services. In many of these cases, NASW joined other professional associations and community groups in the brief, thereby adding to its potential power to influence the court in making a decision.

In addition to the three branches of government, the fourth arena for policy practice is in grassroots and other community organizations that also are involved in delivering human services or advocating for client needs. Social workers may be taking the lead in identifying unmet needs and advocating for changes in these settings (see Table 1.2).

Looking across the rows of Table 1.2, the settings for policy practice are identified for each level of policymaking. At the local level, for example, executive policymaking resides in various boards and commissions as well as in the mayor's office, legislative action is taken by the city council, judicial policies are carried out in the juvenile court, and community advocacy is conducted by a variety of grassroots organizations. In contrast, looking down the columns, the comparable policymaking settings are identified for each level. For example, legislative settings include city councils at the local level, state legislatures at the state level, and Congress at the federal level. Learning how to work in these various settings and levels is an important aspect of learning about policy practice.

Social workers engaged in policy practice frequently begin their work on a problem or an issue at one level in one setting, but find that to achieve their goals, they must move from level to level and setting to setting. Going back to Juan's challenge with helping Mr. Anderson, Juan has many different opportunities to engage in policy practice to address the gap in services he has identified. At the informal level, he may discuss Mr. Anderson's situation (maintaining confidentiality) with colleagues and friends who work in other social service agencies, perhaps finding that Mr. Anderson is not the only older person not receiving the services he needs. As indicated earlier, at the community level Juan may identify other community organizations besides Meals on Wheels that might be in a position to extend or develop services if there is an identified

Table 1.2 Policy Making Organizations by Environmental Level

| Level of Policy Making | Typical Policy Making Organizations by Setting | | | |
	Executive	Legislative	Judicial	Community Activity and Advocacy
Local	Local housing authorities, city and county program offices such as probation office, voter registration, community and family services, local human rights commission, mayors, city managers	City and town councils, county councils, county commissioners, school boards	Circuit court, juvenile court, family court	Nonprofit agency boards, local grassroots organizations such as local gay-rights groups
State	State agencies such as those providing Food Stamps, TANF, Medicaid, emergency housing, etc., State Board of Health, Corrections, vocational rehabilitation, governors	State legislatures	State appeals court, state supreme court	Statewide nonprofit agencies such as Planned Parenthood, or Project Equality
Federal	Social Security Administration, Department of Health and Human Services, U.S. Department of Justice, the president of the U.S.	Congress	Supreme court, federal court system including appeals courts	National affiliate nonprofit agencies such as Big Brother-Big Sister, or the Human Rights Campaign

need. He may work at the local level in letting the locally elected officials know about this need of one of their constituents. When he contacts staff at the state level, he is operating the executive branch of government. When he contacts the state legislator representing this district about a needed change in legislation that would help Mr. Anderson and others like him, he is working in the legislative branch of government. His contact at the federal level might start in the executive branch with the Administration on Aging, but if some changes in federal legislation are required then he may be in touch with the U.S. representative and U.S. senators representing his area and state, the legislative branch. When he finds a need to change federal legislation, he may return to the community and grassroots level to organize a coalition to advocate for such a change. Juan's search for a way to meet Mr. Anderson's need may take him in many different directions through a variety of policy practice settings, depending on the information he finds and what he is able to accomplish.

Policy practice is inclusive of a number of different settings in social work practice at local, state, federal, and even the international levels. Though there may not be comparable bodies in each level (particularly at the international level), the settings for policy practice include citizens advocacy, grassroots-level community organizations, nonprofit agencies (citizen's groups that shape policy and provide valuable community services), and the three branches of

14

Chapter 1

government. These settings across the different levels from local through international are the points of origin for the policies that affect clients and that set the parameters for the services social workers may provide. When social workers understand where the policy originated and where it needs to be changed, then they can plan effective strategies to influence that person or deliberative body. If Juan determines that the gap in services can be resolved in the local community, then he will not need to involve state or federal officials. If, however, he discovers that there are multiple gaps in service delivery due to lack of state and federal funding, then he may need to work at those levels to advocate for increasing funding in this area to meet the needs of vulnerable people. Table 1.3 provides some examples of those policy decision-makers whom

Table 1.3 Policy Examples by Setting and Environmental Level

	Typical Policies by Setting			
Level of Policy Making	Executive	Legislative	Judicial	Community Activity and Advocacy
Local	Local housing authority waitlist policies, local practices of the child protection office, local human rights commission hearing procedures	City and town ordinances banning discrimination based on sexual orientation, county commissioner budgets, school board policy on sex education	City court rulings in municipal drug cases	Local Habitat for Humanity application procedures, local Planned Parenthood clinic policies on service delivery, grassroots organizations' policies, local gay-rights group's stand on gay-rights ordinance
State	State policies on Food Stamp eligibility, TANF, Medicaid, emergency housing; State Board of Health mandates for county services; State Board of Education policies to implement the federal policy of No Child Left Behind	State laws on gay marriage, provision of education to children with disabilities, local taxing authority, etc., plus the state budget funding social services	State appeals court and state supreme court rulings on state and local laws that are challenged	Policies of statewide nonprofit agencies such as Planned Parenthood, or Project Equality that provide guidelines for local group affiliation
Federal	Social Security Administration and Department of Health and Human Services policies that set the broad guidelines for implementing federal programs such as SSI, Food Stamps, TANF, etc.	Federal laws designed to provide services or mandate access to services such as the Civil Rights Act of 1965, No Child Left Behind	Supreme Court and other federal court rulings such as *Brown v. Board of Education* and *Roe v. Wade*	Policies of national affiliates of nonprofit agencies such as Big Brother-Big Sister or Planned Parenthood that set standards for affiliation

social workers may need to target and work with in changing policies to better meet needs identified in communities.

Knowing the origin of a particular policy that is the target of a change effort is critical to designing an effective campaign. For example, if a local social worker discovered that the eligibility criteria for a local free health clinic set at 150 percent of the poverty level still restricted a large number of people in need of health care from using the clinic, one of the first steps in creating an effective campaign would be to identify the organization or body that set this policy. Did the local clinic staff or board set the policy? Have the local conditions and access to health care changed since the clinic eligibility standards were set? Is the clinic part of a network of clinics with state funding from enabling legislation passed last year was signed by the governor? Were the eligibility guidelines written into the law itself or were they promulgated as part of the state agency's rule-making process? Is the clinic receiving federal funds that mandate the eligibility criteria? Discovering exactly where and how the particular policy is made will help social workers as change agents to determine both the level and the setting where action must be focused to change this policy.

Knowing the origin of a particular policy that is the target of a change effort is critical to designing an effective campaign.

Interactivity of Environmental Levels and Settings

Environmental levels (local to international) and settings (the three branches of government plus nongovernmental community organizations) do not exist as separate, discrete entities but rather are interactive components of the entire matrix of policy practice. Sometimes, the ultimate goal may be to bring about change in one setting, but action must first be directed to another. Using the example of the clinic eligibility criteria above, if the social worker discovers that this policy is determined by the federal funding that is being provided, it will be futile to focus change efforts on the director and the board of the local clinic. Although it would be important to bring them into the change process as significant stakeholders (refer back to Box 1.1 for a discussion of "stakeholders"), the primary change efforts will need to be focused at the federal level, either toward Congress (if the eligibility criteria are written into the enabling legislation itself) or toward the executive office charged with implementation (if the eligibility criteria are set by an administrative rule or regulation that has been promulgated). Taking another example, advocates sometimes challenge restrictive laws in the appropriate court system. A local ordinance denying equal protection in employment for gay and lesbian people that could not be overturned even after the next election of the city council might be challenged in the state court system. If upheld by the state supreme court, advocates might then seek to have sexual orientation added as a protected class in state law that would supersede the local ordinance. Currently, several states have passed laws to increase access to health care, particularly by finding some way for providing health care to those who do not have health insurance. Some advocates predict that when enough states have passed laws to demonstrate both the political and economic viability of some version of a single-payer plan, such a plan will be passed by Congress, negating the need for separate state plans. So although the initial goal may be to achieve change at one level, sometimes efforts are more effectively targeted at a different level in the beginning of the change effort.

It may be useful to think about the levels and settings in Table 1.2 as interlocking pieces of a puzzle that must be creatively manipulated during an advocacy campaign to finally create a path toward change. The social worker and allies move through the different levels and settings in a planned but flexible change effort to achieve their policy practice goals. For example, a social worker could learn more about the Conyers bill (HR676) to establish a single-payer system of national health insurance at a national conference. Back in her local community, she could begin to organize social workers through her regional NASW group and then include other professionals and fellow residents concerned about health care. Now she is operating in the local level of the community setting. Later, she uses her NASW network to begin a statewide organizing effort to lobby in the state legislature for a single-payer initiative in the state. Now she is operating at the state level in the legislative arena. At the same time, a national effort is under way to get the Conyers bill moving in Congress again, so this social worker encourages her group to join her in a letter-writing and e-mail campaign; in doing so, she has moved to the national level of the legislative area.

As in the health care SCS, each change effort in each setting at each level will likely require different alignments at different points in time in order to be successful. The policy practitioner who is armed with knowledge and skills to practice at a variety of different levels and settings will be positioned to be successful in achieving policy changes over time.

Foundations of Policy Practice in Generalist Practice

The philosophy and mission of social work are based on a principle of helping people, both in their individual situations and in their collective circumstances. With the person-in-environment perspective situating individuals in the context of their social environments so thoroughly, social workers' attention is directed at both helping individuals change and at helping them change their environmental circumstances as well. This linkage of the person in the environment is found in the origins of the profession with both the settlement house movement and the charity organization societies.

Social justice, one of the core values of social work, serves as the basis for policy practice. The NASW Code of Ethics is clear in its emphasis on "promoting the general welfare" beyond the help offered for individuals. The approach of moving from "case to cause" focuses beyond the individual client to recognize others in similar situations and identify broad community needs in an effort to build support for policy changes. If many people are experiencing similar difficulties, it becomes more difficult to sustain adherence to the belief in the sole solution of personal responsibility; however, this circumstance makes it easier to make the case for a need for more systemic change through the invention of positive social structures to provide and sustain support for a large number of individuals.

Taking this approach, the targets of the change process are not individuals, but that which impedes client development or oppresses clients. Policy practice seeks to remove environmental barriers and to increase opportunities available to individuals and families. Social workers engaging in policy practice are proactively shaping and evaluating new service paradigms and programs to address emergent needs. They are thoughtfully proposing policy-informed service-delivery systems that will be sensitive to the diversity of clients needing services.

Policy practice seeks to remove environmental barriers and to increase opportunities available to individuals and families.

Though policy practice is identified by some[13] as a recent development in social work education, it is in fact central to the history of social work as a profession and has long been part of what community social workers do when they find unmet needs. It could be that scholars are just now identifying and naming policy practice as the profession recognizes the need to focus on skill development in this area in order to prepare social workers for the reality of increasingly complex practice in communities in twenty-first-century United States and as actors on the world stage.

Five Policy Practice Principles

In designing a course to integrate policy discussions and skills with social work practice, Rocha and Johnson articulate the importance of incorporating five policy practice principles[14] to ensure that students acquire the skills both to help clients and to change the policy environment within which they must be able to function. Those principles of policy practice are derived from Iatridis[15] and include

- Determining the effect of social policy, through analysis, assessment, and implementation;
- Linking direct services to social reform efforts through both systems theory and person-in-environment approaches;
- Understanding how organizational policies set the scope and limits of practice;
- Participating directly in the policymaking process at all levels through action steps;
- Increasing social and economic justice in resource distribution in the social environment.

These principles are central to the work of social workers as they help individual clients both directly and indirectly by making their environments more supportive with a variety of resources within social services and beyond in the broader community.

Strategic Use of Power

Social workers, as both professionals and citizens, and their clients have the power to affect policy at all the different stages of the policymaking process, to ensure that communities become more just and equitable in their ability to meet the needs of all the people who live within them. This power to affect policy is at the root of our democratic form of government and policymaking, but too few chose to exercise that power. Some have even suggested that the social work profession has abandoned the policy work that is at its root.[16] Box 1.4 describes the passage of welfare reform when powerful interests were successful in making lasting change in policy.

Box 1.4   Welfare Reform Case Study

The passage of "welfare reform" during the Clinton presidency in 1996 may be a good example of when social work was not successful in using its power to halt a dramatic change in the federal entitlement programs for low-income families. Under pressure from advocates from multiple political persuasions who saw the existing Aid to Families with Dependent Children (AFDC) program as flawed and broken, with many clients "trapped in the system" and oppressed by its policies, many states had already moved to develop reforms of their own state welfare programs, seeking waivers from existing federal regulations in the process. Having vowed to "change welfare as we know it" during his presidential campaign, Clinton proposed moving the AFDC program from an entitlement program to one that was time-limited and that emphasized moving single mothers (the primary caretakers of the children who were the major recipients of AFDC funds) from welfare to work. The resulting legislation created Temporary Assistance to Needy Families, the TANF program. Based on their experiences working with welfare mothers, many practitioners in the states argued for enhancing the state educational and job training opportunities to enable women to move from welfare to employment with wages sufficient to help them support their families and raise them out of poverty. As passed, the educational and job training opportunities were minimal, and child care funding has been cut most recently to reduce costs. Modifications continue to be made to both federal and state level welfare reform efforts, sometimes based on what research shows as most effective in practice in the TANF program. Unfortunately, the bottom-line issue in many states continues to be a reduction in the welfare rolls rather than any appreciable positive change in the outcomes for families. While some follow-up studies report that many former clients are now "better off," there are still substantial numbers of families who are worse off under welfare reform, no matter how states may define success. In fact, in their study of the ten years of the TANF program, Parrott and Sherman assert that while progress was made in both reducing childhood poverty and increasing the number of single mothers in jobs up until 2000, childhood poverty had increased and employment had decreased since 2000. They go on to state that the number of single parents who are both unemployed and not receiving either family or government assistance has increased. TANF, they state, is helping fewer parents who qualify, falling from 80 percent in the early 1990s to 48 percent in 2002.

Startlingly, this drop in TANF participation among eligible families accounts for more than half of the decline in TANF caseloads since 1996. Stated another way, more than half—57 percent—of the caseload decline during the first decade of welfare reform reflects a decline in the extent to which TANF programs serve families that are poor enough to qualify, rather than a reduction in the number of families who are poor enough to qualify for aid.

What is the lesson here? What can be learned from welfare reform about efforts to influence policy? How involved were social workers in trying to influence the outcomes of welfare reform policy? The NASW, social work's professional association, was involved in trying to influence the policymaking process from the first debates on welfare reform and in its reauthorization, but it is challenging to access that legislative advocacy record to understand the process in some detail. The association was involved, but to what extent were they able to mobilize social workers in communities? What changes did they seek? What direct strategies did they use with their allies in Congress to win over the opposition? Welfare reform serves as a reminder of what happens when social workers are not able to achieve policy changes that fit with the social work value base. Learning from past failings, social workers will learn how to involve others in policy practice and stand up to the forces that would seek to implement policies harmful to the most vulnerable people social workers serve.

Source: Parrott, Sharon and Arloc Sherman. "TANF at 10: Program Results Are More Mixed Than Often Understood." Center for Budget and Policy Priorities. 2006. *www.cbpp.org/8-17-06tanf.htm* (accessed June 26, 2007).

THE SOCIAL WORK PERSPECTIVE ON POLICY PRACTICE

Social workers do not have to be in political office or hold positions of power in order to affect policy. Social workers and social work students have both the skills and perspectives (concepts, values, and beliefs) that are important in the policymaking process. These skills and perspectives are rooted in social work's history and experience of working directly with people to address the challenges and needs they face in their daily lives. Now is time to examine these skills and perspectives in more detail to understand the foundation upon which can be built an enhanced skill set for policy practice.

Application of Generalist Practice Skills to Policy Practice

As students learn in their practice classes, the generalist practice skills gained in class and in supervised interactions with people in need can be applied in a variety of settings. This application includes macro-practice settings where the goal is not individual change or access to resources but is rather policy change so that whole groups of people may have access to needed resources. These generalist practice skills that are applicable to policy practice work are discussed below.

Engage Assess Intervene Evaluate

Critical Thinking Question

What could you do specifically to build trust with a state legislator who initially opposes legislation that you support?

- ▶ *Engagement skills*   enable social workers to develop trusting relationships with a wide variety of clients from many different backgrounds and experiences. These same skills, applied in policy practice, foster the development and nurturing of relationships with actors in policy settings including legislators, state agency policy analysts, lobbyists, and representatives of constituent groups. All these participants in the policy process have different personalities and different perspectives on policy goals and the policy process. Building relationships across these different constituencies requires the ability to be open, honest, and respectful to all, while making one's social work perspective clear. As a participant in the process, social workers must earn the trust of others so they are seen as presenting facts and information to others in an honest, straightforward manner, without manipulation or the deliberate withholding of information counter to their own perspectives. That trust is gained when a social worker, while working with a client, acknowledges a variety of perspectives, pointing out the advantages and disadvantages of each of the options available. Although the policy practitioner may suggest that a given direction will achieve the goals in a more fair and equitable or even more efficient manner, the policy decision most probably is not his or hers to make. When a trusting relationship with the policy maker has been developed, the social worker will be able to develop an argument for a particular position with more credibility and salience for the policy maker. Power in the policy process is gained through the relationships that are developed. The interactive skills that help social workers establish and maintain these relationships are elemental to policy practice. Long-time policy practitioners realize that "it is really all about relationship."
- ▶ *Assessment skills*   that social workers use to understand the person in his or her environment can be applied to macro settings to identify strengths upon which change can be launched as well as needs for

resources and opportunities for intervention. Assessment skills are applied to understand problems, analyze proposed solutions for their appropriateness of fit, and develop an implementation plan that takes into account all circumstances for the people involved.

▶ *Communication skills*   are essential to establishing and maintaining relationships with individuals and families. Social workers learn to "start where the client is" with active listening to understand the world from the individual's perspective. So too, in policy practice, they rely on their whole repertoire of communication skills. Social work policy practitioners must be able to communicate with a variety of groups, including those in the opposition and those who are sitting on the fence. There are times when confrontation is important, but equally important is knowing when that time is and how to use confrontation skills judiciously. Being able to testify before a committee and make a case eloquently for a proposed bill is indispensable in some policy practice roles. Policy practitioners also use writing skills to prepare white paper reports on issues, talking points for legislative alert networks, and policy briefs to distribute to policy makers.

▶ *Problem solving and negotiating skills*   are important in direct practice with individuals and families in generating alternative options for new directions and new actions to take. Frequently, in family work, social workers are in the middle, trying to help the "sides" develop solutions that will result in a win-win situation for everyone. Similarly, in policy work, when policy practitioners have identified needs and developed alternative policies to address those needs, they are seldom able to see the details of proposed policies adopted *in toto*. Frequently, they must settle for a watered-down version or a partial step forward that is politically more palatable or fiscally more practical at a given period of time. With continued pressure and persistence, long-term goals may be realized later, but policy practitioners must find ways to negotiate and find common ground in the short term.

▶ *Networking and collaborating skills*   are important in linking clients to needed resources as well as working with other professionals with families experiencing multiple challenges. Wrap-around services that include all the service providers in a team with families are proving to be effective in helping families challenged with being at-risk of abuse and neglect. Many schools use interdisciplinary teams to plan and implement services for students with disabilities. These same skills come into play in policy practice efforts to find allies who will join together in support of legislative initiatives. Endorsements from a variety of perspectives are most helpful in demonstrating broad-based support for bills under consideration in both Congress and the state houses across the country. Using the networks of connections with other constituent groups and coalitions, as demonstrated in later chapters, is often essential to passing legislation. Understanding how to develop and maintain relationships and connections with other groups and individuals with common concerns is a most useful policy practice skill. Being able to find potential allies among traditional opponents can be especially valuable (see Box 1.5).

Box 1.5   A Slice of History

When a family cap was proposed for the federal TANF (Temporary Assistance to Needy Families) program as it was developed to replace the AFDC (Aid to Families with Dependent Children) program, NASW along with a number of other groups opposed the family cap that would not have allowed an increase in a grant if another child was born to a woman already on welfare. Most organizations opposed the family cap based on the restrictions it would impose on income available to raise a family. The Catholic Church and other Catholic organizations joined in this opposition because of a fear that the cap might lead to an increase in the number of women seeking abortions. So organizations with different stances and beliefs on the issue of abortion itself found themselves on the same side of another issue and were able to defeat this restriction in the federal legislation.

Relevance of Generalist Practice Perspectives

Social workers engaged in direct practice with individuals and families in communities not only have skills that are valuable in policy practice activities, but they also have perspectives derived from their education and developed from their engagement in change processes with families, neighborhoods, and communities. Understanding the process of change and learning to be patient with that process is vital for effective policy practice.

Understanding the process of change and learning to be patient with that process is vital for effective policy practice.

> ▶ ***Commitment to and belief in the possibility of change.***   Social work students often become involved in volunteer work with agencies and then get interested in the profession because they want to "help people." When pressed, most will talk about ways in which they want to help others change their lives or the conditions that they live in so that they can realize their dreams. Such help implies the belief in the capacity and will of people to change and to make decisions to change the circumstances of their lives. The belief in the possibility of individual change can be extended to include the possibility for organizational, neighborhood, community, state, and national change, both in the structures of policymaking bodies and in the policies themselves. Indeed, American history is replete with examples of the power of a few to make great changes. Sometimes that change has been sparked by an individual's decision to change or to act differently, much like people like to think of Rosa Park's decision on one day to refuse to give up her seat on the bus, a decision that sparked the civil rights movement and resulted in the passage of the Civil Rights Act of 1965. As in the work for civil rights for African Americans and many other groups, sometimes many individuals have to act in many communities for a long period of time to achieve policy changes. And even then, the work is never completely done.
>
> ▶ ***Commitment for the long haul.***   In developing trust with individual clients, social workers frequently need to convince those with whom they are trying to partner and engage that the social workers will be there for "the long haul." Treating people with dignity and respect means that social workers will "be there" for them when the need arises. In policy practice, social workers are also in it for the long haul. They know that policy change requires persistence and perseverance. Just because a fight for legislation in one session of the legislature is lost does not mean that advocates will not be back to fight the same issue next session. Social workers will recommit their time and energy.

Even when legislation is passed, it is seldom possible to completely relax. Vigilance is important. Monitoring the ongoing implementation of policy requires commitment. Funds may not be allocated. Policies may not be enforced. Rules may be written that undercut the original intent of legislation.

▸ ***Passion for social justice and empowerment.***   Social work's core professional value and belief in the dignity and worth of the individual leads social workers logically into advocacy efforts as they partner with traditionally oppressed populations to realign power structures so that all are represented and have a stake in the well-being of society as a whole. This passion for social justice makes the social work profession, as an organization with its stands on issues, more "left-leaning" politically than some other helping professions. Once people are understood as part of a social environment, social workers are obligated to try to help individual people change and to also help change their environments. After analyzing the barriers that exist in the environments of many people who are poor and vulnerable, social workers realize the need for change in the policies that set parameters around what they can do and achieve. The greater faith the profession seems to place in federal-level interventions to address pervasive social problems may stem from the historical involvement of social workers in the development of federal programs during the New Deal. This perspective makes many social workers fall left of center in the political spectrum.

▸ ***Systems perspective in understanding issues.***   In working with individuals, social workers use the systems perspective to understand how all the elements in the environment interact with one another to facilitate or hinder the individual's ability to develop to his or her potential. The ability to conceptualize the societal issues and challenges from a systems perspective illuminates everyone's stake in creating solutions. The systems perspective also helps social workers understand social problems as not isolated but in a constantly changing interactive environment of problems, solutions, and other factors. Systems thinking also helps identify other overlooked aspects of the environment that can be brought into policy practice efforts.

▸ ***Ability to find common ground in disputes and disagreements.*** Working with individuals and families, social workers are frequently called upon to help settle disputes, sometimes between parents, sometimes between parents and their children, and sometimes among a whole group of family members. Those mediating and negotiating skills can be most helpful in policy practice as well when policy practitioners try to build coalitions around an issue. It is unusual for everyone concerned about an issue to see it from exactly the same perspective. Building a coalition in support of a solution involves getting coalition members involved in the solution-building process from the beginning so that differences can be resolved early.

Fresh perspectives and recent life experiences of the current generation of students will help shape the policy frameworks of the future. As members of the newest generation to enter the workforce, the enthusiasm and engagement of current students and recent graduates will promote policy discussions and deliberations moving into future realms and possibilities that are yet to be dreamed about.

Policy
Practice

Critical Thinking Question

Using the systems perspective to illuminate the problem of childhood poverty, what possible solutions suggest themselves?

A Recommitment to Policy Practice

This chapter identified some key factors that have led social workers to recommit to policy practice:

- Policy practice was a central activity in the profession's historical roots both in micro and macro practice.
- Policy practice is a major feature of the Code of Ethics.
- Policy practice allows social workers to enact their core value of social justice.
- Policy practice enables social workers to partner in the creation of a social environment more supportive of human potential.

Success in policy practice can work to erode social workers' self-doubt and feelings of powerlessness. Publicity about social workers' macro-change efforts can counter the negative public image of social workers and demonstrate their public commitment to positive social change. It is exciting to consider this reconnection with powerful forces for social change in light of the social reforms achieved during the Progressive Era, the New Deal, and the civil rights movement. This revitalization of social workers' roles in social change may attract more activist students to consider entering the profession as well.[17]

PREPARING FOR POLICY PRACTICE ROLES

Some social workers say they are not involved in policy practice because it really is not part of social work. Reviewing the NASW Code of Ethics and some of the discussion in this chapter should help convince any doubters that policy practice is not just part of social work, but an important part of the profession's role in communities. Some social workers say they are not engaged in policy practice because they do not know how to affect policy, do not know enough, and do not have the skills. This book is designed to ensure that you will not belong to that group (see Box 1.6 for one example assignment). Upon completion

---

Box 1.6   To Learn More . . .

Social work faculty regularly require students to form task groups for policy practice projects as a part of their policy or other classes. The range of projects is broad but all are focused on efforts to enhance the principles of social justice so central to social work practice. As Rocha and Johnson detail,

"Projects at the organizational level include working with public housing tenants to change a local HMO's [Health Maintenance Organization's] health care policies, increasing handicapped accessibility in an organization, recommending changes to address disability content more adequately in the curriculum, and using local churches as a resource for pregnancy prevention programs. Projects that have targeted community and state-legislative levels include empowering parent groups to contact state legislators to amend day care legislation, changing transit system policies regarding the location of bus routes in poor neighborhoods, creating a task force to investigate new trends in hunger in a local metropolitan area, and recommending changes in the implementation of child welfare policy."(p. 439)

Other student groups have raised awareness about various issues including homelessness, date rape, and gang violence through informational campaigns. Developing these policy practice skills through social work education allows students to graduate with experience and a sense of self-efficacy that may make it more likely they will engage in policy practice when working as social workers in the community.

Source: Rocha, Cynthia J., and Alice K. Johnson, "Teaching Family Policy through a Policy Practice Framework." *Journal of Social Work Education, 33*(3) (1997), 433–444. *Academic Search Premier,* EBSCO*host* (accessed March 10, 2007).

Critical Thinking Question

What compelling reasons can you give for social workers to be involved in policy practice?

of this text, you will have the necessary skills and knowledge to tackle tough policy issues and exercise your power in thoughtful and ethical approaches to change policies for a more just society. Some social workers say they do not have the time to engage in policy practice. This text will demonstrate the multiple roles available in policy practice, from the caseworker who writes to her state and federal representatives about the need for more affordable housing so that people will no longer be homeless, to the social worker who runs for political office. Social workers can engage in policy practice as part of their social work positions in agencies or in time off by going to community forums, city council meetings, and other venues to voice their opinions. We hope to inspire you about the possibility of change so that you will make the time to engage in policy practice, no matter what your own personal time commitment may be. We hope to inspire some of you enough that you will take the leap and actually try out your policy practice skills in your own communities.

CONCLUSION

This chapter introduced you to how policy practice has been and continues to be a principal focus for social work practice. The roots of policy practice were situated in the beginnings of the profession, primarily in the settlement house movement, which provides a sound foundation for policy practice in the twenty-first century as well. The next chapter will provide a brief history of how social workers have engaged historically in policy practice to increase an understanding about the historical and economic context within which policy practice occurs, a context that must be understood in order to select strategies that are likely to be successful in moving toward the goal of a more just society.

Log onto **MySocialWorkLab** to access a wealth of case studies, videos, and assessment. (*If you did not receive an access code to* **MySocialWorkLab** *with this text and wish to purchase access online, please visit* **www. mysocialworklab.com**.)

1. **Watch the Connecting Core Competency videos on Policy Practice.** Identify the generalist practice skills

(from page 18–19) that Judith Willison demonstrates in the videos, particularly the third one.

2. **Review the Health Care SCS.** Who are the primary stakeholders and how do they try to build a coalition through using their problem solving/negotiating skills?

PRACTICE TEST

The following questions will test your knowledge of the content found within this chapter. For additional assessment, including licensing-exam type questions on applying chapter content to practice, visit **MySocialWorkLab**.

1. Using systems theory in case assessment, social workers:
   a. Recognize whether or not political action should be taken on the macro level.
   b. Continue with the planned intervention and monitoring for a longer period of time to see if change occurs.
   c. Can determine what factors are creating barriers to change.
   d. Focus on only the macro level in order to help more people.

2. The perspective that places the individual in the center surrounded by increasing layers of networks and interactions is referred to as:
   a. The onion perspective
   b. The person-in-environment perspective
   c. The practitioner's perspective
   d. The social network perspective

3. Policy practice:
   a. Did not become a part of social work until the 1960s.
   b. Seeks to ensure social and economic justice in the social environment for all people.
   c. Is focused on federal social policy.
   d. Is implemented only by macro level social workers.

4. Bringing several groups of stakeholders together to advocate for changes in legislation that directly affects them and their client groups is an example of:
   a. Policy analysis
   b. Policy advocacy
   c. Coalition building
   d. The person-in-environment model

5. When developing an effective campaign to change an existing policy:
   a. Historical knowledge of the targeted policy, while interesting, is not critically important.
   b. Understanding how the targeted policy is being implemented is of little relevance.
   c. Understanding why and how the targeted policy was made will help gauge the action that needs to be taken.
   d. Knowing the historic foundation of a policy is important only if a policy is being completely reworked in a new context.

6. No Child Left Behind is a good example of a:
   a. Federal legislative policy.
   b. Federal executive policy.
   c. State court policy.
   d. Local community activity.

7. The power to affect social policy during all stages of the policy-making process:
   a. Is at the root of democratic forms of government.
   b. Is power that only highly influential social workers can wield.
   c. Is only a very small part of policy-making.
   d. Generally rests in the hands of those with the most money.

8. Exercising network and collaborating skills:
   a. Can be of critical value when looking for potential allies among traditional opponents.
   b. Is efficient only when applied at the mezzo level of practice.
   c. Is only done by social workers in political office or in positions of power.
   d. Can yield results only when used with individuals or groups in similar positions.

9. Recommitting and refocusing on policy practice:
   a. Takes time away from critical help that individuals and families need.
   b. Will greatly overburden and possibly alienate some groups of social workers.
   c. Can counter the negative image of the social worker through positive macro level changes.
   d. Should be the endeavor of every agency director.

10. Historically, policy practice has its roots:
   a. Starting in the settlement house movement.
   b. Beginning during the New Deal.
   c. Following the implementation of the Social Security Act of 1953.
   d. In the 1980's.

Log onto **MySocialWorkLab** once you have completed the Practice Test above to access additional study tools and assessment.

Answers

Key: 1) c, 2) b, 3) b, 4) c, 5) c, 6) a, 7) a, 8) a, 9) c, 10) a

History of Policy Practice
in Social Work

CHAPTER OUTLINE

Introduction 27

Historical Roots in Social Work's
    Dual Focus 27
Jane Addams at Hull House
Charity Organization Societies

Progressive Era Reforms 31

Social Work's First Retreat from Policy
    Practice 34

Depression and the New Deal 35

Second Retreat from Activism by the
    Profession 38

Social Reforms of the 1960s 39

Social Workers Doing Policy Practice—Some
    Efforts of the Last Forty Years 42

Today's Social Workers in Policy Practice 45

Looking at Future Policy Practice 45

Conclusion 47

Chapter Review 48

Practice Test 48

 MySocialWorkLab 48
    Connecting Core Competency videos on
    Human Rights and Justice
    Housing SCS

Core Competencies in this Chapter (Check marks indicate which competencies are covered in depth)				
Professional Identity	✓ Ethical Practice	Critical Thinking	Diversity in Practice	Human Rights & Justice
Research Based Practice	Human Behavior	✓ Policy Practice	✓ Practice Contexts	Engage, Assess, Intervene, Evaluate

26

INTRODUCTION

The good we secure for ourselves is precarious and uncertain, is floating in mid-air, until it is secured for all of us and incorporated into our common life.

—Jane Addams[1]

Social workers have often played pivotal roles in the development of American social welfare history. This chapter provides a brief overview of important historical events, legislation, and court decisions that have made significant social welfare history, with examples of how social workers have left their imprint on the U.S. social welfare system. A review of the contributions of social workers to the development of social policies and the advancement of new policy practice strategies for moving the social work policy agenda of social justice forward provides a solid foundation for beginning social work policy practitioners today. The role of social work's professional association, the National Association of Social Workers (NASW), and of its precursors is also relevant to understanding the profession's policy practice efforts, historically and today. The waxing and waning of social work's commitment to policy practice across the major periods and developments in the history of social welfare policy in the United States is illustrated throughout this chapter.

HISTORICAL ROOTS IN SOCIAL WORK'S DUAL FOCUS

From its beginnings, social work has had a dual focus, as exemplified in the work of both mothers of the profession: Mary Richmond and Jane Addams. Jane Addams started Hull House, a settlement house to assist immigrant families, but she is also known as a social reformer who was an active policy practitioner, engaged in what is now called macro practice. Mary Richmond, in developing her theories of interpersonal intervention (now called micro or interpersonal practice), still recognized the need for what she termed *wholesale* work in social work practice. In 1930, she wrote, "Pushed upward in our interest in some retail task toward wholesale remedy for evils of the same class, we are pulled back, our remedy once secured, to the particular again, to complete our work so begun."[2] From the beginning of the profession, there has been this sometimes uneasy recognition of the need to intervene at the system or community level in addition to the personal and family level. Balancing those efforts has continued to be a challenge for the profession, with different degrees of emphasis emerging during different historical eras.

Before examining these two major movements that led to the development of the profession, it is worth taking a brief look at a movement that began during the Civil War era and continued into the Progressive Era that Phyllis Day identifies as the third contributor to the profession.[3] About the time of the Civil War, thousands of children without parental supervision wandered in urban areas, trying to make a way for themselves through begging, stealing, and finding employment at very low wages. Concerned citizens started efforts at "child saving" not only to clear the streets of these undesirable children but also to provide them with safe, supervised surroundings. At that time, children were seen as small adults and expected to start working as soon as possible, and few had the opportunity for an education. They were tried in the adult courts for any crimes they committed. The "child saving" reformers became concerned about protecting abused and neglected children and ensuring their health and safety if they were not able to live at home. This "child saving" movement continued and gained momentum in the Progressive Era and led to the creation of a juvenile court and laws prohibiting child labor.

At the turn of the twentieth century, early social workers were engaged in policy practice, though that practice was not identified as such. Historians frequently mark the beginnings of social work with a discussion of Jane Addams of Hull House and her advocacy on behalf of immigrant populations to improve housing and health conditions in the Chicago neighborhoods surrounding the settlement house. They discuss her involvement in the creation of the first juvenile court in the United States in Cook County, Illinois, but today she would be seen as a policy practitioner. Both of these efforts by Addams are examples of policy practice, working to change policies and services to improve the lives of people. If policy practice was central to early social work efforts, to its roots, then policy practice is at the core of social work itself, and has major significance today as well.

Jane Addams at Hull House

Hull House was part of a great social experiment called the "settlement house movement," which involved upper-income and upper-middle-income college-educated young people moving into and living in immigrant neighborhoods to provide assistance to new immigrants in the "settlement" process. The Hull House residents used a two-pronged approach and intention to helping new immigrants: (1) to improve the individual lives of the immigrants who lived in the tenements surrounding Hull House and (2) to improve the actual conditions of those "walk-ups" and neighborhoods within which the immigrant families lived. Hull House offered English, cooking, sewing, citizenship, and other classes to improve specific skills and promote assimilation into American culture. In addition, the women and men of Hull House carefully documented the challenges and needs of the neighborhood in order to provide the factual basis and rational arguments for the neighborhood improvements for which they advocated, such as better street lighting, ventilation and sanitation of the tenements themselves, and neighborhood parks and green spaces for recreation. As early social workers advocated for these neighborhood changes, they found they had to engage the political power structures of the larger communities within which the neighborhoods were located. Jane Addams, for example, became an influential member of the Chicago Civic Federation, a citywide group concerned with political reform.[4]

As will be seen, however, the impact of Hull House and other settlement houses that were part of this turn-of-the-century movement in the United States reached far beyond the neighborhoods within which the settlement house workers first encountered the immigrant families (see Box 2.1). From a small beginning of six settlement houses in 1891, settlements spread mainly in the Northeast and Midwest to about 100 in 1900 and more than 400 by 1910.[5] They gained somewhat of a reputation for being "hotbeds of radicalism" in their work for community and policy change, but most gradually evolved to more traditional social service agencies and community centers and were able to secure funding from the community chests, the local coordinated fundraising organizations for social services.[6] Some settlement houses continue in operation today as neighborhood and community centers, offering a variety of services to residents.

> ### Box 2.1 Major Legacies of Settlement House Movement
>
> ▶ Establishment of personal relationships between settlement house workers and neighborhood residents by living there.
>
> ▶ Use of systematic research to document human need in neighborhoods.
>
> ▶ Publication of findings such as *Hull House Maps and Papers* about urban and work conditions to demonstrate the need for policy change.
>
> ▶ Advocacy on behalf of citizens in need for policy changes and increased services to neighborhoods.
>
> ▶ Beginning of the recognition of the importance of community organization and policy practice for social change.

In spite of the vast differences between the Hull House workers and the immigrant families in their family backgrounds, ethnicity, religion, income, and education, the settlement house workers effectively reached out to engage and serve immigrant families, while at the same time they worked in the larger systems of the local and state institutions to improve the environment in which families lived and worked. While open to people of many different backgrounds, the settlement workers were not immune to the racism of the dominant culture of that time. In modern social work practice, similar disparities in background persist between social workers from moderately economically comfortable families working with people who are homeless or living on limited means and resources. Sometimes, a hierarchical relationship between worker and client may perpetuate the societal power differential and may get in the way of empowerment processes. In doing community and policy practice, social workers and people in the community can join as equals in the change process. In partnering with people to achieve broader community change, there is less agency-imposed hierarchy, particularly in terms of decision-making power of the social worker over the client's life. We will return to these themes of partnership and equality later in this text.

Julia Lathrop, another Hull House worker, was instrumental in the development of the first juvenile court in the United States in Cook County, Illinois (see Box 2.2). Prior to the initiation of a court specifically designed for children, children who committed crimes and could not be handled by their parents were tried and convicted in adult court. Ms. Lathrop went on to help found, and became the first chief of, the U.S. Children's Bureau at the federal level following the first White House Conference on Children.

Charity Organization Societies

Charity Organization Societies were developed to coordinate both service delivery and eligibility requirements of all the agencies in a city that were helping needy families so that families did not "take advantage of the system." (Use of this current expression demonstrates how this precaution remains an ongoing concern of many public and voluntary assistance programs today.) This community-level coordination was supposed to result in a more equitable distribution of scarce community resources to those in need. Such planning, coordination, and distribution of services are also aspects of policy practice. The first Charity Organization Society was established in Buffalo, New York, in 1877 as a way to bring some order to the chaotic way that relief was provided to people

First, larger cities developed Charity Organization Societies to help coordinate service delivery and investigate need.

Box 2.2   Development of the First Juvenile Court

When asked about the origins of juvenile court, most social workers will respond that the first juvenile court was established in Chicago in the late 1800s through the efforts of the women of Hull House, particularly Julia Lathrop. This statement simplifies a policy practice effort that spanned eight years and involved not only Hull House, but also a variety of other organizations and individuals to achieve the goal of providing better treatment for children in the justice system.

In the late 1800s, several groups in the Chicago area were concerned about how children and families were faring in the midst of increased urbanization and industrialization. The middle-class single women, many with social science college degrees, who had moved to live in Hull House to assist families in the neighborhood, were especially concerned with the welfare of dependent and delinquent children when they became involved with the existing criminal court system. Children were treated as adults without acknowledgement of their unique characteristics and needs. The common practice of the time was to punish or reprimand delinquent children as adults, oftentimes with great severity.

Together with the Chicago Women's Club, the Illinois Board of Public Charities, the Illinois Conference of Charities and Corrections, and the Chicago Bar Association, the women of Chicago's Hull House led by house resident Julia Lathrop, advocated for alternative means for addressing the needs of the community's dependent and delinquent children. Recognizing the unique developmental needs of children, advocates of the juvenile court movement engaged in a political action movement over eight years to introduce the development of an informal child-probation system that ultimately resulted in the establishment of the Juvenile Court Law of 1899. This legislation set forth the ground work for our modern-day family court, juvenile and family courts, and juvenile and domestic relations courts. These systems incorporate the unique needs of the child-family perspective into separate systems of juvenile justice.

The Juvenile Court Law of 1899 represents a sociopolitical movement. The primary organizing groups, with the ongoing support of various community organizations and stakeholders, engaged the political system in social change.

Source: Elizabeth J. Clapp, "The Chicago Juvenile Court Movement in the 1980's." March 17, 1995, www.le.ac.uk/hi/teaching/papers/clapp1.html#fn1 (accessed July 12, 2007).

E.E. Appleby, "An Evolving Juvenile Court: On the Front Lines," *Juvenile Justice, 6*(2) (1999), (retrieved on www.ncjrs.gov/html/ojjdp/jjjournal1299/1.html)(accessed January 14, 2008).

With contributions by Ross Manning, Indiana University School of Social Work Ph.D. Student.

who were destitute.[7] First, larger cities developed Charity Organization Societies to help coordinate service delivery and investigate need. Charity Organization Societies typically recruited volunteer "friendly visitors" (primarily women from middle-income or upper-income families) to visit families to document thoroughly their needs, living conditions, and resources. These friendly visitors were to complete their "assessments" in order to distinguish between the "worthy" and the "unworthy" poor. They were not to dispense alms or relief themselves, but rather to help those in need find ways to achieve self-sufficiency through "moral uplift." At a time of great need, Charity Organization Societies were not only interested in rooting out fraud, abuse, and duplication of services, but they also wanted to address more scientifically and systematically the problem of poverty in their communities (see Box 2.3). They were hampered in this effort because they were operating from an assumption that people were in need due to personal and moral deficits. Though their work was centered clearly on casework with families in helping those families negotiate access to needed services, the volunteers and paid staff became overwhelmed with the desperate needs they found among the families they visited, particularly in times of high unemployment. At those times, it was difficult for the friendly visitors to see the applicability of the individual deficit model of poverty upon which their work was based.

Their inability to respond to widespread need during these times led to their demise, according to historian Michael Katz. He wrote:

> Early in the second decade of the twentieth century, Edward T. Devine, the secretary of the New York COS, confessed failure: "Our use of relief has been most sparing and timid. I am inclined to believe that we have caused more pauperism by our failure to provide for the necessities of life, for the education and training of children, and for the care and convalescence of the sick, than we have by excessive relief, even if we include the indiscriminant alms." With even the leading spokesman for the country's largest COS full of doubt, it is not surprising that radical critics were even much tougher on charity organizations.[8]

Practice
Contexts

Critical Thinking Question

Discuss examples of current social work practices and procedures that demonstrate the legacy of the Charity Organization Societies.

PROGRESSIVE ERA REFORMS

From 1900 to 1920, the population of the United States more than doubled to a total of more than 100 million.[9] This period was a time of great social upheaval in the country as waves of immigrants arrived on the East Coast and then moved into cities in the west, seeking work and increased economic opportunities. Most of the 19 million immigrants who entered the United States before the restrictive Immigration Acts of 1921 and 1924 were from southern and eastern Europe, particularly Italy and Russia.[10] They brought new religious teachings, new languages, new customs, and new foods as they settled into urban and rural areas. Rather than welcoming this new diversity, the dominant groups (Protestant northern and western Europeans) feared the newcomers, particularly those who were Catholic. Immigrants were encouraged to shed their heritage and blend into the "melting pot" and become American. They also experienced discrimination in employment and housing as those who had been here for generations were suspicious of these newcomers and their unfamiliar ways. Discrimination against different ethnic groups was not uncommon; for example, signs in shop windows appeared stating "Help Wanted—Irish Need Not Apply." In addition to the immigration from outside the borders, there was internal migration from the country farms to the cities as people searched for work. More than 2 million African Americans were part of this internal migration as they moved from the rural South to the urban North.[11] Following this internal immigration of over 6 million people from farmland to cities in search of work between 1920 and 1930, over half of the U.S. population resided in cities.[12]

The economy was volatile as well, with rises and falls in the stock market and monetary policy making the value of the currency fluctuate. There was little regulation of business and industry, and workers had few rights. Even in communities that passed local ordinances regarding conditions of work, there was inadequate enforcement. There were no sick days or vacation time. Work days for many were as long as 12 hours with a six-day work week, and conditions were dangerous. Accidents in factories were common where there were few safety measures. Jansson highlights these dangerous conditions with the following powerful comparison: "Approximately, 35,000 Americans were killed and 536,000 injured *each* year during the Progressive Era. In other words, the number of Americans injured in workplace accidents each year was about the same as the total of those killed or injured during the entire Vietnam conflict of the 1960s."[13] A disabled worker unable to return to work had no access to disability insurance or workers' compensation and was unlikely to win a disability lawsuit against an employer. Wages were low and so most families relied on more than one paycheck. Women and children worked in factories alongside men in these dangerous conditions. Steel plants, railroads, and mines were particularly dangerous workplaces.

Both work and living conditions in neighborhoods presented considerable challenges in urban areas. Ethnic gangs in cities added to high crime rates. Wooden tenement housing was crowded with families living together in two or three rooms with no indoor plumbing and poor ventilation. City sanitation was limited. Fires were a constant threat in wooden buildings built close together with limited fire protection from municipal departments. Box 2.4 details one such fire.

Dangerous work conditions led to calls for work-safety regulations.

Fledgling unions had begun organizing for a shorter work day and greater safety in the workplace, but even with modest reforms, the work-environment standards were far from what are accepted as minimal today. The emergent social work profession, unions, and other progressives began to press for greater social controls in the laissez-faire economy to protect individuals from some of the effects of the rapid increase in industrialization and urbanization. Dangerous work conditions led to calls for work-safety regulations. Unions reacted to business efforts toward union-busting by pressing for protections of trade unions. Workers, themselves with no protections, had no sick day or unemployment benefits, leading to efforts to provide greater economic security, such as sick pay, health insurance, and unemployment insurance. Extending economic security to workers' retirement years was a primary goal of reformers, who recognized that there was no social or economic safety net or pension for older citizens who became too frail to work. The passage of child labor laws restricting and regulating the employment of children and the growth of public schools were major achievements of this Progressive Era, resulting in new ways of conceptualizing children and child-development processes as well as the role of women in the raising of families. Box 2.5 lists major developments during this time.

The path set at this time by the two major strands of social work practice—settlement houses with their focus on research, community action, and social reform, and the charity organization societies with their focus on changing individuals and casework—created a false dichotomy within the profession about where the energy and focus of professional activity should be. For a profession that has recognized—from Mary Richmond's first writings—the person-in-environment or person-in-situation perspective, it is indeed a false dichotomy to think the profession can focus only on one (the individual) or the other (the environment). Person-in-environment speaks to the importance of helping both individuals and environments change so there is a better fit between the two. This idea is explored later in the text.

Box 2.4   The Triangle Shirtwaist Company Fire of 1911

The Triangle Waist Company, also known as the Shirtwaist Company, employed primarily Jewish and Italian immigrant workers in the early twentieth century. The Shirtwaist Company occupied the top three levels of the large 10-story Asch Building in downtown Manhattan, New York. Within this space, over 500 women and men (at about a 5:1 ratio) worked in poor sweatshop-like conditions for extended hours for less than adequate wages making women's shirtwaists.

Most workers, some as young as 15, had come with their families to the United States seeking a better life. They encountered grinding poverty and difficult living and working conditions in this urban environment. They were reluctant to join the unions emerging at the time to challenge such unsafe working conditions, fearful of losing even their low-wage jobs. A general strike in 1910 in New York City had established a grievance system for workers, but many employers continued to ignore basic safety considerations.

Just before closing on Saturday, March 25, 1911, a fire started on the top floors of the Asch Building, spreading rapidly. The horror and terror of that fire was forever burned into the memories of both survivors and witnesses on the street, as young women jumped from the top floors trying to escape. Escape routes in the building were blocked (some said deliberately locked to deter theft), ladders from fire trucks did not reach the top stories, and water from the hoses would not reach that high either. In all, 146 of the 500 employees died in the fire, one of the worst disasters in the City's history.

As a result of months of painstaking investigation and testimonials collected by the Women's Trade Union League, a Factory Investigation Commission was appointed to investigate the working conditions of area factories. The work of the commission, with contributions from Francis Perkins, the executive secretary of the New York Committee on Safety who had witnessed the fire, culminated in the awareness of and movement toward improving working conditions. Improvements in fire fighting and fire safety in buildings were additional results.

Still today the U.S. Department of Labor has uncovered an alarming number of violations to current labor and workplace safety laws. For example, 67 percent of garment factories in Los Angeles, CA, and 63 percent of garment factories in New York have been found to violate laws related to wages and overtime. In terms of health and safety, 98 percent of garment factories in Los Angeles, CA, have been recognized as being seriously problematic. New immigrant workers continue to be exploited by unscrupulous employers who put profit above worker safety and living wages.

Sources: The Columbia Electronic Encyclopedia. Triangle Waist Company. Columbia University Press. (2007), www.infoplease.com/ce6/history/A0930651.html (accessed January 25, 2008) and Kheel Center for Labor-Management Documentation and Archives (Online), Cornell University/ILR. "The Triangle Factory Fire." March 2, 2002, www.ilr.cornell.edu/trianglefire/ (accessed January 25, 2008). With contributions by Ross Manning, Indiana University School of Social Work Ph.D. Student.

Box 2.5   Key Events, Court Cases, and Legislation During the Progressive Era

- 1886 The first settlement house established in the United States in New York, patterned after Toynbee Hall in London, England

- 1889 Jane Addams and Ellen Gates Starr opened Hull House in Chicago

- 1896 *Plessy v. Ferguson* established separate services for African Americans

- 1899 Juvenile court first established in Cook County, Illinois; Mary Richmond's handbook for charity workers, *Friendly Visiting Among the Poor,* published

- 1908 Workers' compensation passed by Congress, U.S. first social insurance program

- 1911 Illinois enacted first state mothers' pension program; Washington enacted first workers' compensation program upheld by courts

- 1912 Julia Lathrop became first chief of Children's Bureau

- 1916 Congress passed child labor legislation, later overruled by the Supreme Court; first birth-control clinic opened by Margaret Sanger

- 1917 Illinois opened first department of public welfare

- 1918 Vocational Rehabilitation Act passed for veterans, later extended to civilians

- 1920 Women gained the vote through 19th Amendment to Constitution

SOCIAL WORK'S FIRST RETREAT
FROM POLICY PRACTICE

Subsequent to its beginnings as a profession in the settlement houses and charity organization societies where it was engaged in policy practice work, social work turned its attention inward as leaders worked to establish its identity and recognition as a profession during the greater prosperity of the 1920s. Social work sought to model itself after medicine and engineering, which were successfully applying science to solve practical problems. At a national conference in 1915, Dr. Abraham Flexner, recognized authority on graduate education, had spoken on the topic "Is Social Work a Profession?" and had concluded that it was a calling for good-hearted people, but not a profession since it had no unique method that required advanced education.[14] Not surprisingly, social workers jumped to the defense of the profession in a number of ways.

The first "school" of social work had actually been established by the New York Charity Organization Society when it initiated a summer education program in 1898, the Summer School of Philanthropy, for those already working in the field.[15] That was one year after Mary Richmond had proposed starting a "training school in applied philanthropy"[16] to bring new social workers into the profession. The summer program was expanded to a full year and later became the Columbia University Graduate School of Social Work. Other such schools were developed, and by 1910, the five largest cities in the United States had schools of social work, all but the one in Chicago, developed by charity organization societies, with their focus on casework practices and field work. The Chicago program, with its roots in the settlement house movement, placed greater emphasis on research, policy, and public welfare. Social work leaders from the settlement house tradition pushed for affiliation with universities and curricula more consistent with American higher education. In 1920, the first accrediting body for social work programs was established by the 17 schools then in existence.[17] In June 2010, there were 471 Bachelor in Social Work (BSW) programs and 201 Masters in Social Work (MSW) programs accredited by the Council on Social Work Education.[18]

In 1929, participants at the Milford Conference declared social casework social work's generic method.

Mary Richmond applied the medical model of diagnosis and treatment of disease to social work practice within the context of the charity organizations. Her 500-page book, *Social Diagnosis,* originally published in 1917, was the first effort to document the theory and practice of social work. A tremendous success, "[a]lmost overnight, social diagnosis or casework became the method of social work and the badge of professionalism, overshadowing even to this day all other techniques in the field."[19] In 1929, participants at the Milford Conference declared social casework social work's generic method.[20] This focus on the individual was reinforced when Americans began to learn about the theories of Sigmund Freud. As Katz noted,

> In the 1920s Freudian psychology moved casework away from Richmond's concern with the environment and toward a focus on personality. With Freudian psychology, social work could bypass the new social and economic theories that had undercut scientific charity and return with scientific authority to individual explanations for dependence; it needed only to substitute personality for character and to add sex to drink. Needless to say, any passion for social reform vanished in the process.[21]

Other events contributed to this lack of social activism by the profession. The social unrest that led to Progressive reforms in the United States also had some more radical elements within it that frightened some of those in power. More radical labor unions, such as the International Workers of the World (the Wobblies) had close ties to eastern Europe, with leaders who were recent immigrants from Russia and other eastern European countries and influenced by some of the more radical political movements there. When Russia erupted in its revolution of 1917, those in power in the United States became more fearful about the social unrest here, particularly during the Red Scare of 1919–1920. Reformists were suspect. When many settlement house social workers, Jane Addams most prominently, opposed the United States' entry into World War I and then tried to bring an end to the fighting, they found declining support for the settlements among those who questioned their patriotism.[22] The recession immediately after the war and an upsurge of conservatism made reform and social change less popular in the country and among social workers.

DEPRESSION AND THE NEW DEAL

The next major involvement of social work in policy practice was helping develop the programs designed to alleviate the tremendous needs created by the Great Depression. After the stock market crash of 1929, many people lost their jobs and found they had few ways to support their families. The existing local social service agencies of the time were overwhelmed with the demand for material services, food, and shelter. Some families left communities in the East and Midwest and headed west looking for a more prosperous future, in much the same way that Latino families today come into the United States, both legally and illegally, in search of better lives for themselves and their families. A major drought in the Midwest and the plains intensified this internal migration. "Hoovervilles," shanty encampments named after President Hoover, adjacent to the railroads, became home to the hobos who passed through in search of work. The Hoovervilles contributed to the rising sense of social chaos that spurred the federal authorities to adopt the Social Security Act of 1935.

Many of the young men and women who had learned about social problems and issues through their work in the settlement house movement now began to address the overwhelming need for creating jobs, putting people to work, and giving people a stake in their own futures as well as in society as a whole. Perhaps in the settlements they had learned the lesson that hopelessness and helplessness would only lead to additional social chaos, and so settlement house workers became committed to social change on a societal level, creating a new wave of policy practice.

The list of the people coming out of the settlement house movement who went on to develop lasting social welfare policy at the national level is impressive, suggesting that experience in seeing and understanding the poverty and struggles of particularly hardworking immigrant populations firsthand had a profound impact on the young college-aged people involved. The settlement house experience shaped how young workers understood the roots of poverty and the need for change at the highest levels of government. Florence Kelley, who worked at Hull House, later served as the director of National Consumer League and was a member of the National Child Labor Committee. Lillian Wald and Florence Kelley helped prepare for the 1909 White House Conference on Children. Mary White Ovington helped organize the National Association for the Advancement of Colored People (NAACP) at Henry Street Settlement in Chicago. She authored *Half a Man,* a New York City study that clearly documented

Practice
Contexts

Critical Thinking Question

What experiences could
have influenced so many
former settlement house
workers to see the need
for a federal role in crafting the New Deal?

discrimination against African Americans. Other settlement house workers spoke
out against the discrimination they observed. Former settlement house workers
also helped draft the Progressive Party's 1912 platform, which included a number of "minimums" for an industrialized society, including such provisions as an
eight-hour work day, a six-day work week, prohibitions of child labor and piecework
at home, etc.[23]

The architects of the New Deal legislation that established the federal role
in social welfare policymaking and service delivery were social workers from the
settlement house movement. Harry Hopkins and Frances Perkins (see Box 2.6
for more about Frances Perkins) both had their early training in the settlements.
Frances Perkins became the director of the Council on Immigrant Education and
the first secretary of Labor. Edith Abbott, president of the National Conference
of Social Welfare and dean of University of Chicago School of Social Service
Administration, was a participant in the drafting of the Social Security Act.

Box 2.6   Those Crucial Jobless Benefits? Thank Frances Perkins[i]

BY KIRSTIN DOWNEY
WeNews correspondent

*Editor's Note: The following is a commentary. The opinions expressed are
those of the author and not necessarily the views of Women's Enews.*

(WOMENSENEWS)—At 10 a.m. on a recent chilly
morning, more than 150 workers stood along the side
of the road in Fairfax County, an affluent suburb of
Washington, D.C. They were huddled against the wind,
peering into the windows of passing cars, hoping for
work. Motorists sped by quickly, looking away, to avoid
attracting attention and raising false hopes.

Unemployed laborers are a frightening sight to
those who are still working.

On Friday, the ranks of the still-employed were
found to be thinner than ever when the Department of
Labor reported that unemployment had skyrocketed in
April to 8.9 percent, the highest rate in 25 years, up
from 8.5 percent the previous month. About 13.7 million people in the United States are jobless.

It is in alarming times like these that some of the
key programs of the New Deal demonstrate their continuing significance and highlight how much Americans continue to rely on solutions fashioned then in
response to lessons learned, in times that seem eerily
similar to our own.

It is also in alarming times like these that the system's inadequacies are laid bare.

For U.S. workers, the economic shock absorber
system is unemployment insurance. It is the Federal
Emergency Management Agency of economic hurricanes, and it is keeping more than 6 million individual
workers afloat during these bad times.

Canny Social Worker

The unemployment insurance system was propelled
into existence by Frances Perkins, the canny but little-
known social worker who was President Franklin D.
Roosevelt's secretary of labor.

She had studied the U.S. economy for 20 years
before she took up her Cabinet post and she was
FDR's industrial commissioner from 1928 to 1932
while he was governor of New York. Together they
watched the Great Depression arrive and cast its
shadow across the U.S. landscape.

Perkins is most famous today for her role as primary architect of Social Security.

But in 1933 and 1934, the program she champi-
oned most fiercely of all was unemployment insurance. Now it has become a first line of defense against
capitalism's ruthless pattern of boom and bust cycles.

Perkin's role in establishing a safety net for
unemployed workers is largely forgotten. It's time to
change that.

Millions of people today will pay their bills and eat their
dinner because of her handiwork. Regardless of political
ideology, they have reason to offer her their thanks.

---

[i]From Women's eNews [womensenewstoday@womensenews.org], sent on 5-12-09.

Damping Boom-Bust Cycles

Perkins and FDR had lived through at least three similar boom and bust cycles: in 1893, in 1907, and in the early 1920s. They wanted to blunt the worst of the hardship average people suffered when the downturns hit.

Unemployment insurance is a program designed to help workers who lose their jobs through no fault of their own, so they can keep their families fed while they look for new jobs. It is a short-term program, because Perkins and FDR had complete faith in capitalism's ultimate recovery.

It was part of the package of social safety proposals, including Social Security, engineered by Perkins and FDR and enacted in 1935. Perkins brought her drive and commitment to the effort and FDR won the political support that allowed the package to be piloted to passage.

At the time, unemployment insurance was attacked as a socialist scheme. In some right-wing circles, it continues to be excoriated. But people of every political stripe are usually more than happy to line up for their checks when they find themselves out of work.

Failings to Still Fix

The state-federal unemployment program Perkins and Roosevelt devised is far from perfect though.

Perkins was disappointed in its failings at the end of her life. Some states are generous to their jobless workers; other states give them only a pittance.

The biggest payment a worker in Tennessee can get is $275 a week, but a worker doing the same kind of job in Kentucky can get $415 weekly, according to a recent Labor Department study. Arizona's maximum benefit is $240 weekly, but in neighboring New Mexico, the highest benefit is $455 a week.

In addition, hordes of workers are unfairly excluded from the system by rules that pretend the workers don't exist. Many undocumented immigrants, like some of those day laborers standing along the road in Fairfax County, aren't covered because their employers never paid payroll taxes on their behalf. People mislabeled "independent contractors"—even though they labor side-by-side with payroll employees—are out of luck as well.

The Labor Department's reports highlight the discrepancy.

On top of the 13.7 million workers counted as jobless in April, an additional 2.1 million have become so discouraged in their job hunts that they have stopped looking. That adds up to 15.8 million jobless.

But the unemployment insurance system is providing benefits to only 6.4 million.

Recent news reports, meanwhile, have highlighted crashing computer systems, malfunctioning voicemail trees and bureaucratic snafus in many states that are preventing people from getting benefits in a timely manner.

Frances Perkins would be outraged by reports of workers waiting weeks or months for their checks, by phones ringing unanswered and stories of desperate workers dangling in Internet hell as they try to file claims electronically. Reform is needed. If Perkins were alive today, heads would roll.

Kirstin Downey, a former economics reporter at the *Washington Post,* is the author of "The Woman Behind the New Deal: The Life of Frances Perkins, FDR's Secretary of Labor and His Moral Conscience." For more information, visit www.kirstindowney.com.

Women's eNews welcomes your comments. E-mail us at editors@womensenews.org.

Grace Abbott, organizer of the first White House Conference on Children, also contributed to the drafting of the Social Security Act.[24]

These social work pioneers "cut their social work teeth" in the settlement house movement, working on the community level, and then went on to work for social change efforts at the national level of policy practice. Jane Addams even earned international recognition for her advocacy for peace initiatives when she was awarded the Nobel Peace Prize in 1931. In addition, the number of social workers grew through the 1930s from 31,000 to 70,000. The number of social work professional organizations grew as well, representing medical social workers, school social workers, psychiatric social workers, and others.[25] Box 2.7 lists key policy changes for this era.

- 1929 Crash of the stock market and beginning of the Great Depression
- 1929–1932 Hoover presidency
- 1931 Governor Roosevelt in New York established the Temporary Emergency Relief Administration, prototype for federal relief for unemployed
- 1932 Reconstruction Finance Corporation lent funds to states for relief work
- 1933–1945 Roosevelt presidency
- 1933 Civilian Conservation Corps (CCC) and Federal Emergency Relief Administration (FERA) established
- 1934 Securities and Exchange Commission (SEC) created; first Housing Act passed
- 1935 FERA terminated, Social Security Act passed, including Aid to Dependent Children (ADC), Old Age Assistance (OAA), Aid to the Blind (AB), unemployment insurance, Social Security (retirement), child welfare, and public health programs; Supreme Court declared National Recovery Administration (NRA) unconstitutional; Works Progress Administration established
- 1936 Wagner Act passed establishing the National Labor Relations Board
- 1937 Wagner-Steagall Housing Act passed
- 1938 Fair Labor Standards Act passed
- Early 1940s CCC and WPA ended
- 1941 U.S. entered World War II, Roosevelt prohibited discrimination in war industry with Executive Order 8802

SECOND RETREAT FROM ACTIVISM BY THE PROFESSION

After World War II, many social workers turned away from policy practice and focused more on providing mental health and family social services in local communities, only to reenter policy practice with work on the civil rights movement and the War on Poverty in the 1960s. Important social programs targeting particular groups were developed in the postwar era, including the Veteran's Administration and the GI Bill of Rights (1944) that helped World War II–returning veterans with medical bills, education costs, and housing loans. There was general support for this economic investment in the returning soldiers as the country rebuilt its civilian work force. Having GIs in school earning degrees so they could compete for better-paying jobs also strengthened the economy, serving a macro purpose. Additional legislation of this period included the Vocational Rehabilitation Act of 1954, the National Mental Health Act of 1946, the Hospital Survey and Construction Act (Hill-Burton Act) of 1946, and the National School Lunch Program of 1946. The U.S. Department of Health, Education, and Welfare was established in 1953.

In the post–World War II era, the social work profession turned inward again and worked to unite itself organizationally. The seven professional associations merged in 1955 to form the National Association of Social Workers (NASW)[26] to serve as a united voice for social work professionals working in a wide range of settings and with individuals, groups, families, and communities. While other groups of social workers have formed since that time, NASW has remained the leading voice of the profession, particularly with regard to its advocacy efforts. In recent years, NASW entered into discussions with social work education organizations and others to attempt a "reunification" of professional organizations, but that effort appears to be at a standstill.

SOCIAL REFORMS OF THE 1960s

Social work leaders began calling for a return to activism when new ground was being broken in civil rights in the mid-1950s. The U.S. Supreme Court decision in *Brown v. Board of Education* struck down the "separate but equal" doctrine in public education in 1954. Social worker Whitney Young, later the director of the Nation Urban League, in addressing the National Conference on Social Welfare stated that "social work was born in an atmosphere of righteous indignation," but that "somewhere along the line 'the urge to become professional' had overcome the initial crusading impulse." He called upon the profession to reclaim the "lost heritage" of its founders.[27]

When John F. Kennedy was elected president in 1961, he inspired a new generation of young people to care about the poor and disenfranchised and become involved in community service and social action, in much the same way that the Obama campaign inspired young voters to participate in the political process in 2008. There was a renewed sense of hope about tackling some of the more persistent problems in society.

In the mid-1960s, social workers again took leadership positions by participating in local organizing efforts in the civil rights movement that started with advocacy for local changes (integration of public transportation, schools, restaurants, and other public places) and then developed pressure upward for national change in voting and other rights. Rosa Parks staying in her seat on the bus was initially challenging a local rule about "colored people" sitting in the back of the bus. But used strategically, this local action set off a chain of events leading to national change in civil rights laws. When a critical mass is reached in state and local reforms, it is not unusual then to see the federal government embrace the change as well.

Although Rosa Parks (see Box 2.8) was not a social worker, she was trained at the Highlander School in methods of nonviolent protest and civil disobedience, where many civil rights activists (including social workers) had their training. Michael Schwerner, a social worker and community organizer, was killed during a voter registration drive in Mississippi. Other not-so-famous social workers worked with other civil rights workers on a variety of campaigns and efforts. Whitney Young, Jr., social worker and director of the National Urban League during the 1960s and 1970s, was one of organizers of the 1963 March on Washington where Dr. Martin Luther King, Jr. delivered his famous "I have a dream" speech.

Box 2.8   Slice of History: The True Story of Rosa Parks

"**M**ost historians date the beginning of the modern civil rights movement in the United States to December 1, 1955. That was the day when an unknown seamstress in Montgomery, Alabama, refused to give up her bus seat to a white passenger. This brave woman, Rosa Parks, was arrested and fined for violating a city ordinance, but her lonely act of defiance began a movement that ended legal segregation in America, and made her an inspiration to freedom-loving people everywhere."[1]

Many biographies of Rosa Parks and histories of the civil rights movement start off in a similar manner,

[1]Academy of Achievement. "Rosa Parks Biography: Pioneer of Civil Rights." (Online) November 2, 2005, www.achievement.org/autodoc/page/par0bio-1 (accessed July 7, 2007).

(Continued)

Box 2.8   Slice of History: The True Story of Rosa Parks (*Continued*)

implying that Rosa Parks was a lone woman acting not out of conviction, but on impulse that day in 1955, when she was tired and suddenly became fed up. In reality, Rosa Parks was deeply involved in the beginnings of the civil rights movement in Montgomery along with others in that community who were organizing years before the bus boycott began. As Jon Greenbaum of Metro Justice in Rochester, New York, wrote when Rosa Parks died in 2005, "Rosa Parks was not tired that day. Rosa Parks was a graduate of the legendary Highlander Center for grassroots organizing. Rosa Parks was a leader of a powerful grassroots organization."[2]

Rosa Parks was born on February 4, 1913, in Tuskegee, Alabama. In addition to being a farmer, her father was a carpenter, and her mother was a teacher. She attended rural schools until age 11 when she was able to enroll in a private school that taught a philosophy of self-worth. Later, Rosa had to drop out of high school to help her family when her grandmother became ill, so she did not graduate from high school until she was 21. She attended Alabama State Teachers College and later moved to Montgomery with her husband Raymond Parks. There they joined the National Association for the Advancement of Colored People (NAACP), where her civil rights work started. She helped organize youth and helped with a voter-registration campaign.

Rosa Parks was the secretary in her local chapter of the NAACP and worked on several cases to challenge the system of segregation and the treatment of African Americans in the South. While these previous cases did not gain much publicity, the NAACP had been looking for some time for a test case to challenge the segregation of the races in the public transportation system. In the summer of 1955 Rosa Parks attended a workshop on school integration at the Highlander Folk School in rural Tennessee, founded in 1932 by Myles Horton who believed that the solutions to problems lay in the experiences and skills of the people experiencing the problems.

The day that she refused to give up her seat on the bus was just one in a series of attempts to change the system in Montgomery. At that time, the first four rows of seats on the bus were reserved for whites.

After they paid their fares at the front of the bus, black riders were then required to exit and reboard at the back of the bus. Though 75 percent of the riders were black, they were to give up their seats and stand if more seats were needed for whites. Several confrontations with blacks refusing or complaining about giving up their seats resulted in ejections from the bus, including one in 1943 when Rosa Parks was ejected, ironically by the same man who was driving the bus and had her arrested for her defiance later in 1955.

The local NAACP had planned to challenge the arrest of a 15-year-old girl who had refused to give up her seat, but when the young woman became pregnant the chapter decided they needed a different symbol for their cause. Rosa Parks was seen as a hard-working citizen who was contributing to her community through her work with youth. As it turned out, Rosa's refusal and arrest proved to be the spark needed to galvanize the community. The bus boycott was organized for December 5, the day of Rosa Parks' trial, with 35,000 leaflets being distributed in neighborhoods, an article appearing in the black newspaper, and announcement made from church pulpits urging people to boycott the buses.

The next day some people rode in carpools, some rode in black-owned taxis, but most walked to work. At the rally that evening, the community agreed to keep up the boycott until seating on the buses was on a first-come basis and black drivers were hired. The boycott lasted 381 days. The Supreme Court struck down segregation on buses on November 13, 1956, in *Browder v. Gayle*.

Rosa continued to work as a seamstress until 1965, when she was hired as an aide to Representative John Conyers, Jr. after she and her husband moved to Detroit. She retired in 1988 but continued to make appearances on behalf of civil rights efforts. She died in Detroit on October 24, 2005.

Sources: Shipp, E.R. "Rosa Parks, 92, Founding Symbol of Civil Rights Movement, Dies." *New York Times Online.* October 25, 2005. www.nytimes.com/2005/10/25/national/25parks.html; and Toonari Corporation (Online). "Rosa Parks." July 7, 2007. www.africanaonline.com/rosa_parks.htm.

[2]Posted on Metro Justice website, http://metrojustice.org (accessed October 25, 2005).

Our country has a pattern of finally rectifying oppressive conditions when there is a violent uprising or when such a potential for violence takes hold in communities. The riots in the cities in the 1960s led to the passage of major civil rights legislation, for example. It will be interesting to see if the 2008 economic crisis after the election of President Barack Obama and the subsequent economic bailouts and stimulus plans will create a nonviolent uprising and support for the next opportunity to embrace a positive role for government in social welfare.

Just as the settlement house movement served as the training ground for many who helped to develop the provisions of the Social Security Act, many of those young professionals involved in the New Deal became the leaders in the development of the social programs of the 1960s. For example, Wilbur Cohen, first employee at Social Security Board in 1935, helped design the War on Poverty, and worked on passage of Medicare and Medicaid in 1965. He also served as secretary of the Department of Health, Education, and Welfare during Johnson's administration from 1968 to 1969.[28]

The War on Poverty programs, though they mandated the "maximum feasible participation" of poor people, were nevertheless in the control of the "experts" in most communities and never realized their promise. They were underfunded from the beginning. Head Start, even today, is not funded at a level in most communities to be able to accept all the children who meet income guidelines. In 2006, for example, only 3 percent of eligible children were enrolled in Early Head Start.[29] In summing up the impact of the 1960s (see Box 2.9), Day states, "Perhaps the most enduring lesson is that the threat of rebellion engenders accommodation, but when its force is dissipated, denial of services recurs . . . . [T]he Decade of the Dream—of freedom and social justice—did happen. The shame is that, unless repression becomes severe enough to cause rebellion, it may not happen again."[30]

Policy Practice

Critical Thinking Question

In current policy debates, what are the arguments being made for and against an increased federal role in social welfare and human rights legislation?

Box 2.9   Key Events, Court Cases, and Legislation in Response to the Social and Economic Challenges from World War II Through the 1960s

▶ 1942 Japanese Americans sent to relocation centers

▶ 1954 *Brown v. Board of Education* Supreme Court decision struck down "separate but equal" doctrine and mandated integration in the public schools

▶ 1955 Bus boycott in Montgomery, Alabama, marked the beginning of the civil rights movement

▶ 1956 *Browder v. Gayle* Supreme Court decision struck down segregation in public transportation

▶ 1960–1963 Kennedy presidency

▶ 1961 Juvenile Delinquency and Youth Offenses Control Act passed

▶ 1963 Mental Retardation and Community Mental Health Centers Construction Act passed; civil rights march on Washington

▶ 1964 Economic Opportunity Act, Food Stamps Act, and Civil Rights Act passed

▶ 1965 Social Security amendments (Medicare and Medicaid), Elementary and Secondary Education Act, Civil Rights Act, and Older Americans Act passed

▶ 1965–1969 Chavez began organizing farm workers

▶ 1966 Narcotic Addict Rehabilitation Act passed

▶ 1967 Work amendments added to Aid to Families with Dependent Children, *In re Gault* court decision

▶ 1969 Stonewall riots marked the beginning of the gay rights movement; Nixon proposed the Family Assistance Plan

SOCIAL WORKERS DOING POLICY PRACTICE—SOME EFFORTS OF THE LAST FORTY YEARS

As the country shifted to more conservative stances starting in the early 1970s, social work as a profession again seemed to shift away from active engagement in policy practice and turn inward for the third time. Many state NASW chapters focused on developing state laws and regulations to license social workers to practice in particular fields, particularly the growing area of mental health services. At first, these laws licensed only MSW social workers, but some states found roles for undergraduates as well in their service delivery systems. These developments pushed the Council on Social Work Education (the accrediting body for MSW programs) to begin accrediting BSW programs in 1974. In addition to attempting to protect the public from untrained people calling themselves social workers and practicing without the proper credentials, licensure provided the avenue for third-party (insurance) reimbursements for social work in mental health services. Managed care efforts, such as the institution of the Diagnostic Related Groups (DRGs) (see Box 2.10), began to surface as a way to contain rising health care costs.

Evidence of social work involvement in advocacy during this time, beyond what was carried out at the state level around licensure and other professional issues, is difficult to locate. James Wolk found in his 1981 study that social workers were no more politically active than other professionals, engaging in traditional political activities such as writing letters and participating in political campaigns.[31] In fact, Harry Specht and Mark E. Courtney wrote a critical[32] indictment of the profession, *Unfaithful Angels: How Social Work has Abandoned Its Mission,* in 1994, charging that social work had seriously retreated from its roots in advocacy, particularly advocacy for programs to address the persistent problem of poverty and economic justice. By embracing psychotherapy and clinical models of social work practice, Specht and Courtney asserted that social work

---

Box 2.10   Definition of Diagnostic Related Groups (DRGs)

Diagnostic Related Groups were developed by the federal Health Care Financing Administration to set expectations about the costs of hospital procedures and stays based on common patient characteristics such as diagnoses, specific procedures, age, sex, and discharge status. This standardization of the process was an early attempt to control rising costs of medical care, particularly for those receiving Medicare.

---

had not only lost its mission to work with low-income people, but also lost the community focus that had been central in its early development. They were skeptical about the profession's ability to reform itself and suggested instead a new federal commitment to the development of community care centers to provide services and engender greater community engagement.

Lowe and Reid,[33] in their collection of essays, provided some additional challenges to the profession and its advocacy work. David Stoesz criticized the profession's embrace of welfare statism (modeled on the Western European Social Democratic models of government assistance) as a way to ameliorate the social problems resulting from capitalism and rejecting welfare capitalism (provision of a benefit system of health insurance, pensions, etc.) tied to business and employment. He dates this fateful choice back to the Progressive Era. "In retrospect," he writes, "such romanticism is a little naïve. Yet, despite serious inconsistencies, it continued to guide social work in matters of social policy for decades. In its welfare state utopianism, social work erred in not recognizing that American social programs were located in a capitalist economy. Social Security, for example, mimicked private retirement funds already established by American business."[34] Stoesz then urges social work to regain its voice for social justice by adopting a different policy practice agenda. He states,

> [A] neoprogressive effort to accelerate the upward mobility of the poor, allow them choice in service provision, while dismantling the welfare bureaucracy would have significant and multiple benefits. Poor consumers would know that their perceptions were being respected; the public would appreciate the profession's willingness to make taxpayers' resources more accountable; and politicians would perceive social work and the programs it manages as being an integral component of community development.[35]

Conservative approaches to the provision of social services continued to persist into the 1990s. The passage of Temporary Assistance for Needy Families (TANF), welfare reform, in 1996, moved public policy away from an entitlement program (Aid to Families with Dependent Children [AFDC]) to one that was time-limited in an effort to push single mothers to join the workforce. TANF was passed at a time of growing prosperity; TANF recipients were able to find jobs and leave the welfare rolls, though they did not necessarily succeed in escaping poverty. Average earnings for those leaving TANF have been documented as below the poverty level.[36] Employment rates in the first year of follow-up studies of TANF leavers ranged from 55 to 65 percent.[37] What happens to those who are no longer employed but have used up their benefits is not entirely clear as they are a difficult population to reach in follow-up studies.

The passage of TANF was symbolic of the new approach to social welfare, insisting on "personal responsibility" to force recipients into the low-wage market, frequently without the benefit of health insurance for children or other

Many of those who moved off the welfare roles remained in poverty and struggled with daily life.

benefits considered part of contemporary capitalist welfare programs. Many of those who moved off the welfare roles remained in poverty and struggled with daily life. This new approach diminished ideas about the social responsibility of a society to provide jobs at a living wage or universal access to health care. Box 2.11 lists the major policy changes for this time.

Only gradually have social workers started to respond to the severe cutbacks and dramatic changes in social services of the Reagan-Bush administrations. While efforts at the national level have not been as effective as desired, some local and state efforts have been more successful.[38] Wolk suggested that the profession may not be as effective in legislative advocacy as desired because social workers lack the requisite political skills.[39] He also theorizes that social workers become more involved when the political climate is more receptive to social work values and when there is greater peer group influence.[40] In 1998, Dr. Robert Schneider, then professor at Virginia Commonwealth University School of Social Work, established Influencing State Policy to help social work faculty develop student skills in advocacy work at the state level as a way of increasing the policy practice within the profession. At least one MSW program has developed a concentration in political social work.[41] Recently, the Council on Social Work

Box 2.11 Key Events, Court Cases, and Legislation in Response to the Social and Economic Challenges from 1970s to Present Day

- 1970 Family Planning and Population Research Act and Occupational Safety and Health Act (OSHA) passed
- 1971 Federal eligibility standards for Food Stamps established; Comprehensive Child Development Act passed
- 1972 Social Security indexed to inflation (COLAs) and Supplemental Security Income (SSI) established; Revenue Sharing passed; Equal Employment Opportunity Act passed; *Wyatt v. Stickney* established "right to treatment"
- 1973 Comprehensive Employment and Training Act (CETA) passed, Food Stamps federalized; *Roe v. Wade* decision legalizing abortion
- 1974 Juvenile Justice and Delinquency Prevention Act passed and Title XX (providing social services) added to the Social Security Act
- 1975 Education for All Handicapped Children passed
- 1978 Tax revolt resulted in Proposition 13 passing in California
- 1979 Office of Education created and HEW reorganized to be the Department of Health and Human Services (DHHS)
- 1980 Adoption Assistance and Child Welfare Act and Mental Health Systems Act passed
- 1980–1988 Reagan presidency

- 1981 Omnibus Budget Reconciliation Act cut social services and created block grants to the states; Economic Recovery Tax Act cut corporate and personal income taxes
- 1990 Americans with Disabilities Act passed
- 2001–2009 Bush presidency
- 2001 $1.3 trillion tax cut passed; September 11 attack on World Trade Center towers
- 2002 Office of Faith Based and Community Initiatives created
- 2003 Supreme Court upheld affirmative action and struck down anti-sodomy law; drug benefit added to Medicare, invasion of Iraq
- 2004 Women, Infants, and Children (WIC) program reauthorized
- 2005 *Roper v. Simmons* prohibited death penalty for youth under 18 years, TANF reauthorized
- 2006 Medicare D Prescription Plan began
- 2007 Higher Minimum Wage passed, Head Start expanded, No Child Left Behind reauthorized, State Children's Health Insurance Program (SCHIP) reauthorized after two Bush vetoes
- 2009 Lily Ledbetter Fair Pay Act of 2009 passed
- 2010 Patient Protection and Affordable Care Act (health care reform) passed

---

Box 2.12   Case Study

So what difference can a social worker make as a legislator? Look at some of the bills Representative Joe Micon, MSW, of the Indiana General Assembly authored in the 2007 legislative session that were passed by both chambers and then signed by the governor: extension of the Low Income Heating and Energy Assistance Program, protection against identity theft, and expansion of tax breaks for the use of alternative fuels.

Source: State Representative Joe Micon, News from the Statehouse, www.in.gov/legislative/house_democrats/repsites/r26/R26.html. (accessed May 20, 2007).

Education has mandated policy practice as part of the generalist practice curriculum for all social workers. NASW, at the national level, has increased its advocacy, and some state chapters are doing the same. Mini Abramovitz expressed some hope for future social work advocacy involvement: "Social work now may be better positioned to join those who fight back. It has matured and won the battle for recognition and can devote more resources to social reform . . . . Unlike in the past, social work also has a large membership base, considerable political expertise, and the organizational infrastructure necessary for a proactive stance."[42] Box 2.12 demonstrates the difference a social worker can make.

TODAY'S SOCIAL WORKERS IN POLICY PRACTICE

More than 190 (most likely an under report) social workers were directly involved in policy practice in their roles on local government boards and councils, state legislative bodies, and the U.S. Senate in 2008.[43] Barbara Mikulski, MSW (D-MD) was the first Democratic woman elected to the U.S. Senate in her own right (not serving out a deceased spouse's term), and now Debbie Stabenow (D-MI) is the second social worker elected to the U.S. Senate. Both of these social workers carry their social work values and ethics into their deliberations about the policies that will best serve their constituents' interests. The opportunities for social workers to run for office continue to expand through the financial support of state PACE (Political Action for Candidate Election) committees that endorse candidates who support social work values and provide some financial support in key races. Chapter 12 includes discussion about running for office and working within the legislative process.

As discussed earlier, there are some signs that more social workers are becoming engaged in policy practice, including both legislative activity and political campaigns, but much of that recent evidence is anecdotal and not based on systematic research.

Ethical Practice

Critical Thinking Question

If you were to run for state legislator, what issues would be important and how would the Code of Ethics influence your position on those issues?

LOOKING AT FUTURE POLICY PRACTICE

In making a call for smaller government and government programs more responsive to the needs of people at the end of the twentieth century, Stoesz and others could not foresee the economic downturn of 2008 and the need for government intervention in business as well as human services to stabilize the economy. By deregulating business, reducing taxes, and privatizing many social services during the George W. Bush administration, capitalism became vulnerable and suffered the greatest downturn since the Great Depression. At the same time, there was a decline in direct government programs directed toward those in need during the Reagan and first Bush (George H. W.) administrations, and an effort to grow the entrepreneurial and for-profit human service sector through contracting out social services from government. No doubt this new sector will be an important one in the future of policy development.

Chapter 7 provides a discussion of how the Obama campaign used the new media (e-mail, Web sites, etc.) in the election of 2008 as both a fundraising and campaign tool. Their Web organizing continued after the election, during the transition, and into the new administration as a way to involve supporters in ongoing work in communities and in continued political participation. For example in Bloomington, Indiana, the new Volunteers for Change organization that evolved from the campaign started going door-to-door in neighborhoods collecting canned goods and donations for the Hoosier Hills Food Bank. From November 2008 to May 2009, they collected over 5,500 pounds of food and $5000 in donations.[44] Social workers have been involved in such local grass-roots efforts as well as in efforts to influence a variety of policy issues.

As a newly elected President Barack Obama prepared to take office, NASW presented his transition team with their document: *Turning Priorities into Action: How the Social Work Profession Will Help*.[45] This transition document outlined the policy priorities of the profession and offered the assistance of social workers in their implementation. Box 2.13 summarizes those priorities.

It will be interesting to assess how effective social work will be in this effort to reestablish its role in the national policy development process. As you study policy practice, you will be able to assess how well NASW and other professional associations have energized social work practitioners to become more involved in policy practice. Active engagement by social workers and citizens across the country will make a difference in the policies that are enacted and create a more functional and participatory democracy in the process.

Box 2.13   NASW 2009 Policy Priorities for Obama Administration

- Reviving the economy
  - Enact pay equity for women
  - Reduce child poverty
  - Provide offender re-entry programs
  - Reform immigration policy
- Fixing our health care system[1]
  - Expand the State Children's Health Insurance Program
  - Provide affordable, accessible, and high-quality health care to all
  - Address health inequities
- Fixing our education system
  - Provide increased services to address students, biopsychosocial needs
- Fixing our social security system
  - Preserve Social Security and expand income resources for retirees

- Ending the war in Iraq and finishing our mission in Afghanistan
  - Provide essential behavioral health services to active duty military and veterans
- International peacekeeping and community development
  - Support international exchange
- Utilizing social workers to build communities
- Equality for all

---

[1]On March 23, 2010, President Obama signed the Patient Protection and Affordable Care Act, known as health care reform. This legislation mandates that most people purchase health insurance beginning in 2014, including coverage through health insurance exchanges for those without access to employer-based insurance, and credits for some with limited incomes. In addition, health insurers are prohibited from denying coverage or charging higher premiums due to pre-existing conditions and Medicaid will be expanded to cover those at 133% of the federal poverty level for people under age 65.

(*Source:* The Henry J. Kaiser Family Foundation, Focus on Health Care Reform (2020). http://www.kff.org/healthreform/upload/8023-R.pdf (accessed October 23, 2010). NASW celebrated this health care legislation, stating, "this is a significant step toward a comprehensive and universal health care system for our nation long envisioned by social work pioneer Frances Perkins, Pres. Franklin Roosevelt's Secretary of Labor. NASW also acknowledges that further improvements remain necessary for the system, but the additional coverage of 32 million Americans is a monumental legislative achievement of our time." (*Source*: https://ssl.capwiz.com/socialworkers/issues/alert/?alertid=14849131 (accessed October 23, 2010)).

Source: NASW, *Turning Priorities into Action: How the Social Work Profession Will Help* (2009). www.socialworkers.org (accessed May 5, 2009).

CONCLUSION

After over a century of policy practice work within the social work profession, social workers have made a difference at the national level in creating a more just social and economic environment for families and individuals of all walks of life. Their policy practice efforts nationally have been duplicated on the state and local levels as social workers have proposed legislation and developed state and community services and programs to meet community needs. But the work is far from complete. The next generation of policy practitioners will help address today's issues of the growing income disparity in the United States, the unavailability of affordable housing, lack of affordable and accessible health care, immigration policy issues, and civil rights for all citizens. Learning the policy practice skills outlined in this book will help equip a new generation of social workers for active and involved policy practice and the making of policy change.

Succeed with PEARSON mysocialworklab

Log onto **MySocialWorkLab** to access a wealth of case studies, videos, and assessment. (*If you did not receive an access code to* **MySocialWorkLab** *with this text and wish to purchase access online, please visit* **www. mysocialworklab.com**.)

1. **Watch the Connecting Core Competency videos on Human Rights and Justice.** What gaps or challenges in the service delivery system do you see? If you were Tom, what policy practice efforts might you initiate to address those challenges?

2. **Review the Housing SCS.** At the end of Chapter 2, availability of affordable housing is identified as a policy issue for the next generation of social workers. How did Annette Taylor use some of the policy strategies that have been used historically (coalition building, involvement of people affected, etc.) in her successful efforts?

PRACTICE TEST

The following questions will test your knowledge of the content found within this chapter. For additional assessment, including licensing-exam type questions on applying chapter content to practice, visit **MySocialWorkLab**.

1. The focus of the "child saving" movement that began in the aftermath of the Civil War was to
   a. Remove children from unsafe homes.
   b. Stop the sudden increase in abortions.
   c. Place children wandering the streets into safe surroundings.
   d. Pass legislation to make parents financially responsible for their children.

2. Eligibility determination and social casework are both legacies of which historical social welfare structures and programs?
   a. Settlement houses.
   b. Charity organization societies.
   c. New Deal programs.
   d. Civil rights court cases.

3. The huge influx of immigrants that doubled the U.S. population from 1900 through 1920 brought:
   a. Greater stability to the financial markets with more workers available for jobs.
   b. Discrimination in employment and admonitions to "blend in."
   c. Greater religious tolerance as Protestants learned more about the Catholics moving in.
   d. A decline of urban areas as immigrants spread out into the farmland.

4. One of the major achievements of the Progressive Era was
   a. Passage of unemployment insurance.
   b. Voting rights for African Americans.
   c. Legislation restricting child labor.
   d. Recognition of policy practice as part of generic social work.

5. Harry Hopkins and Francis Perkins were:
   a. The principal organizers of early labor unions.
   b. The social workers who started settlement houses during the Progressive Era.
   c. The primary architects of the New Deal legislation that established a federal role in social welfare.
   d. The first graduates from Mary Richmond's school of applied philanthropy.

6. The introduction of Freudian psychology, fears about ties to radical labor unions, and settlement house leaders expressing opposition to World War I were all factors that contributed to the:
   a. Lack of social activism in the social work profession in the 1920s.
   b. Increase in political awareness of the general population.
   c. Development of radical social workers.
   d. Developing a set curriculum for the new schools of social work.

7. The social worker largely responsible for creating a federal safety net for unemployed workers was
   a. Franklin Roosevelt.
   b. Wilbur Cohen.
   c. Lillian Wald.
   d. Frances Perkins.

8. The national professional association for all social workers, regardless of field of practice, was formed when seven different professional associations merged in
   a. 1917
   b. 1935
   c. 1955
   d. 1982

9. Social work's renewed call to activism starting in the mid-1950s was sparked by:
   a. The end of WWII.
   b. Increased interest in the profession and the beginning of the mental health movement.
   c. New developments in the area of civil rights and the ground breaking case of *Brown vs. Board of Education*.
   d. Whitney Young's leadership of NASW.

10. One of the NASW priorities listed in *Turning Priorities into Action: How the Social Work Profession Will Help*, the document provided to the incoming Obama Administration, was:
    a. Cutting taxes to get the economy working again.
    b. Providing affordable, accessible health care for all.
    c. Privatizing Social Security.
    d. Coordinating homeland security to respond to disasters.

Log onto **MySocialWorkLab** once you have completed the Practice Test above to access additional study tools and assessment.

Answers

Key: 1) c, 2) b, 3) b, 4) c, 5) c, 6) a, 7) d, 8) c, 9) c, 10) b

3

The Politics of Policy Practice

CHAPTER OUTLINE

Introduction 50

Civic and Social Responsibility 50

The Evolution of U.S. Political Parties 53

Political Ideologies and U.S. Political
Parties 67
Conservatives
Liberals

Conclusion—Republican or Democrat? 73

Chapter Review 75

Practice Test 75

 MySocialWorkLab 75
Connecting Core Competency Practice Video:
"Keeping up with shifting contexts"
Gay Marriage SCS

Core Competencies in this Chapter (Check marks indicate which competencies are covered in depth)									
	Professional Identity		Ethical Practice	✓	Critical Thinking	✓	Diversity in Practice	✓	Human Rights & Justice
	Research Based Practice		Human Behavior	✓	Policy Practice		Practice Contexts		Engage, Assess, Intervene, Evaluate

INTRODUCTION

Democracy is based upon the conviction that there are extraordinary possibilities in ordinary people.

HARRY EMERSON FOSDICK, AMERICAN MINISTER

President Barack Obama, a former community organizer in Chicago, ran his 2008 presidential election on the promise of social, political, and economic change, and won the election using broad-based, technologically savvy, grassroots strategies. His campaign has been described as an experiment in street-level democracy (in the style of the 1960s community organizer, Saul Alinksy), which "community organized the nation."[1] Social change occurs within political contexts, regardless of whether it is undertaken at the local, state, or national levels. Policy change efforts, by the nature of their contexts, occur either in cooperation with or in opposition to political power brokers. Knowing the ins and outs of the political arena is essential to successful policy practice. Since the formation of our nation, interest groups have come together around common issues in the hope of gaining enough power and status to see their political vision enacted. The political processes of coalition building, public debates, and voting foster public participation in policy decision making. It is in these American political processes that democracy lives and everyone is assured a voice. Policy practitioners often carry the voice of the most vulnerable and marginalized into the political process in the hopes of influencing policy decisions that will provide some degree of fairness in the distribution of society's resources. To begin to understand the factors that drive and shape political forces, this chapter will introduce the evolution of U.S. political parties, their roles in the democratic process, and how values and belief systems coalesce to form political parties and factions. Political parties decide on and direct the political agenda for cities, states, and the nation. To the extent that policy practitioners understand the political system and how to influence it, they can also influence the political agenda and policy decisions.

CIVIC AND SOCIAL RESPONSIBILITY

Community service and civic and social responsibility had a resurgence under the Obama presidential campaign and later under his administration. Campaigning on a platform of collective good over individual self-interest, President Obama touched a core in the American spirit that had lain dormant since the campaign of President John F. Kennedy (JFK). The idea of civic responsibility brings to mind service to others for the common good and represents a collectivist perspective. During harsh and trying times, such as the Great Depression or the deep recession of 2007 to present, this collectivist approach to community living has historically taken dominance in the country as a matter of survival. Given the national and global economic crises in process as President Obama took office in January 2009, it is not surprising that one of the early pieces of legislation passed reflected his commitment to community service and civic duty. On April 21, 2009, President Obama signed into law a $5.7 billion national service

Box 3.1   For Immediate Release

Monday, March 30, 2009
CONTACT: Sandy Scott Phone: 202–606-6724 Email: sscott@cns.gov

Highlights of the Edward M. Kennedy Serve America Act[1]

H.R. 1388, Senate-passed as of 3–26-2009

Reauthorizes and Expands the Mission of the Corporation for National and Community Service, by:

Increasing Opportunities for Americans of All Ages to Serve

▶ Puts young people onto a path of national service by establishing a Summer of Service program to provide $500 education awards for rising 6th–12th graders, a Semester of Service program for high school students to engage in service-learning, and Youth Empowerment Zones for secondary students and out-of-school youth.

▶ Dramatically increases intensive service opportunities by setting AmeriCorps on a path from 75,000 positions annually to 250,000 by 2017, and focusing that service on education, health, clean energy, veterans, economic opportunity and other national priorities. Ties the Segal AmeriCorps Education Award to the maximum Pell Grant level (now $5,350, but set to increase over time).

▶ Improves service options for experienced Americans by expanding age and income eligibility for Foster Grandparents and Senior Companions, authorizing a Silver Scholars program, under which individuals 55 and older who perform 350 hours of service receive a $1,000 education award, and establishing Serve America Fellowships and Encore Fellowships allowing individuals to choose from among registered service sponsors where to perform service. Also permits individuals aged 55 and older to transfer their education award to a child or grandchild.

▶ Enables millions of working Americans to serve by establishing a nationwide Call to Service Campaign and a September 11 national day of service, and investing in the nonprofit sector's capacity to recruit and manage volunteers.

Supporting Innovation and Strengthening the Nonprofit Sector

▶ Creates a Social Innovation Fund to expand proven initiatives and provide seed funding for experimental initiatives, leveraging Federal dollars to identify and grow ideas that are addressing our most intractable community problems.

▶ Establishes a Volunteer Generation Fund to award grants to states and nonprofits to recruit, manage, and support volunteers and strengthen the nation's volunteer infrastructure.

▶ Authorizes Nonprofit Capacity Building grants to provide organizational development assistance to small and mid-size nonprofit organizations.

▶ Creates a National Service Reserve Corps of former national service participants and veterans who will be trained to deploy, in coordination with FEMA, in the event of disasters.

Strengthening Management, Cost-Effectiveness, and Accountability

▶ Merges funding streams, expands the use of simplified, fixed amount grants, and gives the Corporation flexibility to consolidate application and reporting requirements. Increases support for State Commissions on national and community service. Bolsters the capacity and duties of the Corporation's Board of Directors.

▶ Ensures that programs receiving assistance under national service laws are continuously evaluated for effectiveness in achieving performance and cost goals.

▶ Introduces responsible and balanced competition to the RSVP program.

▶ Authorizes a Civic Health Assessment comprising indicators relating to volunteering, voting, charitable giving, and interest in public service in order to evaluate and compare the civic health of communities.

Box insert taken from Corporation for National and Community Service. Press Release, March 30, 2009, www.nationalservice.gov/about/newsroom/releases_detail.asp?tbl_pr_id=1283 (accessed April 27, 2009).

[1] Corporation for National and Community Service (March 30, 2009). *Highlights from the Edward M. Kennedy Serve America Act of 2009,* www.nationalservice.gov/about/newsroom/releases_detail.asp?tbl_pr_id=1283 (accessed April 27, 2009).

bill, the Edward M. Kennedy Serve America Act of 2009 (see Box 3.1),[2] 75 years after President Roosevelt signed the Civilian Conservation Corps into law, which employed thousands of young men in conservation work at the height of the Great Depression[3] and created the foundation of modern conservation.[4] Similarly, the Edward M. Kennedy Serve America Act of 2009 is expected to engage millions of Americans in responding to Americans' needs and solving local community problems. The act emphasizes civic involvement through community service, and

> reauthorizes and expands national service programs administered by the Corporation for National and Community Service, a federal agency created in 1993. The Corporation engages four million Americans in result-driven service each year, including 75,000 AmeriCorps members, 492,000 Senior Corps volunteers, 1.1 million Learn and Serve America students, and 2.2 million additional community volunteers mobilized and managed through the agency's programs.[5]

Human Rights & Justice

Critical Thinking Question

In what ways does the Edward M. Kennedy Serve America Act support social justice for marginalized populations?

Political commentators have noted the similarities between President Obama's push for public involvement in civic activities for the good of the country and JFK's creation of the Peace Corps.[6] The communitarian perspective of the Obama administration is in stark contrast to the extreme individualism of the previous 20 years that stressed personal responsibility over collective good.[7] During times of economic downturn, volunteerism tends to decline while human needs increase.[8] But regardless of the economic climate, Americans are known to be highly responsive to human need, whether it is the neighbor next door, a community in crisis, a natural disaster, or a foreign nation in need. Consider the nation's outpouring of support following Hurricane Katrina and 9/11. As a nation, we have a history of being civically involved and socially responsible. Civic involvement is at the heart of what it means to be a social worker, historically and today.

Early social workers were primarily women of middle- and upper-class status who moved into the neighborhoods of the poor in order to organize, educate, and help them stabilize and improve their lives. Social work was born out of the idea of civic and social responsibility and was founded through volunteerism. During the late nineteenth century, volunteer "friendly visitors" from charitable organizations visited the poor and determined their eligibility for charitable services.[9] Early social workers developed skill sets and techniques to help improve the quality of life for the poor. As early as 1897, the pioneer social worker Mary Richmond advocated for a university-based training program in "applied philanthropy." By 1904 three schools were established,[10] and since these humble beginnings, social work has evolved into a knowledge-based profession, drawing on empirical research, theoretical frameworks, and practice wisdom to guide practice. The knowledge base of the profession distinguishes professional helping from civic volunteerism. Both volunteers and social workers are often motivated by a sense of collective good, but social workers and other helping professionals (such as psychologists, doctors, nurses, teachers, school counselors, etc.) design their work and interventions using evidence-based approaches that are supported by theoretical and empirical scholarship. The expert knowledge of helping professionals is vital in leading effective helping initiatives, in creating and maintaining social service agencies, and in assessing community needs. All of these helping efforts often involve, and are dependent on, volunteers who work under the direction of social workers (and other helping professionals) to fulfill a professional mission of social justice. Policy practice in social work is fundamentally about promoting social justice for all people, by building strong community networks, garnering relevant and sufficient resources, and enhancing social service delivery systems, especially for agencies serving marginalized populations.

Taking a stand for a client or a community in the form of advocacy and social change embodies the social work value of empowerment that is central to bringing democracy to life for every family and in every community. Social workers involved in policy practice influence the types of policy produced by federal, state, and local governments, the social programs that serve clients, and ultimately, the evolution of democracy.[11]

Social workers involved in policy practice influence the pattern of policy produced, the social programs that serve clients, and ultimately, the evolution of democracy.

THE EVOLUTION OF U.S. POLITICAL PARTIES

To a large extent, the process of social change occurs in the context of the political arena known as government. Government-based social change can occur through executive decision making, court decisions, budgetary decisions, and legislatively through the passage of laws. Social change that becomes institutionalized through legislation is made through a variety of governmental organizations and processes at the local, state, and federal levels. Influencing these processes are the members of legislative bodies that introduce legislation and support their passage and those who oppose new bills. In our democracy, major political parties have evolved to determine whom to put forth as candidates for elected offices, and thus who will influence the legislative, executive, and judicial decision-making processes that constitute our government.

Driven by political parties and their own policy agendas, effective involvement in change efforts requires a working knowledge of governmental systems and also the political parties that seek to dominate and influence policy outcomes. The values of the framers of the Constitution are at the heart of citizen participation and politics in a free society. From the beginning, even before political parties were formed, political factions were at work influencing the structures and processes of government and the policies that would govern the citizenry.

Political parties, as we know them today, did not evolve until the mid-1800s, but politics and political factions have been at the center of government since its inception. In the early days of the nation, political factions were the forces that shaped government and public policy. A faction is a group of people who are united behind some concern, issue, or interest.[12] Members of a faction may differ widely on other issues, but on one central concern they are united. This is one of many distinctions between a faction and a political party. Factions rally around one issue or concern, whereas political parties are more developed, are united on general political philosophy, and put forth agendas to address a wide array of domestic and foreign problems.

The earliest political factions were the Federalist and Anti-Federalist groups that came together at the forming of the nation shortly after the Revolutionary War.[13] Each faction coalesced around one issue: what the structure and composition of the new government would be. The Federalists, led by Alexander Hamilton and made up of primarily wealthy landowners, wanted to protect their property and retain large amounts of political power by creating a strong central government. Conversely, the assumption held by the opposing Anti-Federalists was that public policies that were created by a strong central federal government would serve the interests of the powerful elite and supplant the will of the citizens at large. Wary of the wealthy, the Anti-Federalists feared that a strong central government would undermine the power of the people and would promote corruption.[14] Thus, Anti-Federalists opposed a strong central government and advocated for a government that did not overpower the will of the people as expressed at the state and local levels. They supported a government that encouraged a high rate of citizen participation in the democracy. The debate between the Federalists and Anti-Federalists intensely ensued at the Federal Convention of 1787, a convention authorized for the amendment of the Articles of Confederation (the governing document that had led the young nation for the prior 10 years since the end of the American Revolution), but whose agenda quickly became to adopt a new Constitution giving greater power to a federal government.

The root of the debate between the Federalists and Anti-Federalists lay in the distribution and balance of power between the federal government and state governments. The Federalists, still in the revolutionary mind-set, believed the United States needed a strong central government (1) to secure the nation against foreign invasions; (2) to intervene in quarrels between states and therefore help to solidify a national union; and (3) to defend against encroachments of state governments. Further, the Articles of Confederation did not provide for executive power. Federalists distrusted the public at large and were worried that people responded more to emotions than to rationality. Anti-Federalists such as Patrick Henry and others saw the Constitution as a real threat to the rights and liberties hard won through the Revolutionary War. They feared that a federal constitution would obliterate state constitutions and, with them, the liberties of the individual citizens. Anti-Federalists have been viewed as defenders of the status quo, but they might also be understood as cautious patriots worried about too many changes in the governing document so early in the nation's formation, and who sought some sense of governing stability.

The positions of both the Federalists and Anti-Federalists held great implications for not only the structure and function of government, but also for the level of citizen participation in the democracy and the making of all public policy. Those who held more political power would also hold more influence in the making of public policy. Although the Federalists won the debate at the Federal Convention of 1787 with the drafting of the Constitution, Anti-Federalists, still concerned about what they perceived as an imbalance of power between federal and state governments, pushed for amendments to the Constitution early on to ensure individual liberties. James Madison drafted the Bill of Rights in 1789, which was ratified and became the first 10 amendments to the Constitution in 1791 (see Table 3.1). Herbert J. Storing suggested that this initial debate about the governing structure of our nation began an ongoing political dialogue, so important to a working democracy: "The Political life of community continues to be a dialogue in which Anti-Federalist concerns and principles still play an important part."[15]

Table 3.1 Bill of Rights

"It will be a desirable thing to extinguish from the bosom of every member of the community any apprehensions, that there are those among his countrymen who wish to deprive them of the liberty for which they valiantly fought and honorably bled."

— *James Madison proposing Bill of Rights to the House, June 8, 1789*

Amendment I	Congress shall make no law respecting an establishment of religion, or prohibiting the free exercise thereof; or abridging the freedom of speech, or of the press; or the right of the people peaceably to assemble, and to petition the Government for a redress of grievances.
Amendment II	A well regulated Militia, being necessary to the security of a free State, the right of the people to keep and bear Arms, shall not be infringed.
Amendment III	No Soldier shall, in time of peace be quartered in any house, without the consent of the Owner, nor in time of war, but in a manner to be prescribed by law.
Amendment IV	The right of the people to be secure in their persons, houses, papers, and effects, against unreasonable searches and seizures, shall not be violated, and no Warrants shall issue, but upon probable cause, supported by Oath or affirmation, and particularly describing the place to be searched, and the persons or things to be seized.
Amendment V	No person shall be held to answer for a capital, or otherwise infamous crime, unless on a presentment or indictment of a Grand Jury, except in cases arising in the land or naval forces, or in the Militia, when in actual service in time of War or public danger; nor shall any person be subject for the same offence to be twice put in jeopardy of life or limb; nor shall be compelled in any criminal case to be a witness against himself, nor be deprived of life, liberty, or property, without due process of law; nor shall private property be taken for public use, without just compensation.
Amendment VI	In all criminal prosecutions, the accused shall enjoy the right to a speedy and public trial, by an impartial jury of the State and district wherein the crime shall have been committed, which district shall have been previously ascertained by law, and to be informed of the nature and cause of the accusation; to be confronted with the witnesses against him; to have compulsory process for obtaining witnesses in his favor, and to have the Assistance of Counsel for his defence.
Amendment VII	In suits at common law, where the value in controversy shall exceed twenty dollars, the right of trial by jury shall be preserved, and no fact tried by a jury, shall be otherwise reexamined in any Court of the United States, than according to the rules of the common law.
Amendment VIII	Excessive bail shall not be required, nor excessive fines imposed, nor cruel and unusual punishments inflicted.
Amendment IX	The enumeration in the Constitution, of certain rights, shall not be construed to deny or disparage others retained by the people.
Amendment X	The powers not delegated to the United States by the Constitution, nor prohibited by it to the States, are reserved to the States respectively, or to the people.

Source: James Madison Center, James Madison University, Harrisonburg, VA, www.jmu.edu/madison/center/main_pages/madison_archives/constit_confed/rights/document/document.htm (accessed August 14, 2007).

Over time, political factions have fused and dismantled, taken on different issues and concerns, and changed their perspectives until eventually, well-developed organizations emerged that were grounded in larger philosophies and belief systems beyond the issue of the balance of power between governments (though this debate continues even to this day when we hear discussions of "states rights" or "unfunded federal mandates"). We call these organizations **political parties,** and today their central agendas, beliefs about human nature, and philosophies of government have melded to form distinct identities for each of the two major political parties that govern politics in the United States today: the Democratic Party (considered liberal) and the Republican Party (considered conservative).

Over the span of the 200+ years of our nation's history, only five political parties have evolved to reach major party status, and only the Democrats and the Republicans have been able to sustain that status for over 150 years (see Box 3.2 for a summary of the major U.S. political parties).[16]

The central philosophies and ideologies of the current Democratic and Republican parties[17] have evolved over the past 230 years as early political factions fused around pressing issues and then splintered into new factions when disagreements arose. Although factions have come and gone, their importance in the historical evolution of the two-party system we know today should not go underappreciated.

By the mid-1800s the Democrats and Republicans had become the two major political parties central to U.S. politics and had matured into political organizations that would reflect the characteristics of what constitutes a "true" political party. According to Bailey,[18] fixtures of political parties include the following:

- They are able to attract participation from voters in all parts of the country;
- They hold primary elections to decide on party candidates;
- They put forth viable candidates for the presidency;
- They develop party platforms that can be clearly articulated and that reflect philosophies and positions on specific issues;
- In an effort to appeal to wide sections of the electorate, they avoid radical positions on most issues; and
- There is a tendency to reward loyal party workers with positions when elections are won by party candidates (known as the **spoils system** or **patronage**).

Today, the Democrats and Republicans are concerned about similar issues. They struggle with the same domestic and foreign issues that are prioritized to a large extent by public opinion. The parties differ, however, on how to tackle major issues such as the economy, health care, the war on terror, education, job creation, and foreign affairs. These differences in problem resolution reflect the fundamental differences in party values and vision. Table 3.2 summarizes the party platforms on prominent issues today.

Although political parties may differ on how to get the job done, first and foremost they must hold political power in order to move their political agendas into law. Because political power is the essential ingredient to moving party values into a living reality through legislation, political parties fundamentally serve as election associations and focus on getting their candidates elected to local, state, and national offices. These election associations are driven by a set of ideas and programs for which the party advocates and,

Box 3.2 Major U.S. Political Parties Throughout History

1. **The Federalist Party, 1788–1816.** The champion of the new Constitution and strong national government, it was the first U.S. political institution to resemble a political party, although it was not a full-fledged party. Its strength was rooted in the Northeast and the Atlantic Seaboard, where it attracted the support of shopkeepers, manufacturers, financiers, landowners, and other established families of wealth and status. Limited by its narrow electoral base, it soon fell before the success of the Democratic-Republicans.

2. **The Democratic-Republican Party, 1800–1832.** Many of its leaders had been strong proponents of the Constitution but opposed the extreme nationalism of the Federalists. This was a party of the small farmers, workers, and less-privileged citizens, plus Southern planters, who preferred the authority of the state governments and opposed centralizing power in the national government. Like its leader, Thomas Jefferson, it shared many of the ideals of the French Revolution, especially the extension of the right to vote and the notion of direct popular self-government.

3. **The Democratic Party, 1832–Present.** Growing out of the Jacksonian[*1] wing of the Democratic-Republicans, it was the first really broad-based, popular party in the United States. On behalf of a coalition of less-privileged voters, it opposed such business-friendly policies as national banking and high tariffs. It also welcomed the new immigrants (and sought their votes) and opposed nativist (anti-immigrant) sentiment.

4. **The Whig Party, 1834–1856.** This party, too, had roots in the old Democratic-Republican Party, but in the Clay-Adams faction and in opposition to the Jacksonians. Its greatest leaders, Henry Clay and Daniel Webster, stood for legislative supremacy and protested the strong presidency of Andrew Jackson. For its short life, the Whig Party was an unstable coalition of many interests, among them, nativism, property, and business and commerce.

5. **The Republican Party, 1854-Present.** Born as the Civil War approached, this was the party of northern opposition to slavery and its spread to the new territories. Therefore, it was also the party of the Union, the North, Lincoln, the freeing slaves, victory in the Civil War, and the imposition of Reconstruction on the South. From the Whigs, it also inherited a concern for business and industrial expansion.

---

[*]**Jacksonian** Democrats, also known as the second-party system from 1824–1860, emerged when Andrew Jackson was denied the presidency by the House of Representatives after winning the popular vote and the electoral vote in the 1824 election. Outraged at this "injustice," Jackson mobilized the masses and swept the election in 1828, tripling the voter turnout over 1824. Jackson handed out government contracts and jobs as a way to consolidate power and was referred to by opponents as "King Andrew." The second party system opposed tariffs and national banks and supported the expansion of U.S. territory. Known as the Democracy, Jacksonian Democrats dominated politics until the Civil War and lived by the adage "to the victor belongs the spoils" (thus the name the "spoils system").

[1] Morris P. Fiornina, Paul E. Peterson, Bertam Johnson and D. Stephen Voss, *The New American Democracy*, 4th ed. (Boston: Pearson/Longman, 2005).

Source: *Party Politics in America* (12th ed.) by Marjories Randon Hershey. Used with permission from Pearson-Longman Press.

by doing so, sway voters toward (or away) from specific candidates. To this end, three internal institutions have developed over time that continue to be the mainstay of the Democratic and Republican parties. These institutions are the political parties' (1) national committee, (2) national chairperson, and (3) national convention. These three institutions work in concert to ensure election successes, and thus, the power and survival of the parties. During the 2008 elections, the national committees took unprecedented advantage of technology to promote their candidates. The Democratic National Committee (DNC) offered a 50-state organizing strategy and tools to help local groups organize around local, state, and national elections, making individual citizens feel like an active part of a greater whole. Led by the then Democratic national chairperson, former Vermont governor Howard Dean, the DNC successfully engaged the country in one of its most dynamic

Table 3.2   Major Party Platforms

	Republican Platform[1]	Democrat Platform[2]
Issue		
Abortion	▶ Oppose school based clinics that provide referrals or counseling for abortion and contraception; ▶ The unborn child has a fundamental right to life and it should not be infringed upon; ▶ Prevent unwanted pregnancies.	▶ Supports *Roe v. Wade* and women's right to choose regardless of ability to pay; ▶ Prevent unwanted pregnancies; ▶ Supports access to comprehensive family planning services and age appropriate sex education.
Economy	▶ Government should tax for only essential functions; ▶ Make the 2001 and 2003 tax cuts permanent; ▶ Lower tax burden of families by doubling the exemption for dependents; ▶ Ban Internet tax and stop any new cell phone taxes; ▶ Opposes family death tax on family owned businesses and farms; ▶ Repeal of the Alternative Minimum Tax; ▶ Lower taxes fuel the economy through increased consumption and stimulate economic growth; ▶ Lower taxes increase community ownership; ▶ Supports a major reduction in the corporate tax rates to encourage businesses to keep jobs in the U.S.; ▶ Moderate regulation of business; ▶ Supports "right-to-work" laws; ▶ Legal reform to protect small businesses from lawsuits; ▶ Advocate the creation of Farm Savings Accounts to help farmers manage risk created by drought, floods and other natural events as well as turbulence in the global markets; ▶ Fiscally disciplined government spending promotes the economy and expands prosperity. This is best accomplished through "pay as you go" requirements for mandatory spending; limit spending growth through caps on discretionary spending; and creating a "line-item veto;" ▶ Encourages employers to offer tax deferred savings plans for employees and remove the current limits on tax free savings accounts;	▶ Jump start the economy through stimulus rebates and investment in job creations that repair the nation's infrastructure and creates 5 million green jobs; ▶ Start a National Infrastructure Reinvestment Bank for leveraging private investments into infrastructure improvements and create 2 million new jobs; ▶ Modernize the power grid; ▶ Strengthen the right of workers to organize and support the passage of the Employee Free Choice Act; ▶ Will ensure the right of federal employees to organize; ▶ Oppose the ban on permanent replacement of striking workers; ▶ Opposes "right-to-work" laws; ▶ Seeks to restore and expand overtime rights of workers; ▶ Raise the minimum wage and index it to inflation; ▶ Increase the Earned Income Tax Credit; ▶ Create the Advanced Manufacturing Fund to support job innovators and creators; ▶ Expand the Manufacturing; Extension Partnerships and create new job training programs for clean technologies; ▶ Provide low interest loans to manufacturers investing in creating fuel efficient vehicles; ▶ Reform unemployment insurance to close gaps and extend benefits to workers who are currently excluded; ▶ Will work to expand the Family and Medical Leave Act and make it a paid leave; ▶ Develop transitional jobs program for the unemployed and train them for permanent jobs; ▶ Supports gender pay equity through the Fair Pay Act;

Table 3.2   **(Continued)**

	Republican Platform[1]	Democrat Platform[2]
	● Supports tax reform that simplifies taxes and creates a two-rate flat tax.	● Reform the tax code to close corporate loopholes and eliminate tax havens for the rich; reduce tax liability on seniors; cut taxes for those earning $250,000 or less; expand the Earned Income Tax Credit; and simplify the tax filing process; ● Trade agreements that support the creation of U.S. jobs, and enforce protection of the environment, food safety and health of foreign citizens; ● Fiscal discipline in government spending.
Education	Favors state regulated public education over federal control. Supports: ● Block grants to states as the preferred education funding mechanism; Strengthen schools and families through: ● Child care tax credit for early childhood education and care; ● Promote partnerships between schools and business for learning science, math, technology and engineering; ● Parental choice in educational learning environments through the use of educational vouchers and tax credits; ● Replace "family planning" classes with increased funding for abstinence education; ● Increased funding to cover 40 percent of the cost to states for meeting the mandates of the Individuals with Disabilities Education Act (IDEA); Expand access to higher education by: ● Creating Education Savings Accounts; ● Reform of the federal financial aid system; ● Support for distance learning;	Strengthen education readiness by ● Increased funding for Head Start; ● Expanding child care credits; ● Double funding for after school and summer learning opportunities; ● Creation of the President's Early Learning Council who will be charged with coordinating early education efforts; Improve the quality of public education ● New incentives for teachers to commit to a life of teaching; and mentoring new teachers; ● Create better pay scale in concert with better performance; ● Work with governors and school districts to make education effective, with higher standards; and accountability within the school systems; ● Promote critical thinking, communication, and problem solving in the classroom; ● Encourage parent participation in their child's school; ● Invest in programs to end the school dropout crisis; ● Support full funding of IDEA; ● Support transitional bilingual education and English Language Learner classes; Improve higher education by: ● Invest in community colleges accelerated training and technical certification programs for high demand occupations; ● Support nontraditional methods of education such as distance education and evening and week-end classes for nontraditional students; ● Fully fund joint labor-management apprenticeship programs;

(Continued)

Table 3.2   Major Party Platforms (Continued)

	Republican Platform[1]	Democrat Platform[2]
		▶ Make college affordable for every student by creating the American Opportunity Tax Credit that will ensure the first $4,000 of college education is free; ▶ Simplify the process of applying for federal financial aid;
Energy	▶ Reduce U.S. dependence on foreign fossil fuels while creating new energy related jobs; ▶ Drill more oil from American soil in environmentally responsible ways; ▶ Build new oil refineries; ▶ Supports continued coal production and utilization; ▶ Improve the distribution of natural gas for cooking, heating, and transportation fuel; ▶ Create more nuclear power; ▶ Supports clean coal initiatives such as coal-to-liquid and gasification programs, and carbon capture and storage technologies; ▶ Long term energy tax credits for development and use of renewable power such as wind, solar, geothermal and hydropower; ▶ Invest in new alternative fuels such as bio-fuel; ▶ Create flexible fuel vehicles; ▶ Engage in open energy cooperation and trade with Canada and Mexico.	▶ Enhance government policies that provide incentives for the creation and production of domestic clean and renewable energy; ▶ Eliminate dependence on foreign oil; ▶ Modernize the power grid; ▶ Invest billions of dollars over the next ten years in creating green jobs; ▶ Create an energy-focused youth job program for low-income youth; ▶ Collaborate with business, government, and the American public to make America 50 percent more energy efficient by the year 2030; ▶ Generate revenues through the cap and trade program for reducing greenhouse gases; ▶ Instructs the Federal Trade Commission and Department of Justice to investigate and prosecute those who manipulate the oil market; ▶ Increased funding for low income heating assistance and weatherization programs.
Gay Marriage	▶ Marriage is a sacred bond between a man and a woman; ▶ Supports a national constitutional ban on gay marriage; ▶ In the absence of a national ban on gay marriage, supports state initiatives that ban gay marriage.	▶ Supports the inclusion of same-sex couples in the life of the nation and with equal benefits and protections; ▶ Supports the passage of a bipartisan employment nondiscrimination act; ▶ Opposes the Defense of Marriage Act.
Health Care	Opposes "socialized" health care and government-run health care system. Endorses providing access to affordable high quality health care by giving control of the health care system to health care providers and patients rather than to government by supporting: ▶ Tax credits for medical and health care expenses; ▶ Consumer-driven health care initiatives; ▶ Tax free Health Savings Accounts;	Health care is a right and not a privilege and should be available to every American. Create a national insurance policy that provides all citizens with access to quality, affordable health care insurance. ▶ Health care should be a shared responsibility among employers, workers, insurers, providers, and the government; ▶ End insurance discrimination. All applicants should be accepted without penalty for preexisting conditions;

Table 3.2 (Continued)

	Republican Platform[1]	Democrat Platform[2]
	▶ Associated Health Plans for small employers; ▶ Modernize the healthcare record keeping system; ▶ Medical liability reform; ▶ Strengthening Medicare; ▶ New approaches to Medicaid and State Children's Health Insurance Program; ▶ Health Insurance tax relief.	▶ Family insurance benefits should be similar to those available to members of Congress; ▶ Modernize the health care system to cut cost and improve efficiencies, such as reformed medical record keeping; ▶ Ensure strong health care workforce through training and reimbursement incentives; ▶ End health care disparities among minorities, women, and the poor through culturally sensitive health care practices; ▶ Provide new tax credit for small business that offer quality health insurance to their employees; ▶ Strengthen and expand Medicaid coverage; ▶ Reduce health care inflation; ▶ Protect Medicare and cut prescription drug costs.
Immigration	▶ Immigration is a national security issue; ▶ Improved border security through border fencing and providing agents with new tools and resources to enforce immigration law; ▶ Better enforcement of laws against employers who recruit and hire illegal immigrants; and those who engage in identity fraud and trafficking in fraudulent documents; ▶ Oppose amnesty; ▶ Supports English as the official language of the nation.	▶ Comprehensive immigration reform that provides tough, practical and humane policies; ▶ Secure our borders with additional personnel, infrastructure, and technology, and real-time intelligence; ▶ Dismantle human smuggling organizations; ▶ Promote economic development in migrant-sending nations; ▶ Prosecute employers who hire undocumented immigrants; ▶ Reform and streamline the naturalization process for legal immigrant residents; ▶ Establish a system for illegal immigrants who are otherwise hard working, without criminal records, and playing by the rules a path to full participation in U.S. life. Fines will be imposed and they must meet all the requirements of naturalization.
Social Security	▶ Comprehensive reform of the system which should include the option to privately invest social security fund through Personal Investment Accounts.	▶ Social Security reform that ensure the continuance of the retirement system; ▶ Protect private pensions automatically enrolling workers in a workplace pension plan that can be carried from job to job; ▶ Protect private pensions by barring corporations from investing them in company stock; ▶ Match retirement savings on working families who need the help; ▶ Reform corporate bankruptcy laws to protect workers' pension funds; ▶ Eliminate all federal income taxes for seniors making less than $50,000 a year.

(Continued)

62   *Chapter 3*

Table 3.2 **Major Party Platforms (Continued)**

	Republican Platform[1]	Democrat Platform[2]
Iraq War and the War on Terror	• The United States has declared war on terrorists, and have taken the war to the enemy; the United States will persevere in its mission to keep America safe by using all options available; • Reducing the nation's dependence on foreign oil will guard against underwriting terrorists; • Guard against nuclear terrorism by engaging in nuclear arms reduction at home and in cooperation with other nations; • Guard against bioterrorism and cyberterrorism through investment of human intelligence capabilities; • Support for the Foreign Intelligence Act.	Iraq war: • Bring the Iraq war to a responsible end, keeping a residual force in Iraq to perform specific mission, eliminating terrorists; protecting embassy and civil personnel; and advising and supporting Iraq's Security Forces. War on Terror: • The central front of the war on terror is in Afghanistan and Pakistan where additional troops and resources will be sent to take out terrorist camps, crack down on border insurgents; and help Pakistan develop counter-terrorist and counter-insurgent capacities; • Create the Shared Security Partnership to enhance counter-terrorism cooperation with other countries; • Provide supports to political reformers, democratic institutions, and civil society that uphold human rights and build respect for the law; • Pursue a "no nuclear weapons world" in collaboration with other world leaders to reduce the threat of nuclear terrorism; • Reform intelligence gathering, analysis, and sharing among intelligence entities to guard against all forms of terrorism including bioterrorism and cyberterroism; • Strong diplomatic relations with allies and enemies; • Collaborative global efforts toward common global goals of public safety; • Fully fund and implement the recommendations of the 9–11 commission; • Create the Quadrennial Review at the Department of Homeland Security to fully assess threats the nation faces and our ability to confront them.
Welfare	Help displaced workers through modernizing the retraining and unemployment assistance programs by • Anticipating worker displacement; • Directing a portion of unemployment benefits into a tax free account, the "Lost Earnings Buffer Account" for use in retraining and relocation.	• Expand the Earned Income Tax Credit; • Create "promise neighborhoods" that provide comprehensive in areas of concentrated poverty; • Create good-paying jobs and support parents in work responsibility through health care, transportation, and child care; • Promote responsible fatherhood; • Improve child support enforcement;

Table 3.2 (Continued)

Republican Platform[1]	Democrat Platform[2]
Support individual and family welfare by: ▶ Promoting healthy marriages and responsible fatherhood; ▶ Supporting abstinence; ▶ Promoting work opportunities and work schedule flexibility.	▶ Raise minimum wage and index it to inflation; ▶ Extend child care credits.

[1]Republican Platform Committee (2009), *2008 Republican platform,* www.gop.com/2008Platform/ (accessed April 27, 2009).
[2]Democratic National Convention Committee (2008), *The 2008 Democration national platform: Renewing American's promise,* www.democrats.org/a/party/platform.html (accessed April 27, 2009).

Source: 1. Republican National Committee, 2008 Republican Platform. The Platform Committee, Washington DC. (2008). Available at www.gop.com/2008Platform/.
2. Democratic National Convention Committee. *The 2008 Democratic national platform: Renewing American's promise.* Washington DC: Author. (2008). Available at www.democrats.org/a/party/platform.html.

and well-participated-in elections ever, and was able to recapture the White House and gain a greater margin of control in both the Senate and the House of Representatives as well as win 7 of the 11 governorships up for grabs in that election.[19] The themes, platform, and momentum built up during the election cycle culminated at the Democratic National Convention in August, 2008, in Denver.

Unlike previous election years, both political parties (although more intensely the Democrats) continued to use the same strategies they used in the elections to keep party members (and potential members) and local organizers engaged in the democratic process to help enact the parties' respective political agendas. For example, individuals used tools on the parties' national committee Web sites to find local events to attend, or to create their own events around important issues, such as jobs creation or health care reform. Citizens are also free to use the Web sites to create blogs, or to participate in existing blogs exploring specific social, economic, political, and international issues. Parties are beginning to understand that the more they keep constituents involved between elections, the more likely they will have a sizeable number of people going to the polls to vote for the party's candidates in the next election. The national committee Web sites can also help keep a finger on the pulse of the nation's attitudes and positions regarding specific issues and thus reshape political agendas to be more in line with the constituents of each party.[20]

The national committees are made up of the respective party representatives from state-level parties across the country. The state party leaders work to promote the parties' agendas and to elect the parties' presidential candidates to office. The national committees also assist state-level parties in their fund-raising and political activities, and are especially involved in key state elections. Although the national committee meets only two or three times a year, usually to call media attention to its candidates and party agendas, committee

Policy Practice

Critical Thinking Question

Identify two groups attempting to influence policy today, and the methods used to influence policy outcomes?

members run the national committee on a day-to-day basis from their respective states.[21]

The Democratic and Republican national committees are lead by chairpersons who are elected by the members of their respective national committees. In 2009, Governor Tim Kaine of Virginia was the newly elected DNC chairperson, and Lieutenant Governor Michael Steele of Maryland was the newly elected Republican National Committee (RNC) chairperson. The national committee chairperson coordinates party activities at the national level, manages public relations with the media, coordinates activities with state organizations, and prepares for the national elections. She or he, along with a permanent staff, is the core of the national party organization.[22]

Every four years, the Democratic and Republican parties convene at their respective national conventions, where delegates from across the country (about 5,000) come together to endorse each party's political platform and party statutes, and to nominate[23] the presidential and vice-presidential candidates for the upcoming election.[24]

Third parties have always been a part of the U.S. political landscape, but because they lack some of the important characteristics of established political parties, they are unable to garner much political power, and often fade out of existence.[25] Probably the most successful presidential run from a third party was Theodore Roosevelt in 1912, when he ran as a Progressive Party candidate and captured 27 percent of the popular vote and 88 electoral votes. Since then the influence of third parties has waxed and waned. In recent history, Ross Perot, a self-made Texan billionaire ran as an independent candidate in 1992 against William Jefferson Clinton (Democrat) and incumbent George Herbert Walker Bush and received 19 percent of the popular vote, an astonishing amount in modern-day politics. Political analysts suggest that Perot most likely sealed the election for front-runner Bill Clinton by pulling votes from Republican Bush. Ross went on to form the Reform Party and ran for president again in 1996, but got only half as many votes as he did in 1992. By 2000, the Reform Party had collapsed. In the 2004 election, third parties were hardly noticed, drawing only 1 percent of the popular vote collectively. During the 2008 election, there were a total of 22 third-party candidates, but only one, Ralph Nader—who ran as an independent—was able to capture even 1 percent of the vote. This had effectively no influence on the outcome of the presidential election, as Barack Obama won the race with 53 percent to John McCain's 46 percent in the final count.[26]

In spite of their inability to win presidential elections, third parties still have been able to leave their mark on the country's election outcomes. Consider, for example, the impact of the Green Party and their candidate, Ralph Nader, in the 2000 presidential election. Nader was able to capture 2.9 million votes or 2.7 percent of the national vote. Some contend that the presence of a third-party candidate threw the election to George Walker Bush, because it was speculated that those voting for Nader would have most likely voted for Al Gore, the Democratic candidate, had Nader not run for office. In this example, the third party, the Green Party, changed the course of history.

Critical external events have historically had great influence on the dominance of political parties and the partisanship of parties, often causing a realignment of party membership and a shift in party dominance. For example, during the Great Depression, the Republicans (who had dominated politics

Critical Thinking

Critical Thinking Question

In what critical ways have third parties influenced presidential election outcomes within the last century?

since the late 1860s) downplayed the economic crisis of the time, and took a "wait-and-see" position in regard to the depressed economy and the consequent devastation on people's lives. The Democrats, under the leadership of Franklin Delano Roosevelt, advocated for a more active role for the federal government in boosting the economy and creating employment programs to widen the safety net. These strategies, at such a grave time in our nation's history, attracted to the Democratic Party groups of voters who had previously been aligned with the Republicans. Workers, small business owners, ethnic minorities, and Catholics broke camp and joined the Democrats. The result was a shift in party dominance from the Republicans to the Democrats, which continued until the 1970s.[27]

External critical events, such as the Great Depression, the Vietnam War, 9/11, and the Iraq and Afghan wars, fundamentally change the relationship between the masses and the governing elite, and as a result, change the pattern of policies produced by elected officials.[28] Great national tragedies require extreme responses from the government. The policies resulting from these responses may eventually divide parties on important issues and have the potential for realigning party membership. This was evident on the eve of the 2006 midterm elections as cracks in the Republican Party and disagreements about the Iraq war and the economy became more apparent, and resulted in the Republicans' loss of power in the House of Representatives and the Senate. During the election campaign, Republicans running for reelection began distancing themselves from President Bush as his approval rating dropped to a low of 35 percent.[29] Many loyal Republicans disagreed with Bush's policies on the Iraq war. On another front, the Republican Party's Christian conservative base was calling for accountability regarding the unfolding corruption in Congress and fulfillment of the promises made on moral issues during President Bush's 2004 re-election campaign. As predicted by some political analysts, a realignment of party affiliation began in the fall of 2006 with the midterm elections. Many centrist or conservative Democrats replaced Republicans in the House of Representatives and the Senate, marking a shift in the dominance of power in Congress back to the Democrats. This trend continued as the 2008 presidential election took off in early 2007, with President George W. Bush's approval ratings continuing to be in the mid-30s, the war in Iraq dragging on, and the economy worsening.[30] With two strong democratic presidential candidates—Senator Hillary Clinton, a political powerhouse and women's icon, and Senator Barack Obama with a message of hope—the realignment of political parties became a closely watched phenomenon during the 2008 election. Box 3.3 provides a description of the change in the political landscape during and following the 2008 presidential elections.[31] This shift in power brought to the fore a new policy agenda for domestic and international issues, the most notable of them being ending the Iraq war, jumpstarting the economy, health care reform, focusing on green energy, creating jobs, and education.

Who defines policy has always been determined through an intense interplay of interest groups and their alignment with the dominant political party. This power struggle has historically defined and continues to define who we are as a country and the policies that we adopt and live by. To the extent that we choose to participate in this dynamic and sometimes messy political process, we influence policy and the rules and opportunities of social and economic life for ourselves and the clients that we serve.

External critical events fundamentally change the relationship between the masses and the governing elite, and change the pattern of policies produced.

When we choose to participate in the dynamic and sometimes messy political process, we influence policy and the social and economic lives of clients.

Box 3.3   Was 2008 a Realigning Election?[1]

By Alex Koppelman

April 20, 2009

When University of Virginia professor Larry Sabato speaks about politics, people listen. And by "people" I mean most every political reporter in the country, as Sabato has earned the distinction—by now, it's not really a good thing for him—of being called "probably the most quoted college professor in the land." And given the dramatic predictions in his latest book, "The Year of Obama: How Barack Obama Won the White House," even more people are going to be listening to Sabato as he talks about an election that he believes marks a major shift in U.S. politics.

"The big idea of this book is that 2008 looks to be a realigning election—a very rare event in American history," Sabato told Politico's Mike Allen. "The previous three were 1896, 1932, and 1980. Translation: The Democratic majority is going to last for a while."

To support his contention, Sabato pointed out three demographic trends, according to Allen:

- The young broke more than 2–1 Democratic, and it was an intense preference unlikely to fade quickly. As this group ages and replaces older voters, Democrats will benefit even more since this group's turnout will go up.

- The proportion of minority voters (black, Hispanic, and Asian) shot up and is likely to climb consistently every four years (mainly because of Hispanics). Democrats get about three-quarters of the votes of minorities, taken as a collective group.

- Americans with postgraduate educations have begun to move firmly to the Democrats, not just because of Bush and the economy but also because of the GOP's conservative stance on social issues (abortion, gay rights, etc.)

I think it's probably still a little early for big, sweeping pronouncements about 2008, if only because the 2010 midterm elections will be a good sign of the durability of what we witnessed last fall. But in general, all of this is pretty convincing.

I'm especially interested in the argument about Hispanics and how powerful that demographic group will be for Democrats, as regular readers of this blog will know, but the data about young voters is pretty compelling too. They can probably be expected to shift somewhat rightward as they age, but—as Sabato himself notes—their comparatively social-liberal views will still remain a problem for the GOP, unless the party moves towards the center on issues like same-sex marriage.

---

[1]Alex Koppelman, "Was 2008 a Realigning Election?" *Salon.com* (April 20, 2009), www.salon.com/politics/war_room/2009/04/20/sabato (accessed May 26, 2009).

Source: Salon.com, www.salon.com/politics/war_room/2009/04/20/sabato/ (accessed May 26, 2009). Used with permission

POLITICAL IDEOLOGIES AND U.S. POLITICAL PARTIES

Political parties determine the social welfare of U.S. citizens because they hold the power to set the social policy agenda and thus the direction the country will take in response to selected domestic social issues. Although both parties may identify similar social issues on their political agendas, their approaches to resolving social problems will differ depending on their philosophy of human functioning, their beliefs in economic theories, and the extent to which they believe government should intrude into the market economy and individuals' lives. In short, policy resolutions will be mainly determined by the dominant party's political ideology. These differing belief systems span the political spectrum from the radical (far left) to the ultraconservative (far right) and every position in between. Box 3.4 provides a brief description of various positions on the political-ideological spectrum.[33]

The dominant political parties in the United States occupy the liberal, moderate, and conservative spaces on the political continuum, and at times, differences in party politics are difficult to discern. For example, as many socially conservative Republicans were voted out of office in the midterm elections of 2006, some were replaced with socially conservative Democrats who, like the Republicans they replaced, opposed abortion, stem-cell research, and same-sex marriage. Although similarities can be found across political lines, central differences do exist in the Republican and Democratic camps, and parties are organized around these core belief systems.

Box 3.4   Spanning the Political Spectrum[1]

Very Liberal

Very Conservative

Radical: Seen as being on the far left of the political spectrum, radicals call for wide-sweeping rapid change in the basic structure of the political, social, or economic system. They may be willing to resort to extreme methods to bring about change, including the use of violence and revolution.

Liberal: Liberals believe that the government should be actively involved in the promotion of social welfare of a nation's citizens. Liberals usually call for peaceful, gradual change within the existing political system.

Moderate: Moderates may share viewpoints with both liberals and conservatives. They are seen as tolerant of other people's views, and they do not hold extreme views of their own. They advocate a "go-slow" or "wait-and-see" approach to social or political change.

Conservative: People who hold conservative ideals favor keeping things the way they are or maintaining the status quo if it is what they desire. Conservatives are usually hesitant or cautious about adopting new policies, especially if they involve government activism in some way. They feel that the less government there is, the better. They agree with Jefferson's view that "the best government governs least."

Reactionary: Sitting on the far right of the ideological spectrum, reactionaries want to go back to the way things were—the "good ol' days." Often reactionaries are willing to use extreme methods, such as repressive use of government power, to achieve their goals.

---

[1] USNewsclassroom.com (2006), Political Ideologies, *U.S. News and World Report,* www.usnewsclassroom.com/resources/activities/act010604.html (accessed December 5, 2006).

Source: usnewsclassroom.com, www.usnewsclassroom.com/resources/activities/act010604.html.

Conservatives

Virtually all conservatives will agree on a few central issues: the need for minimal government regulation in business and the economy, devolution of control of government programs to the states, and lower taxes and less government spending.[34] From a philosophical perspective, conservatives believe that government interventions in people's lives crush individual initiative and thus contribute to economic and social problems. Likewise, they believe that the free market works best when left alone, and so they generally oppose regulating the economy, but favor entrepreneurialism. For these reasons, conservatives are proponents of small government. Fundamentally, conservatives believe that social problems are best resolved in the private sector, and they have been major proponents of the privatization of health care, social services, and education. They also support the traditional values of hard work, ambition, and self-reliance. Rather than equality, they pursue the notion of equity, where individual rewards come through individual efforts. Government programs that reflect this perspective are called social insurance programs. They require that individuals pay into a social program before reaping any benefit from it, such as the Social Security (SS) Retirement System.[35] For example, before one can receive any retirement benefits from the SS fund upon reaching retirement age, the person must first contribute 7.65 percent of his or her income to the SS retirement fund for 40 quarters (or 10 years). Although the Social Security Act was passed under the Democratic administration of Franklin D. Roosevelt, the structure of the retirement system included in the act is appealing to conservatives because it uses the concept of equity to award benefits.

Conservatives also promote individual rights and private property. Social conservatives believe in the regulation of private morality by promoting anti-abortion legislation and opposing same-sex marriage.[36]

Like all political ideologies, conservativism runs along a continuum from more conservative to less conservative, creating a rather heterogeneous group. Differences in political ideology often find their origins in fundamental differences in beliefs about human nature. Generally, there are *classic* or *traditional conservatives, economic conservatives* (also known as *neoclassical liberals),* and *social conservatives* (also known as *cultural conservatives).*[37]

Traditional Conservatives

Traditional conservatives (also known as *classic conservatives*) look different from the social conservatives in leadership under the George W. Bush administration from 2001 to 2009. Unlike social conservatives, traditional conservatives have a strong belief in the separation of church and state and do not believe that the government has the right to legislate in the areas of religion, sexuality, and abortion.[38] They believe in small government, ceding most power to the states, and that responsible leaders balance the budget rather than leaving huge federal debt for future generations.[39] Five-time Arizona senator Barry Goldwater (1909–1998) is recognized as the father of the classic conservative movement, and was known as a staunch constitutionalist. A strong supporter of individual freedom and opponent of government interventions for private troubles, Senator Goldwater believed the public needed "to awaken . . . to a realization of how far we had moved from the old constitutional concepts toward a new welfare state."[40]

Economic Conservatives

Support a laissez-faire conservatism that preserves the traditional notion of individualism, and embraces the value of self-interest and self-regulation in pursing individual welfare. Like the classic conservatives, economic conservatives support being fiscally prudent and favor balancing the federal budget.

From an economic conservative's perspective, individuals are responsible for their own well-being and are free to pursue their own destinies. Individuals are perceived as solitary, competitive, rational beings with a singular focus on self-interest. Independence is highly valued (over interdependence), and the economy works best when individuals are left alone to pursue their economic goals and gains without any interference from the government.[41] Noted Noble Prize economist Milton Friedman espoused that social and political freedoms are the result of a free market economy where government has a minimal role.[42]

Social Conservatives

See the well-being of individuals and society as a whole linked to religious beliefs of sin, uncontrolled impulses, and destruction, and therefore believe that the welfare of the country rests in restricting freedoms in order to control the inherent flaws in human nature. Strongly aligned with the Christian Right, social conservatives reject the separation of state and church and believe it is a God-given right to pursue a political agenda that seeks to regulate private lives, especially in the areas of sexuality and abortion rights. For example, in 2003, President Bush prohibited (through executive order) the state department from giving family planning grants to international groups that provide counseling on abortion, because as a social conservative, he and his party's constituents believed abortion to be morally wrong.[43] On a cultural level, social conservatives seek to restore "traditional American values" that they believe have been eroded by feminism, secularism, and cultural relativism.[44] The G. W. Bush presidency came to personify the social conservative movement that often cites God in its policy decisions. The Christian Right was regarded as Bush's political base, and his administration worked to keep them happy by carving out a bigger role for religious organizations in providing social welfare programs, by opposing gay marriage, limiting funding on stem-cell research, and working to overturn the abortion rights decision established by the Supreme Court decision in *Roe v. Wade*. Of legal concern among some conservatives and most Democrats is the practice of involving churches in campaign efforts. For example, one tactic used by the Bush campaign was to encourage churches to send lists of congregation members to the campaign offices. Church members could then be targeted during the election campaign. Involving churches in campaign efforts violates the tax-exempt federal status that most churches hold and is therefore illegal.[45]

Neoconservatives

Are most concerned with foreign policy and believe that world peace is only possible through military strength, military interventions, and, when necessary, the use of preemptive strikes in the face of threats. Neocons, as they are often called, envision the world as a safer place when the United States dominates with military might and actively transforms hostile states into democratic allies with the hope of ending state-supported terrorism. The Neocons had called for the removal of Saddam Hussein since the Gulf War in the early 1990s and were the chief architects of the Iraq war. Ironically, they evolved from a group of socially liberal and militarily conservative intellectuals who became frustrated with the Democrats in the 1960s and 1970s, who espoused cuts in defense spending and increases in social spending. During the Reagan years, the Neocons found an avenue for their aggressive military agenda and most became Republicans, many serving in the Reagan administration. Familiar faces that have pursued a Neocon agenda in key government positions under Republican presidents since the 1980s include former Vice President Dick Cheney; former Defense Secretary Donald Rumsfeld; former deputy secretary of defense and former president of the World Bank, Paul Wolfowitz; former UN Ambassador John Bolton; former chief of staff and national security advisor for Vice President Dick Cheney, Lewis "scooter" Libby; and former Secretary of State Condoleezza Rice.[46]

Liberals

Diversity in Practice

Critical Thinking Question

What core beliefs separate the Republicans from the Democrats?

Liberals believe that government has a social responsibility to provide for the basic welfare of its citizens through government action and promote economic and social justice through social and economic policies.[47] Equality of access and opportunity for all citizens is central to liberal ideology; therefore, government intervention is necessary to ensure equal treatment of citizens by states and institutions, and to provide protections of individual rights and freedoms. Fundamentally, liberals believe that individuals, and thus society, have the capacity for meeting unrealized potential within themselves. Because they believe individual development will promote society as a whole, the government has a stake in promoting and investing in individual growth and the development of individual talents. Liberals are believers in possibility and change, a message central to President Barack Obama's presidential campaign and policy agenda. Although liberals believe in protecting rights, they are opposed to interventions that seek to regulate the private lives of citizens, in the areas of, for example, sexuality and abortion.[48] Liberals, like conservatives, come in various packages and take varying positions on a wide range of issues. Philosophically, liberals can be divided into two general camps: pragmatic liberals and humanistic liberals.

Pragmatic Liberals

Closely resemble laissez-faire conservatives in their views of human nature. They see individuals as capable, competitive, rational, and serving their self-interests. They promote individualism as a means to personal social welfare. However, pragmatic liberals split with the laissez-faire conservatives early in the twentieth century, when they came to understand the impact of capitalism on individuals in a rapidly industrializing nation. They recognized that the benefits of unregulated capitalism are dependent on where individuals start out in life, socially and economically. When starting out in life on an unequal footing (because of differences in class, ability, or social circumstances), individual effort alone is not enough to ensure individuals' equal access to the opportunities provided in American society, and thus the pursuit of happiness and success for those less advantaged is limited. Social conditions affect individuals' lives and their ability to provide for themselves, exercise their rights, and have equal access and opportunities in society. Pragmatic liberals see value and justice in the obligation of the government to intervene in social matters in order to guarantee liberty for everyone.[49]

When starting life on an unequal footing, individual effort alone is not enough to ensure equal access to opportunities, thus success for those less advantaged is limited.

Humanistic Liberals

Understand human beings as holding important interests beyond themselves, including neighbors, family, coworkers, and community. Humanistic liberals place a high value on autonomy, but understand that autonomy is really developed through relationships. One's well-being is promoted and determined by the quality of relationships with others and the interdependence of individuals. From this perspective, government should provide for the collective rather than for the individual, and create environments that support cooperation, mutuality, and a responsibility for each other, rather than promoting individual competitiveness. This approach will secure the collective as well as the individual welfare of citizens, promote equality (economic and social), and reduce social conflicts.[50] Humanistic liberalism best describes the political position of President Barack Obama and is demonstrated in his policy perspectives on how to build strong and safe communities and a strong economy. For example, during the health care reform debate, he made the case that universal access to health care for everyone would be good for business, the economy, health care cost reduction, families, and individuals (see the "Civic and Social Responsibility" section earlier in this chapter for more discussion on Obama's collectivist perspective). Under universal health care, the right to quality health care is no longer dependent on one's job benefits or bank account. Health equality is achieved, which provides many subsequent benefits for everyone in the country. The omission of a public option for health care in the health care reform act signed into law in March, 2010 reflected the still individualistic perspective that the country holds.

Beyond the pragmatic and humanistic liberal, three political factions dominate the Democratic Party: the conservative "Blue Dog Democrats"; moderate "New Democrats"; and, liberal "Progressive Democrats."

Blue Dog Democrats[51]

Comprise a group of 49 House of Representatives economic conservative Democrats and some social conservative Democrats who pursue a moderate-to-conservative fiscal agenda. They also work to build bridges across party lines for greater bipartisan support on important issues. Formed in 1994 under the leadership of Tennessee congressman John Tanner, the name "Blue Dog" emerged in the early days of the fledging coalition when members met in the offices of two Louisiana representatives who displayed "Blue Dog" paintings of Cajun artist George Rodrigue on their walls. John Tanner claims that Blue Dogs are "yellow dogs that have been choked by extremes in both political parties to the point they have turned blue."[52] "Yellow Dog Democrats" are regarded as fiercely loyal to the Democratic Party and hold a strong partisan stance, and would presumably vote for a "dog" over a Republican. The Blue Dog Coalition of conservative Democrats has been persistent in pushing for a balanced budget and reducing the growing national debt. To that end, the coalition called for fiscal accountability and responsibility in the Iraq war in a press release in January 2007, staged to call attention to a new resolution being introduced in the House. The resolution focused on four vital points to improve fiscal responsibility in Iraq:

1. Transparency on how war funds are spent;
2. Forming a "Truman Commission" to investigate how war contracts are awarded;
3. Funding the war through the normal appropriation process rather than through "emergency" supplements; and
4. Focusing U.S. resources on improving Iraq's internal policing operations.

In the area of social policy, Blue Dogs favor welfare reforms like those in the Personal Responsibility and Work Opportunity Reconciliation Act of 1996 passed under President Clinton and take credit for laying the foundation for bipartisan collaboration that has led to welfare reform in recent years. The Blue Dogs were successful in taking House seats from Republicans in the 2006 midterm election, increasing its membership numbers from 37 to 47 and adding substantial political clout to the group. They successfully pushed for and got "pay-go" rules in the House. Pay-go rules mandate that any and all new expenditures (war funds excluded) be matched with tax increases or spending cuts. During the 2008 election, the Blue Dogs picked up two more seats, bringing their numbers to 49. Most voted against the 2009 American Recovery and Reinvestment Act (also known as the stimulus package) in a show of protest against an out-of-control federal deficit and national debt.[53] Their Web site boasts a "national debt clock" showing the current real-time national debt and each taxpayer's share of the debt. At this writing, they reported a $13 trillion debt costing each tax payer $42,350.[54]

New Democrats

Represent a group of Democrats who support a probusiness agenda that will develop new economies and expand opportunities for individual growth and success in the private sector. This moderate group of Democrats has its origins in the 1980s resurgence of pragmatic liberalism, when the neoliberals emerged and moved the party toward a more centrist position on the political spectrum and endorsed more free trade and less regulation of private business. Supporters of a clean and revived environment, New Democrats reject the notion that economic growth and proenvironment policies are mutually exclusive; rather, they call for innovative industries that move the United States toward energy independence. Concerned with the growing economic threats to the middle class, New Democrats are committed to easing the tax burden on the middle class and shifting more of the tax responsibility to the wealthy. Other proposed supports for the middle class include "universal pensions" that workers can take from job to job; better family-leave laws and workplace policies that allow parents to spend more time with their families; strong public schools and increased support for college education; and health care that assures health care coverage for all working Americans and their children. The New Democrat Coalition's focus on the average American garnered its growing support during the 2006 midterm election, and they were able to increase its membership from 47 to 62 by capturing many Republican seats. Following the 2008 elections, its membership grew to 68. Although concerned with the quality of life for the average American, the New Democrats are equally pragmatic about national defense. They believe that safety in the homeland is enhanced by a strong military and the willingness to respond militarily when threatened, but they also rely on the willingness of national leaders to employ diplomatic options and to work closely with international institution in resolving regional conflicts and pursing world peace. The New Democratic Coalition and President Obama appear to be aligned on many issues such as health care, the environment, jobs, economic recovery, regulatory reform, and revitalizing small business.[55]

Progressive Democrats

Fall to the left of the New Democrats on the political spectrum and are more aligned with the humanistic liberal traditions. Born out of Governor George McGovern's campaign for president in the 1970s, the Congressional Progressive Caucus seeks to give voice to the diversity of the U.S. people and support policies that enhance social and economic justice, ensure civil rights and civil liberties, and promote a clean environment through renewable energies and sustainable economies. Ironically, in the seemingly ultraconservative atmosphere of the early twenty-first century, the Progressive Caucus in the House of Representatives is the largest bloc of House Democrats with 75 members and wields significant political power. Its most noted members are former DNC chairman and former governor of Vermont, Howard Dean, and Ohio representative and 2008 presidential candidate Dennis Kucinich. Progressive Democrats propose growing new and sustainable economies by investing in building affordable housing and rebuilding the nation's public schools and physical infrastructure, as well as by investing in creating new renewable energy sources. They view health care, decent housing, and fair and livable wages as rights, and believe that no working family should live in poverty. Preserving civil rights and civil liberties is of utmost importance to progressive democrats, and therefore, they advocate for the expiration of sunset provisions in the Patriot Act and the revision of remaining provisions to meet constitutional standards. In regard to foreign policy, the Progressives promote international cooperation and alliance building, oppose the Iraq war, and are pushing to bring U.S. troops home.[56] Like the New Democrats, the Progressive Democrats find much common ground with President Obama on issues such as sustainable energy and economies, health care, foreign relations, public education, livable wages, and the national infrastructure.

CONCLUSION—REPUBLICAN OR DEMOCRAT?

A range of political ideologies, values, and belief systems span the political spectrum from the far right to the radical left, and these variations occur not just across party lines but within political parties as well. Both Republicans and Democrats are made up of heterogeneous members who come together around common issues to oppose or support party platforms.

Differences between parties are expected, and these differences have long been acknowledged as stumbling blocks to policy progress, especially when the balance of power is near equal in Congress or the state legislature. Diversity of beliefs within a party can also hamper progress in achieving party objectives. Box 3.5 shows how intraparty politics can catch even the most seasoned politician off guard. Former New York senator Hilary Clinton inadvertently offended the liberal arm of her party when speaking at a meeting of moderate Democrats.

The notion that individuals are purely Republican or purely Democrat is a flawed one. Most of us do not fit neatly into either of these general classifications, but adopt varying positions along the political spectrum, depending on the issue at hand.

In policy practice, it is helpful to understand the many political positions that elected and appointed officials may take on any number of important domestic and foreign policy issues, and to recognize that not all Democrats and not all Republicans have unified positions on most issues. Further, it is common for some factions of Democrats to agree with some faction(s) of Republicans on selected issues. For example, New Democrats are similar to Classic Conservatives on economic policies, and many Social Conservative Democrats support the same social policies on abortion and gay marriage that Social Conservative Republicans promote. Likewise, Neoconservatives and New Democrats often align on military issues, but differ on how best to contend with social issues, such as health care. Understanding the diversity of political, social, and economic values and beliefs within and across party lines is valuable when encountering elected and appointed officials in policy practice. It helps to view them as unique individuals with positions and values similar to and different from your own, depending on the issue at hand. This makes it easier to embrace political figures as individuals concerned with providing the best quality of life for his or her constituents, and as such, they share a common goal with social workers— that of improving society. Regardless of political affiliation, the work of policy practice involves dialoguing and negotiating with political leaders and coming to an agreement on how best to meet the common goal of improving society as a

Box 3.5   Clinton Angers Left with Call for Unity

Senator Accused of Siding with Centrists

By Dan Balz

Washington Post Staff Writer

Wednesday, July 27, 2005; Page A03

Sen. Hillary Rodham Clinton's call for an ideological cease-fire in the Democratic Party drew an angry reaction yesterday from liberal bloggers and others on the left, who accused her of siding with the centrist Democratic Leadership Council (DLC) in a long-running dispute over the future of the party.

Long a revered figure by many in the party's liberal wing, Clinton (D-N.Y.) unexpectedly found herself under attack after calling Monday for a cease-fire among the party's quarreling factions and for agreeing to assume the leadership of a DLC-sponsored initiative aimed at developing a more positive policy agenda for the party.

The reaction highlighted the dilemma Democratic politicians face, trying to satisfy energized activists on the left—many of whom are hungering for party leaders to advance a more full-throated agenda and more aggressively confront President Bush—while also cultivating the moderate Democrats and independents whose support is crucial to winning elections. The challenge has become more acute because of the power and importance grass-roots activists, symbolized by groups such as MoveOn.org and liberal bloggers, have assumed since the 2004 election.

The most pointed critique of Clinton came in one of the most influential blogs on the left, Daily Kos out of Berkeley, Calif., which called Clinton's speech "truly disappointing" and said she should not provide cover for an organization that often has instigated conflict within the party.

"If she wanted to give a speech to a centrist organization truly interested in bringing the various factions of the party together, she could've worked with NDN," the blog said in a reference to the New Democrat Network, with which Daily Kos's Markos Moulitsas is associated. "Instead, she plans on working with the DLC to come up with some common party message yadda yadda yadda. Well, that effort is dead on arrival. The DLC is not a credible vehicle for such an effort. Period."

Other blogs noted that the day Clinton was calling for a truce, one DLC-sponsored blog was writing disparagingly of liberals. Marshall Wittman wrote from the DLC meeting in Columbus, "While someone from the daily kosy (misspelling intended) confines of Beserkely might utter ominous McCarthyite warnings about the 'enemy within,' here in Columbus constructive committed crusaders for progressivism are discussing ways to win back the hearts of the heartland."

Roger Hickey, co-director of the liberal Campaign for America's Future, said Clinton had badly miscalculated the current politics inside the Democratic Party and argued that she could pay a price for her DLC association if she runs for president in 2008.

"There has been an activist resurgence in the Democratic Party in recent years, and Hillary risks ensuring that there's a candidate to her left appealing to those activists who don't much like the DLC," he said.

Clinton spokesman Howard Wolfson tried to deflect the criticism. "Her point was simply to say that the goals and issues that divide us are less consequential than are the ones we share in common, and that unity is needed in the face of our shared challenge," Wolfson said.

John D. Podesta, who was White House chief of staff to President Bill Clinton, said he interpreted Clinton's remarks as critical of those on both sides—centrists as much as liberals—who would devote more energy to internal party battles than to confronting the right. But he said Clinton may have underestimated the bad feelings within the party. "I think she was trying to push the DLC back a little bit, but she walked into a crossfire maybe she should have realized was out there," he said.

Meanwhile, Jesse L. Jackson reopened his decades-old battle with the DLC by accusing the group of fronting for corporate interests while ignoring labor and civil rights leaders. "The DLC embraces CAFTA and sells admission to its conference to corporate lobbyists," he said in a speech to the AFL-CIO convention in Chicago.

Source: Used with permission from the *Washington Post,* www.washingtonpost.com/wp-dyn/content/article/2005/07/26/AR2005072601645.html.

whole. In this dynamic process, both social work policy practitioners and political leaders learn and grow in our understanding of the world, its people and their needs, and how best to meet those needs. Policy practitioners are often called to draw upon the social work values of acceptance and tolerance when confronted with fellow policymakers with opposing views, and to translate those values into effective skills of engagement, empowerment, and advocacy.

Log onto **MySocialWorkLab** to access a wealth of case studies, videos, and assessment. (*If you did not receive an access code to* **MySocialWorkLab** *with this text and wish to purchase access online, please visit* **www.mysocialworklab.com.**)

1. **Watch the Connecting Core Competency Practice Contexts video, "Keeping up with Shifting Context".** Assess the political climate of your state and state legislature, noting the state of the budget, and the balance of power among legislators, political parties and government branches. What factors in your state

suggest that policymakers might support a reversal of the budget cuts that impacted adult day care centers; or that they might be open to new funding sources in the budget that would re-fund transportation for adult day care participants. What factors exist that would work against there possible solutions?

2. **Review the Gay Marriage SCS.** What fundamental values and beliefs separated Julia and the show's host Mark Frazier on the position of gay marriage? How did Mark use these differences in the interview to upset Julia and gain political points?

PRACTICE TEST
The following questions will test your knowledge of the content found within this chapter. For additional assessment, including licensing-exam type questions on applying chapter content to practice, visit **MySocialWorkLab**.

1. Of the choices below which would *not* encourage public participation in policy decision making?
   a. Coalition building
   b. Voting
   c. Closed sessions on legislative committee meetings and policy making decisions.
   d. Public debates

2. Social work began to evolve as a profession through:
   a. University based training programs in "applied philanthropy"
   b. The Richmond grant that began funding social work efforts
   c. Informal church groups
   d. Organized charity work

3. Shortly after the Revolutionary War the two main organized political groups were:
   a. The Confederates and the Federalites.
   b. The Patriots and the neo-Federalists.
   c. The Anti-Federalists and the Federalists.
   d. The land owners and the neo-Federalists.

4. The respective national committee chairpersons for the Republican and Democratic parties:
   a. Only exerts the function of chairperson two or three times a year at the large national meetings.
   b. Must relinquish his or her previous job in order to be fully dedicated to the chairperson position.
   c. Can not participate in any foreign travel on behalf of the U.S. during their term as national committee chairperson.
   d. Is the core of the national committee, and among many duties is responsible for managing public relations with the media, and preparing for the national elections.

5. The Republican and Democratic parties of today:
   a. Hold similar party visions and values.
   b. Must hold political power in order to get their agendas passed into law.
   c. List very different issues and concerns on their party platforms.
   d. Adhere to their political agendas regardless of the desires and needs of constituents.

6. Government programs that reflect the conservative perspective of equity, where individual rewards come through individual efforts are called:
   a. Incentive programs
   b. Social insurance programs
   c. Public assistance programs
   d. Pragmatism programs.

7. Which group on the conservative political spectrum supports the ideology of small government, the idea that government should in no way interfere in the personal lives of citizens, and the distinct separation of church and state?
   a. Neo conservatives.
   b. Social conservatives.
   c. Economic conservatives.
   d. Classic conservatives.

8. Which liberal group split with their conservative counterpart in the early part of the twentieth century, promotes individualism, but recognizes that due to unequal standing in society, in some cases individual effort is not enough to ensure equal access to opportunities.
   a. Laissez-Faire conservatives.
   b. Pragmatic liberals.
   c. Blue Dog Democrats.
   d. Humanistic liberals.

Log onto **MySocialWorkLab** once you have completed the Practice Test above to access additional study tools and assessment.

Answers

Key: 1) c, 2) a, 3) c, 4) d, 5) d, 6) b, 7) d, 8) b

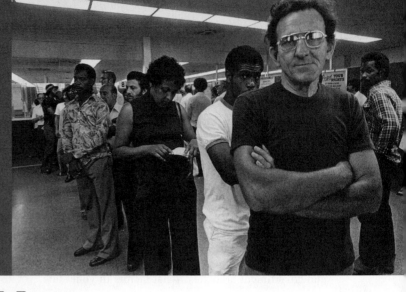

4

The Forces That Move
and Shape Policy

CHAPTER OUTLINE

Defining Policy 77
Types of Public Policy

Policy Formation 79
Social Institutions
Political Economy
Political Forces
Economic Forces

The Social Welfare System in a
Democratic-Capitalist Political
Economy 98

Conclusion 99

Chapter Review 100

Practice Test 100

 MySocialWorkLab 100
Health Care SCS
Gay Marriage SCS

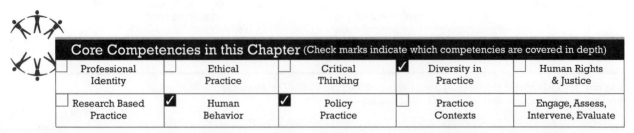

Core Competencies in this Chapter (Check marks indicate which competencies are covered in depth)				
☐ Professional Identity	☐ Ethical Practice	☐ Critical Thinking	☑ Diversity in Practice	☐ Human Rights & Justice
☐ Research Based Practice	☑ Human Behavior	☑ Policy Practice	☐ Practice Contexts	☐ Engage, Assess, Intervene, Evaluate

DEFINING POLICY

Use intelligence to shape policy, not twist intelligence to justify policy.

MADELEINE ALBRIGHT (JULY 29, 2004, DEMOCRATIC NATIONAL CONVENTION)[1]

In the broadest sense, "policy" encompasses all of the invisible forces that guide and direct much of our lives. Policies can take the form of informal tacit rules, such as who sits at the head of the table or who manages the household finances, to formal public policies that dictate what portion of our incomes goes to taxes to support public programs and projects, or whether or not our union with our beloved is considered a "marriage" and is sanctioned by the state of our residence. Policy—whether informal and personal, or formal at the local, state, and federal levels of government—touches all areas of our lives and those of our clients. As such, it is wise and necessary to be informed of existing policies that influence social work practice as well as how to influence policy in the making; and, how to change policies that are not working to the benefit of society or that oppress a particular segment of society.

Generally, one could say that public policy is just a way that the collective of society has found to address problems or potential problems that do or could affect a significant number of people and/or organizations. Policies provide us with a set of principles, intentions, and rules to guide the actions of individuals, communities, and public and private organizations. Policies set the rules of behaviors or actions, which in turn help to establish expectations of our individual behaviors and the actions of organizations and governing bodies. For example, through public policy, the Federal Emergency Management Agency (FEMA) was established to respond to disasters in an organized, effective, and efficient manner. As individuals, communities, and states, we have come to expect this agency to respond in expert ways to those affected by disasters. We find comfort in knowing that such an entity exists, and we depend on it in times of crisis. When a disaster occurs such as Hurricane Katrina or the wildfires in California, then it is the role and duty of FEMA (as sanctioned by public policy) to protect and care for those affected by the disaster. FEMA is held accountable for its actions and inactions and for the well-being of those in need, during and after a disaster. The principles, guidelines, intentions, and rules set forth in public policy are provided to direct actions for the public good, but also provide the criterion against which those sanctioned by public policy fulfill their responsibilities to the public.

The principles, intentions, and rules that guide public policies are grounded in underlying values and philosophies about human nature and how society "ought" to behave. For example, the FEMA policy operates under the assumption that it is right and good that society should respond to those in need during a disaster, rather than leave them on their own. This principle is so engrained in our social values that we (society) have determined that taxes will be collected for the purpose of ensuring the protection and safety of those affected by disasters through the funding of FEMA. Economics, then, also plays a major role in the implementation of public policy. The extent to which the economy can support the taxing of individuals and businesses for the cost of pubic services, hugely influences whether a policy will be adopted and to what extent services will be made available. Finally, political forces, such as the dominant political ideology in play, the presence of government or corporate scandals, the role of the media in portraying the politics of the day, and other events such as national elections,

Policy Practice

Critical Thinking Question

Identify at least one public policy that you take for granted and that touches your life daily. How does this policy serve you, your family, your community, and your state?

play major roles in the adoption, funding, and implementation of public polices and programs.

Types of Public Policy

Public policy takes many forms, such as executive decisions, regulations, laws, and public programs. Public policy is the visible manifestation of strategies and actions taken to address public concerns, and policies tend to be prescriptive in that they provide a set of goals or objectives to be achieved by a designated agency, task force, group, or individual. Public policies are also descriptive in that they seek to explain and delineate the actions being taken by government entities. Public policies are formal policies that contain an explicit intention, policy goal or goals, and a clear policy statement. For example, the Organic Foods Production Act of 1990 stated three broad purposes or goals of the new legislation. The policy goals were

> (1) to establish national standards governing the marketing of certain agricultural products as organically produced products; (2) to assure consumers that organically produced products meet a consistent standard; and (3) to facilitate interstate commerce in fresh and processed food that is organically produced.[2]

To achieve these policy goals, the Organic Foods Production Act of 1990 legislation set forth guidelines for growers of organic food and manufacturers of processed organic foods. These guidelines were then transformed into day-to-day standard operating procedures on organic farms and organic-food-manufacturing plants that ensured that the goals of the policy were fulfilled.

Public policies address any and all areas of concern to the public at large and are under the control of government at the local, state, or national level. Zoning and land use laws, the manufacturing of food, the registration of firearms, the ownership of real estate, the standards of water-treatment plants, and the building and maintenance of roads and bridges are all examples of outcomes of public policies.

Social policies are public policies that focus on improving the quality of life for citizens. Generally, social policies focus on providing the general public access to certain resources that will enrich the lives of citizens. Policies that fund and regulate public libraries and state and national parks are good examples of social policies. Finally, *social welfare policies* are more specific types of social and public policies that aim to address social problems. Social welfare policies are of the greatest concern to social workers, who have a professional commitment to helping people who are challenged by social problems such as poverty, unemployment, lack of health insurance, illnesses such as HIV/AIDS, or teenage pregnancy. Developing skills that will enable social workers to affect social welfare policies that can mitigate or alleviate suffering among large segments of the population and client groups is essential to effective social work practice, and is at the heart of policy practice. To be effective in shaping social welfare policies, social workers must first fully understand all the forces that influence the making of public policy, learn to intersect and participate in the policymaking processes, and know when to act in the midst of the social, economic, and political forces in play that ultimately produce social welfare policies and programs. Practically speaking, social welfare policies are concerned with the transfer of goods—from public funds to individuals and families in need and to organizations equipped with the expertise and infrastructure—to address social problems at the local and state levels of social functioning.

Social welfare policies are of the greatest concern to social workers, who have a professional commitment to helping people who are challenged by social problems.

POLICY FORMATION

To contemplate understanding all the interactions of the social, economic, and political forces in play at any particular time that could influence a particular body of social welfare policy can be daunting to say the least. The model provided in Figure 4.1 helps in compartmentalizing these forces and in understanding interactions among them.

Figure 4.1 depicts the major forces that determine the development, enactment, and funding of social welfare policies. Of significance is the social context within which policymaking occurs. The social context considers the historical era in which policies are made and also the dominant social values, cultural contexts, and the social attitudes toward the target population or issue being addressed in any given policy. It also considers historic or current events that may influence people's attitudes and opinions regarding policy change. For example, since 2000, the topic of legalizing gay marriage has been a prominent topic for state and national legislative bodies, with 40 states passing state laws or constitutional amendments to prohibit same-sex marriage between 2000 and 2008.[3] This initiative occurred in the context of a socially conservative administration whose core supporters were evangelical Christians who view homosexuality as a "sin." Given the prevailing attitudes of the political public, passing legislation to legalize gay marriage has been largely unsuccessful. As the political climate shifted with the campaign and election of Democratic President Barack Obama, so too did the attitudes towards gay marriage begin to change. The shift of political power from far-right toward left-of-center tipped the scales in some states in favor of gay marriage. Between 2008–2009, five states joined Massachusetts in granting same-sex marriage rights (Connecticut, Iowa, Vermont, Maine, and New Hampshire).[4] These policy outcomes are largely reflective of the prevailing attitudes toward gay and lesbian sexual orientation in the social and political contexts of the early twenty-first century. (For more on this fascinating policy topic, see the Simulated Case Study [SCS] on gay marriage, which demonstrates the ongoing struggle between social conservatives and liberals on the

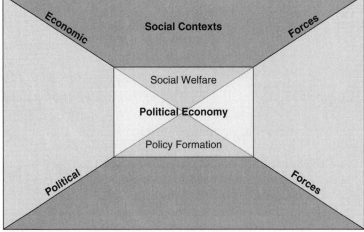

Figure 4.1
Forces Shaping Social Welfare Policy

subject of same-sex marriage; this resource is hosted at Allyn & Bacon's *My Social Work Lab* Web site.)

Social Institutions

Dominant social norms are established and often legislated by the most powerful within the economic and political systems.

Social values, beliefs, practices, and rituals that make up the social context of a society are molded and maintained by five major social institutions: the family, religion, economics, politics, and the social welfare system. While values and beliefs may vary widely from family to family, community to community, and from subculture to subculture, dominant social norms are established and often legislated by the most powerful within the economic and political systems. Generally, social institutions serve to organize social, economic, and political functioning and to maintain society, and when they are functioning at their best, to move society forward. Table 4.1[5] lists the primary social institutions,

Table 4.1   Social Institutions Function and Roles

Institution	Function	Roles
Family	Socialization	Transmits prevailing values, knowledge, and social behaviors to its members.
Religion	Integration	Establishes and maintains relationships among units in social systems such as the family, school, and church. Is responsible for getting members to behave in prescribed ways. Provides social support in times of need.
Economy	Production and distribution of goods and services	Initiates and develops businesses that in turn provide employment and the production of goods. Goods and services are consumed by the public for meeting the basic requirements of life and for establishing and expanding the standard of living (depending on the health of the economy).
Politics/ government	Social control	Laws, edicts, and policies are established in order to bring conformity of behaviors among members of society that are in concert with the established social norms of behavior.
Social Welfare	Mutual support	Provides support to members in the face of loss, increased need, or inadequate functioning of the other social institutions.

Sources: Neil Gilbert and Paul Terrell, *Dimensions of Social Welfare Policy*, 6th ed. (Allyn & Bacon, 2005); Seumas Miller, "Social Institutions," *The Stanford Encyclopedia of Philosophy* (Stanford University, 2007), http://plato.stanford.edu/entries/social-institutions (accessed January 3, 2008).

along with their roles and functions. Be aware that these are not the only forces that shape and influence society, but they are the major ones. For example, while family is identified as being the social institution that socializes the young into the social norms of the times, this also occurs within the educational system. Religion is a primary force in integrating members into society, but so too are voluntary associations, such as neighborhood associations and block clubs; interest group affiliations, such as the American Association of Retired People (AARP) and the National Organization of Women (NOW); and youth programs and organizations, such as the Boys and Girls Club. These are just a few examples of voluntary associations that help integrate people into society and give them a sense of belonging and connectedness to one another.

The economic institution is a central force in most people's lives because it provides them with the income necessary to purchase from the marketplace the goods and services required to meet the basic needs of life—food, shelter, fuel, health care, transportation, etc. Economics has to do with how we produce goods (and create jobs) and how we distribute those goods and services in the market place for consumption. Most people, when they collect their pay checks, take them to the marketplace to pay for groceries, house payment or rent, utilities, doctor bills, car payments and maintenance, and other basic necessities. When the economic institution suffers, most of us will feel it in minor ways that may be financially uncomfortable, but we are still able to function economically well enough to maintain our standard of living. When the economy takes a downturn, it is not uncommon to see an increase in the prices of some basic goods such as fuel, food, and housing as the production of these goods declines but basic demands remain constant. For example, during the economic downturn in 2000, the overall price of goods in the marketplace, as measured by the consumer price index (CPI),[†] rose only 3.4 percent; however, the price of basic products, such as meat, rose 4.5 percent, utilities 7.1 percent, and fuel oil 41.9 percent,[6] while wages for production workers rose less than 1 percent.[7] A more dramatic effect was seen in the recession of 2007 to present, with the bursting of the housing bubble and major losses in the stock market resulting in major job losses as companies downsized or closed. Between December 2007 and July 2009, 6.7 million jobs were lost in the United States, and the unemployment rate rose from 4.9 percent to 9.4 percent.[8] As people lost their jobs and had less money to spend in the marketplace, the demand for goods decreased and so did the price for items that people had to forgo because of job and income loss. For example, the CPI declined 4.9 percent from July 2008 to January 2009 as the population tightened their belts to wait out the recession.[9] Under these circumstances, it could be expected that more families would be faced with limited income and few reserves, and would face considerable difficulties in meeting basic needs; thus a higher demand for social welfare assistance is likely to exist.

When the economic institution is not functioning well, changes in the workplace take place. Wage and hiring freezes may occur for some companies, which may result in increased workloads for individuals when positions go unfilled,

---

[†]The consumer price index in calculated by the U.S. Department of Labor in the Bureau of Labor Statistics (BLS) by sampling products and services in major cities across the country across 8 major categories of products and 180 subcategories. The major categories are: (1) food and beverages, (2) housing, (3) apparel, (4) transportation, (5) medical care, (6) recreation, (7) education and communication, and (8) other goods and services. The BLS reports, on a monthly basis, the percentage of change in overall prices and specific market prices. Monthly and annual reports can be viewed at their Web site at www.bls.gov/home.htm.

and a decrease in real spending power when annual raises are put on hold. Others may experience an unbalanced and low-functioning economic system in more profound ways, such as job loss, as noted above, during the 2007 recession. Major financial insults to the family, and sometimes to whole communities, occur when plants shut down and other local businesses cut back or close, potentially crippling the functioning of individuals and families in a short period of time if the economy does not turn around quickly, or if the social welfare system is not sufficiently responsive to meet society members' basic needs.

Politics, as a social institution, is concerned with the overall social control of individuals, families, businesses, nonprofits, and other organizations. Through the passage of legislation, issuing of executive orders, and handing down of court decisions, society is provided with a set of rules to live by that are intended to keep life well organized, fully functioning, and peaceful. This set of rules reflects a recognized and acceptable set of social norms. For example, adult members of U.S. society are required to pay personal income taxes (assuming a certain level of income), have a valid driver's license when operating a car, observe standard traffic laws, be honest in their dealings with others (no stealing), respect others' persons and property (no harm), provide for one's children, treat people fairly in the workplace (no discrimination), and so on. The lists of "shoulds" and "should nots" are endless, and each prescribed behavior has attached to it a penalty for not conforming to acceptable and mandated standards. Failure to pay taxes may result in cash penalties, the confiscation of personal property, or criminal conviction and imprisonment. Not providing adequately for one's children puts parents at risk of having their children removed and placed in the foster care system; ignoring traffic laws can result in large fines or the loss of a driver's license. Politics is about ensuring that people behave in civil and responsible ways, as defined by the dominant social values of the times, and as interpreted and applied by those elected to power. Politics is almost always connected to economics. The federal income taxes, which residents are mandated to pay by law, fund the federal government, which in turn provides safe roads to drive on, parks to enjoy, student loans and grants for higher education, Supplemental Security Income (SSI) for the poor, elderly, and disabled, and so on. When the economic system suffers, often the political system is called to action in an effort to stimulate the economy. For example, soon after taking office in January 2009, President Obama called on Congress to pass an economic stimulus bill to provide funds to help fledgling businesses, provide tax credits for individuals and financial assistance for states (many of which were facing bankruptcy), and to extend and increase unemployment benefits for those who had lost their jobs due to the recession. Congress responded with the passage of the American Recovery and Reinvestment Act of 2009, which promised to infuse over $600 billion into the economy over a 10-year period.[10] The general purpose of the stimulus bill was to stop the hemorrhage of job losses that had started in 2007 by helping businesses stay open, to increase the amount of money people had to take to the marketplace to spend by providing tax credits, and to ensure that those who had lost jobs had sufficient income through unemployment benefits until they were able to secure other jobs. Putting more money in people's pockets to take to the marketplace increases consumer spending; this, essentially, is a boost to the economic system as it helps to stimulate the production and consumption of goods.

When several social institutions are not functioning well, or when individuals and families suffer major losses (such as during natural disasters) or have increased needs, people may find themselves unable to provide for all of their basic needs. When this occurs, the fifth institution, the social welfare system

Human Behavior

Critical Thinking Question

Review each of the social institutions listed in Table 4.1 and identify how you have personally been influenced by each of these institutions recently and over time.

(see the section "Social Institutions" on page 80), becomes a source of assistance and mutual support by providing income, job training and placement, housing, food, medical care, education, counseling, and other services. Table 4.2 provides an overview of the U.S. social welfare policies, programs, and benefits.

Table 4.2   Overview of U.S. Social Welfare System Policies, Programs, and Benefits

Policy/Program Focus	Policy/Program Name	Types of Benefits Provided
Income Maintenance	Minimum Wage Legislation	Guarantees a minimum hourly wage employers can pay a worker by law.
	State Living Wage Laws	Guarantees a minimum hourly wage that is higher than the federal minimum wage that employers must pay to workers in the state. Some states have attached an annual cost of living adjustment to their minimum wage standards.
	Earned Income Tax Credit	Individuals and families earning below a set annual income are eligible for income tax credits when filing their annual federal and state income taxes. The EITC results in added income in the form of a tax credit added to their tax refund.
	Social Security Income	Cash income paid to those 62 or older who have met the eligibility by paying social security taxes for 40 quarters (ten years) during their work life. Income level is primarily based on number of years worked and earning levels during an individual's work life.
	Unemployment Insurance	Pays a portion of lost income to those who lose their jobs through no fault of their own; for example, when someone is laid off or wrongfully fired.
	Worker's Compensation	Provides income and medical care to those who are injured on the job or become ill because of work conditions.
	Supplemental Security Income (SSI)	Provides cash income to those who are disabled or aged and poor.
	Temporary Assistance for Needy Families (TANF)	Provides cash, job training and placement, and social services to poor families for a limited time.
	General Assistance	Cash income provided by some states for people who are poor who do not have a means of support or income.
Nutrition	Supplemental Nutrition Assistance Program (SNAP) (formerly Food Stamps)	Cash transfer by EBT card for the purpose of purchasing food for low-income individuals and families.
	Food Distribution Programs	Distributes food commodities to low-income individuals and families at the community level.

(Continued)

Table 4.2   Overview of U.S. Social Welfare System Policies, Programs, and Benefits (Continued)

Policy/Program Focus	Policy/Program Name	Types of Benefits Provided
	School lunches, breakfasts, special milk and summer meal programs	Provides reduced or free meals to school children from low-income families.
	Special Supplemental Nutrition Program for Women, Infants, and Children (WIC)	Provides food supplements through cash coupons or by the distribution of food items for low-income pregnant women and children up to five years of age.
	Child and Adult Care Food Program	Provides meals and snacks year round to preschool children in day care and adults with disabilities in adult day care.
	Elderly Nutrition Program	Provides congregate meals and meals on wheels to the elderly.
Health Care	Medicaid	Health care for low-income families and individuals.
	Ryan White Care Act	Provides HIV/AIDS-related health care services.
	Children's Health Insurance Program (CHIP)	Provides health insurance coverage to uninsured low-income children.
	Medicare	Health care for the elderly and disabled.
Social Services	Child protective services	Prevention, investigation, and intervention in child abuse and neglect.
	Substance Abuse Treatment Programs	Provide prevention, treatment, and rehabilitation services to reduce personal and social cost of substance abuse.
	Adult Protective Services	Investigates and intervenes in cases of elder abuse.
	Family preservation services	In home services aimed at keeping families together rather than resorting to out of home placements.
	Community Mental Health Services	A range of community-level mental health care services on sliding scale basis.
	Day care	Day care assistance for low-income working families.
	Independent living and long-term-care services for the elderly and disabled	Provides services that promote independent living.
Employment	Employment Services	Job placement services for the unemployed disabled workers.
	Job Training	Job training and placement for unemployed workers.
	Vocational Rehabilitation	Job rehabilitation for unemployed disabled workers.
Housing	Public Housing	Government housing units for low-income families and disabled persons.

Table 4.2 (Continued)

Policy/Program Focus	Policy/Program Name	Types of Benefits Provided
	Housing vouchers/Section 8	Government vouchers that entitle low-income families to reduced rents.
	Mortgage Assistance	Low-interest loans to first-time low-income home buyers.
Education	Head Start	Preschool education and services to low-income preschool children and their families.
	Pell Grants	Provides educational grants to low-income undergraduate students.
	Public Education	K-12 education for all children.
	No Child Left Behind	Sets standards of learning for all public education students.

Knowledge of the fundamental social institutions in society is important for understanding how society as a whole functions, how individuals become socialized and integrated into society, and how values and beliefs are transferred from one generation to the next. Knowledge of these social systems helps social work practitioners in both the micro and macro areas of practice to (1) understand policy changes needed to help individuals and families find their places in society and (2) to create opportunities to contribute to the well-being of themselves, their families, and communities.

Political Economy

Powerful economic and political forces in play at any given period of time can dramatically influence policy outcomes. It is difficult, if not impossible, to completely separate economic and political forces, except for the purpose of discussion, because in reality they are inextricably linked. Theoretically, the point at which economic and political forces intersect is known as the "political economy," and it is from this point of interaction that social welfare policies emerge. Political economy simply describes the type of political system (e.g., democratic) and economic system (e.g., capitalist) that is operating in any given society. For example, in the United States, we live in a democratic-capitalist political economy that supports a market economy dependent to a large degree on open and free competition. Historically, exceptions to this rule have been made when major industries suffer economic insults (such as the savings and loan industry in 1980s; the Chrysler Corporation in the 1990s; and the airline industry following 9/11). During times such as these, government interventions have occurred in the form of large subsidies and low-interest loans, to guard against the collapse of a large percentage of an industry that in turn would leave many people unemployed. Such a catastrophic event has the potential to cripple the economy. When government interventions use tax payers' dollars to benefit private industry, it is often referred to as *corporate welfare.*

In a democratic-capitalist political economy, workers' wages, types of products, and rates of production are predominantly determined by market demand. As public demand goes up, production goes up and prices fall. As demands for new products are made, the market expands. Open competition in a market economy is the basic reason why there are so many different and affordable products for consumers to choose from.[11] In contrast to the U.S. democratic-capitalist political economy, Cuba has a communist-socialist political economy that supports a command economy that is dependent on government committees to make decisions about workers' wages, what will be produced, and how much will be produced. Consumer influence is minimal in a command economy. Since decisions about production are determined by government committees rather than consumer need or want, command economies often suffer from a shortage of products consumers want or need and a surplus of products consumers do not want.[12]

Each political economy is supported by and is premised on a set of underlying principles and assumptions of the two institutions—politics and economics. These assumptions and principles inform the development of policy. Some of the assumptions inherent in the democratic-capitalist political economy of the United States are that people have access to the policymaking process through free speech, open elections, the right to vote, public information regarding the candidates and policy issues, and access to their elected officials. It also assumes that people have *equal* access to the policymaking process and to the economic market. As a wage earner, I can donate money to my favorite causes or candidates. Another assumption is that in a free-market economy, competition is fair and unbiased. Those who are equally prepared compete on equal terms. Problems arise when these assumptions do not hold true; for example, when men are paid more than women for the same work; when hiring practices favor Caucasians over minorities or able-bodied people over people with disabilities; when income influences access to candidates and information; when reliance on public transportation limits one's ability to get a job and keep it, access the Internet for information, attend political rallies, or meet with their elected officials; then the underlying assumptions of the democratic-capitalist political economy begin to come into question. These are just a few barriers to fully engaging the economic and political systems that people may confront.

Barriers to the political and economic institutions in society limit individual and group influence on policy agendas and policy decisions. The extent to which people are not proportionately represented in government bodies will affect particular groups' access to power and resources. For example, the U.S. Congress continues to be comprised largely of white males, creating governing bodies that overrepresent the interests of white males and underrepresent the interests of women and people of color. Table 4.3 provides a breakdown of the representation of women and minorities in the 110th U.S. Congress (2008–2010) as compared to the groups' representation in the general population. Women were the most underrepresented group in Congress followed by Hispanics/Latinos and Blacks/African Americans, respectively. Females make up over half of the population but have a total representation of only 17.2 percent in Congress, constituting a 66 percent underrepresentation. They held 75 seats out of 435 in the House of Representatives and only 17 seats out of 100 in the Senate. This has significance when debating issues of importance to women such as child care, birth control, health care, pay equity in the workplace, and how to resolve differences in the global village. Women's voices are drowned out when men outnumber women more than 5:1 in the political forum. This argument holds true for minority groups

Diversity in Practice

Critical Thinking Question

How has the composition of Congress influenced policymaking and policy effects on various groups in society?

The extent to which people are not proportionately represented in government bodies will affect particular groups' access to power and resources.

Table 4.3   Underrepresentation of Women and Minorities in Congress (110ᵗʰ Congress)

Group	Percent of Population	Number in House	Percent of House	Number in Senate	Percent in Senate	Total Representation in Congress	Percent of Underrepresentation
Women	50.9%	75	17.2%	17	17%	17.2%	−66%
Hispanics/Latinos	12.5%	25	5.7%	2	2.0%	5.0%	−60%
Blacks/African Americans	12.3%	42	9.6%	1	1.0%	8.0%	−35%

Source: U.S. Census Bureau (2000), *Census 2000 Brief: Overview of Race and Hispanic Origin; Census 2000 Brief: Gender 2000*, Washington DC: Author, www.census.gov/population/www/cen2000/briefs.html (accessed January 3, 2008); and This Nation.com, *The United States Congress Quick Facts* (2008), www.thisnation.com/congress-facts.html (accessed August 29, 2009).

as well. All minority groups remain underrepresented in the U.S. Congress (Blacks, Hispanics, Native Americans, Asians, and Pacific Islanders). Without proportionate representation, the assumptions supporting a democratic-capitalist political economy become skewed toward those holding the balance of power.[13]

As social workers involved in policy practice, we seek to influence policies in ways that advance the core values of the profession. Self-determination, inherent worth and dignity, empowerment, and social justice become the lens through which social workers view the policymaking process when advocating for those who have less access to political and economic power. These groups may include individuals and groups who suffer from underrepresentation among elected officials, who have limited resources, or who are stigmatized in some way by the dominant social and economic class in society. Social work values provide a social justice perspective for policy practitioners to use in influencing social welfare policy changes for the benefit of the most vulnerable and silenced in society.

Political Forces

As discussed in Chapter 3, politics dominates government action whether it is inside the legislative chambers, in the executive office and appointments that emanate from it, in the court system where judges are elected or appointed, in the regulation and rules process, or in service delivery systems that implement policies through social welfare programs. The power of politics cannot be overstated in the construction and evolution (or devolution) of the social welfare state. Core ideological values about constitutional and civil rights, as well as moral grounding, are often rooted in religious beliefs and traditions. These are powerful forces that in many ways influence the future of social welfare as an institution in the United States. The influence of ideology, values, and beliefs frequently finds its way into the public policy debate through the media outlets that have become so important in issue campaigns and elections (more about this in Chapter 7).

Ideally, when one considers the open political system inherent in a democratic society, it is often assumed that the voice of all citizens will find an avenue in which to be heard. It is the belief in the democratic ideal of equal access to the political process that defines the power of a government *for the people, by the people, and of the people* and forms the foundation for the constitutional and civil rights we take for granted. How these rights are defined and distributed is dependent on the political climate of the times. When the more conservative Republican Party is in control, conservative interpretations reign; likewise, when the more liberal Democratic Party holds most of the political power, then more liberal interpretations dominate. For example, when considering the problem of poverty among families headed by single women, the cause of the problem and thus the solutions to the problem will vary, depending on political perspectives. Social conservatives are likely to interpret the problem as a moral failing among women who bear children out of wedlock or who divorce their partners and establish a single-parent household. These moral failings lead to a decline in household income, inadequate supervision of children, and job instability (when parenting demands interfere with work). In contrast, feminist liberals may interpret the problem as an outcome of women living in a patriarchal society that favors men over women in the workplace, does not compensate women for the essential work of raising families, fails to protect women from abusive husbands, does not recognize the value of children by providing affordable and safe child care, and promotes workplace policies that allow women to work and care for their children. These two vastly different understandings of the core issues of poverty among families headed by single women would demand very different policy responses. Conservatives would more likely favor punitive welfare programs that provide low benefits and high work demands (such as Temporary Assistance for Needy Families [TANF] program) and encourage marriage; liberal feminists would favor "equal wages for equal work" for women in the workplace and polices that support both motherhood and gainful employment, such as on-site day care and paid time off to care for sick children.

While this example has used positions at the more extreme ends of the political spectrum for the benefit of making a point, it is important not to polarize the political parties into conservative and liberal. As we discussed in Chapter 3, political views fall along a continuum on the political spectrum. Conservatives (or liberals) may hold the balance of power at any given point in time, but where the dominant values fall on the conservative (or liberal) political spectrum will depend on the power base in the party at the time. This is often determined by who is raising the most money and has connection to the most votes. For example, during the 2008 presidential election campaign, Democratic candidate Barack Obama raised $745 million with donors of both genders, showing a narrow gender split (42% females vs. 58% males), compared to the Republican candidate, John McCain, who raised $370 million but whose donors were predominately males (72% vs. 28% female)[14]. In contemporary elections, the winners have been those who could garner the most support through campaign donations and who were able to attract a wide following. From the demographics of donors from these two candidates, Barack Obama had the advantage on two fronts: He had the most support as represented by dollars raised and he had a wider base of support by gender. This political power, in turn, influences the party platform and political agenda of the newly elected president. As would be expected, those who contribute to a candidate are likely to vote for them. During the 2008 election, 57 percent of women voters cast their vote for Obama vs. 43 percent for McCain. This is consistent with the campaign contributions data that showed women contributing to Obama more often than to McCain. Other constituent groups that were big supporters of Obama during the election included voters under 30 years of age (61%) and nonwhite voters (90%).[15] President Obama will need to be particularly sensitive and responsive to the concerns of women, young constituents, and nonwhite voters to keep their support into the next election cycle.

Campaign donors, especially large donors, expect to have some political access and influence once their candidate gets elected, which is why many corporations and political action committees contribute to major presidential contenders on both sides of the political fence. A new donor demographic emerged during the 2008 presidential campaign, where large numbers of donors were small donors contributing $200 or less. For example, 88 percent of the money raised for the Obama campaign was donated by individual donors (compared to 54% of McCain's funds) and of these individual donors 54 percent contributed $200 or less (compared to 34% of John McCain's donors).[16] This shift in demographics suggests that President Obama is largely beholden to the public at large (individual small donors) rather than to large donors (that often represent special interests) that have dominated election campaign funding in the past. The largest donors for Obama were universities, investment firms, and businesses; while McCain's largest donors represented large banks and investment and security firms. In terms of cumulative contributions by a group, retired individuals or

Table 4.4   2008 Presidential Election Large Contributions

	Obama	McCain
Largest donors	1. University of California 2. Goldman Sachs 3. Harvard University 4. Microsoft Corp. 5. Google, Inc.	1. Merrill Lynch 2. Citigroup, Inc. 3. Morgan Stanley 4. Goldman Sachs 5. JP Morgan Chase & Company
Cumulative donation by a group or industry	1. Lawyers/Law firms 2. Retired 3. Education 4. Business 5. Securities and Investment	1. Retired 2. Lawyers/Law firms 3. Real Estate 4. Securities and Investment 5. Republican/Conservative political groups

Source: Open Secrets.org. Retrieved from www.opensecrets.org/pres08/index.php

organizations (such as AARP) ranked high—for both McCain and Obama (see Table 4.4).[17] Donors will expect to have access to the new president and have significant influence in shaping policies that will impact business, investments, and retired citizens.

Political Agendas

Political agendas can have a major impact (both positive and negative) on the making of social welfare policy. Presidents are generally people who have been heavily invested in the politics and economy of the country prior to being elected president, as a congressperson, state representative, governor, or some other elected or appointed political official. They come to power with ideas of what they want to accomplish as president and as the leader of their political party, which has its own set agenda (see Chapter 3 for an overview of party platforms). These accomplishments usually take the form of policies and often cost significant amounts of money. Presidents and their administrations pressure members of Congress to create and pass legislation that will support their political agenda and then fund the policies at appropriate levels. For example, President John F. Kennedy came to office with a political agenda of creating a public mental health care system. As a result of having a mentally ill sister who was treated with a lobotomy in the 1950s, Kennedy set mental health care as a high priority on his political agenda, which resulted in the passage of the Community Mental Health Act of 1963. The act provided for the construction of community mental health centers (CMHC) around the country, inpatient and outpatient mental health services, and community education.[18] The 1963 mental health legislation began the mental health movement across the country and changed the way the public viewed mental illness and care.

During presidential (and other) campaigns, candidates run on their political agendas and "campaign promises." They are measured by how well they kept these promises and have implemented their agendas after they are voted into office and when reelection time comes around. Presidents and other elected officials are cognizant of the power of political agendas and the necessity of keeping promises. During his election campaign, President Obama was elected on a comprehensive domestic and foreign political agenda that set priorities on

- Ending partisan politics in Washington
- Jump-starting the economy and easing the recession
- Making sure that all Americans have access to affordable, quality health care
- Rebuilding the public education system for global competition
- Restructuring the social security systems to ensure its long-term viability
- Creating a green economy and pursuing energy independence along with tackling climate change
- Ending the war in Iraq and expanding the U.S. presence in Afghanistan to finish our military mission there, and
- Rebuilding foreign relations with our allies to deter Iran in their efforts to develop nuclear weapons.[19]

Policy Practice

Critical Thinking Question

To date, how well do you think President Obama has lived up to his campaign promises?

To move his political agenda from hopes and ideas into reality, President Obama will need to issue executive orders, lobby Congress on legislation, and sign bills into law to create new policies and programs for ameliorating pressing social, economic, and political issues at home and abroad. In fact, his success as a president will, in part, be measured by the extent to which he accomplishes his stated political agenda goals. For example, daily accounts in the media of what's happening with the stock market, unemployment, job creation, and consumer consumption are ways in which the public keeps track of how much the president is accomplishing in his economic goals. New economic policy was made with the passage of the American Recovery and Reinvestment Act of 2009 within one month of President Obama taking office.[20] If the policy does stimulate the economy sufficiently to at least slow and turn around the recession, he will be able to claim a policy success. His ability to pass health care reform legislation allows him to claim some level of success in meeting his campaign promise of affordable health care for everyone.

President Obama's ability to get the stimulus bill passed so quickly after taking office also supported his political agenda of ending partisan politics in Washington. The president was able to bring sufficient members of both parties together to accomplish passing this legislation in record time, indicating that, at least for important and pressing issues like a tumbling economy, he was able to break through old partisan ways of doing things in Congress (at least at this one point in time on this most important issue). He will need to demonstrate his ability to continue this trend on other issues as his presidency continues in order to claim success on this important campaign promise.

Challenges to implementing new policies and to achieving political goals occur frequently in politics, making it difficult to achieve policy goals, regardless of the good intentions of a President or party. For example, as President Obama was working on building momentum for the passage of the health care reform bill, reports issued by the Congressional Budget Office on the projected cost of the health care bill and the accompanying budget deficit of $7–9 trillion by 2019 raised concerns among constituents. Opponents of the bill used this fiscal data to slow down the health care reform movement by claiming that the level of deficit spending that the health care reform bill would create was not sustainable over the long run.[21] Ultimately, opposition forces were able to dilutes some of the core elements of the health care reform bill in its final passage, such as the elimination of a public health insurance option.

Voters who elected President Obama into office in 2008, and who were serious about the *change* he promised during his campaign, will be assessing his success in fulfilling his political agenda until reelection time comes around again in 2012. The extent to which he has been successful in implementing new policies to realize his political agenda will be reflected in his public approval ratings and his ability to get reelected.

Political agendas of governors and state legislators can also have an enormous impact on federal social welfare legislation and programs. As new ideas and programs are developed and implemented at the state level, they can gain momentum when recognized and promoted by the media, or when other states follow suit. Political agendas can be floated to the top and be incorporated into national-level policymaking. For example, Governor Tommy Thompson of Wisconsin (governor from 1987 to 2001) initiated the revamping of the welfare system in his state early in his first term. With the support of the state legislature, new welfare laws were enacted and a waiver to implement and evaluate a new approach to welfare was granted by the federal government. Thus began the new "Wisconsin Works" or "W-2" welfare reform programs that invested in job training and job placement and required that Aid to Families with Dependent Children (AFDC) recipients participate in job training and then find a job; or, if unable to find a job, to participate in a community work program. The new welfare architecture was based on the belief that families were on welfare because they were unable to work or chose not to work, and that dependency is harmful for recipients and their family. The welfare reform of Wisconsin received high marks as AFDC caseloads began to fall. As a national leader in his party (president of the Republican Governor's Association and president of the National Governor's Association), Thompson was able to garner considerable attention to the accomplishments of welfare reform in his state. During the 1990s, with a Republican-controlled Congress, welfare reform was a top priority at the national level. When constructing new legislation to reduce the welfare rolls in the country, members of Congress turned to the "tested" model used in Wisconsin. The influence of Wisconsin's welfare reform programs can be seen throughout the welfare-reform legislation: The Personal Responsibility and Work Opportunity Reconciliation Act of 1996 that "changed welfare as we know it" with greater emphasis on work, fewer benefits, and time limits. Interestingly, assessments of the Wisconsin workfare program, while positive in terms of caseload declines, credited the caseload declines largely to shifts in the state's improved economy as unemployment rates fells from 8.9 percent in 1986 when the workfare programs began, to 3.4 percent two years later.[22]

The Media

There is probably not a more important tool for wielding political power and shaping public opinion than the media. All political strategists are very adept at using the media to shape a message, create a public image, or frame a political issue or campaign (see Chapter 7, "The Media, Public Opinion and Policy Practice"). Media outlets can literally put a face on social problems and point the finger at who or what is to blame, and consequently they have become powerful weapons in the past half century in defining elections and social policy. The "truth" about any particular candidate or policy issue can become irrelevant. For example, in 2006, when President Bush made a deal to sell the operating rights of six ports in the United States to Dubai Ports World of the United Arab Emirates, a ruckus occurred over the sale of U.S. ports to a foreign entity.[23] This occurred at a time when President Bush had reached an all-time low in public approval ratings and contentions over the Iraq war were hot. Public debate over the "sale" of U.S. ports to a Middle Eastern company eventually killed the deal. The media was a useful tool in this debate. What they failed to report was that the operating rights of the six ports were already owned by a British company who was seeking to sell them to Dubai. Only 39 percent of the polled public knew that the ports were already owned by a foreign entity![24] Politically, this played well for Democrats hoping to build support for the fall midterm Congressional elections, where they eventually won and took control of Congress.[25]

Economic Forces

The term "economic forces" covers a lot of ground and includes such things as the state of the national, state, and local economies (which is influenced by international economies); the dominant economic theory in play and therefore the economic strategies used to affect the economy; the employment rate and wage structure, production trends and job structure; the political agenda of the sitting administration; the hiring and firing practices, layoffs, and corporate corruption; the extent to which the public has faith in big business; how secure people feel in their jobs; the performance of the stock market and levels of economic security among the population; the outsourcing of jobs to foreign countries; and globalization in general. With so many possible economic factors influencing social welfare policy, it can be overwhelming to think about having a handle on all of these factors in order to make good policy practice decisions. Many of these factors are linked and have reciprocal relationships, so understanding one factor can help you understand and predict the influence of other economic and political forces. Economics involves the ways in which goods, services, and other resources are produced, distributed, and consumed in a society in order to promote and maintain the material welfare of the country. Material welfare, in turn, influences the overall social welfare of the population. For example, if I am materially well provided for through my job or family money, I can take those monies to the marketplace and purchase what I need to take care of my social welfare needs, such as a house to live in, a car to drive, food to eat, health insurance, vacations and recreation for my family, counseling services in times of crisis, and so on. To the extent that individuals, families, and communities do not have sufficient material welfare, they are limited in their abilities to provide for all of their social welfare needs. In cases where large numbers of individuals, families, and communities are not able to meet their basic social welfare needs because of minimal material wealth, social welfare policies have been put in place with the intention of providing all U.S. citizens with a minimal standard of living. These policies are paid for through individual and corporate income taxes and special taxes such as Medicare taxes or Social Security taxes, and are intended to provide shelter and housing for the poor and homeless, health care for the uninsured, food for the hungry and poor, protection for those victimized, and other social needs. The government becomes a bit like Robin Hood in that it collects from the more materially well-off and distributes these monies to the less materially well-off in the form of cash, goods, and services (see Table 3.2).

Economic Theories[26]
Economic theories attempt to explain how the economy works at its peak performance by laying out some basic underlying assumptions about how healthy economies operate. Capitalist economies have been dominated by two theories over the past 75 years: (1) supply-side economics (a favorite of President Ronald

Reagan's, which he referred to as "trickle-down economics") and (2) Keynesian economic theory, also referred to as consumer-side economics (heavily endorsed by President Franklin Delano Roosevelt).

Supply-side economics works on the age-old assumption that the economy works best when left alone, stressing the concept of a self-regulating economy that is naturally regulated by the perfect competition of a capitalist economy. Producers make a large number of products (supply) available, which then drives down prices so that the public can afford to buy the products. This, in turn, stimulates a continuing demand for a favorable product long after it has been introduced to the market. Based on the beliefs of perfect competition and a self-regulating market, supply-siders view any government interference in the market economy as harmful. Business and economics specialist Robert Hessen defines "perfect competition" as follows:

> Under perfect competition all firms are small scale, products in each industry are homogeneous, consumers are perfectly informed about what is for sale and [at] what price, and all sellers are what economists call price takers (that is, they have to "take" the market price and cannot charge a higher one for their goods).[27]

As the market economy has expanded over the last two centuries and government interventions have increased, this idea of perfect competition has given way to political and economic forces, both at home and globally, that have created a marketplace of big corporations that swallow up small firms. The Antitrust laws first adopted in 1890 with the enactment of the Sherman Act were intended to protect small firms and to guard against the domination of a few large national firms.[28]

Supply-siders see large social welfare programs as detrimental to the economy in two ways. First, the ability to gain income and goods outside the workplace promotes dependency and erodes the work ethic so important to business productivity and a healthy economy. People are needed to go to work in order for the economy to grow and to remain stable. Second, social welfare programs divert money away from the private sector where it could be used to form more businesses and create better products. If business owners are required to pay higher taxes in order to support large social welfare programs, then they will have less money to invest in business growth and product development. Overall, this lack of investment is seen as detrimental to the health of the economy. From this belief structure, it makes most sense for the government to provide supports that reward work over leisure and investment over consumption, which, in turn, fosters the expansion of the economy. Overall, the supply-side argument is that economic growth is good for everyone because it creates more jobs, higher incomes, and more goods for consumption. These benefits eventually filter down to the poor (trickle-down economics). In practical terms, the assumptions supporting supply-side economics translate into economic policies that take the form of:

- Tax breaks for the wealthy. The assumption is that when the wealthy or business owners have more money on hand, they will invest it into businesses, which, in turn, will create more jobs for the masses;
- Cutting social programs, which then requires fewer taxes to support social programs, leaving more money for business investment and development;
- Strict eligibility requirements for using public social welfare programs. Since the use of publicly funded goods and services produces a disincentive to work, then it is in the best interest of the overall economy to apply stringent criteria for participation in welfare programs;

⯈ Little direct responsibility for the social welfare for the citizenry. If the
economy is running strong in an unregulated marketplace with minimal
tax burden on individuals and businesses, then full employment is
possible and wages are sustainable. People will provide for their own
welfare by taking their money to the market and purchasing what they
need. This consumption of private social welfare needs and services, in
turn, fuels the economy and adds to its robustness;

⯈ Deregulation of the market economy. When the government institutes
fewer regulations on the economy, it is able to return to its natural
"perfect competition."

Economic theories inform economic policies and therefore have direct influences on the funding of domestic programs and the military budget. For example, conservative administrations tend to support a supply-side economy that
influences economic, domestic, and defense policies. During the first term of the
George W. Bush administration, the economy hit a rough spot, and President
Bush responded with a series of tax cuts (which primarily benefited the
wealthy)[29] for the theoretical purpose of having more money available to invest
in business expansions and new business starts. Domestic social programs tend
to get cut under supply-side conservative administrations because they are seen
as a diversion of money from business, where jobs are created and where more
people can be employed, and also because welfare programs are believed to
erode the work ethic. For example, in 2007, President Bush vetoed legislation
intended to renew and expand the State Children's Health Insurance Programs
(SCHIP). The Congressional Budget Office estimated the program would cost an
additional $1.2 billion in 2008, but would save the federal government an esti-
mated $500 million in Medicaid costs.[30]

Finally, in a conservative climate where political actors tend to be hawkish,
military might and expenditures tend to expand. For example, under the George
W. Bush administration, war was the highest priority during both terms. This
resulted in a growth of the defense budget from $295 billion in 2000 to $520 billion in 2006 (a 44% increase),[31] as the cost of the Iraq war grew. As of 2007,
$602 billion had been spent on the war in Iraq.[32] Wars have an economic bene-
fit of creating jobs that provide supports in the form of supplies and services for
those in the military theater. As pressure mounts for the war to wind down and
for troops to return home, economic concerns arise as military-related jobs are
predicted to plummet.[33]

Keynesian economics takes a different view of how best to generate a healthy
economy. Developed in the 1930s by the economist John Maynard Keyes in an
effort to explain and understand economic recessions and depressions,[34]
Keynesian economic theory posits that the economy is naturally volatile and in
need of government macrostabilization through regulations. The theory operates
from the assumption that (1) it is not enough to have a strong economy that
works for some, but not for all members of society and that (2) it is equally important that essential services are available and affordable in all geographic locations
and to all socioeconomic classes. Meeting this goal often results in government
interventions that regulate how services are provided and that regulate pricing.
Keynesians do not deny the role of supply and demand in the economy, but
claim that a self-regulating market and perfect competition are not enough to
keep the economy stable, because it is prone to recessions. By the mid-1940s
economists were observing *business cycles* in most developed economies in the
world. Markets experience booms of high production and low unemployment,
and conversely, markets go through recessions or depressions where markets

produce below capacity and unemployment rises. This ebb and flow of market activity is referred to as *business cycles*.[35] Further, Keynesians claim that the attainment of full employment has proven to be elusive at best. Over the past quarter of a century, unemployment rates have ranged from a high of 9.7 percent in 1982 to a low of 4 percent in 2000.[36] In July 2009 the unemployment rate had escalated to 9.4 percent as a result of the lingering recession.[37] Low unemployment rates represent a healthy economy, because most of those wanting to work are able to be employed. However, even with a low rate of 5 percent unemployment, this represents approximately 15 million people who are actively looking for work but unable to find it, demonstrating that the economy is not working well for everyone. To help minimize the impact of a recession on the citizens, Keynesian economists believe that during periods of increased unemployment and inflation, the government should take some corrective action to help restore the economy to stability. Such corrective actions may mean increasing or decreasing the total spending output of the government, which, in turn, adjusts the consumption of individuals through the transfer of public goods and services to those most in need (social welfare). For example, those who lose their jobs and are unemployed for an extended period of time lose the ability to purchase what they need. A decrease in consumption puts a strain on the economy when unemployment is high because overall consumption goes down. To boost consumption, and therefore the economy, the government provides cash relief that individuals take to the marketplace and spend, thereby increasing consumption and stimulating the economy. In addition, if the government purchases goods and services to be provided to those who have lost income due to unemployment, then businesses receive a boost by producing the goods that the government will distribute to those in need. For example, the agriculture and food retail industries get significant boosts from the Food Stamp Program each year, as recipients take their Electronic Benefit Transfer (EBT) cards to the grocery store to purchase essential food stuffs. The U.S. Department of Agriculture estimates that for every $5.00 of food stamp benefits spent, it generates $9.20 in total community spending; and, that $1 billion in retail food demand generated by food stamp recipients supports approximately 3,300 farm jobs each year.[38] This increase in food purchases puts a demand on the agriculture business to provide more goods for consumption. There is also a benefit to the manufacturer and local grocer who will profit from continued sales during a recession. If consumption remains stable, then, as a manufacturer or grocery store owner, they may not have to lay off employees, which would also weaken the economy.

Only 65 percent of those eligible use food stamps. It is estimated that a 5 percent increase of food stamp recipients would result in an additional $971 million/year being funneled into the economy, which, in turn, would generate $1.8 billion in total economic activity.[39] Keynesians see consumption as key to a healthy economy and believe that it is the role of the government to ensure that consumption continues during periods of economic downturn. Eventually, consumption will trigger economic growth, and those who are without work will be called back to their jobs or find new jobs. Then, the need for government assistance will decline, and government expenditures will drop as the economy returns to a healthy level of production. Through these methods of economic regulation, as the economy slows, government spending expands (sometimes called deficit spending); as the economy picks up again, government spending contracts as fewer people need government assistance. Furthermore, the expansion of social welfare expenditures during times of recession is helpful to the overall national income by keeping people healthy so they can return to work when the economy shifts, and by providing jobs through social services and continued production. Keynesian or consumer-side economics is argued to be a more humane way of managing the economy because it does not leave large portions of the population to fend for themselves during economically hard times. Social welfare expenditures are investments in human capital that ultimately increase the national wealth and therefore boost everyone's net income. Economic policies that operate from a Keynesian theoretical perspective provide an increase of government transfer of cash, goods, and services through the expansion of social welfare programs during periods of recession, since stimulating the production of goods through consumption is essential to getting the economy back on track.

Monetarism is another economic theory, developed by Nobel Prize Laureate Milton Friedman, who believed that the market should be regulated using simple monetary rules. First, the role of government should be to keep the money supply steady, growing slowly at a rate that is consistent with stable prices and long-term economic growth. This is believed to be important, because when money growth exceeds the amount of growth of output, then inflation ensues. Friedman recommended that the Federal Reserve regulate the supply of money during the ebb and flow of the business cycles, expanding the supply during recessions and contracting it during booms. The second rule of monetarism is that the government should be inactive in economic affairs and not intervene in the business cycle, limiting the government's interventions to the regulation of the growth of money.[40]

While these two "rules" seem a bit contradictory, Friedman's theory represents a mixed economic approach where government regulation controls money flow through the adjustment of interest rates and exchange rates, but leaves the business of production and consumption to investors, business owners, and consumers. In response to the 2007–present recession, interest rates were cut many times to almost nothing, but with little economic response.[41] This insufficient economic response primed support for the American Recovery and Reinvestment Act of 2009, a $600 billion (plus) stimulus package.[42]

In reality, government interventions extend well beyond monetary policies described in monetarism and include such things as tax exemptions, tariffs, and subsidies to protect and/or boost different segments of the production apparatus. Although social scientists, economists, politicians, and others concerned with economic and business growth and cycles may espouse a particular economic theory, most would agree that the U.S. economy represents a mixed economy—employing principles and practices of all of the dominant theoretical approaches to maintain a stable economy.[43]

Budgets, both federal and state, represent a type of social policy in that funding is required to materialize programs and services at the community and personal levels. The priorities of the elected leadership in state legislations and in Congress can be readily assessed by examining where the money is spent and at what levels programs are funded. For example, in President Bush's proposed 2008 budget, he asked for an increase in defense spending and a cut in discretionary spending, which funds domestic nonentitlement programs such as the Special Supplemental Nutrition Program for Women, Infants, and Children (WIC). This program, which serves low-income pregnant women and their children up to five years of age by providing nutritious foods, has repeatedly shown, through extensive research, to improve pregnancy outcomes, reduce the number of low-birth-weight babies, and improve the nutrition and health of children. President Bush threatened to veto appropriation bills that exceed his recommended levels of spending. Based on the analysis by the Center for Budget and

Table 4.5   Median Income by Gender and Race

	Median Earnings (2006)	
	Men	**Women**
White	$45.727	$34,133
Black	$34,480	$30,398
Hispanic	$27,490	$24,738

Source: U.S. Census Bureau.

Policy Priorities, this would mean a reduction in WIC funding and cutting 500,000 poor women and their families from the WIC program. Poorer states with higher poverty rates, such as Alabama, Louisiana, Texas, New Mexico, and the District of Columbia, would suffer disproportionately compared to other states with healthier economies.[44] As demonstrated here, budget priorities can have a profound impact on the lives of poor women and children.[45]

How Fair Is the Economy?

The US economic system was built on the notion that a free and unregulated marketplace will best meet the needs of the population through the consumption of goods and services in the marketplace. This capitalist theory assumes that all consumers have equal information, equal access, and equal ability to purchase goods and services. As the structure of U.S. families and the diversity of the population have changed over time, these basic assumptions have been demonstrated to be less true for some families and individuals than others. For example, single-headed families on average have lower incomes to provide for the needs of their children, and women still earn less than men doing the same job with the same qualifications. In addition, inherent "isms" in the marketplace influence institutional hiring, promoting, and firing practices, making it easier for some to find livable-wage work than others. For example, the median income for white males is $45,727 compared to $34,480 for black males, and $27,490 for Hispanic males (see Table 3.4). Women consistently earn less than men across all races, with the largest gender gap existing between white men and women, and the smallest gap between Hispanic men and women (see Table 4.5).[46].

Women consistently earn less than men across all races, with the largest gender gap existing between white men and women, and the smallest gap between Hispanic men and women

Many political and economic leaders continue to operate on the definition of the traditional family, historically viewed as a unit made up of two heterosexual spouses—the male as the primary wage-earner, and the female as primary caretaker of their offspring—but in reality, only about half of Americans families live in this traditional family arrangement.[47]

THE SOCIAL WELFARE SYSTEM IN A DEMOCRATIC-CAPITALIST POLITICAL ECONOMY

In a democratic-capitalist political economy where full engagement in the political and economic systems are necessary in order to attain the ideals of a democratic society and to provide well for one's social welfare needs, many are left out. Barriers to the marketplace due to geo-graphic location and the lack of public trans-portation—or because of "isms" that exist in society where attitudes and beliefs regarding certain groups are passed on from one genera-tion to the next and embedded in the structures of our social institutions—keep many people on the margins of society. The social welfare sys-tem contributes to the maintenance and sur-vival of a society by transferring funds from the "haves" to the "have nots" through the collec-tion of taxes and the redistribution through social programs, which ensure a minimum standard of living for all citizens. The notion of equality inherent in democratic ideals can become elusive within a capitalist economy that is out of reach for some. The social welfare system acts as a buffer between these opposing societal mechanisms of democracy and capital-ism, thus counteracting some of the "unequal" effects of the free market on women, children, minorities, disabled, and other vulnerable pop-ulations. Care for vulnerable groups through job training and placement, social services, and income-maintenance programs also helps to appease groups who are not accessing their share of the American Pie, and this also helps to maintain social control, particularly in a society

that tends to fracture along social, political, and economic lines. The U.S. social welfare programs also provide huge subsidies to the market-place that are important to industries such as agriculture, housing, and health care. Finally, social welfare policies and practices are a means for rectifying past injustices. For example, affirmative action was intended to remedy historically racist and sexist practices that have denied minorities and women equal access to eco-nomic opportunities and positions of power. The social welfare system sup-ports not only the poor and marginalized in society, but all members of society through the maintenance of health, order, social and economic justice, and a healthy economy from which we all benefit.

CONCLUSION

Social work policy practitioners are uniquely positioned and prepared to have profound impacts on social policy. Trained in clinical practice, advocacy, and policy formation and implementation, there is probably no other helping pro-fessionals better prepared than social worker to advise policy makers on the impact of current and proposed polices on vulnerable populations. Social workers' knowledge of the roles of policy formation, social welfare service structure and delivery systems, social institutions, and economic and environmental factors in influencing professional practice make them a powerful force in shaping social policy.

Succeed with PEARSON mysocialworklab

Log onto **MySocialWorkLab** to access a wealth of case studies, videos, and assessment. (*If you did not receive an access code to* **MySocialWorkLab** *with this text and wish to purchase access online, please visit* www. mysocialworklab.com.)

1. **Review the Health Care SCS.** In the Health Care SCS, identify one economic and one political factor or force that influenced and shaped the policy platform that the Care4Care task forced adopted.

2. **Review the Gay Marriage SCS.** In the Gay Marriage SCS, social worker Julia Cohen is spearheading an advocacy campaign to support the right of gay and lesbian couples to be married, while her family friend and political opponent, Senator Hawkins opposes gay marriage and blocks efforts to move legislation in this area. What underlying assumptions, values and beliefs support each of the positions these political actors take on the topic of gay marriage? How are these played out in policy options proposed for each side of the issue?

PRACTICE TEST
The following questions will test your knowledge of the content found within this chapter. For additional assessment, including licensing-exam type questions on applying chapter content to practice, visit **MySocialWorkLab**.

1. Explicit intention, policy goals, and a clear policy statement are the essential building blocks for:
   a. Verbal agreements
   b. Any formal public policy
   c. Formal public contracts
   d. Informal contracts between two people.

2. Family, politics, and religion are some examples of:
   a. Social agencies
   b. Social institutions
   c. Informal social groups
   d. Social service vehicles

3. The major social institution responsible for ensuring that people behave in a civil and responsible manner is:
   a. Family
   b. Religion
   c. Social Welfare
   d. Politics

4. Government interventions using tax payer money to assist private industry is referred to as:
   a. Corporate welfare
   b. Industrial welfare
   c. Business bailouts
   d. Private industry welfare

5. Social workers involved in policy practice are constantly looking for ways to advance:
   a. The core values of social work: empowerment, self determination, social justice, and inherent worth and dignity
   b. Existing programs in their area that have proven the most beneficial to the greatest number of people
   c. Interest in social work as a profession and getting new people interested in becoming social workers.
   d. NASW's policy agenda when speaking with any elected official

6. The disparities among wages are most acute between:
   a. White males and Black males
   b. Hispanic males and Hispanic females
   c. Black females and White females
   d. White males and White females

7. Dominant economic theory and related economic strategies, and the state of local, state and national economies are all fundamental elements of:
   a. Stockbroker strategies
   b. Economic forces
   c. Federal Reserve rates
   d. Determining interest rates on loans

8. The concept of "perfect competition" is a cornerstone of what economic theory?
   a. Reaganomics
   b. Socioeconomics
   c. Supply-side economics
   d. Keynesian economics

9. Regulating the market by keeping the money supply steady, and limiting the government's intervention in the economy to growing money, are tenets of what economic theory?
   a. Monetarism
   b. Supply- side economics
   c. Keynesian economics
   d. Friedmanism

10. In order for elected officials to retain their constituents and supporting interest groups they must:
   a. Be gracious and appreciative of the support but strictly following the political agenda they have set out and not permit any outside influences on the agenda or related policies.
   b. Be aware of who contributed to their campaign and be particularly sensitive and responsive to the needs of those groups.
   c. Energetically lobby for contributing groups' needs and bear little mind for any other individuals or groups that did not actively support their campaign.
   d. Capitulate to contributing groups and shift their political agenda to cater to these groups due to their support during the campaign

Log onto **MySocialWorkLab** once you have completed the Practice Test above to access additional study tools and assessment.

Answers

Key: 1) b, 2) b, 3) d, 4) a, 5) a, 6) d, 7) b, 8) c, 9) a, 10) b

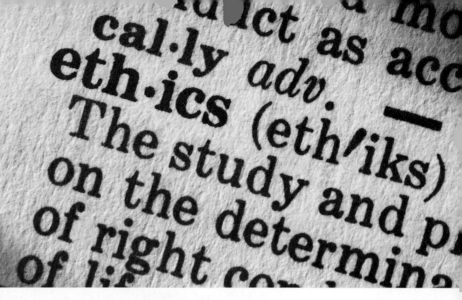

5

Ethics in Policy Practice

CHAPTER OUTLINE

Introduction 102

Ethical Frameworks for Policy Practice 103

Boundaries of Ethical Policy Practice 109
Boundary: The NASW Code of Ethics
Boundary: NASW Standards for Advocacy and
    Political Action
Boundary: Laws
Boundary: Societal Norms and Personal Beliefs

Ethical Decision Making: Application 115
Application of the Model

Conclusion 119

Chapter Review 120

Practice Test 120

 MySocialWorkLab 120
SCS on Health Care Reform
Connecting Core Competency videos on
Affordable Green Housing SCS

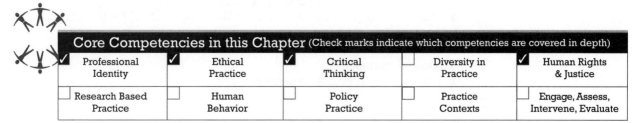

Core Competencies in this Chapter (Check marks indicate which competencies are covered in depth)				
✓ Professional Identity	✓ Ethical Practice	✓ Critical Thinking	☐ Diversity in Practice	✓ Human Rights & Justice
☐ Research Based Practice	☐ Human Behavior	☐ Policy Practice	☐ Practice Contexts	☐ Engage, Assess, Intervene, Evaluate

INTRODUCTION

To care for anyone else enough to make their problems one's own, is ever the beginning of one's real ethical development.

FELIX ADLER

Social work is a practice-oriented profession grounded in the core values of self-determination, empowerment, confidentiality, the right to access basic resources, and a belief in the inherent worth and dignity of all human beings. In microlevel practice, social workers are involved in the lives of people facing difficult and trying problems and circumstances. At the macro level of policy practice, social workers are involved in many of the same types of issues, but on a much larger scale. The actions of social workers in the policy realm can have a profound impact on the quality of life of thousands, if not millions, of individuals, families, and communities. In pursuit of the profession's guiding mission, social workers have a responsibility to promote sound social welfare and economically just policies. Poorly conceived policies can add unnecessary burdens on individuals already struggling to provide for themselves and their families—and ineffective advocacy can prevent or delay good policies from being adopted and hinder the achievement of some measure of social and economic justice for the most vulnerable in society. Social workers working in the area of policy practice can easily add to the hardships of clients' lives if they fail to support and advocate for just policies, or fail to oppose harmful policies whether at the agency, community, state, or federal level. It is, therefore, essential that social workers be aware of the ethical implications of policy practice.

To be a social worker requires that you aspire to the values and mission of the profession.

Social work values are idealistic and can be difficult to attain and sustain in any practice setting, especially in the political arena. To be a social worker requires that you aspire to the values and mission of the profession, that you strive to act on those values in your professional life, and that you recommit to them every day, even when the person across from you is a political adversary who is committed to eliminating social welfare policies that you view as essential to achieving social justice.[1]

This chapter provides a framework for connecting social work values to ethical decision making in policy practice and addresses the following topics as they relate to ethical decision making for the social work policy practitioner:

- Theories that provide a framework for understanding ethical policy practice;
- Connections with social work mission and values;
- Boundaries of ethical policy practice;
- The National Association of Social Workers (NASW) Code of Ethics and Practice Standards;
- Federal and state laws;
- Societal norms; and
- The benefits of ethical reflection.

ETHICAL FRAMEWORKS FOR POLICY PRACTICE

Regardless of the type of practice they are involved in, social workers are regularly confronted with difficult decisions when serving individuals, families, communities, and organizations. It is normal and right that social workers struggle with decisions that will have profound effects on client groups, and difficult practice decisions *ought* to beg for ethical reflection. Ethical reflection prompts big questions:

- Am I doing the right thing?
- What *is* the right thing?
- How do I go about defining the right thing?
- Do the ends justify the means? (Or, does how I do something matter much when my goal is a worthy one?)
- If I'm torn between competing "right things," how do I decide between the two?

Philosophers have developed a variety of ethical frameworks to address these questions. The utilitarian philosophy, developed by nineteenth-century political theorist John Stuart Mill, focuses on the consequences of actions (for this reason it is categorized as a *consequentialist* perspective).[2] A person holding a utilitarian point of view seeks to minimize harm and maximize the good. The phrase "the end justifies the means" is associated with utilitarianism. In policy practice, a utilitarian perspective would prioritize policies that have a positive impact on the largest population, and if some individuals were harmed as a result, that harm would be regarded as an acceptable loss, given the overall benefits to the community. In terms of public policy, vaccination of children is an example of a policy that has an overall positive effect on the vast majority of the population, while a small number may experience adverse effects from being vaccinated.

Philosopher John Rawls proposed another consequentialist approach to ethical decision making: the theory of *distributive justice.* In this approach, one would set aside the consideration of one's own economic and social interests to focus on maximizing the fair allocation of resources to the most disadvantaged members of society.[3] Rawls proposed that ethical decision makers should adopt a "veil of ignorance"—consciously setting aside (veiling) their own interests and striving to impartially determine what would benefit the least advantaged members of society. The metaphorical "veil of ignorance" would ensure that power and privilege do not distort the allocation of resources. A policy practitioner who adopted the distributive justice model would not be as concerned with the overall "greatest good for the greatest number." Rather, from a distributive justice perspective, the practitioner's goal would be to ensure that the poorest of the poor benefit from public policies. Social welfare policies are commonly designed to focus resources on the most needy. For example, the U.S. Census Bureau's poverty threshold (determined to be $22,017 in 2008 for a family of four) is used as a qualifying income level for the U.S. Department of Health and Human Services' Community Services Block Grants, the Head Start Program, Low-Income Home Energy Assistance Program, and the Children's Health Insurance Program.[4]

The *deontological* perspective of ethical decision making was developed by eighteenth-century philosopher Immanuel Kant and focuses on duties or the moral obligations to act because something is inherently the right thing to do.[5] From the viewpoint of *Kantian ethics,* it would not matter how many lives would be positively affected by a policy; if you adhere to the principle that it is wrong to exploit a vulnerable person, then ethically you could not support a policy that could harm some vulnerable individuals, even if the larger population benefited. Kantian ethics and utilitarianism can lead to very different outcomes in ethical decision making. From the Kantian perspective, for example, adhering to the principle that a child must never be harmed could lead to the conclusion that mass vaccination is ethically compromised, even though its overall effect is positive, resulting in fewer deaths and illnesses in a large population of infants and children.

Virtue ethics is another theoretical framework available to policy practitioners. First articulated by the ancient Greek philosopher Aristotle, virtue ethics focuses on how a decision affects the person making the decision.[6] In the realm of policy practice, a goal of virtue ethics would be to preserve a policy practitioner's character as a good member of society by avoiding actions that could diminish the practitioner's integrity. Note that virtue ethics is relative in nature—ethical decision-making outcomes depend on what a given society considers to be "good." Virtue ethics is of particular relevance in political campaigns, which focus attention on an individual's character and integrity.

A fifth perspective considered is the *ethic of care.* Developed by feminist theorists Nel Noddings and Joan C. Tronto, the ethic of care is a comprehensive theoretical framework that offers insight into how people can best live together in a more just society. Tronto defines care as "a species activity that includes everything we do to maintain, continue, and repair our 'world' so that we can live in it as well as possible. That world includes our bodies, our selves and our environments, all of which we seek to interweave in a complex, life-sustaining web."[7] The ethic of care focuses on the development of interdependence among society's members.[8] Most theories of ethics place the individual at the center of things. In contrast, the ethic of care perspective focuses on individuals in relation to one another as members of society (e.g., "I may be an independent adult right now, but I depended on care as a child so that I could reach adulthood, and I may need additional care as I age"). At some level, we all are/have been/will be vulnerable. Other themes in the ethic of care perspective include:

Human Rights & Justice

Critical Thinking Question

To what extent is care equitably distributed in your community?

- ‣ Equality (all people have equal moral worth, and thus the distribution of care in a society should be equitable);
- ‣ The inadvisability of making sweeping generalizations about "human nature" that hold true in all circumstances (in providing care, we should think about the person receiving care as being unique and irreplaceable); and
- ‣ Responsiveness—whose needs must be met, and is the care that is being offered meeting the needs?[9]

The ethic of care perspective bridges the personal, private sphere of activity with the public sphere of politics and civil society. Care is seen as a reflection of the power dynamics within the society: Who receives quality care? How is care distributed across gender, racial, and socioeconomic lines? What is the status of caregivers in the society? By asking whose needs are unmet, the ethic of care perspective pinpoints areas of concern for policy making.[10] Table 5.1

Table 5.1 **Ethic of Care Components**[1]

Component	Value/Virtue	Requirements
Caring about (recognizing that a need exists)	Attentiveness to needs	Ability and willingness to see others' perspectives
Caring for (defining *who* will meet the need and *how* it will be accomplished)	Sense of responsibility	Willingness and capacity to take responsibility for action
Taking care of (caregiving)	Competence	Ability to give care and access to resources needed for care
Care receiving	Responsiveness (from the individual receiving care— caregivers must use that information in determining whether the care is effective)	Interaction between the caregiver and the care recipient

[1]S. Sevenhuijsen, V. Bozalek, A. Gouws, and M. Minnaar-McDonald, "South African Social Welfare Policy: An Analysis Using the Ethic of Care," *Critical Social Policy 23* (2003), 299–321; S. Sevenhuijsen, "The Place of Care: The Relevance of the Feminist Ethic of Care for Social Policy," *Feminist Theory,* 4, no. 2 (2003), 179–197.

outlines the four main components, values, and requirements of ethic of care as a moral framework.

It is important to note, however, that the ethic of care is not solely concerned with vulnerable populations or with health care, child care, or nursing-home care. By grounding policy analysis in an awareness that care is a constant need in any human society, the ethic of care perspective takes into account the full range of social costs that must be part of the cost-benefit analysis for any policy.

For example, transportation policies that favor the construction of freeways over mass transit have immediate implications for ethical policy practice: As companies move toward outer-ring suburbs, inner-city residents lose access to jobs that help stabilize families. In the ethic of care perspective, however, transportation policy must also be considered across the continuum of the lifespan. Does the necessity of long commutes place undue burdens on parents of young children, jeopardizing the quality of early childhood care? Does the dependence on the automobile isolate senior citizens who may not be able to drive? Can the needs of individuals who use wheelchairs be met by a car-focused transportation policy? In this ethical framework, policy effects on those who need greater care, or social supports, must be taken into account when deciding whether to adopt a particular policy. Table 5.2 compares these ethical frameworks along several important dimensions to develop a clear matrix that displays their similarities and differences.

Table 5.2   Ethical Frameworks Compared

	Consequentialism		Deontology	Virtue Ethics	Ethic of Care (Feminist Theories)	NASW Code of Ethics (Professional Ethics)
Example	John Stuart Mills' Utilitarianism (nineteenth century)	John Rawls' Distributive Justice (late twentieth century)	Immanuel Kant's theory of ethics (eighteenth century)	Aristotle's moral theory (ancient Greece)	Nel Noddings and Joan Tronto's Ethic of Care (late twentieth century–present)	NASW (late twentieth century–present)
Primary Focus	Consequences (means versus ends)	Justice—the fair allocation of resources	Duties (moral obligation to act)	Character development (for the person doing the ethical reasoning)	Human interdependency (social obligations of care from birth to death—the individual as part of an interconnected web of relationships)	Enhance human well-being, particularly for those who are vulnerable, oppressed, or living in poverty
A right action	Promotes the best action—depends on result—what is good results in happiness for the greatest number	Protects the interests of the disadvantaged	Is in accordance with a moral principle required by God, natural law, or rationality; a right action is inherently good, regardless of consequences	Is one that a virtuous agent is disposed to make in the circumstances in order to flourish or live well; whatever results from actions of virtuous people	Considers social costs of acting (i.e., nurturing children, caring for the elderly or other vulnerable populations) as a morally inescapable responsibility	Helps individuals meet their basic needs and realize their potential as human beings
Themes	Maximize good, minimize harm; greatest good for the greatest number	Achieving an equitable society	Respect for persons, universality, impartiality, fairness, and justice	Excellence and self-actualization	Regard for others, responsiveness, equality, understanding, and particularity of situation	Empowerment, inherent dignity and worth of all people, and justice
Key Questions	What action will bring about the best outcome for all of those involved?	What action will bring about the best outcome for the most disadvantaged members of society?	What does the duty of respect for persons require? What moral rule should I follow?	What kind of person do I want to be? What kind of life do I want to live?	How do I respond to the particular needs of others?	As a social work professional, how can I best further the well-being of my clients through policy practice levels?

Table 5.2   (Continued)

	Consequentialism		Deontology	Virtue Ethics	Ethic of Care (Feminist Theories)	NASW Code of Ethics (Professional Ethics)
Model of Practical Reasoning	Means-end reasoning: How do I get what I want/what's good?	Adopt the perspective of the least privileged— place a 'veil of ignorance' over one's own interests	How do I determine what's rational?	What habits should I develop?	Whose needs must be met?	Are my actions consistent with the NASW Code of Ethics?

[1]Whetstone, J.T. How virtue fits within business ethics. *Journal of Business Ethics*, 33 (2001): 101–11; Slowther, Johnston, Goodall, and Hope, 2004.

Sources: Adapted from Whetstone, 2001; Slowther, Johnston, Goodall and Hope, 2004.[1]

For the social work policy practitioner, ethical frameworks cannot be considered in isolation, but must be considered in relation to the profession's guiding ethical resource, the National Association of Social Workers (NASW) Code of Ethics. The purpose of social work is to advance the quality of life for all people through the enhancement of mutually beneficial interactions between individuals and society.[11] Social work stands for the social welfare of all people and is committed to social justice through empowerment and social change at the individual, family, community, agency, and structural levels of society. As such, social work has historically been and continues to be in alliance with those members of society who live under difficult or oppressive conditions that keep them disadvantaged and marginalized. The profession of social work envisions a more decent and humane society.[12]

Social work ethics provides social work practitioners with a set of guidelines for practice, translating the abstract values of the profession into action statements, and giving social workers general guidelines for ethical ways of behaving in the practice setting. The first Code of Ethics was adopted in 1960, and was later revised in 1979, 1996, 1999, and mostly recently in 2008 to reflect the changing emphasis and direction of social work practice and changing social and political times.[13] Starting with the 1996/99 revisions, the Code became more explicit about political advocacy, devoting an entire section to the need for social workers to intervene for and with clients at the system level and expanding the section on advocacy in the 2008 revisions.

The Code of Ethics defines the profession's core values, principles, and standards (see Table 5.3). The Code's six standards follow from the ethical principles, identifying social workers' ethical responsibilities to clients and colleagues, in practice settings, as professionals, to the social work profession, and to the broader society. Although much of the Code is focused on clinical practice, there are, in addition to the sixth standard on ethical responsibilities to the broader society, other sections of the Code that apply

Table 5.3   Core Values/Ethical Principles

Core Values	Ethical Principles
Service	Social workers' primary goal is to help people in need and to address social problems.
Social justice	Social workers challenge social injustice.
Dignity and worth of the person	Social workers respect the inherent dignity and worth of the person.
Importance of human relationships	Social workers recognize the central importance of human relationships.
Integrity	Social workers behave in a trustworthy manner.
Competence	Social workers practice within their areas of competence and develop and enhance their professional expertise.

to policy practice. The NASW Practice Standards provide further details on ethical conduct within certain areas of practice. As you consider the NASW Code of Ethics within the context of the various ethical frameworks presented earlier in this chapter, which framework seems most compatible with the social work profession? Review the frameworks in Table 5.2 and compare this with NASW's Code of Ethics.

After comparing these ethical frameworks in relation to the NASW Code of Ethics, which seem most compatible with social work's mission, values, and ethical principles? It is, perhaps, easiest to see the connections with the ethical theories that were developed most recently. Certainly, Rawls's notion of distributive justice, with its concern for the neediest, resonates with social work's historical focus on those at society's margins. The ethic of care is also closely aligned with the social work agenda, because it looks at policy through a continuum-of-care lens that reveals the policy implications of human dependencies. If, as a society, we were to follow through on that vision, our political and policy landscape would look different from what we see today. For example, the individualistic strand in American public life would be tempered by the realization that the presumption of the individual-as-autonomous-actor only holds true for a portion of the lifespan, at best. Instead of having a subset of policies that address the needs of working families, the elderly, those with disabilities, etc., *all* policies would factor in the needs of vulnerable segments of the population.

Yet it can also be argued that each of the ethical frameworks has relevant insights to bring to the consideration of social work policy practice ethics. The utilitarian emphasis on the greatest good for the greatest number can be found in the cost-benefit analyses that are part of the policy evaluation process.[14] And a Kantian assertion of absolute moral principles is found in the NASW Code's core values and ethical principles. Virtue ethics would seem to have the least to contribute to the ethics of policy practice—it focuses on the decision maker, instead of articulating a vision of a just society. However, virtue ethics *is* relevant to the political arena. The norms of politics can be at odds with ethical policy practice, and having a clear moral center is an asset for the policy practitioner.

BOUNDARIES OF ETHICAL POLICY PRACTICE

To take ethics from ideals into actions requires knowledge of the boundaries of ethically encouraged/permissible action. Those boundaries are defined by the NASW Code of Ethics and Practice Standards, laws, and societal norms related to political campaigning and public advocacy. Figure 5.1 outlines these boundaries.

Note that between the center (actions that advance the social work mission) and the outer area (illegal/unethical actions) lies a gray area, where ethical dilemmas arise.

Boundary: The NASW Code of Ethics

Section 6 of the NASW Code of Ethics addresses the relationship of social work to society in general (see Box 5.1). As this section makes clear, policy practice and advocacy are core ethical obligations of the social work profession.

Policy practice and advocacy are core ethical obligations of the social work profession.

Social work's role in developing and enacting policies extends beyond social work professionals. Social workers also seek to empower client populations in the policymaking process. When social workers empower their clients, those clients become more able to exercise control over their own life circumstances. Social workers assist in this process by providing information and assisting client populations in connecting to like-minded groups to build coalitions. Social workers help clients find a public voice for their private troubles.

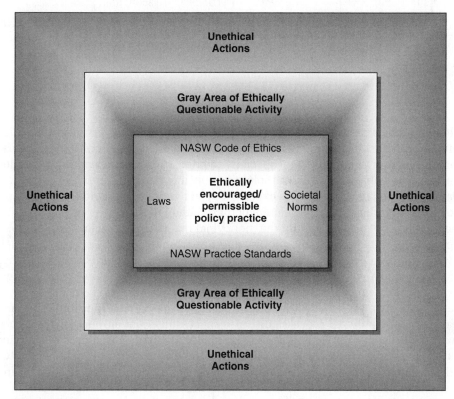

Figure 5.1
The boundaries of ethical policy practice

Box 5.1   Social Workers' Ethical Responsibilities to the Broader Society; Section 6 of the NASW Code of Ethics

6.01 Social Welfare

Social workers should promote the general welfare of society, from local to global levels, and the development of people, their communities, and their environments. Social workers should advocate for living conditions conducive to the fulfillment of basic human needs and should promote social, economic, political, and cultural values and institutions that are compatible with the realization of social justice.

6.02 Public Participation

Social workers should facilitate informed participation by the public in shaping social policies and institutions.

6.04 Social and Political Action

a. Social workers should engage in social and political action that seeks to ensure that all people have equal access to the resources, employment, services, and opportunities they require to meet their basic human needs and to develop fully. Social workers should be aware of the impact of the political arena on practice and should advocate for changes in policy and legislation to improve social conditions in order to meet basic human needs and promote social justice.

b. Social workers should act to expand choice and opportunity for all people, with special regard for vulnerable, disadvantaged, oppressed, and exploited people and groups.

c. Social workers should promote conditions that encourage respect for cultural and social diversity within the United States and globally. Social workers should promote policies and practices that demonstrate respect for difference, support the expansion of cultural knowledge and resources, advocate for programs and institutions that demonstrate cultural competence, and promote policies that safeguard the rights of and confirm equity and social justice for all people.

d. Social workers should act to prevent and eliminate domination of, exploitation of, and discrimination against any person, group, or class on the basis of race, ethnicity, national origin, color, sex, sexual orientation, gender identity or expression, age, marital status, political belief, religion, immigration status, or mental or physical disability.

Source: NASW Code of Ethics, 2008.

Professional Identity

Critical Thinking Question

What skills do social workers need to facilitate informed public participation in policymaking?

On the surface, empowerment sounds like a fairly simple process. In reality, involving clients in the policymaking process is challenging. Public speaking can be intimidating to anyone, but especially to clients who have been downtrodden and made to believe that they are solely responsible for their lot in life. Even more daunting is giving voice to one's experiences and views to powerful agency heads, government officials, and legislative bodies. Although the power of personal stories cannot be minimized in the policymaking process, social workers who approach clients with this possibility and opportunity must be sensitive to their own power in potentially "using" a client to promote a cause or issue. Knowledge is a fundamental ingredient of empowerment. But knowledge alone is not enough. Social workers must also train clients in the skills necessary to be effective advocates on their own behalf. Training in public speaking, coalition building, and navigating the political process cultivates successful client empowerment. Social workers impart new information and knowledge to clients, teach problem-solving skills, and foster clients' self-determination. As clients learn to seek out knowledge, solve problems, and advocate for themselves, they will reap the benefits and responsibilities that come with self-determination. When clients are able and willing to take these steps, they have empowered themselves. These are the steps taken by an MSW student, Kirk, whose clients were empowered by participating in the legislative process (see Box 5.2).

Box 5.2   Empowering Clients in the Policy Arena

Kirk, an MSW student, and director of a program that helps youth who have aged out of foster care, was introduced to policy practice in his foundation policy class during his first semester in graduate school. He, along with all of his classmates, was invited to participate in the state's Social Work Lobby Day. As part of his class assignment, Kirk examined policies being introduced to the state legislature and selected one he could get passionate about: a bill proposing to provide much-needed resources (like rent vouchers, education vouchers, and health care) to teens aging out foster care so that they could make the transition from foster care to stable self-care. At the time, the state's unofficial policy was to transport foster youth to the nearest homeless shelter when they turned 18. Kirk was determined to help his young clients make a difference in their own lives. He began by teaching them about the legislative process and the proposed bill that would have a major impact on their lives and the lives of thousands of other youth just like them. He trained and coached them in public speaking. One

month before lobby day, he drove them to the state capital (8 hours away) and took them on a tour of the statehouse, allowed them to witness the legislative process, and introduced them to legislators. When Social Work Lobby Day arrived, again Kirk drove his clients to the state capital to talk to legislators. He had made appointments with critical legislators to lobby for the passage of the foster care bill, including Senator Campbell, chairman of the human services and social welfare committee. During their conversation, the senator invited the youth to attend the committee meeting later that afternoon and to share their stories with the committee members. The young clients decided that they were ready to speak up for themselves and agreed to testify. At the beginning of the meeting, the committee favored killing the bill, 5–3. After hearing the impassioned and well-informed testimony of the foster youth, the committee passed the bill out of committee, 7–1 in favor of its passage. Kirk understood the power of teaching clients to advocate for themselves.

Boundary: NASW Standards for Advocacy and Political Action

Today, social workers are facing more complex issues in practice. The changes in the social, economic, and political landscape of the United States have created a context of social work practice that has more ethical challenges than in the past. In response to these societal changes, the 1996 NASW revised Code covered more areas of practice and provided more specificity in professional behaviors. In all, the Code now consists of 156 Practice Standards. Some of the new standards expand on old practice issues but in a new context; others address practice issues for the first time.[15]

Box 5.3 excerpts the advocacy and public empowerment expectations from the NASW Standards for Social Work Practice with Clients with Substance Use Disorders (SUD). As you read the excerpt, consider the following: What advocacy skills might be needed in countering the stigma attached to clients with SUD? What types of knowledge would SUD social work policy advocates need to possess to be effective?

Whether the focus of practice is child welfare, end-of-life-care, or civil rights, social workers are called to be an effective presence in the public arena. As noted in several of the standards, social workers possess "unique, in-depth knowledge" that brings a special responsibility to their roles in advocacy and in the political arena. By virtue of their interactions with vulnerable populations, social workers are more informed than most about the needs that public policy is designed to address. Social work's rigorous, evidence-based approach to social problems means that social workers have the capacity to raise the level of public debate and to represent a "voice of reason" when others may be resorting to unfounded emotional appeals to self-interest (as opposed to the common good).

By virtue of their interactions with vulnerable populations, social workers are more informed than most about the needs that public policy is designed to address.

Box 5.3   NASW Standards for Social Work Practice with Clients with Substance Use Disorders

Standard 5. Advocacy and Collaboration

Social workers who provide services to clients with substance use disorders (SUDs) shall advocate, when appropriate, for the needs, decisions, and rights of clients. The social worker shall promote collaboration among service providers and seek to ensure that individuals with SUDs and their family members have access to services that support their treatment needs.

Interpretation

The stigma associated with SUDs requires special attention to empowerment and advocacy. **Social workers who provide services to these individuals and their families shall use their empowerment and advocacy skills to educate clinicians, policymakers, researchers, and community members about SUDs and related problems. Social workers shall advocate for changes that provide effective responses to the treatment of SUDs and promote social justice for individuals struggling with SUDs.** Empowerment and advocacy also require that social workers assist clients and their family members in learning to advocate for themselves in obtaining necessary services within various community agencies (schools, health care, criminal justice), and to oppose discrimination in employment, health care, or other settings. In addition, social workers shall

advocate in support of their clients' choices of treatments, when appropriate. This includes making clients aware of the range and combinations of treatments, including psychosocial treatments, culturally specific treatments, and medications. Social workers shall be open to discussing with clients spiritual, indigenous, and self/mutual- help methods of addressing SUDs. The social worker shall advocate with educational providers for adequate education and continuing-education opportunities. The social worker shall advocate with researchers for research agendas that truly address the full range of research development needs of practitioners. Community empowerment is an important component in reducing the impact of chronic substance abuse. Social workers shall help community leaders and members understand that alcohol, tobacco, and other drugs adversely affect communities and seek to engage community members in prevention, treatment, and long-term recovery efforts. **Social workers shall use their advocacy and political skills to address issues such as insurance parity for SUDs, increased funding for accessible treatment, harm reduction, and abstinence strategies, when appropriate.**

Source: NASW Practice Standards at www.socialworkers.org/practice/Default.asp. Emphasis added.

The empowerment tradition in social work is another thread that runs through the Practice Standards. Although social workers are expected to engage in direct political action, fostering clients' "ability to do for themselves" is equally important. For example, effective policy practice would increase parents' ability— to navigate the complexities of city government to advocate for stiffer penalties— to ensure that landlords are in compliance with lead-abatement regulations.

A third theme evident in the Practice Standards is the multidimensional nature of the social work profession. Microlevel practice, administration, educating clients, decision makers, and the public, and policy practice are intermingled in the professional life of the social worker. The dictum "stay current" is all the more essential because a social worker may never know when she is called upon to express an informed opinion on a policy matter. This rich "stew" of activity is an asset—experience in direct practice informs policy work, whereas the ability to intervene at the system level through policy practice can potentially address clients' needs at the level of root causes (e.g., a raise in the minimum wage may reduce family stressors).

Although the post–1996 NASW Policy Practice Standards provide more guidance on political and advocacy work than was the case in the past, the standards do not cover every aspect of policy practice. For example, there are no standards for policy practice related to working with the mentally ill, gender equity issues, housing, environmental health, or political campaigns.

Boundary: Laws

Federal and state laws place another boundary on policy practice. The law that has the greatest effect on policy practice is the Hatch Act. Passed in 1939, the Hatch Act places significant restrictions on political activity for federal employees. It was amended in 1940 to extend these restrictions to state and local government employees whose salaries depend, in all or in part, on federal funds.

Table 5.4 summarizes legal and illegal political activity for federal, state, and local government employees.

Table 5.4   The Hatch Act: Federal Employees . . .

may be candidates for public office in nonpartisan elections; *EXAMPLE: An employee may run for school board in the District of Columbia because school board elections in the District are nonpartisan.*	**may** join and be an active member of a political party or club; *EXAMPLE: An employee may serve as a delegate, alternate, or proxy to a state or national party convention.*
may register and vote as they choose; *EXAMPLE: An employee may register to vote Republican and vote for a Republican candidate even though his boss is a Democratic political appointee.*	**may** sign and circulate nominating petitions; *EXAMPLE: An employee may collect signatures for the nominating petitions of individuals who are running for public office.*
may assist in voter registration drives; *EXAMPLE: An employee may assist in a voter registration drive sponsored by the League of Women Voters.*	**may** campaign for or against referendum questions, constitutional amendments, and municipal ordinances; *EXAMPLE: An employee may be politically active in connection with a referendum question that seeks to ban smoking in eating establishments.*
may express opinions about candidates and issues; *EXAMPLE: An employee may write a letter to the editor at the* Washington Post *which expresses her personal opinion on a candidate or political issue.*	**may** campaign for or against candidates in partisan elections; *EXAMPLE: An employee may walk around his neighborhood and introduce a candidate, who is running in a partisan election, to his neighbors.*
may contribute money to political organizations; *EXAMPLE: An employee may make a monetary contribution to any candidate, political party, club, or organization of her choosing.*	**may** distribute campaign literature in partisan elections; *EXAMPLE: An employee may stand outside of a polling place on election day and hand out brochures on behalf of a partisan political candidate or political party.*
may attend and give a speech at a political fundraiser, rally or meeting; *EXAMPLE: When an employee is off duty she may attend and give a speech or keynote address at a political fundraiser.*	**may** hold office in political clubs or parties; *EXAMPLE: An employee may serve as a vice president of a political action committee, as long as the position does not involve personal solicitation, acceptance, or receipt of political contribution.*
There continue to be important restrictions on employees' political activity. Whether on or off duty, federal employees . . .	
may not use official authority or influence to interfere with an election; *EXAMPLE: An employee who signs a letter seeking volunteer services from individuals may not identify himself by using his official title.*	**may not** engage in political activity while on duty, in a government office, while wearing an official uniform, or while using a government vehicle; *EXAMPLE: An employee may not display a political poster, bumper sticker, or campaign button in his or her office or in the common areas of a federal building.*

(Continued)

Table 5.4   The Hatch Act: Federal Employees . . . (Continued)

may not solicit or discourage political activity of anyone with business before her agency;
EXAMPLE: An employee with agency wide responsibility may address a large, diverse group to seek support for a partisan political candidate as long as the group has not been specifically targeted as having matters before the employing agency.

may not become a candidate in a partisan election;
EXAMPLE: An employee may not become a candidate in an election where any of the candidates are running as representatives of political parties, usually the Democratic or Republican parties.

may not solicit, accept, or receive political contributions (may be done in certain limited situations by federal labor or other employee organizations);
EXAMPLE: An employee may not host a fundraiser at his home or solicit funds at any other fundraiser for a partisan candidate.

The Hatch Act restricts the political activity of individuals principally employed by state, county or municipal executive agencies who work in connection with programs financed in whole or in part by federal loans or grants. An officer or employee of a state or local agency is covered by the Hatch Act, if he or she has duties in connection with an activity financed in whole or in part by federal funds. These state and local employees . . .

may be candidates for public office in nonpartisan elections, which, in other words, is an election where no candidates are running with party affiliation;
EXAMPLE: An employee may run for the school board in Washington, D.C., as long as the school board elections in Washington, D.C., remain nonpartisan.

may hold elective office in political parties, clubs, and organizations;
EXAMPLE: An employee may serve as the vice president of the local Democratic or Republican party.

may be appointed to fill a vacancy for an elective office;
EXAMPLE: An employee may be appointed to finish the unexpired term of an elected officeholder. The employee may not run for reelection if the election is partisan.

may actively campaign for candidates for public office in partisan and nonpartisan elections;
EXAMPLE: An employee may campaign for candidates by making speeches, writing letters, working at the polls on election day and organizing political rallies and meetings.

may contribute money to political organizations;
EXAMPLE: An employee may make a monetary contribution to any candidate, political party, club, or organization.

may attend and give a speech at a political fundraiser, rally, or meeting.
EXAMPLE: An employee may attend and give a speech or keynote address at a political fundraiser.

There continue to be important restrictions on employees' political activity. State and local employees . . .

may not be candidates for public office in partisan elections;
EXAMPLE: An employee may not run for office in an election where any of the candidates are running as representatives of a political party, for example, the Democratic or Republican party.

may not use official authority or influence for the purpose of interfering with or affecting the result of an election or nomination for office;
EXAMPLE: A supervisor should not ask a subordinate employee to volunteer for a political party.

may not directly or indirectly coerce contributions from other state or local employees;
EXAMPLE: A supervisor should not advise employees that they may purchase tickets to a fundraising event.

may not orchestrate a "write-in" candidacy during a partisan election;
EXAMPLE: An employee may not solicit voters to write his name on the ballot on election day.

Sources: www.osc.gov/documents/hatchact/haflyer.htm; www.osc.gov/documents/hatchact/haflyer2.htm; www.osc.gov/ha_state.htm.

Note that the Hatch Act applies to employees of private nonprofit organizations "only if the statute through which the organization derives its federal funding contains a provision, which states that recipient organizations shall be deemed to be state or local government agencies for purposes of the Hatch Act." Practicing social workers are responsible for knowing whether the Hatch Act applies to their place of employment.

Federal laws and regulations on lobbying by nonprofit organizations also affect policy practice at the national level. Although lobbying can be a powerful force for social change, there are stringent rules defining the boundaries of legal lobbying activity and there are also financial-reporting requirements for nonprofit organizations. Chapter 10 outlines lobbying laws and regulations, as well as strategies for effective, ethical lobbying.

Boundary: Societal Norms and Personal Beliefs

The fourth boundary of ethical policy practice is challenging to discern—sometimes we are so close to our beliefs and so immersed in our cultural context that it can be difficult to recognize their influence on our behavior.

The practice of self-reflection can help you identify your values and beliefs. In policy practice, having a strong sense of self—knowing your personal boundaries—will be a definite asset. (For a tip on how to access self-assessment diagnostic tools, see the Discussion Questions and Exercises at the end of this chapter.)

Societal norms in the policy practice arena include the social work values of service, social justice, dignity and worth of the person, importance of human relationships, integrity, and competence, as well as other idealistic expressions of politics as true public service—but they also include, at the other extreme, dirty tricks and the expectation that anything goes as long as you don't get caught. One of the pitfalls of policy practice is falling victim to the insider mentality in politics. This view, summed up in the phrase "everyone does it," is contrary to ethical policy practice. This cynical perspective focuses on staying in power and on staying close to those in power—often at the public's expense.

The American public's attitude toward politics has grown increasingly cynical over the past 40 years. Surveys such as the Government Trust Index, a national survey conducted by the American National Election Studies group at Stanford University and the University of Michigan, show a long-term downward trend (61% in 1966 to 37% in 2004) in the extent to which members of the public express trust in government institutions and politicians.[16] Likewise, there has been an increase in the percentage of people who believe politics serves special interests (33% in 1966; 56% in 2004) and in the percentage that agree with the statement "Public officials don't care much what people like me think" (34% in 1966; 50% in 2004).[17]

An example of positive societal norms is reproduced below. This newsletter from the City of Livermore, California, outlines the boundaries of fair versus unfair campaign practices (Box 5.4). This document can serve as a guide to what the public should expect of those in public life.

Critical Thinking

Critical Thinking Question
Why do you think public trust in government is declining?

ETHICAL DECISION MAKING: APPLICATION

Resolving ethical dilemmas in policy practice is not a simple task. It requires knowledge of the boundaries of ethical behavior, a close analysis of all the relationships involved in the situation, the imagination to visualize the probable

Resolving ethical dilemmas in policy practice is not a simple task.

Box 5.4   City of Livermore, CA, 2005 Newsletter, "Campaign Ethics & Voter Guidelines"

What's Fair & Unfair

Campaigning that's Fair & Ethical: Campaigns can be highly critical and hard-hitting and still be fair and ethical. Staying true to a Code of Ethics and values does not mean that a candidate is limited to making only nice statements about an opponent. America's political process is founded upon the Constitutional guarantee of free speech and democracy, which is not weakened by rough and tumble campaigning that stays within ethical boundaries. Ethical, but hard-hitting campaign message that focuses on the issues and the future rather than on personal short-comings and petty bickering can strengthen the democratic process.

Evaluating How Candidates Behave Toward Opponents:
If your alarm bell goes off when you read or hear messages that criticize candidates, the following guidelines may help you make informed decisions:

What's Fair?	What's Unfair?
Criticism of a voting record	Personal attacks
Criticism of a policy position	Rumors and innuendos
Comparison of experience	Distortions and lies
Questions about leadership ability	Unsubstantiated charges of misconduct
Debate of tough political issues	

☑Checklist for Evaluating Candidates

The Livermore City Council and candidates who attended the September 19, 2005 Campaign Ethics workshop signed a pledge to demonstrate the ethical qualities listed below during their campaigns and incumbencies. This checklist may help you evaluate the ethical qualities of candidates you are considering on the November ballot:

1. Write each candidate's name on the dashed lines at the top of checklist.
2. Place a checkmark under the candidate's name of each ethical quality or value you believe the candidate has demonstrated (a checked box means "yes" –a blank box means "no").

CANDIDATES' NAMES ☞	1	2	3	4	5	6	7
TRUTHFUL							
FAIR							
ACTS WITH INTEGRITY							
ACCOUNTABLE							
HONEST							
RESPECTFUL							
RESPONSIBLE							
RELEVANT							
OPEN							
APPROACHABLE							
HONORS/RESPECTS POSITION AS INCUMBENT							

Source: www.ci.livermore.ca.us/city_newsletters/LivNews21_Ethics_6_sprds.pdf.

consequences of different courses of action, and a commitment to take the time needed to think through all of the above. Figure 5.2 outlines a process you can use to work your way through the ethically questionable "gray areas" of policy practice.

In some cases, policy practitioners will need to draw on the collective wisdom of colleagues and other professionals, as noted in the Code of Ethics:

> [Social workers] should be aware of any conflicts between personal and professional values and deal with them responsibly. For additional guidance social workers should consult the relevant literature on professional ethics and ethical decision making and seek appropriate consultation when faced with ethical dilemmas. This may involve consultation with an agency-based or social work organization's ethics committee, a regulatory body, knowledgeable colleagues, supervisors, or legal counsel.[19]

It is important to understand that models are simple versions of a more complex reality. In practice, ethical problem solving will be a messier process that only approximates the decision-making stages outlined in Figure 5.2. The purpose of presenting the model is to set the expectation that as a future policy practitioner you will be alert to the ethical implications of your actions, know the relevant boundaries, and reflect on how to best proceed, seeking guidance from colleagues as needed.

Application of the Model

Maria is a human services aide to a U.S. Representative. She is working on a large federal earmark to expand badly needed job-training programs for Temporary Assistance for Needy Families (TANF) recipients in her home district. Tom, a friend and an aide for another representative, offers to persuade his boss to support the earmark if Maria agrees to do the same for his top project—keeping

Steps for Resolving Ethical Dilemmas

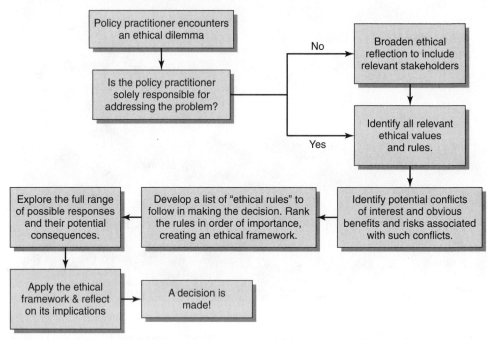

Figure 5.2

Steps for Resolving Ethical Dilemmas

Note: Adapted from D. Hardina, "Guidelines for Ethical Practice in Community Operation," *Social Work,* 49, no. 4 (2004), 595–604; and Reisch, M., and J. I. Lowe, "Of Means an Ends Revisited: Teaching Ethical Community Organizing in an Unethical Society," *Journal of Community Practice,* 7, no. 1, 19–38.

states from "buying Canadian" to reduce drug prices. Tom has close ties with a lobbying group for large drug companies. The drug companies are playing hardball on this measure and have run a series of advertisements in national outlets that cast doubt on the quality of Canadian drugs.

Maria brings the issue to the weekly staff meeting—this is a proposal that needs to be vetted with her boss and with other staffers (but Maria's opinion as the human services/health subject matter expert is usually the most influential in discussions such as this one). In discussion and through personal reflection, Maria and her colleagues identify the relevant ethical values and rules. Maria draws on her knowledge of the NASW Code of Ethics and Practice Standards. In this case the Practice Standard for Social Work Practice in Health Care Settings and the Standard for Social Work Practice in Child Welfare indicate that advocacy for access to quality health care is a professional obligation.

Maria also assesses whether the offer violates the norms of the political environment. As a seasoned policy practitioner, Maria recognizes that while bargaining is an accepted political practice, she is uncomfortable with a media campaign that distorts information in communicating with the public.

In weighing a course of action, Maria also identifies potential conflicts of interest and obvious benefits and risks associated with such conflicts. In this case, her personal friendship with Tom is a potential conflict of interest. There is also considerable risk involved, because Maria does not know the extent of Tom's involvement with drug company lobbyists; if he is violating federal lobbying laws, she and her boss may be affected if a scandal develops.

Here is a list of the ethical rules that emerged from the reflection process:

1. Basic human needs take priority.
2. Define social costs—who would be most harmed if Maria's or Tom's measures didn't pass—children of the unemployed in one U.S. House district, or the elderly across the country (national scope)?
3. Follow lobbying laws.
4. Avoid association with those who work against informed public participation in the political process.

In exploring the full range of possible responses and their potential consequences two options emerge:

▶ Option 1: agree to Tom's deal → jobs program advances in one community; access to prescription drugs remains limited nationally
▶ Option 2: decline Tom's deal → no jobs program, expanded access to health care

As Maria's ethical stance becomes clearer to her, it begins to align with the ethic-of-care framework in that Maria recognizes the responsibility of ensuring that the most vulnerable members of society have their needs met by preserving equitable access to an affordable source of prescription drugs.

After reflection, Maria declines Tom's offer. The benefits of expanding the jobs program are outweighed by the social cost of denying equal access to health care, a basic human need.

Seeing the steps in an ethical decision-making process outlined in this way may seem overly mechanical to you and divorced from the practical, internal reasoning processes we all use in our day-to-day lives. The process described in this chapter is intended as a learning tool; by breaking things down into steps, it helps to demonstrate a pattern of thinking that will help you develop your ethical decision making.

Ethical Practice

Critical Thinking Question
What would you do, if you were in Maria's place?

CONCLUSION

Social work researchers Miriam Hirschfeld and Daniel Wikler argue that the consideration of ethics results in a higher quality of decision making in policy practice:

> There should be a space for ethics in policy making to recognize the value of a deliberative process in which arguments are advanced and carefully evaluated. By examining and evaluating ethical considerations and remaining open to policy revisions in light of criticism and experience, policy makers, whether at the local or national level, create a context in which their strategies can be more fully understood. . . . Incorporating ethics into planning conveys a respect not only for the importance of weighing options and choosing among them, but also for the process of doing so. The hoped-for result is a reasoned dialogue that illuminates questions of social justice from different angles.[20]

Thus, a key benefit of ethics to policy practice is that an ethical framework imposes a deliberative process on decision making. This process helps ensure that the full implications of policies are considered prior to their adoption by social work policy advocates and that policies reflect the values and mission of the profession.

Succeed with PEARSON mysocialworklab

Log onto **MySocialWorkLab** to access a wealth of case studies, videos, and assessment. (*If you did not receive an access code to* **MySocialWorkLab** *with this text and wish to purchase access online, please visit* www.mysocialworklab.com.)

1. **Review the Healthcare Reform SCS.** Answer the 'Key Questions' from Table 5.2, exploring how each ethical framework (utilitarianism, distributive justice, Kant's theory of ethics, virtue ethics, ethic of care, and the NASW Code of Ethics) could be applied to the SCS.

2. **Review the Affordable Green Housing SCS.** How does social worker Annette Taylor meet her ethical responsibilities to the broader society? In particular, how does she facilitate a public role for her client, Serena Honesta?

PRACTICE TEST The following questions will test your knowledge of the content found within this chapter. For additional assessment, including licensing-exam type questions on applying chapter content to practice, visit **MySocialWorkLab**.

1. The ethical decision-making approach that emphasizes maximizing the greatest good for the most disadvantaged of society, setting aside one's own social and economic interests is referred to as:
   a. The martyr approach
   b. The virtue ethics perspective
   c. The distributive justice approach
   d. The ethic of care perspective

2. The Consequentialist perspective or utilitarian approach is most associated with:
   a. Acting on moral obligations or duties because it is inherently the right thing to do.
   b. Prioritizing policies that do the greatest amount of good for the greatest number of people, even if a few individuals are harmed in the process.
   c. The Robin Hood syndrome, taking from the rich and giving to the poor
   d. Decision making that is relative in nature and has as its focus how the decision will primarily effect the decision maker and their integrity

3. Identifying a need, defining who will meet the need / how it will be satisfied, caregiving and care receiving are:
   a. Ethic of Care components
   b. Some standards set out and defined in the NASW Code of Ethics
   c. Sole responsibilities of those people working in the medical professions
   d. Basic tenets that are followed in large non profit charity organizations

4. The NASW Code of Ethics is:
   a. A general set of guidelines for social work practitioners that may or may not be followed
   b. Was developed in the 1960's and while interesting to know from a historical perspective, the code is not relevant in today's society
   c. Is vague and utopian in its perspective, and difficult to apply to today's real life situations
   d. Defines the profession's core values, principles, and standards

5. Section 6 in the NASW code of ethics addresses the relationship between social work and society in general, and stresses that social work practitioners should:
   a. Put the interests of their agency or target population as top priority
   b. Join a social workers association and advocate for social workers' rights
   c. Act to expand choice and opportunity for all people, especially the most vulnerable in society
   d. Make political action a top priority and run for elected office as much as possible

6. The law that sets the clearest guidelines for and boundaries of policy practice is:
   a. The Social Security Act of 1935
   b. The Harrison Act
   c. The Hatch Act
   d. The Patriot Act

7. Under the Hatch Act federal employees may not:
   a. Solicit, accept or receive political contributions
   b. Contribute money to political organizations
   c. Give a speech at a political fundraiser
   d. Sign or circulate nominating petitions

8. Social justice, integrity, the importance of human relationships, and competence are some examples of:
   a. Grassroots organizational guidelines
   b. Societal norms in the policy practice arena
   c. Normal ethical behavior of politicians
   d. Guidelines for ethical political activity

9. According to the text, when a policy practitioner encounters an ethical dilemma the first step to take in resolving any such dilemma is:
   a. Decide what the easiest solution is – the path of least resistance
   b. Identify the solution that will most benefit the policy practitioner
   c. Identify if the policy practitioner is the solely responsible for handling the dilemma
   d. Figure out the solution with the greatest economic benefit for the programs for which the policy practitioner is responsible

---

Log onto **MySocialWorkLab** once you have completed the Practice Test above to access additional study tools and assessment.

Answers

Key: 1) c, 2) b, 3) a, 4) d, 5) c, 6) c, 7) a, 8) b, 9) c

6

Entering the Policy Practice Arena

CHAPTER OUTLINE

Introduction 122

Case Study 122

Ecology of Policy Practice Across Policy
    Settings 126
Overview of Social Worker Roles in Policy Practice

Social Work Careers in Policy Practice 127

Executive Settings 127
Elected Executive
Appointed Executive Policymaker
Role of Agency Board in Making Policy
Advisor/Staff to Policymaker
Agency Policymaking at the Direct Service Worker
    Level—The Case for Street-Level Bureaucrats

Legislative Settings 131
Legislative Policymaker
Legislative Assistant/Constituent Services

Judicial Settings 134
Expert Witness
Amicus Curiae Briefs

Consultants in Judge Education Programs
Elected Judge
Advocate in Judge Appointment Processes

Community Settings 136
Campaign Director or Worker on a Campaign
Part-Time or Volunteer Policy Advocate
Lobbyist
Research/Policy Analysis Positions
Policy Practitioner/Educator
Grass Roots Organizer of Community Groups
Policy Practice Roles for Direct Service
    Practitioners
Informal Opportunities to be a Policy Advocate
Policy Practice by Professional Associations

Conclusion 141

Chapter Review 142

Practice Test 142

 MySocialWorkLab 142
Connecting Core Competency Series on Engage,
Assess, Intervene, and Evaluate
Health Care SCS

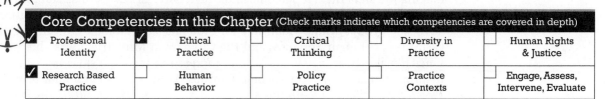

Core Competencies in this Chapter (Check marks indicate which competencies are covered in depth)				
✓ Professional Identity	✓ Ethical Practice	☐ Critical Thinking	☐ Diversity in Practice	☐ Human Rights & Justice
✓ Research Based Practice	☐ Human Behavior	☐ Policy Practice	☐ Practice Contexts	☐ Engage, Assess, Intervene, Evaluate

INTRODUCTION

My dream? Everyone should be guaranteed some minimum above subsistence.

SOCIAL WORKER ADVOCATE

This chapter starts with a case study of Shaniqua Abrams, a social worker who has had a number of policy practice roles during her career. After a brief review of the centrality of policy practice to social work's ethical stance, the chapter explores a variety of policy practice roles to consider for your own social work career. In discussing each role, likely tasks, activities, and associated projects as well as necessary skills are highlighted. In addition, likely ethical considerations and challenges are identified. This chapter will provide a clear understanding of the range of skills involved in policy practice and how those skills are used in a variety of roles. Subsequent chapters will explore those skills in some depth.

There is little systematic research on the efficacy of policy practice skills or policy roles in changing or enacting new social welfare policies. Certainly, as noted in previous chapters, the settings where policy practice occurs are complex and constantly changing and, therefore, challenging to study in a systematic way. Because of the limited research available on policy practice, evidence in this chapter comes from some limited survey research and post hoc reflections and evaluations of policy change efforts. In addition, the authors conducted a series of interviews with social work policy practitioners from a variety of settings. Comments from these interviews are included throughout this discussion.

CASE STUDY

As a policy analyst with a statewide nonprofit agency advocating for low-income families, Shaniqua Abrams (a pseudonym with permission to use her story), MSW, is most proud of helping to create the state's Earned Income Tax Credit (EITC). Though she says it is still not perfect, she relays how the law was passed in the state legislature. "Back in 1999, the state was about $15 million short in its MOE (Maintenance of Effort) funding for TANF (Temporary Assistance for Needy Families). We brought in some national policy people to work behind the scenes with us and the state staff. We created a hybrid EITC that was structured so that the less you made, the more you got back." The state was running short by about $15 million in their MOE from the previous year. The group realized that they could use the EITC for the state's MOE and, therefore, help low-income families at the same time they saved the state from having to pay potential fines and from suffering cuts in TANF funding in the future (See Box 6.1 for a full definition of terms and acronyms used in this paragraph.)

"Several years later, we came back to the state legislature to advocate for making the state EITC a percentage of the federal EITC. To raise state revenue, legislators were considering an increase in the state sales tax. A coalition of advocacy groups (State Coalition for Housing and Homeless Issues, United Coalition of Human Services, and Big City Urban Ministries) was able to convince a majority of legislators that an increase in the state sales tax would fall disproportionately on low-income families. We used research data from *Who Pays? A Distributional Analysis of the Tax Systems in All 50 States* from the

Box 6.1   Definitions of Terms

Earned Income Tax Credit (EITC) is a tax credit for low-income people with children who have earned income. The amount of the credit depends on income and family size. Taxpayers who qualify for the EITC may reduce their taxes or actually receive a refund larger than the taxes they paid. The Internal Revenue Service operates the federal EITC program. Many states also have their own EITC programs that reduce state taxes for low-wage workers.

Maintenance of Effort (MOE) is the federal mandate instituted when the Clinton administration passed "welfare reform" requiring that states expend funds to maintain the services and benefits they were providing for low-income families prior to the new law. A number of services and benefits can count toward a state's MOE. The MOE for each state is set at 80 percent (or 75% if certain requirements are met) of their historic level of funding for services and benefits. The penalty for noncompliance is a dollar-for-dollar reduction in the federal grant to the state for its Temporary Assistance for Needy Families (TANF) program.

Temporary Assistance for Needy Families (TANF) is the "welfare reform" passed in 1996 that changed Aid to Families with Dependent Children (AFDC) from an entitlement program to a time-limited program for very low-income families with children. New work requirements were instituted, and restrictions on benefits were imposed, so that many families no longer were able to qualify or had their benefits reduced. States were given new latitude in creating their own policies to address needs in their states.

Additional information about all these programs is available on federal and state government Web sites and on Web sites of policy analysis organizations with different perspectives, such as the Center for Budget and Policy Priorities, the Heritage Foundation, and the Center for Law and Social Policy, among others.

Citizens for Tax Justice and reports from the Center on Budget and Policy Priorities (CBPP) to make our case. The CBPP prepared papers for us based on their 2000 earned income credits reports, demonstrating the potential impact of an EITC on the state tax income and on low-income families. We convinced the legislators that if they were going to pass this tax increase, they had to give poor people something back. The administration balked at this prospect, but they knew that if they did not pass the EITC we would come down on them hard in the media. They could not afford that political fallout."

"I am a social worker but I can talk like an economist. I had to help legislators understand the concept of 'tax burden.' I remember talking to one senator who kept insisting that poor people do not pay taxes, even though they certainly pay sales taxes, and indirectly pay property taxes as well through their rents. And our state is one that taxes family income under the poverty line. What was most difficult was making the concept real to people. We knew that we risked losing everything by opening the issue up. We did not have the same circumstances as when the EITC was originally created and the issue was how to make sure we could document MOE or risk losing our federal funding for TANF and paying penalties. We were able to push things, even though we were afraid sometimes that the bottom might fall out."

As the above example illustrates, Shaniqua had built credibility as an advocate with both the legislators and the administrators in the executive branch of government. She had developed a good working relationship with the director of the state agency for social services through honest, direct communication. The director came to trust Shaniqua's assessment of the implications and possible impacts of various policy initiatives under consideration. She had provided research information from the Center for Budget and Policy Priorities and other nationally respected think tanks for the policy changes she advocated.

With a state-agency director committed to trying to help low-income people and open to the use of research data to inform policy decisions, Shaniqua had been able to demonstrate innovative ways to create opportunities for low-income families within the context of TANF and federal funding mechanisms. So it should not have been surprising when she later became a staff member of the state agency to manage and oversee these same programs at the state level. Not only did she bring a clear understanding of these complex programs, but she also understood how the state legislature worked from her lobbying days and could provide suggestions of how to work for policy change at that level.

When Shaniqua agreed to join the state agency, she made the change in her policy practice role clear. "I told the director that I expected that he would listen to my input when he asked for my advice about policy decisions. And I also said that I would leave if I felt I could not carry out a decision that I disagreed with from an ethical standpoint. Later I told my staff that as an administrator I was hired to carry out and implement the law. I said I would make sure that the policies of these programs would be implemented faithfully. If someone was not able to get on Medicaid because he or she did not qualify and later died, that was not my problem as an administrator but a problem for those who make the laws. But if someone who was eligible for Medicaid died because we were not doing our job, then that's my problem, that's our problem."

Shaniqua stayed at the state agency for almost two years. In her position, she was in charge of 22 different social service programs in the state. She asked her TANF policy staff whether they had ideas about how to change the implementation to better serve clients and was surprised to learn that no one before had ever asked them for their views on implementation. When she arrived, the Food Stamp staff did not talk to the staff in Commodities. "When I walked in the door, the staff there did not think they were doing anything. They saw themselves as pushing paper and preparing reports. I helped them see that what they were doing was important. I asked them what they wanted to do that would be more empowering for them and would keep them learning. I helped them figure out what they could do in positive ways to prevent horrible things from happening. I am really proud of being able to change the internal culture while I was there, because I think that translates into better services for people in communities. I am also proud of being part of passing the earned income tax deduction. We were able to change our own state EITC in 1999 for those earning $12,000 or less from a refundable portion credited to MOE into a real EITC in 2001."

Shaniqua hardly expected to be working for the state agency when she started college. Originally a forestry major because she liked the outdoors, she switched to psychology when she found those concepts easier to grasp and more interesting than how to calculate the number of board feet for a lot of timber. Combining her interest in the outdoors and psychology, she went to work for a boot camp for youth where she was quickly promoted to positions of greater responsibility. Then she worked at a crisis center for two-and-a-half years, where she saw people under great stress with long-term mental illnesses.

"I liked the aspect of crisis work, of not knowing what each day would bring, the nonroutine nature of the work, but I questioned whether I could really force people to change their behavior. People have choices, and what I want to encourage them to do may not be the choice they will make. I remember seeing a woman who was suicidal, and I was trying to get her into an inpatient facility. About a month later she was discharged, but seven hours later, she was back at our center. She felt she had 'failed,' but she had not failed. The system had failed her. I realized we needed to look at what we are doing as a society and provide more than Band-Aids. That was when I decided I needed to get into policy work, even though I was not a policy wonk yet, and went back for my MSW."

When a new governor was elected and another political party came into power, Shaniqua was let go from her position with the state agency. New governors, like new presidents, frequently bring in their own agency directors, but this governor went much farther down in the organizational chart in mandating changes in leadership. As an independent consultant since then, Shaniqua has worked with other policy projects, including one with a nonprofit advocacy organization that monitored the state's privatization of its social services eligibility process. She is continuing her career in policy practice.

Shaniqua's path to policy practice is not unusual. She did not start off thinking she would be a social worker engaged in policy practice. Though many people enter social work because they want to make a difference, they frequently think of that "difference" as being a difference in the lives of individuals. Some have seen the suffering and oppression of individuals in their own communities, and even their own families, and want to alleviate that suffering by getting people the help and resources that they need, much as Shaniqua wanted to help the woman who was thinking about committing suicide. Some may have already made the connection between individual troubles and social problems and want to ensure that social services and opportunities are available and accessible to the people who need them. And so those social work students may see the need to be involved as an advocate and supporter of social welfare policies in their communities. Direct service practitioners also need to engage in policy practice. Some policy practice roles are full-time positions, such as the ones that Shaniqua has held in her social work career. Other policy practice roles are an outgrowth of work with individuals and a desire to help a large number of people who are suffering from the same problem. For example, a social work clinician may involve herself in a statewide legislative process to pass a mental health parity bill for expanded mental health insurance coverage, in order to help individual clients gain access to the mental health care that they need.

Direct service practitioners also need to engage in policy practice.

In the Health Care Simulated Case Study that accompanies this book, the alumni newsletter highlights the variety of roles that social workers can play in policy practice. Buck Hoffman works for a foster care agency, but is concerned about shrinking budgets and changing regulations that adversely affect the youth he serves. His concern about lack of health insurance for some of the youth aging out of the foster care system catapults him into policy practice, in an effort to change policies and improve the prospects of youth. As assistant to the governor in charge of keeping him abreast of health and welfare issues, Annie Haskins is in a position to influence state-level policymaking through her relationship with the governor. Governors can determine policies through executive action within the current statutes, but they also can use their leadership skills to launch legislative initiatives of their own. Then they work to convince legislative leaders to support their initiatives. A social work policy practitioner, like Annie, can help collect information about issues affecting constituents and assist in the formulation of social policy emanating from the governor's office. These are just two examples of social workers in the policy practice roles discussed in this chapter. Shaniqua, in the case study at the beginning of this chapter, has actually served in multiple policy practice roles within both the public and nonprofit sectors of the policy practice arena.

ECOLOGY OF POLICY PRACTICE ACROSS POLICY SETTINGS

Overview of Social Worker Roles in Policy Practice

Social work uses an ecological perspective as evidenced in the person-in-environment perspective, whether applied to direct practice with clients or applied to policy practice in a variety of political settings. The concept map in Figure 6.1 illustrates the organic nature of policy practice roles in the variety of settings. Though the discussion here may focus on a role in a particular setting, most roles have counterparts in all three levels of governmental policy practice (local, state, and federal). For example, lobbyists at the federal level seek to influence federal legislation on everything from tax policy to environmental actions to social welfare concerns. Similarly, lobbyists for some of the same for-profit and nonprofit organizations as well as others work at the state level to influence state legislation on similar issues. State-level lobbyists may not have as many resources or as broad a sphere of influence as those at the federal level, but they successfully seek to influence policy nonetheless. Even at the local level, representatives of various community

Figure 6.1
Concept map of social work policy practice roles

groups may attempt to "lobby" the city council to pass or defeat particular ordinances or initiatives that are of interest to them and their constituencies. Local "lobbying" may look very different from the images of backroom wheeling and dealing in state houses and Congress. It may be a conversation on Saturday morning at the local farmer's market with a county commissioner about a proposed juvenile detention and treatment center for the county, or a phone call or e-mail to a school board member about a current "Just say no" sex education program. As discussed later in the chapter, there are even policy practice roles to be performed within local agencies.

The skill sets identified and discussed will be very similar across different levels of policy practice. In order to be effective in a variety of settings, practitioners must understand the specific context of policy practice and the differential skills needed. The skills needed and the specific strategies developed depend on the characteristics of the settings within which practitioners work and their specific roles as defined within those settings. The exploration of different policy practice roles in this chapter will include identifying specific defining characteristics of the settings and people for each setting and then discussing the skills needed for the roles within those settings. The case studies of real social workers presented later in this chapter will illustrate how social workers adapt and respond to different dimensions of different settings to achieve their policy practice goals.

SOCIAL WORK CAREERS IN POLICY PRACTICE

The concept map in Figure 6.1 is an organic way to illustrate the variety of roles that social workers may play in the policy area, including work at the local, state, or national level in roles as varied as elected legislator or other policymaker, lobbyist, and campaign director. Another way to conceptualize this variety of roles is configured in Table 6.1, which identifies examples of different roles across settings as they intersect with the different levels of policymaking. Roles presented here are meant to be illustrative rather than exhaustive of all the roles possible.

EXECUTIVE SETTINGS

Social work policy practice roles in executive settings are similar in the tasks and skills required across the different environmental levels, even though the particular tasks may be more complex and have broader potential impact at the national level. Some executive settings include the offices of elected officials such as mayors and governors, but most also include staff who are appointed or hired for their particular expertise. Some policy roles, such as serving on boards of nonprofit organizations, are volunteer positions.

Elected Executive

Social workers could be mayors, governors, and the president of the United States, all examples of policy practice roles in executive settings. Though there have yet to be social workers serving as governors or president, social workers have been elected to local executive political offices, including mayors and county commission members. In running for political office, candidates attempt

Table 6.1   Policy Practice Roles by Setting and Environmental Level

Typical Policy Practice Roles by Setting

Level of Policy Making	Executive	Legislative	Judicial	Community Agencies
Local	Local street-level bureaucrat and direct-service practitioner such as child welfare caseworker, probation officer, domestic violence shelter worker, executive director, and any other administrator of a local agency providing social services	Elected member of school board, town council, city council, county commissioners and other local legislative groups, and local constituent services representative for federal office holder	Local community practitioner providing expert testimony about best practices with particular populations and problems	Grassroots organizer developing neighborhood and local groups concerned about policy issues, participant in local initiatives such as development of new programs or services, Get Out the Vote (GOTV) and other local political work
State	Governor, state-level public program manager or agency administrator, director of statewide advocacy organization or nonprofit agency	State legislator, aide to state legislator	Expert witness in state court, participants in friend-of-the-court briefs	Lobbyist at the state level for social service agencies, participant in statewide organizing for issue or political campaign
Federal	Administrator or manager in Social Security Administration, and Department of Health and Human Services that administers federal programs such as SSI, Food Stamps, TANF, etc.	Member of Congress—senator or representative, staff of member of Congress	Participant in federal friend-of-the-court briefs	Staff of national nonprofit advocacy organizations, staff of "think tanks" providing policy analysis information

to assess the needs of the community and articulate a platform to address those needs, thereby winning the majority of the votes cast. Candidates must have the whole range of policy practice skills we have identified, including the ability to develop relationships or form connections with potential voters and campaign contributors. Once elected, though the tasks and duties of these roles vary across the different levels, most of these roles involve the implementation of the laws and policies set by the corresponding legislative bodies, including the preparation and monitoring of budgets. Some of those policies are usually ones developed and proposed by the executive and are related to both the issues raised in the political campaign and the reality encountered once inaugurated in office.

Appointed Executive Policymaker

Appointed executive policymakers may serve in government agencies or in nonprofit agencies. If the appointed executive policymaker is within the executive branch of government, that person may have been appointed by the elected executive discussed above and then will serve at his or her "pleasure." Within both state and federal government, as we saw in the case study of Shaniqua earlier in this chapter, the newly elected executive may be able to discharge the appointees of previous administrations and replace them with staff more closely aligned with his or her political values and orientation. These appointed policymakers may be in charge of particular policy areas or programs within the administration. In addition to the knowledge and skills needed to provide competent program administration and oversight, such a policy practitioner will also need to be able to negotiate the political climate of the administration within which he or she works. Sometimes, persuasive arguments about pursuing particular policy options may need to include an assessment of what is politically feasible and acceptable as well as the more rational arguments about what the research may show as being the most effective approaches to meeting needs in local communities. An ethical dilemma could arise if an appointed policymaker is asked to implement a policy that he or she sees as violating his or her professional ethics or values. Policymakers have resigned in protest rather than be forced to carry out such policies. For example, in 1996 when President Clinton signed the Personal Responsibility and Work Opportunity Reconciliation Act (PRWORA), creating Temporary Assistance for Needy Families (TANF), thus ending the entitlement program Aid to Families with Dependent Children (AFDC) and setting time limits for welfare receipt and mandating work, three of his top administration officials quit in protest. Wendell Primus resigned as deputy assistant secretary for human service policy at the department of Health and Human Services (HHS), stating that "to remain would be to disown all the analysis my office has produced regarding the impact of the bill."[1] His own research indicated that the law might result in over a million more children becoming poor. One month later, two assistant secretaries in HHS, Mary Jo Bane and Peter B. Edelman, also resigned. Writing about his decision later, Peter Edelman stated, ". . . the bill President Clinton signed is not welfare reform. It does not promote work effectively, and it will hurt millions of poor children by the time it is fully implemented."[2] He pointed out that the bill went well beyond "welfare reform" in cutting Food Stamp and Supplemental Security Income for legal immigrants, among other cuts. Edelman concluded, "The best that can be said about this terrible legislation is that perhaps we will learn from it and eventually arrive at a better approach. I am afraid, though, that along the way we will do some serious injury to American children, who should not have had to suffer from our national backlash."[3]

In the case of the appointed agency executive in a nonprofit organization, whether at the local, state, or national level, the role is one of implementing the policies set by the agency's governing body, in most cases a board of directors. Hired by the board, the agency director is responsible for hiring the staff to carry out the policies and programs of the board. Staff supervision and budget monitoring are among the director's tasks. Skills required by the agency director include relationship-building skills with both the board for vision and strategic planning and with the staff for implementing policy and providing data for policymaking. A director with a vision for the future for both the agency and the clients served will be a transformational leader, not merely a manager of the status quo. Such a vision presupposes an ability to assess the community and its needs as well as determine the agency resources required to meet that need.

Ethical Practice

Critical Thinking Question

What contextual and other factors would you consider if you were asked to implement a policy with which you had ethical concerns?

Role of Agency Board in Making Policy

In nonprofit agencies, the volunteer board of directors is selected (through a nomination and election process that involves the board and/or community members of the agency at an annual meeting) from the broader community served by the agency. Board members are usually selected for some expertise they may bring to the agency, such as an accountant with financial planning and budgeting skills, a business woman from a public-relations firm who can help with the agency's public image, and a social worker from a partnering agency working with the same population. With their community representation, boards may bring the local community concerns to the agency in a boundary-spanning role. The board is generally responsible for setting the broad policy and direction of the agency, hiring and evaluating the executive director, and approving the agency budget. Board members typically serve a two- to four-year term, so they need the ability to analyze the agency functioning and understand how best to help it achieve its organizational goals. Board members may be asked to make policy decisions such as how to best expand services to reach more clients, what legislation to support in the upcoming state legislature, and what funding agencies to approach with grant proposals. Boards vote on their decisions but typically work to develop a consensus on issues before moving toward a formal vote, to ensure the support of more than just a simple majority of board members. Working on a board requires the time and commitment of volunteer board members who develop and then analyze policy proposals from board committees and engage in collaborative decision-making and consensus-building activities for successful agency change. Resolving policy conflicts among board members and between board members and staff can sometimes be challenging processes for agency board members.

Advisor/Staff to Policymaker

Both governmental and nonprofit agency executives may have policy staff to advise them about new programs and policies to meet the needs of people in their service areas. These staff members are frequently chosen for their expertise in the particular content area, so, for example, a social worker with experience working with health care organizations might become the health policy analyst for the governor as Annie Haskins does in the health care simulated case study that accompanies this book. With expertise in a particular area, the staff person may be responsible for staying abreast of the research in this area so that programs can be updated to standards corresponding to what social scientists are discovering works best in meeting particular human needs. Being able to translate that more esoteric research into terms and policies more readily understood by the executive is an important analytical skill. Clearly, communication and relationship-building skills are important in this linking role between the agency and the practice community. Sometimes, too, this person's relationship to the executive may be helpful in getting information or new proposals into the mix of those under consideration. When executives must make decisions about a wide range of issues, they may rely more on the trusted judgments of their advisors in particular areas where they lack expertise and experience. Access to the staff members who advise executives is sometimes critical for policy advocates.

Agency Policymaking at the Direct Service Worker Level— The Case for Street-Level Bureaucrats

Street-level bureaucrats are those social workers in agencies who carry out the policies of an agency, and direct service workers engaged in micro practice. The vast majority of social workers are in roles of street-level bureaucrats vis-a-vis the clients they serve. The policymaking aspects of these roles are not often considered. Social workers in these roles are often regarded as distant from policy and the policymaking process. But the reality is that they frequently have a great deal of discretion in how they implement agency policy. Many agency policies regarding the kinds of referrals that will be made, for example, have some degree of leeway in their definitions, so that the social workers' professional judgments may be used in determining the best match between a particular client and a variety of community agencies. In addition, there is a qualitative policy difference and possible outcome difference between simply giving a client a name of a food pantry on a piece of paper as a referral and giving the person a contact person at the pantry, their phone number, street address and directions, plus information about the intake process at the pantry and any documentation the client may need to bring. The second referral process is more likely to end in a client receiving the needed services. Street-level bureaucrats are boundary spanners, linking the executive aspect of the agency back to the community it is committed to serve.

The vast majority of social workers are in roles of street-level bureaucrats vis-a-vis the clients they serve.

LEGISLATIVE SETTINGS

Social workers are employed and volunteer in a variety of roles within legislative settings. Some of these positions are elected and, therefore, are clearly connected to political processes. Other positions are appointed, based on particular expertise and skills or based on political connections and networks. Numerically, more social workers serve in these roles at the local level than at the state and federal levels, as there are more opportunities to serve locally. Those who are successful in gaining positions at the federal level sometimes have a start at the local level in their policy practice careers.

Legislative Policymaker

Legislators at all levels of government are elected by their constituents to represent their views and interests in the legislative body. At the federal level, social workers can be elected to Congress either as a representative from their congressional districts or as one of the two senators from their states. Chapter 12 provides detailed information about the skills and strategies needed to run a successful campaign. Currently, Debbie Stabenow (D-MI) and Barbara Mikulski (D-MD) are social workers serving in the U.S. Senate.

For Barbara Mikulski, running for political office (Baltimore City Council) for the first time in 1971 was a natural extension of her community organizing work as a social worker. Daughter of a grocery store owner, she became a social worker to address community needs, including those of at-risk children and older people. "Social work evolved into community activism when Mikulski successfully organized communities against a plan to build a 16-lane highway through Baltimore's Fells Point neighborhood. She helped stop the road, saving Fells Point and Baltimore's Inner Harbor, both thriving residential and commercial communities today."[4]

Similar to many others, Senator Barbara Mikulski (D-MD) started her political career at the local level. She served on the Baltimore City Council for five years, and then successfully ran for Congress in 1976. She served in the U.S. House of Representatives for 10 years before running for the Senate in 1986. She was the first woman elected to the Senate in her own right (previously some women had served out their deceased husbands' terms). She has served there for over 20 years. In her political work, Senator Mikulski puts her social work values into action. "Mikulski's experiences as a social worker and activist provided valuable lessons that she draws on as a United States Senator. She believes her constituents have a right to know, a right to be heard, and a right to be represented. She listens to her constituents and makes the personal, political."[5] Her top legislative concerns (education, services for older people, health research, women's health, and services for veterans) demonstrate the social work influence.

Senator Mikulski was one of the initial sponsors of the Children's Health Insurance Program (SCHIP) in 1997. This program, now CHIP, instead of SCHIP, is a joint federal and state program providing low-cost health insurance to children from low-income families who earn too much to qualify for Medicaid. With more children becoming eligible for CHIP recently and increased costs, CHIP has become a target for budget cuts. Discussing her support of SCHIP in August 2007, Senator Mikulski referenced her social work background: "I have fought for children's health care for a very long time, going back to my days as a social worker and as a young member of the U.S. House. This bill is what we have hoped and dreamed for. This program fills the gap for children who might otherwise have to go without any health care at all. The funding is critical to ensure our children have access to the health care they need and deserve."[6]

Senator Debbie Stabenow (D-MI) was first elected to office (County Commissioners) in 1974 when the closing of a nursing home inspired her to become involved in the policymaking process, a year before she earned her MSW degree from Michigan State University. Similar to Senator Mikulski, she continued to serve in local office until she ran for and won a seat in the state House of Representatives in 1979. There she became the first woman to become the Speaker of the House in Michigan. Before being elected to the U.S. Senate in 2000, she served in both the Michigan Senate and the U. S. House of Representatives. Key issues for Senator Stabenow include affordable health care and environmental concerns.[7]

As indicated in Chapter 1, Senators Mikulski and Stabenow are 2 of at least 191 social workers currently in direct policymaking roles in public office.[8] At the state level, as of 2008 there were 71 social workers elected to state legislatures. As legislators at either level, social workers must read and learn about hundreds, even thousands, of bills each year and become informed about the issues underlying the proposed legislation. They use their assessment skills to analyze the proposed policies and do the research to determine how well the proposed policies will address the issues or problems within the context of their own political value system. They rely on staff (though staff in many state legislatures is quite limited) to help them stay informed about constituent views on the issues as well as learning what lobbyists and experts in the relevant fields have to say. They research and propose legislation themselves to promote the agendas of their constituents. When the legislative body is not in session, they are back at home in their districts, meeting with ordinary citizens, local business people, advocacy groups, and others with an interest in pending legislation and attending local public events, including parades, public forums, and community meetings. They also must spend time fundraising for the next election. The use of these skills in legislative settings is discussed in more detail in Chapter 10.

Social workers' engagement, communication, and active listening skills help them interact and "hear" the variety of views of the people living in their districts. They also have the assessment and analytical skills to look at community or national issues and problems, understand their complexities, and help craft solutions to address them in a way that meets most needs and that capitalizes on underutilized strengths. Legislators must also be skilled negotiators to bring about enough support "from both sides of the aisle" in order to pass legislation. Most successful legislation requires the cooperation of both major political parties to pass and to avoid a veto by the executive branch. Legislators use their networking and collaboration skills to build broad coalitions to support proposed legislation to advance social welfare and social justice concerns. Ethical dilemmas are sometimes posed when a legislator must make a decision to support a piece of legislation that may not be the best, and may even have some egregious aspects, but it is a step in the right direction and the best that may be possible under the current political realities. Being able to explain these difficult choices to constituents who are not happy with their elected official's vote can be a particular challenge. The debate and discussion about health care reform at the federal level during the 2008 presidential election campaign and into Obama's presidency in 2009 brought such challenges into the discussions of whether to pursue a single-payer system, an array of options that included a public option, or a completely private health insurance system with a government mandate, similar to the mandate to purchase automobile insurance.

Professional
Identity

Critical Thinking Question

If social workers have the skills necessary for political office, what are the barriers to electing more social workers to higher offices?

Legislative Assistant/Constituent Services

Those who work for legislators, whether at the state or federal level, have many opportunities to exercise their social work skills, whether working in the legislator's governmental office or in the office "back home" in the district. Members of Congress have more funding to hire aides and may even have specialized staff to follow social welfare legislation specifically. Those in state legislatures have fewer aides and may even share staff among several legislators. They may not have an office back home in the district, but may operate from their homes, meeting constituents in coffee shops or other local establishments. In either context, legislative assistants are involved in a wide range of tasks to support the work of the legislator. They use assessment and analytical skills to research a variety of policy proposals and bills in order to brief the legislator about the pros and cons from the legislator's perspective, the likely consequences, and degree of constituent support for particular proposals. They are involved in constituent services work, helping constituents access federal or state benefit programs such as Social Security or Medicaid, or determining how best to address a local issue brought to the legislator's attention. A good understanding of the social service delivery system is critical to this role, as well as case-management skills from engagement to evaluation. Good communication skills, both written and oral, are also important for composing written responses to constituent letters and e-mails and also for talking with some constituents, both in person and over the telephone, who may be upset about how a policy is affecting them and their families. Legislative staff also help arrange local political events and public forums, visits to the state house or U.S. Capitol, or interviews or press conferences with the legislator for the media. Jason Carnes, BSW, former constituent caseworker for Representative Baron Hill (IN) and recently promoted to field representative for about five counties in southern Indiana, states, "I use my social work skills in interacting with people every day."

JUDICIAL SETTINGS

Policy practice roles in judicial settings are limited for social workers, but there are several important roles that can be very influential in policy practice.

Expert Witness

In judicial proceedings, whether in a local, state, district, or federal court, both prosecutors and defense attorneys may call social workers as expert witnesses to testify as to the research, accepted practice standards, or state of knowledge and skills of social work practice. Social workers can be called to testify regarding individual clients in some cases, but they may also be called to testify when the court hearing is about an accepted procedure used with both a particular client and other clients as well. For example, a social worker with expertise in working with families that are at risk of child abuse and neglect might be called to testify as to the accepted practice in determining when a child should be removed from biological parents in a lawsuit alleging inappropriate removal.

Amicus Curiae Briefs

Social work and advocacy organizations, represented by their attorneys, may join with plaintiffs as "friends of the court" in filing briefs challenging court decisions related to policy issues of concern. As noted in Chapter 1, the National Association of Social Workers (NASW) has joined with other professional organizations on a number of occasions in an effort to influence a court decision. Though briefs are legal documents, social workers will work with their attorneys to substantiate the rationale for the social work position on an issue, citing the relevant practice research as well as the value position and history of the profession. Analytical skill in developing a logical argument as well as written skills in using persuasive language with reference to relevant precedent cases is important. In *NASW News,* Rufus Sylvester Lynch, NASW member and principal investigator with the Institute for the Advancement of Working Families, summarized the importance of these briefs for social policy: "Courts make the final social policy. They make the final decision about many issues that social workers are most concerned about, and it is crucial to facilitate the legal process."[9] Amicus curiae briefs filed by NASW are always consistent with NASW policy as delineated in *NASW Speaks,* the evolving policy statements created by the Delegate Assembly of NASW elected members. In *Kennedy v. Louisiana,* NASW "argued that the death penalty for child rape actually hurts the victims it aims to help. Last October [2008], the U.S. Supreme Court upheld the ban on capital punishment for child rape as a matter of constitutional law. In making its decision, the Court referred to NASW's brief in noting that the

Courts make the final social policy.

death penalty offers an incentive for the criminal to murder his victim who is the single witness, is likely to cause the victim to suffer more emotionally due to repeated court testimony about brutal acts, and could cause more child sexual abuse cases to go unreported since perpetrators of child rape are often family members."[10] This example highlights the influence on court cases that social work involvement and expertise can achieve.[11]

Consultants in Judge Education Programs

Social workers are sometimes called upon to provide continuing education programs for judges on topics such as the implications for sentencing policies on families and decisions made in domestic court regarding family matters such as divorce, visitation, child support, and intimate partner abuse. In this instance, policy practitioners must be able to span the boundary between the social work and legal professions, and start where the judge is. Having knowledge of the legal system, the degree of discretion that the judge actually has, and the family dynamics in cases where a parent is sentenced are important. Communication skills are critical in any educational program. Ethical issues can emerge when mandatory sentencing, regardless of the individual family circumstances, is being discussed under the rubric of "fairness."

Elected Judge

Many local judges in family and juvenile courts are elected rather than appointed. As more social workers interested in policy go on to pursue their law degrees through joint MSW/JD programs or sequentially earning their JD degrees after their MSWs, they will be particularly well qualified to pursue these elected offices. Understanding both the law and how families function and how families can best be served would help such judges make good professional decisions on the bench. Assessment and analytical skills are important in being able to understand the complexity of both the offenses and the circumstances under which they were committed. Oral communication and engagement skills are particularly important in being able to establish relationships with all parties involved in a case, including the attorneys. Negotiation skills may help parties find informal solutions to challenges in a case. Judges sometimes might have to carry out judgments that are "legal" but not satisfactory from an ethical perspective when the law (such as laws requiring mandatory sentences for particular offenses) does not really allow the judge to take all the circumstances into account.

Advocate in Judge Appointment Processes

Judges at some levels are appointed, rather than elected. For example, the justices of the United States Supreme Court are appointed by the president to serve until they retire or die in office. Such appointments are extremely important as Supreme Court decisions have set definitive social welfare policy through interpreting the Constitution, such as *Brown v. Board of Education* (1954), which ended segregation in the schools, *Roe v. Wade* (1973), which guaranteed a woman's right to choose abortion as an alternative, and *Grutter v. Bollinger* (2003), which upheld the use of race as one of many factors to be considered in university admissions processes. When the president nominates someone to fill a vacancy on the Court, the Senate must consent, and it is not unusual for advocacy groups and other organizations to weigh in about the qualifications of the nominee and his or her judicial temperament and philosophy. For example, in 2009 NASW approved the nomination of Appellate Judge Sonia Sotomayor, nominated by President Obama to the Supreme Court. In its endorsement, NASW highlighted Judge Sotomayor's support of the "rights of citizens to sue corporations acting on behalf of the federal government when the corporation in question has violated the citizen's rights . . . [and] the rights of adolescent girls whom she believed were needlessly strip searched in juvenile detention centers."[12]

COMMUNITY SETTINGS

Campaign Director or Worker on a Campaign

Agency-based social workers can engage in policy practice roles in at least four different ways.

One important grassroots organizing role for policy practitioners is working on a political or advocacy campaign. These roles and the specific skills involved are discussed in much more detail in Chapter 12. Here it is worth noting that social workers can get their start in politics by helping others get elected whose views and positions are close to those espoused by the social work profession. Campaign workers typically start by doing such mundane tasks as stuffing envelopes for a direct-mail campaign to counteract an opponent's attack, to arranging for a media event in a community agency, to holding a fund-raising event in their own homes. Campaign workers go "door knocking" to identify possible supporters for later Get Out the Vote (GOTV)

efforts for their candidate. Some campaign workers work at party headquarters on the phone banks, making sure voters from their party know where their voting station is located, have a ride to the polls, or have already sent in their ballots. All these grassroots activities use many of social work's interactive skills as workers identify how best to appeal to certain voters and what arguments in favor of their candidate seem most persuasive. With more experience, campaign workers develop the political networks that may help in their own future community work as they become more involved politically. There are some paid positions for political policy practice with the major political parties and with the high-profile state and federal political candidate campaigns. Most state and local campaigns, however, rely fairly extensively on volunteers.

Part-Time or Volunteer Policy Advocate

Some policy advocates are hired by social service agencies or coalitions of agencies as lobbyists. Some such advocates in larger agencies have full-time policy roles, while others in smaller organizations may have only a portion of their jobs devoted to advocacy efforts. Many social workers also volunteer their time to work on advocacy efforts in a volunteer capacity, not as part of their paid jobs. The restrictions on lobbying (urging a legislator to vote in a particular way on a particular bill) for agency employees is discussed fully in Chapter 10. Social workers can, as private citizens, engage in all variety of advocacy efforts, including writing letters and meeting with their representatives. Using communication and engagement skills are particularly important in these efforts.

Lobbyist

In the case study at the beginning of this chapter, we learned about Shaniqua Abrams and her various policy practice roles, including that of lobbyist for a statewide advocacy organization. Advocacy organizations that represent the interests of vulnerable populations, including older people (American Association of Retired People), children (Children's Defense Fund), and low-income citizens (Coalition for Human Needs), may employ social workers with advocacy experience to fill positions as lobbyists. Effective lobbyists for social welfare policies and populations do not have the budgets to "wine and dine" legislators to help win their support for public policy positions. Instead, they rely upon developing relationships with policymakers, much as Shaniqua did, so that the decision makers learn to trust the information that social workers provide to facilitate the policymaking process. Those social work engagement skills are additionally helpful in framing the policy debate in terms and values that resonate with the legislative decision maker. Lobbyists use their analytical skills to understand the complexities of pending legislation and determine how the proposals fit with their organizations' values and issue positions. Additionally, lobbyists must be skilled in collaboration to reach out to other organizations and their lobbyists who are potential allies on a legislative issue even if they have been on the opposite side on other issues. In addition, lobbyists must be able to be objective and see the worth of the individuals who are opposed to their views. As one social work lobbyist confided, "It is difficult to listen to them and their rhetoric. I have to listen though to see where I might be able to help them see something differently, see it from my perspective." Using the social work mantra of "starting where the other is" can be very helpful in discovering the "hook" or connection that will allow the advocate to make a point the legislator will listen to.

Research/Policy Analysis Positions

Some community organizations, particularly those at a state or national level, have staff to conduct research and make policy recommendations. Some of these organizations are nationally well-known think tanks such as the Center for Budget and Policy Priorities, while others are well known in their own states. Some remain nonpartisan but are linked to advocacy issues such as homelessness or health care reform. Staff may be engaged in research projects that entail actual data collection from people using surveys or interviews, or secondary data analysis of large data sets such as the Survey of Income and Program Participation (SIPP) of the U. S. Census Bureau. Others may

Research Based Practice

Critical Thinking Question
What are some current research projects in policy research organizations working in a field of practice of interest to you?

complete meta-analyses of other social science research to draw the broader conclusions and policy recommendations. Skills needed include research, analytical skills, and statistical and qualitative data analysis. Good writing skills are essential, especially when translating research into meaningful terms for policy practitioners. Ethical issues can emerge in this work when the data seem to suggest results that challenge the dominant ideology. How to then frame issues so they will be heard in a meaningful way can be a challenge. For example, when some initial research on Head Start found that the gains children experienced did not last over time, advocates suggested that these results demonstrated problems with the public school systems, which did not provide the resources that students needed to maintain their achievement levels, and not failures of Head Start.

Policy Practitioner/Educator

Some social work faculty are actively engaged in policy practice themselves through their own organizing efforts, on either issue or political campaigns. In this way, they continue to hone their own policy practice skills and bring their own active experiences into the classroom to model for student learning. Hull writes that as his students were involved in a local political campaign with him as their faculty mentor and guide, they became more interested in political events and more active in other political campaigns.[13] Other social work faculty members have found additional ways to get students more engaged in policy and policy practice, as noted in the profiles 6.1 and 6.2 below.

Faculty Profile 6.1   Faculty Profile—Radio Talk Show Host

Ruth White describes herself as a "ranter." "I am always ranting about something," she says. She teaches social policy courses at Seattle University's BSW program. She already had several venues for her advocacy efforts, including a column in a parenting magazine and frequent commentaries in the Seattle papers with her op-ed pieces. She had always wanted to have a radio talk show, particularly when she heard others on the radio expressing their views. She expressed the thought out loud and was overheard by the manager of the student radio station at Seattle University, KSUB, Seattle. The manager agreed it was a good idea and asked Dr. White to e-mail her ideas for the show. Before she had a chance to do so, the manager e-mailed her, stating the management team had discussed the idea and wanted her to proceed. And so she was off and running with her own radio show, *Policy Brief,* airing on Wednesdays at 9:00 A.M. Pacific Time, online at www.ksubseattle.org or FM 96.

Ruth White's goal in hosting a radio show on social policy was to engage more young people in policy practice issues and get them involved. She structured the show around current policy issues, the first one

being organized around the Farm Bill pending in Congress and issues of hunger. Another program was on the challenge of AIDS. She invited a panel for each hour-long show to address the particular issue from a variety of perspectives: service provider, client or consumer, activist, and policymaker. She always tried to include a student on each panel who was involved in the issue in some way, to help make the connections with her student audience. Her time slot saw an increase in the number of listeners, despite the limitation of being available online only for some time.

Ruth's other goal was to educate the public in general about social policy issues and how they can help change policy and get involved in the policymaking process. At first she was challenged by some of the technology of "running the board" in her role as producer, but she laughed when she said she thought she mastered that and did not push any "wrong buttons." Though Ruth had to suspend the program in 2009 due to the work involved in hosting the program and other responsibilities, she found it to be a valuable experience.

Ruth White serves as an outstanding model for her students as she "did" policy practice, live on the air, on *Policy Brief.* She continues to help students connect to issues and, in class, she helps them connect with community agencies and advocacy groups where their assignments are to develop policy briefs, write letters to policymakers, write letters to the editor, and complete a policy analysis on a policy or issue of concern to the agency. She happily reports that students are pleased when their letters to the editor are published. Learning by doing policy practice in the real world can make such a difference in student learning. Dr. Ruth White practices her own "doing" and channels her "rants" in ways that will contribute to both student and community engagement.

Faculty Profile 6.2   Faculty Profile—Organization Initiator

On a Saturday night in Chicago, during a Council on Social Work Education Conference in 1997, when there were plenty of other "things" for attendees to do, 27 faculty members gathered at the invitation of Dr. Robert Schneider of Virginia Commonwealth University, in a hotel meeting room. Dr. Schneider laid out his concerns that with the 1996 welfare-reform legislation, much of social policy was devolving to the states. He thought that social work educators, students, and practitioners were ill-prepared to handle this shift since much of the focus of social welfare policy had been at the federal level up to that time. He proposed starting an organization to promote and support teaching students how to influence state-level policy. The group brainstormed and became excited about the possibilities. Someone passed the hat, literally, to collect contributions to get the enterprise off the ground. And so was born Influencing State Policy (ISP).

ISP has grown substantially since 1997. In 2009, there were over 1,200 members on the mailing list. ISP has a Web site (www.statepolicy.org) with links to state as well as federal policy Web sites, descriptions of the six videos on policy practice skills that ISP has produced, and additional resources. A DVD of the ISP videos is available to all members. ISP sponsors contests at the BSW, MSW, and PhD levels to encourage more student engagement in state policy work.

When Bob Schneider recalls how he himself became interested in policy, he talks about being in the Washington, D.C., area during the 1970s, when there was a great deal of political turmoil over the war in Vietnam and civil rights. "The Great Society [President Johnson's anti-poverty programs] inspired me. I wanted to become an activist and help people," he said. For his MSW, he started with group work, but finished in community organization at Tulane University and then continued into their accelerated doctoral program.

Reflecting on his initiative in creating and nurturing ISP, Dr. Schneider is most pleased about the significant work he has been able to accomplish. "The notion of ISP has struck a chord with people. It really took off because a lot of social work faculty members were thinking about the changes in how policy was being made. ISP gave some structure and form to our participation in state policy work. If we don't get involved and stay involved, we will just be implementing, not formulating, policy," he said. "We were able to highlight that we need to be at the table at the state level, not just the national level. And we became part of a national consciousness that it does not take that much activity to influence state-level policy."

And what is Bob Schneider most proud of in his work with ISP? "I love the notion of what students have done, what faculty have inspired them to do." His hope is that students will continue to use the policy practice skills that they learn in their educational programs when they become practitioners in communities. In honor of Dr. Schneider's commitment to student involvement, the PhD award was named after him, starting in 2009.

In 2008, Dr. Schneider retired, and Dr. Kathy Byers of Indiana University became the new chair of ISP. Dr. Schneider hopes that ISP will continue its contests that get students involved in the policymaking process at the state level. He also hopes that ISP will inspire social workers to become more active in policy practice, getting back to the roots of the profession. He would like to see more research in state-level policy and for social work to create a stronger voice in policy development. He sees the connection between direct practice and policy practice and hopes ISP can continue to help students recognize that important connection. As he says and as the ISP buttons proudly proclaim, "Policy affects practice; practitioners affect policy."

Grass Roots Organizer of Community Groups

The roles of community organizer and coalition builder will be discussed in some detail in Chapter 11. People in these roles are frequently employed by an issue-based agency seeking to organize coalitions in support of an issue, for example, current efforts to organize around immigration and health care reform. In other cases, the community organizers are from neighborhoods themselves and are not professionally trained organizers. A wide range of engagement skills is necessary for those in community organizing roles in order to attract other individuals and groups to the cause. In addition, analytical skills are important in order to be able to assess community needs and the political climate, and to match organizing strategies appropriately. More specifics about these skills are discussed in later chapters.

Policy Practice Roles for Direct Service Practitioners

Professional Identity

Critical Thinking Question

Which policy practice roles would you find the most rewarding and what challenges would they present for you personally?

Agency-based social workers can engage in policy practice roles in at least four different ways. First, when they notice that a number of people are not getting services or resources that they need, social workers can propose new programs to fill gaps in services. Second, social workers remember that client empowerment includes political empowerment. They can help clients develop political empowerment by developing voter registration, education, and GOTV drives, all without telling clients how to vote but simply encouraging their participation in the political process. Social workers can also help clients mobilize for legislative activity and help them speak up about their concerns in ways that are safe for them to do. The disability movement, for example, includes large numbers of people with disabilities themselves who have learned how to be effective self-advocates.[14] Partnering with social workers and other advocates has made this group a very important political force.

Third, social workers can become involved themselves, as they help clients in the legislative process, by speaking with legislators, inviting policymakers to visit agencies to learn about services, writing letters to legislators and other policymakers, calling and e-mailing when crucial votes are imminent, and organizing and attending Lobby Day events. And fourth, social workers can find ways to educate the general public on legislative issues by speaking up at public forums, writing letters to the editor and opinion columns for the local paper, serving as a guest on local radio talk shows, providing press releases about the impact of current or proposed legislation on agency services, organizing a speakers bureau, and organizing community forums. Details of the skills necessary to take on these activist roles are covered in later chapters in this book.

Informal Opportunities to be a Policy Advocate

Social welfare policies are regularly the topic of conversation in social gatherings, whether it is discussing U.S. immigration policy, taxes, global competition for manufacturing jobs, or homelessness. Social workers can be alert to opportunities to dispel myths about some of these policies with friends in casual conversations. Several years ago, one of the authors was at a party when the topic of welfare reform came up. One of the other guests started talking about all the "lazy mothers on welfare who were just having more children so they could get more money without working." The author took the opportunity to explain how TANF operates with work and training requirements and even family caps in some states. She also talked about her own previous work with mothers on welfare and what she had observed about their motivation to improve their family circumstances through hard work. If social workers let comments like the one above about "lazy mothers on welfare" stand unchallenged, then they are complicit in the perpetuation of myths and erroneous public views that can lead to support of public policies detrimental to social justice goals. Using their active listening skills to help "start where the other is" and then framing responses so that the other person can see the social worker's point is indeed a challenge. But it is a challenge that social workers must address or risk losing some important opportunities to educate others about the social justice issues of concern.

Policy Practice by Professional Associations

With over 150,000 members, the NASW (Web site accessible at ww.socialworkers.org) is social work's largest professional association and, as such, plays an important role in policy practice at the federal, state, and sometimes local levels. For example, NASW at the national level has advocated for a single-payer health insurance program for many years. It has been instrumental in the development of the Title IV-E Child Welfare Training program that helps so many social work students pursue their education and work in the field of child welfare. At the state level, NASW state chapters have worked hard to establish licensing laws and other efforts to regulate the profession and protect the public from unethical and unprofessional practitioners. Multiple volunteer roles within NASW are outlined in Appendix A at the back of the book.

Many social workers belong to other professional organizations that also play roles in policy practice, such as the National Association for Black Social Workers, the National Association of Christian Social Workers, the Council on Social Work Education, and the Social Welfare Action Alliance, formerly the Bertha Capen Reynolds Society.

In addition to other social work professional associations, there are any number of local, state, and national advocacy groups for a whole variety of issues that would be happy to have volunteers to assist in their efforts. Working with an existing advocacy group that is focused on a population or issue is a much better strategy than trying to start a new organization. At the end of this chapter is a list of a few Web sites for such organizations.

CONCLUSION

This chapter provided an environmental scan of the variety of roles that social workers play in policy practice from paid positions as legislators, policy analysts, or lobbyists, to volunteer work as a member of an advocacy organization such as NASW or other professional associations, or as a private citizen. There are more opportunities to begin policy practice work at the local level. Most social workers who are active in policy practice at the state and national levels have started their work at the local level. The specific skills needed for each policy practice role are described in subsequent chapters.

Succeed with PEARSON mysocialworklab

Log onto **MySocialWorkLab** to access a wealth of case studies, videos, and assessment. (*If you did not receive an access code to* **MySocialWorkLab** *with this text and wish to purchase access online, please visit* www.mysocialworklab.com.)

1. **Watch the Connecting Core Competency videos on Engage, Assess, Intervene, Evaluate;** pay special attention to video during which social worker Michael Melendez reviews the progress a client has made in returning to sobriety and regaining custody of her son. In reviewing what she has done to come to this point, the client mentions a variety of community services she has used. If you were Michael Melendez providing testimony as an expert witness about the importance of this array of services and programs in a state budget hearing, what would you emphasize to convince legislators about the need to continue funding?

2. **Review Health Care SCS.** Compare and contrast the sources of power (both personal and role-related) for Buck Hoffman, Marta Madison, and Annie Haskins in the Health Care SCS as they begin to organize for health care reform. After you have read the whole SCS, think of different actions that they might have taken in their practice roles to lead to greater success. Identify the constraints and limitations that each of them have in their roles.

PRACTICE TEST

The following questions will test your knowledge of the content found within this chapter. For additional assessment, including licensing-exam type questions on applying chapter content to practice, visit **MySocialWorkLab**.

1. Talking to a councilman at a community event, or emailing the county commissioner about a proposed program are examples of:
   a. Local lobbying
   b. Judicial education
   c. Influencing state policy
   d. Executive policy making

2. Appointed executive policymakers in non-profit agencies:
   a. Follow the direction of elected executives in most agency contexts.
   b. Are free to make their own independent policy decisions with little accountability.
   c. Must request board review before any decisions implementing policy are made.
   d. Follow the broad policies set by the board and hire the staff necessary to accomplish agency's goals.

3. Stuffing envelopes, organizing a media event, making sure that voters know where to vote, and making sure they have a way to get there are duties that would be done by a:
   a. Policymaker's assistant
   b. Campaign worker
   c. Advocate in judge appointment process
   d. Street-level bureaucrat

4. Good writing skills, analytical and research skills, and statistical and qualitative analysis skills are needed in order to be an effective:
   a. Elected executive
   b. Appointed judge
   c. Research / Policy Analyst
   d. Lobbyist

5. An example of local level policy practice would be:
   a. Participant in the friend of the court briefs
   b. Grassroots organizer of community policy groups
   c. Expert witness in state court
   d. A governor's advisor on health care

6. The responsibilities of nonprofit agency boards include:
   a. Hiring and evaluating the executive director, and setting broad agency policy directions
   b. Approving the agency budget, and all hiring and firing for all agency positions
   c. Handling all agency public relations and setting broad policy objectives
   d. Actively lobbying and advocating for the agency, and evaluating the agency staff

7. The type of policy practitioner responsible for determining the best match between individual clients and community agencies is:
   a. An administrative social worker
   b. A street-level bureaucrat
   c. An agency board member
   d. Appointed executive director

8. A social worker giving a presentation to judges on the effects of sentencing in domestic court decisions about family matters such as child support, visitation, and divorce is an example of:
   a. Judge's assistant
   b. Judicial advocate
   c. Consultant in judge education programs
   d. Consultant to the judicial board

Log onto **MySocialWorkLab** once you have completed the Practice Test above to access additional study tools and assessment.

Answers

Key: 1) a, 2) d, 3) b, 4) c, 5) b, 6) a, 7) b, 8) c

7

The Media and Public Opinion in Policy Practice

CHAPTER OUTLINE

Introduction 144

The Basics 145
Understanding the News Media
Working with the News Media

Communication Strategies for Policy
    Campaigns 151
Summary Model

New Media Advocacy 155
E-mail
Advocacy Web Sites
Blogs
Podcasts

Evaluating Advocacy Communication 166

Conclusion 167

Chapter Review 168

Practice Test 168

 MySocialWorkLab 168
SCS on Health Care Reform
SCS on Gay Marriage

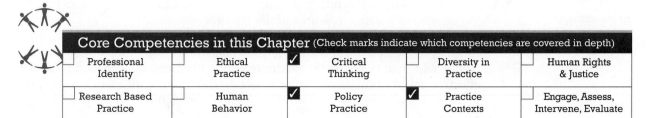

Core Competencies in this Chapter (Check marks indicate which competencies are covered in depth)				
☐ Professional Identity	☐ Ethical Practice	✓ Critical Thinking	☐ Diversity in Practice	☐ Human Rights & Justice
☐ Research Based Practice	☐ Human Behavior	✓ Policy Practice	✓ Practice Contexts	☐ Engage, Assess, Intervene, Evaluate

INTRODUCTION

If you don't exist in the media, for all practical purposes, you don't exist.

DANIEL SCHORR, COMMENTATOR, National Public Radio

Policy practice is the public stage of social work, where the lessons learned from micro, mezzo, and macro practice and social work research are translated into public policy. One of the core competencies of policy practice is advocating effectively in the media. Presented below are two examples of mediated communication from the Simulated Case Studies (SCS). In the first example, from the Gay Marriage SCS, policy practitioner Julia Cohen struggles to get her message across. In response to an escalating series of attack questions from a right-wing radio talk-show host, Julia loses her temper:

> Mark Frazier, you are THE argument against intelligent design . . . you are a leech, a bloodsucker, sucking the blood out of civilized discourse. I now understand the true meaning of "Jesus wept." He took one look at you and was filled with the despair I feel.

After her blow up, Julia slams out of the studio, cutting the interview short. In a subsequent e-mail, Julia realizes that "I blew it. . . . I've created lots of deadly ammunition for the opposition by losing my cool." Other coalition members assess the damage (which includes derisive bumper stickers such as "Jesus wept when we did nothing to stop the gay agenda" and clips from the interview circulating around the Internet). The situation is ultimately turned around, but it requires extra effort and the potentially draining deployment of organizational resources.

The second example, taken from the Health Care Reform SCS, provides a more positive example of interaction between a policy practitioner and the press. Reporter Paul Stutzbach e-mails Care4Care member Buck Hoffman:

> Hey, thanks for sharing those case studies, and thanks especially for helping us get them before TV did. The stories were compelling, and your people gave excellent interviews. We have had a tremendous response to our pieces. Also, thanks for the phone call clarifying why there are two meetings on the same night about healthcare. You really helped me not to misinterpret what was going on there. We will have someone at both meetings.

Policy practitioners need to know about news values, how news is produced, and how abstract policy issues can become newsworthy.

Communicative competence entails knowing how to work with members of the media and knowing when and how to mobilize public support for policy initiatives. Policy practitioners need to know about news values, how news is produced, and how abstract policy issues can become newsworthy. In our communication-saturated society, with audience attention so split across multiple forms of media, it is imperative that policy practitioners stay current with the latest technological trends, and understand their implications for capturing the increasingly scarce resource of the public's attention.

This chapter will provide an overview of these topics, beginning with routine, ongoing communications between the policy practitioner and the media, and then covering the communicative competencies needed to mount effective policy campaigns. The final section concludes with an analysis of how the Web, e-mail, and other new technologies are reshaping policy practice.

THE BASICS

The foundation of good public communication is ongoing, routine interaction with journalists. If these relationships are nurtured over the long term, it is easier to attract coverage when needed such as when involved in a local, statewide, or national issues campaign.

Understanding the News Media

As in any social relationship, success in public communication will be, in part, a function of how well the policy practitioner understands the conditions under which they operate. A social worker would never think of entering into a direct practice relationship with a client from another cultural background without first acquiring the cultural competence needed to engage in a productive relationship. Likewise, it is the responsibility of the policy practitioner to understand the world of the journalist—to acquire the degree of cultural competence that will lead to a productive relationship.

In order for something to become news, it must be compatible with journalistic news values. Fishman[1] asserts that "what is known and knowable by the media depends on the information-gathering and information-processing resources" of the news organization. Table 7.1 lists factors that increase or decrease the likelihood of news coverage.

It may surprise you that "predictable and routine events" are on the list. Why isn't "news" simply the coverage of "new things"? The answer lies in the sociology of the news organization. Because potential news stories vastly outnumber the capacity for coverage, news organizations focus their reporting

Table 7.1 News Selection Factors

Factors that increase coverage
- Power and fame of individuals involved in events
- Personal contacts of reporters
- Location of events
- Location of power
- Predictable and routine events
- Proximity to the audience of people and events in the news
- Recency and timeliness of events
- Timing in relation to the news cycle (the period between releases of the medium—24 hours for a daily newspaper)
- Novelty
- Shock
- Conflict
- New data
- Simplicity
- Kids
- Social issues or prominent figure involved
- Humor
- Outdoor location
- Action
- Bright props and images
- News stories about the event published in advance
- Local impact
- A symbol of a trend
- Holidays, anniversaries

Factors that inhibit news coverage
- Indoor location
- People reading scripts
- A private, profit-oriented goal
- Complexity
- Unknown participants
- Bad timing or remote location

Sources: McQuail. 2000, p. 284; Salzman. 1998, pp. 16–17.

resources on certain areas, or beats. Possible beats that can be relevant to policy practice include city government, the courts, human services, health, and the environment.

Far from being a simple mirror on the day's events, the news is a social construction[2] that emerges from the interpretive frames of journalistic news values.[3] A journalistic frame is "a central organizing idea for news content that supplies a context and suggests what the issue is through the use of selection, emphasis, exclusion, and elaboration. The result of these journalistic frames is news that reflects political and economic power, news that is heavy on personalized human-interest stories, and news that focuses on the horse race of politics—who's ahead, who's behind, often at the expense of more substantive coverage of issues.

How powerful are the media in influencing members of the public? Research indicates that there is no "magic bullet" of media effects that directly determines how people think—interpersonal communication is more powerful.[4] However, the media *are* gatekeepers, acting as a filter on information that enters the public sphere.[5] Although the advent of the World Wide Web has broadened access to information, the traditional news media (newspapers, broadcast television, radio, and cable news) are still the predominant news source for the majority. In the 2006 midterm elections, for example, 69 percent of respondents got most of their political news from television; 34 percent relied the most on newspapers, and only 15 percent obtained most of their news from the Internet.[6] Of that 15 percent, a majority (60%) relied mostly on online versions of mainstream media (i.e., CNN.com).[7] For the 2008 presidential election, though, there are indications that the Internet may one day eclipse mainstream media as a source for political news. Television remained the predominant source for election news (77% of respondents in a national survey relied on television for election news), but 55 percent of those surveyed went online to access election coverage, this being the first time a majority of adults used the Internet to follow a political campaign.[8]

While the long-term trend may be toward some erosion of influence of the mainstream media, it is still the case that the media functions as gatekeepers, setting the political agenda for the public. Research on agenda setting demonstrates that although the media may not tell people what to think, it does tell them what to think *about*.[9] The media defines the set of issues that are considered "the issues of the day"—in a sense, providing a policy "top ten" list. The public salience of such issues as global warming, health care reform, crime, or pollution is largely a function of where the media spotlight shines (see Figure 7.1). There are, of course, issues that would merit coverage that do not get sufficient play in the news media, including prison conditions, white-collar crime, and the social consequences of urban sprawl.

Agenda-Setting News Flow

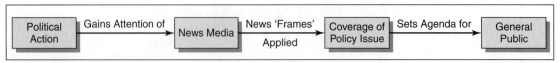

Figure 7.1
Agenda-Setting News Flow

Working with the News Media

Policy practitioners should develop ongoing relationships with key reporters and news outlets. Create a media list that includes all possible contacts made with area media and identify the likely beats that connect to a particular area of policy practice. For example, education, government, children, and housing are news beats that may be relevant to policy practice work with families. To determine which reporters cover which beats, contact the newspaper, radio (especially the local National Public Radio affiliate), or TV station assignment editor.

Policy practitioners should develop ongoing relationships with key reporters and news outlets.

After identifying the most promising journalists and media outlets, the policy practitioner can start seeking news coverage. Here are some common tactics to help ensure success.

- Pitching story ideas: Keep in mind the news values listed in Table 7.1 and focus on story topics that are aligned with them. Reporters are busy and will ignore calls or e-mails that don't seem to lead to a story; even if you strike out on several rounds of pitching stories, your persistence may help to access the reporter when you have a legitimate news story.
- Meeting with the newspaper's editorial board: In setting their editorial direction, editorial-section staff members generally meet with key community stakeholders such as universities, businesses, and social service agencies. This can be an effective strategy for educating reporters about an important issue from a macro perspective. Editorial boards are most likely to meet with policy practitioners based in large, well-known community agencies or with representatives of coalitions that bring together a wide range of relevant stakeholders around a single issue.
- Writing an opinion-editorial (op-ed) piece for the newspaper's editorial section: Generally, 700 words is the ideal length for an op-ed article, although guidelines vary from paper to paper. The likelihood of getting a piece published will be greater if you present a local angle on the issue and if you personalize the piece by including examples of the issue's human impact.
- Writing a letter to the editor: Keep the letter short and to the point, at about 200 words. Box 7.1 is an example of a letter to the editor that effectively utilizes professional expertise to educate the public and advocate for passage of a bill to address the needs of a particularly vulnerable group—victims of child abuse.

Practice Contexts

Critical Thinking Question
Why do you think the local angle is so important to journalists?

If you have a particularly newsworthy event—and note that "event" can be construed broadly to include the publication of new data in a report, an anniversary of a milestone event, or the formation of a task force to address a social problem—a press release should be issued to the media. Do not issue press releases for mundane activities such as your organization's board meeting or new staff hires—unless there is an interesting angle that can be played up (for example, "our new board member is a CEO whose mother utilized our services in her climb out of poverty").

Press releases should be sent one week in advance of the event, and can be followed up with a call to reporters on your media list. In his book *Making the News: A Guide for Nonprofits and Activists,* Jason Salzman[10] recommends making calls to reporters one day prior to the event. Call in the morning to ensure that you don't get in the way of reporters working under the day's story deadline (usually after 3 P.M.). Note that reporters often prefer to receive press releases via e-mail—make the effort to identify the preferences of those on your media list.

If you anticipate a high degree of interest in your release, consider holding a press conference, which is a simultaneous briefing for reporters from multiple

Box 7.1   A Letter to the Editor

Child Victims Act is Needed in the State

I am quite surprised at the lack of public response to the March 28 editorial "Helping the victims" regarding enacting a Wisconsin Child Victims Act. As a psychotherapist in private practice for 20 years, I have had the honor of serving adults who bravely work to confront their sexual abuse, which occurred in childhood and/or adolescence. Some of the clients recovered memories of abuse later in their lives. Others never had blocked their memories but were too terrified and ashamed to tell anyone when they were younger. And, sadly, some did try to tell what happened to them early on but were ignored and dismissed.

For any readers concerned about "false memory syndrome," let me say that the majority of abuse cases I have handled have been substantiated either by the perpetrators themselves, other witnesses, or others who independently reported abuse by the same perpetrator. Sexual abuse is not uncommon in our society and more often happens within families and with acquaintances.

Seeking legal solutions and pursuing financial compensation are not the answers needed for some survivors of abuse. But there are some people whose lives have been so badly damaged, who cannot afford treatment, and they deserve their day in court or at the bargaining table. Let's pass the Child Victims Act so justice can be served.

PEG BACKUS-WALLNER
MSW, LCSW Greendale

Source: Milwaukee Journal Sentinel. April 9, 2009. www.jsonline.com/news/opinion/42771862.html.

news outlets. Here are a few policy practice examples that would warrant a press conference:

- The formation of a high-profile coalition to tackle the hot-button issue of the day;
- Release of a significant policy report with strong supporting data that connects to newsworthy policy topics; or,
- To accommodate a high degree of media interest if your policy activities relate to a breaking story (such as a policy proposal to increase housing options for the mentally ill following a highly publicized beating to death of a mentally ill homeless person).

Press conferences require significant organizational staff time to coordinate—only use this strategy if you are confident that reporters will actually attend. Prepare a press packet to distribute at the conference that contains the press release, background information on your organization, and relevant supporting materials such as tables, charts, and survey results. Timing is important—the best chance to obtain media coverage for any type of event is Monday through Thursday, 10 A.M. to 2 P.M.[11] Box 7.2 is a sample news release put out by the National Low Income Housing Coalition to mark the anniversary of the McKinney-Vento Homeless Assistance Act.

Analysis of this press release demonstrates how the National Low Income Housing Coalition has maximized the news appeal of its reform agenda. The release headline, "Homeless Advocacy Organizations Mark Bittersweet Anniversary," connects to the well-established news "peg" of an anniversary. However, framing it as "bittersweet" cleverly emphasizes how far we still have to go to meet the intent of the original act. This adds novelty (another news value), and it provides a symbolic "hook" that is used to good effect, later in the release. All of the standard features of a press release are also present, including a release date, indication of when the news can be made public ("for

Box 7.2   Sample Press Release

PRESS RELEASE: Homeless Advocacy Organizations Mark Bittersweet Anniversary

July 18, 2007

**Press Release
for Immediate Release:** July 18, 2007
Contact: Name: _____

Phone Number: _____

Homeless Advocacy Organizations Mark Bittersweet Anniversary

WASHINGTON, DC—The twentieth anniversary of passage of the McKinney-Vento Homeless Assistance Act is July 22. To celebrate this bittersweet anniversary, organizations that fight homelessness, including the National Low-Income Housing Coalition (NLIHC), will join together with Members of Congress at a press conference tomorrow on Capitol Hill to highlight the importance of a balanced reauthorization of the McKinney-Vento Act.

NLIHC is concerned about the housing circumstances of all low-income people, but focuses most particularly on solving the housing problems of the lowest-income people, including people who are homeless.

The July 19th press conference will be held at 9:30 A.M. in Room 402 of the Cannon House Office Building. Members of Congress and the organizations will stress that in order to truly end homelessness in America, Congress must complement the McKinney-Vento Act with substantially increased investments in safe, decent and affordable housing.

The McKinney-Vento Homeless Assistance Act authorizes the bulk of federal spending for shelter and services for people who are homeless. The anniversary presents an opportunity to recognize the significant strides made in addressing homelessness using McKinney funds. But the milestone is also a cause for reflection.

"The McKinney-Vento Act has helped to ameliorate the suffering of countless homeless people, but it cannot and was never intended to prevent or end homelessness in the United States," Sheila Crowley, president of NLIHC, said. "Observance of this anniversary should be used to spotlight the growth in homelessness in America in the last two decades as a consequence of decreasing federal investment in affordable housing."

Maria Foscarinis, executive director of the National Law Center on Homelessness and Poverty, will moderate the event during which all participants will receive bittersweet chocolate bars, with labels declaring the "Bittersweet Anniversary." Following the event, chocolate bars will be distributed to each congressional office to raise awareness about the McKinney-Vento Act and the continuing homeless crisis. The candy bar labels will include a list of 10 steps that Congress and the administration could take now to help address homelessness.

The 10 steps are:

1. Assist currently homeless people by reauthorizing and doubling funds for HUD McKinney-Vento programs.
2. Create housing for low-income households by enacting a National Housing Trust Fund.
3. Protect, preserve, and expand existing federal housing programs that serve the lowest-income people.
4. Appropriate funds for at least 5,000 Section 8 housing vouchers for homeless veterans through the HUD—Veterans Affairs Supportive Housing program.
5. Expand access to addiction and mental health services for people experiencing homelessness through reauthorization of the Substance Abuse and Mental Health Services Administration.
6. Increase homeless and low-income persons' access to healthcare by reauthorizing and expanding the Consolidated Health Centers program.
7. Increase homeless persons' access to mainstream disability income, temporary assistance, and workforce investment services.
8. Provide homeless children and youth with increased services and support by reauthorizing the Education for Homeless Children and Youth program within the No Child Left Behind Act and the Runaway and Homeless Youth Act.
9. Require the administration to develop and publish a coordinated federal plan to end homelessness.
10. Require jurisdictions receiving federal housing funds to protect the civil rights of homeless persons.

Organizations sponsoring the anniversary press conference and activities are the Corporation for Supportive Housing, Family Promise, Mercy Housing, National Alliance to End Homelessness, National Center on Family Homelessness, National Coalition for Homeless Veterans, National Coalition for the Homeless, National

(*Continued*)

Health Care for the Homeless Council, National Law Center on Homelessness & Poverty, National Policy and Advocacy Council on Homelessness, NLIHC, and National Network for Youth.

NLIHC's sole mission is to end the affordable housing crisis in America. NLIHC educates, organizes, and advocates to ensure decent, affordable housing within healthy neighborhoods for everyone.

* * *

National Low-Income Housing Coalition (NLIHC)
727 15th Street NW, 6th Floor, Washington, D.C. 20005 202/662–1530; Fax 202/393–1973; info@nlihc.org; www.nlihc.org
©2007 National Low-Income Housing Coalition

immediate release"), a contact person, and the city where the news event will happen. In keeping with the reverse-pyramid journalistic writing style, the most important information is in the first paragraph of the release, which outlines *what* the event is (a press conference to mark a legislative anniversary); *who* is involved (National Low Income Housing Coalition and Members of Congress); and *when* and *where* the event will take place as well as *why* (to "highlight the importance of a balanced reauthorization of the McKinney-Vento Act").

The release has a clear call to action, advocating for "substantially increased investments in safe, decent, and affordable housing" and listing "10 steps that Congress and the Administration could take now to help address homelessness." Bittersweet chocolate bars are used as a symbol to "raise awareness about the McKinney-Vento Act and the continuing homeless crisis." The bars were distributed to congressional offices, with the wrappers listing the 10 action steps needed to address homelessness.

The press release ends with four standard elements: (1) more detailed background information on participants; (2) a boilerplate paragraph describing the organization; (3) a set of hash marks (###) to indicate the end of the release text; and (4) organizational contact information.

If strategies to attract media attention work, the policy practitioner will then face the challenge of being interviewed by a reporter. Although there is professional media training available to those who are frequently in the public eye, here are some simple techniques that can help to effectively communicate a policy message:

- Craft a simple, sound-bite-worthy message. Identify your core message and be sure to include elements of that core message in your responses to interview questions. It is important to frame the issue and to put the message in language that everyone can understand, rather than using professional jargon. Watch and analyze the news and C-SPAN for models of how to communicate abstract policy information in the short-attention-span public arena.
- Anticipate questions and come prepared with supporting information. Do mock interviews with colleagues if you are new to the process or if you are being interviewed on a new or particularly delicate subject.
- Never ask to go "off the record" or say "no comment." Both strategies will backfire. If you don't know the answer to a question, say you'll get back to the reporter—and then do so in a timely manner. If a reporter calls, respond promptly. Sensitivity toward a reporter's deadline is expected, and if you are untrustworthy in this respect the reporter will go to another source the next time.[12]

Understand that there are risks in sharing information with the media—once the press release has gone out or the interview has been completed, you have no control. In interviews, you have to be careful about off-hand remarks that might be taken out of context. Remember that a reporter can put a different spin on your comments than what you intended, picking up on a small point that he or she sees as newsworthy and emphasizing that over other items that you think are more important. Also remember that your news can be eclipsed by other events or could be highlighted on a slow news days.

Choose the best spokesperson, one who will advance your cause. It may not always be the leader of the group. Try to create your own sound bites so that you have some control over what is reported. (Communicating with reporters via e-mail can help in this regard, because you can be more thoughtful about your word choice.) Try to paint visual pictures with your words, bring the issue down to the human level so that people listening will see how it affects them and their families. You need to look relaxed, use humor if appropriate, and look at the interviewer—not the camera.

Choose the best spokesperson, one who will advance your cause.

If the interview or event results in a story, feature the coverage in your organization's Web site, which will enhance the legitimacy of your organization and its policy positions. You can also forward stories (with a personal note) to policymakers, which can help build relationships. Nurturing ongoing contacts with the news media—developing and updating a media list, becoming a "known quantity" to media outlets through editorial board meetings and by writing op-ed pieces or letters to the editor, and promoting your organization through newsworthy press releases—lays the foundation for policy campaign communications.

COMMUNICATION STRATEGIES FOR POLICY CAMPAIGNS

Policy campaigns are intense, goal-focused high points in a policy practitioner's career. To succeed in the public arena, policy practitioners must be "on top of their game," utilizing every resource at their command to effectively reach the public, the media, and the governmental decision-making bodies they hope to sway.

Why are policy campaigns such a test of acumen? Why isn't "being right" enough to have an impact in the public sphere? Humans have a bias against change, and indeed, generally fear the unknown.[13] Policy campaigns often revolve around the proposed adoption of a social innovation. Historical examples include such issues as a 40-hour workweek, women's right to vote, or an end to child labor. All of these social policies seem unquestionably right from today's perspective, yet they were only achieved after hard-fought campaigns against entrenched interests—for example, employers/big business, social traditionalists, parents who needed the income from working children.[14] Social change movements must overcome the inertia of the status quo, and they must also counteract the public's suspicion of change and the related suspicion that social movements are somehow outside the "mainstream" of society. In this regard, the relationship of the media to policy practice can be a difficult one. Social work policy practitioners depend on the media to get the word out—to publicize their cause. At the same time, the structures of the mass media—the news net, the beat system, etc.—all rely on official, established sources of information such as government officials, the courts, the police, and other news sources that have already been vetted by prior coverage, such as prominent business interests, educational institutions, and long-established social service agencies. Analysis of media coverage of social movements indicates a tendency for movements to be marginalized.[15] Common distorting effects include a focus on "worthy" v. "unworthy" populations affected by the issue, biased language that sensationalizes events, elevation of a few individuals disproportionate to their level of influence on events (and the exclusion of less "mediagenic" individuals), and the preferential treatment of mainstream officials as quoted sources.[16]

To be effective in this challenging environment, successful policy practitioners have developed an understanding of the dynamics of power and how to move people to action at every stage of the policymaking process.

The policy campaign media is the roadmap you will follow in communicating the issues of your policy campaign and developing strategies that will move people to action. Elements of the media plan include the following:

- Analysis of target audiences and the media most likely to reach them;
- Identification of core messages and how they will be framed;
- Timing and intensity of media outreach;
- Pacing—whether communications will be constant in nature or build up in intensity to a climactic point;
- Media mix (balance of different types of media you intend to use, paid versus free media, audience-generated versus organizationally controlled media); and
- Budgets and assigned responsibilities.[17]

Media plans need to be nimble to take advantage of unanticipated opportunities or problems that arise in the course of the campaign, but preliminary planning will help ensure that organizational resources are expended to greatest effect.

One of the greatest resources is the institutional legitimacy the organization confers to the policy campaign. A policy practitioner's connection to a "legitimate" organization can be a real advantage in policy advocacy. For example, a policy practitioner advocating co-housing (that is, collaborative housing in which residents actively participate in the design and operation of their own neighborhoods—a more communal living arrangement than is the norm in U.S. society) will be seen as more legitimate in the eyes of reporters, the government, and members of the public if the practitioner is connected to a social service agency with long-standing community roots, a board made up of highly respected community leaders, and a mission that directly speaks of a commitment to improved housing for all. Conversely, advocates who operate on their own, with no organizational backing, will find it more difficult to attract media attention. Although an individual can gain coverage through a stunt (e.g., laying down in front of a bulldozer about to break ground for a traditional, sprawling subdivision), the story that has "legs," or the potential for longer term coverage, is one that can be authoritatively sourced back to a legitimate advocacy organization.[18]

Policy practitioners can also mobilize their advocacy publics as a key campaign resource. An advocacy public is a group of people who share a past or current connection to the advocacy organization. Note that the general public is not considered an advocacy public from the standpoint of resource mobilization. The general public does play a role in the policy campaign, but it must be

Critical Thinking Question

Are there any ways in which a media plan is similar to a client treatment plan? How are they different?

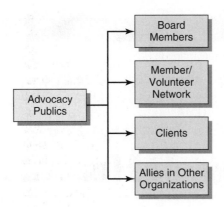

Figure 7.2
Advocacy Publics

reached secondarily through either the media or through the actions of the advocacy publics.

Figure 7.2 identifies four types of advocacy publics: (1) members of the organization's board; (2) members and volunteers who have a current or past connection to the organization; (3) clients served by the organization; and (4) allies at other organizations.

Boards are typically composed of well-connected community members, who may have direct access to government decision makers. These power brokers can be a critical resource in the policy process.[19] Individuals who have a current or past voluntary association with the organization—for example, through being members, charitable giving, volunteering time, or subscribing to a newsletter—are another type of advocacy public. Clients served by the organization are potential advocates as well—they can be very effective at demonstrating the human dimension of a policy issue, and tapping them as advocates can further their self-determination. (From an ethical perspective, however, it is vital to fully inform clients of any possible negative consequences to "going public.")

The nonprofit organization serves as a recruitment network, mobilizing individuals who are likely to respond to a call to action. Organizations nurture their constituent groups with regular events and communications so that they can be called on to act at the opportune moment (see Figure 7.3).

Remember to keep advocacy publics informed about the progress of the campaign. Box 7.3 is a sample e-mail that clearly provides activists with a sense of accomplishment in helping achieve reforms.

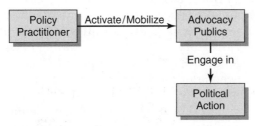

Figure 7.3
Mobilization of Advocacy Publics

Box 7.3   Updating Supporters

From: Coalition on Human Needs [chn@mail.democracyinaction.org]
Sent: Friday, August 04, 2006 10:49 AM
To: Byers, Katharine V.
Subject: YOU STOPPED THE GUTTING OF THE ESTATE TAX!

Your Calls Made the Difference. Thank You!

Last night the Senate defeated a motion to proceed on H.R. 5970, the bill that sought to blackmail supporters of a minimum wage increase into voting to gut the estate tax. But the $750 billion cost to the exclusive benefit of multi-millionaires was too high. Proponents needed 60 votes to move the bill forward. The vote was 42–56.

Majority Leader Frist is a committed supporter of repealing or gutting the estate tax but changed his vote to "no" in order to give him the right to bring the bill up again in September. All other Republicans voted in favor of the motion to proceed except Chafee (RI) and Voinovich (OH). All Democrats voted against the motion except Byrd (WV), Lincoln (AR), Nelson (FL) and Nelson (FL). Not voting were Baucus (D-MT) and Lieberman (D-CT).

This was a difficult vote for many Senators who, like the Coalition on Human Needs, strongly support an increase in the minimum wage. Our real satisfaction at stopping this cynical legislation is tempered by disappointment that poor workers must continue to wait for a much-deserved raise.

Thank your Senators who voted with us. You can find the roll call vote record here: http://www.senate.gov/legislative/LIS/roll_call_lists/roll_call_vote_cfm.cfm?congress=109&session=2&vote=00229

This fight is not over. It is clear that some want the estate tax gone at almost any cost. Thanking the Senators who voted the right way is especially important because the pressure on them will likely intensify over the coming months.

Look for more details in our ***Human Needs Report*** coming soon.

Summary Model

To this point, we have considered individual pieces of mediated policy advocacy. Figure 7.4, Policy campaign communications process, connects the individual pieces to describe the whole. Beginning in the center with the policy practitioner are numerous vectors of influence that reveal the direct and indirect ways in which the practitioner (and the supporting organization) affects policy outcomes.

Using organizational resources such as staff time, funding, advocacy skills and organizational legitimacy, the policy practitioner mobilizes advocacy publics to engage in political action (e.g., attending public meetings, contacting government officials, participating in a protest march). If the political action aligns with news values and captures the attention of the news media, journalists will cover the story. If the story has strong news appeal that leads to continued coverage, then the underlying policy issue may become part of the general public's agenda of most salient issues. Politicians and other governmental decision makers are attentive to trends in public opinion, which is monitored through polls and by tracking phone calls, e-mails, and other contacts. Other pathways of influence include the following:

- ▶ Direct influence of the policy practitioner through public testimony to governmental bodies, position papers, consulting, and interpersonal communication with decision makers;

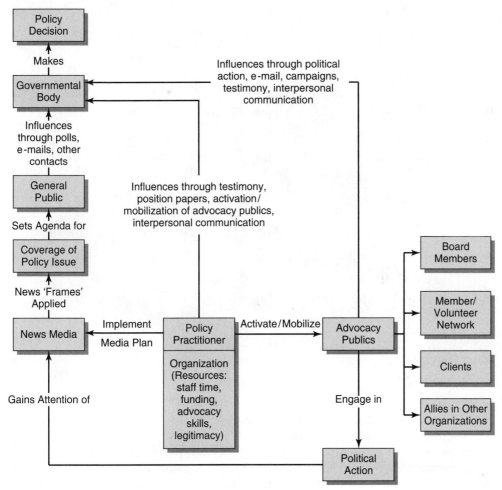

Figure 7.4
Policy Campaign Communications Process

> ● Indirect influence of the policy practitioner through implementation of the media plan; as with public opinion, news media are monitored by politicians and other governmental decision makers; and,
>
> ● Advocacy publics influence politicians and other governmental decision makers through political action, e-mails, interpersonal communication, etc.

If all the pieces come together, the result is a policy decision. Of course, the policy practitioner is not always victorious—policy campaigns can sometimes take decades to achieve their goals, and campaigns do fail. Nonetheless, the model provides a framework for understanding how policy issues become salient to the public and to policymakers.

NEW MEDIA ADVOCACY

New media and new technologies are having a profound impact on policy campaigns. The now well-established "Web 1.0" technologies of Web sites and e-mail plus the new, user-generated "Web 2.0" media—blogs, wikis, social networks,

New media and new technologies are having a profound impact on policy campaigns.

virtual worlds—are reshaping the landscape of policy practice. This is an area of rapid change, and the innovations outlined in this section may be superseded by other technologies within a year or two—but there is an underlying shift in thinking about communication in the policy campaign, and understanding this paradigm change is the most important point to gain from this section.

Alison Fine[20] observed that successful nonprofit organizations are making a transition from a mass media model of social activism to a networked model of activism. In the older model, activists used the "one to many" traditional mass media to connect with the public, and information and solutions were concentrated within the nonprofit organization. The networked model uses "many to many" strategies to mobilize resources:

> In connected activism, information is widely and freely distributed and discussions are open to everyone. Social media, which offer simultaneous connections between, among, and by many people at the time of their choosing, facilitate connected activism. People are encouraged to partici-pate in decisions and actions regardless of their position inside or outside the organization. Resources within social networks, connecting webs of people who are voluntarily associated with one another, are put to work creatively. There are no prescriptions, no right or wrong answers, simply enormous opportunities for participation and change if we engage in the process of connecting with one another.[21]

Since the mid-1990s, the trend has been toward an increasing use of tech-nology to engage advocacy publics and to interact with members of the media. Howard Dean's 2004 presidential campaign was a watershed event in demon-strating the political potential of the Internet. While Dean was not ultimately successful in winning the Democratic nomination, his ability to raise funds quickly and mobilize youthful supporters has influenced subsequent campaigns, particularly Barack Obama's technologically savvy "youth vote" campaign in the 2008 Iowa primary, which was the catalyst for his subsequent primary victory.[22]

E-mail

Now an indispensable communications tool, e-mail is supplanting letters with both internal and external audiences in policy campaigns (see Box 7.4).

Table 7.2 shows the steep increase in the use of e-mail in citizen communication with the U.S. Congress and a decline in postal communications.

A 2006 study of 30 nonprofits using e-mail in their advocacy campaigns found increasing sophistication in the use of e-mail as follows:

- The greater the investment in e-mail support infrastructure, the better the results;
- 47 percent of e-mail subscribers took at least one e-mail action (in other words, they sent an e-mail to a legislator, signed a petition, submitted their comments, etc.);
- The best time to send a message is Thursday or Friday, with a 6 percent higher click-through rate on those days (the click-through rate is measured by the number of times e-mail recipients click on a link in the e-mail);
- Targeting by geography is particularly effective; targeting by issue subgroup (in other words, based on the interests of user profile of interests) also led to higher click-through rates.[23]

E-mail is also a vital communication tool in working with reporters. Most journalists now complement face-to-face and phone interviews with e-mail to

---

Box 7.4   An E-mail Case Study

Viral List Building: Online List Growth Can Be Contagious

Kevin Suer, GetActive Software

The Humane Society of the United States (HSUS) experienced major list growth success with the Petition for Poultry, an online petition that took advantage of a highly effective list growth technique known as "viral list building."

Viral list building puts recruitment tools into the hands of existing online constituents, enabling them to recruit other subscribers themselves. The term "viral" is used because recruitment is self-propagating—as new constituents join, they are in turn acting as recruiters themselves. Viral list building generally requires little-to-no cost to recruit new audiences.

A key ingredient to successful viral list building is the coordinated use of a message or call to action that is appealing, timely and topical. The Petition for Poultry illustrates this approach. In 2004, just

weeks before Thanksgiving, HSUS launched the Petition for Poultry demanding protection of poultry under the federal Humane Methods of Slaughter Act. Launched just before Thanksgiving, the petition was especially timely and topical. Petition signers could join HSUS's e-mail list and use a tell-a-friend feature to encourage signers to send the petition to other people.

This action resonated deeply with its audience, and viral list building results were impressive. The Petition for Poultry grew HSUS's e-mail list virally by over 16,000 new members (7 percent) in just three weeks. Thousands signed the petition, surpassing its original goal of 25,000 signatures to reach more than 57,000 signatures by Thanksgiving, and 146,000 signers to date.

HSUS's viral list building success hinges on a fundamental tenet: Generate excitement and passion for your campaign, and leverage tools that allow your subscribers to tap into their social networks, promoting and sharing that passion.

Source: M + R Strategic Services & the Advocacy Institute, 2006.

Table 7.2   Postal and E-mail Communications to Capitol Hill: 1995–2004

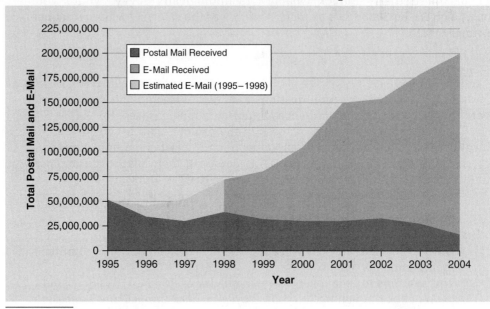

Source: Congressional Management Foundation, http://www.cmfweb.org/index.php?option=com_
content&task=view&id=65&Itemid=

gather information. For the policy advocate, e-mail interviews allow for greater control over responses, but there is less opportunity to make a connection with a reporter, to gauge the reporter's immediate response to your ideas, and to build a relationship.

Advocacy Web Sites

Over the course of a decade, Web sites went from being a nice "extra" to being a core communications tool for the policy organization. Research on how Web site visitors evaluate sites highlights the importance of an attractive, professional design for advocacy Web sites. As a medium, the Web seems to encourage a more superficial level of engagement than print media such as books or newspapers. Fogg notes that "Web users typically spend small amounts of time at any given page, moving from page to page quickly"[24] The terminology of the Web—"surfers" and "browsers"—conveys this sense of information quickly scanned and evaluated. In the absence of detailed analysis, Web users rely instead on features that are immediately apparent for cues as to the quality of information being presented. The primary features that have been found to increase a Web site's credibility with users are the overall design, look and appearance, the logical organization of information into a navigational structure, and information focus, or how readily users can discern a site's purpose.[25] For nonprofit sites, trustworthiness is an important component of credibility. Users want to know who is behind a site, as well as the underlying motivation for the site.[26] Policy advocacy Web sites must establish their legitimacy to overcome users' innate suspicions of advocacy communications. For those Web site visitors whose only experience of an organization is through a Web site, the web site *is* the organization. A poorly designed site communicates that the organization itself is lacking in professional standing and credibility.

Because Web sites are more flexible than other media, site content can address the information needs of multiple audiences, such as members of advocacy publics as well as reporters. Effective advocacy Web sites serve as a springboard to action for supporters and as an access point to authoritative sources for members of the news media.

Box 7.5 presents the advocacy Web site of the Crittenton Women's Union, a Boston-based organization that helps women climb out of poverty, and an analysis of the Web site. Take a moment to examine the Web site screenshot closely. Which features stand out? What are your first impressions of this organization?

In addition to e-mail and Web sites, policy advocates can employ newer user-generated "Web 2.0" media such as blogs, podcasts, and social networks to activate advocacy publics and raise awareness of their cause.

Box 7.5   An Advocacy Web Site

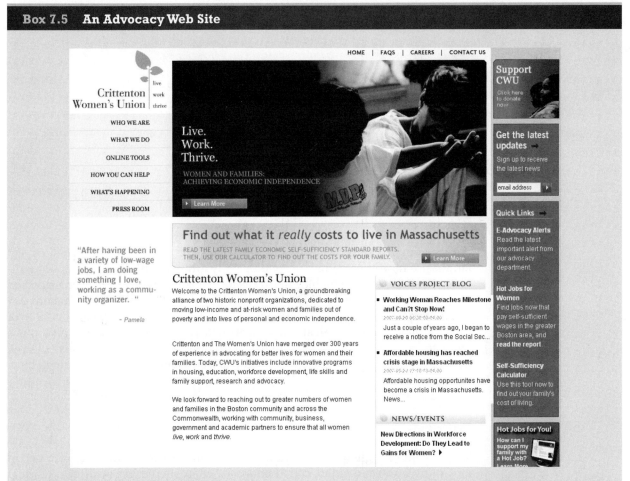

Features that **make the site credible** include the attractive, well-organized layout, compelling images, the "Who We Are" section and "Welcome" at the center of the page, both of which establish legitimacy, and current content with date of creation visible on home page. Features that would **attract a journalist** include the "Press Room" section for the media, the first-person quote (aligned with news values), and the News section. Features that **work from an advocacy standpoint** include the "How You Can Help" call to action, as well as innovative features such as the interactive tools, the opportunity to subscribe to receive latest news, the Voices Project blog, and the e-advocacy alerts.

(Continued)

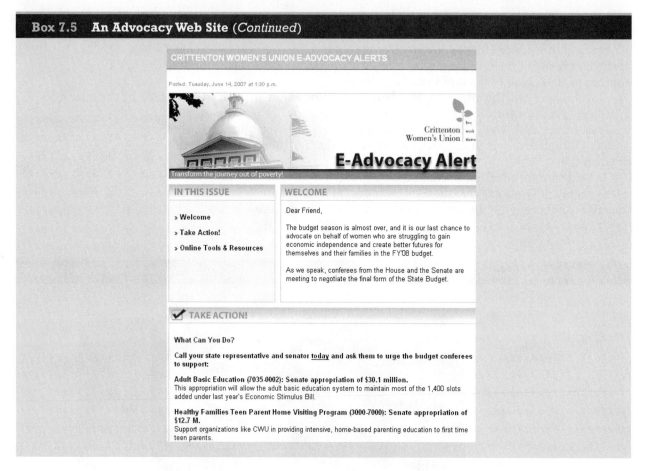

CRITTENTON WOMEN'S UNION E-ADVOCACY ALERTS

Posted: Tuesday, June 14, 2007 at 1:30 p.m.

Crittenton
Women's Union

live
work
thrive

E-Advocacy Alert

Transform the journey out of poverty!

IN THIS ISSUE

» Welcome

» Take Action!

» Online Tools & Resources

WELCOME

Dear Friend,

The budget season is almost over, and it is our last chance to advocate on behalf of women who are struggling to gain economic independence and create better futures for themselves and their families in the FY'08 budget.

As we speak, conferees from the House and the Senate are meeting to negotiate the final form of the State Budget.

✔ TAKE ACTION!

What Can You Do?

Call your state representative and senator today and ask them to urge the budget conferees to support:

Adult Basic Education (7035-0002): Senate appropriation of $30.1 million.
This appropriation will allow the adult basic education system to maintain most of the 1,400 slots added under last year's Economic Stimulus Bill.

Healthy Families Teen Parent Home Visiting Program (3000-7000): Senate appropriation of $12.7 M.
Support organizations like CWU in providing intensive, home-based parenting education to first time teen parents.

Blogs

A variant on the static Web site concept, blogs are frequently updated sites that emphasise new information, chronologically arranged. Blogs are generally written in the first person, and blogging tools have made it easy for the average person to create his or her own blog. Organizations can also use blogs to create a more personal connection with their audience (e.g., a state social service agency director using a blog to communicate organizational priorities). Blogs can also put a "human face" on abstract issues, telling the stories of those who are most affected by social problems. The blog phenomenon is well established: the Technorati blog-tracking Web site currently tracks 100 million blogs worldwide.[27] Box 7.6 features the Voices Project blog, which focuses on women's economic self-sufficiency.

Podcasts

The advent of high-speed Internet connections has made possible the use of streaming audio and video, called podcasts when offered in a syndicated format for download and subscription to media devices such as iPods. In the example featured above, the blog post promoted the Project Hope-sponsored podcast—"Sound Proof: Stories of Transformation." Luz's story of her search for a decent place to live and a stable job, gives voice to the dispossessed, facilitating social work's core value of empowerment (see Box 7.6). Hearing Luz's story in Luz's voice makes it more immediate and powerful.

New media such as blogs and podcasts have great potential to humanize complex issues and to increase access to the public sphere for people who

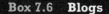

Box 7.6   Blogs

Note the chronological organization, which is typical of blogs. The right-side "Categories" menu and the calendar on the left help visitors find blog content, and there is an opportunity to subscribe to alerts of new postings. The blog post, "Sound Proof: Stories of Transformation," is written in a breezy, brief, and personal style that is best suited to the blog format.

would otherwise be statistics in a report or passive consumers of news produced by someone else. These social media are integral to Fine's vision of connected activism that uses the power of the "crowd" to effect social change.[28]

Web 2.0 technologies are characterized by Brown[29] as collaborative online tools that enable users to shape their own environment. Web 2.0 technologies are deployed by policy practitioners in conjunction with e-mail and Web sites to move advocacy publics to action. In the early days of e-mail advocacy, recipients were urged to action by "signing" e-mail petitions and by forwarding boilerplate e-mails to elected officials. Although informative as an indicator of public opinion, such generic e-mails are a low-involvement form of advocacy. In the example provided in Box 7.7, e-mail is made more interactive by connecting it to a Web site where recipients can add their unique perspectives to the policy debate.

Here is another example of how e-mail can provide the gateway to rich media resources for advocacy on the Web. The e-mail in Box 7.8 was used to generate traffic to a YouTube video, and also provides a powerful example of the use of this popular media to inform the public about the destructive nature of intolerance in society, and how to advance legislation that takes action against hate crimes. Embedded in an e-mail, this video serves as an example of a useful tool for promoting connected activism for achieving a specific policy goal.

Social networking tools such as MySpace and Facebook also offer powerful ways to engage supporters in political activism. One example of how widely

---

Box 7.7   Web 2.0 User-Generated Advocacy

Below is the text of an e-mail mobilizing abortion rights supporters:

From: PPAN.Indiana@ppin.org
Sent: Thursday, April 26, 2007 8:39 AM
To: Byers, Katharine V.
Subject: Express your outrage!

Dear Katharine,

Make Hoosier voices heard!

Join me at the Planned Parenthood Wall of Protest

It has already begun. Less than one week after the U.S. Supreme Court upheld the federal abortion ban, North Dakota has become the first state to pass legislation that will not allow women to access abortion services in that state if the Supreme Court overturns Roe v. Wade.

This news is not unexpected, but only adds to the outrage and frustration I feel because of the Supreme Court's blatant disregard for women's health and safety. But the messages I've received from thousands of you across the country have given me hope.

One common thread in your words of support is a desire to speak out, tell personal stories, and express frustration with the Supreme Court's decision.

We have now created a communal space for our outrage: the Planned Parenthood Wall of Protest.

Like the March for Women's Lives, where three years ago one million of us joined together and raised our voices in support of women's health and safety, www.wallofprotest.com is a place for us to gather—to express our anger, share our stories, and renew our strength.

This virtual wall illustrates the widespread outrage at the court's decision, and is available online for the world to see. We've added a few photos from Indiana—please add your own! You can make your voice heard by uploading a picture or posting a YouTube video now and sharing your comments.

Show the world that we will not allow politics to trump women's health.

In the next few weeks, we will be taking your voices from the Wall of Protest and bringing them to Capitol Hill. When we demand action from our leaders in Congress, we will be able to show them that hundreds of thousands of Americans stand together for women and women's health.

Continue to be a part of the movement. Join the protest. Go to www.wallofprotest.com.

Thanks so much for all that you do. In solidarity,

Planned Parenthood Advocates of Indiana

Planned Parenthood of Indiana

If you would like to unsubscribe from the Planned Parenthood

Action Network of Indiana click here.

Take a moment to read this call-to-action e-mail closely. Is the message persuasive to you? Why? Notice how many opportunities there are for the e-mail recipient to act by clicking through to the Wall of Protest, and how the message has been tailored to include an Indiana angle. Finally, note the 'opt-out' message at the bottom, which is best practice for e-mail advocacy.

Here is a screen shot of the Wall of Protest:

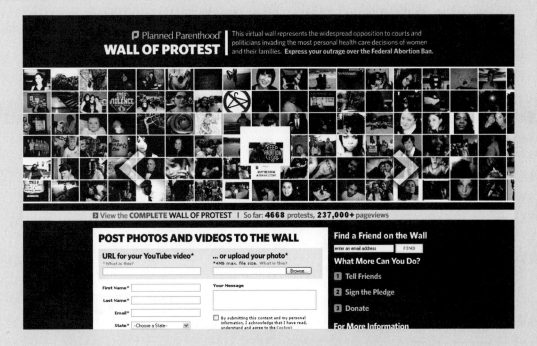

Members of the pro–choice advocacy public have been mobilized to generate this electronic protest. Here are sample postings:

I want the right to choose my future and the future of my children. Every type of federal aid has been subject to cuts and now our rights as well. NO welfare, NO foodstamps, NO healthcare! Now no choice!

Hey! What about OUR family values?!?

ideas can diffuse through social networks is MySpace's OurPlanet project, which encourages MySpace users to submit their own tips and feedback about environmental causes. There are now roughly 160,000 individuals and organizations that have added OurPlanet to their friends list on MySpace (meaning that these 160,000 will see updates from OurPlanet when they visit their personal MySpace page).

Box 7.8　E-Mail and YouTube Advocacy

Subject: something for us to do
Importance: High

Dear Kathy,

Please view this video and contact the Senate:
http://www.youtube.com/watch?v=GOqlrHgrSgc

Thanks, Jeff

Here is a screen shot of the video:

Note: Note that more than 493,332 people had viewed the video as of July 16, 2009. The Director box provides a link to the sponsoring organization, the Human Rights Campaign, as well as a way to take action. Also note the extensive use of tags to categorize the video, which increases the likelihood of target audiences finding the clip. YouTube also provides an 'embed code' functionality so that bloggers can insert videos right into their blogs. You can view this video at www.youtube.com/watch?v=GOqlrHgrSgc.

Many nonprofits have a presence in MySpace, including Oxfam, Kiva (an international microloan nonprofit), and the Natural Resources Defense Council. MySpace also features the Impact Channel, an online group that serves as a clearinghouse for information on nonprofits in MySpace. All of these sites are highly interactive, enabling visitors to add the site to their social network as a friend, post content, respond to polls, and learn how to get engaged in social activism.

Adult Internet users' membership in online social networks such as MySpace and Facebook is climbing rapidly—from 2005 to 2008, Facebook membership more than quadrupled, from 8 to 35 percent of Internet users.[30] Teenagers are particularly attracted to social networking: More than half of American teenagers now use MySpace, Facebook, or a similar site.[31] For advocacy groups looking to attract young supporters, familiarity with these new tools is essential. Facebook was an important tool for attracting young voters in the 2008 elections. Since the election, President Obama and his new media team are continuing to use these social networking technologies (and other new media) to keep supporters from the election campaign engaged in the administration's policy agenda and to build support for high-priority policy changes such as health reform legislation (see Box 7.9).

Policy Practice

Critical Thinking Question

Reflect on how you might use Facebook in policy practice. Are there any potential conflicts with what you currently post to Facebook? If so, how might you resolve those conflicts?

Box 7.9   White House Takes Web 2.0 Leap

The White House took a major leap into the Web 2.0 world, launching pages on social networks MySpace and Facebook and sending its first "tweets" on hot micro-blogging service Twitter.

Content from President Barack Obama's Web site, WhiteHouse.gov, is being fed in real time to White House profile pages on MySpace and Facebook and members of the communities can sign up as Facebook "fans" or MySpace "friends."

The White House had more than 60,000 fans on Facebook and more than 8,000 friends on MySpace within a few hours of the pages going online while more than 14,500 people had signed up as "followers" of the White House Twitter stream.

"Technology has profoundly impacted how—and where—we all consume information and communicate with one another," the White House said in a blog post titled "WhiteHouse 2.0."

"WhiteHouse.gov is an important part of the administration's effort to use the Internet to reach the public quickly and effectively—but it isn't the only place," it said, pointing to the new online destinations.

. . .

MySpace said the official White House page will allow users to "connect directly with the Obama administration on a daily basis to stay informed and educated about the priorities and activities of the United States government.

"The community also provides users the opportunity to voice their thoughts and concerns directly to the White House by leaving comments and participating in discussion forums," MySpace said in a statement.

Obama relied heavily on the Web during his presidential campaign for organizing, fundraising and communicating and created pages on MySpace and Facebook that attracted hundreds of thousands of followers.

On January 21, his first full day in office, he issued a memo pledging to use the Internet to help make government more "transparent, participatory and collaborative."

Besides revamping WhiteHouse.gov, the Obama administration has created several other websites including recovery.gov to track the economic stimulus bill and transparency.gov to monitor spending.

It has also announced plans to launch data.gov, a site which will "make a broad array of US government data" available to the public.

Obama's "New Media" team created a channel on YouTube upon his taking office and the White House is also present on photo-sharing site Flickr, video-sharing site Vimeo and on Apple's iTunes.

The White House on Wednesday posted hundreds of pictures on Flickr chronicling Obama's first 100 days in office.

The new White House sites can be found at Facebook.com/WhiteHouse, MySpace.com/ WhiteHouse, and Twitter.com/WhiteHouse.

---

[1]AFP, (2009). "White House Takes Web 2.0 Leap," www.google.com/hostednews/afp/article/ALeqM5ik1WzCUcAlqihQDFUaZkhFASZCTg (accessed May 4, 2009).

Source: AFP. May 1, 2009.[1]

Given its newness, there is a paucity of research on the impact of Web 2.0 technologies on activism. One commonsense guideline is to avoid getting too far out in front of the publics you are trying to reach. Blogs can be a great way to mobilize advocacy publics, but if your target audience is older or lacks the economic means to participate in online advocacy, consider more traditional strategies. Some new technologies can be time and resource intensive to implement. Virtual worlds such as Second Life, for example, have significant entry barriers in terms of cost and expertise for the average nonprofit, making it a better choice for deep-pocket advocacy groups (such as presidential campaigns) that may benefit from media coverage of their innovative approach to campaigning.

EVALUATING ADVOCACY COMMUNICATION

Critical Thinking

Critical Thinking Question

In evaluating advocacy communications, which outcomes are more immediate and which, in your opinion, would take longer to become apparent?

Although the complex interplay of variables makes it difficult to tease out the reasons why one policy communications campaign succeeds and why another fails, there are some tools you can use to gauge the effectiveness of a communications campaign. Reisman, Gienapp, and Stachowiak[32] have developed a set of guidelines for the Annie E. Casey Foundation, identifying six broad outcomes for advocacy and policy work. Outcomes include a shift in social norms, strengthened organizational capacity, strengthened alliances, a strengthened base of support, improved politics, and changes in impact (the policy change has the desired effect on social conditions). The success of the communications strategies that are commonly used to help achieve these outcomes can, in many cases, be measured.

For example, to gauge whether policy advocacy has achieved a desired shift in social norms, public opinion polls can be conducted to measure changes in beliefs, attitudes, values or issue saliency that have occurred. While causality is difficult to determine, if members of the public, opinion leaders, or policy makers increasingly adopt the frame articulated in your policy advocacy message, then your message is having an impact. A strengthened base of support is reflected in public actions such as voting, attending rallies, and writing letters to the newspaper. The effectiveness of your interaction with the media can be determined by monitoring media coverage. For example, has there been an increase in the quantity, prominence, or extent of coverage? Is your core policy message echoed in media coverage of the issue?[33] There is also a wealth of data that can be used to gauge the effectiveness of Web-based media. Site visit statistics, click-through rates from e-mail links to Web pages, the number of people adding your advocacy page as a friend in social networking sites, and your Web site's rating in Google search results on terms related to your advocacy issue are all ways to concretely measure success in getting your message out. Public meetings sponsored by your advocacy organization should be evaluated as well. Create an evaluation form as a handout or as a Web link that can be e-mailed to attendees. The evaluation form results can help you assess whether participants felt they learned about the issues and what overall messages they retained. Evaluation forms can help create a connection with event attendees—for example, would they participate in future advocacy events or campaigns? Every policy advocacy campaign should include a postmortem meeting to retrospectively assess which strategies were most effective, to better inform future campaigns.

CONCLUSION

For too many people in our society, politics is just something that happens. The daily newspaper and the nightly TV broadcast showcase events that unfold one after the other, like scenes in a play the audience passively watches. For the social work policy practitioner, *for you and for those you seek to empower,* politics is active, not passive. Understanding how to employ various media in moving a broader constituency to action is a prerequisite for achieving social change in the twenty-first century. The next time you read a newspaper, visit a blog, or watch the headline news, take a moment to think about the many individual actions that have resulted in these particular stories and issues achieving sufficient prominence to be placed before you.

There are many variables at work in the interaction of the media, public opinion, and policy practice. The social work policy practitioner can employ communication strategies to influence policy outcomes in a number of ways, including mobilizing advocacy publics and developing a keen sense of how to frame and create events to draw media attention. New technologies offer intriguing possibilities in this work, potentially increasing the effectiveness of policy campaigns. The challenge for the policy practitioner is knowing when and how to act. When a window of opportunity arises—a moment when attention is drawn to a particular policy topic—the social work policy practitioner will need to know which strategy to use to maximize the opportunity and to give voice to those for whom they speak.

Log onto **MySocialWorkLab** to access a wealth of case studies, videos, and assessment. (*If you did not receive an access code to* **MySocialWorkLab** *with this text and wish to purchase access online, please visit* www.mysocialworklab.com.)

1. **Review the Health Care Reform SCS.** What Web 2.0 communication strategies are used in the Health Care Reform SCS to mobilize advocacy publics?

2. **Review the Gay Marriage SCS.** Policy practitioner Julia Cohen e-mails guidelines for LGBT supporters who are planning to attend a rally. Analyze the e-mails (subject line "The Date is Truly Set," dated Mon. May 2, 2005) and identify Julia's strategies for 'mainstreaming' her cause to increase media coverage and avoid marginalization as an outsider group.

PRACTICE TEST

The following questions will test your knowledge of the content found within this chapter. For additional assessment, including licensing-exam type questions on applying chapter content to practice, visit **MySocialWorkLab**.

1. The central idea for news content that supplies context and implies the issue being discussed via selection, exclusion, emphasis and elaboration is referred to as:
   a. The lead story
   b. Hype
   c. Journalistic frame
   d. News outline

2. Some actions that policy practitioners can take to ensure successful news coverage are:
   a. Write a letter to the editor, and meet with the newspaper's editorial board
   b. Take the senior editor of the newspaper out to dinner, and pitch story ideas
   c. Write an opinion editorial, and shadow reporters and newspaper investigators
   d. Meet with the newspaper owner and figure out what tactics to use to influence the owner in covering the story you are pitching

3. Clients, allies in other organizations, member boards, and volunteer/member network are all examples of:
   a. Policymaking bodies
   b. Recipients of blanket e-mails
   c. Advocacy public
   d. Media outlet influencers

4. Self propagating recruitment and the coordinated use of a call to action appealing message are key components in:
   a. Running for elected office
   b. Coordinating a petition campaign
   c. Being a good web coordinator for a social work agency
   d. Viral list building

5. Web 2.0 tools, e-mails, and websites are often used by policy practitioners to effectively:
   a. Communicate with other policy practitioners and policymakers
   b. Show other social work practitioners their web design skills and savvy
   c. Move advocacy publics into action
   d. Communicate with politicians and lobbyists

6. Social Networking sites such as Facebook and MySpace are especially important tools for advocacy groups in order to:
   a. Effectively communicate with other advocacy groups and politicians
   b. Communicate with elderly supporters
   c. Figure out the correct angle from which to run particular campaigns
   d. Attract young supporters

7. Key features for an effective website are:
   a. Logical organization of information, information focus and overall design
   b. Ease in locating website with Google, color of opening webpage, and font
   c. Larger, easy to read font, background music and information focus
   d. Logical organization of information, ease in finding site on a search engine, color of opening page

8. Detailed background information on participants, paragraph summarizing the organization, a set of hashmarks, and the organization's contact information are:
   a. The correct way to end all official organization emails
   b. The four standard elements for concluding a press release
   c. Components in official media-policymaker communications
   d. Key opening elements to use when crafting a press release

9. Blogs and podcasts are powerful policy practice tools because:
   a. Everybody uses a computer now, so podcasts and blogs make communications easier and faster
   b. They humanize complex issues to a level everyone can identify with and offer a face what would otherwise be a faceless statistic
   c. They reach a large portion of the younger generation
   d. They are the main forms of communication for the most influential lobbyists

Log onto **MySocialWorkLab** once you have completed the Practice Test above to access additional study tools and assessment.

Answers

Key: 1) c, 2) a, 3) c, 4) d, 5) c, 6) d, 7) a, 8) d, 9) b

8

The Stages of Policymaking: Integrating Knowledge and Action

CHAPTER OUTLINE

Introduction 170

Social Workers as Policymakers 175

Approaches to Policymaking 179
Rational Model
Political Model
Incremental Model

The Policymaking Process 186
Stage One: Problem Identification and Case Finding
Stage Two: Data Collection and Analysis
Stage Three: Informing the Public and Identifying
   Stakeholders

Stage Four: Selecting Policy Options and
   Developing Policy Goals
Stage Five: Building Public Support and
   Developing Coalitions
Stage Six: Program Design
Stage Seven: Policy Implementation
Stage Eight: Policy Evaluation

Conclusion 207

Chapter Review 208

Practice Test 208

MySocialWorkLab 208
Health Care SCS

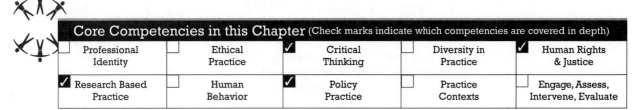

Core Competencies in this Chapter (Check marks indicate which competencies are covered in depth)									
	Professional Identity		Ethical Practice	✓	Critical Thinking		Diversity in Practice	✓	Human Rights & Justice
✓	Research Based Practice		Human Behavior	✓	Policy Practice		Practice Contexts		Engage, Assess, Intervene, Evaluate

INTRODUCTION

There is no such thing as a fixed policy, because policy like all organic entities is always in the making.

LORD SALISBURY, Prime Minister of England, 1895–1902

Policy practitioners are concerned with bringing about change through the effective use of advocacy efforts that consider political, social, and economic elements of change and depend on sound rationale for policy practice decisions to guide the change effort. The use of political and analytical skills in the application of multipronged policymaking models can be maximized by asking pointed and appropriate questions regarding the policy change effort at hand and seeking the answers that will ultimately inform the policy practitioners' strategies for a successful policy change. Questions that are worth entertaining when beginning a change effort are:

Is major change needed, or will a smaller incremental change work?

What objective data are available to present a rational foundation for change?

If no data are available, how could such information be generated?

What is the political climate for the topic of change being considered?

Is the timing right for change in terms of political agendas, economic conditions, and public attitudes?

What would be the most expedient course of action to take with the highest probability of success to achieve the change needed?

Is it possible to get an executive decision from an agency head, city or state department director, or city mayor or state governor?

Is this a legal issue that needs to be tested in court for precedence to be set in order for policy to be made? Or does a legislative agenda need to be pursued?

Perhaps the issue is just about money. Would increasing the budget for needed services provide sufficient change?

Strategic policy practitioners will explore each of these questions, and based on the answers, assess how each type of change will affect the target population, considering both positive outcomes and possible unintended effects or residual effects. Approaches to policy change should take into consideration the following elements:

- The context of the policy practice effort;
- The stakeholders on both sides of the issues;
- The political "hotness" of the issue;
- The impact on local, state, and national economies and on vulnerable populations;
- The timing of the effort;
- The public and personal agendas of important political actors;
- The most effective route to change (i.e. executive decision, legislation, court cases [judicial], budget changes, and agency, local, state or national levels of change); and
- What is at stake for the target population.

Using multidimensional approaches to policymaking is particularly appropriate for social workers in the political arena since they are trained to understand the personal and environmental factors influencing social problems; to see the connections between policy and practice; and to understand the significance of executive, legislative, and court policy decisions for vulnerable populations. Recognizing that individual problems have their roots in the larger social context (structural, cultural, and economic factors), effective policy practitioners are acutely aware of, and actively participate in, political and economic institutions at the local, state, and/or national levels. Active social work policy practitioners have the power to influence social welfare policies and to shape and direct social work practice. Social work policy practitioners must put into action their understandings of political, economic, and social forces that impact the families and communities that they serve and they should also make efforts to change institutional and social policies that marginalize people and strip them of their human dignity and civil and legal rights. Social workers are uniquely positioned to facilitate the movement of historically silent groups into positions of power where their voices can be heard.[1]

To advance flexible and contextual approaches to policy practice, knowledge of policymaking models is essential, as is an understanding of the eight stages of policymaking, the critical roles that social workers play in the policymaking process, and Key tasks to be completed within each stage. Social work policy practice and policy change is based on the belief that well-planned and appropriate interventions with vulnerable populations in the policy field are the natural outgrowths of social work's ecological knowledge base. Just as environmental factors are considered at the individual level, so too must they be considered at the community, state, and national levels where interventions take the form of policy interventions.

This chapter reviews three common approaches to policymaking, the stages of policymaking, and explores elements that social workers need to attend to when engaged in the policymaking process. The complexity of policymaking necessitates that social work policy practitioners adopt a mind-set for strategic planning during the policymaking process, aligning necessary resources, identifying key stakeholders and political actors, discovering opportune moments for building support for change, and creating opportunities for gaining momentum in the change effort. Social work policy practitioners will often need to develop a long vision and commitment to policy change, as it is not unusual for policy issue campaigns to repeat themselves many times over before achieving desired outcomes. Long campaigns are especially true for major changes, such as equal rights for women. As you review Box 8.1, notice the long history of gaining equal rights for women and what types of actions and policies have been incrementally taken to achieve gender equality over the last 200 years. Women organized to gain consensus on the issues and to map out agendas for action. In the fight for equality, women made inroads in education, employment, sexual freedom, holding public office, voting, and legal protections from harm. Some changes were small and incremental. Other changes, such as the passage of the Nineteenth Amendment to the Constitution giving women the right to vote, were large and life altering. Policy changes for women's equality occurred at the local, state, and national levels and were initiated by executive orders, court decisions, and legislative action. All of these were heavily influenced by grassroots activism, public speaking, writing, and pushing the envelope to the point of breaking the law and enduring imprisonment. These are the sacrifices some women made on behalf of all women. So, as

Box 8.1   The History of the U.S. Women's Rights Movement Timeline 1792 - Present

1792 British author Mary Wollstonecraft argues for the equality of the sexes in her book, the *Vindication of the Rights of Women.*

1821 Emma Willard founded the Troy Female Seminary in Troy, NY, the first school to offer girls college-level classical and scientific studies.

1828 Scottish woman Frances Wright, was the first woman to address an American audience composed of both men and women, at the courthouse in Cincinnati, OH, on "The Nature of Knowledge."

1833 Oberlin College is founded as the first coeducational institution of higher learning, in Oberlin, OH.

1837 Mount Holyoke, the first college for women, is founded by Mary Lyon in South Hadley, MA.

1845 Margaret Fuller publishes *Woman in the Nineteenth Century,* and influences the development of American feminist theory.

1848 The first woman's rights convention is called by Lucretia Mott and Elizabeth Cady Stanton. Amelia Bush is chosen chair.

1848 NY State Legislature passes a law that gives women the right to retain possession of property owned prior to marriage.

1849 Elizabeth Blackwell graduates from Geneva College in NY with the first medical degree awarded to a woman.

1850 The first National Women's Rights Convention takes place in Worcester, MA. More than 1,000 attend.

1851 Amelia Bloomer publishes in her Seneca Falls newspaper, *The Lily,* a description of a comfortable, loose-fitting costume consisting of a short skirt worn over pantaloons. It becomes known as the "Bloomer."

1851 Elizabeth Cady Stanton and Susan B. Anthony meet and begin their 50-year collaboration to win for women their economic, educational, social, and civil rights.

1851 Sojourner Truth delivers her "And Ain't I a Woman" speech at the Woman's Rights Convention in Akron, OH.

1853 Antoinette Brown Blackwell, first woman ordained in the U.S. by First Congregational Church in Butler and Savannah, NY.

1855 Elizabeth Cady Stanton speaks before the NY State Legislature; speaks on expanding Married Woman's Property Law.

1866 The American Equal Rights Association is founded to secure for all Americans their civil rights irrespective of race, color, or sex. Lucretia Mott is elected president.

1866 To test women's constitutional right to hold public office, Stanton runs for Congress receiving 24 of 12,000 votes cast.

1867 Stanton, Anthony and Lucy Stone address a subcommittee of the NY State Constitutional Convention requesting that the revised constitution include woman suffrage.

1867 Lucy Stone, Susan B. Anthony, and Elizabeth Stanton traverse Kansas supporting women suffrage. Women suffrage is voted down.

1868 Stanton and Anthony launch their women's rights newspaper, *The Revolution,* in New York City.

1868 Anthony organizes the Working Women's Association; encourages women to form unions for higher wages and shorter hours.

1868 The Fourteenth Amendment adopted; grants suffrage to former male African American slaves, but not to women.

1869 National Woman Suffrage Association (NWSA) is founded. Elizabeth Stanton is president.

1869 American Woman Suffrage Association (AWSA) is founded. Henry Ward Beecher is president.

1869 Wyoming Territory grants suffrage to women.

1870 Utah Territory grants suffrage to women.

1870 First issue of the *Woman's Journal* is published with Lucy Stone and her husband Henry Blackwell as editors.

1871 Victoria Woodhull addresses the Judiciary Committee of the House of Representatives arguing that women have the right to vote under the Fourteenth Amendment. The Committee issues a negative report.

1872 In Rochester, NY, Susan B. Anthony registers and votes. Several days later she is arrested.

1873 At Anthony's trial, judge denies her testimony, dismisses the jury, rules her guilty, and fines her $100. She refuses to pay.

1874 In *Minor v. Happersett,* the Supreme Court decides that citizenship does not give women the right to vote and that woman's political rights are under the jurisdiction of each individual state.

1876 Stanton writes a Declaration and Protest of the Women of the United States to be read at the centennial celebration in Philadelphia. When the request to present is denied, Anthony and four other women charge the speakers' rostrum and thrust the document into the hands of Vice-President Thomas W. Ferry.

1879 Belva Lockwood becomes the first woman lawyer admitted to practice before the Supreme Court.

1880   NY state grants school suffrage to women.

1882   The House of Representatives and the Senate appoint Select Committees on Woman Suffrage.

1887   The first three volumes of the *History of Woman Suffrage,* edited by Susan B. Anthony, Matilda Joslyn Gage, and Elizabeth Cady Stanton, are published.

1888   The International Council for Women is founded and holds its first meeting in Washington, DC.

1890   The NWSA and the AWSA merge to form the National American Woman Suffrage Association (NAWSA) with Stanton, Anthony, and Stone as officers.

1890   Wyoming joins the union as the first state with voting rights for women. By 1900 women have suffrage in UT, CO, and ID.

1895   Stanton publishes *The Woman's Bible,* which critically examines biblical teaching about women.

1896   The National Association of Colored Women is formed, bringing together more than 100 black women's clubs. The black women's movement includes Josephine St. Pierre Ruffin, Mary Church Terrell, and Anna Julia Cooper.

1903   The National Women's Trade Union League (WTUL) formed. Advocates for better wages and working conditions.

1907   Harriet Stanton Blatch, daughter of Elizabeth Cady Stanton, founds the Equality League of Self-Supporting Women, later called the Women's Political Union.

1912   Suffrage referendums are passed in AZ, KS, and OR.

1914   MT and NV grant voting rights to women. Alice Paul and Lucy Burns organize the Congressional Union for Woman Suffrage. It merges in 1917 with the Woman's Party to become the National Woman's Party.

1915   Suffrage referendum in NY state is defeated. Carrie Chapman Catt is elected president of the NAWSA.

1916   Jeannette Rankin (R), from Montana, becomes the first woman to serve in Congress, elected to the House. President Wilson addresses NAWSA. Margaret Sanger opens first U.S. birth-control clinic in Brooklyn, NY. The clinic is shut down 10 days later and Sanger is arrested.

1917   Members of the National Woman's Party picket the White House. Alice Paul and 96 other suffragists are arrested and jailed for "obstructing traffic." When they go on a hunger strike to protest their arrest and treatment, they are force-fed.

1917   Women win the right to vote in ND, OH, IN, RI, NB, MI, NY, and AK.

1918   House of Representatives passes a resolution in favor of a woman suffrage amendment, but is defeated in the Senate.

1919   The Nineteenth Amendment granting women the vote adopted by joint resolution of Congress; sent to states for ratification July 2.

1920   Henry Burn casts the deciding vote that makes Tennessee the thirty-sixth, and final state, to ratify the Nineteenth Amendment.

1920   The Women's Bureau of the Department of Labor is formed to collect information about women in the workforce.

1921   Margaret Sanger founds the American Birth Control League; this becomes Planned Parenthood Federation of America in 1942.

1923   At the 75th anniversary of the Seneca Falls convention, Alice Paul proposes an Equal Rights Amendment to remedy inequalities not addressed in the Nineteenth Amendment.

Late 1920s   Many states continue to bar women from jury duty and public office. Widows succeed their husbands as governors of Texas and Wyoming. Middle-class women attend college and enter labor force. "Women's vote" fails to materialize.

1933   Frances Perkins is appointed first female secretary of Labor by FDR.

1935   Mary McLeod Bethune organizes National Council of Negro Women; lobbies against racism, and sexism in the workplace.

1936   Federal court rules birth control legal for its own sake, rather than solely for prevention of disease.

1941   United States enters World War II. Millions of women are recruited for defense industry jobs.

1941   WAC and WAVE are established as first women's military corps.

1947   Percentage of women in the labor force declines as women leave jobs to marry and to make way for returning soldiers.

1952   Democratic and Republican parties eliminate women's divisions.

1955   Civil rights movement escalates in the South; Septima Clark and others lead sit-ins and demonstrations.

1955   The Daughters of Bilitis (DOB), the first lesbian organization in the United States, is founded.

1960   FDA approves birth control pills.

1961   President's Commission on the Status of Women is established, headed by Eleanor Roosevelt.

(Continued)

Box 8.1   The History of the U.S. Women's Rights Movement Timeline 1792 - Present *(Continued)*

1963   Commission on the Status of Women success-fully pushes for passage of Equal Pay Act.

1963   Betty Friedan's *The Feminine Mystique* articulates dissatisfaction about limits on women.

1964   Civil Rights Act prohibits job discrimination on the basis of race or sex and establishes.

1965   In *Griswold v. Connecticut,* Supreme Court strikes down state law prohibiting the use of contraceptives by married couples.

1966   National Organization for Women, founded by Betty Friedan, promotes child care for working mothers, abortion rights, the equal rights amendment, and "full participation in the mainstream of American society now."

1967   Executive order 11375 expands President Lyndon Johnson's affirmative action policy of 1965 to include gender.

1968   The EEOC rules that sex-segregated help-wanted ads in newspapers are illegal.

1969   California becomes the first state to adopt a "no fault" divorce law, which allows couples to divorce by mutual consent.

1971   *Ms. Magazine* is first published as a sample insert in *New York* magazine; 300,000 copies are sold out in eight days. The first regular issue is published July 1972; becomes major forum for feminist voices; Gloria Steinem is the cofounder and editor.

1972   After nearly 50 years, the Equal Rights Amendment passes both houses and is signed by President Richard Nixon.

1972   Shirley Chisholm becomes the first African American candidate for president of a major political party when her name was placed in nomination at the Democratic National Convention and she received 152 votes on the first ballot.

1973   In *Roe v. Wade,* U.S. Supreme Court affirms women's right to first-trimester abortions.

1974   Ella Grasso of Connecticut becomes the first woman governor elected in her own right.

1974   The Equal Credit Opportunity Act prohibits discrimination in consumer credit practices on the basis of sex, race, marital status, religion, national origin, age, or receipt of public assistance.

1974   In *Corning Glass Works v. Brennan,* the U.S. Supreme Court rules that employers cannot justify paying women lower wages because that is what they traditionally received under the "going market rate."

1976   The first marital rape law is enacted in Nebraska, making it illegal for a husband to rape his wife.

1978   The Pregnancy Discrimination Act bans employment discrimination against pregnant women.

1981   Sandra Day O'Connor is appointed first woman U.S. Supreme Court justice.

1982   Deadline for ERA ratification expires; final count is three states short of adoption.

1984   Geraldine Ferraro is first woman from a major political party nominated as vice president.

1984   EMILY's List (Early Money Is Like Yeast) established as a financial network for pro-choice Democratic women running for national political office.

1986   *Meritor Savings Bank v. Vinson,* the Supreme Court finds that sexual harassment is a form of illegal job discrimination.

1992   More women run for and are elected to public office than in any other year in United States history.

1992   Mae Jemison becomes the first woman of color to go into space.

1992   In *Planned Parenthood v. Casey,* the Supreme Court reaffirms the validity of a woman's right to abortion under *Roe v. Wade.*

1993   Ruth Bader Ginsburg becomes the second female member of the Supreme Court.

1994   Violence Against Women Act of 1994 signed into law.

1996   *United States v. Virginia* affirms that the male-only admissions policy Virginia Military Institute violates 14th Amendment.

1997   Supreme Court rules: college athletics programs must have equal numbers of men and women to qualify for federal support.

1998   Mitsubishi Motor Manufacturing of America agrees to pay $34 million to settle an E.E.O.C. lawsuit contending that hundreds of women were sexually harassed.

2000   CBS Broadcasting agrees to pay $8 million to settle a sex discrimination lawsuit by the E.E.O.C. on behalf of 200 women.

2003   *Nevada Department of Human Resources v. Hibbs,* Supreme Court rules that states can be sued in federal court for violations of the Family Leave Medical Act.

2008   First woman from a major political party, Hillary Rodham Clinton, campaigns for the Democratic nomination for President of the United States.

2009   Sonia Sotomayor becomes the first femaile Hispanic Justice of the U.S. Supreme Court.

Sources: Anthony Center for Women's Leadership (2006). "The History of U.S. Suffrage Movement Timeline 1792 to Present."

Rochester," NY: University of Rochester. www.rochester.edu/sba/suffragetimeline.html (accessed April 22, 2008); National Women's History Museum (n.d.). "Emma Hart Willard." *The History of Women and Education: Biographies.* www.nwhm.org/exhibits/education/Biographies_Willard.htm (accessed April 22, 2008). Connors, R.J. "Frances Wright: First female civic rhetor in America." *College English*, 62, no. 1, (1999). 30–57. National Women's History Project (n.d.). "Timeline of Legal History of Women in the United States

A Timeline of the Women's Rights Movement 1848–1998." www.legacy98.org/timeline.html (accessed April 22, 2008). American Women through Time (2007). "American Women Through Time 1970–2001." www.mtsu.edu/∼kmiddlet/history/women/time/wh-recent.html (accessed April 22, 2008). Imbornoni, M.A. (2007). Women's Rights Movement in the U.S. Timeline of Key Events in the American Women's Rights Movement. www.infoplease.com/spot/womenstimeline1.html#WHM-1980 (accessed April 22, 2008).

you enter the policy arena, do not be discouraged if on your first attempt to change policy, you are not successful. Use each failure to learn from and to build on as you construct future strategies for improving social policies for those for whom you advocate. Take the time to experience policy change from a historical perspective to get an idea of the resourcefulness, ingenuity, and courage it often takes to advocate for those who are treated less than equally or less than justly by our current systems and institutions of government. Visit your libraries and view films that depict historical events that helped marginalized groups in society overcome barriers to equality and justice. One movie, *Iron Jawed Angels,* provides a moving and accurate account on the life of suffragette Alice Paul and her fellow suffragettes at the turn of the twentieth century.

SOCIAL WORKERS AS POLICYMAKERS

Chapter 6 explored a wide variety of career positions social workers might consider as policy practitioners, but even social workers who are employed in more traditional social work jobs, such as direct service workers, supervisors, or agency directors often find themselves involved in policy change. Regardless of whether social workers are in a policy practice position or a more traditional social work position, they are likely to be engaged in policy practice in some capacity. In this section, common roles of social workers in the policymaking process are examined, and essential tasks often associated with these roles are explored.

Human Rights & Justice

Critical Thinking Question

What policy changes can you identify that lead to greater equality for one selected group?

Direct service workers are distinctively aware of agency-level policy issues that affect client groups and are usually the first to suspect a problem within the agency. As such, they are uniquely positioned to engage in several important tasks during the early stages of policymaking, such as: (1) documenting recurring issues with clients; (2) identifying cases (case finding) that represent a suspected general problem; and (3) beginning to describe a practice or community problem by delineating its common elements. These are a few usual activities direct service workers may find themselves involved in. For example, a direct practice worker in a family-counseling agency in a Latino neighborhood noticed that several of her clients had cancelled their appointments over the past month. When she contacted her clients to reschedule, she subtly inquired as to the reasons for the missed appointments, and learned that child care was a problem. To determine whether this was a problem unique to her clients or a problem with clients throughout the agency, she informally discussed it with her colleagues and discovered that they too had noticed a similar pattern, and with increasing frequency. Over the course of the day, the social worker identified 12 clients within the agency who had a pattern of canceling appointments. The direct service worker identified a potential problem and had begun to identify cases across the agency.

Advocates can speak on behalf of client groups in identifying and resolving problems of importance to clients, their families, and neighborhoods. Once a problem is recognized and cases identified, advocates can speak on behalf of target populations, communicating their desires for policy and program changes. Social workers can advocate for client groups within an agency or community, in court settings, at city council meetings, and within legislative processes. To carry the example forward from the previous paragraph, as a result of identifying a significant number of clients needing child care in order to come to the agency and receive services, the direct service worker may decide to talk to each client, or to organize a group meeting to discuss with them what options for child care might be available through the agency, community, or their own mother's care group. Based on the group's decision, as a frontline social worker and a policy practitioner, she may choose to take on the role of advocate within the agency or community, or help the mothers empower themselves to resolve their child care issue.

Policy Practice

Critical Thinking Question

What policy practice roles have you taken on in your employment or internships?

The ability to conduct research is an important skill in the policymaking effort. *Researchers* locate or generate objective data upon which to base policy decisions, as well as subjective data from clients about how they experience a particular problem, agency setting, or service delivery system. Social work researchers in the policymaking process are often involved in: (1) collecting and analyzing data to substantiate a problem and define the problem by size, context, and target group; (2) establishing a factual database upon which to build a policy-change effort; (3) attending to the subjective lived experiences of clients who know the problem first hand; (4) assessing the cost/benefit ratio of policy options under consideration when developing a plan for policy change; (5) evaluating the impact of a new policy/program on the target population; and (6) making recommendations for courses of action based on available data.

Returning to the child care needs of Latino clients' example, imagine that the frontline worker decided to discuss with her supervisor her concerns about clients missing appointments. As a result of reporting the outcomes of her initial inquiry into the problem and case finding, she was able to communicate effectively the existence of a real problem that was interfering with the effective delivery of agency services to Latino clients. The supervisor shared the worker's concerns, and decided to conduct an in-agency survey with all direct service workers to assess the extent to which clients were missing appointments. She constructed a brief online survey asking workers to count how many cancelled appointments or "no shows" each had experienced over the past three months, and how many individual clients were involved. Next, the supervisor sent the survey out to workers through e-mail, requesting a reply within three days. Results indicated that over the previous three months, social work counselors had 57 cancelled appointments or "no shows" involving 35 clients of the 150 active agency clients. Through research, the social work supervisor determined the extent of the problem (23% of clients had missed appointments), and recognized that this problem not only interrupted the helping process, but also had an economic impact on the agency in terms of missed payments, down time for workers, and lost productivity. Notice that there are interconnected micro and macro effects of clients missing appointments.

The next step in the research endeavor is to determine the nature of the problem; in other words, to identify factors or conditions that are keeping clients from showing up for their appointments. The direct service worker reported a common response of "child care needs" in the few cases into which she inquired. The supervisor next sought to substantiate the initial finding through a more systematic interview with clients, in which she also attempted to uncover other factors that may be contributing to the problem of missed appointments. The supervisor developed a brief interview that contained three open-ended questions for the agency social workers to ask clients who have missed appointments. The questions were:

1. I notice that you have missed your last _____ (number) appointments. I'm calling to see if there is anything we can do here at the agency to help you make it to your next appointment?

2. What do you think is the biggest obstacle to keeping your counseling appointments?

3. Is there anything else that keeps you away from the agency?

During a staff meeting the supervisor shared her finding from the online survey of agency social workers, and requested that all workers contact their clients who had missed appointments and conduct a brief telephone interview. She presented the three open-ended interview questions that she had constructed and instructed each worker to use these questions in conducting the telephone interviews. She also requested that each worker complete the interviews within two weeks and forward the client responses to her. To help prepare the frontline social workers for conducting the interviews, during the staff meeting, the supervisor asked workers to role play interviews with client in order to help avoid any problems in the interview process. She also used this opportunity to train workers in how to inform clients that they were participating in a phone research survey, and to stress the importance of obtaining verbal consent to participate in the study from clients before beginning the data collection interview.

At the end of two weeks, all seven social workers had completed their client interviews and sent their interview results to their supervisor. After analyzing the data, the supervisor identified three major themes that emerged from the client interviews that interfered with clients keeping their appointments at the agency. In a memo to the staff, she listed these factors in order of priority as indicated by client responses. They were:

1. Unreliable child care arrangements

2. Inconvenient agency hours

3. Embarrassment about poor English skills and the lack of Spanish-speaking counselors and staff at the agency as well as the absence of signs in Spanish.

Based on the online survey and telephone-interview findings, at the next monthly staff meeting, the supervisor led a discussion on what recommendations they should make to the agency director for policy changes to meet the needs of the clients. The preliminary recommendations included:

1. Explore options for supporting child care for clients;

2. Explore options for increasing agency hours to include some evening and some weekend hours;

3. Explore the option of developing agency resources more appropriate to a Latino community, including hiring Spanish-speaking counselors and creating agency signs (inside and outside the building) written in Spanish.

In the case example presented here, the frontline social workers and the supervisor played pivotal roles in factually defining an agency problem and generating possible responses to client and community needs. Because of their close proximity to the clients, their trust-based working relationships with clients, and their commitment to serving clients, the traditional social work counselors were able and willing to initiate a policy change. It is unlikely that any agency personnel not directly linked to the clients would have noticed the signs of an underlying problem in the agency's service delivery system. The importance of direct social work practitioners working in the problem identifier, case finder, and researcher capacities in the policy-change effort cannot be overstated. Direct service workers are essential to keeping service delivery systems working effectively, efficiently, and in the best interests of the clients.

Community organizers attempt to bring client groups, social workers, and other community members together to address a problem and consider change effort strategies. Building on the previous case example, consider the supervisor's perspective on the agency's problem in serving clients. After spending two months identifying the agency problem, doing research, and making recommendations to the agency director about what actions should be taken to help the agency's clients become more fully engaged in the counseling process, the supervisor began wondering if this problem was unique to her agency or if other human service agencies were also experiencing similar problems. At the next meeting of the County Coalition on Human Services, the supervisor reported on the obstacles they had discovered to clients keeping appointments and asked if other agencies had encountered similar problems. At first, members of the coalition were reluctant to speak, but one by one they acknowledged that this was in fact a problem and that it was becoming a serious economic issue for some agencies. The supervisor suggested that the coalition take a look at this issue from a countywide perspective and begin to organize and plan for action across agencies. She volunteered to organize a subcommittee of the coalition that would (1) conduct research across all agencies; (2) form focus groups of clients across agencies to discuss barriers to accessing agency services; and (3) consider asking some clients to join the ad hoc organizing committee.

Planners work with others in creating a plan for policy change, developing policy goals, and determining strategies for policy change. These were essentially the charges of the ad hoc committee of the County Coalition on Human Services for meeting Latino service needs. After organizing the committee and recruiting client members, the committee returned to the research process and collected data from agencies across the county. This data collection allowed them to create a more representative database from which to make a plan for action. The ad hoc group made several observations and recommendations from the additional data collected and reported it at the next bimonthly coalition meeting. These observations and recommendations included:

1. A need for a community-wide child care center that was accessible (located on public transportation lines); affordable (subsidized); and sensitive to Latino culture;

2. Agencies across the county collectively employed only three Spanish-speaking workers. The ad hoc committee concluded that such a cultural gap in the service delivery system resulted in a continuum of care system that replicated the hierarchical power structure of the larger society, and was an obstacle to client and neighborhood engagement and empowerment. The group recommended filling 20 percent of agency positions with Spanish speaking people over the next three years, and to engage in active advertising and recruiting of staff members with Spanish-speaking ability;

> *Direct service workers are essential to keeping service delivery systems working effectively, efficiently, and in the best interests of the clients.*

3. Within the next year, all agencies would add/replace signs inside and outside their agencies with signs written in Spanish as well as English;

4. Each agency reconstitutes its board of directors with 20 percent Spanish-speaking members within the next two years to make them more representative of the communities that they served.

Managers of community events or initiatives engage the public in building support, and in coordinating stakeholders in the change effort. The County Coalition for Human Services adopted the recommendations of the ad hoc group on methods to increase access to community services and selected two members of the coalition to manage the implementation of the plan. After several weeks of working together, the managers determined that to accomplish the goals of the coalition and to implement the plan, they would need an initial budget of $250,000 to create a child care center and staff it, and to support advertising and recruiting of Spanish-speaking staff members and board members. The managers had identified several community, state, and federal resources for potential funding as well as individuals and organizations within the community who could be approached for sizeable donations to support the change effort. Community-wide fund raisers were also being considered as a means of both raising needed money and building community cohesion and support.

Administrators implement new policies through the development and delivery of programs, and also oversee and authorize the evaluation of program effectiveness. Social workers working in administrative roles may act as monitors of the implementation process, or as supervisors and agency directors overseeing the operations of a new program that is an outgrowth of policy change. For the County Coalition for Human Services to be successful in implementing the community-wide plan for change, it will be necessary to get the endorsement of the directors of most, if not all, community agencies and to get them involved in developing an implementation plan for their individual agencies. In addition, agency administrators will need to develop methods of monitoring the implementation of the community-based plan and to periodically report on their accomplishments.

Social workers may take on one or several roles in creating policy change. Policy practitioner roles will change or expand with each stage in the policymaking process, and within diverse professional and social contexts. Flexibility and adaptability are important skills for social work policy practitioners to develop in order to optimize opportunities in the change process and to ensure its success. Further, it is also important to understand the context of policy change (cultural, social, economic, and political) and to be aware of various policymaking models that take into account these contextual factors when launching a policy change effort.

APPROACHES TO POLICYMAKING

Scholars have long attempted to make sense of the complex process of policymaking. While many models of policymaking have been put forth, for the most part they describe what "ought" to take place when making decisions that will affect millions of people's lives, or the models are able to partially describe what happens, at least in some instances. While many models of policymaking exist,[3] in this section, only three commonly recognized models of policymaking are presented with examples of how they might be applied in practice. Table 8.1 provides highlights from each model. While the models are presented discretely, life in the policy arena is never so precise or predictable.

Table 8.1   Policymaking Models

Model	Assumptions	Policy Question
Rational Model	1. The cost and benefits of a policy intervention can be known and calculated prior to being implemented and evaluated 2. All policy alternatives must be identified and assessed, and are available 3. All policy consequences can be known, identified, and measured 4. Cost/benefit ratios can be calculated.	What are the short- and long-term costs and benefits of instituting a national children's allowance for all children in the United States?
Political Model	1. Few social values can be agreed upon 2. People cannot agree on how to define social problems 3. Conflicting costs and values cannot be compared or weighted 4. Policymakers cannot accurately forecast the consequences of various policy options 5. The political environment of policymakers with its many power groups and influences, make it impossible to discern all social values 6. Policymakers often seek to maximize their own rewards of power, status, reelection, and money 7. The bureaucratic structure of government and agencies create barriers to coordinated policymaking.	What policy alternative can be adopted to reduce the number of uninsured citizens in the country while holding spending constant and satisfying most of the voting public?
Incremental Model	1. A complete analysis of a social problem is not possible 2. Aspiring to complete information about a social problem is an obstacle to any policy action 3. Existing policies are fundamentally adequate, needing only small adjustments 4. Small change is desirable because it is doable and maintains a level of stability that is not possible with extreme change 5. The existing government and agency organizational arrangements and power relations are adequate for addressing social problems using existing and future policies.	Will removing TANF welfare benefits for unwed teen mothers reduce the number of teen pregnancies, and thus, the demands on TANF?

Most often a mixture of many models comes into play when policy is actually being made.

Rational Model

Rational policymaking (also referred to as synoptic approach) is a linear and scientific approach to policymaking that progresses in a systematic fashion in identifying and assessing the most logical policy response to a presenting problem. Like the scientific process, the rational model follows a problem-solving process that includes five general steps. These include:

1. Objectively define the problem;
2. Generate a list of possible alternatives to resolve the problem;
3. Assess probable outcomes for each alternative (both positive and negative);
4. Gather and analyze available data related to each policy alternative; and,
5. Select the policy alternative that best resolves the problem with greatest efficiency.[4]

As reflected in the five-step process above, the rational approach to policymaking is concerned with efficiency, is based on the analysis of objective data, and incorporates business techniques such as cost/benefit analysis, and program policy budgeting systems.[5] The rational model of policymaking attempts (as much as possible) to eliminate or avoid common factors that tend to make policymaking "irrational"—such as politics, personal and political agendas, motivations, emotions, and sensory stimuli.[6] Policymakers using the rational approach strive to maximize the policy outputs while minimizing the policy inputs. To put it another way, rational policymakers are concerned with cost/benefit ratios and seek to get the biggest bang for the buck. In other words they consider *how to effectively address the presenting social issue at the lowest cost while achieving the greatest benefit.* In many ways, the rational model aligns with the utilitarian ethical framework of policymaking discussed in Chapter 5 that seeks the greatest good at the lowest cost while minimizing any unintended harmful effects of the policy.[7]

The policy with the highest cost/benefit ratio is identified as the most rational choice. However, it should be noted that cost assessment should go beyond dollars and include such things as social, political, and value costs as well. It is possible to make rational cost-effective policy choices that sacrifice social and value costs, which can result in short-term savings but long-term costs since social and value costs are ultimately converted to monetary costs. For example, it may be economically cost-effective to reduce the welfare rolls by making the eligibility criteria more stringent and by imposing time limits; however, policymakers also need to be aware of the value and social cost of this economically minded policy. What are the long-term effects of such a policy on children born into poverty when their families lose the benefits of Temporary Assistance for Needy Families (TANF), possibly pushing the family deeper into poverty? This circumstance could force families into homelessness, which in turn may cause interruptions in the education of children in displaced families and may ultimately interfere with children's cognitive, social, and academic development. Some advocates might conclude that the potential long-term costs are not worth the short-term benefits of reduced caseloads.

The 1996 welfare reform law, the Personal Responsibility and Work Opportunity Reconciliation Act (PRWORA), removed the entitlement status of Aid to Families with Dependent Children (AFDC), increased work requirements, and set time limits for welfare assistance through its replacement program, TANF. The intention of the policy was to reduce the welfare rolls, and to encourage self-sufficiency. Between 1996 and 2006, welfare caseloads were reduced by 60 percent, indicating an achievement of one of the policy goals.[8] But consider the cost of this policy. A meta-analysis of research on TANF recipients and TANF leavers revealed that TANF recipients experienced a significant decline in income between 1996 and 2001, and that TANF leavers experienced significant increases in deep poverty growing from 24.4 percent to 33.3 percent between 1996 and 2001 in one national data set (Survey of Income and Program Participation [SIPP]), and from 25.3 percent to 31.6 percent between 2000 and 2005 in a second national data set (Current Population

*Rational policy making
considers not only the
immediate monetary
cost of a policy but also
the long-term social and
value costs to families
and communities.*

Survey).[9] The association between poverty and child well-being has long been established, but children who live in extreme poverty for multiple years suffer the worst outcomes in terms of physical health, developmental delays and learning disabilities, school achievement, and emotional and behavioral problems. Young children living in poverty are particularly vulnerable to poor outcomes.[10] Rational policy decision making regarding family assistance policies would necessitate considering not only the immediate monetary cost of the policy but also the long-term social and value costs to families, communities, and the nation. These social and value costs will ultimately convert to economic costs as more children require early childhood interventions and long-term supports. There is an additional opportunity cost in the loss of contributions to society these children might have made had they not succumbed to the ravages of poverty in terms of underdevelopment and underachievement in school and subsequently in the marketplace.

When approaching policymaking from a rational perspective, policymakers consider all of the policy choices, conduct a cost/benefit analysis of each one (short- and long-term analyses are critical), and based on outcomes of these analyses, choose the most efficient policy intervention.

Several assumptions direct the rational policymaking process.

- First, it is assumed that all of the cost and benefits of a policy intervention can be known and calculated prior to it being implemented and evaluated;
- Second, the model assumes that all policy alternatives can be identified and assessed, and are available; and
- Third, the rational model assumes that all policy consequences can be known, identified, and measured.[11]

An example of a rational policymaking question would be:

What are the short- and long-term costs and benefits of instituting a national children's allowance for all children in the U.S.?

The assumptions that support the rational model for policymaking are clear and concrete, but hardly ever attainable in the real world. Predicting human outcomes is often an exercise in futility. Therefore, calculating meaningful cost/benefit analyses can often be elusive. Another challenge with the rational model is that it is frequently not possible to identify and know all possible policy alternatives. Even if it were possible, assessing each one for cost/benefit ratios would be very time-consuming. Furthermore, all policy decision makers are not equally capable of taking in, assessing, and analyzing data and coming to optimal decisions regarding policy options. Finally, human beings are not purely rational by nature. Policymakers come to the policymaking process with prior experiences and clear preferences that can and often do influence their policy decisions even while pursuing a rational policymaking process.[12] The impracticality of comprehensive rational policymaking is obvious. If policymakers sought to meet all the assumptions of the rational model, they might well get left out of the decision-making process altogether because of the delays due to multiple and extensive policy analyses. Other real-world policymakers using less-demanding models would be making timely policy decisions using available, but incomplete information.

Attempting to work purely from a rational model when developing policy can be problematic, and often not very practical. In response to the impracticality of comprehensive rational policymaking, 1978 Nobel prize winner Herbert

Simon developed the concept of *bounded rationality,* which he described as " rational choice that takes into account the cognitive limitations of the decision maker—limitations of both knowledge and computational capacity."[13] While Simon was an economist, when his concept of bounded rationality is applied to less fixed circumstances, such as social policies predicting human behaviors, the limitations of the decision maker can be considerable, and attempting to gather information on all possible outcomes endless. In the context of social policy, bounded rationality has come to be understood as an approach to policymaking that considers a limited number of options (versus all possible options), predicting policy outcomes of this limited number of options using the available and appropriate data (as opposed to all data) and recognizing that there will still be a considerable margin of error. Policymakers make the best possible choices given the limited information available.[14]

Political Model

The political approach to policymaking recognizes that values largely influence policy decisions, and that gaining consensus on social values among stakeholders in the policymaking process is unlikely. Value conflict is the norm in policymaking. Furthermore, social problems are difficult to define because people view the causes of social problems from many different philosophical and ideological perspectives. What one group of policymakers sees as a problem may not be a concern to another group, and may actually benefit yet a third group. Because of these differences in values and perspectives, it is believed that the costs and values of any policy option cannot be known and compared, which makes predicting policy outcomes within so many diverse social, economic, and political value contexts difficult at best.[15] This is often played out in House and Senate floor debates over important legislative issues where partisanship is high and the values inherent in the Republican and the Democratic ideologies heat up these Congressional debates. It is not surprising that political ideology (and the values that support it) is predictive of how Congressional members will vote on bills passing through their chambers.[16]

Policymaking is further complicated by the political system of power and influence, which is invariably linked to money.[17] Policymakers are bombarded daily by interest groups and lobbyists who want to influence their policy decisions to benefit the clients they represent (e.g., big business concerned with government regulations, environmental groups concerned with manufacturing pollutants, or social work lobbyists concerned with child abuse). How can policymakers possibly get a balanced perspective of what is best for the target population, whose voices are often not even present in the policymaking process? Furthermore, policymakers can easily become more motivated by their own rewards of power, status, reelection, and money, causing them to neglect the values and needs of those whom they were elected or appointed to serve. The very nature of government, with its large bureaucracies, is an obstacle to well-informed, coordinated, and intentional policymaking.[18] Politicians make quick decisions on a multitude of policies from zoning laws, road repairs, trade policies, and health care for all children. The range of topics they are expected to have sufficient knowledge about to make informed policy decisions is vast. They make the best decisions they can, attempting to represent their constituents' preferences, while considering their own political viability, and somewhere in the process, determine what policy decisions would provide some positive outcomes without causing more harm than good. They use information that comes to them through lobbyists, constituents, staff, and others, such as professionals and experts, as the basis for their policy decisions. With so many political actors vying for the policy decision makers' attention and trying to influence his or her decisions, it is not difficult to see how policymaking can become very irrational at times. DiNitto concluded that a political approach indeed raises issues about the rationality of policymaking, noting that it suggests:

- Few social values are agreed upon;
- Problems cannot be defined because people cannot agree on what the problems are;
- Conflicting costs and values cannot be compared or weighted;
- Policymakers cannot accurately forecast the consequences of various policy options because of so many diverse social, economic, and political values;
- The political environment of policymakers with its many power groups and influences makes it impossible to discern all social values, especially those that are not represented in the policymaking setting;
- Policymakers are not necessarily motivated to make decisions on the basis of social values. Instead they often seek to maximize their own rewards of power, status, reelection, and money; and,
- Given the pervasiveness of politics and influence within government in general, the bureaucratic structure of government and agencies creates barriers to coordinated policymaking.[19]

A policy question posed from a political approach to policymaking might be:

What policy alternative can be adopted to reduce the number of uninsured citizens while holding spending constant and satisfying most of the voting public?

The political policymaking model reflects a reality within decision-making bodies (legislatures, courts, executive offices) that politics is present, alive, and well and will invariably interfere with rational policymaking processes. Politics and its inherent conflicts also slow the policymaking process and interfere with the making of radical or large-scale policy changes. The combination of the political reality of policymaking and the impracticality of comprehensive policymaking made way for the emergence of a third policymaking approach, the incremental model.[20]

Incremental Model

Incrementalism was first introduced by Charles Lindblom in 1959 to describe the process of policymaking as it has most often occurred in the United States. He called this process and the title of his seminal work "The science of muddling through."[21] Lindblom's incremental model for policymaking was a response to what he viewed as the impracticality of a comprehensive rational model. His conservative incremental model describes the evolution of social policy as largely a continuation of past policies with only small or incremental changes. Based on the challenges of the political model, and the impossible demands of a comprehensive rational model, incrementalism recognizes the constraints of time, money, information, intelligence, and politics that make rational policymaking impossible. Lindblom noted that even aspiring to a comprehensive rational approach to policymaking is in itself an obstacle to change. Focusing on more limited and bounded change provides a context where policy choices can quickly be assessed and policy decisions made.[22] Incremental changes prevent drastic swings in social policies and will guarantee a certain level of social, economic, and political stability. Others have described incrementalism as a method for ensuring that the status quo is maintained; however, Lindblom asserts that "a fast-moving sequence of small changes can more speedily accomplish a drastic alteration of the status quo than can an only infrequent major policy change."[23] Rather than introduce sweeping new policies, incrementalists favor tinkering and finessing current policies that improve policy outputs and reduce costs. An example of an incremental policy question would be:

> Will removing TANF welfare benefits for unwed teen mothers reduce the number of teen pregnancies and, thus, the demands on TANF?

The incremental model fundamentally accepts the existing organizational and structural arrangements for the development and implementation of policies, the delivery of programs, and the power relations within these systems. While large-scale policy changes are possible within an incremental model, such changes usually occur only in response to a crisis.[24] For example, in response to the Great Depression, President Franklin D. Roosevelt was able to engineer and pass massive legislation that produced the infrastructure of the current social welfare system. The crisis of high unemployment rates and massive numbers of citizens without homes and living on the edge of existence provided FDR the opportunity for major social policy change, but consider that was 75 years ago, and while we have been tinkering with the social welfare system ever since, changes of this scope have not occurred since.

This section on policymaking models has provided an overview of three discrete approaches to policymaking, but in reality, elements of each of these models can be found in day-to-day policymaking. From the analysis of objective data, a social problem may be identified (rational model); and, with political pressure from the public and professionals in the field trying to address the identified problem, it finds a place on the political agenda (political model). Policymakers come to the table to assess what can be done within the existing governing and agency structures to respond to the problem in an effective yet limited way (incremental model). Often, one model will dominate the process, but elements of the other two models can be seen. For example, during President Clinton's second administration, it was clear that the Republicans who dominated Congress at the time were pushing for welfare reform. Clinton had made a campaign promise to "end welfare as we know it," but had put welfare reform as a priority behind health care reform during his first administration. As a result of the Republicans sweeping the mid-term elections in 1994, the Clinton administration had no choice but to make welfare reform its top priority.[25]

Clinton objected to many components of the Republicans' welfare reform bill, such as provisions eliminating all AFDC and housing benefits for children born out of wedlock to mothers under 18 years of age, and barring these children from AFDC for life. The Clinton administration was also concerned with the Republican plan to ban aid to legal immigrants and to tie Medicaid to welfare reform. The assessment by policy analysts that the Republican welfare reform plan would put 1 million more children in poverty was a grave concern. Given the shift in power in Congress and the public polls that put welfare reform as the number one issue among U.S. citizens, President Clinton was politically pressured to make some compromises and move forward with welfare reform measures.[26] Rationally, there was concern about the growing number on welfare. Between 1981 and 1994, the welfare rolls had increased from 3.9 million to 5 million (rational objective data). What is often not reported is that in 1994, only 83 percent of eligible families participated in AFDC.[27] In the end, Clinton negotiated a deal with the Republican Congress on the provisions of the new welfare legislation (political model), and endorsed the Personal Responsibility and Work Opportunity Reconciliation Act of 1996, also referred to as the welfare reform bill. In essence, TANF was a reworking of the existing AFDC program (incrementalism). It increased the work requirement (which was already a part of AFDC), and imposed a lifetime limit for families receiving benefits, thus removing the entitlement status of AFDC, and cut funding for Food Stamps, and Medicaid and Supplement Security Income (SSI) for children with disabilities. This was a bitter pill to swallow for the Clinton administration, and two top Health and Human Services executives resigned when President Clinton signed the bill. But President Clinton was not finished with welfare reform. In negotiating the budget reconciliation bill with Congress that year, President Clinton was able to extend Medicaid and SSI benefits to legal immigrants, restore funding to the Food Stamp program and to disabled children for SSI and Medicaid, and provide $3 billion for welfare to work programs. All of this political maneuvering over the budget bill helped to restore some of the losses President Clinton agreed to in the original welfare reform legislation.[28] In the making of welfare reform policy in 1996, rational, political, and incremental policymaking was at work, but the political policymaking model dominated the process.

It could be argued that the elimination of the entitlement status of welfare under AFDC went beyond incremental change and constituted a major policy shift; conversely, a more conservative assessment may regard it as incremental, arguing that even though entitlement status of AFDC was removed under TANF, the same institutional structures at the state and federal levels that administered AFDC were also the auspices for the new TANF program. The TANF policy was fundamentally the same in many ways as its predecessor policy, AFDC. For example recipients were still required to meet poverty-eligibility standards, and to be involved in work activities (albeit more hours). The position that individual policy practitioners and analysts take on this point will be influenced by the political ideology they embrace, the assumptions they hold about welfare recipients, and the role(s) they hold within the policymaking and service delivery systems.

THE POLICYMAKING PROCESS[29]

The effective application of political, rationale and incremental models of policymaking requires knowledge of the process of policymaking. While some policies can be swiftly made through executive decisions, others require more effort and the building of support to realize. Generally, policymaking progresses through eight stages (not necessarily in a linear fashion) with the change effort building momentum and the change strategies developing in greater detail as the process moves forward. This section explores each stage of the policymaking process, the essential tasks that require completion in each stage, and the roles that social worker policy practitioners need to master to be effective change agents in responding to agency, community, and social problems.

Social welfare policies are collective ways to respond to social problems or potential problems. Policy change is often initiated as a result of public or organizational pressure to respond to an unmet need. But who decides when there is a problem or impending problem? What constitutes a social problem, who decides how it is defined, and what factors guide the development of its policy solution? How a problem is defined will directly shape the policy response.

Blau contends that social problems are constructed and influenced by the values and dominant ideologies of those with the most power. Values and preferences influence what problems are addressed and which problems are ignored. The agreed-upon cause of the problem and the theory adopted to explain its presence are also influenced by values and ideologies. Collectively, these factors determine how the problem is framed and defined and, subsequently, the architecture of the policy that responds to it.[30] For example, homelessness is a growing social problem in the United States, especially among members of households with children.[31] While rates of homelessness are impossible to measure exactly, according to a review of available research by the National Coalition for the Homeless that is based on the increase in number of shelter beds, homelessness increased threefold between 1981 and 1989, and doubled between 1987 and 1997.[32] These conservative figures do not take into account homeless people who do not use shelters, but instead double up with friends or relatives or stay out in the open. The causes of homelessness have been hotly debated for nearly three decades. Those advocating on behalf of people who are homeless argue that the most salient factor in the growing number of homeless people is the significant loss of affordable housing, and the near-elimination of the federal government's commitment to providing affordable housing, as a major cause of homelessness.[33] However, social scientists have identified addiction and mental illness as major contributors to homelessness,[34] and some government officials have adopted the stance that people are homeless because they fail to take responsibility for their lives. Notice that the policy response to each of these "causes" of homelessness would be very different and would range from policies that funded the construction of more low-income housing, to more funding for treatment of drug and alcohol addiction and mental illness among those earning low incomes, to more punitive policies that required job training and work requirements for welfare benefits, and case management to teach homeless individuals how to effectively manage their lives. The first cause (lack of affordable housing) suggests a social structural cause of homelessness (housing) and implies that the responsibility for the problem resides not with homeless individuals but with society and governmental institutions; the second cause defines the problem within a medical model of pathology (mental illness and addiction) and suggests a moral responsibility to respond to the medical needs of the poor; and the third cause indicates a moral failing of the individual and suggests a personal reform and accountability policy as the most appropriate response to the problem of homelessness.

So who gets to decide which understanding of causality dominates and, in turn, directs the policy response? Whether a social problem publicly recognized is influenced by the sheer number of people affected by the problem, and the power and status of those seeking to define the problem and respond to it by appropriating public resources to remediate or alleviate the problem.[35] Also influencing the policy response will be the public attitude toward the target population affected and the power they possess as a group. Groups that are marginalized outside the political and economic systems will often be ignored until politicians are morally embarrassed into recognizing a serious problem, or until the problem begins to affect the more politically and economically connected. Consider that the problem of HIV/AIDS came to the attention of the public in 1980 and was defined as a gay disease.[36] The government's response was to ignore the problem, and some groups even framed the disease as God's response to a sinful lifestyle. It was not until the disease started affecting those outside the gay community and, in particular, middle-class teens, that the government provided a significant policy response to HIV/AIDS. Teen Ryan White was diagnosed with HIV in 1984 as a result of blood transfusions. Ryan spent his remaining life

**Research
Based Practice**

Critical Thinking Question

Compare the value assumptions about homelessness with the available research evidence.

Table 8.2   Stages of the Policy Formation Process

Stage	Essential Tasks	Social Worker Roles
One: Problem identification and case finding	Case finding documentation	▶ Direct Service Worker ▶ Advocate
Two: Data collection and data analysis	Develop factual knowledge base	▶ Researcher ▶ Organizer
Three: Inform the public and identify stakeholders	Present the problem in a forum to relevant parties	▶ Community organizer ▶ Communication planner/spokesperson
Four: Select policy options and develop policy goals	Develop broad-based goals in a policy statement	▶ Planner ▶ Cost/benefit analyst
Five: Build public support and develop coalitions	Bargain with groups in the larger system to cultivate leadership and consensus	▶ Community organizer ▶ Communication planner/spokesperson
Six: Program design	Plan the allocation of responsibility, organizational structure, and program operations	▶ Planner ▶ Organizer ▶ Manager
Seven: Policy implementation	Deliver services to client groups	▶ Administrator ▶ Direct service worker ▶ Monitor implementation
Eight: Policy evaluation	Assess the effectiveness of the program	▶ Researcher ▶ Direct service worker

until he died in 1990 campaigning for people to have compassion for individuals with HIV/AIDS and was instrumental in setting school policies for the education of children with HIV/AIDS.[37] The changing demographics of those contracting HIV/AIDS and the efforts of Ryan White resulted in the passage of the Ryan White Care Act in 1990 which provided $2.1 billion in health care and other services to individuals living with HIV and AIDS in 2008.[38]

As the examples above indicate, moral values, ideologies, objective data, politics, and power brokering all play a part in whether or not a social problem is recognized, how the problem is defined, and the public investment made into the policy response aimed to resolve the problem. The level of commitment to a particular social problem can be best assessed by the amount of money the government invests in resolving it. Government budgets are instructive in assessing social problem priorities among policymakers.

In the section that follows, the eight stages of the policymaking process are presented while integrating the multiple roles that social workers perform at each stage. While the policymaking process is described as a linear course of action here, it is important to recognize that in the real world of policy practice, the stages often overlap, and policymakers often return to earlier stages more than once in order to clarify problems and issues, or to include key stakeholders in the process. Table 8.2 summarizes the stages of the policymaking process, social worker roles, and the essential tasks that need to be completed in each stage.

Stage One: Problem Identification and Case Finding

Identifying a problem in human services can occur in many contexts. It may be an observation that an individual worker makes about her client base that is later linked to a general pattern within an agency or community, as in the example presented earlier in this chapter. But it can also be a social problem that affects a whole city, state, or the nation. Policymaking takes place in small offices, city council meetings, large state agencies, in the state legislature, in budget hearings, in the courts, in Congress, and in executive branches of government. But, first and foremost, a problem is identified and a decision is made to address the problem. At this stage of policymaking the important task at hand is *case finding* and *documentation* to substantiate the problem and to begin to define the pervasiveness of the problem: who it affects, and how it affects individuals, agencies, and communities. In the human services, case finding and documentation often falls to the *direct service workers* as discussed earlier in this chapter. The identification of a larger problem that affects a particular group of people or that affects a large geographic area usually begins with the identification of individual cases. As discussed earlier, the first case of HIV/AIDS was identified in 1980. Thereafter, cases presenting similar characteristics were reported and tracked. Over the course of a few years, the Centers for Disease Control had developed a sophisticated system for tracking and recording information about the number of cases in the population and who was affected by the disease. This tracking data enabled epidemiologists to define the size and dimensions of the problem. Scientists studied the problem and determined the cause and how it was transmitted. We now know a great deal about the worldwide problem of HIV/AIDS, but our current understanding of HIV/AIDS began with the identification of one case in 1980.[39]

To demonstrate how stage one is operationalized in policy practice, consider some of the problems with meeting client needs and with organizational functioning in service delivery found in the health care Simulated Case Study (SCS) accompanying this text (located on the Allyn & Bacon *My Social Work Lab* Web site). In response to the high cost of prescription drugs under the Medicare Modernization Act of 2003 (also known as the Medicare part D law), in e-mail #22 in Part I of the SCS, six grandmothers picketed a drug store in protest. After exhausting the modest minimum coverage provided by the new prescription drug law, the grandmothers entered the "doughnut hole" and were facing high drug costs, similar to the amount they paid prior to the passage of the Medicare part D legislation. The term *doughnut hole* was applied to the gap in prescription drug coverage after initial benefits had been exhausted, and seniors began to pay all drug costs out of pocket until they had spent up to a certain amount; then, they became eligible again for benefits under "catastrophic coverage" (see Table 8.3). Identifying the problem and then taking local, state, and national action on it resulted in Congress agreeing to close the doughnut hole with provisions included in the Affordable Health Care Act of 2010, otherwise known as the Health Care Reform Bill. Box 8.2 summarizes how the new legislation eliminates the problem of the doughnut hole over a ten-year period. Table 8.3 demonstrates how the doughnut hole was projected to expand over time. For example, in 2006 beneficiaries had a benefit limit of $2,250. After exhausting this benefit, seniors paid out of pocket for their medication until they spent $3,600, at which point catastrophic coverage kicked in and covered 95 percent of seniors' medications cost. By 2015, seniors would have been required to pay $6,850 out of pocket before reaching catastrophic coverage. The doughnut hole was a serious problem for seniors because

Table 8.3   The Ever-Growing Doughnut Hole

Year	Average Beneficiary Premium	Deductible	Initial Benefit Limit	Catastrophic Threshold	Out-of-Pocket Spending at Threshold
2006	$23	$250	$2250	$5100	$3600
2007	$35.86	$265	$2400	$5451.25	$3850
2008	$37.19	$285	$2580	$5871.25	$4150
2009	$39.64	$310	$2770	$6295	$4450
2010	$42.39	$330	$2980	$6737.50	$4750
2011	$45.36	$355	$3200	$7233.75	$5100
2012	$48.52	$380	$3440	$7795	$5500
2013	$52.04	$410	$3700	$8367.50	$5900
2014	$55.82	$445	$3990	$9058.75	$6400
2015	$59.88	$475	$4290	$9711.25	$6850

Source: NCPSSM calculation based on data from *The Annual 2006 Report of the Boards of Trustees of the Federal Hospital Insurance and Federal Supplementary Medical Insurance Trust Funds* & U.S. Department of Health and Human Services, Centers for Medicare and Medicaid Services, *Fact Sheet: Drug Benefit Enrollment Up, Costs Down from Competition and Beneficiary Choices,* June 8, 2006.
Note: Out-of-pocket spending at threshold does not include amounts paid in monthly premiums.

Box 8.2   The New Health Care Law: $250 Rebate for Medicare Part D Beneficiaries

Most Medicare part D prescription drug plans have a coverage gap - often called the "donut hole" - during which beneficiaries must pay the entire cost of their prescription drugs while at the same time continuing to pay their full Part D premium. One of the immediate changes which will result from enactment of the historic 2010 health care reform laws will be a one-time $250 payment to help Medicare beneficiaries who fall into the "donut hole." An estimated four million Part D beneficiaries will be responsible for all of their drug costs when they enter the drug coverage gap known as the "donut hole" in 2010. To help these beneficiaries afford their medications, one-time $250 rebate checks will begin mailing on June 10, 2010 (and about every six weeks after to cover beneficiaries that fall into the gap after that date).

Beginning in 2011, 50 percent discounts will apply for brand-name drugs and a small discount for generics. These discounts will be increased annually through 2020, when the donut hole will be completely closed.

Source: National Committee to Preserve Social Security and Medicare. http://www.ncpssm.org/news/archive/donut_hole_facts/

many are on fixed incomes, and high out-of-pocket costs were prohibitive. As people age they tend to have more than one chronic health condition, such as high blood pressure and diabetes, and are often on several medications that they must take to maintain their health and a good quality of life.[40] Social workers, nurses, physicians, and other human service workers as well as the elderly and their advocates persistently brought attention to the doughnut hole problem and eventually resolved it within the health care reform law.

In the health care SCS, a group of human service professionals came together to address the problem of uninsured citizens. A major issue that emerged was the poor functioning of the current health care system. At this level, the problem is bureaucratic rather than client centered. Individual professionals in the group had each identified bureaucratic problems with the health care system in their individual practices. The group, as a whole, decided that they needed to point out the flaws in the system, and also recommend alternative systems of care. As the providers and the frontline workers who were trying to deliver services every day could not afford to leave the formulation of policy solely in the hands of law-makers who are heavily lobbied by pharmaceutical and insurance companies. Without the voice of service providers working within the health care system, policymakers may be persuaded by the reasoning of lobbyists hired by the pharmaceutical and insurance companies rather than reaching decisions that meet the needs of the poor, elderly, and uninsured.

Stage Two: Data Collection and Analysis

Once documentation of the problem has been established and the problem broadly defined, the extent and nature of the problem needs to be delineated. Collection of both objective and subjective data provides a means for understanding the causes of the problem and how people experience the problem. These types of data are needed to support and direct an appropriate policy approach to the problem. Research data also help in determining who is affected by the problem and in what ways the problem affects them. In the health care SCS, the small group of professionals who came together to address the problem of uninsured citizens began to get an idea of the size of the problem they faced when they examined statistical data about the uninsured in the fictitious state of Factoria. They discovered that Factoria ranked near the top of states in uninsured individuals (20%), compared to the U.S. national uninsured rate of 16 percent. When they compared themselves with other states, they discovered that Minnesota had an uninsured rate of 9 percent and Texas a rate of 24 percent (see Table 8.4).[41] Surprisingly, they also discovered that the major cause of individual bankruptcy in the state of Factoria was medical costs. These conditions of bankruptcy for Factoria are reflected in United States too. Researchers report that over half of individual bankruptcy cases were due to high medical costs in 2001, and that 75 percent of those filing medical bankruptcies had health insurance at the outset of their illness.[42]

In addition to locating statistical data regarding uninsured rates, the group began to collect qualitative data through interviews with uninsured people in order to better understand the circumstances that led to individuals being uninsured and how it affected them and their families. Hector was one such case:

> Hector, age 48, is Mexican and has worked in the States for 15 years. He has a wife and four children aged 9–15. He has paid social security, taxes, and income taxes; he owns a car, and has a perfect credit history. He is, however, technically and legally, an "illegal." He has no health insurance though he is a skilled mason and regularly employed by local contractors. He has taken care of all his family's medical needs through out-of-pocket payments and visits to the emergency room. To pay for insurance would be $1200 a month. That is not possible on his salary. He recently discovered that his 15-year-old daughter has ovarian cysts, but is relying on folk remedies rather than a doctor's care because of lack of funds.

Hector's story demonstrates the personal nature of being uninsured and provides insight on at least one path to being uninsured. Other case studies from the health care SCS are presented in Box 8.3. The richness of this type of qualitative data provides important information to consider when constructing policy responses.

Critical Thinking

Critical Thinking Question

How many factors can you identify in Box 8.3 cases that contributed to being uninsured?

Table 8.4   Uninsured Citizens by State

Uninsured Citizens by State					
State	# Uninsured	% Uninsured	State	# Uninsured	% Uninsured
Total U.S. Pop.	45,657,193	15.3			
Alabama	618,913	13.6	Montana	153,006	16.4
Alaska	115,824	17.7	Nebraska	224,689	12.8
Arizona	1,237,322	19.6	Nevada	468,808	18.4
Arkansas	485,849	17.5	New Hampshire	143,754	11.0
California	6,701,890	18.5	New Jersey	1,344,323	15.6
Colorado	813,188	16.9	New Mexico	441,351	22.8
Connecticut	325,516	9.4	New York	2,590,364	13.6
Delaware	100,560	11.7	North Carolina	1,547,212	17.2
District of Columbia	60,803	10.6	North Dakota	68,412	11.2
Florida	3,738,230	20.7	Ohio	1,229,769	10.9
Georgia	1,660,156	17.7	Oklahoma	646,363	18.5
Hawaii	103,025	8.3	Oregon	648,169	17.4
Idaho	217,759	14.7	Pennsylvania	1,206,115	9.8
Illinois	1,737,876	13.7	Rhode Island	101,869	9.7
Indiana	732,256	11.6	South Carolina	696,484	16.2
Iowa	291,009	9.9	South Dakota	85,566	11.0
Kansas	340,373	12.9	Tennessee	845,728	14.1
Kentucky	604,929	14.6	Texas	5,832,884	24.9
Louisiana	848,463	20.2	Utah	391,392	15.1
Maine	118,935	9.1	Vermont	66,140	10.7
Maryland	769,007	13.8	Virginia	1,070,636	14.2
Massachusetts	498,451	7.9	Washington	741,450	11.7
Michigan	1,096,821	11.0	West Virginia	249,384	13.8
Minnesota	453,544	8.8	Wisconsin	465,762	8.5
Mississippi	572,555	19.8	Wyoming	72,811	14.2
Missouri	750,218	13.0			

Source: The Kaiser Family Foundation. Health Insurance Coverage of the Total Population, States (2006–2007), U.S. (2007). www.statehealthfacts.org/comparebar.jsp?ind=125&cat=3 (accessed July 22, 2009).

Box 8.3   Case Studies of the Uninsured from the Health Care Simulated Case Study

Gus and Ellen

Gus is a white male, 37, with a family of three. He worked for a parts manufacturing company and made $70,000 a year with full benefits. Because of a declining market and outsourcing of jobs, Gus was laid off. After his union and unemployment benefits ran out, he took three part-time jobs in desperation. He works 15 hours a week at a big box retailer; 20 hours for a fast oil-change automotive shop; and 20 hours for a fast food outlet. His total earnings are around $25,000. His wife, Ellen, has had to return to work after being at home with the kids. She earns approximately $24,000 a year as a "domestic" at a local hotel. Neither Gus nor Ellen has health care benefits, and now they have the additional expense of child care. They can "make it" as long as there are no medical needs. Preventive care has disappeared from their radar, and emergency room visits have replaced visits to the doctor's office.

Chloe and Frank

Chloe is a professional African American female, 32, with a family of three. She works for a major paper-manufacturing company as a customer service manager. She works a 40 hour week, has full benefits, and earns $60,000 a year. She is very aware that the paper industry is a shrinking one with plants closing nationwide and jobs like hers are being shipped abroad. She is training at night to get new skills in computer technology in anticipation of the possibility of losing her job. Her husband, Frank, has one year left to receive his master's in business accounting. He earns nothing except a tuition grant, but the flexibility of his degree program allows him to provide the bulk of the child care for their 5-year-old son and 3-year-old daughter. Frank has no insurance with his degree program so Chloe wants to include him and the two children on her plan. To do so, however, will cost an additional $990 per month. They are "riding" hoping that no major medical problems occur.

Alicia

Alicia is a single mother, 25, with one child, 5. She has worked hard to get off of public assistance. She completed her associate's degree in computer science and has a job offer, but it includes no insurance. She feels she has to stay on public assistance to protect her child and to medicate and monitor her own hypoglycemia. She says: "I've tried playing by the rules, but they want me to stay right where I am."

As a social work policy practitioner, research skills become essential in building factual databases upon which to build a policy response. Important research skills that policy practitioners need to be proficient in include how to:

1. Do library research to find important research articles that support and document various policy options;

2. Locate and utilize existing databases that contain data to help define the problem at hand and the successes and failures of different policies in the past;

3. Construct surveys and conduct survey research to establish local databases on the target population of concern;

4. Conduct cost/benefit analyses of viable policy options to help determine which policy option is most responsive to individuals' needs while at the same time assessing fiscal feasibility;

5. Use the Internet to locate research-data sources and position perspectives, and analyze and interpret data once they have been collected (primary data) and/or located as an existing source of data (secondary data).

The factual information the policy practitioner is able to locate or create becomes invaluable in determining the policy responses in future stages of the policymaking process.

Stage Three: Informing the Public
and Identifying Stakeholders

Once the social problem of concern has been identified and documented, and defined and supported with factual data, the policy practitioner, working in collaboration with others concerned about the problem, informs the "public" about the issue. First and foremost, it is important to define the appropriate "public" and then determine how best to inform them about the problem. The "public" will change from problem to problem and location to location. The size and make up of the "public" will depend on the nature and extent of the problem. Returning to the heath care SCS, the "public" becomes the citizens of Factoria who are affected by the problem of inaccessible health care due to the lack of coverage, and also those who may not be personally affected, but are professionally affected, such as hospitals and other health care providers. The "public" will also include anyone in the state who may become uninsured in the future. Because the costs of treating those without insurance are passed on to the rest of the Factoria citizens in the form of higher insurance premiums, doctor payments and hospital bills, the "public" then encompasses everyone in the state's population.

Key to beginning the process of informing the public is the inclusion of important stakeholders in an ongoing dialogue about how to address the problem of uninsured citizens. A stakeholder is anyone who has a "stake" in the outcome of the policy response. In the example of healthcare reform, some of the stakeholders would include professional health care providers; private, nonprofit, and government agencies who provide health care such as hospitals, clinics, and public health departments; city, county and state departments of health and human services; businesses such as pharmacies and medical equipment companies that provide prescription drugs and other medical aids to consumers; advocacy organizations for vulnerable groups such as children; human service agencies that rely on health insurance payments to remain fiscally viable; business owners who provide health care benefits; insurance companies, elected public officials such as mayors, council members, legislators, and the governor; and community members needing health care.

Informing the public and gaining their input is a crucial step in launching a policy issue campaign. Shaw surveyed 257 state officials (these included elected and nonelected individuals such as state legislators, social service agency directors, and senior advisors to governors) about the extent to which they used public input when forming new policies. The results were dramatic. Eighty-five percent of respondents indicated that informing the public and getting the public's thoughts and suggestions on policy issues was an important part of the policymaking process that they actively engaged in, and that they utilized diverse strategies for involving the public.[43] Public education can involve different strategies and venues. Bear in mind that informing the public can involve a variety of techniques and stretch over a long period of time. The extent of the information campaign to educate the public will be influenced by the seriousness of the problem, how many people are involved, the geographic area affected, and the amount of resistance a policy issue may face from citizens, stakeholders, and elected and appointed officials. Respondents in Shaw's study conducted in 2000 reported regularly using eight venues for dispersing information and gathering input about a policy concern. These included:

- Public hearings;
- Appointed study groups or task forces;
- Advocacy group contacts;

> ◗ Meetings with other state officials;
> ◗ Meetings with community leaders and groups;
> ◗ Public-initiated contacts such as phone calls or letters;
> ◗ News media; and,
> ◗ Professional conferences, journals, and newsletters.[44]

The methods of contacting the public listed above are just a few possibilities for public engagement. Using natural venues in local communities are also common vehicles for disseminating information and gathering additional input, such as churches, schools, and community centers. Consider the steps the small group of health care professionals took in the health care SCS to begin to inform the public about the issue on uninsured citizens in the state of Factoria. After the small organizing group of health care professionals gathered information about the problem, they organized a public open forum to discuss the issue, and announced the forum in the local newspaper:

> Please join us for an evening of talk and planning to try to do something to solve this health care mess that is affecting every one of us personally and professionally. We are meeting at 6:00 PM at the Greencorners Neighborhood Center (5th and Montclair) next Thursday on the 15th.

This approach was simple, straightforward, inexpensive, and likely to be seen by a large number of local citizens. The large turnout for the first policy forum indicated the effectiveness of the newspaper advertisement in disseminating the information about the public forum, and the intense interest of local citizens.

Historically, face-to-face gatherings such as town hall meetings have been the primary way in which policy organizers informed the public, but today, technology is used more and more to connect with interested citizens and stakeholders. The use of e-mails, Web sites, Web cast, and podcast has become increasingly important in getting out important public policy information. Technology also creates greater accessibility to public forums for those individuals who are not physically able to attend the public forums. Remember Tony from the health care SCS who was disabled. As a new and somewhat marginal member of the health-care reform group, but also technologically savvy, he reminded the able-bodied members of the importance of providing access by offering to institute some technological solutions in an e-mail he sent to group members:

> I wondered if you couldn't do something for somebody like me who can't attend because of our disabilities (another one of those words I choke on). how about putting a couple of web cams in the meeting room and having a web broadcast of your meetings? It wouldn't have to be tv quality, but sure could help people like me who have a strong interest in knowing all we can know and be able to participate in the meeting either by microphone or IM. I'm no tech wiz for sure, but me and a couple friends could get you set up for next to nothing. web cams are dirt cheap these days. And, btw, people "like me" have too much time. Why don't you let me set up and maintain your website/blog? I know you'll want those. They won't be beautiful like the Insurance Underwriters of America, but the content would be a bit more useful to us average Joes.

Tony was also able to set up an interactive blog where the group posted their meeting minutes, had an ongoing dialogue with citizens and members of interested organizations, creating an ongoing virtual "meeting" that continued to richly define the problem, recruit supporters, and provide direction for the policy initiative. While technology has become a way of life for many people today and has done wonders for increasing accessibility to information for people with and without disabilities alike, to rely exclusively on technology for an education campaign would be a mistake. There are many citizens who do not use technology, or do not have access to it because of cost factors. Many still rely on traditional methods of getting important information, such as the newspaper, local radio and TV. More personal approaches also reach another sector of the population. Local forums in places where people gather, such as community centers, public libraries, and churches and at popular events, such as county fairs, are important venues for bringing policy information to the public. These more intimate methods of delivery are especially important in rural areas. Knowledge about the geographic context of the educational campaign, the most-often used media outlets in specific areas, and important local, regional, and state events should inform the policy practitioners' strategies for informing the public. Initial public forums, particularly if well advertised, can generate new outlets for disseminating information about the policy effort. In the heath care SCS, a reporter picked up on the public forum announcement and attended the meeting. The resulting small article about the group in the local newspaper, *The Ledger,* was an unplanned but helpful avenue for reaching the public.

Initial public forums and ongoing blogs are two-way interactions that serve many purposes, beyond informing the public. They not only raise community awareness of the problem at hand, but can also be vehicles for gathering additional data about the problem, are useful in identifying key stakeholders in the policymaking process, and can also help identify those who might oppose the policy initiative. Such public education events are important vehicles for identifying potential collaborators and negotiating their "buy in" for the policy initiatives. They also provide an opportunity to build and extend relationships that can lead to coalition building.

Being able to work effectively as a community organizer is vital for informing the public of a social problem. Having technical expertise with computers and the Internet and being able to network with the press are also fundamental to effectively connect with the public, especially when reaching out to younger populations who have been raised on fast-paced technologies. While many social workers may possess these technical skills, sometimes other group members donate these skills or they are a purchased service. For example, most campaigns will hire a Web master, or find a stakeholder to donate funds to hire a Web master, or donate the technical services of the staff at their business or agency. For more information on the use of technology in the policymaking process, see Chapter 7, *The Media and Public Opinion in Policy Practice.*

Stage Four: Selecting Policy Options and Developing Policy Goals

In dialogue with community members, key stakeholders, and elected officials, policy options for addressing the social problem begin to emerge, and are considered and debated. Often this process can be a bit bumpy. People get involved in social problems largely because in some way they are affected by the issue, either personally or professionally. This involvement often means that individuals come to the process with preconceived ideas of what needs to be done. A good organizer will know how to create a working atmosphere where group members can share their ideas, yet not dominate the process or shut down other members who may see things differently. To complicate the process a bit more, it is not uncommon for people to come to the policymaking process with some emotional connection to the problem. Emotionally charged meetings may be energizing but can also become chaotic and nonproductive. This emotional connection was reflected in the healthcare SCS in an e-mail from Buck, a Coalition member. Following a meeting, he was left confused about what the group had determined as its primary policy goal. Buck wrote:

> Despite the agenda and good facilitating by Marta and Ravi, I'm *a bit concerned* that we had sort of a shotgun scatter of ideas and issues with no clear direction of what we're after. This is such an emotional issue for so many people, we can't waste this energy. Too many people have so little time between them and disaster. So where are we going from here? The discussion at the meeting also helped me realize something. I'm unclear if our overarching goal is to (1) Present actual healthcare alternative plans to lawmakers; or, (2) Highlight the problems and what needs to be fixed without offering a solution. This makes a huge difference in how we proceed and in whom we involve as stakeholders.

As the social problem being addressed becomes more finely tuned, and more data are gathered to add depth of understanding to the social problem, individuals, groups, and coalitions involved in the policy initiative begin to voice policy goals that they consider important to be achieved by the policy option adopted. Once policy goals are agreed upon, determination of the best policy intervention can be made. Policy goals should focus on outcomes for the target population as well as the process for achieving those goals. Policy goals must have a strong connection to the social problem. When individuals come together for advancing a policy change, they usually clarify their purpose by developing a mission statement. Policy goals should reflect the policy change organization's stated mission.

Ultimately, the Factoria Care4Care Coalition agreed upon a set of goals and presented their goals in a way that tightly connected them to the social problem (see Box 8.4). Notice how the first goal, *provide access to healthcare for all citizens,* is a broad overarching goal, and the goals that follow it are more specific and supporting of the overarching goal. Furthermore, the mission of the Care4Care Coalition was clearly reflected in the policy goals they set forth:

> *Care4Care mission:* The Care4Care Healthcare Coalition of Factoria is a group of individuals, families, businesses, community organizations, and government bodies, committed to understanding and correcting the problems of our current health care delivery. Our commitment is to every

---

Box 8.4 Factoria Care4Care Coalition Policy Goals from the Health Care Simulated Case Study

1. *Provide Access to Healthcare for All Citizens.* 15.9 percent of Americans are without health care coverage, the majority being young adults aged 18–34. Twenty percent of Factoria residents are uninsured.

2. *Make Health Coverage Portable.* Health care coverage should not be tied to a job. It should follow people from job to job as well as during periods of unemployment.

3. *Make It Easier for Small Businesses to Provide Health Care for Their Employees.* Of the more than 45–47 million Americans who are uninsured, nearly 60 percent of those are employed by small businesses.

4. *Reduce Emergency Room Visits.* Many ER visits are a result of poor preventive care and lack of access to a primary care physician due to no insurance coverage.

5. *Increase Access to Affordable Prescription Drugs.* Twenty-five percent of the elderly population has no insurance coverage for prescription drugs. In recent years, growth in prescription drug spending has outpaced that of every other category of health expenditures.

individual of every age and income level. We support no political party, no interest group, other than the common good. Our simple goal is to have medical services both preventive and palliative available and affordable to all citizens of Factoria. We seek to accomplish this by education, individual and group discourse, government and business involvement and dialogue. We will succeed when comprehensive health care is available and affordable to all.

Stage four of policymaking is also concerned with examining the various policy options available to determine which will best meet the stated policy goals. There may well be many policy options that can achieve the stated policy goals. The best policy options are grounded in the theoretical and empirical knowledge, and reflect best practices. Policy practitioners should guard against policy options that are ideologically inspired rather than empirically based, and are geared more toward political goals rather than ameliorating the social problem of concern. Policy options should also translate the policy goals into concrete services and structures; reflect the best fit with the context and the target population being served, and be achievable within the constraints of the local, state, or federal budgets. Policy options will need to be assessed in terms of (1) theoretical and empirical soundness; (2) acceptability to key players involved; (3) feasibility in terms of federal, state, and local budget demands, and state and local agency capabilities; (4) the willingness of the target population and key stakeholders to participate in the option; and (5) the amount of community support that can be garnered for the option. Ultimately, stage four should result in the selection of a policy option that is best able to achieve the policy goals set forth, and is balanced with the constraints and opportunities noted above. In the process of moving the policy initiative forward by selecting a policy option, social work policy practitioners function in the roles of both planners and cost/benefit analysts.

In the process of moving the policy initiative forward, social work policy practitioners function in the roles of both planners and cost/benefit analysts.

Stage Five: Building Public Support and Developing Coalitions

It is rare that everyone involved in a policy change effort will fully endorse the policy option selected or even agree with how the problem has been defined. In order to increase the probability of successful implementation of the intervention strategy, it is necessary to build toward consensus on the selected plan of action, including as many stakeholders as possible. Consensus building is central to creating a successful policy initiative campaign at all stages of the policymaking process, from defining the problem, to designing a public education campaign, and developing policy goals, but is most critical in selecting the policy option to be put forward and agreeing on a standard message for "selling" the plan. All stakeholders will not agree with all details and components of the plan, but reaching consensus simply means that all parties involved support the plan of action to the extent that they will not oppose it. The greater the support, the more likely the plan will be successfully implemented. It is not unusual for policy initiatives to fizzle and die when conflict intensifies within a change effort if consensus on the issue and policy response is not obtained from key stakeholders. In a number of states, for example, licensure for social workers was delayed when groups within the profession disagreed publicly on the specifics of the licensure bill that was introduced by legislators working with the state chapter of the National Association of Social Workers. Building consensus on the key elements of a policy initiative is fundamental to its success. Approaching policy change with an open and nonpartisan stance helps in the consensus building process, and also tends to maximize inclusion of stakeholders.

Stage five of the policymaking process is vital to the survival of the change effort. Building support in numbers is important, but gaining the support of key individuals and organizations who are power brokers in the policy and program arena is absolutely necessary for the survival of the policy movement. Constructing a list of key stakeholders is helpful when beginning to develop a plan of action for recruiting key players. A list of key actors will often includes client groups and client advocacy groups; formal and informal community leaders; directors and staff from social service agencies; budgetary stakeholders; members of the business community; members of the religious community, and citizen groups.

Including some people with political savvy involved in the policymaking process helps to ensure success of the change effort. Those with political experience recognize that people bring their own values, ideologies, and agendas to the policy formation process. Understanding what each person seeks to gain from supporting the action plan helps to secure his or her support. Of equal importance is the ability to assess and understand potential fears that stakeholders may harbor of losing resources or power as a result of the implementation of the policy plan. Helping people understand that their perceived short-term loss often results in greater long-term gains for themselves, their organizations, and the community is the basis for building public support.

Establishing a communication plan that keeps supporters in the loop helps to keep people energized and makes them feel that their presence and contributions are important to the success of the policymaking process, as indeed they are. During stage four of the policymaking process, communication with the public and key stakeholders is manageable because the number of people involved is limited. By stage five, the growth of the initiative is such that a well organized, far-reaching, effective, and efficient communication system is necessary. A well-managed communication system ensures that all communication mechanisms are working and up-to-the minute information is available to the entire change-effort community or coalition. Having an ill-defined and poorly managed communication system can undermine the success of a policy campaign. When interested members and key stakeholders are not consulted or responded to in a timely fashion, they can lose interest and fail to support the effort. In addition, repeated offenses such as neglecting timely communication can mark a change organization as unfocused and unorganized, which can have the effect of repelling potential supporters. The Factoria Care4Care Coalition experienced these communication challenges early in their policy campaign when the support of interested members grew faster than that the organization could keep up with. It quickly became clear how important it was to have someone managing their communications. In frustration, one of the core members of the coalition, Buck, sent an e-mail to his fellow members voicing his concerns, and urging for some reorganization that would put someone in charge of communications.

Our success and the enormity of the problems may be our undoing. I've received numerous e-mails from people who just happened to "hear" or "know" I was connected with the Care4Care Group. And I know every one of you has had the same experience. Plus, I checked with Tony, and between blog postings and mail to the address announced in the paper, we have opportunities and needs piling up. There are some people with specific political agendas, others just in dire medical/financial need, and organizations interested in working together. These people can't be left hanging out there. We need somebody to contact them, to negotiate and to coalesce this coalition. Tony has been great alerting us to the numbers and communications, but he can't follow up. We need to get somebody in charge of coalition building and liaisoning.

Failing to communicate effectively can not only cost the policy organizing effort key stakeholders and support, it can cost it significant material resources. In the heath care SCS, the representative from the state American Association of Retired People (AARP) made several attempts to join the Care4Care Coalition offering "formidable resources." When coalition members failed to respond on numerous attempts, AARP took their support and resources to a rival organizing group also interested in reforming health care.

Avenues of communication can include community forums, organizational forums, listservs and e-mail distribution lists, cells phones and phone trees, text messages, press releases, press conferences, blogs, Web sites, Web casts, podcasts, radio and TV ads, and appearances on radio and local television talk shows. With so much communication going on, staying on message and being consistent across messages is vital. Public perception of conflict within the policy campaign organization or a shift in policy goals can quickly undermine the campaign. Appointing a spokesperson (sometimes called a press secretary or chief information officer) for the policy initiative can help to minimize the risk of inconsistent or confusing messages. All messages should come from or be approved by the appointed spokesperson, who assures that the messages reflect the policy goals and policy option agreed upon by the policy coalition members.

Gauging coalition members' commitment to the policy change initiative must go beyond words. When the commitment is strong, it shows up in concrete ways. Committed members show their support by contributing to and being involved in the planning of an initiative, and campaigning on behalf of a policy change. Individuals who are actively involved in the policy change effort are those who make contributions of time, ideas and resources, and make public statements of support. They demonstrate their support in ways that can be counted on. When the majority of the stakeholders commit through substantive actions, legitimacy of the intervention strategy has been accomplished. Effective social work policy practitioners rely on a diverse set of skills for building public support and developing coalitions. Core skills include bargaining, compromise, and persuasion. The application of these skills is key to completing a number of tasks, including:

- Working toward consensus in a policy initiative group;
- Seeking to maximize every member's contributions;
- Organizing, participating, and conducting policy coalition and public meetings;
- Building support for the selected policy option;
- Cultivating leadership in the policy initiative effort; and
- Getting the issue on the public agenda as a legitimate social problem and policy option.

Stage Six: Program Design

When a policy issue campaign reaches stage six, it has garnered considerable support, and those holding the purse strings will want to know not only what the outcome of the policy change is projected to be, but they will also want to have a specific plan of how policy goals will be achieved. A program design is required to prepare for implementation of the policy, to bring it to life, and to convince key financial and administrative players that the policy option being supported is fiscally feasible and administratively practical. In stage six, the goals and objectives identified in stages four and five are translated into an action plan that describes specific elements of the program, and what will be done to prepare for implementation. Several important questions help detail the elements of a program design:

1. What is the program and its delivery structure?
2. Who will be responsible for the program?
3. Under whose auspices will it be formed?
4. What are the benefits of the program?
5. Who is eligible for the program?
6. When will the program be available?
7. When and where will the program be delivered?
8. How will the program be funded?
9. How will the program be monitored and evaluated?[45]

Box 8.5 shows a press release from the Kansas Health Policy Authority describing the state program design for a new health care program called "Kansas Healthy Choices" for low-income families. As you read the case example, notice how the press release includes information on timing, responsibility, eligibility, benefit levels, and funding mechanisms (see Table 8.5).

The press release depicted in Box 8.5 includes many critical elements of a policy design. For example, it announces a new "initiative" to expand health care for low-income families (what) to become available in January 2009 (when). The program will be delivered through employers and state health care plans (who) to low-income families earning $17,000 or less for a family of three (who is eligible). Benefits will be similar to insurance available to state employees (benefit levels), and will have a shared funding structure involving state and federal governments, employers, and individual recipients (funding). This very brief press release provides information sufficient to grasp all the program design elements of how the plan will work (see Table 8.5), but also points to more detailed information at their Web site for stakeholders wishing to understand the design in more depth.

Policy practitioners play important roles (in collaboration with other key stakeholders) in preparing and presenting policy program designs. The development of a policy design involves policy practitioners in multiple roles: planner in the creation of the design; organizer in getting key players involved in the design and in presenting the design to a broader audience; and manager in delegating tasks and overseeing the design operations.

Stage Seven: Policy Implementation

In stage seven, policy practitioners oversee the implementation of the policy and its related programs. Here, the policy design created in stage six is put into action, and services are actually delivered to the target population. In the Kansas Health

Box 8.5   Sample Program Design

Coordinating Health & Health Care for a Thriving Kansas

KHPA
   KANSAS HEALTH POLICY AUTHORITY
   For Immediate Release: Barb Langner,
   Director of Policy
   January 23, 2008 785-291-3310

***Kansas Health Policy Authority Announces the
Program Design for the "Kansas Healthy Choices"
Premium Assistance Program***

The Kansas Health Policy Authority (KHPA) announced today program design details for a new initiative to expand private health insurance to thousands of very low income uninsured Kansas families, beginning in January 2009.

For eligible low-income families (earning less than $17,000 per year for a family of three and under), the new "Kansas Healthy Choices" program will provide private health insurance coverage either through employers, where possible, or through competitively bid state-procured health plans. Program funding will be shared by individuals, participating employers, the State, and federal government. Health care benefits will be similar to those offered through the state employee health plan. Benefit levels for children and adults currently enrolled in Health Wave will not change.

There will also be a pilot program in two counties to provide low income families with a combination of a high-deductible health plan and a funded health opportunity account for families to use for health related expenses.

Once approved by the Centers for Medicare and Medicaid Services, the next steps in the implementation of Kansas Healthy Choices are to contract with three health plans to provide participants with a choice of both carrier and benefits. KHPA remains on track to meet the original implementation date of January 2009, when the first of approximately 20,000 current and 24,500 newly-eligible parents and their children will begin enrolling in this new private market alternative to a traditional Medicaid program.

Governor Sebelius included funding for the new program in the fiscal year 2009 budget proposal released last week.

KHPA is appreciative of the Governor's support and looks forward to working with the legislature to secure funding for premium assistance, as well as to address the comprehensive set of health reforms forwarded to the legislature by the KHPA Board last fall," said Executive Director Marci Nielsen.

For additional details on the Kansas Healthy Choices plan, go to www.khpa.ks.gov.

Source: KHPA Press Release. www.khpa.ks.gov/PressReleases/Kansas%20Healthy%20Choices%20Press%20Release%2001-23-08.pdf (accessed May 2, 2008).

Choices example (see Box 8.5), the policy director identified several behind-the-scene steps to be completed before service delivery could begin (see Table 8.6). The state must receive approval from the Medicaid and Medicare centers in Washington, D.C., before the first client could be issued an insurance policy and be seen by a health care provider. In order to give low-income families choices about their health coverage, the state had to contract with existing insurance companies and service providers to guarantee insurance and health care at reasonable rates for employers and individuals. State legislators had to approve the governor's spending plan for the Kansas Healthy Choices program so that costs would be covered and funding would be made available to pay providers of insurance and health care, and to subsidize employers and low-income recipients in gaining access to care.

It is common for implementation to take place in stages, especially when a new policy involves a large target population and/or geographic area such as a statewide health care program. Notice in the Kansas Health Choices example that the state planned to pilot the program in two counties before expanding it across the state. This slow roll out allowed the state agency to work out any problems with the program in the implementation process in a small, controlled area, and thus reduce the cost of implementation when adjustments had to be made. What often looks perfect on paper (policy design) is less than perfect when put into action, and adjustments are always necessary. In addition, implementation in an

Table 8.5   Kansas Health Choices Program Design Elements[1]

	Program Design Elements
What	*New initiative to expand private health insurance to thousands of very low-income uninsured Kansas families. This new private market plan is an alternative to a traditional Medicaid program.*
When	*Begins January 2009.*
Who	*Kansas state government will provided private health insurance coverage either through employers, where possible, or through competitively bid state-procured health plans.*
Who is eligible	*Low-income families earning less than $17,000 per year for a family of three and under. Approximately 20,000 current and 24,500 newly-eligible parents and their children will begin enrolling in January.*
Benefits	*Health care benefits will be similar to those offered through the state-employee health plan. Benefit levels for children and adults currently enrolled in Health Wave (Medicaid) will not change.*
Funding	*Program funding will be shared by individuals, participating employers, the state, and federal government.*
More details	www.khpa.ks.gov.

[1]*Note: KHPA Press Release.* www.khpa.ks.gov/PressReleases/Kansas%20Healthy%20Choices%20Press%20Release%2001-23-08.pdf (accessed May 2, 2008).

Table 8.6   Kansas Healthy Choices Implementation Steps

Step 1	*Request and receive approval from the Centers for Medicare and Medicaid Services.*
Step 2	*Contract with three health plans to provide participants with a choice of both carrier and benefits.*
Step 3	*Obtain legislative approval of the governor's 2009 budget proposal including the Kansas Healthy Choices initiative.*
Step 4	*Begin pilot program in two counties to provide low-income families with access to health insurance and health care.*

urban county may be quite different from implementation in a rural county. Flexibility in policy design and implementation processes is essential for creating service delivery systems that meet the needs of local residents, and that fit well with existing service delivery structures in a given area.

Normally, those who implement a policy (administrators, supervisors, and direct service workers, for example) are not the same people who designed the policy and its accompanying programs. For this reason, it is not uncommon for some of the intention of the policy and its goals to become lost in translation. Monitoring the implementation of a policy becomes vital to ensuring that implementation remains true to the intent and purposes of the policy change.

Common barriers to effective policy implementation include: (1) inadequate resources to fully support the policy, such as inadequate funding or infrastructures; (2) poor policy coordination, especially when implementation must occur across federal, state, and local levels, and geographically diverse regions; and (3) intentional sabotage of the policy implementation process, which may occur when bureaucrats responsible for implementing the policy are opposed to the policy.[46]

Program implementation can be a complex process requiring the coordination of actors and organizations in order to successfully deliver services to clients in need. Policy practitioners often act in the roles of administrators, supervisors, and direct service workers in establishing a smoothly working and accessible delivery system for clients. Optimal implementation, especially when implementing complex policies, depends on cooperation within and across agencies and governmental organizations in order to effectively put policy into practice.[47] The policy practitioners' ability to effectively use political and interactional skills in the implementation process can help to improve cooperation among service delivery personnel and organizations, and to overcome common barriers to the implementation process.[48] For more on policy implementation, see chapter 13, Evaluating Policy Implementation and Outcomes.

Stage Eight: Policy Evaluation

Policy evaluation is about determining the effectiveness of a particular policy and its related programs in achieving policy goals. Policy evaluators want to know how successfully a policy intervention has addressed the social problem it was designed to alleviate. When a policy is assessed as meeting its policy goals and ameliorating the social problem to which it was directed, it is deemed a successful policy. Realistically, most policies do not experience 100 percent success, but experience success in some areas, and small change in other areas and failure in other areas. Policy evaluations tell policymakers where to make changes in the policy in order to improve policy outcomes. In this sense then, policy evaluation leads us back to stage one of the policymaking processes of problem identification. Policy evaluators seek to know what dimensions of the social problem still linger, and where problems exist within the policy structure, implementation process, and service delivery systems that interfere with optimal effectiveness. Identifying shortfalls of a policy and its programs allows policymakers to amend existing policies either through legislation or changes in rules and regulations, in order to improve policy outcomes. For more on policy evaluation, see chapter 13, Evaluating Policy Implementation and Outcomes.

Social welfare policies can and do evolve over decades. For example, the current TANF policy is an evolution of a policy that has its origins in the Aid to Dependent Children (ADC) (Title IV) of the Social Security Act of 1935 (see Table 8.7). Prior to the Great Depression, many states had enacted programs to assist poor widows and their children to provide a resource, given the dangerous working conditions that many faced in the factories and mines of the day. In response to the growing number of poor and dependent children during the Great Depression, the federal government designed Title IV of the Social Security Act to assist poor mothers (primarily widows at the time) in raising their children. Since its creation in 1935, the ADC policy has seen many changes in response to unexpected and unintended "spillover" effects of the policy or because the policy did not meet its stated policy goals. Some of the challenges with the ADC program and its derivatives were also related to the changing nature of the "problem" of single motherhood, which can be linked to the changing roles of women and mothers in the workplace and changes in family structure related to an increase in the divorce rate and the number of unwed mothers. Initially, the family cash benefits under the ADC program were available only to families headed by single women (believed to be mothers who were widowed or abandoned). Families with a father present were deemed ineligible for assistance. By the 1950s policymakers became concerned that the "man in the house" rule was contributing to the breakup of families. An unemployed father unable to support his family made his family ineligible for assistance if he remained living with his family. Some believed this policy encouraged fathers to abandon their families in order for the wife and children to gain ADC assistance (however, empirical studies showed little impact of welfare on family structure).[49] In 1961, the "man in the house" rule was removed from the policy, and families with unemployed fathers were eligible for assistance (Aid to Dependent Children-Unemployed Parent [ADC-UP] program); but, if fathers refused work without a good cause, the family would lose eligibility. In 1962 the name of the ADC program was changed to AFDC to emphasize the family unit, and unemployed and incapacitated second parents became eligible for assistance (AFDC-UP program). And in 1968 the U.S. Supreme Court ruled that children could not be denied benefits solely because the mother lived with a man to whom she was not married (see Table 8.7).[50] The expanding eligibility for assistance from 1935 to 1968 contributed to the growing welfare caseloads and to public concern about the erosion of the work ethic among welfare families. Policy changes over the next 30 years after 1968 would shift focus from cash relief to work and training, in order to encourage workplace participation and self-sufficiency. The growing concern about welfare dependency heavily influenced policy changes that occurred with the Personal Responsibility and Work Opportunities Reconciliation Act (PRWORA) of 1996 that replaced the AFDC program with TANF. The policy intent to lower caseloads and to improve self-sufficiency among welfare families dramatically changed the structure of the welfare program. Most notably, welfare was no longer a right of entitlement, but a time-limited benefit that set more stringent work requirements for fathers and mothers.

Historically, welfare policy changes have reflected values and public beliefs about welfare recipients that were not necessarily supported by empirical studies. Today, policy evaluation is a crucial part of assessing policy outcomes and plays a much bigger role in the making of policy decisions, although it should be understood that the interpretation of research data is highly influenced by the values and ideological perspectives of the readers of the research.[51] Empirical research suggests that it seems to be human nature for people to ignore or discount research data that is contradictory to their own beliefs and values.[52]

CONCLUSION

Social workers play significant roles in the development, implementation, and evaluation of social welfare policies and programs at the local, state, and federal levels of government. Social workers weld significant power within the policymaking process to inform best practices by supporting and advocating for evidence based and rational "best policies." Social work practitioners are beholden to the clients and communities they serve and, as such, have an obligation to be involved in the shaping of social work practice through active participation in policymaking, defining policy rules and regulations, informing program designs, monitoring program implementation, and evaluating current and new programs. As direct service workers, supervisors, agency administrators, outreach workers, and community educators, social workers have extensive knowledge of program and policy needs, and opportunities for improving social programs for those in need. As advocates for the silent and marginalized groups in society, social workers bring voice to the policymaking process that would otherwise go unheard.

As advocates for the silent and marginalized groups in society, social workers bring voice to the policymaking process that would otherwise go unheard.

Table 8.7 Policy Evaluation and Policy Change

Example: ADC/AFDC/AFDC-UP/TANF

Welfare Program	Date	Provisions	Rules and Regulations	Policy Spillover Effect
Aid to Dependent Children (ADC)	1935—Title IV of the Social Security Act	Cash relief	1. State participation voluntary; 2. Federal benefit equal to 1/3 of state benefit payment; 3. Open-ended appropriations—entitlement status; 4. Child must live with parent of close relative; 5. Families with fathers residing in the home not eligible.	Encouraged family break-up
	1950	Cash relief	1. Resident parent becomes eligible for assistance; 2. State participation voluntary.	
	1950s		1. Nineteen states exclude children from eligibility if born to an unwed mother after she began receiving benefits.	
ADC-UP (unemployed parent)	1961		1. Families eligible if an unemployed father in home; 2. States can deny benefits if unemployed parent refused to accept work without a "good cause."	
Aid to Families with Dependent Children (AFDC)	1962		1. Program name changed to emphasize the family unit	
AFDC-UP	1962	Cash relief	1. Second unemployed parent eligible for cash benefits; 2. State participation voluntary.	Few states elect to offer UP option
	1962	Work and training	1. Community Work and Training (CWT) begins; 2. States can deny benefits if unemployed parent refuses to accept training assignment.	
	1962		1. Federal government allows waivers of specific parts of AFDC law to encourage state program experimentation.	
	1967		1. States required to establish paternity for all AFDC children.	
	1968	Cash relief	1. Supreme Court rules that "man-in-the-house rule" cannot be used to deny children assistance because of living with a man, unmarried. See *King v. Smith*.	
	1968	Work and training	1. Work Incentive (WIN) training program begins; 2. State required to participate in WIN program and enroll all "appropriate" AFDC recipients.	

			Caseloads double*
1960–1970			
1971	Work and training	1. AFDC parents required to register with WIN program except mothers with children under the age of six years	
1984	Cash relief; Work and training	1. States required to offer AFDC-UP program option.	
1988	Work and training	1. WIN replaced by Job Opportunities and Basic Skills Training program (JOBS); 2. All unemployed AFDC fathers must be enrolled in JOBS; 3. AFDC mothers required to be enrolled in JOBS unless have child under three years.	
1990s			Growth in caseloads; More able-bodied parents receiving benefits; Belief that AFDC-UP erodes work ethic and encourages out of wed-lock births.
1995			Forty states received waivers for experimental welfare programs.
Temporary Aid to Needy Families (TANF)	1996	Cash relief; Work and training	1. Entitlement status removed; 2. Funding changed to block grant to states; 3. Five-year limit on benefits; 4. Denial of benefits to immigrants; 5. TANF recipients required to be in the workforce within two years of receiving benefits; 6. By 2000, recipients required to work 35 hours per week; single parents with children under six years only required to work 20 hours per week.	Dramatic caseload reduction, in part attributable to the expansion of the economy and increase in low-wage jobs in the service sector.

*The growth in caseloads during this period were linked not only to expanding eligibility during the 1960s but also to the welfare rights movement of the era that encouraged the poor to apply for AFDC benefits.

Sources: Blank, S. W., and Blum, B. B. "A Brief History of Work Expectations for Welfare Mothers." *The Future of Children,* 7, no. 1 (1997), 28–38; U. S. Department of Health and Human Services (n.d.). *A Brief History of AFDC.* http://aspe.hhs.gov/hsp/AFDC/baseline/1history.pdf (accessed June 26, 2008); Lectric Law Library's stacks. *The ACLU's Most Important Supreme Court Victories* (1996). www.lectlaw.com/files/cur59.htm (accessed June 30, 2008); DiNitto, D. M. (w/Cummins, L. K.). *Social welfare: Politics and Public Policy.* Boston: Allyn & Bacon, 2005.

Log onto **MySocialWorkLab** to access a wealth of case studies, videos, and assessment. (*If you did not receive an access code to* **MySocialWorkLab** *with this text and wish to purchase access online, please visit* **www.mysocialworklab.com.**)

1. **Review the Health Care SCS.** Identify the stages of policy making that the Care4Care coalition was involved in and the roles that social workers played in the policy initiative.

2. Identify the key stakeholders in the Care4Care policy initiative and the personal and political agendas that they brought to the process.

PRACTICE TEST

The following questions will test your knowledge of the content found within this chapter. For additional assessment, including licensing-exam type questions on applying chapter content to practice, visit **MySocialWorkLab**.

1. Direct service workers are uniquely positioned for critical tasks in policy making such as:
   a. Writing proposals and legislation, and organizing advocacy groups
   b. Lobbying influential politicians and organizing grassroots campaigns
   c. Documenting recurring issues with clients, and identifying cases that indicate a general problem
   d. Organizing agencies for large advocacy campaigns and lobbying to local politicians

2. Working with others to create a plan for policy change, developing policy goals, and ascertaining strategies for policy change are primary tasks for:
   a. Community organizers
   b. Planners
   c. Direct service workers
   d. Researchers

3. A summary definition for the rational model of policy-making might be:
   a. A policymaking model that seeks to do the greatest good at the lowest cost with the least amount of unintended consequences.
   b. "The science of muddling through"
   c. A model that seeks to create the best policy possible with the resources given, and in accordance with the donors' wishes.
   d. "The ends justify the means – even if a few individuals are harmed in the process"

4. The policy model that emphasizes tinkering with current polices in order to achieve improved policy outputs and reduce costs rather than implementing sweeping changes is:
   a. Rational model
   b. Political model
   c. Incremental model
   d. Social model

5. Core skills for coalition building and garnering support include:
   a. Bargaining, small talk and threatening
   b. Persuasion, compromise and bargaining
   c. Filibustering, posturing, compromising
   d. Demanding, compromising, bargaining

6. The gap between when initial medical benefits for prescription drugs have run out, and before catastrophic coverage begins is referred to as the _____, and was eliminated by _____.
   a. Pastry gap, Stimulus Package
   b. Deductible, Jobs Benefit Bill
   c. Beneficiary bind, Reconciliation Act of 2010
   d. Doughnut hole, Health Care Reform Bill

7. An effective way to inform the public of a policy issue that has been identified is:
   a. Having a dinner party and telling friends about it
   b. Holding public forums
   c. Meeting with state officials and community leaders
   d. Facebooking your fantasy golf club

8. Critical roles in developing a policy program design include:
   a. Planner, organizer, and manager
   b. Advocate, administrator, and manager
   c. Direct service worker, organizer, and planner
   d. Organizer, advocate and administrator

9. Poor policy coordination and insufficient resources to fully support the policy are:
   a. Issues that do not affect efficient policy implementation
   b. Issues that policymakers complain about all the time
   c. Common barriers to efficient policy implementation
   d. Actions that opposing politicians take to sabotage the implementation of an unwanted policy

10. Policy evaluation is important because it:
    a. It is required by most funders of human services
    b. Elevates the social workers' role in policy practice and adds prestige to the profession.
    c. Helps in training social work students for cases they are likely to encounter in the field
    d. Assesses and identifies where problems exist in the policy structure, implementation, and delivery systems so that changes can be made to correct these short comings.

Log onto **MySocialWorkLab** once you have completed the Practice Test above to access additional study tools and assessment.

Answers

Key: 1) c, 2) b, 3) a, 4) c, 5) b, 6) d, 7) b, 8) a, 9) c, 10) d

9

Social Problem and Policy Analysis: An Ethic of Care Approach

CHAPTER OUTLINE

Introduction 210

Theoretical Analysis 211

Budget Analysis 212

Value Perspectives: Adequacy, Equity, and Equality 213
Ethic of Care Values: Collaboration, Inclusion, Interdependence

Policy Interventions: Preventive, Alleviative, and Curative Interventions 219

Social Problem Analysis 222
The Usefulness of Social Problem Analysis

Policy Analysis 228

An Ethic of Care Policy Analysis Framework 230
Elements of Care
The Framework
Application of the Model

Conclusion 239

Chapter Review 240

Practice Test 240

MySocialWorkLab 240
Housing SCS
Gay marriage SCS

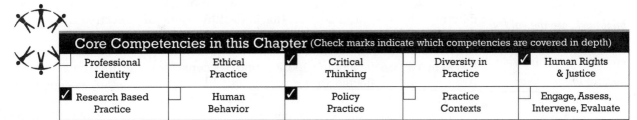

Core Competencies in this Chapter (Check marks indicate which competencies are covered in depth)				
☐ Professional Identity	☐ Ethical Practice	✓ Critical Thinking	☐ Diversity in Practice	✓ Human Rights & Justice
✓ Research Based Practice	☐ Human Behavior	✓ Policy Practice	☐ Practice Contexts	☐ Engage, Assess, Intervene, Evaluate

INTRODUCTION

Justice is itself the great standing policy of civil society; and any eminent departure from it, under any circumstances, lies under the suspicion of being no policy at all.

Edmund Burke (British Statesman),
Reflections on the Revolution in France, 1790.

Social welfare policies are public responses to social problems deemed worthy of a government investment of public dollars. This chapter explores criteria often used by policy analysts for assessing the value of a proposed or current policy, and offers a new ethic of care model for analyzing the appropriateness and effectiveness of a policy from an integrated and comprehensive perspective that considers the short- and long-term consequences of social problems and the wisdom of attending to these concerns from an inclusive point of view. While criteria for policy analysis can vary depending on the area of policy being assessed, the policy outcome being sought, and the focus of the policy analyst engaged in the analysis, being responsive to the needs of the whole (individual, family, and community) positions the social work policy practitioner and policy analyst to see the integrated web of life that affects us all, and provides an understanding that when we care well for others (from the policy development perspective) we care for ourselves as well.

Policy analysts are concerned with many policy issues, such as theoretical soundness, client provisions, client outcomes, rules of eligibility, and funding levels. Social work policy practitioners examine the theoretical consistency between the empirically supported understanding of the social problem and those affected, and the provisions and intervention provided by the policy response. Holistically, this should also include the effect of the policy not only on the client but also on the client's family, community, and any organizations with which they are associated. Establishing this connection is important to assess the validity of a policy option, and requires skills in detecting ideologies that may be driving a policy response rather than evidence-based practice and policy knowledge. Related to this is the assessment of the values that guide the policy response. Common values related to social policy responses are adequacy, equity, and equality or social justice, discussed later in this chapter. From a social work perspective the values of self-determination, inherent worth and dignity, and empowerment are important. From an ethic of care perspective the values of caring, collaboration, inclusion, and interdependence become significant, and are in harmony with the social work values of social justice, empowerment, and inherent worth and dignity.

The value analysis of a policy is important because policies can have the effect (intentionally or unintentionally) of valuing some individuals and groups over others, or limiting the roles (and therefore the potential) of some groups. These values may be apparent, for example, in policies that assign specific roles to women in society, that reflect the value of education over work, the value of business profit over services to those in need, and the worthiness of people in different income brackets, living conditions, and employment status. When assessing a policy, policy analysts consider value questions such as: Are the values reflected in the policy broad based and generally accepted by society at large, or are they derived from views held by a small segment of the country? From an ethic of care perspective, a social work policy analyst might

From an ethic of care perspective, a social work policy analyst might ask, are the values that guide this policy inclusive and comprehensive in their treatment of individuals?

ask, are the values that guide this policy inclusive and comprehensive in their treatment of individuals or do they relegate some groups to a position outside the access to care or to a position of lesser care?

Policy analysts are also concerned with the types of provisions and interventions that a policy provides and the impact of provisions on client, family, organization, and community outcomes. Policy practitioners make judgments as to the appropriateness of the level and type of policy interventions that these programs provide. Three types of interventions common in policy and program responses are preventive measures; alleviative provisions; and curative approaches to the social problem. The policy analyst may ask: Does the policy response seek to prevent a problem, alleviate suffering related to a problem, or cure a problem, or is it a mixture of all three elements? Comprehensive and inclusive policies would contain elements of all of these. Ultimately, the policy practitioner wants to know what the policy outcomes are, as they relate to client, family, organization, and community well-being and empowerment.

Finally, policies need to be gauged as to their political, economic, and administrative feasibility. Will the current political climate support the passage and implementation of the selected policy alternative? Are the necessary funds available to fully implement the policy and thus ensure greater success? Is there an appropriate and adequate administrative infrastructure for translating the policy into programs and services? An ethic of care question might be, in what ways can care be structured that provides for comprehensive and inclusive care, while reducing the cost of the policy over the long run by building capacities, integration, and interdependence?

This chapter presents a framework for analyzing social problems and the policy responses to those problems that can be used by social work students and beginning policy practitioners to gain a deeper understanding of a particular policy. Using analytical frameworks for understanding a social problem and assessing the appropriateness and effectiveness of a policy response is helpful in remaining objective in the policy and problem analysis, staying steeped in empirical knowledge and best practice wisdom, and keeping one's personal biases and ideological preferences at bay. Having said that, social workers are clear about the values they espouse, and the social work policy analyst will also critique policies for values and interventions that support the growth and empowerment of individuals, families, organizations, and communities.

THEORETICAL ANALYSIS

Theoretically, it's important to know whether the provisions of a policy are appropriately linked to the empirically grounded and theoretically accepted causes of the problem. For example, it has been established by social scientists that child abuse in children under five years of age is highly correlated with social stress, such as single parenthood, low income, social isolation, and lack of social supports.[1] Given this empirically supported knowledge, which of the following policy interventions would be the most appropriate policy provisions for mothers at risk of abuse?

- Providing financial supports
- Teaching networking skills with other young mothers to build supports
- Providing educational and child care supports to ensure future income levels that would adequately care for mother and child(ren)

- ⬧ Risk-screening in the hospital for all new mothers; Linking new at-risk mothers to community resources
- ⬧ Neighborhood parenting co-ops where new mothers are mentored by knowledgeable and experienced mothers
- ⬧ Or perhaps, providing home visits to monitor new mothers and teach new baby care

Being knowledgeable about the current theories for explaining a social problem is crucial to assessing the appropriateness or inappropriateness of provisions included in the policy. The theoretical framework of the policy reveals the extent to which policy construction was guided by empirical evidence, as opposed to myths, outdated research, or ideologies. For example, consider the prevalent myth that parents who were abused as children will grow up to be abusive parents. Rigorous research does not support this thesis. While parents who were abused as children have been shown to be at greater risk of abusing their children, in fact, two-thirds of parents who were abused as children, *do not* abuse their own children.[2]

Research Based Practice

Critical Thinking Question

Find two empirical research articles that help to explain the cause of a selected social problem.

While it is commonly believed that the environmental factors such as single parenthood, low income, social isolation, lack of social supports, and history of abuse are responsible for child abuse, and indeed empirical studies have supported these beliefs in the past, more recent studies suggest that any one of these factors alone cannot explain child abuse, and that even simply counting factors additively is not sufficient to explain the problem of child abuse today. Based on a recent qualitative study of abuse among adults who are receiving welfare relief, John Frederick and Chris Goddard argued that child abuse occurs within a complex web of factors and that understanding the interaction of factors within the child, the abuser, the family, and community more accurately explains the persistence and prevalence of child abuse. An ecological perspective that "locates and organizes multiple causal factors at individual and environmental levels,"[3] rather than only psychological traits or sociological factors better captures the complexity of child abuse. They warn against simplistic explanations for a very complex problem.[4] The evolution of knowledge about the causes of child abuse should also help policymakers consider how best to establish policies and programs to effectively prevent and treat child abuse.

BUDGET ANALYSIS

A policy practitioner may be interested in analyzing policy outputs against cost of investment, as discussed in rational policymaking in Chapter 8, and cost/benefit evaluation in Chapter 13. Budget analysis is an important part of any policy analysis. A perfectly designed policy is useless if there are insufficient funds to support its implementation. Once the decision has been made to expend dollars for a social welfare policy and its subsequent programs, important accountability questions should be considered, such as: What is the public getting for its money? How can we assess the public's return on its investment? How does the money invested in this policy support the integration of care at the family, organization, and community levels? In what ways does the money invested increase individual, family, organization, and community capacities, and thus provide a return on the initial investment in the form of social cohesiveness, interdependence, and contributions to the family and community, and to society as a whole?

A budget analyst may examine the trends in abuse cases for children under five years of age since the implementation of a policy to determine whether abuse cases have declined, stayed the same, or increased. Another approach may be to count the number of risk-screening programs that have been implemented in a geographic area and the number of home visits on average that new mothers receive and then compare changes to abuse rates or other indicators of family–child problems. Some assessments may count inputs, such as the number of home visits, or the number of family parenting coops created; while others may count policy or program outputs, such as the reduction in the number of children reportedly abused, or the severity of abuse and compare these measureable elements to conditions and programs that existed before the policy was implemented. Another important area regarding budget and policy is the adequacy of the funding appropriated for delivering the programs and services specified in the policy. For example, an analyst may conclude that the policy is implementing appropriate programs and getting good results; however, the funding level is such that the amount of services or number of caseworkers needed to address the entire target population is inadequate. From this focused analysis the analyst may conclude that policy change needs to occur only at the level of budget appropriations.

VALUE PERSPECTIVES: ADEQUACY, EQUITY, AND EQUALITY

Policy analysts are often concerned about value perspectives that policies reflect, and whether a policy responds adequately, equitably, and/or equally to the problem and the target populations affected by the problem. An ethic of care perspective will also consider the values of inclusiveness reflected in the policy and the extent to which it supports collaboration and interdependence among families, communities, and service providers (see Table 9.2 for a summary of these policy values).

Adequacy refers to meeting a set standard of need that has been established for a county, state, or country. For example, the U.S. poverty threshold for a family of four in 2008 was $21,200. This level of income was considered adequate to meet the basic needs of a family in the United States in 2008.[5] Antipoverty policies may be assessed as to the extent to which they have met a minimum standard of need. The context of a problem and the target population can (and some believe should) influence minimum standards of need. For example, the value or spending power of $21,200 is very different in Tennessee, which had the lowest cost of living in the 4th quarter of 2007 at 89 percent of the national average, and California, which had the highest cost of living during the same period at 137 percent of the national average.[6] Under federal poverty guidelines, a person living in Tennessee making $21,200 will be more "adequately" provided for than someone living in California making the same wages. But even $21,200 may not be sufficient to meet the needs of a particular family who may still need to rely on some government assistance programs (See Box 9.1 for a discussion on the adequacy of the current federal poverty line.)

One method to assess the adequacy of the federal poverty guideline policy is to calculate the cost of basic necessities for a family of four. Table 9.1 provides a guesstimate of these costs based on available data using national averages. These costs will be more if the family lives in California, and may be less if the family lives in Tennessee. A family of four living at the poverty level of $21,500

Box 9.1   "Raise Poverty Line to Reflect Economic Reality"

BY JOHN E. SCHWARZ

Newsday September 18, 2007

Senior Fellow John Schwarz *explains* why the official poverty measure fails to reflect the reality of this nation's working poor.

Raise Poverty Line to Reflect Economic Reality

John E. Schwarz is a senior fellow at Demos, a national public policy organization in Manhattan, and the author of "Freedom Reclaimed."

Last week, a group of religious leaders launched MICAH—the Mobilized Interfaith Coalition Against Hunger—a yearlong effort to address poverty on Long Island. The effort comes on the heels of the release of the nation's most recent poverty figures.

For the millions of Americans struggling to make ends meet despite news of economic growth, the Census Bureau numbers released late last month may have been encouraging. They show that the poverty rate dropped last year for the first time since President George W. Bush took office. About 36.5 million Americans were living in poverty, down 0.3 percent from the previous year.

But in Suffolk County the poverty rate rose, from 4.8 percent to 6.5 percent, while in Nassau the 5.2 percent rate remained unchanged.

And regardless of where you live, there are reasons to be worried: The official poverty measure belies the reality of working-poor Americans who don't fit neatly into the government's outdated formula.

The official poverty measure originally considered "income adequacy," especially the ability of individuals and families to afford the bottom level of the prevailing standard of living. It identified how many Americans were beneath the bottom of that scale. The first poverty figures, published four decades ago, were right on target. But since then, the measure has been updated only for inflation. It doesn't reflect the real, basic costs of the living standard we experience now.

The measure today reports how many 2007 dollars it takes to live at the 1955 poverty level, the base year for the first measurement. That year, many American families still had no private telephone or a car.

Applying the same formula as the poverty measure does, but using 2007 as the base year rather than 1955, the updated poverty line today would be $34,000 annually for a family of four—instead of the $20,000 that the official measure currently dictates.

When it was first applied, the poverty line stood at just about 50 percent of the median family income—as is currently the case for most of the world's developed nations and would be the case here, too, if the poverty measure had been updated appropriately. Instead, in the United States the official poverty threshold has fallen to barely 29 percent of the $69,000 median income for a family of four.

The implications of our nation's misleading poverty line are enormous. It drives the argument that people can pull themselves out of poverty by finding a steady job, regardless of the wage. Nationwide, two earners must earn about $10.50 per hour to attain the $34,000 in income necessary to avoid poverty. Yet, more than 40 million employed Americans—nearly 30 percent of all workers—are in jobs paying beneath that wage, many of them well beneath it. In sharp contrast, according to the outdated official poverty measurement, only 8 million workers are paid beneath a poverty wage.

The artificially low measurement diminishes the income ceiling for assistance from federal and state programs, including the earned-income tax credit, food stamps, housing assistance, Medicaid and more. It means that many steadily employed Americans facing real economic hardship get very little help—or none at all—from public programs. Such income ceilings are significant; for example, in 2006 an estimated 448,000 Long Islanders lacked health insurance.

Finally, a mistaken poverty line assists in keeping the minimum wage low—now, barely over $6 per hour nationally and $7.15 in New York State. By a valid poverty measure attuned to the household economy of 2007, pay falling beneath $10.50 per hour is a poverty wage. Not coincidentally, $10.50 per hour is the current minimum wage in our world peers, including Great Britain and the Netherlands.

Had it been adjusted simply to reflect the real rise in the base productivity of our workers over the past two decades, our own minimum wage would be well over $10 per hour today.

Of course, even that is inadequate in high cost-of-living areas like Long Island. According to the 2007 Long Island Index, two earners of a family of four would each need to make $20.78 per hour in order to meet their basic needs.

The country's poverty measure masks the true economic conditions that American workers and families face. More than 40 million Americans are earning poverty wages. Another 20 million are right on the edge. On Long Island between 1996 and 2005, real incomes for the bottom 10 percent actually dropped 1 percent, while they rose in double digits for the top 10 percent.

It's estimated that more than 300,000 Long Island workers are on the edge of, or below, a $10.50-per-hour wage. Another 500,000 workers are just on the cusp of, or below, the minimum to adequately cover the basics.

This widening income gap is a symptom of a larger problem, and we must examine the economic realities that hardworking Americans actually confront. That is the essential first step to changing those realities and making our country the nation it claims to be, one in which all workers can attain a decent and dignified living through work.

Source: Used with permission from: www.demos.org/pub1496.cfm.

Table 9.1 Low-Income Family Costs for Basic Needs

Item	Average Cost to Low Income Families
Housing	$ 645
Food	$ 705
Child Care	$ 287
Health Care	$ 147
Transportation	$ 92
Total	**$1876**

Table notes: A family of four living at the poverty level of $21,500 would have a gross monthly income of $1,792. Housing costs were calculated on 36 percent rate recommended as the top limit by mortgage lenders; however, a growing number of low-income families are spending 50 percent or more of the disposable income on housing. Food costs were based on the USDA Thrifty Food Plan—the lowest cost version—for a family of four. Nationally, low-income families spend 16 percent of their income on child care. Health care expenses were based on the average monthly of out-of-pocket expenditures for low-income families, although some reports indicate low-income families are spending 15–20 percent of their income on health care. Transportation cost are based on the average driving of 109 miles per month @ 20 miles per gallon and $4.10 per gallon; a monthly insurance cost of $50 and repair cost of $20. Notably these are low projections. This table does not include other basic needs such as, clothing, heating costs, other utilities, payroll taxes, and federal and state income taxes. Nor does it include any Earned Income Tax Credit, child care credits or vouchers, food stamps, or access to food pantries that families may be eligible for.

Sources: Galbraith, A. A., S. T. Wong, S. E. Kim, and P. W. Newacheck, "Out of Pocket Financial Burden for Low Income Families with Children: Socioeconomic Disparities and Effects of Insurance", *Health Services Research*, 40, no. 6.1 (2005): 1722–1736; Social Security Online. Social Security and Medicare tax rates. Trust Fund Data (December, 2007). www.ssa.gov/OACT/ProgData/taxRates.html (accessed May 12, 2008); Tax Foundation. U.S. Federal Individual Income Tax Rates History, 1913–2008 (January, 2008). www.taxfoundation.org/taxdata/show/151.html (accessed May 12, 2008); USDA. Official USDA food plans: Cost of Food at Home at Four Levels, US Average, August, 2007. Center for Nutrition, Policy and Promotion (September, 2007). www.cnpp.usda.gov/Publications/FoodPlans/2007/CostofFoodAug07.pdf (accessed May 12, 2008); Urban Institute. Child Care is a Major Expense for America's Working Families (2001). www.urban.org/url.cfm?ID=900031&renderforprint=1&CFID=33015803&CFTOKEN=91629257 (accessed May 12, 2008).

would have a gross monthly income of $1,792 (after withholdings). In order to avoid excessive housing expenses, experts recommend that families spend no more than 30 percent of their income on rent or house payments. However, as income goes down, percentage of housing costs goes up and many low-income families are devoting more than 50 percent of their income to housing. According to the U.S. Department of Agriculture, it would cost a family of four (with two young children) using the lowest cost food plan providing the recommended nutrition values about $705 per month to feed their family.[7] Low-income families may have access to Food Stamps and food pantries that could reduce their food costs. Nationally, low-income families spend 16 percent of their income on child care. Low-income families may also be eligible for child care vouchers or child care credits.[8] On average, low-income families spend about $147 a month for health care expenses, although some reports indicate that low-income families are spending 15–20 percent of their income on this basic need.[9] (Families can supplement health care expenses if they meet the eligibility requirements for Medicaid or the State Children Health Insurance Program [SCHIP]). Transportation cost includes car maintenance, gasoline, and car insurance, but some families may be able to cut this cost by carpooling or using public transportation if they live in areas where it is available. Most of the cost estimates in this example are modest at best and do not include other basic needs such as clothing, heating costs and other utilities, tax requirements such as payroll taxes, federal and state income taxes, and other emergency expenses. Low-income families can get some financial breaks by applying for the Earned Income Tax Credit (EITC). The U.S. General Accounting Office (GAO) reported that most (93%) low-income families with two children participate in EITC.[10]

What is evident from this preliminary analysis is that it would be virtually impossible to provide the basic needs of a family of four on an annual salary of $21,500 without the use of social welfare benefits, and other community and family supports.[11] The Wider Opportunities for Women (WOW) developed a self-sufficiency standard in 1995 that takes into consideration family composition, actual market costs of items, and the cost of living in a given geographic location (see Box 9.2).[12] Many advocacy and policy organizations are now using the sufficiency standard to more accurately assess basic needs among the poor.

Box 9.2   The Self-Sufficiency Standard

The self-sufficiency standard calculates how much money working adults need to meet their basic needs without subsidies of any kind. Unlike the federal poverty standard, the self-sufficiency standard accounts for the costs of living and working as they vary by family size and composition and by geographic location. While both the self-sufficiency standard and the official federal poverty measure assess income adequacy, the standard differs from the official poverty measure in several important ways.

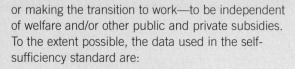

The standard defines the amount of income necessary to meet basic needs (including paying taxes) in the regular "marketplace" without public subsidies—such as public housing, Food Stamps, Medicaid or child care—or private/informal subsidies—such as free babysitting by a relative or friend, food provided by churches or local food banks, or shared housing. The standard, therefore, estimates the level of income necessary for a given family type—whether working now or making the transition to work—to be independent of welfare and/or other public and private subsidies. To the extent possible, the data used in the self-sufficiency standard are:

- collected or calculated using standardized or equivalent methodology nationwide;
- obtained from scholarly or credible sources such as the U.S. Census Bureau;
- updated annually (or as soon as updates are available); and
- geographically- and/or age-specific (where appropriate).

The standard provides important guidance for policymakers and program providers regarding how to target their education, job training, workforce development, and welfare-to-work resources. It helps individuals choose among occupations for work experience and educational training. It also shows policymakers how subsidizing child care, transportation or health care impacts the wages necessary for working families to make ends meet.

The self-sufficiency standard is relevant to a range of issues and arenas, providing crucial information about wage adequacy to help design strategies for self-sufficiency. The standard can be used in a variety of settings—from the welfare client choosing the best path out of poverty for herself and her family, to organizations weighing investment in various education and training opportunities, to state-level policymakers facing critical policy choices on tax policy, subsidies,

welfare-to-work programs, economic development plans, education, and training.

The self-sufficiency standard was created by Wider Opportunities for Women and Dr. Diana Pearce, founder of the Women and Poverty Project at WOW, and a professor at the University of Washington, School of Social Work.

The standard also offers the relevant data to provide further analysis on the modeling of work supports, wage adequacy, and local high-growth self-sufficient jobs.

Table 9.2 Value Standards for Assessing Policy Effectiveness

Policy Evaluation Criteria	Definition	Sample Policy Questions
Value Perspectives: Adequacy	A minimum standard of need is established and the provisions within a policy meet that need.	Will expanding the state Medicaid eligibility to 250 percent of the poverty line be sufficient to cover all those who want health insurance but cannot afford it?
Equity	Concerned with fairness in the distribution of resources. The allocation of benefits is differentiated based on contribution or another criteria.	Are Social Security retirement payments fairly distributed to women (as compared to men) when institutional sexism and unpaid work at home are taken into consideration?
Equality	To all an equal share; Equal opportunities and access to basic needs and rights such as housing, education, and employment; Implies equal treatment. All citizens meeting the eligibility of a policy provision have equal access to the benefit and the benefit formula is applied equally across individuals and subgroups.	Do women receive equal protection under the law from abusive spouses/ partners in rural v. metropolitan counties across the country?
Collaboration	We are more effective in pursuing a quality of life in support of each other that in separation from each other.	In what ways does the policy support those who "care about" those in need, and include them in the caring process?
Inclusion	Connotes the understanding that "we are all in this together." What touches one touches all, and has immediate and long-term consequences for each element of the human web.	What social constructions of "otherness" undermine the infusion of collaboration and interdependence? How do these constructions of "otherness" promote separation and fragmentation of the web of human life?

(Continued)

Table 9.2   Value Standards for Assessing Policy Effectiveness (Continued)

Policy Evaluation Criteria	Definition	Sample Policy Questions
Interdependence	Appreciates that we can't look "outside" of ourselves for the target population of those served. As human beings, we all are/have been/will be vulnerable.	How does the policy support the whole of care giving and care receiving for individuals, families, organizations, and communities? How does it recognize and honor the contributions of each in the process of caring? How does the interdependence of caring contribute to the quality of life for all involved?

Sources: Hugman, R. (2003). "Professional ethics in social work: Living with the legacy. "*Australian Social Work,* 56, no. 1. 5–15; Meahger, G., and N. Parton. "Modernising Social Work and the Ethics of Care." *Social Work and Society,* 2, no. 1, (2004): 10–27; Tronto, J." Care as a Basis for Radical Political Judgments. "*Hypatia,* 10, no. 2, (1995): 141–149; Tronto, J. "An Ethic of Care." *Generations,* 22, no. 3 (1998): 15–21; Tronto, J. "Care Ethics: Moving Forward." *Hypatia,* 14, no. 1 (1999): 113–119. Sevenhuijsen, S. "The Place of Care." *Feminist Theory,* 4, no. 2 (2003): 179–197. Gilbert, N., and P. Terrell. *Dimensions of Social Welfare Policy.* Boston: Allyn & Bacon, 2005; Chambers, D. E., and K. R Wedel. *Social Policy and Social Programs: A Method for the Practical Public Policy Analyst.* Boston: Allyn & Bacon, 2005.

Equity is concerned with a sense of fair treatment and getting what one deserves based on one's personal contributions. This value is most often reflected in social insurance programs such as unemployment insurance and the social security retirement program, which requires that individuals and/or employers first contribute to the program before being eligible for benefits.[13] For example, employers and employees pay payroll taxes to cover the cost of these two programs. Those with the greater investment into a social welfare program will receive the greater benefit. The more an individual pays in social security taxes because of higher income or a longer work life, the higher the retirement benefits for that individual.

Equality means that, from a distribution or resources perspective, all receive an equal share. To assure that everyone gets their basic needs met and a share of society's resources, social welfare serves as a mechanism for redistributing goods in society from those that have much to those most in need such as the aged, the sick, disabled, and marginalized. Benefits are distributed as provisions in the form of services, cash, and opportunities, which in turn equalizes the distribution of society's resources and opportunities. Social welfare programs that provide cash (such as Social Security income, TANF, unemployment benefits, and Supplemental Security Income [SSI]) and in-kind goods (such as Food Stamps, WIC, Medicare, Medicaid, and social services) provide a share of society's resources to those who have the least.

Social welfare policies that remove barriers to basic rights and needs such as housing, education and employment, provide opportunities for accessing society's resources through the marketplace. Policies such as the Fair Housing Act, the Equal Pay Act, and the Civil Rights Act are examples of policies that provide opportunities to those who have been historically discriminated against by society's mainstream institutions. Affirmative Action policies attempt to make restitution for those who have suffered discrimination in the past by providing greater opportunities in the present for education and employment. The provisions of rights and goods to those who have been denied access or who cannot access them because of barriers to full participation in mainstream society are reflective of the concept of distributive justice discussed in Chapter 5. Those most in need are provided with goods and opportunities to meet their basic needs.[14]

Equality suggests equal treatment among those using public services. All citizens meeting the eligibility of a policy provision should have equal access to the benefits and the benefit-rationing formula is applied equally across individuals and subgroups. The formulas embedded in the distribution of policy provisions provide equal or proportional benefits across target populations, representing the concept of "to each according to his need."

Critical Thinking Question

How do you see the values of adequacy, equity, and equality reflected in the current TANF policy?

Ethic of Care Values: Collaboration, Inclusion, Interdependence

The ethic of care focuses on the development of interdependence among society's members. Most social welfare policy analysis models places the target population at the center of analysis and seeks to evaluate problem resolution with a specific population. In contrast, the ethic of care perspective focuses on individuals in relation to one another as members of society, and appreciates that vulnerability is part of the human condition for everyone. For example, "I may be an independent adult right now, but I depended on care as a child so that I could reach adulthood, and I may need additional care as I age." At some level, we all are/have been/will be vulnerable. The recognition of this common denominator in life compels a position of inclusion and collaboration in the caring of each other and the creating of quality life for all when making and evaluating policies.

POLICY INTERVENTIONS: PREVENTIVE, ALLEVIATIVE, AND CURATIVE INTERVENTIONS

When assessing the value and effectiveness of social welfare policies, analysts also examine the level of intervention a policy supports in addressing the targeted social problem. Do the goals of the policy and its provisions aim at curing the problem (bring to an end a chronic and persistent problem), alleviating the problem (reduce human suffering), or preventing the problem (keeps the problem from manifesting itself in the future), or some combination of these three levels of intervention? (See Table 9.3). From a comprehensive approach, a policy that contains all of these elements is for the ideal. Preventing problems tends to be much more cost effective than alleviating a problem once it has developed and, on the face of it, it may appear to be a good investment of money. However, when large numbers of people are suffering from a widespread acute problem, such as homelessness following a natural disaster, then investing money in the immediate provision of temporary housing seems like the most humane response, in the short term. Curing a social problem will usually take a considerable investment of money and a long-term commitment, such as President George W. Bush's collaborative initiative to help end chronic homelessness. This policy goal has a commitment of $70 million in new dollars targeted toward homeless initiatives per year starting in 2005 and a target of achieving the goal of ending chronic homelessness in 10 years or by 2015, by

Table 9.3   Policy Approaches to Social Problem Resolution

Approach	Focus	Policy Example
Preventive	Aims at keeping a problem from manifesting itself in the future.	Providing public education as an entitlement and mandating education of children aged 5–16 (in most states) prevents massive illiteracy.
Curative	Concerned with ending a chronic and persistent problem	Addiction treatment policies that promote comprehensive treatment of drug and alcohol addictions including outreach, active treatment, and follow-up care are efforts to cure drug and alcohol addiction in affected populations.
Alleviative	Concerned with easing human suffering	The provisions of temporary shelter, food, health care, and counseling following the destruction of Hurricane Katrina in 2005 was intended to provide some measure of immediate relief for the hurricane victims.

Sources: Chambers, D. E., and K. R. Wedel. Social Policy and Social Programs 4th ed. Boston: Allyn & Bacon, 2005; Gilbert, N., and P. Terrell. *Dimensions of Social Welfare Policy,* 6th ed. Boston: Allyn & Bacon, 2005; Karger, H. J., and D. Stoesz. *American Social Welfare Policy: A Pluralist Approach.* Boston: Allyn & Bacon, 2006.

providing access to permanent housing and appropriate treatment to the 150,000 chronic homeless in the country (about 10% of the homeless population). (See Box 9.3 for further information.)[15] Chronic homelessness is defined by the federal government as "an unaccompanied homeless individual with a disabling condition who has either been continuously homeless for a year or more, or has had at least four episodes of homelessness in the past three years." The chronic homeless reportedly consume approximately 50 percent of the homeless resources.[16]

Ideally, social policies will reflect all three approaches, prevention, alleviation of suffering, and long-term goals for curing or eliminating the problem. The balance of investment of these three approaches will depend on the size, context, and immediate needs of the target population. HIV/AIDS is a global social problem that provides a balance of preventive, alleviative, and curative approaches to this epidemic. Funding for fighting HIV/AIDS provides public education about the disease and high risk behaviors to help in the prevention of future cases. Likewise the distribution of condoms, safe-sex education, and abstinence education are also preventive methods for limiting the spread of the disease. For individuals who already are infected with HIV, advances in medical treatment and the provision of funds through the Ryan White Act provide access to medical treatment, help to extend life, and alleviate suffering among those infected with the HIV virus. Funding is also made available to medical scientists who work to develop a cure for those infected, and a vaccine to prevent contracting the illness if one comes in contact with the deadly virus.

Understanding the nature and extent of social problems will influence analysts' assessment of policy approaches, provisions, and effectiveness. Social problem analysis is the starting point for conducting a policy analysis.

Box 9.3   Initiative Helps End Chronic Homelessness

Initiative Helps End Chronic Homelessness

BY REBECCA A. CLAY

When you're in and out of psychiatric wards, said Gayle Scarbrough, it's hard to maintain a place to live. Suffering from schizoaffective disorder and a drug addiction that only made her hallucinations more terrifying, Ms. Scarbrough slept in parks, under bridges, in shelters, anywhere she could. "My family's kind of messed up, so they couldn't provide any support," she explained. "As for friends, a person can only take so much when I'm having mental issues and drug problems. I didn't really have anywhere to go."

Then Ms. Scarbrough heard about an innovative program called Project Coming Home at Contra Costa County Health Services in nearby Martinez, CA. Project Coming Home is one of 11 sites across the Nation participating in a unique collaboration among the U. S. Department of Health and Human Services (HHS)—with participation by SAMHSA and the Health Resources and Services Administration (HRSA)—the U. S. Department of Housing and Urban Development (HUD), and the U. S. Department of Veterans Affairs (VA). Launched in 2003, the 3-year collaborative initiative to help end chronic homelessness is designed to bring a comprehensive approach to bear on the problem.

Each Federal agency is tackling a different piece of the puzzle. Within HHS, SAMHSA is funding substance abuse treatment, mental health care, and related supportive services, and HRSA is funding primary health care services. HUD is funding permanent housing. The VA is offering medical services to homeless veterans. The U.S. Interagency Council on Homelessness, which coordinates the Federal Government's response to homelessness, is helping to coordinate the $55 million effort.

"With this project, SAMHSA and its partners are providing a model at the federal level of the kind of collaborative relationship we encourage at the local level," said SAMHSA Chief of Staff Gail P. Hutchings, M.P.A. "Working together to help homeless people overcome their multiple problems is the only way to help these individuals move off the streets, into housing, and back into productive lives."

Today, the 28-year-old Ms. Scarbrough is living in a subsidized one-bedroom duplex that the program's staff found for her. She's receiving mental health services. (She has been off drugs for four years now.) A caseworker calls and visits frequently to see if she needs food, makes sure she's taking her medicine, and helps her tackle the new challenges of running a household.

A Complex Problem

According to a series of fact sheets available from SAMHSA's National Resource and Training Center on

(Continued)

Box 9.3   Initiative Helps End Chronic Homelessness (*Continued*)

Homelessness and Mental Illness, as many as 2 to 3 million Americans experience homelessness at some point each year. Most homelessness is short term. However, about 10 percent of these individuals experience chronic, long-term homelessness.

Lacking a home isn't the only problem. An estimated 20 to 25 percent of homeless people have a serious mental illness, and up to half of those with a serious mental illness also have alcohol and/or drug problems. These problems often go untreated.

Navigating the multiple systems offering services to homeless people can be difficult even for those who don't have a major disability like serious mental illness, said Project Officer Lawrence D. Rickards, Ph.D., Acting Chief of the Homeless Programs Branch of the Division of Service and Systems Improvement at SAMHSA's Center for Mental Health Services.

Some chronically homeless people with mental illnesses initially may not even want treatment. Their priorities are often more concrete—housing, food, health care. "Many of these individuals are distrustful of a system that hasn't treated them well in the past," explained Dr. Rickards. "They may have gone through institutional treatment and been treated poorly, for example. Or they may have been treated with some of the older drug regimens that had many negative side effects or just weren't effective. And often their substance abuse issues were not addressed at all."

Substance abuse also plays a major role in chronic homelessness, said Project Officer Richard E. Lopez, M.A., Ph.D., J.D., a social science analyst in the Co-Occurring and Homeless Activities Branch of the Division of State and Community Assistance in SAMHSA's Center for Substance Abuse Treatment. "When you're on drugs, just about all your focus is on finding drugs and getting high," said Dr. Lopez. "You start losing

focus about what it takes to keep an apartment or house of your own."

According to Dr. Rickards, substance abusers may also have cognitive problems as a result of their drug use and they can be difficult roommates, neighbors, or tenants. Family members, friends, and other potential sources of support often become alienated.

Many chronically homeless individuals also have physical disabilities like tuberculosis, heart disease, diabetes, or HIV. Treating such diseases in homeless populations can be especially challenging, said Dr. Rickards. These patients can have a hard time refrigerating medications, for example, or remembering to take them at the right time of day.

As a result of all these untreated conditions, as well as a range of systems barriers, chronically homeless people often land in hospital emergency departments, acute behavioral health facilities, or jails. Because services in these settings are costly, chronically homeless people consume more than half of the resources devoted to the homeless population as a whole.

To tackle this complex interplay of problems, grantees of the Collaborative Initiative to Help End Chronic Homelessness pull together community resources to address comprehensively the housing, mental health, substance abuse, and primary health care needs of the chronically homeless people they serve.

Although each of the 11 grantees takes a slightly different approach, all share a philosophy of housing people as quickly as possible, a goal of making it easy for individuals to get all the services they need, and a strategy of aggressive outreach.

Source: U.S. Substance Abuse and Mental Health Services Administration. *SAMASHA NEWS*, 13, no. 2. www.samhsa.gov/SAMHSA_NEWS/_VolumeXIII_2/index.htm (accessed August 7, 2008).

SOCIAL PROBLEM ANALYSIS

Social problem analysis is the starting point for conducting a policy analysis.

Many factors come into play before a social problem is recognized as a social problem worthy of government response. As discussed in Chapter 8, social problems get recognized as "real" problems, or ignored, based on a number of factors. Some common factors include:

- The number of people affected by the problem;
- The position those affected by the problem hold in society;
- Social and organizational pressures to respond to the problem;
- The power and status of those seeking to define the problem; and,
- The price tag of the policy remedy.

All of the above elements are heavily influenced by the values and ideological perspectives held by those in power, which, in turn, determine the relevance and significance of the problem. Empirical research can provide data that help in defining a social problem and in establishing social facts, but social facts can be interpreted in any number of ways. Interpretations of social facts are highly determined by the values and ideologies of those doing the interpretations. Values and ideology play an important part in the interpretation of social events. For example, collectively, it is agreed by most human service workers and social scientists that poverty is a social problem, and the research data based on the federal poverty guidelines have established the level of poverty in the country in the general population as well as among subgroups. While the problem of poverty has been statistically established, the interpretation of the problem and why it exists varies widely by social values, political ideologies, and economic perspectives. For example, a single mother of two small children working full time at $6.00 per hour will earn an annual income of $12,000, far below the federal poverty guidelines of $17,600 for a family of three in 2008.[17] Clearly she and her family live in poverty. No one would dispute this social fact. The meaning of this social fact can have many interpretations from a liberal structural interpretation to a conservative personal responsibility interpretation. A liberal structuralist may look to the need for a livable wage for working Americans, while a social conservative may argue that single parenthood is the problem and promote social policies that encourage the formation of two-parent families; one social problem, two interpretations, and two diverse policies. Which is right? Better yet, which social policy provides the best resolution to the problem? Both would probably provide some relief on the preventive, alleviative, and curative levels of intervention. If successful, livable wages would prevent poverty for those entering the work force; alleviate poverty for those in the workplace, and together cure the problem of poverty among the working class, just as social-security retirement income greatly reduced and nearly cured the problem of poverty among the elderly. Similarly, a successful policy that encouraged the formation of two-parent families could have a preventive function in reducing the number of single-parent families living in poverty by the fact that two parents earn more than one. It could alleviate poverty by lifting single-parent families out of poverty as a result of marriage and adding a second income to the household. Together, these effects could reduce poverty among families in general and perhaps reduce the number of single-parent families. The more immediate and far reaching policy would be raising the livable wage because this would reach all parents, regardless of marital status, and promote the values of self-determination, empowerment, and social justice. One policy is more driven by a moral standard supporting the institution of marriage, while the other is value-driven by a notion of economic justice: Working wages provide income adequate to support one's family (regardless of the family structure) and lift them out of poverty. Frequently, policymakers are not faced with "either-or" decisions about policy. They might do both, enact standards for a livable wage and develop policies that support marriage and parents remaining together with their children. Creating multiple policies to address the problem of poverty recognizes that there are, in fact, multiple causal factors that contribute to the problem of poverty, not just a single cause.

As demonstrated by the previous example, problem identification and problem analysis are the first steps toward designing a policy response, or in reassessing a problem and making policy adjustments. Policymaking is an ongoing process wherein policy provisions are provided to ameliorate a particular problem. Provisions are then implemented in the form of programs and services, and finally evaluated for impact and effectiveness. Evaluation outcomes will direct policymakers to change policy provisions based on how well the initial policy (or its latest version) has worked. Generally, policies will get tinkered with (incremental change) to keep up with the changing nature of the problem and the changing target population. Attentive, effective, and responsible policy changes are grounded in a sound policy analysis which begins with detailed problem analysis.

Social problems evolve over time, necessitating an ongoing evolution of policy responses. For example, the antecedent events and theoretical understandings of the causes of homelessness in the 1930s during the Great Depression were dramatically different from the antecedent events and theoretical understandings of the causes of homelessness that reasserted itself in the 1980s and continues today. During the Depression, homelessness was understood as a failing of the economic structures in the country—a macrostructural problem demanding policy responses that created jobs, regulated wages, and put people to work (curative and preventive approaches), while at the same time providing for immediate needs through cash relief payments, commodities distributions, and soup kitchens to feed the masses (alleviative approach). Today, homelessness is largely understood, on the one hand, as a personal failing attributed to mental illness, substance abuse, and a culture of poverty mentality; and on the other hand, many contend that a lack of affordable housing and stagnation of wages are to blame for homelessness today.[18] These identified "causes" of homelessness demand policy responses that include access to neighborhood mental health and substance abuse treatment, case management for tracking and monitoring clients; providing services within the clients' environments versus the agency setting; job rehabilitation; the construction of safe low-income housing; and the funding for housing subsidy vouchers. The differences in the causes of social problems in different historical eras demand different policy responses. Ongoing problem and policy analyses are crucial to developing and adapting current and relevant social welfare policies.

Well formed and relevant policy responses are grounded in a full understanding of the social problem it seeks to alleviate, ameliorate, remediate, or eliminate. Problem analysis develops from the general to the specific. A set of general questions to begin the inquiry might include:

- What is the nature of the problem?
- How does it first appear?
- What does it look like?
- How do I know it when I see it?
- What are the signs and symptoms of the problem?
- Who does it affect and how?
- How many does it affect?
- Are there different levels of severity of the problem?
- What are the antecedent events that lead to the problem?
- What are the consequences of these antecedent events?
- Do the antecedent events and consequences vary by target population?

Critical Thinking

Critical Thinking Question

What elements would you include in a causal chain for it?

Lack of clarity and concreteness in understanding the social problem are obstacles to determining antecedents that led to the problem under study. The empirical literature provides answers to these social problem questions and will lead to a clear and concrete understanding of the social problem.

Box 9.4   Steps in Conducting a Social Problem Analysis

Using the available empirical and theoretical literature the policy practitioner follows the following steps:

1. Identify the social problem
2. Conduct a literature search using key words
3. Collect articles, reports, and books that have been written within the past five years plus any classic materials that continue to be at the foundation of knowledge around the social issue; include both qualitative and quantitative studies so that the contextual nature of the problem is understood as well as the lived experiences of those who experience the problem
4. Define the social problem in terms of size, characteristics, symptoms, and target populations from the literature review; define the context of the problem in terms of relationship to others (family, friends, social service providers, volunteer organizations, work, community, etc.)
5. Identify antecedent events or conditions and risk factors for developing the social problem

6. Evaluate existing interventions based on evidence of effectiveness
7. Evaluate the values that are imbedded in the interventions:
   a. To what extent are the values of adequacy, equity, and equality present in current interventions?
   b. To what extent are the values of self-determination, inherent worth and dignity, empowerment, and social justice evident in the programs and interventions?
   c. How are the interventions inclusive and collaborative and how do they recognize and support interdependence?
8. Construct a causal chain, indicating logical points of policy interventions for preventions, alleviation, and cure of the social problem
9. Apply the problem analysis and causal chain to assess the appropriateness of the proposed policy change or existing policy interventions

The outcome of this literature review should produce a causal chain that indicates the causal factors that contribute to the existence of the problem, the interactions among factors, and areas where policy interventions would likely be successful. Box 9.4 outlines the necessary steps in constructing a social problem analysis and causal chain.

The Usefulness of Social Problem Analysis

Social problem analyses are used to inform new policy responses and in evaluating the goodness of fit between existing policy responses and current social problems. For example, the problem analysis will identify those most affected by the problem and those who are connected with those affected (see Box 9.5). Therefore, the target population identified in the policy should be congruent with those identified as most affected by the problem in the problem analysis. The eligibility rules of a policy should readily include those most affected with the social problem into the target population who will receive the provisions of the policy. A causal analysis is useful in linking types and levels of policy interventions, such as preventive, alleviative, and curative approaches, to particular aspect of a social problem. For example, in the case of homelessness among the mentally ill, policy interventions that prevent the recurrence of homelessness might include discharge planning from the mental health facility that coordinated community care with outpatient mental health providers; outreach efforts from the local community mental health center (CMHC); transitional housing from the hospital to low-income permanent housing; and home visits from CMHC workers to ensure the safety and stability of client living circumstances and to assess the extent to which

Box 9.5   Sample: Social Problem Analysis

Social Problem: Chronic Homelessness

Definition of the Problem "An unaccompanied home-less individual with a disabling condition who has either been continuously homeless for a year or more, or has had at least four episodes of home-lessness in the past three years.[1]

How many are affected? 150,000

How are people affected? Periods of homelessness for one year or more; or frequent episodes of home-lessness. Limited or no access to appropriate care/treatment.

Target populations: Those with disabling conditions such as mental illness; drug and alcohol addicts; physically ill and disabled, and those that care about them.

Risk factors and interactions: Disconnected from a community of care—loss of contact with health care providers; loss of contact with family and friends. Suffers from one or more debilitating conditions—chronic mental illness, disability, or drug and alcohol addiction. Disconnected from the work force—unable to work due to disability; loss of employment. Difficulty navigating a fragmented system of

care—housing eviction; loss of welfare benefits such as housing vouchers, SSI, food stamps, or TANF.

Antecedent events: Disconnected from a community of care followed by (1)Acute mental health crisis; (2) loss of sobriety; (3) loss of employment; (4) eviction; or (5) a combination of these events.

Prevalent intervention and results: Discharge planning from mental health, substance abuse, and physical health facilities; transitional housing to permanent low-income housing; case management that links clients to social welfare benefits at the federal, state, and local levels; mental health treatment; substance abuse treatment; physical health treat-ment; mental and physical rehabilitation; job train-ing; employment supports; long-term counseling, development of community-building skills, and the importance of the context of community in receiv-ing services and care.

[1]U.S. National Archives and Records Administration (January 27, 2003), "Notice of funding availability (NOFA) for the Collaborative Initiative to Help End Chronic Homelessness," *Federal Register*, 68, no. 17, 4019. http://edocket.access.gpo.gov/2003/pdf/03-1801.pdf (accessed August 7, 2008).

Comprehensive policy responses provide policy provisions that are tai-lored to the needs of the target population and those who care for and about them.

patients are maintaining their medications (See figure 9.1). From an ethic of care perspective, preventive care might also include promoting the social connections with family and friends to maximize informal observation and care of the client. This type of intervention would also support the client's inclusion into the com-munity, promote collaborative care between informal care givers and professional care givers, and provide opportunities for the client to be valued as a unique con-tributor to the community. Alleviative care could include outreach teams to iden-tify mentally ill community members who had lost their housing; and linking the homeless mentally ill back into transitioning housing to minimize the length of time homeless. Informal care from family might include providing a cell phone to the mentally ill family member so that they could be located if they dropped out of their routine contacts with family and friends; and providing temporary hous-ing until transitional or permanent housing could be arranged. Curative care of homelessness among the mentally ill might involve supervised residential group homes. Ideally, these group homes would be integrated into the local community that on some level could become an informal element that improved the quality of life for the mentally ill residents. Trips to the library, sheltered workshops, attend-ing activities at the local Young Men's Christian Association (YMCA), or exploring nature in local parks and recreation areas are community activities that would improve the quality of life for mentally ill group home residents. Comprehensive policy responses provide policy benefits, services, and provisions that are tailored to the specific needs of the target population and those who care for and about them; and, deliver services using methods that maximize accessibility to care, sup-port the integration of care, and value the uniqueness of each individual.

Ideology and values that influence the interpretation of the social problem analysis will also influence the manner in which the provisions and eligibility

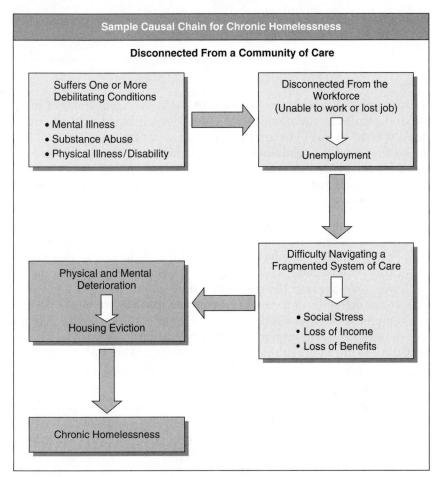

Figure 9.1
Sample Causal Chain for Chronic Homelessness

standards are determined—for example, a social problem analysis of the problem of homelessness and housing insecurity may have concluded that affordable and accessible housing is essential to effectively addressing the social problem of homelessness. As interpreters of the social problem analysis, policymakers may conclude that housing should be a "right" that all citizens are entitled to, but also conclude that housing benefits should be provided in way that does not create a disincentive to work. These values and beliefs may result in a policy that provides more low-income housing through construction of new subsidized units, but also uses a means tested method for determining eligibility for housing assistance. From an ethic of care perspective, low-income public housing should also integrate the poor into the community, be accessible via public transportation, provide a pleasing environment for growing children and families (such as the inclusion of play areas, nature parks, and public gathering spaces), be well lighted at night, and be build with quality, safe materials, and also be sensitive to environmental issues such as global warming (and energy use) and environmental pollutants. In the long run, such housing interventions would promote healthy families, encourage the building of natural social networks, promote access to transportation, and thus work and services, and save money on repairs and energy. In the low-income sustainable housing Simulated Case Study (SCS), housing authority social worker Annette argues this point in an e-mail to Erik, a local "green" developer, seeking a public housing contract, but who is hampered in his effort to secure the city contract by a local policy requiring that the "lowest bidder" get the contract:

ERIK,

I'm sure you agree with me that the lowest bidder requirement for our housing results in the creation of houses of a quality neither you nor I would want to buy. The way the system is set up now, we will build houses that meet the minimal building standards by law, but do not meet wise investment standards for the city or individuals.

As we prepare our proposal for the affordable housing, I think we need to emphasize two policy issues.

1. The lowest bidder requirement results in just that—the least expensive housing, and the least durable, never mind the least energy efficient, the least green. Isn't it time to review this policy? Surely the council is aware of the new opportunities our city faces. We can lead the way with affordable housing that is also construction-built to last and to protect the environment. We must emphasize that low bidder equals higher long term costs in maintenance and energy. Green is finally a better investment—the bidding requirements should reflect that.

2. As an investment with a calculable ROI (Return On Investment), it makes sense to consider how soon solar panels, more efficient insulation, energy friendly siding, roof overhangs for shade, and the like actually pay for themselves and add long-term benefits. We are speaking to businessmen, and I think with the right presentation we can help them see that current limitations are short-sighted, short-term savings.

Thanks, I look forward to your thoughts.
Annette

The policy response may also require work and job training participation for those using the housing benefits, and the location of the housing site should be such that these requirements are readily accessible. These policy elements reflect the values and ideologies that framed the interpretation of the social problem analysis.

POLICY ANALYSIS

Public policy analysis is a systematic process of discovering, describing, and explaining the processes and effects of government policy on social problems and those affected by them. Social welfare policy analysis examines the actions taken by governmental bodies to resolve a social problem, and the consequences of that action (both good and bad) on individuals, families, organizations, and communities. Most often analysts want to know to what extent the policy met its stated goals, to what extent has the target problem been resolved, and what values does the policy advance in society. Policy analysis is an important skill for social work policy practitioners to develop because it arms them with the ability to assess, in a systematic manner, the extent to which a current policy or a proposed policy has the potential to empower marginalized groups in society or conversely, to create obstacles to realizing their potential.

A number of social policy scholars have put forward policy analysis frameworks for understanding social welfare policies. Policy analysis frameworks vary by the elements of a policy or policymaking process they seek to examine: products, processes, outcomes, and values are common elements of focus. For example, some frameworks explore the social, economic and political theories, values and perspectives embedded in a policy, and how they impact program design, service delivery, and provisions. Neil Gilbert and Paul Terrell proposed an analysis model that looked at policy choices in the design of social welfare policies, and examined dimensions of choice for program eligibility, social provisions, service delivery mechanisms, and financing of the policy.[19] Others have been concerned with policy outcomes, or how well the policy responds to the social problem it was designed to address. Karger and Stoesz offer a policy outcome framework that incorporates an assessment of the social, economic, and political contexts of policies.[20] And Popple and Leighninger incorporated dimensions of choice and policy outcomes into their framework.[21] Still other frameworks are value directed and assess policies for the extent to which they promote a certain set of values. In their value-critical model of policy and program analysis Chambers and Wedel contend that all policy judgments are value laden; and, that being the case, suggest that policy analysts select the value criteria against which the policy will be assessed at the outset.[22] Dolgoff and Feldstein test policy outcomes for the measure of social justice delivered to those most in need.[23] Other examples of value criteria for assessing social welfare policies are: (1) traditional values of family, work, and self-sufficiency; (2) humanistic values of adequacy, equity, and equality; (3) social work values of inherent worth and dignity, empowerment, self-determination, and social justice; and (4) ethic of care values of inclusion, collaboration, integration, and interdependence. Figure 9.2 portrays these four value sets along a continuum from prescriptive to flexible values, with prescriptive values being more limiting in their applications across populations and flexile values being more inclusive. For example, the traditional values of family, work, and self-sufficiency are positive values that will work well for some in society, but do not provide a good fit for others. A lesbian couple would not fit the traditional definition of family. Therefore, policies grounded in these traditional values would exclude them from participating in the benefits that heterosexual couples enjoy, such as marriage, tax benefits, and employee health care coverage of a partner. Conversely, a policy reflective of the values of inclusion, collaboration, integration, and interdependence would recognize alternative family structures and include them in the benefits currently reserved for traditionally married couples, promote a sense of equality among all family types, and support an integration of society through acceptance of other.

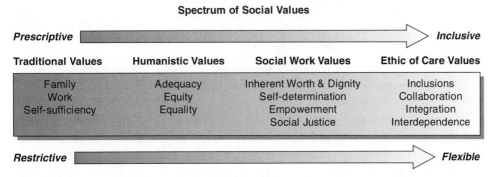

Figure 9.2
Spectrum of Social Values

It is argued that the values sets presented in Figure 9.2 represent a continuum of values from individual to collective; and from a dependence/independence paradigm tone of interdependence. While all of the values sets on the continuum hold positive possibilities for those in need, those at the left of the continuum are more prescriptive and limiting in life choices, while those at the right end of the continuum are inclusive of all the sets that preceded them and offer endless possibilities for creating a quality web of life for everyone.

AN ETHIC OF CARE POLICY ANALYSIS FRAMEWORK

The social welfare policy analysis framework offered here is intended to build on the value traditions of social work that have contributed much to the evolution of just policies over the past century and, in some way, to progress the value foundation of social work toward a more inclusive perspective of value difference in the making, designing, and implementing of social welfare policy. The ethic of care perspective compels social work policy practitioners to recognize the worth of those who bring value sets to the policymaking process that appear contrary to social work values. In doing so, the profession becomes more philosophically, ideologically, and principally inclusive of others involved in the business of policymaking, more willing to collaborate with those who think and see the world differently, and more likely to create policies that are responsive to a continuum of value perspectives rather than in opposition to some. From this standpoint, the social construction of "other" dissolves and political opponents become colleagues and collaborators in securing a higher quality of life for all.

The ethic of care policy analysis framework builds on the ethic of care work of Sevenhuijsen,[24] Tronto,[25] Meagher & Parton,[26] Hugman,[27] and Fisher.[28] Fisher and Tronto defined care as "a species activity that includes everything that we do to maintain, continue, and repair our "world" so that we can live in it as well as possible. That world includes our bodies, our selves, and our environment, all of which we seek to interweave in a complex, life-sustaining web."[29] Society as an interwoven web implies that what touches one touches all, and has immediate and long-term consequences for each element of the human web. Policy analysis working from an ethic of care perspective considers: (1) the impact of policies on target populations and those touched by them, and (2) the number of generations impacted, including individuals, families, communities (both those in need and those who care for them) and (3) the surrounding environment. The framework takes an inclusive perspective, rather than a marginalized v. mainstream approach currently held by most policy analysis frameworks.

The ethic of care reflects the moral judgment that all have equal worth and are worthy of care.[30] As such, the ethic of care policy analysis framework is grounded in the following assumptions:

1. All humans are dependent on others; therefore, interdependence and a responsibility for each other should be reflected in the policies and programs created;

2. Care in the form of policies and programs should attend to others with compassion, and respond to each person as unique and irreplaceable, and as essential components of the human fabric;

3. Social welfare policies and programs should foster the growth of participants and create caring relationships between participants and caregivers/social welfare personnel;

Table 9.4 Comparison of Policy Analysis Language Traditional Language v. Ethic of Care Language

Traditional Frameworks	Ethic of Care Framework
Problem identification	Attentiveness
Auspices of policy oversight	Responsibility for caring
Evaluation of quality of policy outcomes	Competence in care giving
Evaluation of access to services	Responsiveness of care givers
Care fragmented across agencies and professions	Seeks an integration of care
Agency, provider, case manager, counselor	Care giver
Client, patient, resident	Care receiver
Dependence/independence	Interdependence

Sources: Hugman, R. "Professional Ethics in Social Work: Living with the Legacy." *Australian Social Work,* 56, no. 1 (2003): 5–15. Tronto, J. "Care As a Basis for Radical Political Judgments." *Hypatia,* 10, no. 2 (1995): 141–149. Meahger, G. and N. Parton. "Modernising social work and the ethics of care." *Social Work and Society,* 2, no. 1, (2004): 10–27. Tronto, J. "Care ethics: Moving forward." *Hypatia,* 14, no. 1, (1999): 113–119; Sevenhuijsen, S. A Place of Care: The Relevance of the Feminist Ethic of Care for Social Policy. *Feminist Theory,* 4, no. 2 (2003), 179–197.

4. Analysis should consider how class, gender, ability, race, and other measures of "difference" intersect and influence how programs are delivered and how benefits are received by participants;

5. Policy and program flexibility is an essential component for their application across cultures and settings;

6. Both subjective and objective evaluations of policies and programs are needed to determine not only the outcomes but also how participants and those providing services experienced the delivery system as a care giver, and as a care receiver.[31]

The ethic of care approach places the process of caring at the center of the construction, implementation, and assessment of policy.

The ethic of care policy analysis framework is concerned with elements of care, and attempts to redefine policy analysis from a purely rational and technical exercise, to one that takes into account the nature of relationships between and among those receiving care and those providing care, the context of service delivery, and the overall impact of the quality of life for all.[32]

As discussed earlier in this chapter, elements of policy analysis have traditionally focused on performance, process, outcome, and values. While these components are important to any policy analysis, the ethic of care approach places the process of caring at the center of the construction, implementation, and assessment policy. Placing caring at the center of analysis transforms the language commonly used in policy analysis and encompasses the relational aspects of care as it is captured in program designs, service delivery systems, and interpersonal relationships between those being served (care receivers) and those providing services (care givers). Table 9.4 contrasts the traditional policy analysis language with ethic of care language.

Elements of Care

Attentiveness

From an ethic of care perspective, policy in relation to the social problem is understood not only as a response to fill an unmet social need, but also something that includes an element of environmental scanning as a part of the stewardship process that attends to the vulnerable population. The environmental scan attends to not only the target population, but also to those who care for them, the communities they live in, and the impact of the unmet needs on the human web of life. For example, a policy that targets inner-city juvenile delinquents would attend not only to the behavior and needs of the youth, but also the needs of the family and community, and consider the impact of the problem on juvenile delinquency on younger generations in the vicinity and for how many generations to come? What is the effect on the crime rate and economic cost; the loss of human capital because youth do not meet their potential; and separation of communities by levels of need rather than integration of communities through caring. Attentiveness considers: Who is in need of care? What basic care is required to meet their needs? How comprehensive is the need response? Does the need response consider the physical needs, emotional needs, psychological needs, and political needs of individuals, families, and communities?[33]

Responsibility

Under traditional analysis frameworks responsibility of care is assigned to a government agency that is deemed most appropriate for implementing a particular policy. For example, the responsibility for meeting the educational needs of children falls under the auspices of the Department of Education at the federal and state levels. In the ethic of care approach, the responsibility for care is inclusive of family, friends, community, and government agencies. Responsibility for care considers: Who determines who is responsible for providing care to those in need? And what is the balance of responsibility and the appropriateness of the distribution of responsibility across those connected to the ones in need of care. Who is overly responsible? Who is left out of the responsibility of care that could, and ethically should, be included?[34] For example, historically, the education system has had primary responsibility for providing for the education needs of our children, and has exerted power over parents in a number of areas of care connected to, or that influences, children's ability to learn in the traditional school setting. School attendance is mandatory, court judgments have been sought by schools to medicate unruly children, and changing parenting standards at time infringes on culturally based parenting practices. All of these regulations and actions suggest that government had taken on an unbalanced responsibility for caring for the nation's children. In recent years, the power balance has begun to shift with more parents choosing to home school their children, and the government providing policies that legitimize home school education. Flexible social policies encourage inclusiveness of care givers and enhances the collaboration of care givers.[35]

Competence

Competence is regarded as the ability of caregivers, both informal and formal, to provide appropriate and quality care to those in need, and to provide it in a manner that those in need are able and willing to receive. Competence includes professional skills in physical caring, psychological caring, and emotional caring, as well as competence in advocating for care receivers who are unable to make their own voices heard. Competence also attends to the ability of care givers (both individual care givers and organizations as care givers) to "be" with the care receivers. Competent care givers are able to recognize conflicts between care givers and care receivers that may arise, and move quickly to identify the conflict, and garner the resources to resolve the conflict in a process that demonstrates acceptance and inclusion rather than fault and blame. Competence is supported by care giving organizations through the provision of appropriate and adequate resources to family members, friends, and professionals providing the direct service and care.

Resources that match the need and the context of care are more likely to produce caring that can be readily received (physically, emotionally, and culturally) by those being cared for. Competence is measured by not only the standards set by best practices of professions and agencies, and by legal standards, but also assessed against community and family standards that may reflect unique geographic and cultural ways of caring. Competent care giving is flexible and fluid, and attuned to the changing needs of those in care. An ethic of care avoids static care goals that do not account for the dynamic nature of life.[36]

Responsiveness

Responsiveness gives more agency to the receiver of care or program benefits than does the traditional policy evaluation process. Responsiveness considers: How do care receivers respond to the care that they are given physically, emotionally, psychologically, and culturally? How well does the care process match the needs of the care receiver in terms of unique preferences, for example privacy, social interaction, the need to feel valued as opposed to a burden, the need to be cared for in a manner that acknowledges and respects cultural identity and customs? Care giving should also make room for the inclusion of valued people in lives of those being cared for. Other concerns of responsiveness include: If needs of the care receiver conflict with one another, how readily is it recognized, and how quickly is it resolved and by whom? Are the methods of conflict resolution inclusive of the care receivers' preferences or are the methods imposed by the care givers?[37]

Integration of Care

Integrated, seamless care is experienced by care receivers as complete, dependable, and predictable. There is confidence that if the needs for care change, the integrated system of care givers (from individuals to agencies) will respond in a manner that reflect the worth and value of the care receiver, and recognizes their uniqueness in the human web of life. Integrated systems of care work together to promote individual, family, and community empowerment, and are aware that care receivers are also care givers to others in their environment. Integration of care acknowledges the cycles of care giving and care receiving that naturally occur across the life span and accepts and values both roles on personal, agency, and community levels. Integrated care allows for and explores variations in ways of caring that engage cultural practices of care giving, and resist static prescriptive ways of caring that may not be responsive to the needs of care receivers. Care givers in integrated systems embrace the opportunity to collaborate with other care givers, appreciate the expertise and experiences they bring to the care giving process, and resist the old practices of protecting professional "turf"; thus, the deconstruction of "otherness" allows for the infusion of collective caring, collaboration, inclusion, and the development of interdependence in a caring society.[38]

The Framework

In this first effort to create an ethic of care policy analysis framework for assessing social welfare policies and how well they care for those in need (which is all of us at some point), including our communities, our institutions, and our environment, we have posed a series of questions to be pondered at when exploring a policy's imprint across these domains of caring. Policy imprints can be positive or negative and last for a brief time or across generations. It is hoped that positive imprints on society will carry forward for many generations while negative imprints are quickly attended to and leave no noticeable trace beyond the here and now. Table 9.5 suggests ways to consider the attentiveness, responsibility,

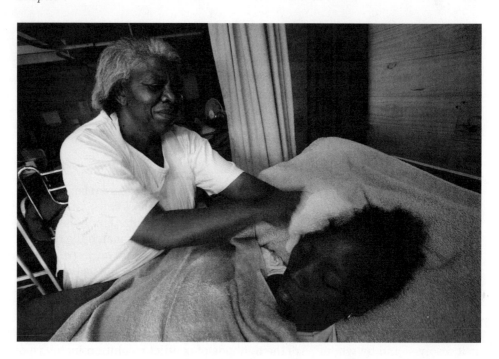

Table 9.5   Ethic of Care Policy Analysis Framework

Areas of Caring to Assess	Questions to Consider

Attentiveness	1. Who is in need of care?
	2. What basic care is required to meet the need of those in need? Consider the
	   a. physical needs,
	   b. emotional needs,
	   c. psychological needs,
	   d. economic needs, and
	   e. political needs.
	3. What maximal care is desired for those in need of care? Consider the
	   a. physical needs,
	   b. emotional needs,
	   c. psychological needs,
	   d. economic needs, and
	   e. political needs.
	4. How attentive is the policy to the needs of those in need of care in terms of
	   a. access to care,
	   b. affordability of care, and
	   c. goodness of fit of care provided with care needed?

Responsibility	1. Who is responsible for providing care to those in need? This should be inclusive of family, community, and government responsibilities. What is the balance of responsibility and is it appropriate? Who is overly responsible? Who is left out of the responsibility of care that could and ethically should be included? 2. Who determines who is responsible for providing care to those in need? Who else should be involved in determining who should provide care?

Table 9.5   (Continued)

Areas of Caring to Assess	Questions to Consider
	3. What are the power relations between those in need of care and those providing care (individual to organizational)?
	4. What forms of power and privilege reside in the caring process? How do they shape the nature and adequacy of care?
	5. In what ways does the policy encourage and enhance the collaboration of care across the responsible units?
Competence	1. How competent are those responsible for providing care (individuals to administration; lay care givers to professional practitioners, agencies, and organizations) in meeting the basic care needs of those in need of care, in terms of best practices and cultural competence?
	2. Who actually provides the care, and how competent are the informal and formal systems of care in meeting the physically, emotionally, psychologically, and politically needs of those in need of care? How well do they meet the standards of care of the family, the community, the agency, and legal standards?
	3. Are there resources that caregivers need to more competently do their work that is currently not provided by the policy? What are they?
	4. Who attends to the changing needs of those in need of care?
	5. What conflicts, if any, exist between the care givers and the care receivers?
Responsiveness	1. How responsive are the care givers (individual, family, community, agency, and organization) to the needs of the care receiver (physically, emotionally, psychologically, and politically)?
	2. How do those in need respond to the care that is given (by individuals, family, community, agencies, and organizations)?
	3. What is the proximity of care giver and care receiver, and how does this support or disrupt the integration of comprehensive care?
	4. Are caregivers (individual, family, community, agency, and organization) more responsive to some in need than others? Who is left out or marginalized?
	5. What are the consequences of low responsiveness or unresponsiveness to the needs of those in need of care in terms of access to care and quality of care for the care receiver? The family? The community? Who suffers and in what ways?
Integration of Care	1. In what ways does the policy allow for the integration of cultural practices of care giving?
	2. How does the policy reflect the values of self-determination; inherent worth and dignity, and empowerment?
	3. How empowering is the policy for the care receivers? For the care providers? For institutions responsible for regulating and monitoring care?
	4. How does this policy reflect the values of caring, collaboration, inclusion, and interdependence? What social constructions of "otherness" undermine the infusion of these values?
	5. In what ways does the policy support those who "care about" those in need, and include them in the caring process?

(Continued)

Table 9.5   Ethic of Care Policy Analysis Framework (Continued)

Areas of Caring to Assess	Questions to Consider
	6. What challenges to comprehensive and integrated care does the policy present? What gaps in care remain?
	7. What ethical issues does this policy raise in the delivery of care, and in the maintaining or creation of care disparities?

Sources: Hugman, R. "Professional Ethics in Social Work: Living with the Legacy." *Australian Social Work,* 56, no. 1 (2003): 5–15; Meahger, G. and N. Parton. "Modernising Social Work and the Ethics of Care." *Social Work and Society,* 2, no. 1 (2004): 10–27; Tronto, J. Care as a Basis for Radical Political Judgments. *Hypatia,* 10, no. 2 (1995): 141–149; Tronto, J. "An Ethic of Care." *Generations,* 22, no. 3 (1998): 15–21; Tronto, J. "Care Ethics: Moving Forward." *Hypatia,* 14, no. 1 (1999): 113–119. Sevenhuijsen. S. "The Place of Care." *Feminist Theory,* 4, no. 2 (2003): 179–197; A Place of Care: The Relevance of the Feminist Ethic of Care for Social Policy. *Feminist Theory,* 4, no. 2, 179–197.

---

competence, and responsiveness of social welfare policies, and to assess their potential for integrated care and fostering interdependence. Ultimately, the model makes the following inquiry: Does the policy elevate the role of caring in society across private and public spheres and deconstruct the old notions about who provides care and the value of caring? This is a working model and we are hopeful that others will join us in evolving it so that it reflects the values and intentions of the caring professions.

Application of the Model

The low-income sustainable housing Simulated Case Study (SCS) that accompanies this book (located on the Allyn & Bacon *My Social Work Lab* Web site) provides an opportunity for applying the ethic of care model of policy analysis. As you recall from the social problem analysis section of this chapter the housing authority social worker, Annette, and her collaborator, "green" housing developer Erik, faced a policy obstacle to getting the funding and city approval for developing environmentally friendly and energy-efficient low-income housing. City policy required that the lowest bidder on the low-income housing project receive the building contract (see Box 9.6). Erik and Annette needed to make the case to local policymakers (mayor and city council) that a policy that mandated the lowest bidder rule is ineffective in improving the quality of life for those most in need, and the community as a whole; and in the long run is more costly than the "green" alternative. Using the ethic of care model to assess the "lowest bidder" policy and to assess a proposed new policy of removing the restriction of the lowest bidder rule, Annette and Erik could explore the long-term benefits of a low-income sustainable and energy-efficient housing development. Such an attentive, responsible, competent, and responsive policy was only possible outside the restriction of the low-bidder policy rule. Table 9.6 provides an analysis of the "lowest bidder policy" and arguments from an ethic of care perspective that the "lowest bidder policy" undermined the quality of life for the community as a whole, the city's budget, and for the health and well-being of the low-income residents in need of quality housing.

In the low-income sustainable housing SCS, Annette and Erik were successful in getting the "lowest bidder rule" removed from the city ordinances by using the ethic of care approach in their analysis of the policy and their presentation to city leaders. This opened the door for Erik to secure the public

Box 9.6   Sustainable Low Income Housing SCS

Email from Annette to Erik

ERIK,

I'm sure you agree with me that the lowest bidder requirement for our housing results in the creation of houses of a quality neither you nor I would want to buy. The way the system is set up now, we will build houses that meet the minimal building standards by law, but do not meet wise investment standards for the city or individuals.

As we prepare our proposal for the affordable housing, I think we need to emphasize two policy issues.

1. The lowest bidder requirement results in just that—the least expensive housing, and the least durable, never mind the least energy efficient, the least green. Isn't it time to review this policy? Surely the council is aware of the new opportunities our city faces. We can lead the way with affordable housing that is also construction built to last and to protect the environment. We must emphasize that low bidder equals higher long term costs in maintenance and energy. Green is finally a better investment— the bidding requirements should reflect that.

2. As an investment with a calculable ROI (Return On Investment), it makes sense to consider how soon solar panels, more efficient insulation, energy friendly siding, roof overhangs for shade and the like actually pay for themselves and add long-term benefits. We are speaking to businessmen, and I think with the right presentation we can help them see that current limitations are short-sighted, short-term savings.

Thanks, I look forward to your thoughts.
Annette

Table 9.6   Ethic of Care Policy Analysis for Rescinding the "Lowest Bidder" Rule' for Low-Income Housing Developers

Element of Care	Policy Analysis
Attentiveness	Attentive housing policies recognize the value for the vulnerable as well as the community when they attend to the physical, psychological, and development needs of low-income residents with quality, well-situated housing. Such policies consider the health of the residents which can be compromised with low-cost pollutant-treated building material, or building on polluted land; the psychological effects of restricting the poor to designated areas in poor quality housing; and the developmental losses that occur when the most vulnerable are marginalized rather than integrated into communities of diverse families, incomes, experiences, and cultures. Housing policies that attend to these dimensions of care improve the quality of life for the whole community and reduce city spending for frequent repairs and housing replacements, subsidize health care for the poor, increased crime, and lost human potential. The imposition of the lowest bidder rule precludes the city from adequately attending to the needs of the community as a whole, and to the needs of the most vulnerable, specifically.
Responsibility	A responsible housing policy will consider the well-being of its low-income residents and the health of the city's budget over the long run. While "green" housing may require more cost up front, in the long run it provides more quality product dollar for dollar and saves money and improves quality of life. Low-income residents who live in quality housing are more likely to: ▶ feel a sense of pride in their home and to care for it; ▶ feel valued as community members, and as a consequence respond to opportunities for community participation and be more integrated into the fabric of the community; and ▶ achieve a sense of belonging in their community and be protective of it. *(Continued)*

Table 9.6   Ethic of Care Policy Analysis for Rescinding the "Lowest Bidder" Rule' for Low-Income Housing Developers (Continued)

Element of Care	Policy Analysis
	Low-income residents who feel a sense of inclusion in the community are less likely to be involved in criminal and destructive activities, and more likely to be involved in activities that promote self growth, such as finishing high school, engaging in job training, and taking advantage of employment and learning opportunities. Responsible housing policies provide for the physical, psychological, and development needs of low-income residents which in turn provides for the community's quality of life, and reduces city spending for preventable consequences. The lowest-bidder rule interferes with the city leaders' abilities to provide care for the community in a responsible manner.
Competence	Competent builders of publicly funded housing have a demonstrated record of building quality, environmental friendly housing that maximized on renewable energy, and reduces the need for costly public resource expenditures. Competent low-income housing developers provide quality, safe, and energy efficient housing that reduces the need for frequent repairs due to poor workmanship and low-quality material in construction of housing; circumvents high utility bills for low-income residents (which are subsidized with public funds) through the use of passive renewable energy such as solar panels; and reduces the need for publicly funded medical care for low-income residents who suffer from living in poor quality housing. The lowest-bidder rule eliminates the most competent housing developers in the competitive bidding process by attending to initial cost of construction only, and ignoring the long-term cost of construction, repair, and care of residents, community and the environment.
Responsiveness	Responsive policy makers, who are the care givers to the community, consider the comprehensive needs of the most vulnerable in their community and recognize that preventing insults to the most vulnerable, in the long run prevents insults to the community as a whole. Low-income residents in need of housing are valued for their potential contributions and care giving to the community now and in the future, and as such, responsive policy makers move quickly to adjust policies that will reduce human loss (psychological, health, developmental, economic), and maximize future contributions to the community. Responsive community caregivers recognize the consequences of low responsiveness or unresponsiveness to the needs of low-income residents in terms of housing costs, social costs, economic cost, and cost to quality of life to the community as a whole. The lowest bidder rule relegate the city policy makers to low responsive care givers, which has short and long-term consequences for the low-income residents and the community as a whole.
Integration of care	The removal of the lowest bidder rule opens the way for providing quality low-income sustainable eco-friendly housing that supports growth and health of the community through the integration of low-income residents into the community. Integration of all community members benefits all emotionally, psychologically, physically, economically, and politically.

housing development contract, and to ultimately build the high-quality sustainable housing development, Sunstar Terrace, for the city and its low-income residents. In time the city will evaluate the ability of the sustainable low-income housing project to provide well for low income residents, to promote community integration, and to reduce city expenditures on long-term maintenance and other public costs often related to low-income public housing units and their residents. In analyzing the housing project's imprint on the life of the residents, the community, and the city budgets, the social work housing

Box 9.7	Housing Policy Analysis Questions for SCS

1. How attentive is the policy to the needs of the low-income citizens at Sunstar Terrace? Is housing accessible, affordable, and appropriate?

2. Who is responsible for ensuring that housing is available to those most in need of safe affordable housing? In what ways do they meet this responsibility? In what ways do they fall short?

3. How competent is the system that is responsible for the delivery of safe housing on all levels (individual staff to administration).

4. How responsive is the housing authority and city government to those in need of safe, affordable housing? Is the system more responsive to some than others? Who gets left out?

5. What are the consequences of the current housing policy in terms of quality and access to housing? Who suffers and in what ways?

6. How well does the policy reflect community values of caring, inclusion, collaboration, and collectivity?

7. What are the power relations between those in need of housing and those providing housing (both the institutions and its individual members)? How empowering is the policy for low-income citizens? For housing providers? For institutions involved in the regulation and monitoring of housing policy?

8. To what extent does the current housing policy and practices support the provision of comprehensive housing (safety, affordability, location of inclusion, quality, etc)? To what extent does it fragment and/or exclude the low-income members of the community?

9. What challenges to safe, affordable housing or gaps in housing access does this policy present?

authority policy practitioner, Annette, may want to consider the policy analysis questions in Box 9.7. As you read through the policy analysis questions, can you think of other ethic of care policy analysis questions that would assess the attentiveness, responsibility, competence, and responsiveness of the project to the low-income residents and the community as a whole? In what ways might integration of care and integration of low-income residents into the community be assessed?

Human Rights & Justice

Critical Thinking Question

What analysis questions would reflect the inclusive ethic of care perspective for a single parent in need of/or using food stamps?

CONCLUSION

Social workers are uniquely prepared and positioned to examine policies and assess the extent to which policies reflect an accurate understanding of the social problem they address and the values of those affected by the policies. Social workers' ecological training, practice experience, and practice wisdom provide a sound value base consistent with the ethic of care framework for evaluating the appropriateness of the policy provisions and their responsiveness to those in need of care. Training in diversity and work with diverse populations endows social workers with multiple cultural lenses for understanding the importance of culturally responsive care. In addition, social works are prepared to assess the organizational structures and processes of care for their attentiveness to those in needs and their willingness to balance the roles of care giving across formal and informal care givers at the individual, family, and community levels of care. In providing responsible, competent, and integrated systems of care, social workers support the inherent worth and dignity of those in need and those who care about them, and encourages their empowerment. Ultimately, integrated systems of care invite those on the fringes to fully embrace the web of life.

Log onto **MySocialWorkLab** to access a wealth of case studies, videos, and assessment. (*If you did not receive an access code to* **MySocialWorkLab** *with this text and wish to purchase access online, please visit* **www. mysocialworklab.com.**)

1. **Review the Housing SCS.** Answer the ethic of care policy analysis questions in box 9.7 in the text on page 256. What ethic of care values are reflected in the housing policies adopted by Shoreacres and for SunTerrace in the SCS?

2. **Review the Gay Marriage SCS.** Develop a set of ethic of care policy analysis questions to assess the extent to which this policy reflects the ethic of care values of inclusion, collaboration, integration, and interdependence.

PRACTICE TEST
The following questions will test your knowledge of the content found within this chapter. For additional assessment, including licensing-exam type questions on applying chapter content to practice, visit **MySocialWorkLab**.

1. When analyzing the provisions of a policy, one must look at the theoretical framework in order to decipher:
   a. If there is an adequate amount of staff allocated in the policy
   b. If the target population will be sufficiently served
   c. The extent to which the framework is based on empirical data, versus myths, ideologies, or outdated research
   d. The amount of certified social workers to implement the policy

2. Meeting a set standard of need as established by a county, state, or country is referred to as:
   a. Adequacy
   b. Welfare
   c. Equity
   d. Charity

3. Paying into social security old age fund while working and then receiving social security checks after retirement age is an example of:
   a. Adequacy
   b. Investment
   c. Equity
   d. Equality

4. The calculation or standard used to measure how much income working adults need to meet basic needs, accounting for family size, geographic location, and costs of living is:
   a. The federal poverty standard
   b. The self-sufficiency standard
   c. The government standard
   d. The Standard and Poor measure

5. The element of care that resists the old practice of protecting professional "turf" and focuses on inclusion, collaboration and interdependence is referred to as:
   a. Integration of care
   b. Responsiveness
   c. Prescriptiveness
   d. Curativeness

6. The three approaches social problems that an ideal social policy would include are:
   a. Preventative, alleviative, and curative
   b. Pre-emptive, reactive and inclusive
   c. Reactive, inclusive and curative
   d. Alleviative, Interdependence, curative

7. The first two steps in designing a policy response are:
   a. Problem identification and policy analysis
   b. Policy identification and problem analysis
   c. Problem identification and problem analysis
   d. Policy identification and policy analysis

8. The type of values that focus on including the largest number of populations and the least number of limitations in policy responses is:
   a. Prescriptive values
   b. Flexible values
   c. Collective values
   d. Inclusive values

9. Within the ethic of care framework, the ability of caregivers to provide appropriate, quality care in a way that the person receiving care is willing and able to accept is referred to as:
   a. Attentiveness
   b. Responsiveness
   c. Integration of care
   d. Competence

10. According to the federal government's definition, a person is considered chronically homeless if:
    a. The person does not have a fixed mailing address
    b. The person with a disabling condition that has been continuously homeless for at least six months
    c. The person has moved twice in the space of one year
    d. The person has a disabling condition and has been continuously homeless for one year or more or has had at least four episodes of homelessness in three years.

Log onto **MySocialWorkLab** once you have completed the Practice Test above to access additional study tools and assessment.

Answers

Key: 1) c, 2) a, 3) c, 4) b, 5) a, 6) a, 7) c, 8) b, 9) d, 10) d

10

The Legislative Process, Interest Groups, and Lobbying

CHAPTER OUTLINE

Introduction 242

The Legislative Process 243
Advocacy Roles in the Legislative Process

Defining Interest Groups 256
Theoretical Approaches to Understanding Interest
    Groups
The Recent Growth of Interest Groups
Sources of Power

Lobbying 262
Ethical Lobbying
Social Workers as Lobbyists
How to Lobby

Involvement of Clients in the Advocacy
    Effort 278

Conclusion 279

Chapter Review 280

Practice Test 280

MySocialWorkLab 280
Connecting Core Competency videos on
Policy Practice
SCS on Gay Marriage

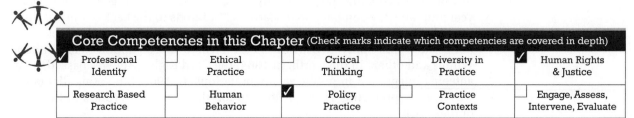

Core Competencies in this Chapter (Check marks indicate which competencies are covered in depth)				
✔ Professional Identity	Ethical Practice	Critical Thinking	Diversity in Practice	✔ Human Rights & Justice
Research Based Practice	Human Behavior	✔ Policy Practice	Practice Contexts	Engage, Assess, Intervene, Evaluate

INTRODUCTION

Nothing could be worse than the fear that one had given up too soon, and left one unexpended effort that might have saved the world.

—JANE ADDAMS

In the fight for voting and other civil rights in the South during the 1960s, the National Association of Social Workers (NASW) and its social workers joined other interest groups on the front lines of the demonstrations and the marches and in the back rooms for the hard work of lobbying for needed legislation. Social workers were not in the lead, but they worked along with civil rights organizations such as the National Association for the Advancement of Colored People (NAACP), the Southern Christian Leadership Conference, and Student Nonviolent Coordinating Committee. This coalition of civil rights interest groups pursued advocacy efforts through multiple venues: in the Southern state legislatures, in the federal courts, in the halls of Congress, through boycotts and marches to gain public attention, and in the streets of Selma, Montgomery, and other cities throughout the north and south. In 1961, social worker Whitney Young became the fourth executive director of the National Urban League. Planning meetings for the historic 1963 March on Washington for civil rights were held at the Urban League offices, and Young's call for a domestic Marshall Plan influenced the development of Johnson's War on Poverty programs.[1] The president of the NASW, Howard Gustafson, took part in the 1965 Selma to Montgomery March, an experience that led him to reflect on the profession's need to advocate for social justice:

> On the way back home, I tried to analyze what the civil rights struggle means to our Association. . . . I was wondering whether social workers, and NASW in particular, are really prepared to act on social issues in their own communities and in their own Agencies. . . . This is what I've been thinking about since returning home from Montgomery.[2]

There were social workers, both black and white, in cities who helped keep the peace when riots threatened. There were social workers who went door-to-door to help people register to vote.

The interest groups advocating integration and equal rights were not wealthy or politically powerful at the beginning of the civil rights movement. They were not the business elites of the Southern cities. They were people from churches, neighborhoods, colleges, and other groups without much money or many resources but who believed in the cause of civil rights so strongly that they put their lives on the line, in some cases. They may not have had the political and economic power of the entrenched powers, but these civil rights groups learned to use their economic power to boycott lunch counters and other businesses that refused service to African Americans. They learned to use their economic power to boycott the buses in Montgomery for over a year and force the company to discard its "Coloreds to the back of the bus" policy. The television coverage of peaceable demonstrators being attacked by police dogs and sprayed with fire hoses created more support among liberal Whites and others in the North. In 1964, the Civil Rights Act was passed, guaranteeing integration in public accommodations. In 1965, the Voting Rights Act was passed, protecting the right to vote for all citizens regardless of the color of their skin.

Although many of the battles and challenges after that shifted to the courts and some continue to this day, the passage of civil rights legislation stands as testimony to the power of people working in coalitions of interest groups triumphing over those entrenched in powerful positions in the community. Much of policy practice occurs within the context of various interest groups, so it is important to understand them and how they function in our political system.

This chapter will cover three topics relevant to interest groups and policy practice: first, legislative processes, particularly as they relate to policy practice interventions by interest groups; second, the characteristics, functions, and broad evolution of interest groups in American politics; and third, lobbying as a subset of interest group activities. After learning the material in this chapter, you will have an understanding of the positive and negative aspects of interest groups; you will be able to identify ways in which social workers intervene in legislative and other policymaking processes through participation in interest groups and lobbying activities; and you will understand how to engage in lobbying activities on behalf of vulnerable populations and to access publicly available Internet resources to monitor the lobbying activity of others.

THE LEGISLATIVE PROCESS

Interest groups play an important role in the legislative arena, from the identification of problems and issues warranting legislative attention to the final passage of a bill into law and its subsequent implementation and evaluation. Using appropriate strategies at each stage in the legislative process is critical to finally enacting bills that maintain the integrity of core values and perspectives even though compromises have to be made to build viable political support. Before successful influence strategies can be designed, the legislative process must be clearly understood. Each state is somewhat different in how the legislative process works at the state level, and how Congress develops and passes legislation differs from what happens in the states. The outline presented here is based on Congressional processes, with some notes about how states may differ. Even though the specifics of the process may vary from state to state, the broad outlines are still similar.

Legislation, whether at the state or federal level, starts with an idea or an issue that someone thinks requires legislation to remedy or address in some way. Formulated by a legislator, usually with the help of aides and others, into a bill, the legislation is introduced into one chamber of the legislative body and then is assigned to a committee (see Figure 10.1 Advocacy as a Bill Becomes a Law Flowchart[3] on page 246). It is important to note here that all state legislatures but one, Nebraska, are bicameral, meaning they have two chambers. Nebraska is unicameral and has only one legislative chamber. Although the flowchart was designed as an aid to those advocating specifically for after-school programs, by following the arrows you can clearly see the different steps in the Congressional legislative process and where advocates can have an impact on the process.

The bill's author is the primary sponsor, meaning that legislator will actively work for passage of the bill within the legislative chamber. (Note that at the state level, sponsors may not be required, depending on each state's laws and practices.) One of the first activities is to find other legislators in the chamber willing to sign onto the bill as sponsors. Gaining the endorsement of influential legislators will enhance the bill's chances of passage.

When the bill is first introduced, assignment to a committee is a crucial step in the process. Both the House and the Senate have standing committees to which bills are assigned for more detailed initial hearings and consideration. See Table 10.1 for a comparative listing of all the Congressional committees.

Table 10.1   Comparison of Congressional Standing Committees[1]

House Committees	Senate Committees
	Aging
Agriculture	Agriculture, Nutrition, and Forestry
Appropriations	Appropriations
Armed Services	Armed Services
	Banking, Housing, and Urban Affairs
	Commerce, Science, and Transportation
Education and Labor	
Energy and Commerce	
	Energy and Natural Resources
	Environmental and Public Works
Ethics	Ethics
Foreign Affairs	Foreign Relations
Finance Services	
Ways and Means	Finance
	Governmental Affairs
	Health, Education, Labor, and Pensions
	Indian Affairs
Homeland Security	
House Administration	
Intelligence	Intelligence
Judiciary	Judiciary
	Labor and Human Resources
Oversight and Government Reform	
Rules	Rules and Administration
Small Business	Small Business
Science and Technology	
Standard of Official Conduct	
Transportation and Infrastructure	

Table 10.1 (Continued)

House Committees	Senate Committees
Veterans' Affairs	Veterans' Affairs
National Resources	

To see examples of Congressional committee reports go to
http://thomas.loc.gov/cp110/cp110query.html

[1]For more information on Congressional committees, visit
www.senate.gov/pagelayout/committees/d_three_sections_with_teasers/committees_home.htm and
www.house.gov/house/CommitteeWWW.shtml.

Committee assignment may determine to a large degree the fate of the bill. Assignment to a committee whose chair is opposed to the intent of the bill will likely result in the bill being "buried" in the committee without a hearing and vote. It will then be dead for that legislative session. On the other hand, assignment to a committee whose chair is favorable to the bill may result in scheduling a hearing and vote on the bill in a timely fashion so that the bill may then be sent to the full chamber for a vote. Typically, bills are assigned to committees that consider legislation relevant their particular expertise. So, the Senate Agriculture, Nutrition, and Forestry Committee would consider bills related to farming, forestry, and other agriculture-related issues. Sometimes, the logic of committee assignment may be harder to discern. For example, bills related to Food Stamps are also typically considered by the Senate Agriculture Committee, since the Food Stamp program was initially conceived of as a way to increase the consumption of agricultural and farming products by low-income families, thereby aiding farmers who needed to sell their products as well as the needy families who consumed them.

Committee assignment may determine to a large degree the fate of the bill.

The committee, then, must consider the legislation, schedule hearings, offer amendments to change details or the language in the bill, and then report it out to the full chamber for a vote, after various opportunities for amendments or "readings" before the final vote is cast. If the legislation passes the first chamber, then it is considered in the second chamber through its committee structure and voting processes. If the bill that emerged from the first chamber is different from the version that comes through the other chamber, then the two versions will be considered in a conference committee composed of members from each chamber. In the conference committee, compromises are reached between the two versions. Once the final version of the bill is agreed upon by all the committee members, the bill is sent back to both chambers for approval. It then must be signed by the president (in the case of federal legislation) or by the governor (in the case of state legislation) in order for it to become law. This process is clearly laid out in Figure 10.1, but this flowchart does not illustrate how legislation can be derailed along the way. The next section will consider those derailment possibilities before examining each stage in this process for potential points of influence.

Thousands of bills across the country are introduced in state legislatures and in Congress each year, but very few of them become law. Box 10.1 identifies information sources for state legislature and Box 10.2 identifies sources for Congress. It is sometimes helpful to think of the legislative process as a funnel that bills pass through, with few emerging at the end as laws that govern public

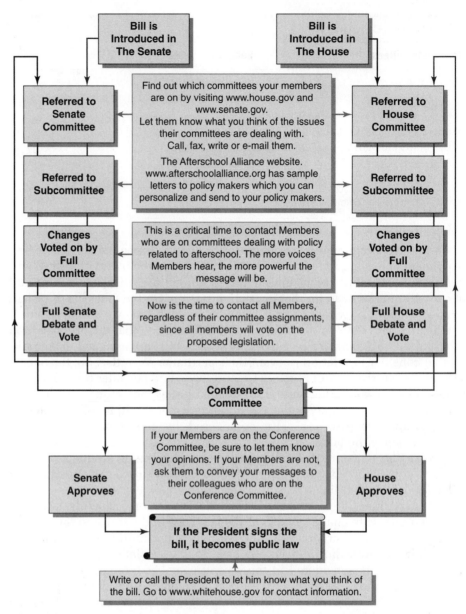

Figure 10.1

Advocacy as a Bill Becomes a Law Flowchart[1]

[1]Used with permission from www.afterschoolalliance.org/prog_docs/advoc_chart.pdf.

policy. So, how can a bill become derailed in this process? First, some ideas promoted to legislators are never developed into bills. Why might a legislator refrain from taking an idea and developing it into legislation? He or she might not agree with the idea that has been offered by a constituent, a lobbyist, or someone else. While the problem might be one that is of concern to the legislator, the proposed legislative solution might be too expensive in the current political climate or not popular for other reasons with other legislators and, therefore, unlikely to develop any traction in the legislative process. So, some ideas do not even make it to the stage of being developed into bills. For example, though some communities (such as Sante Fe in California and Detroit and

---

Box 10.1 Understanding Your State Legislature

Visit your state legislature's Web site for a detailed description of the specific process followed in your state. You will find not only the legislative process described, but also postings of actual bills under consideration, their legislative sponsors, and where they are in the legislative process. Tracking legislation via these Web sites can give you more detailed information than what is on the nightly news or in the local press. Forty-six states and the District of Columbia provide either audio or video or both types of webcasts of legislative proceedings, live or archived, so citizens have access to legislative processes.[1] To understand more about state legislatures in general, visit the National Conference of State Legislatures Web site: www.ncsl.org/. There you will begin to understand the variability in state legislatures in size, frequency of sessions, session length, political party representation, level of professionalism, and other variables salient to their functioning and policymaking processes.

---

[1] National Conference of State Legislatures Web site, www.ncsl.org/programs/lis/webcasts.htm (accessed May 15, 2008).

Box 10.2 Understanding the U.S. Congress

Your understanding of Congressional processes will be enhanced with two Web sites. The Library of Congress Web site (http://thomas.loc.gov/) provides extensive information about current and previous Congressional sessions, including bills under consideration, committee reports, and schedules of hearings, as well as detailed information about the legislative process. The Center on Congress at Indiana University (http://congress.indiana.edu/) attempts to bring the legislative process to life for students of all ages. If you think that Congress is a remote organization that has little to do with your life, use the site's interactive module on the Impact of Congress to see what difference Congress may make in your own daily life.

Box 10.3 The Death of the Gay Marriage Amendment in Committee

In the spring 2004 Indiana General Assembly, the Democrats controlled the House by a slim 51–49 majority, and the Republicans controlled the Senate. It was an election year, and partisan feelings were running high. An amendment to the State Constitution banning gay marriage (SJR-7) had passed quickly and overwhelmingly in the Senate 42–7 and was then referred to the House. There it was assigned to the Committee on Rules and Legislative Procedures, where it sat and sat and sat, without a hearing despite various efforts on the part of the Republicans, including using a "blast" procedure that would have allowed it to come out of the committee directly onto the floor of the House without a committee hearing or vote. In addition, the Republicans made reference to the bottled up bill at every opportunity in speaking about other bills that were brought to the floor for votes. They made statements such as, "I speak against this bill, which the Democrats think is more important than securing the sanctity of marriage as we would be able to do if we could bring SJR-7 to the floor for a vote." This tactic continued all session while important fiscal issues, such as the state budget and property tax reform, languished for weeks. The session ended with headlines in the newspapers such as "Rancorous session draws to a close," "Partisan session saw many battles, few approved bills," and "In Indiana, do-nothing session a reason for thanks."

Grand Rapids, Michigan)[4] have passed "living wage" ordinances, Congress is not likely to adopt a living wage in lieu of the current minimum wage due to arguments that small businesses, in particular, would not be able to sustain themselves under this heavy burden. The power of the business lobby makes it politically impossible to introduce and pass living wage legislation at this time. Box 10.3 is an example of how the legislative process can be stopped.

Once a bill is written, the measure is introduced into the first chamber by its legislative sponsor(s), the legislators who have agreed to help guide the bill through the process. The bill must be assigned to a committee before it can be considered. In the U.S. House of Representatives, the speaker of the House refers bills to specific committees. See Table 10.1 for a listing of standing Congressional committees. Visit your own state legislative Web site to identify your state standing legislative committees to which bills are referred. Note the chairs of those committees and visit their Web sites to find out more about their legislative interests and positions.

Bills with a fiscal impact or that require budgetary appropriations will be referred to the Senate Finance Committee and the House Ways and Means Committee in addition to a committee concerned with the substance of the bill. Referral to more than one committee means that bills may have more difficulty getting through the legislative process with more legislative hurdles to overcome. If a bill does not get referred to a committee, it "dies"—a testament to the power of the speaker. The majority party in the House selects the speaker and is, therefore, in control of the flow of legislation to a large degree. The speaker can assign a bill to a "friendly" or "unfriendly" committee, thus either speeding passage of the bill or slowing it down. The committee chair is able to exert a great deal of power and control in this process. Chairs of committees are determined in most cases by the political party in control of the chamber with some recognition of seniority as well. Some committees, such as Ways and Means in the House and Finance in the Senate, are considered particularly prestigious and powerful, since they control the state or federal budgets and how funds are allocated across the different programs. Appointment to these committees and achieving the "in line" status for chair is a goal for many legislators. In addition, legislators may seek appointment to committees that oversee public policy topics of particular concern to them. A legislator who was a former teacher may seek appointment to the Education Committee, or a returning Iraq veteran may be particularly drawn to Veteran's Affairs.

Bills may be amended and changed in committees and then are voted upon. If a bill does not pass out of the committee, it is "dead" for that session, though in many legislative settings it could be offered and accepted as an amendment to another piece of legislation that is moving through the process. One thing that advocates learn is that "it is not over until it is over," because there are so many ways that legislation that looked to be "dead" can reemerge in a new form and move toward passage. Advocates who might oppose such legislation need to maintain their vigilance until the very end. Box 10.4 provides an example of how a "window of opportunity" can open and allow passage of legislation.

Box 10.4   How Legislation Can Change and How "Windows of Opportunity" May Open

For 12 years, social workers have worked for mental health parity, coverage for mental health conditions equal to the coverage provided in insurance policies for physical health conditions. Many insurance policies, for example, have limited the number of visits in a year to a mental health practitioner, while not imposing those same limits on visits to a medical doctor. Most states have achieved some mental health parity, but coverage has been piecemeal and limited in the disorders covered.

At the federal level, the 1996 law on mental health parity was not adequate as it permitted managed care to limit both access to mental health care and reimbursements. But, all that changed on October 3, 2008, when President Bush signed the $700 billion Emergency Economic Stabilization Act of 2008

(EESA), the bailout for failing Wall Street firms and mortgage companies, passed by Congress. Senators Edward Kennedy (D-MA) and Pete Domenici (R-NM) and representatives Patrick Kennedy (D-RI) and James Ramstad (R-MN) had been working in both chambers on passage of the Paul Wellstone and Pete Domenici Mental Health Parity and Addiction Equity Act, a more comprehensive mental health parity law, for some time. They saw the bailout legislation as a good opportunity to make sure that mental health coverage was available to people during the economic downturn. Stress levels and mental health needs do increase when people are faced with financial crises, such as losing their jobs and their homes. So the almost guaranteed passage of EESA provided that "window of opportunity" for mental health parity to be passed as well.

This federal mental health parity law, that goes into effect on January 1, 2010, does not mandate that all insurance must cover mental health and addiction services. It does require that those plans that do offer such coverage must provide coverage that is equitable to the coverage for medical care. Also, there will no longer be caps or limits on mental health services. It does exempt health plans with 50 or fewer employees.

The text of the full Bill is at http://banking.senate.gov/public/_files/latestversionAYO08C32_xml.pdf. Look at page 310 for the mental health parity section. A summary of the legislation is available at http://banking.senate.gov_files/latestversionEESAsummary.pdf.[1]

[1]Sherri Morgan and Carolyn Polowy, "Social Workers and the Mental Health Parity Act of 2008," *NASW Indiana Update* (Winter 2009), 15–16; and "Mental Health Parity included in bailout," *NASW Indiana Update* (Winter 2009), 13.

Bills that pass out of committee are then eligible to be called for a vote on the floor of the first chamber. Again, the majority party in the chamber is in charge of the legislative calendar and can schedule time for both debate and votes on bills, speeding up the legislative process or slowing it down depending on their stances on particular pieces of legislation. During the debate process on the floor, amendments may be offered and then submitted for a vote. Some amendments may strengthen a piece of legislation and indicate broader support for the bill. At other times, amendments may be offered to weaken legislation or make it less palatable to its supporters so that they "kill" the legislation themselves. These killing amendments are sometimes called "poison pills."

A bill may easily pass through all the processes in one chamber and then run into roadblocks and difficulties in the other, as did the Gay Marriage Amendment example discussed in Box 10.3. Sometimes, that difficulty is based on differences in the power of the political parties between the two chambers. Sometimes, that difficulty can be due to rapidly changing circumstances in the economy, politics, or other aspects of the external environment that occur during the legislative process. And sometimes that difficulty can be due to the mobilization of constituencies or stakeholders and their increasing voices attempting to influence the legislative process.

If two different versions of the same bill pass out of the two chambers, compromises that are agreeable to both sides may not be possible in the conference committee, and then the legislation will die. If the governor or the president threatens a veto, sometimes the conference committee will attempt to come up with a version that will be "veto proof" (have enough support in both chambers to override the threatened veto) or contain language or provisions that are agreeable to the executive. A governor or a president may veto the legislation so that it will not become a law.

Advocacy Roles in the Legislative Process

At each stage in the legislative process reviewed above, advocates have points of leverage where they can take action and make a difference in keeping legislation alive and in helping it move through the process with its overall coherence

Table 10.2   Overview of Advocacy Roles at Major Stages in Legislative Process

Stages in Legislative Process	Roles and Strategies for Advocacy Groups
Identify and frame an issue	Bring issues relevant to clients and agency practice to attention of policymakers
	Frame in language and values orientation to foster best reception
	Identify other potentially supportive groups and develop collaborations
Assess and analyze data	Collect existing and new data related to the issue
	Develop analysis of data in formats readily accessible to policymakers
Generate a proposal—write a bill	Identify possible policy options and assess potential impact to identify best approach
	Develop potential arguments to counter opposition
Develop, support, and present proposal—introduce bill in first and then second chambers and guide through the process	Identify groups in support of initiative using networks and develop strong coalitions
	Contact legislators regarding support or opposition to pending legislation and potential impact on constituents
	Testify
	Generate public support to reinforce political feasibility
When bill passes both chambers, work out compromises in conference committee	Determine how far willing to compromise without jeopardizing principles and values
Bill either signed into law or vetoed by executive	Identify key supporters who can make a difference
	Mobilize public support
Monitor the rule making and implementation processes	Engage executive branch in clarification of rules for implementation to maintain intent of policy
Identify changes needed in policy over time congruent with changing circumstances	Monitor implementation processes through contact with clients and agencies in touch with policy
	Make suggestions for changes in implementation or in policy itself back to relevant executive agency

intact. Table 10.2 outlines the appropriate roles at each stage that will be described in some detail in the following section. This legislative process mirrors the policymaking process discussed in Chapter 8, though the policy making in the legislative arena will have unique processes and characteristics that differ from policymaking in the executive or judicial branches of government.

Identify and Frame an Issue

The first stage in the legislative process occurs long before Congress or the state legislature convenes. Someone has to identify an issue or problem that affects people and requires legislative action in order to remedy. Issues can be those that affect a large number of people such as a more progressive state tax structuring policy or those that affect only a small number of people such as allowing the appointment of a juvenile judge in a particular county. Issues can be present for a considerable time before they are identified as warranting action. Domestic violence, for example, has only recently been identified as a social problem requiring specialized programs for prevention and treatment, for both women and their partners. Federal legislation and funding to support treatment and prevention was first passed in the 1994 Violence Against Women's Act. Box 10.5 details how domestic violence finally emerged as a social issue warranting attention and legislation.

Once an interest group or individual has identified an issue needing legislative attention, the issue must be "framed" to maximize its appeal to both legislators and large groups of their constituents.[5] For example, proponents of an increase in Temporary Assistance for Needy Families (TANF) payments might frame the issue around children, highlighting how current levels of aid to needy families cause some children to go hungry and to perform poorly in school; conversely, opponents of the increase might frame the issue as an example of a liberal "tax and spend" raid on voters' checkbooks. A bill's ultimate success may depend on the power of its frame to shape discourse. See Box 10.5 for another example of how an issue emerges.

A bill's ultimate success may depend on the power of its frame to shape discourse.

Relationships with lawmakers are a crucial part of issue identification. Policy practitioners can invite legislators to visit agencies so that they can see services in operation and talk to staff about client needs, agency structure, and funding. These latter discussions are not lobbying activities but rather educational in nature, because they concern overall needs and not specific legislation or bills. Policy practitioners can identify needs that are important to address and help increase legislators' awareness of the impact of policies on

---

Box 10.5   Issue Identification: The Emergence of Domestic Violence as a Social Issue

While battering wives was considered a crime as early as 1871,[1] violence against women in marriage in the United States was widely ignored by police and prosecutors, unless permanent, serious injury or death resulted.[2] It was not until the early 1960s that police started to receive training in how to respond to domestic disturbances that escalated into violence. Police responses seldom resulted in arrests or prosecution. Only with the growth of the women's movement in this country did the laws begin to address domestic violence. Beatings, if a "sufficient" number occurred, became grounds for divorce in New York in 1966,[3] and one of the first shelters for women opened in Maine in 1967.[4] In 1992, the U.S. Surgeon General found that spousal abuse was the leading cause of death for women aged 15 to 44,[5] and that same year the American Medical Association developed domestic violence screening guidelines for physicians to use. Finally, in 1994 Congress passed the Violence Against Women Act, which provides funding for shelters and other programs to address domestic violence against women. Violence between same-sex partners is only now beginning to gain some attention.[6]

---

[1]Massachusetts first declared wife beating illegal in 1871 (Susan Schechter, *Women and Male Violence* (Boston, MA: South End Press, 1982).

[2]Del Martin, *Battered wives* (New York: Pocket Books, 1976).

[3]Ibid.

[4]Nancy Lemon, *Domestic Violence Law: A Comprehensive Overview of Cases and Sources* (San Francisco, CA: Austin and Winfield, 1996).

[5]Kate Sproul, *California's Response to Domestic Violence* (California Legislature, CA: Senate Office of Research, 1996).

[6]Tod W. Burke and Stephen S. Owen, "Same-Sex Domestic Violence: Is anyone Listening?" *Gay & Lesbian Review Worldwide* (January 2006) 6–7. *Academic Search Premier*, EBSCO *host* (accessed May 9, 2008). And Sheila Seelau and Eric Seelau, "Gender-Role Stereotypes and Percepts of Heterosexual, Gay and Lesbian Domestic Violence," *Journal of Family Violence*, 20, no. 6 (2005), 363–371. *Academic Search Premier*, EBSCO *host* (accessed May 9, 2008).

Policy Practice

Critical Thinking Question

If you are interning or volunteering at a local community agency, what activities could they initiate to inform city, state, and federal legislative policy makers about their clients and services?

constituents in their districts. In this process, social workers develop a relationship with legislators, learning about their priorities and concerns, and helping them understand clients' needs in the context of the community they represent. Social workers understand how to form relationships, starting where the other person is and framing issues in ways that the other will most clearly understand. In this way, developing relationships based on trust and openness with legislators is no different from developing such relationships with other people as a part of generalist social work practice. The difference is in the purpose of the relationships.

This early part of the process is also a good time to reach out to other groups that may also be concerned about the same issues and that may be supportive of the proposed legislation. Identifying other stakeholding groups fosters the development of effective coalitions (discussed in more detail in the next chapter). Bringing other groups on board early in the process provides the opportunity for them to "buy in" by helping to shape the legislation. Their ideas can be incorporated early so as to avoid opposition from groups that sit on the same side of the issue but perhaps see slightly different ways to resolve it.

Assess and Analyze Data

Although legislative decisions are seldom completely data-driven rational processes, data about the problem and the issue must be collected to bolster the arguments in favor of the proposal. Advocates can collect data from their agencies that help identify need. For example, in advocating increased funding to maintain more older people in their own homes and, therefore, to reduce the cost of nursing home placement, social workers can identify the number of elderly people currently on the waiting lists for home health care and/or the number of elderly currently in nursing homes or assisted living facilities who could have remained at home had home health care, shopping services, and other such supports been available at an affordable cost. Data currently collected by agencies for reports to funders or annual reports may already be available. If new information is needed, it can be collected through interviews or surveys. Having a working understanding of how to collect and analyze data in community settings is, therefore, an important skill for policy advocates. Data collection can also be a coalition-wide activity, generating data from a variety of settings, demonstrating the widespread nature or diversity of the need.

When the raw data are collected, policy practitioners analyze it to understand both the community context and the broader state and federal contexts. Comparing local data to state and federal statistics helps contextualize the issue. In addition, trends over time are significant. Is the problem increasing in magnitude and affecting more people? So, for example, is the poverty rate going up? Or is the problem increasing in intensity so that the affected people are experiencing greater stress? Or is the poverty rate remaining constant but the number of people in extreme poverty is increasing? The next step in this process is putting the data analysis into a fact sheet or white paper that is easily accessible to policymakers. Poorly presented data will be ignored or misunderstood. Legislators must grapple with hundreds, or even thousands of pieces of legislation each year, from technical pollution standards that require some degree of scientific literacy, to recognition of the rights of gay people to marry, which is based more on ethical and moral standards. Data should be presented in a clear format using nontechnical language. The example in Box 10.6 from the Consortium for Citizens with Disabilities follows a "myth" versus "reality" format in dispelling arguments about the increase in lawsuits following enactment of the Individuals with Disabilities Education Act (IDEA).

Generate a Proposal—Write a Bill

Before the legislative session, policy practitioners can talk with their "home state" legislators about issues of concern and consult with them about authoring legislation to address community needs that arise in social work practice. Sometimes, advocacy groups or lobbyists may suggest the outlines or provisions of legislation (or actually draft the bill) and then identify legislators who might be likely to "carry" such legislation as sponsors because of their previous voting record or known stances on particular issues. Those legislators may then put their own personal stamp on the draft legislation prior to introducing it in the session. They may or may not keep the initial groups in the loop, as they work on passing the legislation through the process.

Based on research, the policy practitioner should be able to identify some of the available policy options. Each option will have potential positive and negative consequences, benefiting some groups and generating costs for others. For example, increasing the earned income tax credit for low-income families in a state will allow them to keep more of the money that they earn. But that reduction in the state revenue will have to be made up somewhere else by someone else if the budget is to remain the same. Understanding where the political will and support will come from, both in terms of legislators and other advocacy groups, is important, as the political feasibility of a proposal is weighed.

Research is what enables policy practitioners to develop arguments in favor of a proposal as well as arguments to counter the opposition. Policy practitioners must be able to anticipate the arguments that will be used to discredit or undermine a proposal and be prepared to counter them. See the Health Care Reform Simulated Case Study (SCS) for examples of how the Care4Care organization countered some of the arguments they anticipated for their health care reform agenda. Box 10.6 provides another example.

Box 10.6   Data Presentation: Countering Negative Perceptions

ATTORNEYS' FEES AND THE INDIVIDUALS WITH DISABILITIES EDUCATION ACT MYTHS AND REALITIES—JANUARY 27, 2004

In 1986, Congress added provisions to the Individuals with Disabilities Education Act (IDEA) that allow parents of students with disabilities to receive reimbursement for their attorneys' fees when a court or hearing officer determines that their child has been denied a free, appropriate public education. In a 2000 publication, *Back to School on Civil Rights,* the National Council on Disability affirmed the reality that parents are the primary enforcers of IDEA. The attorneys' fees provision in the law is among the most important tool parents have to secure an appropriate education for their child. This document seeks to respond to concerns that have been raised about the attorneys' fees provisions in IDEA.

Myth # 1: The attorneys' fees provisions have resulted in an explosion of litigation.

Reality: IDEA litigation is decreasing.

A recent GAO study www.c-c-d.org/press_room/attyfee-mythfact.htm-_edn1 found that requests for hearings, generally the first step in any IDEA litigation, decreased between 1996 and 2000, the last year for which we have data. Overall, dispute resolution activity was relatively low, with only five due process hearings held per 10,000 students in special education. A small percentage of due process hearings proceed further to court (2%) www.c-c-d.org/press_room/_attyfeemythfact.htm-_edn2. Often a case must proceed all the way to

(*Continued*)

Box 10.6   Data Presentation: Countering Negative Perceptions (*Continued*)

court in-order for parents of a student to obtain attorneys' fees unless the state education agency (SEA) or local education agency (LEA) agrees to pay them as part of a settlement.

Myth # 2: Financially strapped schools are reducing classroom services because they have to pay attorneys' fees.

Reality: Schools spend less than one-half of one percent of their special education resources on dispute resolution, including attorneys' fees.

For the 1999–2000 school year, total spending on the entire dispute resolution process for special education,

including mediation costs, was less than one-half of one percent of the total spending on special education (0.03%). //www.c-c-d.org/press_room/attyfeemythfact.htm_edn3. There are no data on the amount spent specifically on attorneys' fees for students who are prevailing parties. However, as students only obtain fees when they win and little money is spent on due process overall, it simply cannot be the case that paying attorneys' fees to students who are prevailing parties is an unreasonable expense that is taking funds out of the classroom.[1]

---

[1]www.c-c-d.org/press_room/attyfeemythfact.htm (accessed May 15, 2008).

Sometimes an interest group and legislators will know that their proposal has little chance of passage, but they want to introduce it anyway to begin to educate legislators on the issue. It may take several sessions before enough support has been gained for a measure to pass. Sometimes the political and economic context shifts, creating an opportune moment for a particular piece of legislation. For example, as more and more companies find that the cost of health care for workers drives up the cost of manufacturing in the United States, they may pressure the government for universal health care coverage, threatening to move more of their plants overseas. This action would create a favorable environment for passage of a universal national health insurance reform package.

Develop, Support, and Present the Proposal

Bills can change dramatically over the course of the legislative process and so must be monitored constantly.

Once there is a bill that can be used as a rallying point, it is time to generate public support for the proposal as it is introduced in the legislative session. Policy practitioners need to develop a network of contacts to generate e-mails, letters, and phone calls to legislators quickly at various points in the legislative process. If the bill is not being heard in committee, policy practitioners need to urge the committee chair to schedule hearings for the bill to be considered and to contact members of the committee, volunteering to speak from their agency experience about how the legislation will affect clients and services. Policy practitioners can appear at the hearing and testify on behalf of a bill or against a bill to try to stop it in a committee. Because amendments may be offered and adopted in committee, bills should be tracked closely to make sure that they still are worthy of support or should be opposed. Bills can change dramatically over the course of the legislative process and so must be monitored constantly.

As a bill moves out of committee and comes up for consideration on the floor of either chamber, policy practitioners can contact their home district legislator to let him or her know about their position on the bill and rally their network members before crucial votes on the floor to make sure that all the legislators hear from their constituents on the issue. Surprisingly, few constituents contact their state legislators, so legislators pay close attention when they receive even a dozen phone calls and e-mails on a particular issue. Assume that those opposing the bill in the legislative process are rallying their troops as well—it's important that legislators realize the strength of support (or opposition) for a bill under consideration.

The Conference Committee

A great deal can change in the conference committee when slightly different versions of a bill have passed in each chamber. The original sponsors of the legislation from each chamber are frequently assigned to the conference committee where differences are ironed out and compromises are made. It is important to inform members of the committee about the group's stand on the choices and options before the committee. The advocacy group must be clear about the principles that cannot be compromised away in this process and convey that stance to committee members.

Signing the Bill Into Law or Vetoing It

In addition to voicing the group's stand to the governor or the president through letters and e-mails, the group can identify influential or connected supporters who may have the governor's "ear" and can be persuasive in presenting the position of either support or opposition to the bill. The executive branch of government is sensitive to political pressure and the voices of constituents, as these decisions are being made.

Monitoring Rule Making and Implementation

The work of advocacy does not stop with the passage of a bill. Rules are then developed at the federal level, and implementation of policies at the state level that facilitate the law is being put into practice. The rules may strengthen or weaken the legislative intent. Sometimes, the rules and procedures may discriminate against some individuals. The American Civil Liberties Union filed a class-action lawsuit against Indiana's Family and Social Service Administration in May 2008 for "allegedly terminating or denying Medicaid and food stamp assistance based on minor technicalities."[6] This lawsuit was based on case finding by a number of advocacy groups that were monitoring Indiana's privatization of the eligibility determination of its programs for low-income families, Medicaid, Food Stamps, and TANF. For example, when clients were available by telephone during the prearranged two-hour window on one day, but not available the following morning when the case manager made a scheduled call, clients were terminated for "failure to cooperate." In addition, one client was terminated for "failure to cooperate" when two pages of a document she faxed were blurred.[7] Social work roles in monitoring and evaluating the impact of policies are discussed in more detail in Chapter 13.

Ongoing Monitoring to Detect Changes in Need

Advocacy groups remain vigilant in their identification of client needs. In economic recessions, client needs typically increase as people are laid off from their jobs. In those same difficult times, state revenues may decrease due to decline in sales (if the state uses a sales tax for substantial revenue generation) and declines in income due to layoffs. Fewer people working means that fewer people are paying state income taxes as well. So at a time when there is greater need, the state may also be experiencing a belt-tightening that may not bode well for the expansion of needed social services. Such changes in the economy require advocates to make the argument that the investment in social services is an investment in the citizens of the state and will have an economic payoff down the road.

This overview of the legislative process has helped clarify the roles that advocates can play in advancing legislation they deem of interest. It is now time to take a more in-depth look at the groups that are engaged in these efforts to influence the legislative process.

DEFINING INTEREST GROUPS

Voters and politicians alike decry the power of "special interest groups" that have undue influence on politicians and political deliberations.[8] The excesses of "K Street lobbyists" who provide perks to legislators in return for access and legislative favors have attracted widespread negative coverage by the news media, as detailed in Box 10.7.[9]

In light of these scandals, public interest advocates have called for campaign finance reform and other legal measures to protect the legislative process from the undue influence of large corporations and moneyed interests.[10] Who are these "special" interest groups that exert such a corrupting influence on political and legislative processes? It might surprise you to know that included in this much-maligned characterization are groups as far ranging as the National Rifle Association, the Sierra Club, Planned Parenthood, the Catholic Church, state governmental departments, the League of Women Voters, motorcycle enthusiasts, senior citizens, the Urban League, and even the NASW. All are involved in trying to influence policy at the federal, state, and even local levels. We encounter many such formal organizations or informal citizen groups in our social welfare policy work, just as Julia does in the gay marriage SCS and Tony does in the health care SCS (the simulated case studies that accompany this book can be located on the Allyn & Bacon *My Social Work Lab* Web site). As detailed in this chapter, such interest groups actually perform some valuable functions in the legislative process and are the vehicles whereby

---

Box 10.7   The K Street Project

K Street, a busy street in Washington, DC, which is lined with prominent lobbying firms, has become a symbol of the strong influence of lobbyists on the legislative process. In 1995, Grover Norquist, president of the Americans for Tax Reform, and then-U.S. House Representative Tom DeLay began the K Street Project. Their goal was to increase the number of Republicans in high-level positions within lobbying firms and to increase access for lobbyists to important law makers and the White House. The K Street Project facilitated the revolving door within the American political landscape, whereby lawmakers and special interest groups continuously exchange favors as a way to meet personal and political interest objectives, with lawmakers or staff joining lobbying firms at the end of their public service. Scandals involving lobbyists and legislators in early 2006 may signal some changes in these relationships.[1] The most publicized scandal involved lobbyist Jack Abramoff who pleaded guilty to bribery and fraud in the case filed against him. Others associated with Abramoff's effort were also convicted of efforts to "buy" political influence. In addition, Representative Tom DeLay and Representative Robert Ney were forced to give up their leadership posts in Congress.[2]

---

[1]Unraveling Abramoff: Key Players in the Investigation of Lobbyist Jack Abramoff, Compiled by Washingtonpost.com, Updated June 26, 2007. www.washingtonpost.com/wp-dyn/content/custom/2005/12/23/CU2005122300939.html (accessed July 8, 2009).

[2]Republicans Track Politics of Lobbyists, *The New York Times,* June 10, 2002, www.lexisnexis.com/us/lnacademic/api/version1/sr?csi=6742&sr=headline(Republicans+Track+Politics+Of+Lobbyists.)+and+date+is+June+10%2C+2002&secondRedirectIndicator=true (accessed July 6, 2009). Stolberg, Sheryl Gay. Push to Control Lobbying Produces Unexpected Shifts and Alliances, The New York Times, January 18, 2006.www.lexisnexis.com/us/lnacademic/api/version1/sr?csi=6742&sr=headline(Push+to+Control+Lobbying+Produces+Unexpected+Shifts+and+Alliances.)+and+date+is+January+18%2C+2006&secondRedirectIndicator=true (accessed July 6, 2009).

many individuals are able to voice their preferences about policy issues and decisions. So, perhaps when we hear about curtailing the "special" interest groups, we ought to ask which "special" interests and whose voices are some attempting to still? We prefer the more general and less politically charged term *interest group* to *special interest group* though you will see the latter term used frequently in the media. Sometimes the term *pressure group* is used as well.

Interest groups have been identified as sources of influence in the legislative process from the beginnings of the federal government. In 1787, James Madison first noted the potential of "factions" to operate in their own special interest instead of the common good when he wrote, "By a faction, I understand a number of citizens, whether amounting to a majority or a minority of the whole, who are united and actuated by some common impulse of passion, or of interest, adverse to the rights of other citizens, or to the permanent and aggregate interests of the community" in the *Federalist No. 10*.[11] Factions were discussed extensively in Chapter 3 in the context of the development of the political party system. Most interest groups, such as those listed above, have broad missions or goals to serve their members in a variety of ways. For example, Planned Parenthood provides a variety of health services for low-income women, educational services for community members, and other preventative services to carry out its mission of "every child a wanted child." It has become involved in some legislative advocacy efforts in order to ensure that a broad range of family planning and other health and medical services for women remain available and financially accessible. For most interest groups, legislative activity is not the primary mission of the organization, but is just one arm of activity used to pursue its overarching mission.

In the context of our democracy, Thomas defines an interest group as "an association of individuals or organizations or a public or private institution that, on the basis of one or more shared concerns, attempts to influence public policy in its favor."[12] This definition includes organizations of organizations such as the Chamber of Commerce, labor unions, and statewide coalitions for social service agencies. It includes institutions that attempt to influence policy as well, including public governmental entities and organizations and private for-profit and not-for-profit organizations. While the term *lobbyist* can be applied to all members of an interest group who are active in seeking to influence governmental decisions, for the purposes of clarity, this textbook will refer to such interest group members as *advocates*, reserving the term *lobbyist* for individuals who are required to register as lobbyists by law (see the next section in this chapter for more on the legal parameters of lobbying). One could say that interest groups are engaged in legislative or other lobbying activities to promote their self-interests, except perhaps those, like the League of Women Voters and Common Cause, whose concerns are to promote the public interest in general.

Theoretical Approaches to Understanding Interest Groups

Scholars have outlined two primary theories to explain how interest groups influence the policymaking process in democratic societies: (1) pluralism and (2) neocorporatism or corporatism. According to the pluralism paradigm, everyone is free to organize and attempt to gain access to governmental processes where decisions are made through competition, bargaining, and compromise in a free market of ideas and groups. By joining these interest groups and by working in coalitions, individuals then have the strength to compete with the large

Human Rights & Justice

Critical Thinking Question

If interest groups wield such power with government, how can the voices of clients and vulnerable populations be heard by legislators?

corporations and government to have their own political interests represented. The hope is that the "common good" will emerge through this competitive process of specific interest groups. In the United States, political scientists have mainly accepted this pluralistic perspective as orthodoxy, but some question how well the theory reflects the reality on the ground since some groups are historically not represented in political processes.[13] Many of those traditionally unrepresented groups are the very groups that social work advocates are most concerned about. As this discussion of the role of interest groups in electoral, legislative, and judicial systems continues, you can make your own determination about the applicability of the pluralism model to the interest group functioning and the policymaking process.

Neocorporatism or the earlier version, corporatism, assumes a structured collaboration between government and business/labor interests in order to maintain a stable economy. In this model of interest group activity, government, business interests, and labor negotiate together to reach agreement on economic and social policies. In addition, business and labor organizations may actually carry out the policies that result, strengthening the partnership with government with the end of a more stable economy. Scholars point to the model of corporatism in conservative, authoritarian regimes such as Franco's Spain and the neocorporatism model prevalent in modern West European democracies such as Sweden and Switzerland.[14] As Williamson notes, "Corporatism opened up an important debate about the wider nature of close and structured relationships between public authorities and seemingly independent organized interests."[15] This discussion about the relationships of interest groups to government policymakers is one that continues despite the decline of efforts to regulate the U. S. economy through policies other than those that are market based. In our current more global market, there is less effort and ability to influence market forces through agreements with U.S. business and labor. As noted in Chapter 4, broader political economy approaches to understanding interest groups and how they function are gaining more salience.

The Recent Growth of Interest Groups

Why do people join and participate in interest group activities? Scholars have found that people join interest groups for a variety of reasons. Some researchers, like Olson,[16] posit that people join interest groups as part of a rational decision-making process about their own economic self-interest. Using this perspective of economic self-interest, Olson suggests that interest groups have the ongoing challenge of trying to keep members involved and contributing, rather than just remaining on the sidelines to wait for the economic benefits once they are achieved. Moe[17] found other motivations for interest group membership, including belief in the group's goals and specific benefits from group participation. Benefits from participation could include opportunities for networking and skill development, as well as new challenges and growth experiences.

Interest groups form at the nexus of power in the political process, so in the United States, we see interest groups operating at both the federal and state levels, and in local communities as well. The number of interest groups as well as the memberships of some of the most prominent groups has grown substantially in the last 40 years.[18] The number of national associations grew from 5,483 in 1959 to 23,298 by 1995.[19] Multiple groups form to address similar concerns in this interest group proliferation process. For example, groups such as the Children's Defense Fund, the Child Welfare League of America, and the Children's Bureau have similar missions to advance and protect the welfare of children in this country. Interest groups, though they may cooperate and collaborate in their lobbying efforts, may also vie for members in their direct mail and Internet fundraising efforts. While there has been some leveling out of the numbers of associations since the 1980s, memberships in some organizations have grown dramatically. For example, while the National Audubon Society and the Wilderness Society have seen memberships remain steady since the mid-1990s, the Sierra Club, the Natural Resources Defense Council, and the Nature Conservancy have seen memberships increase substantially.[20]

Why this surge in the number of interest groups? The increase could be related to a number of factors and circumstances. Businesses have expanded their use of lobbyists and trade associations in order to influence the policy-making process, and many interest groups, including business and labor, have formed political action committees (PACs) in order to channel contributions to political campaigns ($5,000 per candidate committee per election). For more on PACs, see Chapter 12, Campaigns.

Changes in our two-party system may have led to some of the growth in interest groups. Parties have to have a broad base of supporters with a variety of views on issues in order to win elections. In contrast, by their very nature, interest groups are very narrowly focused. Some researchers suggest that the centrist orientations that both the Democratic and the Republican parties have traditionally adopted in an attempt to attract the moderate Independents needed to win elections have led to the formation of more citizen groups to address the more polarizing issues and interests of the day. In more recent years though, the political parties have become more polarized in their views on a variety of issues, while interest groups have continued to gain membership.

The amount of money spent on both lobbying and contributions to political campaigns is also increasing, demonstrating an increase in efforts to influence public policy processes. The amount of PAC funds supporting candidates rose by 86 percent between 1985 ($139M) and 2000 ($259M).[21]

Role of Interest Groups in U.S. Political and Economic Contexts

Thomas Jefferson was one of the first to observe that although interest groups have a positive outcome on public life, it is "a paradoxical by-product of the sum of their selfish interests."[22] Special interest groups are often portrayed in a negative light in the media, but with their organization, membership, and financial resources, interest groups play an important role in the political process. Berry and Wilcox[23] and Thomas[24] outline the major functions of interest groups in our political system. Interest groups

- Link citizens to the government by organizing diverse voices to be heard in both the electoral process and the policymaking process;
- Facilitate governmental processes by providing relevant information, policy options, and bases for compromises and assist in policy implementation;
- Serve as a vehicle for citizen participation in governmental processes through writing letters and other campaign efforts;

- Educate both their members and the general public about policy issues, both problems and proposed solutions;
- Frame political issues based on their value orientation and serve as a voice for that perspective;
- Bring issues to light and help build the agenda for policy initiatives;
- Assist in candidate recruitment;
- Provide both important monetary and human resources in political campaigns; and
- Monitor program implementation to evaluate progress and report short-comings.

Interest groups provide an avenue for two-way communication between citizens and the policymaking bodies within the government. Teater's 2008 qualitative study of nine state legislators identified the importance of interest groups for helping get the groups' agendas before the legislators.[25] Where the lone citizen's voice may not be heard among all the other "voices" clamoring for attention, joined with others who share the same perspective in a public effort, that citizen will potentially have greater influence in the policymaking process at legislative, executive, and judicial levels of government.

For example, preceding a 2007 vote to extend the legislation and increase the funding for the S-CHIP (State Children's Health Insurance Program), many child advocates and those working with low-income children expressed concerns that the U.S. House of Representatives might not support this important program because of its cost. A number of organizations, led by the Coalition for Human Needs, initiated an e-mail campaign asking members to write and call their representatives about the issue. Although the increase ultimately failed to pass, the efforts of many citizens acting together resulted in changing some representatives' votes, so the S-CHIP bill was defeated by a much narrower margin than was anticipated. Taking the long view of policy practice, convincing a few more legislators of the need for the S-CHIP program may, in retrospect, prove to be a milestone on the path toward truly universal access to health care for children. In February 2009, President Barack Obama signed the Children's Health Insurance Program Reauthorization Act (CHIPRA), which extended the CHIP program to an additional 4.1 million children and to pregnant women.[26]

In today's political landscape, the two major political parties, Democrats and Republicans, largely determine legislative and executive governmental directions and efforts. Through their appointments to the courts, they also shape the stance and approaches of the courts as well, in the cases brought before them. It should, therefore, come as no surprise that interest groups work closely with the political parties. Political parties and interest groups need each other to accomplish their goals. Berry and Wilcox describe their similarities, differences, and relationship in these terms:

> Both interest groups and parties represent citizens, facilitate their participation in the political process, educate the public, put issues on the agendas of Congress and varied agencies, and monitor program performance, yet parties and groups are linked together in our system not simply because their functions overlap but also because they need each other to accomplish their most important goals. Groups cannot enact policy or formulate regulations on their own. Parties need the political support of interest groups, which can provide campaign donations, mobilize voters

on election day, activate their membership on behalf of a bill, and influence the general public's attitudes.[27]

Sources of Power

Interest groups have many sources of power that make them attractive to both political parties and to politicians. The big corporate lobbies at the federal level, particularly, for social policy, include those in the rapidly growing health care industry, such as insurance companies, pharmaceutical companies, hospitals, and nursing home associations. But interest groups have not only the power associated with money but also the power associated with their memberships when those may be translated into votes. Those running for political office need both money and votes, so even the interest group with few monetary resources may have considerable power if its members are known to regularly show up at the polls to exercise their right to vote.

Professional Identity

Critical Thinking Question

As an interest group, what sources of power and influence does the NASW have?

Money

The financial resources of interest groups vary widely, and they may elect to expend those resources in a variety of ways, including gifts and perks to legislators and other policymakers, luncheons, receptions, development of promotional materials, research related to policy initiatives, and, through separate PAC organizations, contributions to political campaigns. Large corporations may be able to afford to retain law firms to engage in a lobbying strategy to advance the interests of the corporation and others engaged in a similar business or industry. For years, the tobacco lobby resisted efforts to restrict smoking in public places and advertising with cartoon figures until the court judgments against them in the form of the Tobacco Settlements that paid for both treatment and prevention programs proliferated through the states. Public opinion at this time shifted as the truth about the dangers of smoking and secondhand smoke became more widely known. Small not-for-profit organizations usually do not have the funds to hire law firms or even one full-time staff member to engage in lobbying efforts. The NASW does not have the same financial resources available to expend on lobbying activities as more affluent professional associations, such as the American Medical Association (AMA). Landa (2001) reported that the AMA had the third highest federal lobbying expenditures in the last six months of 2000, tallying $8.76 million.[28] In 2007, the AMA spent over $22 million on federal lobbying, dropping to third place behind the U.S. Chamber of Commerce and the Pharmaceutical Research and Manufacturers of America.[29]

Interest groups raise funds in a variety of ways, including direct mail and Web solicitation of memberships and special donations. Some people who support a cause, but do not themselves have time to take on advocacy efforts, invest in the interest group by engaging in "checkbook activism." Their financial support is appreciated, but they may not be counted on to become actively engaged in a campaign on the issue beyond the computer-generated e-mail letter or signature on a petition.

Endorsements

As mentioned above, interest groups may provide endorsements without financial contributions, and sometimes the endorsement is more important than the financial contribution. For example, endorsement by a large group of older people, such as the PAC of the American Association for Retired Persons (AARP), in a presidential election is highly sought after by candidates. Older Americans are more likely to vote in elections than younger voters. In the 2000 election, 84 percent of eligible Iowa voters in the 65-to-74 age bracket voted—20 percent higher than the statewide average of 64 percent. In the same election, Missouri seniors outvoted younger voters by 16 percent.[30] Endorsements by unions, such as the Service Employees International Union (SEIU), the largest labor union in the country, are also coveted because labor unions have a history of turning out their members to vote. Typically, an executive committee or board of the PAC or interest group makes the final decision about possible endorsements.

Information/Expertise in Areas of Specialization

Interest groups are focused on rather narrow topics of interest and have considerable expertise in that area that has been developed over time. Given the sheer volume of legislation that is considered in each Congressional or state legislative session, legislators cannot possibly begin to develop expertise in such divergent areas as water pollution, tax policy, health care reform, and bank regulation. As our laws have become more technical and more complex, legislators have become increasingly dependent on lobbyists and interest groups for information about bills under consideration.[31]

Because of their access to financial resources, ability to mobilize members and endorse candidates, and policy expertise, interest groups are a powerful influence in American politics. That power is often expressed through lobbying.

LOBBYING

At the national and state levels, across the legislative, executive, and judicial branches of government, lobbying is a common aspect of policy practice. Defined as "the practice of attempting to influence the decisions of government,"[32] lobbying ranges in scope from the large national association with offices in Washington, DC, and a dedicated team of professional lobbyists who work the halls of Congress throughout the year to the local social service agency that sends a program director to meet with a state legislator's aide for a briefing on how a proposed human services bill will affect area constituents.

The practice of attempting to influence the decisions of government takes many forms, including personal meetings with legislators and governmental agency administrators, testimony before congressional committees, drafting bills and providing policy expertise to legislators, filing "amicus curiae" friend-of-the-court briefs in legal cases, and mobilizing grassroots activity to influence a congressional vote. Lobbying can be proactive or defensive in nature. Proactive lobbying is about working for change. For example, the policy practitioners in the health care SCS are working toward passage of legislation at the state level that would increase access to basic health care. Conversely, defensive lobbying aims to stop change from occurring—in the social work realm, to prevent legislation or administrative actions that would harm vulnerable populations or be counter to the core values of the profession. In the gay marriage SCS, the character of Julia is engaged in defensive lobbying when she meets with Senator Hawkins to persuade him to end his support for a law that would ban gay marriage.

While every citizen can engage in lobbying activities, the definition of a *lobbyist* is narrower in scope. A lobbyist is a "person who lobbies on behalf of an organized interest (or numerous organized interests)".[33] Lobbyists work for professional associations such as the NASW, citizen groups such as the AARP, charities such as the Children's Defense Fund, think tanks such as the Center for Progressive Politics, or for coalitions such as the National Coalition for the Homeless. Lobbyists may also work for dedicated lobbying firms that have a variety of clients (although this is more typical of corporate interests—nonprofits often cannot afford the services of dedicated lobbying firms).

In the post–World War II era of continuous governmental expansion, lobbying activity has increased steadily.[34] It is not the sheer size of government that has led to more lobbyists, but the expansion of policy areas (today covering every area of social work practice, including family services, welfare, homelessness, nutrition, retirement, education, and housing) within government that has driven increased lobbying activity:

> Government activity acts as a magnet, pulling groups of all kinds to become active. More so than direct federal spending or the number of business firms in various areas of the economy, government attention, as measured by Congressional hearings, draws groups to Washington. . . . As government has grown, becoming more active in various areas of the economy and in social life, groups of all kinds have found that they must be present in Washington.[35]

It is estimated that 90,000 lobbyists are active in the nation's capitol, and that an additional 200,000 lobbyists work at the state level throughout the nation.[36]

Ethical Lobbying

Policy practitioners employed by organizations that qualify for 501(c)3 nonprofit status must know the boundaries of allowed lobbying activity. Figure 10.2 applies the Boundaries of Ethical Policy Practice diagram from Chapter 5 to lobbying activities.

While the social work profession's Code of Ethics and Practice Standards explicitly encourage social workers' participation in public life, and while our societal norms favor transparency in government, when it comes to lobbying, *laws* form the critical boundary that most defines allowed lobbying activity. The Lobbying Act of 1976, which was clarified in 1990 when the Internal Revenue Service (IRS) issued detailed guidelines for its implementation, and the Honest Leadership and Open Government Act of 2007 (HLOGA) together define legal lobbying activity at the federal level. Nonprofits can elect (choose) to register with the IRS as a 501(h) organization—a subcategory of 501(c)3 nonprofit status that sets clear monetary limits on lobbying expenditures. Broadly stated, a nonprofit organization with a budget of $500,000 can spend 20 percent, or $100,000, on lobbying per year; larger organizations can spend more, but the percentage they can spend drops with each budget increment of

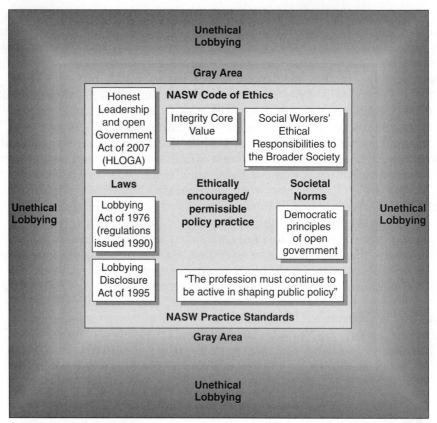

Figure 10.2
Boundaries of Ethical Lobbying

$500,000. There is also a total cap on lobbying expenditures of $1 million per year for 501(c)3 organizations.

The IRS has established an important distinction between direct lobbying and grassroots lobbying. *Direct lobbying* occurs when an organization communicates with a legislator about its position on a specific piece of legislation. *Grassroots lobbying* is communicating with the general public to express a view about specific legislation and includes a call to action such as urging citizens to e-mail their legislators.[37] Grassroots lobbying can only constitute one-fourth of an organization's lobbying expenditures in a given reporting period. However, mobilizing the organization's membership is not defined as grassroots lobbying, but as direct lobbying. For example, it is direct lobbying when the Mental Health America (MHA) organization (formerly the National Mental Health Association) sends out an action e-mail alert urging members to speak out in support of a particular bill, but it is grassroots lobbying when MHA takes out an advertisement in the *New York Times* to urge members of the general public to support the bill. Again, this is a useful distinction because organizations can spend more on activities defined as direct lobbying.

Federal lobbying law lists five types of communications that are not considered to be lobbying activities:

1. *Self-defense:* communication on any legislation that would affect an organization's existence, powers and duties, tax-exempt status, or deductibility of contributions.

2. ***Technical advice:*** providing technical advice to a governmental body in response to a written communication.

3. ***Nonpartisan analysis or research:*** studying community problems and their potential solutions is considered nonpartisan if it is "an independent and objective exposition of a particular subject matter . . . (which) may advocate a particular position or viewpoint so long as there is a sufficiently full and fair exposition of pertinent facts to enable the public or an individual to form an independent opinion or conclusion."[38]

4. ***Examinations and discussions of broad social, economic, and similar problems:*** communication with the organization's own members with respect to legislation that is of direct interest to them, so long as the discussion does not address the merits of a specific legislative proposal and makes no call for action.

5. ***Regulatory and administrative issues:*** communication with governmental officials or employees on nonlegislative (i.e., administrative) matters such as rule making.[39]

The National Council of Nonprofit Associations provides the following guidance on examples of activities that would count toward an organization's expenditures on lobbying:

- paid staff time spent meeting legislators, preparing testimony, or encouraging others to testify;
- printing, copying, or mailing expenses to get the organization's message to legislators;
- prorated cost of any newsletter article urging the organization's members to speak out on legislation (prorating based on the space the lobbying message takes in the newsletter); and
- prorated share of rented space used in support of lobbying (a good way to handle this is to prorate the cost based on the percentage of staff time spent lobbying).[40]

The Lobbying Disclosure Act of 1995 (and its subsequent amendments) requires lobbying firms to register with the government if the time they spend lobbying for a client is more than 20 percent of their overall work for the client over a six-month period. Lobbying firms and other organizations that employ in-house lobbyists (such as the NASW) must also register if the amount spent on lobbying activities is more than $10,000 per year.

Largely in response to the lobbying scandals referred to earlier in this chapter, lobbying laws were tightened in 2007 with the passage of the HLOGA, which lowered the threshold for when lobbyists are required to register; increased restrictions on gifts to lawmakers; extended the prohibition on senators and high-level executive branch officials taking employment as lobbyists from one to two years (senate staffers, House representatives, and staff members are banned from lobbying employment for one year after leaving government service); tightened travel rules; and banned "K Street Project" types of initiatives, whereby legislators actively work to influence employment decisions in nongovernmental entities such as lobbying firms.[41] Upon taking office, President Barack Obama enacted still stricter lobbying guidelines, including placing a ban on staffers working on issues they had formerly lobbied to support and a measure that restricts members of his administration from lobbying the government for a two-year period after leaving government service.[42] While most organizations will have access to legal counsel who will keep them within the evolving legal boundaries of lobbying activity, policy practitioners must know the basic laws that govern interactions with elected officials.

Social Workers as Lobbyists

Social workers lobby at both the state and national levels. While social workers lack the financial resources of large corporate interests, their professional expertise (not only in the policy arena, but also in interpersonal communications and social movement strategy) is a great asset in this type of policy practice work.

Many state NASW chapters coordinate annual (or biennial, depending on the state's legislative calendar) Social Work Lobby Days at the State House or with state legislatures to serve several purposes: to demonstrate the magnitude of social work support for particular legislative initiatives or opposition to current legislative efforts, to thank legislators for their work on behalf of social justice and social work professional goals, to educate social work practitioners and students about the legislative process and effective ways to influence legislation, and to provide a sense of solidarity with other social workers on issues of concern. Organizing a Social Work Lobby Day takes a great amount of planning and networking with social workers who are actively involved in state house activities. Looking at one state's efforts may be instructive to others wanting to learn about that organizing process.

Indiana, according to Influencing State Policy figures tabulated each year by members and compiled by the chair,[43] has one of the most successful lobby days in the country in terms of the number of students and practitioners who are involved in the event. In 2007, 650 people participated, and a little more than 600 participated in 2008. Indiana's lobby day was initiated in 1999 by a collaborative group of social work educators originally brought together by one of the authors (Byers) and Pam Miller, currently of Calgary University but at the time at Ball State University. Over coffee at a local coffee shop, they discussed the need to have an increased social work lobbying presence at the state level in light of the devolution of social policy from the federal to the state level. In addition, they were looking for an opportunity to empower social workers and social work students to engage in more policy practice roles. They also recognized that teaching *about* policy practice was very different from teaching the *skills* of policy practice. Creating a lobby day experience for their students and for social workers seemed a logical intervention, so they decided to call a meeting to include the NASW, social workers involved in the legislature, and policy teachers in the largest social work programs in the state. That initial group, despite some discouragement by the state NASW staff at the time, invited participants from all the social work education programs in the state to plan the event. They investigated the lobby day formats used in other states: a daylong event with a luncheon, half-day events of going to the State House to meet with legislators in small groups, and other formats. The basic model adopted as most feasible for Indiana was a morning session to help educate students on lobbying strategies and specific issues followed by a march to the State House and a rally there, with legislators speaking to the crowd about current legislative efforts. That first year for Lobby Day 2000, no one knew how many students and practitioners to expect since relationships with the social work programs were not well established yet and the NASW did little advertising of the event among its membership. But almost 400 people came to the February event, much to the satisfaction of the organizers. There were not enough seats or handouts, but the organizers said, "This is a good problem to have."

Over the years, the format has changed somewhat due to increasing student participation. More policy educators are including policy practice principles and lobbying strategies in their courses. Legislative Education and Advocacy Development, or LEAD as it is now called, is seen now as a process and not just a one-day event, and can focus more on specific issues of concern during the session, covering topics such as child welfare, gay rights, and housing. As LEAD has changed, fund-raising strategies to support it have become more creative, with a T-shirt contest; sales of exhibit space for supporting agencies; contributions from social work programs, the NASW, and other organizations; charges for practitioners earning CEUs; and passing the hat at various social work events. Now students who participated the previous year are actively involved in the planning process in subsequent years. Box 10.8 includes student comments. After six years of increasingly successful events, LEAD became a standing committee of the Indiana State NASW Chapter, thus ensuring its institutional home. Organizers hope that participation in LEAD continues to help make the legislative process more "real" for students, enabling them to become more comfortable after graduation in using the policy practice skills they are learning as a normal part of their professional lives.

If your state has a Social Work Lobby Day or a Social Work Day at the Legislature, participate to experience this same sense of empowerment. Volunteer to assist with the planning whether the event is one sponsored by the NASW or your school or another social work group. If your state does not currently have a Social Work Lobby Day, then begin to talk about the idea for your state with other students, faculty and your NASW chapter volunteers and staff. Remember the Indiana LEAD event started when two friends were having coffee. You can do it, too!

In addition to sponsoring a Lobby Day or other such events in many states, NASW state chapters are involved in monitoring the legislative sessions in their states to identify policy issues of concern to social workers, including licensure of social workers, child welfare, and services to other vulnerable

---

Box 10.8   Students Speak Out About Lobby Day

"As everyone gathered in the hall at the Westin Hotel, the mood was one of optimism, excitement, and anticipation, and even I began to be swept up in it. Lobby Day forced me to confront my irrational fears and uninformed ideas about the legislative process. I was lucky to have the opportunity to learn some valuable lessons first hand. Even though I am still focused on becoming an interpersonal social worker, I now feel responsible for helping pass legislation that will help not only my clients, but also potential clients all over the state."

"Taking part in Lobby Day was one of the largest group efforts I have been involved in. It was a positive feeling to see such numbers with a united purpose and passion. I was reminded of just how much the principles and mission of social work parallel the core of who I am and what I stand for."

"I found Lobby Day to be educating, empowering, and motivating. The turnout of social workers from around the state showed a commitment to the oppressed populations that we speak on behalf of. The rally was powerful. I now realize the importance of the social work role in legislation and that more social work professionals need to take part in the lobbying process and also run for legislative office."

"It was exciting to see so many social workers in full force on Lobby Day. I felt a unity and bond with the profession. I would definitely do this again."

"There is an emotional component to lobbying, in that one must feel the passion about the issues and process, to understand fully the power of lobbying. I believe I experienced for the first time what it feels like to be a social worker."[1]

---

[1]Unpublished paper, Katharine Byers; Marion Wagner and Dwight Hymans, "400 Voices at the State House: Empowering Students in Policy Practice."

populations. The chapter executive and board members may be called upon to testify at hearings, but they will also help mobilize networks of concerned social workers in the state to also testify, to write letters and e-mails, and to talk individually with their respective legislators to help move legislation at those key points in the legislative process discussed earlier in this chapter. NASW state chapters have legislative committees composed of NASW members interested in public policy work who help determine the chapter's legislative agenda for each session and plan strategy during the session. For most successful campaigns, state chapters may also join coalitions of other organizations concerned about human services and their lobbying efforts. This united voice of social workers and other human service professionals has the greater likelihood of success, as will be discussed in the chapter on building coalitions.

At the national level, the NASW is the primary professional association for social workers. The NASW develops a legislative agenda each year. For the 111th Congress from January 2009 to December 2010, the following issues were the advocacy focus for the NASW:

- *Social Work Reinvestment Initiative:* in support of education and training for social workers;
- *Addressing health care for all, physical and behavioral:* universal access to the full continuum of health and mental health services for all individuals;
- *Addressing the needs of an aging population:* insuring full funding for services as the baby boomers continue to age;
- *Strengthening families:* adequate funding and improvements in child welfare programs and the TANF program;
- *Educating our nation's youth:* full funding for programs to reduce dropout rates and other challenges facing the public schools;
- *Financing higher education:* full funding for loan forgiveness programs for social workers;
- *Economic security:* tax, budget, and spending programs to increase economic resources to the most vulnerable and promotion of livable wages and equal pay for equal work;
- *Protecting civil and human rights:* "NASW supports full civil and human rights for all people and opposes public policies that alienate individuals by race, ethnicity, national origin, gender, age, physical or mental abilities, marital status, sexual orientation, or religious belief;"[44] and
- *Supporting members of the military and veterans:* supportive programs to address the mental health needs of military personnel and veterans and their families as they cope with deployments and mental and physical disabilities.[45]

The NASW employed five lobbyists/government relations staff at its Washington, DC, headquarters; in 2007, the NASW spent $468,801 on lobbying the branches of the federal government. NASW lobbyists advocated for the legislative agenda by lobbying for a variety of bills and issues in 2007, including the DC Voting Rights Act, the Elder Justice Act, the Genetic Information Nondiscrimination Act, Head Start, judicial nominations, Departments of Labor and HHS appropriations, Medicaid foster care, the Minority Health Improvement and Health Disparity Elimination Act, and social work research and training.

Some of this information on NASW's political activities is available on the NASW Web site at www.nasw.org, but the data on the amount spent on lobbying and the specific nature of the lobbying activity were obtained from an invaluable resource: the U.S. government's Lobbying Disclosure Web site at http://ldsearch.house.gov/. This database, which came into being as part of the Lobbying Disclosure Act, is searchable by topic, organization, lobbyist, or governmental body being lobbied.

How to Lobby

There are well-established practices that are employed for effective advocacy. Face-to-face meetings, e-mail, and phone conversations are core lobbying activities. Whether a lobbyist or advocate is alerting legislators about how a bill might affect their constituents or is consulting with officials to plan legislative strategies, communication skills are essential. Successful lobbyists are persuaders who are attuned to the interpersonal dynamics of the lobbying situation. People skills, experience, knowledge of the issue, intuition, political judgment, negotiating skills, and reputation are all vital assets in lobbying.[46] Lobbyists understand the importance of being "on the ground" and available to act on their interests. Figure 10.3 illustrates critical points for lobbying in the legislative process. A lobbyist engaged in advocating for a bill that is being considered by the U.S. House of Representatives, for example, will know when the bill is going to the committee, and she will be in contact with the representative and/or members of her staff to make her case. A good lobbyist is persistent, but not annoying. In making the case, lobbyists' presentations are brief and information is tailored to meet the needs of the individual (or individuals) being lobbied.

Successful lobbyists are persuaders who are attuned to the interpersonal dynamics of the lobbying situation.

Talking Points

This brief list of key points that defines an advocacy position is useful in staying on message when meeting with legislators, and can be left with legislators as the meeting "takeaway." The influence of well-crafted talking points was evident when, several years ago, one of the authors' students gave a list of talking points to a Florida state legislator at a Lobby Day meeting. Imagine that student's surprise, when, watching the evening news that night, she saw the legislator being interviewed and discussing an issue by quoting verbatim from the students' talking points! This was a very instructive moment in terms of the "power of one" and the value of talking points. Box 10.9 is an example of talking points.

The NASW has produced a list of "dos and don'ts"[47] that summarizes how to best approach the lobbying relationship:

Do

1. Do learn members' committee assignments and where their specialties lie.
2. Do present the need for what you're asking the member of Congress to do. Use data or cases you know.
3. Do relate situations in his/her home state or district.
4. Do ask the representative's or senator's position and why.
5. Do—in case of voting records—ask why he/she voted a particular way.
6. Do show openness to the knowledge of counterarguments and respond to them.
7. Do admit that you don't know. Offer to try to find out the answer and send information back to the office.
8. Do spend time with members whose position is against yours. You can lessen the intensity of the opposition and perhaps change it.
9. Do spend time in developing relationships with Congressional staff.
10. Do thank them for stands the member has taken which you support.

Box 10.9   Sample Talking Points

Assuring Quality Special Education for Children with Visual Impairments[1]

The American Foundation for the Blind has prepared the following sample talking points to illustrate how to succinctly convey an advocacy position.

Summary of Recommendations

To ensure that children who are blind or visually impaired receive a high-quality education with related services, Congress must

▶ ensure that blind or visually impaired students are provided with timely access to classroom instructional materials and technology equal to their nondisabled classmates;

▶ require that assessments of students with visual impairments are designed with sensitivity to their unique needs, are administered by personnel with knowledge of those needs, and are provided in individually appropriate reading media;

▶ dramatically increase the availability of teachers and related services personnel trained to meet the unique needs of students who are blind or visually impaired;

▶ provide for a complete and accurate identification of students with visual impairments in need of special education and related services;

▶ address the need for a full range of appropriate transition services ensuring successful progress from school to work;

▶ guarantee placement of students with visual impairments in educational settings based on individual students' needs.

For More Information: [Add Contact Information]

Talking points analysis:

Note the use of verbs to convey that action is required by Congress and the legalistic phrasing, which reinforces the legislative action being sought. Phrases such as "timely access," "full range of appropriate transition services," and "administered by personnel with knowledge" can all be defined in more detail in a bill. While human interest stories are an effective component of advocacy campaigns, particularly in demonstrating an issue's impact, talking points should focus on the core ideas that define an advocacy position.

[1]www.afb.org/Section.asp?SectionID=3&TopicID=237&DocumentID=2368 (accessed June 1, 2008).

Don't

1. Don't overload a Congressional visit with too many issues.
2. Don't confront, threaten, pressure, or beg.
3. Don't be argumentative. Speak with calmness and commitment so as not to put him/her on the defensive.
4. Don't overstate the case. Members are very busy, and you're apt to lose their attention if you are too wordy.
5. Don't expect members of Congress to be specialists. Their schedules and workloads tend to make them generalists.
6. Don't be put off by smokescreens or long-winded answers. Bring the members back to the point. Maintain control of the meetings.
7. Don't make promises you can't deliver.
8. Don't be afraid to take a stand on the issues.
9. Don't shy away from meetings with legislators with known views opposite your own.
10. Don't be offended if a legislator is unable to meet and requests that you meet with his/her staff.

The NASW also has a Legislative Office Visit Follow-Up Report Form on their Web site[48] for members to report back to the organization on issues discussed, the legislator's position on the issue(s), and whether the NASW should provide any specific follow-up, including calls from NASW lobbyists and Steering Committee members to the legislator and activation of the NASW's membership to generate phone calls/letters from social work constituents.

Letter Writing and E-mails

Whether writing a formal letter or an e-mail to a legislator, the same guidelines apply. Letters that are short and clear are more effective than ones that are rambling and disorganized. The letter should focus on one topic, issue, or piece of legislation. If it is a piece of legislation, make sure that you have the full name of the bill or the bill number so that the legislator has a clear point of reference. While form letters and petitions sent out from advocacy organizations may give some indication of support or opposition to an issue, the most effective letters are the personal ones that relate your own experiences with a policy or how it is affecting clients in your agency. Use the talking points that you develop as the starting point for developing your letter. Decide which of those points you want to emphasize within the letter through the use of examples, data, and further elaboration. Box 10.10 lists specific tips for writing effective letters.

Testimony

During the fourth stage of the legislative process, when bills are publicly presented, policy practitioners can provide testimony to support or oppose a measure under consideration. Typically, testimony can be provided during congressional committee or subcommittee meetings or hearings (see illustration below).

Policy practitioners seek out opportunities to testify at all levels of policy practice, from the local town council meeting to the U.S. Congress. At whatever level testimony takes place, policy practitioners understand the importance of knowing the committee members: What is their political orientation? Which issues are they passionate about? How likely are they to be receptive to the practitioner's testimony? Policy practitioners know the procedures for being included in the process of providing testimony, such as whom to contact about

---

Box 10.10 Tips on Writing Effective Letters to Legislators

1. Make sure to address the letter correctly ("The Honorable Sam Jones").

2. Remind the legislator of any past contact you may have had, assuming it was a positive interchange. ("I met with you last week at Social Work Lobby Day and wanted to follow-up. . .")

3. Compose the letter in your own words, even if you are writing in response to an alert from an advocacy organization.

4. Handwrite or type your letter, so it is neat and legible.

5. Be sure to identify the bill (and provide the number) or subject in the first sentence.

6. Ask for specific action—to support, oppose, etc. This request should be in both the first and last paragraphs.

7. Personalize the letter with your own experiences and reasons for writing. You can make appeals to both logic and emotion.

8. Always be courteous and respectful. Never attack or threaten—that is not a good way to influence people.

9. Always sign the letter and provide your own contact information (address, phone, and e-mail), so the legislator can follow up with you if he or she has questions.

10. Timing is important in the legislative process, and so e-mails sometimes can be effective in getting information about your position to legislators more quickly. You do not want your e-mail or letter to arrive after a crucial vote has been taken.

(Continued)

Box 10.10   Tips on Writing Effective Letters to Legislators (*Continued*)

11. Always be factual and accurate in any data you include.

12. Only write once on a particular bill, unless you are trying to provide new information or to counter the arguments being used by the other side.

13. Always thank the legislator for his or her time and for efforts to provide services and assistance for constituents.

14. If the legislator votes as you wish, then follow up with a note thanking him or her for the support.

testifying (for Congress, either the member of Congress or a member of his or her staff); rules about the length and format of testimony; and they keep apprised of when hearings or committee meetings are announced (for the U.S. House and Senate, meetings must be announced at least one week in advance of the meeting).

Here are some tips for effective policy practice testimony:

▶ Public testimony should be written out in advance. The text should be of a high quality and brief—no more than several pages. Every word must count as there are usually time limits on how long each person may speak. In addition, your audience has a limited attention span and will appreciate someone who gets to the point rather than rambling.

▶ A written copy of the testimony should be provided at the time to members of the committee or body to which the testimony is provided as well as to the media with your contact information for any follow-up questions.

▶ Start by introducing yourself and by establishing your credentials. What in your background or experience provides you with the expertise to speak to the issue? It could be your professional experience or your personal experience.

▶ Begin with a clear statement of your position on the policy under consideration.

▶ Provide a rationale for your position that includes both data and a personal face or story that reveals the human context of the problem or issue.

▶ Information provided should grab the audience's attention and be framed to show how your position fits with values and approach of policymakers.

▶ Main points should be listed so that the focus and substance of your proposal is clear to the audience.

▶ Speaking to how the proposal or initiative will or does affect the committee's constituents is usually an important part of testimony.

▶ Be prepared for questions, some of which may be hostile to your position. All questions need to be addressed honestly and rationally, sticking to the major points of the testimony.

▶ If you don't know the answer to a question, admit that you do not know and promise to get back to the committee on the issue. Then be sure to follow up as quickly as possible with an e-mail or a note with the requested information.

▶ If orchestrating a series of people testifying on an issue, determine in advance who will be making which points and the best order for those points to be made for the greatest impact.

The Affordable Green Housing SCS (located on the Allyn & Bacon *My Social Work Lab* Web site) provides an example of how well-crafted public testimony can be effective at the local level. Sustainable housing developer Erik

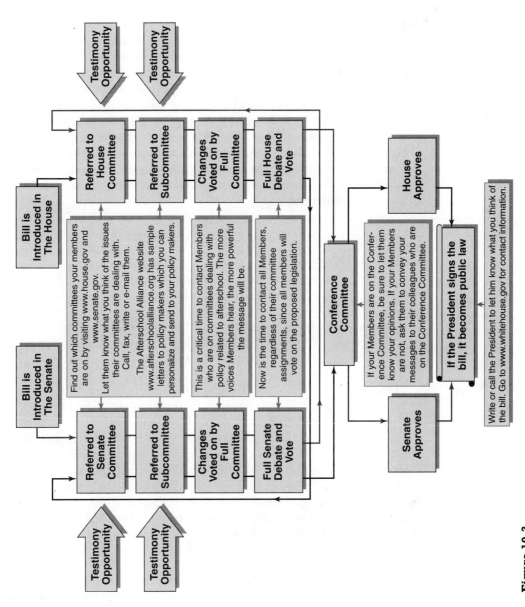

Figure 10.3
Testimony Opportunities

Shorte and Housing Authority social worker Annette Taylor face a hostile-to-indifferent audience at a County Planning Commission meeting when they testify on a proposal to develop a green housing complex for low-income county residents. Their careful and calm rebuttal of negative questions, along with a focus on how the development would improve not only the lives of the residents but also the economic standing of the county (by locating housing near jobs and by stabilizing an area in need of redevelopment), is persuasive to the commissioners. Their testimony is a key factor in the ultimate approval of the development.

In addition to interpersonal communication and public testimony, lobbyists also provide expertise in drafting legislation; engage in relationship-building activities, such as volunteering in electoral campaigns; and spend a good deal of time monitoring government bodies to be ready to lobby against measures that might negatively affect the issues they support. Lobbyists "follow the money" by attending very closely to the budget process. Social service programs commonly face budget cuts. Policy practice advocates must be prepared to act swiftly in the event that a program they support is threatened by legislative or regulatory action. The following case study illustrates how one organization lobbied and mobilized its grassroots network of supporters when their program was threatened.

Case Study: The Foster Grandparents Program Fights Proposed Budget Cuts

The disclosure form (Box 10.11) indicates that Van Scoyoc Associates, acting on behalf of the National Association of Foster Grandparent Directors (NAFGPD), lobbied the House, the Senate, and the Corporation for National and Community Service regarding appropriations for the federally funded Foster Grandparents Program (FGP), which provides volunteer opportunities for seniors (and small stipends for low-income seniors) to mentor, tutor, and support at-risk children.

President George Bush's 2008 budget initially called for significant budget cuts to the program. In response to the looming cuts, the NAFGPD's lobbyist mobilized grassroots support targeting Congress.

In addition to generating more than 1,000 letters of support, the lobbying effort led to the Association's president and a volunteer foster grandparent testifying before Congress. Their congressional testimony demonstrates the power of making a well-crafted public speech before a legislative body. Excerpts from their testimony are presented in boxes 10.12 and 10.13. As you read the two testimonies, compare and contrast that of the Association's president (Box 10.12) with that of a foster grandparent volunteer (Box 10.13). How are the testimonies different? What does each achieve, from a persuasive viewpoint?

The Association's lobbying efforts were successful: The FGP funding was restored, as indicated in this communiqué from the NAFGPD president:

Both the House and Senate restored our $13.387M cut that the President proposed in his FY 2008 budget. This occurred because we were relentless, diligent, and methodical in letting Congress know the effect that the cut would have on our programs and beneficiaries—the volunteers, children/youth, and our communities. NAFGPD wants to thank each of you for the phone call, letters, and e-mails that you sent. And we want to thank our Washington Representative, who delivered more than 1,000

Policy Practice

Critical Thinking Question

What are the most powerful points this volunteer makes in her testimony? How do they complement and contrast with the testimony of the professional?

Box 10.11 Lobbying Disclosure Form

The excerpt below from a lobbying disclosure form illustrates the type of information lobbyists must provide to the government.

Registrant <u>Van Scoyoc Associates</u>   Client Name <u>National Association of Foster Grandparent Directors</u>

Lobbying Activity. Select as many codes as necessary to reflect the general issue areas in which the registrant engaged in lobbying on behalf of the client during the reporting period. Using a separate page for each code, provide information as requested. Attach additional page(s) as needed.

15. General issue area code   BUD Budget/Appropriations   (one per page)

16. Specific lobbying issues

> H.R.3043/S.1710, Departments of Labor, Health and Human Services, and Related Agencies Appropriations Act,
> FY2008, Foster grandparent program.
> H.R.2857, Generations Invigorating Volunteerism and Education "GIVE" Act, National Service Programs.
> H.R.2764, Consolidated Appropriations Act, FY2008, Foster grandparent program.

17. House(s) of Congress and Federal agencies   ☐ Check if None ☑ House
                                                 ☑ Senate   ☑ Other

> Corporation for National and Community Service

Box 10.12 Congressional Testimony: The Professional

TESTIMONY OF JANE WATKINS
SUBMITTED TO THE
SUBCOMMITTEE ON LABOR, HEALTH AND HUMAN SERVICES, EDUCATION
AND RELATED AGENCIES APPROPRIATIONS
UNITED STATES HOUSE OF REPRESENTATIVES

SUBJECT: FISCAL YEAR 2008 APPROPRIATIONS FOR
THE FOSTER GRANDPARENT PROGRAM
A Program of the Corporation for National and Community Service

March 29, 2007
2:00 PM

Mr. Chairman and Members of the Subcommittee, thank you for the opportunity to submit this testimony in support of FY 2008 funding for the Foster Grandparent Program (FGP), the oldest and largest of the three programs known collectively as the National Senior Volunteer Corps. . . . NAFGPD is a membership-supported professional organization whose roster includes the majority of more than 350 directors, who administer Foster Grandparent Programs nationwide, as well as local sponsoring agencies and others who value and support the work of FGP.

(Continued)

Box 10.12   Congressional Testimony: The Professional (*Continued*)

Mr. Chairman, I would like to begin by thanking you and the distinguished members of the Subcommittee for your steadfast support of the Foster Grandparent Program. No matter what the circumstances, this Subcommittee has always been there to protect the integrity and mission of our programs. Our volunteers and the children they serve across the country are the beneficiaries of your commitment to FGP, and for that we thank you. I also want to acknowledge your outstanding staff for their tireless work and very difficult job they have to "make the numbers fit"—an increasingly difficult task in this budget environment.

ADMINISTRATION'S REQUEST FOR FGP

Although the number of older people in America eligible to serve as Foster Grandparent volunteers is increasing by leaps and bounds as the "Baby Boomer" cohort ages, we were extremely disappointed to learn that—instead of seeking an increase for FGP to enable FGP to engage more low-income seniors in service—the Administration has proposed slashing funding for FGP by $13.387 million—a 12.1% cut.

IMPACT OF THE ADMINISTRATION'S PROPOSED FUNDING CUT

FGP is the only program in existence today that actively seeks out, trains, enables, places, and supports the elderly poor in contributing to their communities by changing the lives of children who desperately need one-on-one attention. If enacted, this request will have a devastating effect on FGP programs nationwide:

- 3,150 low-income Foster Grandparent volunteers—over 10% of the current volunteer complement—will be cut permanently, slashing the total number of Foster Grandparent volunteers from 30,550 to 27,400. This will happen at a time when the number of FGP volunteers has not increased appreciably in 10 years!
- Local communities will lose over 3.3 million hours of volunteer service annually.
- Approximately 35,000 fewer children with special needs will receive the critical services provided by Foster Grandparents.

****

[TEXT OUTLINES SCOPE OF PROGRAM, CLIENTS SERVED, VOLUNTEER NETWORK OF FOSTER GRANDPARENTS, VOLUNTEER SITES]

FGP: COST-EFFECTIVE SERVICE

The Foster Grandparent Program serves local communities in a high quality, efficient and cost-effective manner, saving local communities money by helping our older volunteers stay independent and healthy and out of expensive in-home or institutional care. Using the Independent Sector's 2005 valuation for one hour of volunteer service ($18.03/hour), the value of the service given by Foster Grandparents annually is over $503 million, and represents a 4-fold return on the federal dollars invested in FGP. The annual federal cost for one Foster Grandparent is $3,960—less than $4.00 per hour.

****

The message is clear: (1) The population of low-income seniors available to volunteer 15 to 40 hours every week is increasing; (2) communities need and want more Foster Grandparent volunteers and more Foster Grandparent programs. The subcommittee's continued investment in FGP now will pay off in savings realized later, as more seniors stay healthy and independent through volunteer service, as communities save tax dollars, and as children with special needs are helped to become contributing members of society.

Mr. Chairman, in closing I would like to again thank you for the subcommittee's support and leadership for FGP over the years. NAFGPD believes that you and your colleagues in Congress appreciate what our low-income senior volunteers accomplish every day in communities across the country.

Box 10.13 Congressional Testimony: The Volunteer

ORAL TESTIMONY OF LUCILLE STOUT
GIVEN BEFORE THE
SUBCOMMITTEE ON LABOR, HEALTH AND HUMAN SERVICES, EDUCATION
AND RELATED AGENCIES APPROPRIATIONS

UNITED STATES HOUSE OF REPRESENTATIVES

SUBJECT: FISCAL YEAR 2008 APPROPRIATIONS FOR
THE FOSTER GRANDPARENT PROGRAM
A Program of the Corporation for National and Community Service

March 29, 2007
2:00 PM

Hi, my name is Lucille Stout (Foster Grandparent with the Foster Grandparent Program of Central Florida). I have been a Foster Grandparent for four (4) years. I have not been involved in anything as worthwhile, fulfilling, or rewarding as this program.

****

It [the Foster Grandparent Program] had all the right ingredients to make a person happy. The training and support I received from the program staff was very helpful. I was assigned to an elementary school close to my home. It is here (Dream Lake Elementary School) that I get to help over 160 children in 8 different classrooms and mentor 6 specific children who are in need of added help in reading and math. The smiles and hugs I get from these children are all the thanks I need.

Of course knowing how much the teachers appreciate my help is a blessing as well.

I would hope and pray that if anything the Foster Grandparents would be on the increase to accommodate all the new children moving into Orlando. I have heard about 1,200 people are moving into this area every week.

It would be a very sad day for me and for my "kids" if I was one of the 12 percent who got cut from this wonderful program. Thank you!

P.S. One of the nicest compliments I ever received from a school administrator was "we could never pay you enough for all you do for our children."

letters to the Hill, followed up on the contacts that we had made in both the House and the Senate, and worked tirelessly with Congress to ensure that our programs did not suffer a devastating 12+% cut.

Immediately, we will begin developing a strategy for working with CNCS and Congress on an increase for our programs in the FY 2009 appropriations (www.nafgpd.org/presMsg.cfm).

Whether the lobbying campaign is defensive in nature, as in the FGP example, or proactive in attempting to change current laws and regulation, the effects of lobbying can be enhanced when paired with a strong mobilization effort. (See Chapter 7 to learn more about mobilizing strategies.)

INVOLVEMENT OF CLIENTS
IN THE ADVOCACY EFFORT

The volunteer's testimony (Box 10.13) in the case example of the FGP above illustrates the power of the client speaking for herself. Advocates frequently write letters, send e-mails, and provide testimony *on behalf* of those who use social services or benefits designed to address "social problems." Who, though, is in the best position to discuss how a policy or a problem affects an individual, but that individual himself or herself? As indicated earlier in this chapter, it takes only a relatively few letters or e-mails to gain the attention of a legislator. And if those letters come from ordinary people instead of advocates and others whose professional roles include advocacy functions, policymakers tend to pay special attention. Advocates regularly write, but the average citizen must be particularly affected or moved to take the time and energy to communicate with legislators. If clients or marginalized populations come to testify in a committee hearing, then policymakers have a unique opportunity for dialogue. Policymakers can then ask those affected to provide more detail about their specific needs and circumstances. Such testimony can have a powerful impact on how policymakers view the "problem" as well as the proposed policy solution. While facts and figures can be persuasive, hearing the story of one or two people and how they are affected by a current policy or problem and what they see as the best way to address the issue can be extremely powerful as was the testimony of Lucille Stout above.

In addition to the powerful, persuasive arguments that clients can make, participation in the legislative process can be empowering for them, just as it is for beginning policy advocates. Most people believe that what they have to say will not make a difference, but policymakers want to do what is best for their constituents. After all, if their constituents are pleased with the legislator's performance, they may reelect him or her to another term of office. So as clients or citizens begin to participate as politically involved persons, they will gain more confidence about their ability to speak with legislators. They will realize that while they may not be "experts," they are still experts in their own lives and can speak their minds about the circumstances they face, both their strengths and their challenges.

As was highlighted in the health care SCS, when involving clients in the legislative process, it is important to guard against any potential exploitation of the client and his or her situation and potential vulnerability. Being covered in the media may expose the client to unforeseen risks and complications that must be considered beforehand. In addition, clients may be exploited when others ask them to speak *on behalf of* all members of a particular group, such as Latinos, gays, or women. Preparing for testimony may help avoid some of these potential problems and alleviate natural fears about such a new experience.

The social work profession stresses the importance of client empowerment, in making decisions about his or her own life. Too often, however, empowerment does not include political empowerment. Participating as a citizen in the legislative process is part of developing a sense of political empowerment. While there may be many obstacles to participation in the legislative process by low-income and other marginalized groups, there are also organizations (welfare rights organizations, for example, and neighborhood associations) that are finding ways to get some people involved.[49] Reflecting on her work with mothers on welfare in the days just before TANF went into effect, Rickie Solinger notes the motivation that keeps the women involved in the struggle, "[K]eep pushing, keep organizing; that's what gives birth to the next great wave of activism. Some of the members of Women United are standing up and speaking out for the first time. They say the experience makes them feel strong."[50] And that is what client empowerment is all about.

CONCLUSION

In American society, politics can be described as both an open and a closed system. Politics is an open system, because all citizens can participate. Politics can also be described as a closed system, or as a subculture with its own boundaries that create "insiders" and "outsiders." Policy practitioners are obligated to work on the inside of the political system, gaining knowledge of legislative processes; building relationships with legislators, legislative staff, and other government officials; and mobilizing their policy practice resources to act as agents for social change or as a protective barrier defending governmental programs that serve society's most vulnerable populations. At each stage of the legislative process, from issue identification to bill writing, to shepherding a bill through committee, policy practitioners can exert influence.

In the hubbub of state capitols and Washington, DC, where "money talks" and power and privilege are readily apparent, one might have predicted that the social work profession would be a minor player, given its comparative lack of financial resources and entrenched power. However, the public spirit at the profession's core has given social work an larger impact on U.S. legislative history, at both the state and national levels. As you take up your own policy practice, you will be joining a cadre of dedicated women and men who have worked against the odds to make a difference in the lives of those they serve.

Log onto **MySocialWorkLab** to access a wealth of case studies, videos, and assessment. (*If you did not receive an access code to* **MySocialWorkLab** *with this text and wish to purchase access online, please visit* www.mysocialworklab.com.)

1. **Watch the Connecting Core Competency videos on Policy Practice.** How is the issue framed at first by

the correctional officer and then by the social worker? How does the social worker help the correctional officer see the issue from another perspective as they approach the administrator?

2. **Review the Gay Marriage SCS.** What would be the best way to frame the issue for the broadest appeal in a lobbying effort?

PRACTICE TEST
The following questions will test your knowledge of the content found within this chapter. For additional assessment, including licensing-exam type questions on applying chapter content to practice, visit **MySocialWorkLab**.

1. Bills sent to a committee whose chair does not concur with the bill's intent frequently end up:
   a. Being voted down in the committee
   b. Buried in the committee without a hearing or vote
   c. Being sent back to the sponsors to be reworked
   d. Forwarded to the second chamber for changes and resubmission

2. If the two chambers of a legislature pass two slightly different versions of a bill,
   a. The authors sit down with the caucus leaders to work out the differences
   b. The two chambers vote on each other's versions
   c. The bill is sent to a conference committee to come up with a compromise
   d. The bill dies for lack of a positive vote

3. Once a social issue or problem has been identified and framed, a variety of policy options to address the issue may be identified by using
   a. Research about what approaches work best in similar situations
   b. Party ideology that identifies the values and ends to be pursued
   c. Surveys of what the public thinks would be best
   d. Historical and traditional approaches to solving problems.

4. Most interest groups
   a. Exert undue influence on the legislative process and undermine democracy
   b. Purport to represent vulnerable populations though they really represent business interests
   c. Operate on the periphery of the legislative process having little impact
   d. Promote their own self-interests in the legislative process.

5. Two sources of power interest groups have in influencing legislators and policymaking are:
   a. Money and threatening litigation
   b. Media campaigns and votes
   c. Gifts to legislators and information/expertise
   d. Votes and money

6. Neocorporatism is a theory of
   a. The way business is organized today and has changed historically.
   b. How all people in a democracy are free to organize into interest groups.
   c. The collaboration between business and government to create economic stability.
   d. The Neocons, who want less government regulation and greater freedom for business.

7. Expressing a view on specific legislation to the general public that includes a call to action is the hallmark of:
   a. Direct lobbying
   b. Grassroots lobbying
   c. Indirect lobbying
   d. Community lobbying

8. The brief list of key points in an advocacy position that can be left with legislators is called
   a. Policy brief
   b. White paper
   c. Talking points
   d. Summary

9. In the legislative process, when bills are publicly presented, normally testimony is heard during:
   a. Special chamber hearings
   b. Committee meetings closed to public
   c. Committee or subcommittee hearings
   d. Federal judicial hearings

10. Some positive outcomes of direct client testimony on an issue are:
   a. Increased self esteem for the client and a fast track on issue resolution begins
   b. Issue less likely to become bogged down in committee and client feels empowered
   c. Policymakers' view of the issue is powerfully framed and a fast track on issue resolution begins
   d. The client generally feels empowered and policymakers' view of the issue is powerfully framed

---

Log onto **MySocialWorkLab** once you have completed the Practice Test above to access additional study tools and assessment.

Answers

Key: 1) b, 2) c, 3) a, 4) d, 5) d, 6) c, 7) b, 8) c, 9) c, 10) d

11

Building a Coalition to Create Change

CHAPTER OUTLINE

Introduction 282

Forming Coalitions 283
Defining Coalitions
Advantages and Drawbacks of Coalition
    Membership
Identifying Likely Allies to Form Coalitions
Have Some Problem or Broad Goals in Mind
Recruitment Strategies

Generating the Agenda for Inclusion 293
Finding Common Ground
Continuing to Expand the Circle by Inviting Others
    to Attend Meetings
Integrating New Members

Coalition Developmental Stages 296
Build the Group's Expertise
Develop an Identity
Engage Participants in Action
Involving Members in the Organizational Structure

Meeting the Challenges in Coalitions 305
Handling Disagreements
Sharing Power
Staying Organized
Raising Funds

Creating Ongoing Networks of Influence—
    Moving from Ad Hoc to Ongoing 308

Characteristics of Successful Coalitions 310

Importance of Coalition Leadership 315

Celebrate the Small Victories and Have Fun
    as Part of the Process 316

Conclusion 316

Chapter Review 317

Practice Test 317

MySocialWorkLab 317
    Core Competency Series videos on Policy
    Practice
    Gay Marriage Amendment SCS

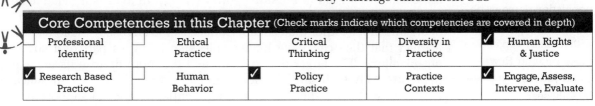

Core Competencies in this Chapter (Check marks indicate which competencies are covered in depth)				
☐ Professional Identity	☐ Ethical Practice	☐ Critical Thinking	☐ Diversity in Practice	☑ Human Rights & Justice
☑ Research Based Practice	☐ Human Behavior	☑ Policy Practice	☐ Practice Contexts	☑ Engage, Assess, Intervene, Evaluate

INTRODUCTION

Politics makes strange bedfellows.

CHARLES DUDLEY WARNER, American Editor and Author, 1829–1900

In the debate over welfare reform in the 1990s, one of the major points of contention was the idea of instituting a "family cap"—so that once a woman and her child(ren) became eligible for welfare benefits, those benefits would not increase if she had any additional children. Proponents of the family cap claimed that the Aid to Families with Dependent Children (AFDC) rules at the time actually encouraged women to have more children to increase their welfare checks. The family cap, they said, would reduce out of wedlock births and decrease welfare expenditures. "Sen. Phil Gramm (R.-Tex.) warned that striking the family cap would 'perpetuate a system which subsidizes illegitimacy, which gives cash bonuses to people who have more and more people on welfare.' 'Do not tell the states how to spend their own money,' said Gramm, 'but set a few basic moral Principles for the use of federal funds.'"[1] The Christian Coalition supported many of the harsher provisions of welfare reform, including the family cap as a way to reduce the number of births out of wedlock. By contrast, Catholic Charities joined with the American Civil Liberties Union, the National Association of Social Workers, the National Right to Life Committee, and Planned Parenthood in opposing the family cap and other more punitive provisions of welfare reform.[2] The Roman Catholic bishops opposed the family cap from their faith and stance on the sanctity of life and because they feared the family cap might lead to increased abortions among low-income women. In contrast, Planned Parenthood presented its analysis in opposition to the family cap, highlighting the lack of "conclusive impact data" on potential changes in abortion rates, the negligible impact it would have on overall out-of-wedlock birth rates, and the severe hardship it would impose on individual affected families in terms of hunger and homelessness.[3] Though Catholic Charities and the Catholic bishops disagreed with Planned Parenthood's position on access to abortion, on the issue of the "family cap," they found common ground to oppose this aspect of welfare reform. Politics does indeed make for strange bedfellows. The coalition was successful in keeping a mandated family cap from becoming part of the federal 1996 Temporary Assistance for Needy Families (TANF) legislation.

Coalitions, like all advocacy groups, must remain vigilant with regard to ongoing policy developments around their issues. Though the mandatory federal family cap was defeated, family caps remain an option at the state level. In 2006, 22 states had a family cap. Interestingly enough, 70.6 percent of those states with high African American populations had a family cap while only 29.4 percent of those states with low African American populations had a family cap.[4]

This chapter explores the nature of coalitions, how they come about and operate in the political environment of advocacy efforts, and how they can be most effectively used in pursuing policy change. In today's legislative climate, just as advocates have learned they can have a louder voice speaking on behalf of organizations rather than as individuals, so too advocacy organizations have learned that they can have louder voices speaking as part of a coalition of organizations. The larger the coalition and the more diverse its membership, the more likely their united voices will be heard and have an influence since they represent a broad constituency of potential voters and supporters.

Research Based Practice

Critical Thinking Question

What hypotheses might you generate regarding the differences noted in population demographics between the states with a family cap and those without? How could you test out those hypotheses?

Policy practitioners involved in creating coalitions will find it important to attend to particular stages in the coalition-building process, and essential steps in growing vibrant, diverse, and influential coalitions. These fundamental focal points in coalition building and management include: forming coalitions, generating the agenda for inclusion, engaging participants in action, meeting the challenges in coalitions, creating ongoing networks of influence, and successful coalitions.

This chapter provides students with a basic understanding of how to build and maintain a successful coalition focused on advocacy and change, as well as foundation knowledge of empirical research on coalition building, including examples of successful strategies for coalition-based advocacy action. Essential skills for successful coalition building are discussed, and students are provided with an opportunity to critique coalition building efforts in a Simulated Case Study (SCS) included with this text.

FORMING COALITIONS

Defining Coalitions

Coalitions have distinct characteristics that differentiate them from networks and other groupings of organizations as they are more activist oriented in their pursuit of social policy change. Table 11.1 provides an overview of the salient features of coalitions that are discussed below.

The primary purpose of networks is to help member organizations gather and disseminate information through the connections that are created among member organizations. Though they may take advocacy stances from time to time on important issues, advocacy and organizing for change are not their primary goals. Coalitions, on the other hand, are formed with a more action-oriented purpose. Sometimes networks may be mobilized in a crisis to take action and, therefore, may behave more like coalitions. So the definitional line between networks and coalitions can be fuzzy at times when comparing the above criteria to real organizations in communities. Be careful about relying on the name alone to distinguish between networks and coalitions. Look instead to their stated goals and where they invest their resources and activities.

Social work practitioners understand the importance of developing professional networks to have good contacts at a number of social service agencies

Table 11.1 Comparing Coalition and Network Features

	Type of Organization	
	Network	**Coalition**
Focus or Purpose (from Most Important to Least Important)	▶ Transfer of information ▶ Provision of support ▶ Advocacy at times	▶ United action to change policy ▶ Transfer of information ▶ Mutual support & reciprocity
Membership	Fee, but no major commitment of resources	Invited, fee, and commitment of staff, time, and other resources
Duration	Generally long-term	Both short-term and long-term

and other organizations to facilitate the referral process and to make sure that clients are able to get their needs met. Social workers also acknowledge the importance of these professional networks for mutual support around personal and professional issues that emerge in practice. Sometimes it is helpful to talk about a difficult situation at work with a trusted colleague who is not directly involved in the situation but who can help find a solution to the problem. So practitioners are encouraged to build both personal and professional networks that contribute to their work in a number of ways.

Organizations, as well as individuals, need networks to facilitate referrals, to share information and opportunities, to discuss common problems and issues, and to provide support to one another in numerous ways. Some communities have an organization similar to the Chamber of Commerce for social service agencies. Instead of being for business and the support of businesses as the Chamber is, the organization is for social service agencies, to enhance communication and build some opportunities for collaboration and sharing. These organizations or networks may be "loosely coupled"[5] in that they are connected to one another rather tenuously, but they are still useful as networks of communication. Others, like the Human Services Coalition of Prince George's County, are well organized with a board of directors and a clear structure. From looking at their Web site listing of activities (http://hscofpgc.org), their advocacy role seems less prominent than that of the Seattle Human Services Coalition (http://shscoalition.org/) that self-identifies as "an assertive and unified voice helping people shape public policy to meet basic human needs in Seattle and King County, Washington." For over twenty years, this coalition has set yearly priorities with the long-range goal of meeting "basic human needs in King County, including eliminating institutional racism, by the year 2020."[6] Their Web site identifies a number of successes, such as $59 million in funding for community health and social services in the region from 2002 to 2006 and the creation of a set of tools for human service organizations to use in identifying and eliminating institutional racism in their agencies.

Coalitions form when organizations or interest groups develop alliances to take action with a specific mutually beneficial purpose in mind. The purpose may be to support or oppose a particular policy, similar to the family cap discussed earlier, or more broadly focused such as making social services a funding priority at the state legislature. Coalitions are sometimes formed to sponsor or conduct a particular event, such as a march in favor of a living wage, or may be long-term, such as reducing the number of poor people. So some coalitions are ad hoc, while others are relatively stable over time. Both of the local coalitions identified earlier, the Human Services Coalition of Prince George's County and the Seattle Human Services Coalition, have been operating for a number of years. Some coalitions, like these two, are formed of like-minded organizations, while others, like the one formed temporarily around the family cap issue in the welfare reform debate include strange bedfellows or unlikely partners.

Research shows that more effective advocacy groups at the federal level form coalitions, among other strategies.

Coalitions operate in local communities, at the state level, and at the national level and have become increasingly important in the last twenty years. Bailey and Koney[7] pointed out the potential of "interorganizational community-based collaboratives," a kind of coalition, when they discussed the devolution of policy making to the state level in the 1990s. Research shows that more effective advocacy groups at the federal level form coalitions, among other strategies.[8] Hoefer notes that human service advocacy groups listed coalition building as their most important strategy in their efforts to influence the rule-making process in the executive branch of the federal government in a survey reported in 2000.[9] A good number of states have state coalitions of social service advocacy groups, but forming coalitions does not appear to be consistently linked with the success of human service interest groups in every state.[10] The Indiana Coalition for Human Services celebrated it twenty-fifth anniversary in 2006.[11] One of the largest coalitions in Florida is the Clearinghouse on Human Services, meeting weekly with about fifty members.[12] The mission statement of the Human Services Coalition of Oregon makes clear the value of collective rather than disparate action on legislative outcomes:

> The Human Services Coalition of Oregon (HSCO) is comprised of organizations and individuals whose purpose is to educate and advocate in the Oregon Legislature for vulnerable Oregonians. During the legislative session, we meet weekly to share information, strategies, and to present a supportive, united front on our issues to the legislature and to the media. In doing this, we honor our commitment as members of HSCO to avoid pitting ourselves and our programs, and most importantly—vulnerable Oregonians—against each other. Mission Statement: The Human Services Coalition of Oregon promotes the dignity of all Oregonians through improved public policy and strengthened support for human services.[13]

Too often in the past in human services, when social service budgets had to be cut, advocates for children's services found themselves fighting advocates for housing for homeless people, advocates for employment services for people with disabilities, and advocates for home-based support services for elderly people, among others. The growth of human service coalitions over the past twenty years has reflected, in part, recognition of how counter-productive such fighting with each other has been, particularly when social service funding is threatened with significant reductions across the board. Now state and regional coalitions are presenting a united front to state legislatures to argue that the pie must be made larger for human services, that tax monies spent on human services are investments in the human resources and the human infrastructure of the state, not a drain on the public coffers. The Indiana Coalition for Human Services, for example, included the following goal in its 2007 public policy statement: "Invest in human capital through health and human services as part of Indiana's economic development plan."[14]

The Coalition on Human Needs (see Box 11.1 for list of members) is an example of a "mega" coalition operating at the national level as "an alliance of national organizations working together to promote public policies that address the needs of low-income and other vulnerable people,"[15] and working since 1981 on a variety of issues, including the federal budget and taxes, housing, food and nutrition, and immigrants.

It is sometimes difficult to assess the degree to which the activities of advocates impact policy making processes, but here are three recent accomplishments by the Coalition on Human Needs at the national level:

▶ By narrow vote of 216 to 214, the U.S. House of Representatives passed a budget bill on February 1, 2006; though it cut funding for students, families, children, older people, and people with disabilities, it still was a "major improvement" over the president's original proposal. Advocates sponsored more than 300 events in January across the United States. Representatives received hundreds of thousands of calls from citizens over a four-month period. Hundreds of groups met with their representatives to talk about how the bill would hurt their communities.[16] This massive advocacy effort resulted in persuading four Republicans

Human Rights & Justice

Critical Thinking Question

If there are organizations with which you are not familiar in the membership list of the Coalition on Human Needs in Box 11.1, visit their Web sites. Are you surprised by any of the members? Why do you think they might belong to the Coalition?

Box 11.1   Members of the Coalition on Human Needs

As of March 2007

ACORN, AFSCME, Alliance for Children and Families, American Association of People with Disabilities, American Association of University Women, American Friends Service Committee, American Jewish Committee, American Network of Community Options and Resources, American Psychological Association, Americans for Democratic Action, America's Second Harvest, The Arc and UCP Disability Policy Collaboration, Association for Career and Technical Education, Association of Maternal and Child Health Programs, Bread for the World, Campaign for America's Future, Campaign for Youth Justice, Catholic Charities USA, Center for American Progress, Center for Community Change, Center for Economic and Policy Research, Center for Law and Social Policy, Center for People in Need, Center for Women Policy Studies, Center on Budget & Policy Priorities, Child Welfare League of America, Children's Defense Fund, Church Women United, Cities for Progress/Cities for Peace, Citizens for Tax Justice, Community Action Partnership, Congressional Black Caucus Foundation, Inc., Congressional Hunger Center, Consortium for Citizens with Disabilities, Corporation for Enterprise Development, Craig Associates, Easter Seals, Inc., Economic Policy Institute, Evangelical Lutheran Church in America, Every Child Matters Foundation, Families USA, First Focus, Food Research & Action Center, Friends Committee on National Legislation, General Board of Church & Society (United Methodist Church), General Board of Global Ministries (United Methodist Church), Generations United, Housing Assistance Council, Human Services Coalition of Oregon, Illinois Facilities Fund, Inclusion Foundation, Institute for Children and Poverty, Institute for Women's Policy Research, Jewish Council for Public Affairs, Joni B Goodman (Washington Representative), Legal Momentum, Lutheran Services in America, Mennonite Central Committee, National Advocacy Center of the Sisters of the Good Shepherd, National Alliance to End Homelessness, National Association for State Community Services Programs, National Association for the

Education of Young Children, National Association of School Psychologists, National Association of Social Workers, National Coalition for the Homeless, National Committee to Preserve Social Security & Medicare, National Community Action Foundation, National Community Reinvestment Coalition, National Consumer Law Center, National Council of Jewish Women, National Council of La Raza, National Council of the Churches of Christ in the USA, National Disability Rights Network, National Education Association, National Head Start Association, National Housing Trust, National Human Services Assembly, National Immigration Law Center, National Low Income Housing Coalition, National Ministries, American Baptist Churches USA, National Neighborhood Coalition, National Partnership for Women and Families, National Priorities Project, National WIC Association, National Women's Law Center, National Youth Employment Coalition, NETWORK (A National Catholic Social Justice Lobby), OMB Watch, Oregon Food Bank, Parents' Action for Children, People for the American Way, policyAmerica, Poverty and Race Research Action Council, Presbyterian Church (U.S.A.) Washington Office, Religious Action Center, Research Institute for Independent Living, RESULTS, Salvation Army (National Social Services Office), Sargent Shriver National Center on Poverty Law, Seekers Church, Service Employee International Union, Sisters of Mercy of the Americas, Inc., U.S. Conference of Catholic Bishops, Unitarian Universalist Service Committee, United Church of Christ - Justice and Witness Ministries, United Jewish Communities, United Way of America, Voices for America's Children, Volunteers of America, Wider Opportunities for Women, The Workforce Alliance, Work, Welfare, and Families and YWCA USA.

Coalition on Human Needs
1120 Connecticut Ave. NW Suite 910 Washington, DC 20036 phone: (202) 223-2532
fax: (202) 223-2538 email: info@chn.org
Retrieved from www.chn.org July 5, 2008.

who had supported the bill to change their votes to "no." Though advocates were not satisfied with the final outcome, they recognized that their actions had made a difference.

▶ After many months of negotiation and compromise, the Older Americans Act was reauthorized for another five years by voice vote on September 10, 2006 in the House of Representatives and then in the U.S.

Senate on September 30, also by voice vote. Advocates had worked hard on improvements in the bill, including more funding for outreach efforts to low-income seniors to enroll them in underutilized government programs,[17] including Food Stamps, Medicaid, and assistance with Medicare premiums.

▶ The work of advocates, plus bad economic news, was credited with turning around Republican opposition to the extension of Unemployment Insurance for another 13 weeks that was attached to the bill providing continued funding for the wars in Iraq and Afghanistan signed by President Bush on June 30, 2008. Additionally, funding for veterans' education benefits and disaster relief were included.[18]

Advantages and Drawbacks of Coalition Membership

As member organizations work together and achieve their goals, they begin to see beyond their individual and parochial needs of older people, children, or people with disabilities, for example, to the greater human service need. In this way, one possible consequence of working actively in a coalition is the reduction of human service organizations fighting with each other for limited funds. The coalition challenge is how to increase the funds overall so that all organizations will realize some benefit.

Lowery and Brasher[19] identify four advantages for interest groups that join coalitions as part of their legislative advocacy effort: (1) sharing the cost of lobbying; (2) presenting a united front that puts the interest groups in greater control of the shape of the legislation; (3) creating greater legitimacy for the interest group's cause; and (4) increasing the organization's influence as it will be seen as equal to the most active member of the coalition. Rosenthal notes, "Coalition building is not easy, but it is well worth the effort. From a legislative perspective, its value is clear. The greater and more broad-based the support, the more likely that legislators will see the wisdom of a particular policy direction."[20] Such broad support is difficult to oppose and provides the political "cover" that legislators sometimes need to support the coalition's cause.

In spite of these clear potential advantages of affiliating with a coalition, Lowery and Brasher also point out there can be a down-side to coalitions as well. Sometimes other members of a coalition may be potential competitors for members and resources such as when the American Association of People with Disabilities and UCP Disability Policy Collaboration are both members of the Coalition on Human Needs. Having to come to some consensus on the coalition goals may mean having to compromise on particular organizational policy goals and also agreeing to not disagree or "fight" among coalition members in public. Such sacrifices of organizational autonomy may be difficult to make. Giving up this autonomy may not be worth the potential value of a coalition when organizations are in fierce competition with each other for membership or resources. So when are organizations more likely to join coalitions? Lowery and Brasher summarize the research demonstrating that if there is strong opposition or an opposing coalition, then organizations are more likely to join coalitions. If the issue is being considered across several legislative committees, then coalitions are more likely to be formed. And lastly, organizations that have a history of affiliating with each other are more likely to form similar coalitions again on another issue.

Simply bringing groups together around a common concern does not necessarily result in the creation of a coalition. In recognition of the aging of people with developmental disabilities, providers serving both the aging population and people with developmental disabilities in Georgia came together to share information and discuss common concerns. Though participants reported an increased awareness of the challenges faced by people with disabilities who were aging, the group did not move beyond that information sharing stage to form a coalition.[21]

Identifying Likely Allies to Form Coalitions

As an organization begins to work on developing a coalition, the first step is to identify potential allies for collaboration on this particular effort or goal. Organizations already in the "network" of regular contacts and information exchange systems of the initiating organization will be important. In the health care SCS that accompanies this book (located on Allyn & Bacon's *MySocialWorkLab* Web site), Marta Madison invited her colleague Dr. Ravi Singh to join the group, knowing his perspective coming from Vancouver would be supportive of the emerging efforts of the social work group. Later, Buck Hoffman expressed disappointment when Ricardo Gomez was not able to come to some initial meetings as he recognized his input from a "minority" perspective would be valuable and he would not be treated as a token. He also valued Ricardo's connections and network that he would bring to the work of the group. Identifying those who have a broad circle of connections can be of great assistance, and Marta points to the importance of everyone helping to identify potentially interested groups.

> Marta writes: 2006/09/23 Wed, 1:30 pm—Also, we need to expand our circle. Remember the list of steps on coalition building that Buck gave us? We need everyone to go to the blog to identify more stakeholders they want to attend, like AARP [American Association of Retired People], plus indicate contacts. Remember, expanding the circle doesn't have to be that formal. If you're in a carpool, talk. If you're in the coffee room, talk. If you're at a Tigers game watching, or waiting, or yet again questioning the wisdom of their inexplicable affection for the T formation, mention the coalition.

Using all the resources at their disposal, the initial group in a coalition can expand the group rapidly. Here the goal is to build a coalition that will be in place for some time. In the gay marriage SCS, the coalition building occurred in planning the strategy for the rally. Representation from Parents, Families, and Friends of Lesbians and Gays (P-FLAG), the Unitarians, other churches, the American Civil Liberties Union (ACLU), and National Association of Social Workers (NASW) was highlighted in attempting to build a strong and broad coalition to demonstrate the varied but united opposition to the Gay Marriage Amendment being considered for the state constitution. Having a diverse group at such a rally demonstrates the broad opposition to such an amendment. Organizers want to make the point that the opposition comes from people who are straight, Christian, and mainstream standing in solidarity with gay and lesbian friends and neighbors.

Have Some Problem or Broad Goals in Mind

While the initiating organization will already have a focus or issue in mind, bringing in new partners may require some reframing or redefinition of that focus or issue. Usually the coalition umbrella goal or mission must be broad and inclusive enough so that all member organizations can feel they comfortably fit within the coalition without having to compromise any of their basic values. So, for example, the Seattle Human Services Coalition seeks to shape "public policy to help people meet their basic human needs" which the Web site delineates as including "homelessness, hunger, domestic violence, childcare, literacy, aging, disabilities, sexual assault, health care, employment, racial equity, and child/youth development."[22] A wide range of human service organizations could be comfortable under this broad umbrella. Even their 2008 priorities are broad and inclusive of many human services, as noted in Box 11.2. It is worth noting that the first two priorities are clearly connected to their overall goal and organizational mission. The second two priorities are focused on internal organizational maintenance needs and point to two common challenges that coalitions face: learning how to collaborate effectively as a coalition rather than fighting with each other for limited resources and securing ongoing funding for the coalition itself through membership dues and other fundraising efforts.

These examples have illustrated coalitions that are broadly focused on human needs and social services. Other coalitions may be focused more narrowly on a specific event, legislative initiative, or community issue in an effort to target a change effort. In these targeted coalitions like the one that focused on the family-cap issue at the beginning of this chapter, the participating organizations may not share anything in common with each other except for the common concern about the targeted issue. In the health care SCS, the group wants to gather a diverse set of organizations and individuals who are concerned about health care in their community. So Annie Haskins writes about the mission statement:

> 2006/09/23 Wed, 1:30 pm—Our mission statement should make clear that we are not party driven, nor are we solution pre-determined. That we are not favoring a privately funded system nor a publicly funded system, but rather that we are seeking a system that works for all people and all employers and for all governments, both state and local in Factoria.

The coalition of organizations that came together in Seattle to protest against the World Trade Organization (WTO) and its policies during its Ministerial Conference in late November 1999 is an example of such a targeted coalition. The WTO includes representatives from trading nations and sets international trading policies to facilitate free trade among countries of the world. The developing and developed countries sometimes see different impacts of these free trade policies. About 1,400 labor and social justice organizations united to

---

Box 11.2 Seattle Human Services Coalition (SHSC) 2008 Priorities

▶ Develop support for stable, adequate funding for community health and human services to assist residents of King County to meet their basic human needs.

▶ Monitor, analyze, and educate on City of Seattle policies that affect residents' abilities to meet their basic human needs.

▶ Coalition building to strengthen SHSC members' abilities to work collaboratively.

▶ Develop adequate, stable funding for SHSC functions.

Source: Seattle Human Services Coalition, http://shscoalition.org/priorities.htm (accessed July 2, 2008).

protest the policies of the WTO at the conference. From all over the world, these organizations united in standing up for third world countries, strengthening social services, increasing food security, and other environmental and social issues they contended were jeopardized by WTO policies. When police intervened in the massive protests, the resulting violence had repercussions beyond the issue of free trade and caused some to question whether rights to free speech had been trampled. The WTO failed to come to agreement on any resolutions at the meeting, and there were political ramifications in Seattle afterwards, including the resignation of the chief of police.

Whether a targeted or a more long-term effort, developing an effective coalition involves a number of steps and much attention to detail as Buck makes explicit in his notes on how to create "a powerhouse coalition" in the health care SCS (Box 11.3). The discussion presented here includes much of the theoretical and research documentation that suggests the power of the steps Buck lists. Some examples from the SCS are included as well to further illustrate how these steps may be enacted in actual policy practice.

Box 11.3   Buck's Notes on "Creating a Powerhouse Coalition" from Health Care SCS

1. Be sure all participants understand the problem and the broad goals.
2. Brainstorm on stakeholders.
3. Involve as many stakeholders as possible.
4. Study the problem and possible solutions so that the coalition becomes the best resource for information on the problem.
5. Constantly expand the circle by extending more and more invitations.
6. "Listen" to stakeholders' concerns rather than being sure you all agree.
7. Develop a name, a Website, an e-mail list, and open a bank account.
8. Create a dynamite PowerPoint presentation on the problems and goals of the group.
9. Train members on effective presentation skills.
10. Publicize a speakers' bureau on health care issues.
11. Speak whenever/wherever possible.
12. Hold regular meetings so people can plan the coalition into their calendars.
13. Create a FEW key committees so coalition members can offer their expertise to the right people.
14. DO STUFF! Letters to editor, op ed pieces, speak—not to just civic groups, but to classes. Have a booth at public events and fairs.
15. Understand the media: Develop contacts, nourish contacts, and provide news to those who hunger for news, that is, reporters.
16. Be sure we have a problem resolution process firmly in place so that as inevitable disagreements occur within the group, we can work it out.
17. Be transparent. Have minutes of meetings. (They don't need to be boring!)
18. Recruit talent where needed. We soc. work types often assume that the facts will speak for themselves, but, we often could use a good data analyst and graphic artist to help us make our point in a more compelling way.
19. Involve politicians from all parties with no favoritism and no promises.
20. When other groups join, be sure they get visibility as specific, unique players. They must not be "lost" in the coalition. If they are lost, they will drop out.
21. Be certain where we can compromise—and where process and outcome are set in concrete.
22. Understand opponents and their positions as well as we understand our own process and goals.
23. Help everyone remember that progress will be slow. Change will not be dramatic. Celebrate small victories and accomplishments so that "fun" is a part of the process and so that morale is never in the basement. (One guy in the basement—named Buck—is one too many. But I'm expecting all of you to help me end my burnout by means of a coalition that has IMPACT!)

Recruitment Strategies

Coalitions come into being when a few people from key organizations who share a concern come together and determine they are more likely to be successful if they join forces and pool some resources to reach their common goals. When the decision is made to form a coalition with a particular or more generalized goal in mind, the group will then brainstorm to identify other stakeholders or potential allies to involve from among their own networks of organizational contacts. They will identify other potential coalition members from among those whom they have encountered in their previous lobbying or community organizing efforts. Box 11.4 points out some of the issues to be considered when identifying potential new coalition members.

There may be times when a decision is made to deliberately exclude a particular group from the coalition. Perhaps the group has a "radical" or controversial reputation in the community that may hurt the coalition's cause and acceptance by key legislators.[23] On the other hand, as Rosenthal points out, having more radical groups involved may enable the more moderate groups to gain more of what they want. "Despite the problems of dissension, when Greenpeace joins in a coalition with the more moderate Audubon Society and Sierra Club, the former's radical position enables the latter groups to get more."[24] Staying focused on the issue can help diverse coalitions stay together, but a diversion may lead to splintering the coalition. A coalition of organizations representing people with mental illness, their parents, and mental health professionals can agree, for example, on the need for increased funding for community services. If they get diverted by the issue of involuntary commitments to mental health facilities, the coalition is unlikely to be able to continue as a united force.[25] Deciding which groups to include or exclude from a coalition requires thoughtfulness and reflection. A more homogeneous coalition may have less difficulty reaching consensus, but may sacrifice some diversity of perspectives and views that could be useful in advancing its issue.

Decisions will need to be made about how and who will approach potential new members. Using already existing networks of relationships may mean that different people will be making the contacts to invite different organizations to participate. For example, in seeking additional organizational endorsers for its

---

Box 11.4   Issues for a Coalition to Consider in Inviting New Members to Join:

- Is the potential new partner organization striving to accomplish the same goals?

- Does the new organization use processes that are compatible with coalition processes as well? If offering a different perspective or orientation, can the coalition tolerate or even use the differences to its advantage?

- What resources (funding, power and influence, reputation, leadership, constituents, and linkages to other organizations) could the new organization bring to the coalition?

- What reasons might the new organization have for joining the coalition? Could any of these motivations run at cross-purposes to the goals of the coalition?

- Is the leadership of the new organization willing and able to commit to the nitty-gritty work of the coalition?

- Could the new organization bring a potentially disruptive "hidden agenda" to the coalition that might distract it from its goal and consume unnecessary energy?

- If this organization is a member of the coalition, will other potential member organizations become alienated?

- Are there any risks the coalition may be assuming in asking this new partner organization to join the coalition? If so, are they outweighed by the potential benefits?

single-payer health insurance initiative in Indiana in 2007, Hoosiers for a Commonsense Health Plan looked to a current member who was a minister to contact the local ministerial alliance and a member social worker to contact the Indiana Chapter of the NASW.

Sometimes, a visit to the potential organizational member will be appropriate, to invite participation and gauge interest. Representatives of two of the already committed organizations can plan on making the call to invite the participation of the new agency. Selecting representatives carefully is important at this stage in the process. People who are already "known" to the potential new member or who are looked up to or influential in the potential new member's circle of contacts may be viewed with greater trust and, therefore, receive a warmer reception. Coalitions are built among organizations, but they ultimately depend on forging human relationships built on mutual trust and understanding. As in all social work practice, strong coalitions depend on strong relationships among the representatives of the participating organizations. This issue will be addressed in more depth later in this chapter. Where visits are not possible due to distance and expense or timeliness, telephone conversations may serve equally well as a way to dialogue with potential participating organizations. E-mail may be a useful auxiliary method to guarantee consistency in message and information sent. E-mail might serve to broach the subject initially with the suggestion of a follow-up phone contact or in-person interview. Documents clarifying the coalition mission and goals can easily be transmitted by e-mail. Because e-mail can be so easily misinterpreted though, it does require some personal follow-up that will engage the representative of the new organization in a dialogue with a real person who can respond to questions and concerns.

The initiating organization and the others to first join the coalition must reach out to other potential organizational members and convince them to get involved in the action effort. A general recruitment strategy will be developed or will evolve as the initiating organization encounters success. Box 11.5 highlights steps and considerations in developing a coalition recruitment strategy.

Involving a number of people in this outreach effort will strengthen the coalition as they articulate the reasons that their own organizations have

---

Box 11.5   Considerations in Developing a Coalition Recruitment Strategy

Recruitment Method – Could be the responsibility of the membership committee to develop the process and then seek board approval or coalition consensus.

- Determine which other organizations will be approached (using criteria discussed in Box 10.5).
- Find out the decision-maker and the decision-making process in the target organizations.
- Determine how contact will be initiated (phone call, e-mail, formal letter) and who will make that contact—it may vary from organization to organization.
- Match the discussion format (phone conversation, in-person discussion, video conference) with the target organization and the resources of the coalition, plus practical considerations such as distance

and time. If, for example, the target organization is already familiar with the coalition and its work and is "on board" with its values and approach, a short phone call may be all that is needed to solidify the membership recruitment effort. On the other hand, when the target organization has many questions about the ramifications of membership and the level of commitment expected, an in-person conversation may be best.

- Once format is determined, identify the coalition members (best to have two for an in-person visit) who will "make the pitch" during the discussion. Coalition members who already have positive working relationships with decision-makers in the target organization can capitalize on those relationships in the discussion meeting where the development of trust is important.

▸ Carry out the discussion as planned with the message points developed.

▸ Regardless of the outcome of the discussion, be sure to send a note thanking the decision-maker for meeting and considering affiliation with the coalition. If the decision is to not join now, remember that times change and the organization may want to join the coalition later.

Crafting the Message—Remember our previous discussion about thinking about your target audience as you frame an issue. Those same principles are valid in this context as well.

▸ Be clear about the coalition's goal and purpose.

▸ Discuss the coalition's history and accomplishments to date.

▸ Identify the benefits for the organization if it joins the coalition.

▸ Be specific about the costs of joining, including membership fees, expectations of staff involvement, and other resource commitments.

▸ Be clear about the expectations for coalition members participating in the activities of the coalition.

▸ Discuss any restrictions with regard to speaking out on the coalition issues that the organization will need to abide by.

▸ Clarify the process by which the target organization will decide on membership, including board approvals needed.

▸ Offer to provide a presentation about the coalition to a board meeting or other venue that would facilitate the decision-making process.

▸ Be sure to thank the decision-maker for his or her time and consideration.

Box 11.6   Issues for Organizations to Consider in Joining Coalitions:

▸ Is the coalition aligned to work on the same goals as the organization?

▸ Are its values and ways of working compatible with those of the organization? If not, is the common goal worth potential conflicts on other issues? Can the organization live with the incompatibility?

▸ What degree of autonomy on what issues may the organization have to give up in joining the coalition?

▸ What resources and power may the organization gain around the target goal? Are these gains worth the potential costs?

▸ What other organizations are members of this coalition and will an association with them enhance or damage the image and/or reputation of the organization?

▸ Having joined the coalition, how difficult may it be to disassociate from the organization if an impasse is reached on either a goal or process issue?

---

determined to sign on. In most cases, the organizational representative will need to take the invitation to join the coalition to the organization's governing body or board of directors for approval. Depending on the frequency of meetings and the time and process for getting on the board's agenda, this process could take some months. In the meantime, the initiating organization can make sure that this potential new member receives regular information about the coalition and other new members who are affiliating. Sometimes this growing sense of momentum and the specifics of who else is joining the coalition may make the decision to join an easier one for the new organization to make. Box 11.6 highlights considerations for those invited organizations.

GENERATING THE AGENDA FOR INCLUSION

As new organizations join the emerging coalition, first they need to be integrated into the fabric of the coalition by letting them find common ground, and then the coalition can focus on expanding the number and variety of organizations that become affiliated. Expansion of the coalition provides an opportunity to build the group's expertise and to develop new connections and new understandings as members continue to study the problem or issue they are attempting to address.

Finding Common Ground

As was noted in the beginning of this chapter, organizations considering joining together in a coalition must find common ground in order to sustain their work together. Sometimes that means working on some issues together as the Catholic groups did with Planned Parenthood on the family cap, while they agree to disagree on other issues. Korgen writes about the importance of this sort of flexibility rather than rigidity in making coalitions effective in Catholic social action efforts:

> There are those who suggest that Catholics will subject coalition partners to a pro-life litmus test before working with them on any issue. My experience does not support this. The question is usually "What's the issue at hand?" or in the case of formal and lasting coalitions, "What's the scope of this organization?" When I was lead organizer for the Brockton Interfaith Community (BIC) in Brockton, Massachusetts, a leader explained it to me like this: "We don't take on issues that will divide us." Now there's an understanding of power![26]

Disagreements between purists and pragmatists can threaten the unity of a coalition unless handled adroitly.

Even when coalitions can steer clear of controversial issues, there will be disagreements on both the substance of issues and the strategies and tactics to be used in lobbying and public attention efforts. Disagreements between purists and pragmatists can threaten the unity of a coalition unless handled adroitly. Compromises will have to be made among those who disagree with each party determining how much to compromise and for what end. Consensus building is essentially a bargaining process among coalition members.[27] Sometimes the compromise will be worth the goal that is within grasp, while other times an interest group may refuse to compromise, even to the point of withdrawing from the coalition. In the gay marriage SCS that accompanies this book (located on Allyn & Bacon's *MySocialWorkLab* Web site), Josh Stevens, a Log Cabin Republican, does not agree with the timing of the issue:

> Wed. Apr 27, 2005 9:49 am—Gay Republicans believe just as strongly in their beliefs as you do. Your underlying attitude with me last night was that I was wrong and you were right. If I'd been allowed to finish a few sentences, I would have told you that I believe that—of course!—gays should be allowed to marry. I just don't think the country's ready for it just yet, and it's not the fight we need to pick right now.

This situation also points out the importance of taking the time to really "listen" to various stakeholders to insure that such misunderstandings do not take place. In building a coalition with other organizations, it is critical that areas of both agreement and disagreement are clear.

Continuing to Expand the Circle by Inviting Others to Attend Meetings

Most coalitions remain open to new members, thereby continuing to expand their potential influence. If twenty interest groups in a coalition can speak with a powerful, united voice that legislators will pay attention to, a coalition of thirty organizations becomes even more powerful. For different purposes, there may be an "optimal" size for a coalition. While more members bring resources, they also bring opportunities for conflict. Getting the commitment of new members to join then is only the first step in this process of integration. New members will need to be integrated into the "culture" of the coalition. Experienced members will need to reach out so new members feel welcomed and learn how best to interact and become involved in the work of the coalition. Finding out the new member's motivation for joining the coalition may assist in finding the best niche for them to invest their energy. All members need to feel they are contributing to the coalition in order to stay engaged and committed. This engagement needs to start as soon as possible.

Integrating New Members

Learning how the coalition handles potential conflict will be especially important for new members. Many coalitions tolerate a great deal of conflict over strategy and tactics within the context of coalition internal discussions but are adamant about having a united voice to the press and policy makers once decisions have been made within the coalition. Some coalitions operate with Roberts Rules of Order and vote on decisions to be made. Other coalitions may be much more informal in their decision-making processes and work toward a consensus. Even those coalitions with formal voting procedures may not bring issues to a vote until they are sure that they have reached a consensus on the issue. This approach makes the coalition stronger since members commit to a workable compromise rather than having some members angry with the outcome and upset that their voices were not heard.

The addition of new member organizations means access to their memberships, data bases, networks, and financial resources for the coalition. Alerts sent to the members of thirty organizations will yield more letters, e-mails, and phone calls in support of legislation in any grassroots campaign. New member organizations may have expertise, data, and reports about the problem issue that they will make available for the coalition to use in its problem/solution analysis process. This additional information and resident expertise may also be useful in developing the issue campaign. The staff members of new member organizations may possess research, policy proposal development, fundraising, and organizing skills that the coalition may find useful in its work. When a new organization joins the coalition, that organization also brings its network of contacts into the coalition. Perhaps members of the new organization have previously developed a solid working relationship with legislators on a key legislative committee. Now, when those members approach the legislators as representatives of the coalition they can build on the previously positive relationship they have already developed. Lastly, when new organizations join the coalition, they bring additional financial resources including their membership dues to assist the coalition. Even coalitions that are informal and short-lived may need financial or in-kind contributions from member organizations to print policy briefs and other materials for distribution to the press and legislators. Those coalitions that are more permanent and maintain an office and staff, including paid lobbyists, will require much more extensive funding from either their member organizations or other sources.

As each new member organization joins the coalition, the coalition must determine both the new organization's concerns regarding the issue and the extent to which the coalition can count on the commitment of the new organization's resources to the coalition effort. Making sure that implicit understandings are made explicit is critical at this juncture to avoid any unnecessary misunderstandings in expectations. Even when goodness of fit has been determined before inviting an organization to join, some fine tuning and adjustments may need to be made when joining has become a reality. In the health care SCS, when AARP expresses interest in joining the coalition, the group indicates its particular interest:

> FROM THE CARE4CARE BLOG MAILBOX—AARP of the Tri-Cities is looking for relationships to improve health care across the state. We bring formidable resources if we can get a good match of interests. Our primary concern is reform of the Prescription Drug Act. If you can commit to making this a major goal, we would be very interested in pooling our resources.

If their goal does not fit well with that of the Care4Care coalition, then the alliance may not be one that will be workable, even though their considerable resources would make them very attractive. Much depends on the flow of the legislative process and what can be worked on when. If attention is diluted into issues that distract from the main focus, then the goal will be more difficult to achieve.

With an increase in membership comes an increase in the potential for disagreement and dissent among the members. Having leaders who are skilled at negotiating these differences will facilitate a larger coalition maintaining its sense of unity around core issues. This skill at negotiation is discussed in more detail a little later in this chapter. Even so, coalition alliances are often quite tenuous. Two organizations in a coalition may vie for leadership. Sometimes members of a coalition may defect to another coalition working toward somewhat the same goal because it seems better positioned to be successful. Even in those coalitions that do form, the strength of the bond with the coalition may not be that strong, as Browne and Ringquist point out in their research on Michigan interest groups. "The relationships that hold these alliances together are too informal, too dependent on voluntary cooperation, and too undisciplined to subjugate private interests to common efforts for very long."[28] This statement suggests the very hard work that must go on behind the scenes of those coalitions that do manage to overcome this tendency to fly apart and become successful in working together effectively for social change. Some of these long-standing and effective coalitions are highlighted in this chapter. The chapter ends with some discussion of what makes those coalitions particularly successful.

COALITION DEVELOPMENTAL STAGES

Coalitions, like all groups, generally experience predictable stages of growth and development. The forming, storming, norming, and performing stages that are commonly discussed in group process outlines are observable in the development of coalitions. All sustainable groups are based on relationships among group members with a foundation of trust that evolves over time. Using the stages identified by Butterfloss and colleagues[29] (formation, implementation, maintenance, and outcomes), Downey and her colleagues provide probably the most useful comprehensive analysis of the critical indicators for each developmental stage based on their research of four community coalitions focused on public health and safety.[30] Table 11.2 adapts their critical indicators and stages model to the current discussion of policy practice coalitions to suggest the developmental tasks that may be specific to advocacy coalitions.

Table 11.2   Critical Indicators of Developmental Progress of Coalitions[1]

Core Components	Formation	Implementation	Maintenance	Outcomes
Funding	Collaborate with partners to obtain funding	Secure funding for coalition continuation	Monitor ongoing funding sources to maintain budget	Coalition has sustainable funding
Data	Identify available data and data still needed	Collect and analyze additional data	Guide efforts with data	Data updated and continues to drive coalition
Coalition Structure	Create coalition vision and structure	Formalize coalition structure	Monitor ongoing implementation of organizational structure	Goals achieved by adhering to structure, modifying over time as needed
Membership and Partnerships	Recruit members with similar interests	Empower current members for action while continuing recruitment	Continue to expand coalition with new members	Coalition includes members from all key organizations to ensure success
Leadership	Notify social service community about coalition to identify new members and potential leaders	Network with other groups with similar interests and select members for leadership roles	Delegate tasks to appropriate people	Coalition has a plan to mentor and develop new leadership in the coalition to take over
Coalition Enhancement	Structure and facilitate effective meetings	Ensure that active members all have roles in coalition	Use strategic planning to identify future directions	Coalition becomes a learning organization that sustains itself
Broader Support	Announce coalition to social service and policy leaders	Seek broader community support for initiatives	Maintain relationships by keeping coalition agenda in front of supporters	Broader community recognizes the success and impact of the coalition
Education	Identify education needed about the issue	Channel messages through most effective media to reach audiences	Maintain effective channels while taking advantage of new ones that emerge	Community is aware and supportive of coalition position on issue
Outreach Advocacy	Link with partners to get messages out	Try new outreach venues	Identify future opportunities to disseminate messages	Educational and advocacy programs reach targeted groups

(Continued)

Table 11.2   Critical Indicators of Developmental Progress of Coalitions (Continued)

Core Components	Formation	Implementation	Maintenance	Outcomes
Publicity	Develop relationships with media to disseminate information	Keep coalition efforts in the news	Continue to communicate agenda to the media	Coalition is effective in disseminating information to the broader community
Evaluation	Develop an evaluation plan to assess coalition efforts	Evaluate process and outcomes of coalition work on a regular basis	Create a learning organization that uses evaluation data to make improvements	Evaluation helps the coalition to refine its efforts.

[1]Laura M. Downey, Carol L. Ireson, Svetla Slavova, and Genia McKee, "Defining Elements of Success: A Critical Pathway of Coalition Development," *Health Promotion Practice,* 9, no. 2 (2008), 130–139, http://hpp.sagepub.com (accessed July 9, 2008).

These indicators demonstrate how an organization may grow and develop across a number of core components over time to become strong, effective, and sustainable. As the original researchers propose, these components are not ordered in a strict temporal sequence, and, in fact, some are actually concurrent and interdependent. Attention to both the internal functioning and the external advocacy activities are critical to organizational success as will be detailed in the following sections that highlight some of these developmental tasks.

Build the Group's Expertise

As new interest groups join the coalition and as the coalition matures, members can study the issue and the alternative solutions in more depth to create additional expertise within the coalition. Those participating in the coalition can pool their knowledge resources to have a more complete understanding of the issue and possible alternative solutions. Understanding and being able to articulate the pros and cons of each of the alternative solutions will assist the coalition in presenting its case to the legislature or other policymaking body. Building expertise becomes an ongoing process of staying on top of the latest research and the ever-expanding knowledgebase about a particular issue. A research committee of the coalition may be charged with reviewing the literature on the issue and monitoring legislative proposals in other states to stay apprised of emergent trends in the policymaking process. But all members of the coalition may be encouraged to stay alert to any new information or articles they encounter and to pass those along to the research committee or the broader membership. Keeping the coalition membership informed of the research and emergent data in the field is important. E-mail or electronic newsletters, such as Box 11.7 from the Coalition on Human Needs, can serve this information dissemination function as well as alerting members to pending legislation and mobilizing grassroots lobbying efforts.

Sometimes a coalition will realize that local or state-based knowledge about a particular problem or issue will be more persuasive than a national

Box 11.7   Coalition Electronic Newsletter

COALITION ON HUMAN NEEDS

The Human Needs Report

April 29, 2008
Complete Human Needs Report: www.chn.org/pdf/
2008/080429hnr.pdf (pdf) www.chn.org/humanneeds/
080429.html (html)

In This Edition

▶ House May Include Anti-Recession Measures in Supplemental Appropriations Bill Congressional leaders want to send the President supplemental appropriations legislation covering both war and domestic spending before their Memorial Day recess.

▶ *Congress Continues Push to Suspend Harmful Medicaid Regulations* A bill to keep a set of harmful Medicaid regulations from taking effect passed the House with overwhelming veto-proof support.

We Appreciate Your Input

Give us your thoughts on our Human Needs Report or any of our other services at feedback@chn.org.

Job Announcements and Calendar of Events

Please visit the Coalition on Human Needs Job Announcements page about employment opportunities and the Calendar of Events on upcoming conferences, briefings, and meetings. If you would like us to post a job announcement or an event, please contact Maricela Donahue at mdonahue@chn.org.

Please forward this e-mail!

Above e-mail received by one of authors on April 29, 2008.

study or one conducted in another state. If such research data is unavailable, the coalition may decide to undertake its own research project. Member organizations may lend staff to this effort or contribute additional resources. Such research could be as "simple" as mining existing databases such as Census Data (available at www.census.gov/) or the Survey of Income and Program Participation (SIPP) (available at www.census.gov/sipp/) for information about the extent of the problem or issue in the state or more local area. Or the research could be as involved and complex as conducting a mail, e-mail, or telephone survey of service providers to determine increases in demands for services or new presenting problems. For example, the increasing need for specialized community health and rehabilitative services (including mental health services) for veterans returning from Iraq and Afghanistan is not yet well documented in government statistics or the social service literature, so a survey of community service agencies in addition to Veterans Administration Hospitals might be useful in documenting this emergent need. Learning to create and use databases to enhance information available about the extent of the problem include research skills that are useful in policy practice.

Identifying potential resources to fill in gaps in both coalition resources and expertise can prove very useful. Sometimes local and state-level organizations may be able to assist the coalition though they may not be appropriate as members of the coalition. For example, departments or institutes within universities may be able to provide some pro bono help in accessing a data base and producing a report or providing a graduate student intern to assist in the research process. Coalitions have sometimes served as practicum sites for social work students who want to learn more about how to influence public policy. Brainstorming a list of resources to be tapped to fill knowledge gaps can be an early step in the process of developing the coalition. Coalition members can then be on the alert for additional resources as they go about their work.

Develop an Identity

As the coalition develops itself internally with new members, it must also be concerned with "branding" or developing its public image and identity. Expertise in public relations or advertising from a member organization may be helpful here in developing a public image for the coalition that will be reflective of its mission. The name of the coalition itself is important to indicate the breadth of its concern. It is not by chance that we have seen many coalitions in the human services with names that include the term "coalition" to indicate that the organization represents a group of organizations and therefore wields a certain degree of power. In addition, the names include terms such as "basic human needs," "human needs," or "human services" to indicate their inclusion of a variety of services for all people, across the dimensions of age, race, ability, and others.

If the coalition becomes a formal organization, it will also need to incorporate, file with the IRS, and maintain financial and other records in accordance with its tax-filing status. Articles of incorporation to be agreed upon by member organizations include such items as the governance structure and officers for the coalition, frequency of membership meetings, provisions for changing the articles and any bylaws adopted, and provisions for dissolution of the coalition. Incorporating as a nonprofit, the coalition will probably file as 501(c)3 or a 501(c)4 organization, terms deriving from the federal Internal Revenue Service tax code. A 501(c)3 is a nonprofit to which donations are tax-deductible on contributors' individual federal returns and which is limited in the amount of lobbying it may do. A 501(c)4 is also a nonprofit allowed to engage in unlimited lobbying, but to which donations are not tax-deductible. Setting up a bookkeeping system to facilitate the tracking of income and expenses in accordance with any state and federal tax filing regulations is also important. In some cases, a small coalition may contract with one of its member organizations to perform this bookkeeping function under the direction of the coalition treasurer, rather than hire its own staff to perform this organizational maintenance task.

In today's electronic environment, developing and maintaining the coalition's Web site is a critical aspect of maintaining the coalition's public image. Increasingly, people are going to the Web for basic information, bypassing libraries, phone books, and other more traditional sources of information. It is becoming hard to establish a credible organization today without having a Web presence. An attractive, easy to navigate Web site with current information becomes a necessity. Paying for Web site design, periodic upgrades, and regular updating may be a critical investment for the coalition. Generally Web sites for coalitions of human service advocates include pictures or graphics to create a sympathetic affect regarding the human need and social services related to the coalition's issue. Web sites are also loaded with information such as mission statements, legislative priorities, lists of member organizations, detailed position papers and policy briefs, membership applications, and contact information as well as links to other useful resources.

The final aspect of identity development to consider is the creation of an e-mail list, listserv, membership based blog, Facebook page, or some way to regularly communicate with members about the coalition and its activities. Some coalitions have developed electronic newsletters (discussed earlier) that are distributed monthly as a vehicle for information dissemination, for both legislative and research information. But in the rapidly changing environment of legislative politics, coalitions must be able to communicate quickly and effectively with their membership organizations and their individual members in order to maximize opportune moments in the legislative process. Having an e-mail alert system gets important information, including sample advocacy messages, out to members in a timely manner. Making it as easy as possible for members to respond is important to ensure a high response rate. Some e-mail alerts include direct links to legislators' e-mail addresses or include phone numbers for calls, since the research shows that more people will respond to the alert the fewer steps they have to take in completing that response. Analyze the effectiveness of Box 11.8, an alert from the Coalition on Human Needs. Notice that the alert includes all the information that

Engage Assess Intervene Evaluate

Critical Thinking Question

What makes the email alert in Box 11.8 a good example of how to keep members informed and involved in taking action?

Box 11.8   An E-mail Alert from the Coalition on Human Needs

COALITION ON HUMAN NEEDS

From Our Friends at the Food Research and Action Center

Take Two Actions Now on Behalf of Hungry People

1) Call your Members of Congress (Senators and Representatives) to urge passage of a final Farm Bill conference agreement with the strongest nutrition title.
Use the toll-free number (**1-800-826-9624**) made available by AARP to connect to the U.S. Capitol switchboard. (You will be connected after listening to a short message). Share the toll-free number with your allies.

MESSAGE TO DELIVER: Please tell your Member that hungry people can't wait; it is crucial that the final Farm Bill include new investments to improve food stamp benefits and food stamp access for needy people and to increase funding for The Emergency Food Assistance Program (TEFAP) to stock shelves in local food banks.

SIGN ON TO THE JOINT LETTER IN SUPPORT OF A STRONG NUTRITION TITLE OF THE FARM BILL   circulated by FRAC and America's Second Harvest—The Nation's Food Bank Network. (Click here for the letter text and for the list of organizations already signed on; to sign on, contact Etienne Melcher at FRAC: emelcher@frac.org or Eleanor Thompson at America's Second Harvest: ethompson@secondharvest.org.)

WHY Now? Breaking Developments

House Agriculture Committee leaders are expected to put a Farm Bill proposal on the table in a meeting of

Senate and House Farm Bill conferees on February 13th, according to an open letter from House Agriculture Committee Chairman Collin Peterson (D-MN) and Ranking Member Bob Goodlatte (R-VA). The letter was posted on the House Agriculture Committee Web site on February 10th. Key decisions about the amount of the Farm Bill (H.R. 2419) funding for the Food Stamp Program and TEFAP improvements may be on a very fast track.

What is at Stake

More than 35.5 million people in the U.S. live in households that face a constant struggle against hunger. Food stamp benefits average a mere $1 a person a meal; the minimum monthly food stamp benefit has been stuck at $10 for three decades. Many food bank shelves are empty. The pending Farm Bill nutrition title would make significant investments in both the Food Stamp Program and TEFAP.

Feedback and Technical Assistance

For feedback, suggestions and/or technical assistance on the Farm Bill, contact evollinger@frac.org or eteller@frac.org

Please forward this e-mail!
Email received by one Author on February 12, 2008.

a person would need in order to act: who to call, phone number, and talking points to pinpoint the message. Students may want to role play this phone call to practice their persuasive skills.

In the health care SCS, when Annie Haskins realizes the level of organization needed to carry out the activist mission of their coalition, she expresses a concern of many who do not want to lose sight of the goal in the midst of the minutiae of setting up a new organization. She writes:

> Week 6, Day 1, 8:22 am, Monday—Somehow our talk of teams, coalitions, kinds of attendees, and goals both encourages and concerns me. I'm encouraged because we do need the coalition of various "interest" groups representing individual needs to bring about change. Concerned, because it is so easy to get caught up in a bureaucratic web and forget the people. Believe me, as a government worker I UNDERSTAND bureaucracy. I have to work hard not to sound like a heartless bureaucrat.

Creating that balance between internal organizational tasks and external actions that helps the coalition reach its advocacy goals is critical to the success of the coalition and its ability to sustain its work. Some coalition members will be better at performing the institutional maintenance tasks, while others will excel in some of the external action tasks like speaking before groups, testifying, writing position statements, and making contacts with other organizations to seek new members or financial support. Good leadership will help coalition members find the best opportunities for using their own individual and organizational talents and strengths.

Engage Participants in Action

To reach agreement on actions to take, coalitions typically hold regular meetings that people can plan to attend. When state legislatures are in session, many coalitions like the Indiana Coalition for Human Services and the Human Service Coalition of Oregon meet on a weekly basis to update their member organizations on legislative developments and pool resources, including legislative contacts, and determine the next action steps to take. Otherwise, coalitions may have monthly board meetings and annual membership meetings, as provided in their bylaws. With phone and video-conferencing capabilities (see Box 11.9) extending to nonprofit human services, more coalitions are able to include members from a distance in their deliberations without the expense and time involved in traveling a long distance to attend a meeting. E-mail contacts and phone calls may need to be made when more immediate responses and decisions are needed.

Box 11.9   The Use of Web Conferencing

Even coalitions on a tight budget can afford some commercially available Web conferencing technologies. TypePad.com (at www.typepad.com/) has a blog format available for a small monthly fee that is particularly useful when coalitions are working on documents collaboratively and sharing other electronic resources. GoToMeeting.com (www1.gotomeeting.com/?Portal = www.gotomeeting.com) has a useful Web-based conferencing technology for a monthly fee. LiveMeeting is another conferencing technology (office. microsoft.com/en-us/livemeeting/default.aspx? ofcresset=1), but with a video component. Adobe Acrobat Connect Pro (www.adobe.com/products/acrobatconnectpro/) provides an integrated Web-conferencing technology based on Flash player.

Involving Members in the Organizational Structure

Coalitions develop their own structures based on how members think the coalition can best be configured to accomplish its tasks as part of the overall mission. The bylaws of a coalition will specify the officers who will form the core decision-making group, or executive committee. Each person on the executive committee will be from a different organizational member of the coalition. The president or chair of the coalition provides leadership to the coalition and is typically responsible for calling the meetings to order, moving the group through the agenda at meetings, writing a president's message for the annual report, and other such organizational duties. The vice president or vice chair is usually empowered to serve in the absence of the president and perform those duties when needed. The vice president may have other designated duties, such as chairing the planning committee for the annual meeting. The secretary of the coalition will usually be responsible for sending out notices of meetings, writing up minutes of meetings and decisions made, and writing any other correspondence for the coalition. The coalition treasurer is responsible for overseeing the organizational budgetary and bookkeeping processes and for filing any financial reports that are required. Frequently, these four people serve as the executive committee that is empowered to make decisions when the full board of directors is not able to meet. In some coalitions, the executive committee is expanded to include representatives of other coalition organizations as at-large members. The selection process for the officers, as well as the term of office, is designated in the bylaws. Frequently, officers are either elected by a vote of the board of directors or a vote of the membership at the annual meeting. Board members are usually nominated by the nominating committee of the coalition who identify those from within the coalition interested and able to provide volunteer time to the coalition. A slate of board members is then presented and voted on, either by the board or by the membership.

Work of the coalition must be done outside the board meetings and most coalitions find that having committees that focus on particular tasks (or some of the core components listed in Box 11.2) allows the coalition to be more efficient and effective. The structure of committees developed by the coalition provides an opportunity for new people to become involved and use their specific interests and talents for the advancement of the coalition's goals. Possible committees, in addition to a research committee discussed earlier in this chapter, include a membership committee to recruit new member organizations, a fundraising committee to identify additional sources of income besides membership fees, a legislative committee to draft the legislative priorities and strategies for board approval each year, an education committee to develop educational programs for target groups, including legislators and other policymakers, a nominating committee to identify new and emerging leaders to serve in designated roles, and a publicity or public-relations committee to develop and nurture the important contacts with the press. These committees may be designated as standing committees in the bylaws, where their particular roles and functions will be outlined. In addition, the coalition may decide to form ad hoc committees from time to time to focus on particular nonrecurrent issues. For example, every five years or so, a strategic-planning committee may be formed to help focus the coalition's attention to reexamining its mission and vision in light of the changing realities related to the issue of concern.

In addition to being an efficient way to get focused work done, committees provide an avenue for involvement of organizational members directly in the

A coalition has power only by exercising that power through action.

work of the coalition. The more people who can become involved in the internal processes of the coalition, the greater their commitment to the organization and its efforts. When organizational members are involved in committee work, they develop deeper understanding about the core component or task their committee is charged with. In addition, committee work provides an opportunity to hone leadership skills. Someone who has been active in a committee is likely to be asked to replace the chair of that committee when he or she steps down. By the same token, serving as a committee chair for several years is good preparation for serving as an officer of the coalition later. The leadership of many coalitions is composed of volunteers, people who are employed by their member organizations in a variety of roles with multiple responsibilities. In order to keep them engaged in the coalition as volunteers, their work for the coalition must be rewarding to them in some way. They must enjoy working with the other people. They must enjoy the challenges of the work. They must appreciate the opportunity to practice new leadership or other skills. As volunteers with busy lives, coalition members must have internal motivations for continuing their involvement and investment in the coalition, beyond the importance that their own organization places on their involvement. Working on these committees or as officers whose work is then recognized and valued by the coalition and their own organizations can fulfill that motivational need.

A coalition has power only by exercising that power through action. Putting strategies into action has a number of positive benefits for the coalition, including creating greater visibility for the coalition and its goals, providing an opportunity for member organizations to act together and create a sense of solidarity, and actually influencing policy in a desired direction. Members become more encouraged about the value of the coalition when they experience some sense of success. Chapter 7 highlighted some of the theoretical underpinnings for the development of a communications plan. Now the importance of such a communications plan becomes apparent in a very practical way for a coalition. Based on an overall strategy of a communications plan, the coalition could initiate a campaign to write letters to the editor and op ed pieces and could develop a speakers bureau to be available to speak to groups and classes about coalition issues. In some cases, when a public information campaign might be important, the coalition could have a booth at public events and fairs to get its name out there among the broader community. In situations demanding more radical action, the coalition might sponsor a demonstration or a march. Action and involvement are at the heart of coalition work.

A good communication plan with solid implementation can sometimes be effective in stopping legislation before it even gets started as well. When one author was an intern policy analyst for a Midwest governor, legislation was planned to be introduced to significantly limit the resources individuals with developmental disabilities could have and still be eligible for housing assistance. Parents, friends, and family members came together and formed a coalition to nix the legislation. Boxes of letters were delivered to the governor's office, but went unread and ignored. The day the legislation was to be introduced, bus-loads of parents, citizens with developmental disabilities, advocates, and others showed up and picketed the statehouse, with press coverage and all . . . needless to say the legislation never was introduced!

As part of its legislative strategy, a coalition may approach potential opposition groups to learn more about their positions on the issue and work out compromises amongst themselves, rather than testifying against one another. When Indiana's social work licensing bill was stalled due to opposition by other mental health professionals, the coalition favoring social work licensure that included NASW, universities with social work programs, and social service agencies, sat down with the opposition and hammered out compromise language for the bill. They then took that language to the legislators and had no difficulty getting a social work licensure bill that all could live with. The compromise was not ideal, but it enabled the legislation to move forward when the various stakeholders were able to agree.

Understanding the opposition is critical even if compromises cannot be developed. In the gay marriage SCS, opponents of the gay marriage amendment develop a Web site to counter the arguments being used in support of the amendment:

> Julia Cohen writes: Tue. May 03, 2005 9:02 am—Here is our new site dedicated to serious analysis of what the supporters of the Marriage Protection Act are saying. It takes the points from Marriageissacred.com (the most serious analysis of the issues), and we then post our respectful comments.

This is an excellent example about how to use the Web to disseminate important information to clarify an issue. By countering the opposition's arguments, the advocacy group is able to get ahead of their arguments and position. This strategy strengthens their position.

Like other organizations that depend on the media to transmit accurate information about them and their issues, coalitions need to develop and nurture media contacts at newspapers, radio and television stations. Press packets that inform reporters about the issues, provide background research information for in depth reporting, and contacts for further information provide a good way to introduce the coalition to the media. Following up with a contact to answer questions is always helpful. Thinking like a reporter looking for a story, the coalition can provide press releases of anything news-worthy that will help inform both the public and the policymakers of the event or issue. The media chapter in this text (Chapter 7) provides a blueprint for how to cultivate and use the media to the advocacy group's advantage. Obviously these insights apply to coalitions as well.

MEETING THE CHALLENGES IN COALITIONS

As discussed earlier, for all their advantages in terms of pooled resources, enhanced talent, and increased clout in the policymaking process, coalitions, particularly those that aim to become stable and long lasting, face a number of challenges: handling disagreements, sharing power, and raising the funds to sustain a presence. How a coalition handles and resolves each of these ongoing challenges will determine, to a large degree, its ongoing success.

Handling Disagreements

All organizations need to learn to handle disagreements within the group and work toward consensus if possible. This process is just more complex when the organization is a coalition of organizations, each with its own approach and philosophy that may differ from others in the coalition. A common conflict is

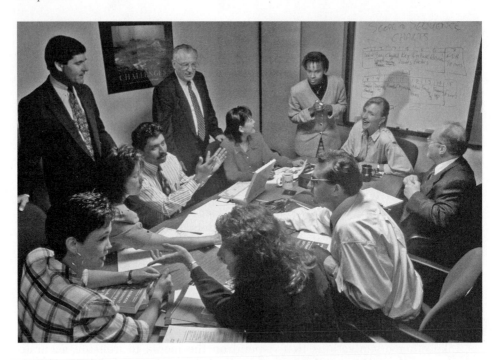

that between the purists who want to hold firm to a principle and the pragmatists who are willing to settle for the "possible."[31] This conflict between the purists and the pragmatists can occur with regard to both the substance of an issue and the policy proposal to address it and the strategies and tactics used to influence the policymaking process. For example, the purist advocate for universal single-payer health care may not be willing to settle for legislation that provides government subsidies to insurance companies to cover the uninsured. A purist pursuing a traditional legislative strategy of lobbying legislators through information exchanged in direct conversations with key legislators may have difficulty supporting coalition involvement in a rather spontaneous grass-roots demonstration at the state house of state employees protesting dramatic increases in insurance premiums.

Conflicts in coalitions are bound to occur, so the question becomes how to use negotiating strategies to address and resolve those conflicts. Keeping the conflict at a professional level, without letting it deteriorate to a personal level, helps lead to a faster resolution. The member organization in conflict with the coalition's position on an issue must be clear about what can be compromised and where the group stands firm on both process and outcomes. Identifying the areas of potential compromise can facilitate resolution. Both the coalition and the member organization must be willing to compromise on some points to create that "win-win" outcome so important to successful negotiation. Sometimes a neutral party can help facilitate this negotiation process. As was noted earlier in this chapter, the process of offering motions and voting on actions is one way to resolve conflicts and disagreements. Many coalitions prefer to work toward consensus when possible so that members will be highly committed to the compromises that are worked out. If a satisfactory compromise cannot be reached after considerable effort, the member organization in conflict may need to consider withdrawing from the coalition.

Sharing Power

Organizations accustomed to autonomous decision making and planning may have difficulty sharing power with other organizations in a coalition. Deciding on priorities for the year for the coalition requires considering the needs of one's own organization as well as the needs and legislative initiatives of other organizations in the coalition. Depending on the legislative agenda that emerges in the session, different member organizations' needs and priorities may be highlighted. Priorities shift and change with changing circumstances in communities. The jump in home foreclosures in April 2008, up 65 percent over the previous year,[33] for example, shifted legislative attention in many states toward issues such as affordable housing, aggressive mortgage plans being offered to high-risk borrowers, and home buyer education programs. So coalition members focused on housing issues may have received more coalition assistance on their legislative issues than members focused on services for people with disabilities. Coordinating member organization efforts with those of the coalition becomes important as part of sharing power. If coalition members are not speaking with a united and coordinated voice, then they are undercutting the potential power of the coalition to rally around a cause. Speaking with one voice does not always come easily. Being clear about who makes what decisions, who can speak on behalf of the coalition, and how others will be informed are all procedural policies that must be understood and followed for a coalition to remain united. As others have said, "When in doubt, talk it out."[33]

Staying Organized

With all sorts of external activities going on, it is easy to neglect some internal organizational issues. In the health care SCS, the organizers do not respond to the blog quickly enough and lose some potential supporters. In addition, Marta senses that they have a "shotgun scatter of ideas and issues with no clear direction of what we're after." In the gay marriage SCS, Julia Cohen tries to take on too much and becomes overwhelmed:

> Date: Thu, Apr 28, 2005 8:17 am—It is time for a moment of sober reflection. I know that in my commitment to the cause I have madly been trying to cover all bases, talk to all people, and in the process have hurt and alienated friends and supporters, seen our group splinter, made newbie type errors (aka Mark Frazier Show), and given lots of unintended comfort to our opponents.

In both these case studies, the policy advocates are trying to do too much too fast with too few resources. When the Health Care4Care group finds a retired volunteer to organize the blog, the minutes, and contacts as well as other routine office tasks, it is on the road to becoming more organized. Having a clear division of labor and accountability for accomplishing particular tasks will help insure that those tasks will be done in a timely manner. Using the expertise in the group to assign tasks can give everyone a sense of worthwhile participation. A core leadership group that can make rapid decisions, when those need to be made, and can guide the coalition toward its goals is important as well.[34]

Raising Funds

If coalitions use in-kind contributions of member organizations, such as book-keeping assistance, designing and printing materials, e-mail alert networks and press release networks, their direct expenses will be reduced. Even so, some funds will be needed. The Indiana Coalition for Human Services, with no full-time staff, for example, has an operating budget of under $20,000, with 95 percent of that income generated from memberships. Organizations with larger annual budgets pay a higher membership fee than those with smaller budgets. In addition, there are different levels of membership. In some coalitions, only those who pay full membership have access to the weekly legislative meetings where important information is shared and contacts are made. Coalitions may also invite members of the public to join and show their support by paying for a membership or making a contribution. Sometimes coalitions may have events to raise funds such as a nationally known speaker on an issue of concern. Other creative fund raising activities by coalitions include dinners, auctions, house parties, and other events that draw attention to the coalition issue as well as seek financial support.

CREATING ONGOING NETWORKS OF INFLUENCE—MOVING FROM AD HOC TO ONGOING

When a coalition determines to have a more permanent presence in the policy practice arena, it will need to pay greater attention to the organizational development tasks as well as the coalition advocacy action tasks. Investing energy in the organization itself should result in greater capacity to take action, but coalitions could become so focused on the internal institutional maintenance tasks that they lose the capacity to respond to the quickly changing legislative and executive branch developments that require the capacity to respond quickly to an ever-changing political scene.

One internal organizational maintenance task is to continue to build relationships and invite others to join the coalition. As other groups sign on, the coalition can give them visibility and roles in the coalition structure as discussed earlier. They will have "buy in" and a stake in the efforts of the coalition. Making expectations clear from the beginning leads to an increase in commitment. Some groups may just want to endorse the coalition's efforts while others may want to get directly involved as part of a collaborative team. Minutes of meetings and other communications circulated to the coalition members will keep everyone involved and up-to-date. Maintaining transparency and openness so that the coalition's agenda is clear to everyone will attract and keep member organizations. As the work of the coalition continues, it will be able to use the talent it has and recruit the talent it needs—someone skilled in graphics, someone knowledgeable about statistics, someone who can make complex topics easier to grasp, someone with expertise in the issue, etc. The coalition will continue to grow if more people in the coalition will take on responsibilities and assume new roles.

Externally, the coalition will develop strategies of how to launch and maintain its campaign, planning events and activities, but also taking advantage of opportunities that present themselves. An example of a successful coalition will help illustrate these points. In 1994, the Missouri Association of Social Workers (MASW) formed a collaborative group of social work researchers, practitioners, advocates, and students "to examine changes in welfare policy and the potential for asset-based strategies to combat poverty."[35] With federal changes in welfare reform devolving much of the decision making to the state level, policy advocates and others saw an opportunity to create a state program from a community economic development (CED) perspective to help combat the problem of poverty. This five-year project, in which students learned the policy development process as they enacted it, resulted in passage of an IDA bill (a bill establishing individual development accounts, a subsidized savings program for low-income families designed to encourage savings for home ownership, business ventures or post–secondary education) attached to a welfare reform bill on the last day of the legislative session in 1999. Along the way, the coalition used the strengths of the participants in carrying out a variety of roles and tasks. As a statewide organization already engaged in advocacy work at the state legislature, the MASW was well-positioned to initiate the coalition and help organize the effort. MASW helped develop information and disseminated it to legislators, state officials and the public. Members of the coalition drafted legislation and fact sheets that were then disseminated in a variety of ways throughout the state, including public forums, statewide conferences, and workshops. An electronic legislative alert network was also established to facilitate communication. "The email system, called "TAKE FIVE," informed coalition members and others about the week-to-week progress of the bills and encouraged them to take five minutes to write or call their legislators at crucial moments during the session."[36] Social work researchers understood the effects of a variety of asset-building strategies, including IDAs.[37] Their "expert testimony on asset theory and evidence of policy successes elsewhere helped convince legislators in Missouri that they should pay attention to the . . . project's proposals."[38] The social work practitioners brought their experiences with clients to the coalition. Students brought energy, person-power, and time as this legislative activity became part of their practicum experience. They were primarily involved in "legislation development, coalition building, liaison activities with the legislature and government officials, lobbying, and survey development and analysis"[39] as part of the research efforts associated with the project. With their understanding of how IDAs work, they were able to help the bill sponsors understand where compromises could be made in the bill as it wound its way through the legislative process. They were also quite involved in developing the "strategies and scripts for answers to critical questions that might surface in floor debate or behind closed doors"[40] that were then incorporated into FAQ sheets to be distributed to legislators.

Some attention will need to be given to developing relationships with key politicians and keeping them abreast of coalition's efforts and concerns. Identifying allies and opponents among both legislators and other groups and coalitions is an ongoing process. Then the coalition is able to reach out to potential allies to coordinate efforts. Outreach to opponents, as indicated earlier, can help work out conflicts and develop compromises on the sidelines where the interest groups have more potential control over the outcome. In other cases, such sideline negotiations can result in completely turning someone around on the issue. In the Missouri project above, students specifically courted one legislator for a whole year after he voted against the IDA bill. After attending one of the coalition's meetings, he became a supporter of the legislation.[41]

Critical Thinking Question

Using the characteristics of successful coalitions identified, assess the degree of success of a coalition with which you are familiar or the coalition in the Health Care SCS.

CHARACTERISTICS OF SUCCESSFUL COALITIONS

Lewis[42] makes a useful distinction between networks and coalitions. Networks, she says, help shape policy through the nodes or contacts and their interactions or communications. Only when that network of contacts has been mobilized for targeted action does it become a true coalition with a goal and purpose. So, successful coalitions are those that take action and whose actions make a difference in the policy development process. What characteristics do successful coalitions share, if any?

Bailey and Koney[43] identify eight core components of "interorganizational collaboration" or coalition building: leadership, membership, environmental linkages, strategy, purpose, tasks, structure, and system, indicating that they are all interconnected in such a way that changes in one will result in changes in another. The leadership and the membership of the collaboration are the primary stakeholders, but they are connected to other organizations and stakeholders in the broader social and political context through their environmental linkages. The strategy is the general approach the collaborative takes in reaching its goal or purpose, with the tasks being the specific activities that the collaborative completes to lead to its desired end state. The structure is the way in which the collaborative is organized and the system is the way that organizational parts are connected with one another and communicate. One approach to evaluating the effectiveness of a coalition might be to examine how these different components function together. Are there common components shared by successful coalitions? It is helpful to remember that specific activities and even systems associated with success may change with time. For example, having a Web presence and using some form of electronic communication as part of a coalition's system is becoming more of a necessity today than the luxury it was only a few years ago. MASW faced a challenge that many coalitions face, that of staying connected with individuals and small agencies that do not have computer access. "More work is needed to insure that the technological infrastructure is available in advocacy and human service organizations."[44]

In summarizing the key dimensions related to coalition success, Wolff identifies the following characteristics: coalition readiness, intentionality, structure and organizational capacity, taking action, membership, leadership, dollars and resources, relationships, and technical assistance.[45] With these factors as important, he identifies best practices based on an overview of successful coalitions. Taking the time to build relationships based on the initial environmental scan is important. Visioning exercises and annual retreats may help increase intentionality and strengthen the shared vision for coalition members. Clear structures with adequate staffing and sufficient resources contribute to coalition success. Coalitions that take action through task forces or committees are more effective in achieving success. In recruiting members, the coalition needs to create an environment that encourages and rewards participation. Leaders look to develop new leaders and delegate responsibility to broaden the participation base. The resources need to be adequate to the tasks at hand to ensure success. In addition to funds, in-kind resources can supplement limited funds. Coalition building is about building relationships. Leaders and members all work together in a sense of community to build a well-functioning coalition.

Leaders look to develop new leaders and delegate responsibility to broaden the participation base.

The National Organizations Responding to AIDS (NORA), a coalition of 125 different organizations, many of whom had previously worked under the auspices of the Consortium for Citizens with Disabilities on the passage of the Americans with Disabilities Act of 1990 (P.L. 101–336), is largely credited with the successful passage of the Ryan White Comprehensive AIDS Resources Emergency (CARE) Act of 1990 (P.L. 101–381).[46] Members of NORA included traditional service providers and professional associations (including NASW), specialized advocates (including the National Council on La Raza), AIDS organizations, and many other religious and secular organizations.

> Clearly, a national level coalition that included the PTA, La Raza, and the National Gay and Lesbian Task Force could wield power across a broad range of domains. The effectiveness of NORA seemed to stem from three facts: (1) The large number of national groups gave weight to the concern at hand; (2) the presence of mainstream and long-respected agencies lent legitimacy to the issue; and (3) the passion and knowledge of less traditional activist organizations helped to fuel the sense of urgency and outrage.[47]

This coalition would certainly have been difficult to dismiss.

In addition to using a broad and respected coalition as the central organizing group, advocates in NORA used a number of strategies and tactics designed to maximize success. First, they sought support from both political parties, with the two major sponsors of the Ryan White legislation being Senators Edward Kennedy (D-MA) and Orin Hatch (R-UT). By the time the legislation reached the floor of the Senate for a vote, it had 67 sponsors. It passed with only four voting in opposition. Second, they used celebrities to bring public attention to both the problem of AIDS and the solutions. Elizabeth Taylor "spoke forcefully in support of the bill during her testimony to the Budget Committee, playing a vocal and visible role in its introduction."[48] Third, advocates framed AIDS as a problem affecting all people, not just particular segments of the population, and, therefore, as a "national disaster." At that time, some in the opposition tried to marginalize AIDS as a "gay disease" that was God's punishment for a moral failing. But the climate shifted with recognition that the populations at risk of contracting the disease included children, people with hemophilia, and heterosexual women. Naming the bill after Ryan White, an adolescent who contracted the disease through blood transfusions, and using the same disaster terminology that rallied government support for relief from hurricanes and earthquakes "was helpful in normalizing a government response and in focusing the media attention."[49] Poindexter concludes that

> NORA is an example of what advocates in a coalition can accomplish. These social policy advocates recognized a policy window of opportunity, crafted model legislation, mobilized groups across a broad spectrum of interests, and educated legislators. With a social worker as head and NASW as a member, NORA embodied the spirit of social work's commitment to social justice. The development of the CARE Act is a success story about social change, coalition building, positive government action, a pluralistic movement, and social work intervention on the national level. Constituency and coalitions were broad based, legislators were highly committed, and value conflicts were resolved through compromise.[50]

An effective coalition certainly can accomplish a great deal by putting in all the necessary conceptual and logistical work in the initial planning phases and orchestrating all the members to come together as one.

In reflecting on the success of the MASW coalition that was able to get IDA legislation passed in Missouri, Sherraden, Slosar, and Sherraden attribute their success to a number of factors, including the appeal of the policy/program across partisan lines, the availability of resources including the staff of an ongoing advocacy organization, the involvement of partners from a number of perspectives, and the energy and talent of the students involved. They conclude:

> Legislative success would have eluded the CED [community economic development] committee without the involvement of a broad range of people and organizations from all over the state. In legislative work, support came from across the political spectrum, beginning with bill sponsors recruited from both political parties. An urban-rural split in the legislature dooms many worthy proposals, thus great efforts were made to work with legislators from urban and rural districts. Constituents, especially those involved in pilot CED projects, and practitioners who work with consumers, were helpful in articulating the importance of these initiatives at the ground level. In the case of CED policy, which crosses the social and economic divide, the business sector as well as the social service sector were brought on board. Finally, it was important to gain support from the state agencies that would be responsible for implementing the CED programs.[51]

Successful campaigns frequently require persistence. In Connecticut, another successful statewide effort using coalitions, over a 17-year period, culminated in 1991 in the passage of a civil rights law protecting people from discrimination on the basis of sexual orientation. In this case,[52] gay rights advocates developed strong alliances by actively working in two electoral political coalitions and on several electoral campaigns, including one for town committee person and another for a state legislator. Working on these campaigns along with other groups helped the gay rights advocates build political expertise but also helped them develop relationships with straight progressives and created positive visibility. Gay activists, including Bonelli, an MSW student whose field placement was with People for Change (PFC), worked prominently as members of a third party, PFC, that operated in Hartford from 1987 to 1994. The student's work "enabled the gay, lesbian, and bisexual community to gain increased respect within PFC and the broader Hartford activist community."[53] Using community organizing strategies, including phone banking, door knocking, and fundraising, the PFC won two seats on the Hartford City Council in 1987. The coalition of progressive organizations then determined to elect Juan Figueroa as Hartford's first state representative from Puerto Rican heritage. "The campaign also provided the Coalition a chance to show its strength by helping elect a pro-gay state representative to the General Assembly and an opportunity to build stronger alliances with the Puerto Rican community. It has been a long-standing desire of progressive gays to build a multicultural gay rights movement and work in coalition with progressive allies of color."[54] When Figueroa was elected, another voice for gay rights was added to the legislature. Later, gay civil rights was reframed as a workers' rights issue. One International Association of Machinists official, who had experience working with a Coalition leader, helped provide additional support for gay rights legislation from organized labor. When Bonelli ran unsuccessfully for city council, his candidacy as an openly gay man still galvanized many voters and raised the issue of gay civil rights to the forefront again. In addition, his "campaign forced the political establishment to take the gay community seriously and dramatically illustrated the organizing capabilities of this community."[55] Each foray into the political process increased the coalition's expertise in organizing and developing strategy to achieve long-range goals.

In addition, through the relationships they developed working on progressive campaigns together, straight organizations began to understand better the issues related to gay civil rights, creating new allies. So when the gay rights legislation was before the Connecticut legislature yet again in 1991, several new developments created the conditions for successful passage. More legislators were educated on the issue. The Coalition set up chapters across the state and hired a lobbyist to help monitor the progress of the legislation, thereby putting more resources into the effort. In addition, a campaign of direct action and civil disobedience, reminiscent of the civil rights demonstrations in the 1960s, brought media attention to the issue. Support by other groups also contributed to the successful passage of the bill and its signing into law by Governor Lowell Weicker in 1991.

At the local community level, the passage of the Fairness Ordinance in Lexington-Fayette County, Kentucky, in 1999 represents another instance of a successful coalition, the Fairness Alliance, a coalition of leaders from the lesbian, gay, bisexual, and transgendered (LGBT) community, business and civic organizations, political parties, and community and religious organizations.[56] The Fairness Ordinance "added protection based on real or perceived sexual orientation or gender identity, to existing civil rights protection related to housing, employment, and public accommodations."[57] The lead organization in this effort was the Bluegrass chapter of the Kentucky Fairness Alliance (KFA-Bluegrass), a grassroots organization advocating for LGBT rights. KFA-Bluegrass brought together representatives from a variety of fields to assist in the effort, including social work, law, journalism, and local businesses. The actual campaign only lasted 17 days, though planning efforts began months in advance. When a similar ordinance passed in Louisville, the Bluegrass group sensed a window of opportunity and went into action. The group developed an e-mail alert network to facilitate rapid communication within the group. Selecting the name "Fairness Campaign" was carefully thought out with great attention to the power of words. The name "also provided an interesting antithesis for opponents who were often referred to as the anti-Fairness position. Further, the name conveyed the important message that this was a discussion of social justice, not of perspectives on sexual orientation. The fact that the language resonated with the community as a whole became evident as the local city council quickly began to refer to the proposal as the Fairness Ordinance."[58]

Identifying potential coalition partners required the KFA-Bluegrass to find common ground within this social justice framework. In a Bible-belt community, support from religious leaders is important and all that may be needed is education on the connection between religious views and the social justice perspective on this issue. At time of the vote on the ordinance, 13 religious leaders had sent letters of support, and three testified in favor of the ordinance. Letters from the business community pointed out the economic impact of nondiscriminatory policies as well as compatibility with the current hiring policies of local companies. Coalition members were also sought from other social justice organizations. The coalition provided educational materials on the ordinance to interested organizations so they could speak knowledgably about the ordinance. In turn, KFA members were called upon to support other social justice organizations in their own issue efforts, an example of the important principle of reciprocity that solidifies the relationships among coalition members.

The campaign started quietly with educating the city council members on the issue. Starting quietly helped reduce the resources needed to mount a successful lobbying effort and caught the opposition a bit off-guard. The primary strategy used by both the KFA and opposition was to rally constituents to contact the city council members. The message from the Fairness Ordinance supporters was consistently focused on the social justice issue. The opposition appealed to religious concerns, but sometimes disintegrated into political and personal threats. "The gravity of the lobbying efforts was quite evident in the council chambers, as some council members spoke with sometimes angry, sometimes strained, voices about the threatening phone calls they had received. In two cases, the council members indicated that the vehement reactions of some opponents of the ordinance helped to solidify their support by making evident the need for such protection in the community."[59] Once they were successful, coalition members recognized the importance of maintaining their focus for future efforts as there is a tendency for coalitions to disperse once the initial goal has been achieved. As with the example from the Ryan White bill though, a new incarnation of the coalition may be needed for the next policy battle.

Many of the examples in this chapter have shown how coalitions can be effective in the legislative process, but it is important to remember their power when trying to influence executive decisions as well. Here's just one example of a coalition affecting an executive decision. After a two year campaign to get the Illinois state legislature to increase funding for homeless youth shelters (there were only nine in the entire state to serve an approximately 30,000 homeless youth), it became increasingly clear that the Illinois Coalition for the Homeless was close to getting a new line item in the state budget for homeless youth. This development created political pressure on the director of the department of juvenile justice, who did not want to lose budgetary control, into agreeing to commit $20 million to homeless youth shelters over the following five years. Part of the agreement was that the funding commitment be made public, thereby making it more difficult to rescind the commitment in the future. One of the things that made this policy issue campaign so successful was the coalition's involvement of youth (homeless and college) stakeholders, and very well developed relationships with the media across the state. Legislators and executive branch administrators do listen when constituents speak about how policies are affecting them.

Coalitions do not always persist in their success though. Pittsburgh's Alliance for Progressive Action (APA) was founded in 1991 and included 34–50 social movement organizations with the goal of opposing "racism, sexism, militarism, exploitation of the poor, and advocacy for environmental protection, civil rights and civil liberties."[60] Membership included organized labor, peace and justice groups, environmental groups, and groups representing the rights of various marginalized populations. Started as an information clearinghouse, or network, the organization evolved into an advocacy coalition and secured funding to hire staff. APA mounted three campaigns: establishing a community review board to investigate cases of police misconduct, keeping the public television station from becoming commercial, and establishing a living wage in the western part of the state. When Starr interviewed key leaders[61] in 1998, they had succeeded in creating an Independent Citizens Police Review Board and had defeated the public television station's effort to win Federal Communications Commission (FCC) approval to become a commercial station. Despite these successes, the coalition no longer is functioning. What caused its demise? We would need to research and investigate possible causes, but Starr pointed at some potential problems in his 2001 account of APA. Its diverse membership may have made it more challenging to hold the coalition together under the pressure of some of the campaigns and subsequent publicity. The more conservative organizations provided the most resources, so if they withdrew, the organization would be in greater jeopardy. Starr noted at the time that getting involvement from membership organizations was difficult even if their representatives were enthusiastic. A former staff member posted a notice[62] in 2004 about APA's end, noting both the ultimate failure of all of the campaigns (the television station was privatized, the police review board was perceived as ineffective, and the living wage campaign failed), withdrawal of member organizations over the living wage campaign, and internal staff and volunteer conflicts. Despite all their work on commitment and trust within the group, the leaders were not able to sustain it over time, particularly during discouraging times when all their efforts ended in failure. Coalition builders can learn a great deal from the successes and failures of other coalitions. We do know that coalition leadership is critical.

IMPORTANCE OF COALITION LEADERSHIP

The previous examples of successful coalitions demonstrate the importance of strong, but flexible leadership capable of helping coalition members forge alliances and work through differences. All of the research on factors that are essential for coalition success points to the central role of coalition leadership.[63] Leadership of any organization can be challenging, but leading a diverse group of organizations toward a common goal can be especially challenging. Leaders of large, well-funded coalitions are paid staff members. Leaders in smaller coalitions are volunteers who serve as presidents or chairs of the coalition organizations. Frequently, coalitions rely on multiple leaders within the coalition to assist in the many tasks that must be completed. Particular skills that are important for leaders include the ability to share leadership and to build bridges,[64] in creating the collaborative partnerships that are central to coalition development.

This empowering leadership style is also credited with resulting in higher levels of participation by member organizations.[65] Empowering leadership "seeks out and utilizes the views, skills, and expertise of all coalition members and provides ample praise and recognition of their contributions. It also works collaboratively with membership in decision making by seeking to balance interests and build consensus on key issues."[66] Empowering leadership style seeks to share power rather than impose it in a hierarchy. A key leadership task is to bring the coalition together around a shared vision that serves as both a guide or compass for the coalition's tasks and activities but also as the glue[67] that helps hold the coalition together. An empowering leader also helps participants believe in their sense of self-efficacy or influence through the experience of their engagement and higher level of participation. Having a committed leader who is trusted by the coalition and who has the necessary skills to negotiate differences within the coalition and new contacts within the broader community will more likely be seen as helping the coalition achieve its goals.[68]

CELEBRATE THE SMALL VICTORIES AND HAVE FUN AS PART OF THE PROCESS

As progress is made on the tasks to be accomplished in moving toward goals, it is important to take time out to celebrate and savor those small steps that move the coalition closer to its goal. Even the most seasoned advocates need encouragement and a sense of accomplishment in the hard work of trying to secure change. In the health care SCS, participants recognize the need for a celebratory pause in this e-mail when Pam Baker reminds the group of their successes.

> Week 14, Day 3, 11:01 am, Wednesday—In other words, we are on a roll. Michael has certainly been valuable in reminding us of the importance of a clear and strong message. Plus, Ricardo and Buck have both been regular reminders that we must be the voice for the ordinary person.

And once Buck Hoffman has read the case studies of people struggling with health care, he reflects:

> Week 14, Day 3, 3:36 pm, Wednesday—I think this is great. These personal stories will speak to everybody. This will expand our coalition, guarantee media coverage, and bring in people like Ricardo who have been concerned that we are too business oriented. Featuring these stories on our blog will make clear our commitment across the board, as it will demonstrate once again that the grassroots movements now get their power not only from the people, but from the Internet. I can get some pro bono TV shooting and air time, for starters. The paper and online press will be easy to bring along. Let's get a game plan and run our plays!

CONCLUSION

Coalition building is both rewarding and challenging, in a constantly changing environment. Organizations join coalitions to coalesce their power and increase their influence in attempting to have an impact on the policy development process. Few major policy changes have come about without the work of powerful coalitions, both behind the scenes and out front in the streets where all can see. Social workers, with our negotiation and collaborative skills, are well suited to become active in coalitions seeking social justice.

Log onto **MySocialWorkLab** to access a wealth of case studies, videos, and assessment. (*If you did not receive an access code to* **MySocialWorkLab** *with this text and wish to purchase access online, please visit* www.mysocialworklab.com.)

1. **Watch the Connecting Core Competency videos on Policy Practice.** If the social worker in the Policy Practice video was not successful in achieving the policy change by working within the prison, what external organizations might she bring together in

a coalition to bring pressure on the prison to make changes? What initial approach could she take in inviting other organizations to be part of the coalition?

2. **Review Gay Marriage SCS.** If you were Julia Cohen in the Gay Marriage SCS, what are some organizations you would invite to be part of a coalition opposing the Gay Marriage Amendment? What would be your rationale and how would you approach them to increase the likelihood they would join with you?

PRACTICE TEST The following questions will test your knowledge of the content found within this chapter. For additional assessment, including licensing-exam type questions on applying chapter content to practice, visit **MySocialWorkLab**.

1. Unlike networks, the primary purpose of coalitions is to:
   a. Transfer information.
   b. Raise funds.
   c. Develop mutual support.
   d. Take united action to change policy.

2. When considering the inclusion of radical groups as coalition members, coalition organizers should keep in mind that radical groups:
   a. Have the potential to harm the coalition's cause and its acceptance by legislators.
   b. Are always poor choices for coalitions and lead to problems.
   c. Can occasionally be beneficial if the radical group can be convinced to modify its views and tactics.
   d. Have the potential then to invite other radical groups into the coalition and completely subvert its purpose.

3. Strong, successful coalitions are founded upon:
   a. Going to social functions together, and good communication skills
   b. Strong relationships with member organizations, as well as mutual trust and understanding
   c. Good communication and frequent meetings of member organizations
   d. Member organizations following the same value system and excellent organizational skills

4. When considering joining a coalition, an invited organization will need to
   a. Have only the approval of the executive director.
   b. Have all the details about the purpose and plan for the coalition worked out in advance.
   c. Have goals that are compatible with the mission of the coalition.
   d. Know that no funding will be required from member organizations.

5. When a coalition has sustainable funding, a clear structure, membership inclusive of key organizations, and a good information dissemination system, it is probably at what stage in its development?
   a. Implementation
   b. Integration
   c. Maintenance
   d. Outcomes

6. Important elements in developing a "name" or "brand" for a coalition identity include:
   a. A good name for the coalition and holding frequent community social events
   b. Creating and maintaining a Website and an e-mail list, or listserv
   c. Developing a social networking page and hiring powerful lobbyists
   d. Filing the proper IRS paperwork and finding a good accountant

7. Committee work in coalitions
   a. Is usually a waste of time since most of the important work is done at public hearings.
   b. Is an efficient way to get work done and involve more members in active work for the coalition.
   c. Is frequently an opportunity for social interaction with membership organizations.
   d. Seldom involves the most influential coalition members since they are more involved in public roles and functions.

8. Since strong but flexible leadership is a keystone for a successful coalition, critical skills for coalition leaders are:
   a. Strong opinions and charisma
   b. Persuasiveness and connections with legislators
   c. The ability to share leadership and build bridges
   d. The ability to energize members and organize meetings

Log onto **MySocialWorkLab** once you have completed the Practice Test above to access additional study tools and assessment.

Answers

Key: 1) d, 2) a, 3) b, 4) c, 5) d, 6) b, 7) b, 8) c

12

Campaigns

CHAPTER OUTLINE

Introduction 319

Overview of Campaign Processes 320
Resources

Campaign Roles for Social Workers 327

Campaign Roles for the Social Work
Profession 336

Laws and Ethics of Campaigning 337
Campaign Finance Reform

Conclusion 344

Chapter Review 345

Practice Test 345

 MySocialWorkLab 345
SCS on Gay Marriage
Connecting Core Competency videos on
Career Exploration

Core Competencies in this Chapter (Check marks indicate which competencies are covered in depth)									
✓	Professional Identity		Ethical Practice	✓	Critical Thinking	✓	Diversity in Practice	✓	Human Rights & Justice
	Research Based Practice		Human Behavior		Policy Practice		Practice Contexts		Engage, Assess, Intervene, Evaluate

INTRODUCTION

The sooner social workers achieve an understanding of the importance of the relationship between community and client systems, the faster the number of social workers involved in electoral politics and government relations will increase.

JAMES L. WOLK

Compared to members of the general public, social workers are remarkably engaged in the political system. A study of social workers' political participation in 11 states found that "social workers are twice as active [as] the public when it comes to advertising for a party or candidate during an election year; three times as active in contributing financially to a candidate or party; and four times as active when it comes to attending political meetings or rallies and volunteering for political campaigns."[1] While a majority of social workers are politically engaged, the highest levels of participation are in lower commitment areas such as voting (97%) and discussing politics (72.5%).[2] Unfortunately, when it comes to electoral campaign participation, "four times as active" means that 13.1 percent of social workers are involved in campaigns, versus 3 percent for the general public.[3] Given the assets social workers bring to public life (firsthand knowledge of the social problems of vulnerable, politically marginalized groups in society; excellent communication, mediation, and problem-solving skills; and data and policy analysis abilities), and the profession's historic orientation toward social justice, it is not unreasonable to expect much higher levels of social worker involvement in the electoral process.

The National Association of Social Workers (NASW) has outlined the benefits of social worker political participation (Figure 12.1).

The social workers who give "time, money, and their valuable perspective" to election campaigns have a clear and lasting impact on public policy, addressing the structural community barriers that clients face in their paths toward self-determination.

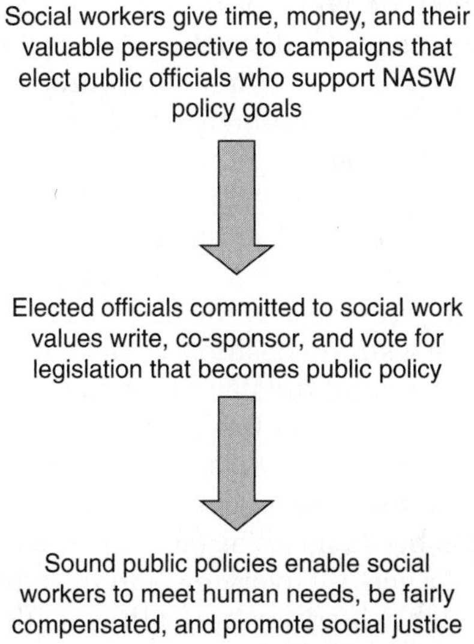

Social workers give time, money, and their valuable perspective to campaigns that elect public officials who support NASW policy goals

Elected officials committed to social work values write, co-sponsor, and vote for legislation that becomes public policy

Sound public policies enable social workers to meet human needs, be fairly compensated, and promote social justice

Figure 12.1

Political Change Starts with the Social Worker in Campaigns and Elections[1]
[1]www.socialworkers.org/pace/why_involved.asp (accessed June 25, 2008).

A central theme of this text is that policy practice is a core activity for *all* social workers. Politically engaged social workers tend to be those with a strong sense of political efficacy (the belief in one's own ability to have an impact on political outcomes).[4] Efficacy stems from the knowledge that you possess both an understanding of policy and the policy practice skills to influence the policy process, both of which can be learned. The Simulated Case Studies (SCS) that accompany this text (you can find these in *MySocialWorkLab* on the Allyn & Bacon Web site) are designed to illustrate the application of these skills across the spectrum of policy practice—from analyzing policy to mobilizing networks of supporters to working with the media. As this chapter illustrates, these policy practice skills are assets when it comes to the campaign trail.

This chapter will explore roles that policy practitioners can play in campaigns, including volunteer, advisor, empowerer of others, and candidate. By the end of the chapter students will understand how each role functions and how to apply policy practice skills to electoral campaigns in all stages of campaigning, from the precampaign exploratory phase to the final "get out the vote"activities.

OVERVIEW OF CAMPAIGN PROCESSES

Campaigns are intense and exhilarating experiences for those who are actively involved. Each campaign is a unique mix of circumstances: Is the race at the local, state or national level? Is an incumbent running, or is it an "open" race? How much money have the candidates raised? What are the hot-button issues with the voters? What is the demographic makeup of the precinct, district, or the state? Can the candidate rally people to her cause? While the interplay of these variables adds to the complexity of U.S. politics, there are some core elements that apply to all campaigns.

Some of the most critical activities take place before the campaign begins. During the exploratory/precampaign period, potential candidates assess the possibility of winning the election and decide whether to run for office. Factors affecting that decision include whether or not an incumbent will be running, whether past voting patterns in the district or state favor the candidate's party, and whether the candidate can tap sufficient resources needed to win.[5] Once a candidate decides to run, the development of a campaign plan is a key task.

Having a written campaign plan ensures that the campaign stays on message.

The campaign plan is the roadmap for running the campaign. In the midst of a frenetic, rapidly changing campaign, there is always the temptation to react to every turn of events—to strike back at the negative attack advertisement or to let the news of the day dominate strategic thinking about how to win the election. For example, focusing speeches on the need to enforce building codes after a major fire may seem like a strong position to stake out, but what if the voters are more interested in how the candidate will address economic issues? Having a written campaign plan ensures that the campaign stays on message and that, to the extent possible, there is structure and coherence to campaign activities. Components of a campaign plan are outlined in Table 12.1.

Each of the items in Table 12.1 can be (and has been!) the subject of its own book. For the purposes of a general overview and introduction to political campaigns, three areas are highlighted for in-depth consideration in this chapter: resources, staffing, and media. Visit the Allyn & Bacon Web site of *My Social Work Lab* for additional information and exercises on other topics such as researching a district, Get-Out-The-Vote (GOTV) activities, and polling.

Table 12.1 Campaign Plan Components[1]

Contextual Information:

District Profile: relatively stable characteristics such as geography, housing patterns, leading employers, transportation infrastructure

Demographic Profile: characteristics of the population, including race/ethnicity, income levels, occupation, union membership

Past Voter Behavior: voting patterns; extent of partisan identification

Candidate Qualifications and Background

Opposition Profile: fact sheet on the opposing candidate, identifying weaknesses

Resources and Staffing

Budget

Fundraising Plan and Schedule (connected to Candidate Activities, below)

Staffing

Organizational Requirements: headquarters, equipment (computers, phones and faxes, cars)

Audience Considerations

Issue Papers: Summaries of the candidate's key positions on important issues; used in developing brochures, press materials, website content; may be created from longer, more detailed position papers

Polling Plan and Schedule: identifies dates, techniques, budget for conducting polls

Voter Concerns: culled from prior voting behavior, news coverage, polling results

Strategy and Tactics

Campaign Theme: derived from "what the voters want, what the candidate has to offer, and what the opponent has to offer;" for example, a theme of "the Candidate of Change" would work best for a younger, "outsider" candidate

Stages of Voter Decision-making: strategy for how the campaign will address three stages of voter decision-making: (1) cognition/generating awareness of the campaign and the candidate; (2) affect, when voters form opinions about the candidate; and (3) evaluation, when they reach a decision and are motivated to get out and vote

Paid Media (advertising)/Voter Contact Schedule: plan for placing ads in newspapers, radio, TV, web plus individual voter contacts such as direct mail, canvas of neighborhoods, and calls; aligned with stages of voter decision-making and phases of campaign

Earned Media: plan to generate news coverage, including press conferences, staged events, debates

Candidate Activities: broad outline of candidate schedule, including debates, appearances, meetings with newspaper editorial board, other obligations, such as a congressperson running for reelection needing to be in Washington for key votes

[1]Adapted from Daniel M. Shea, *Campaign Craft: The Strategies, Tactics, and Art of Political Campaign Management.* (Westport, CN: Praeger, 1996), 22–23.

Resources

Dollars fuel campaigns. All campaigns require financial resources to pay for staff, advertising, polls, consultants, and other expenses, but the importance of money increases when challengers face incumbents. Being the sitting office-holder confers a large advantage on the incumbent: between 1946 and 2006, 90 percent of U.S. House and Senate races included incumbents, who then went on to win 90 percent of the races.[6] Money's power to offset incumbency is evident in the statistics on U.S. House elections between 1972 and 2006: 54 percent of those challenging incumbents raised less than $100,000, and their odds of winning were 1 in 3,027; challengers who spent $1M or more increased their likelihood of winning to 1 in 3.[7]

In 2006, the average contributions to a U.S. House race were $953,044 (54% from individuals, 1% from parties, 35% from Political Action Committees [PACs], 5% from candidates, and 5% unknown).[8] For Senate races in 2006, the average contribution was $7,943,400 (68% from individuals, 0.3% from parties, 13% from PACs, 13% from candidates, and 5% unknown).[9] In political campaigns, the financial contributions of supporters are important and many small contributors may be more important in building a grassroots movement than a few generous contributors. During the 2007–2008 presidential primary season, for example, Democratic candidate Barack Obama's campaign was largely fueled by grassroots donors who were highly engaged in his campaign. According to data from the Federal Election Commission, "Cumulatively from January 1, 2007 through April 30, 2008 Obama raised 47% of his funds in amounts of $200 or less, Clinton 33% and McCain 23%."[10]

Political action committees (PACs) have been in existence since 1944, when the Congress of Industrial Organizations (CIO) formed a PAC to support President Franklin D. Roosevelt's campaign.[11] Monetary restrictions were set in place by the Federal Election Campaign Act (FECA), passed in 1972 and amended in 1974. By the end of 1974, 89 corporate PACs and 201 labor PACs were operating.[12] Six years later, more than 1,200 business PACs were operating to labor's less than 300.[13] As of 2006, there were 1,622 corporate PACs and 290 labor PACs in existence.[14] Clearly, more interest groups (and particularly, corporate interest groups) understand the importance of electing politicians sympathetic to their views and so are becoming more involved politically as well as legislatively.

Part of this increase in interest groups was the growth of the so-called "527" committees. The term *527* refers a section of the Internal Revenue Service's tax code, which provides a tax-exemption to organizations that can accept unlimited contributions from individuals in order to influence federal elections, as long as they do not endorse or oppose a particular candidate. These organizations can engage in general political activities such as issue campaigns or voter mobilization efforts that frequently will attempt to influence recipients' views of candidates, without explicit endorsements. Their contributions and expenditures are reported to the Internal Revenue Service IRS. Opensecrets.org, a project of the Pew Charitable Trusts, and other organizations access and compile the IRS data and make it available to the public. In the 2004 election cycle, 527s spent over $600 million attempting to influence the outcomes of elections.[15]

While 527 groups are criticized for their corrosive effects on political discourse (see Box 12.1), most 527s are more innocuous. Among the top 527 committee spenders in 2004 were five labor unions, College Republicans, several other political party-related organizations, the Sierra Club, EMILY's List (an organization that supports pro-choice Democratic women running for Congress and governor—EMILY is an acronym for "Early Money Is Like Yeast" (it helps the dough rise), and the Gay and Lesbian Victory Fund.[16]

A subset of supporters will contribute to the PAC associated with an interest group, generally those who understand the importance of electing the people whose views are most compatible with those held by the interest group. PACs use a variety of methods to determine how to distribute their financial resources. Sometimes they survey candidates, asking a series of questions related to issues of concern to the group. With respect to incumbent officeholders,

It was a 527, Swift Boat Veterans for Truth that created the advertising campaign attacking Senator John Kerry's heroism in his swift boat during his tour of Vietnam, contributing to his defeat for the Presidency in 2004. The group was financed by Sam Fox, a conservative Texas billionaire and political activist.

While the claims of the Swift Vets group have been widely rebutted, the Kerry campaign was unable to overcome the negative impressions caused by the attack ads.[1]

JOHN KERRY SECRETLY MET ENEMY LEADERS.

John Kerry : Testimony
United States Senate Committee on Foreign Relations, April 22, 1971
www.swiftvets.com

[1]www.swiftvets.com/index.php?topic=Ads, the Swift Vets and POWs for Truth website (accessed May 15, 2008); Sourcewatch, a Project of the Center for Media and Democracy, www.sourcewatch.org/index.php?title=Swift_Boat_Veterans_for_Truth (accessed May 15, 2008).

PACs examine the candidate's voting record and willingness to work with the group (or coalition with other groups) on legislation in determining whether to support a candidate for another term. Generally, the PACs realize that politicians are unlikely to agree with the interest group on all issues, so they must prioritize which issues are nonnegotiable. So a women's rights group might decide that having a pro-choice stance was nonnegotiable, while a health care group might decide that they could live with a candidate with a pro-life stance but who strongly supported a single-payer government-funded health insurance program. Some groups with little money may provide endorsements to candidates in "safe" districts (where they are expected to be elected because they are from the majority party in the district) without contributing to their campaigns. They thus save their limited financial contributions for those candidates in hotly contested races, where even their relatively small contributions may make a difference. Members of the interest groups may offer to have fundraising events in their homes for candidates endorsed by the group, inviting other friends from outside the interest group.

For all campaign contributions, it is important for both individuals and interest groups to follow campaign financing laws (see the last section in this chapter, Laws and Ethics in Campaigning).

Staffing

From an organizational standpoint, all campaigns need a staff to schedule the candidate and plan events (including fundraisers), reach out to key constituencies, conduct research, mobilize supporters, direct volunteer activity, interact with the press, and create and maintain a campaign Web site and other new media such as having a presence in MySpace and Facebook. Table 12.2 outlines Barack Obama's 2008 presidential campaign organization for the state of New Hampshire. While presidential race organizations are certainly more complex than other races (in lower-level campaigns many of the positions would be combined or be fewer in number, or staffed by volunteers), the list offers a clear example of the various functions needed in a modern campaign organization.

Note the prominence of press and new media functions, the number of interns, and how key constituencies have dedicated political staff. Presidential

Table 12.2   Barack Obama's 2008 New Hampshire Campaign Organization[1]

LEADERSHIP STAFF
State Director
Deputy State Director
Assistant to the Directors and
Multimedia Producer
4 State Co-Chairs
2 National Co-Chairs

POLITICAL STAFF
(constituencies)
Women, Education, Child Advocacy
Lawyers, Republicans, Independents, Businesspeople, Faith,
Progressives, People of Color, GLBT, Health Care, Environment,
Disabilities, Sportsmen, Veterans, Seniors, Labor, Political Staff
Assistant

FIELD STAFF
Field Director
Deputy Field Director
New England Field Director
Regional Field Directors
16 Offices Across the State
Statewide Volunteer Coordinator

COLLEGE STAFF
NE College Organizer
College Organizer (Keene)
College Organizer (Plymouth)

PRESS STAFF
Communications Director
Press Secretary
Deputy Press Secretary
Press Assistant
Press Assistant
Rapid Responder

NEW MEDIA STAFF
Director of New Media
Online Organizer
Blogger
Videographer

**SCHEDULING AND ADVANCE
STAFF**
Director of Scheduling
Deputy Director of Scheduling
Assistant to the Scheduler
Assistant to the Scheduler
Advance Staff

OTHER STAFF
Director of Operations
Voter File Director
IT Support Specialist
Tracker
Receptionist
65 interns

[1]www.gwu.edu/~action/2008/obama/obamaorgnh.html (accessed June 10, 2008).

candidate John McCain's New Hampshire organization, while leaner, also focuses on key supporters, college students, and connections with the state's counties and cities (see Table 12.3).

Compare and contrast Obama's constituent groups with McCain's—in what ways are they similar? Different? What might account for the differences?

Table 12.3   John McCain's 2008 New Hampshire Campaign Organization

Chairman
Campaign Manager
Deputy Campaign Manager

Field Organizers
Coos and Grafton Counties
Hillsborough County
Strafford and Merrimack
Rockingham County
Belknap and Carroll Counties
Cheshire and Sullivan

Veterans Director
Coalitions Director
Office Manager/Volunteer Coordinator
Press Secretary
Senior Advisor
Honorary Chairman
Co-Chair
7 Vice-Chairs
TOWN CHAIRS–county-level committees—15–30 members each
COUNTY LEADERSHIP–6–8, includes some elected officials

COALITIONS
Chairman of Educators for McCain
Chairman of Conservative Outreach
New Hampshire Business Leaders for McCain Leadership
Chairmen of the Sportsmen Coalition
New Hampshire "Women for McCain" Leadership Team New Hampshire
Veterans Advisory Coalition: more than 200 Granite State veterans
New Hampshire Law Enforcement Advisory Coalition
New Hampshire Legislative Caucus for McCain
Conservation Advisory Committee
Conservatives for McCain Steering Committee
New Hampshire First Responders Coalition
New Hampshire Independents for McCain Coalition

New Hampshire Students for McCain Leadership
New Hampshire Youth Chairman: Rivier College
New Hampshire Students for McCain Co-Chair: Keene State College
New Hampshire Students for McCain Co-Chair: UNH Durham
Student Organizations at 15 New Hampshire colleges
National Co-Chairman

www.gwu.edu/~action/2008/mccain/mccainorgnh.html (accessed January 10, 2008).

Media

The media plan is the roadmap the campaign will follow in communicating about the issues and the candidate. As noted in Chapter 7, elements of the media plan include the following:

- Analysis of your target audiences and the media most likely to reach them;
- Identification of core messages and how they will be framed;
- Timing and intensity of media outreach;
- Pacing—whether communications will be constant in nature or build up in intensity to a climactic point;
- Media mix (balance of different types of media, paid v. free media, audience-generated versus organizationally controlled media); and,
- Budgets and assigned responsibilities.

Media plans need to be nimble to take advantage of unanticipated opportunities or problems that arise in the course of the campaign, but preliminary planning will help ensure that organizational resources are expended to greatest effect.

New technologies are having a great impact on how campaigns communicate with the public. These technologies are evolving quickly. Some of the newest applications for advocacy communications include the use of text messaging in GOTV efforts (Box 12.2).

Box 12.2   Instant Messaging and the Youth Vote

The Student PIRGs' New Voters Project and Working Assets, in cooperation with researchers from the University of Michigan and Princeton University, recently released a study demonstrating the effectiveness of using text/SMS messages to mobile phones to mobilize young voters in the November 2006 elections. The study found that text message reminders to new voters increased an individual's likelihood of voting by 4.2 percentage points.

The Study

On the day before the election in November 2006, researchers sent text message voting reminders to over 4,000 mobile phone numbers chosen at random from a pool of over 8,000 mostly young people who had completed voter registration applications. Afterward, participants were matched to voter records to determine if they had voted in the election, and a sample was surveyed to gauge their reaction to the messages.

Important Results

- Across the board, text message reminders increased the likelihood of an individual voting by 4.2 percentage points.
- Of the different messages tested, a short, to-the-point reminder was most effective, with a boost of nearly 5 percentage points.
- In a follow up survey, 59 percent of recipients reported that the reminder was helpful, versus only 23 percent who found it bothersome.
- Hispanics had especially positive feelings about the reminders.
- At just $1.56 per additional vote generated, text messaging was extremely cost-effective.

Comparison with Other Mobilization Tactics

Tactic	Mobilization Effect	Cost/Vote Generated
Text/SMS Messages	4–5%	$1.56
"Quality" Phone Calls	4–5%	$20
Door-to-Door Canvassing	7–9%	~$30
Leafleting	1.2%	$32
Direct Mail	~0.6%	$67

Source: New Voters Project, www.newvotersproject.org/text-messaging.

Second Life is another emerging Web 2.0 application that is being used for online advocacy. Second Life is an online social world where visitors interact through their avatars (online personas). The Clinton and Obama campaigns capitalized on this exciting technology during the 2008 election season by creating and showcasing the virtual campaign headquarters of Hillary Clinton and Barack Obama. New media can be used to reinforce voter support, both to build a relationship that can lead to additional campaign contributions, and to prevent the voter from losing interest in the race and failing to actually vote. The Obama campaign kept voters engaged and informed through the use of e-mails with embedded videos that were sent out to millions of potential voters with regularity before the 2008 presidential election. Embedding video in an e-mail is characteristic of the ascendancy of new media strategies, which have attracted record numbers of relatively small donors, whose collective impact has had a major impact on campaign finances. Refer back to Chapter 7 for additional information on framing issues to attract press coverage, how the media operate, and the use of traditional and new media in mobilizing supporters.

Securing sufficient resources, developing an organization that functions effectively, and getting the public on board are requisites of the twenty-first century political campaign. There are certainly parallels with social service agency management, community organizing, and other organizing efforts. The next section explores how policy practitioners use their skills to elect social justice-oriented candidates to public office.

Securing sufficient resources, developing an organization that functions effectively, and getting the public on board are requisites for winning elections.

CAMPAIGN ROLES FOR SOCIAL WORKERS

Social workers play a variety of roles in political campaigns, including serving as campaign volunteers, as senior advisors, as empowerers who help marginalized groups achieve a public voice, and as candidates themselves. While social workers can be found across the political spectrum, the majority traditionally align themselves with the Democratic Party—just 13 percent identify as Republican, with 21 percent describing themselves as conservative.[17] Those most likely to be active include NASW members, city dwellers, and those socially connected to the "recruitment networks" of politically active people.[18]

Volunteering (making calls, canvassing neighborhoods, stuffing envelopes, etc.) is a way to get started in working on political campaigns, an experience that can serve as a springboard to other positions in the campaign or in future campaigns. Also, political connections developed through NASW state-chapter participation can be useful in securing higher-level campaign positions. When social workers serve as campaign advisors, their policy practice skills come to the fore. Policy analysis; conducting research, and knowing how to frame an issue; understanding historical forces that have led to the current situation; coalition building and interpersonal communication skills; working across varied groups and possessing cultural competence; and in general, having an ecological, holistic perspective are all assets in the complex and rapidly changing world of the political campaign.

Social workers also bring their focus on empowerment to the political arena. Section 6 of the NASW Code of Ethics, on ethical responsibilities to the broader society, stipulates that "social workers should act to expand choice and opportunity for all people, with special regard for vulnerable, disadvantaged, oppressed, and exploited people and groups." Similarly, the Cultural Competence Practice Standard 6 on Empowerment and Advocacy[19] requires

Critical Thinking

Critical Thinking Question
What are some possible reasons for social workers' historical tendency to align themselves with the Democratic Party?

that "**s**ocial workers shall be aware of the effect of social policies and programs on diverse client populations, advocating for and with clients whenever appropriate" (emphasis added).

Empowerment processes are "the mechanisms through which people, organizations, and communities gain mastery and control over issues that concern them, develop a critical awareness of their environment, and participate in decisions that affect their lives."[20]

One type of action used by policy practitioners to enable marginalized groups to participate in decisions that affect their lives is the voter-registration drive: "Registration is a beginning step in obtaining political empowerment for everyone. Social workers are encouraged to help educate clients to be informed voters and to mobilize them to vote in elections."[21]

The following example is taken from a study of a social worker-led voter-registration drive at a psychiatric institution:

> A patient with a paranoid schizophrenic diagnosis … filled out the [voter] registration form on his own, and then discussed with the [social] worker his belief that voting was not just a right of every citizen, but was, in fact, a responsibility. He said that although many people believed that their vote made no difference, he believed that his vote counted. Prior to his hospitalization, this patient had lived on the streets for a period of over a year. In this case, a previously disaffiliated patient's desire to participate in his social environment was supported in a concrete way.[22]

There were multiple benefits to this empowering action:

> As they registered to vote, the patients had an opportunity that drew them outside of themselves and the autistic preoccupation that accompanies severe psychiatric illness. With political involvement came increased social contact and opportunities to practice social skills. Improved organizational capacity, cooperation, and delayed gratification were all lessons to be learned from political activity. Finally, participation in politics at the local level integrated the patients into a network of environmental supports.[23]

Another example of empowerment occurred within the context of one of the author's policy classes. Students in the course engaged in a comprehensive voter education and turnout effort, focusing on a local precinct (selected because of its low voter turnout in previous elections). The students developed nonpartisan materials on candidates running for office and distributed them door to door, engaging residents in conversations. The majority of the neighborhood's residents were low-income African Americans, and many had never voted in their lives. While some were interested, many were angry at the suggestion that their vote would make a difference. After weeks of working the neighborhood, students then organized a GOTV campaign and drove voters to the polls. They set up a headquarters (the author's office) where people could call if they needed a ride on election day. The stories of empowerment that the students heard were inspiring. Many older voters were voting for the first time (some of these were the ones who were angry initially) and were moved to tears as they cast their first ballot.

In addition to voter registration drives, policy practitioners can politically empower individuals and groups by providing leadership opportunities for the community, and by encouraging clients to volunteer in campaigns and to run for office. Policy practitioners' empowerment activities emerge from direct

Policy practitioners can politically empower individuals and groups by providing leadership opportunities for the community and by encouraging clients to volunteer in campaigns and to run for office.

Box 12.3   Social Worker on the Campaign Trail: Karen Persichilli Keogh

As the director of New York operations for Senator Hillary Rodham Clinton, and her senior adviser on local matters, Karen Persichilli Keogh keeps Senator Clinton's New York City headquarters on the ball and on message.

She has been the operational backbone behind the scenes for a string of disparate Democrats, from the maverick Councilman Sal F. Albanese to the former Council speaker and mayoral/gubernatorial contender Peter F. Vallone to Albany's dapper mayor, Jerry Jennings.

"What I do on behalf of the senator is a big deal, but I don't feel like a big deal," Ms. Persichilli Keogh says.

She grew up in Baldwin, on Long Island, intent on becoming a nurse until she found out, two years into the nursing program at the State University at Stony Brook, that she was too squeamish. (Don't they say politics is a blood sport?)

Instead, she earned a master's in social work from Columbia University in 1989 and worked for District Council 37, the city's largest municipal union, before moving to City Hall in 1993 as chief of staff to Councilman Albanese. She liked the renegade chutzpah that relegated him to the back row of Council chamber seats alongside a fellow outcast, Thomas K. Duane. Christine C. Quinn, now the Council speaker, was her counterpart on Mr. Duane's staff. Ms. Quinn and Mr. Duane were, she says, her mentors in the art of urban campaigning. Tenacious.

When you believe in people and work for people who are fantastic public servants, you are impacting change in a wonderful way," she adds. "Politics is all about the future, and in a way, it is a kind of social work."

Her job covers staff recruitment, communications, constituent services, community outreach, and the senator's in-state schedule and travel. The senator is, to put it mildly, a hot ticket: "We averaged about 50,000 requests for appearances per year, and now that she's announced for president, it's gone up to 60,000."

Ms. Persichilli Keogh, who as campaign director for Senator Clinton's 2006 reelection effort supervised the strategy that yielded a winning margin of 67 percent, has been a campaign addict since she worked the phones and banged on doors for David N. Dinkins in 1989.

"That was when I got the bug," she says. "I will do anything to help Hillary Rodham Clinton run for president. I consider myself a feminist. And it means something extra when your own 12-year-old daughter says, 'Wow, she's running for president? A girl can do that? That's cool.' "

The "collaborative, inspirational, nuts-and-bolts" (her words) politician Ms. Persichilli Keogh refers to as "the senator" expressed, via e-mail, an effusive tribute toward her home state touchstone. "I love KPK," Senator Clinton wrote. "In a city known worldwide by its initials, she is a political star known by hers. She is a compassionate public servant who works hard for New Yorkers each and every day."

So does she think she's a carbon copy of the boss? Ms. Persichilli Keogh notes that she would, if asked, decline to run. "I'm behind the scenes," she says. "Believe me, I see more than enough action."

Robin Finn. "While Clinton Runs, She Minds the Store" New York Times, March 23, 2008. www.nytimes.com/2007/03/23/nyregion/23lives.html?n=Top/Reference/Times%20Topics/People/C/Clinton,%20Hillary%20Rodham (accessed July 20, 2008).

contact with groups who lack power and influence in society. Working with them to gain access to public power is truly meeting the goals of the profession.

Many policy practitioners have used their involvement in campaigns as a springboard to elected office. As of 2005, there were 177 social workers holding public office: 6 in the U.S. Congress, 69 in state legislatures, 30 serving at the county/borough level, 44 in city office, and 28 on school boards.[24]

Box 12.4   Social Worker on the Campaign Trail: Jason Carnes

It was a hot day in July when Jason Carnes sat down to discuss his work on United States Representative Baron Hill's campaign and already the campaign in Indiana's Ninth Congressional district was heating up. With a district that includes both conservative and liberal constituencies that are politically active, it has long been a battleground between the Republicans and Democrats. In 2004, Hill, the incumbent, lost by 1,500 votes, but he came back to win in 2006 by about 9,600 votes.[1]

Now in 2008, Baron Hill is running for reelection. As a volunteer on the campaign, but also a constituent caseworker in Hill's district office for a year and a half in Bloomington, Indiana, Jason has two perspectives on the candidate and the Congressman. In his work during the week, Jason helps constituents access services that they need to meet their needs. He describes his role as helping people who "fall through the cracks" or who need help faster than the pace of some social agency bureaucracies. Through his networks, he can get answers to questions about eligibility or services faster than the general public. He uses his social work skills daily as he takes constituent calls and extracts the essence of the problem. With his social service systems knowledge from his BSW degree, he is able to link people with the resources that they need. He says, "I get them started, but then I want them to do some of the work on their own so that they will be empowered to take the steps the next time without my help."

In addition, Jason is able to inform the Congressman of gaps in the service delivery system or policies that are not being implemented as designed or that are having unintended negative consequences. His case finding and documentation may lead to future legislative proposals or efforts to change policy at the executive level.

How did Jason get into politics? He wanted to "make a difference" and debated about the best major (psychology, telecommunications, political science) when he decided to attend college a few years after high school. He settled on social work because he saw the opportunity in the profession for "hands-on advocacy." He said he was not happy with the general direction the country was taking and wanted to become more involved politically.

He completed a practicum in Representative Hill's office and after graduation he was hired to help set up the 211 program with the Area Agency on Aging. There he developed a program to help those on Medicare to select the best Part D insurance program to meet their specific prescription needs. During the next year and a half he learned a great deal about the whole network of social welfare services and policies, information that has been very useful in his current position in Congressman Hill's office.

Jason volunteers for the Hill campaign as much as he can and speaks with enthusiasm about meeting constituents and talking with them about their concerns. Whether he is at a booth at a county fair or going door-to-door in a neighborhood, Jason says he always starts conversations by finding out what matters to the person, what issues are of most importance to him or her. He then can explain Hill's stand on the issues and get feedback from the constituent. He sees these discussions as a "two-way street," a dialogue in which he learns a great deal about the concerns of constituents. He wants to have polite and nonaggressive debate when he finds different perspectives. Respectful conversation may open the door to causing some constituents to pause to think, and maybe even reevaluate their own stances. He is not trying to convince those who support Hill's opponent but rather is trying to appeal to those voters who are on the fence and not sure of how they may vote. After a day of campaigning, he and other campaign workers can also inform the campaign staff about what they are hearing so that the candidate can make sure his position is clearly articulated.

Jason uses his generalist practice social work skills in these campaign interactions as well when he "starts where the voter is" in his discussions about issues. Though he hears that people are not happy with Congress, they are favorable toward Congressman Hill. Jason thinks that part of that favorable rating is because Hill is back home in the district every weekend. "People feel connected to him." The issues that concern voters the most are the price of gas and the economy. In some counties, there are concerns about immigration. He is hearing less concern about the war in Iraq. He shares Representative Hill's positions in a nonthreatening way, wanting to present information to help voters make their own decisions about who to support.

Jason says that political work may not seem like a "natural fit" with social work but he has found a good place to practice his social work skills and it feels natural to him. He sees government as designing programs to help people. So it is important to have people, in government and in politics, who are trained to understand people and listen to what they are saying so these systems can be responsive and not turn into rigid uncaring bureaucracies. "Politics absolutely is where social workers need to be involved. We just need to reframe things to understand that the "client" can be a cause and not just a person."[2]

[1]Midwest: Illinois, 50-state roundup, Thursday, November 9, 2006; A36; www.washingtonpost.com/wp-dyn/content/article/2006/11/08/ AR2006110802553_pf.html (accessed July 15, 2008).
[2]Personal interview July 22, 2008.

Box 12.5   Why Social Workers Should Run for Office[1]

National Association of Social Workers (NASW) encourages social workers to run for office because social workers are a profession of trained communicators with concrete ideas about how to empower communities. Social workers understand social problems and know human relations, and the commitment to improving the quality of life brings a vital perspective to public decision-making.

Social workers across the country serve in a range of political institutions, from school boards to city and county offices and state legislatures. There are six social workers in the U.S. House and Senate.

Social workers make good political candidates because they:

- are well educated
- are articulate and experienced in public speaking
- are comfortable at persuasion
- are knowledgeable about their communities
- understand social problems and are committed to social justice
- understand how policies affect individuals and communities

- Social workers run for public office because they:
- are attracted to politics through an issue or cause.
- realize they are just as capable as many officeholders.
- see the opportunity to make changes on a broader scale.
- want to provide leadership to improve their community.

NASW also encourages social workers to offer their professional expertise to campaigns. Social workers can use their skills as campaign managers, volunteer coordinators, and political directors. These jobs can also translate into legislative jobs in which social workers can shape policy, and help constituents by working with federal, state and local agencies to get individuals appropriate assistance. Social workers can also translate their involvement in campaigns into key appointments in state and local agencies in which they can oversee key government agencies to influence the practice of social work and seek social justice.

[1]www.socialworkers.org/pace/why_run.asp (accessed June 20, 2008).

Professional Identity

Critical Thinking Question

How does Jason Carnes
combine micro and
macro-level skills in
performing his job and in
campaign volunteering?

Special Section—Social Workers in Elected Office

Social Worker in Office: Tamara Grigsby

Tamara Grigsby joined the Wisconsin Legislature in January of 2005 as a representative to the 18th Assembly District in Milwaukee.

Representative Grigsby received her B.S. from Howard University in Washington, D.C., in 1997 and her Master's in Social Work from University of Wisconsin-Madison in 2000. Upon receiving her master's degree, Representative Grigsby worked as a family social worker focusing on youth, parents involved in the child welfare system, and families in crises.

As a complement to her family social work practice, Representative Grigsby joined the Wisconsin Council on Children & Families in Milwaukee as a Program Manager where she worked from 1999 until her election in November 2004. There she worked on reducing racial disparities in child well-being and improving systems that serve children and families. Through her work at the Council, Representative Grigsby was very involved in advocating for change in the Child Welfare, W-2, Educational and Criminal Justice systems. In addition to her advocacy work, Representative Grigsby taught at the University of Wisconsin-Milwaukee in the Helen Bader School of Social Welfare from 2001 to 2004.

Representative Grigsby has a strong interest in social and economic justice, racial equality, and issues that impact children, youth, and families. Her civic and volunteer activities include: youth mentoring, membership in the National Association for the Advancement of Colored People, Sherman Park Neighborhood Association and National Association of Social Workers. Representative Grigsby is enthusiastic about her new responsibilities in Madison and sees her role as being a "voice for the people" and an advocate for our state's most vulnerable populations.

Representative Grigsby's legislative committee assignments for the 2007–08 legislative session are: Children and Family Law; Criminal Justice, and Workforce Development. She was selected by her colleagues to serve as the vice-chairperson of the Assembly Democratic Caucus, putting her in a leadership position in the legislature.

Representative Grigsby also serves on the following boards: Interstate Adult Offender Supervision Board; Milwaukee Child Welfare Partnership Council; W-2 Monitoring Task Force; Family Impact Seminars Advisory Board; American Civil Liberties Union (ACLU); Wisconsin Women in Government; the Felmers Chaney Pre-Release Correctional Center Community Advisory Board; and the Mentoring Connection Advisory Panel.[1]

---

[1]www.legis.state.wi.us/assembly/asm18/news/bio.htm (accessed June 25, 2008).

Social Worker in Office: Bill Rosendahl

Los Angeles Councilman Bill Rosendahl won election in May 2005. He serves as chair of the Council's Transportation Committee, and was the immediate past-chair of the Public Works Committee, which has oversight of most essential city services, such as tree-trimming, street-repair, street-lighting, and street-beautification projects and capital improvements.

He serves as vice-chair of the Commerce Committee, which oversees Los Angeles World Airports, including Los Angeles International Airport. Bill is also a member of the council's Budget & Finance Committee, and Ad Hoc Committee on Homelessness, which he co-founded.

Since taking office in July 2005, Councilman Rosendahl has focused on: stopping the expansion of Los Angeles International Airport (LAX), promoting mass transit, enhancing public safety, curbing overdevelopment, standing up for tenants' rights and for affordable housing, seeking solutions to the problem of homelessness, and giving our neighborhoods a greater voice in city decision-making. His most notable achievement so far has been the historic agreement between LAX and airport neighbors, ending airport expansion and promoting regional aviation.

A resident of Mar Vista, the largest community in the 11th District, Bill is the first openly gay man elected to the Los Angeles City Council, and is the city's highest-ranking GLBT official.

Prior to his election, Bill was an educator and an award-winning television broadcaster with a long record as a leader in Los Angeles civic affairs.

While he served as distinguished professor at Cal State Dominguez Hills until his election, Bill is best known as producer and moderator of critically acclaimed public-affairs television shows. As host of "Local Talk," "Week in Review," and "Beyond the Beltway," Bill created a needed forum for discussion of public affairs. An advocate of empowering people through information, Bill produced more than 3,000 programs over 16 years, opening the airwaves to all viewpoints and steering thoughtful dialogue on the most complex and controversial issues.

Prior to his cable-TV career, Bill was a White-House appointee to the state department as chief of operations for the U.S. Trade and Development Program, served as an associate in philanthropic work for John D. Rockefeller, III and worked on many political campaigns, including Robert Kennedy's 1968 presidential bid.

A Vietnam-era veteran, Bill served in the U.S. Army from 1969 to 1971, spending a year as a psychiatric social worker, counseling troops returning from combat. As special assistant to the commanding general at Ft. Carson, Colorado, he won national recognition for reorganizing the base and boosting morale of the service people. Bill is currently a member of The American Legion, Post 283, in Pacific Palisades.

Bill holds a Master's of Social Work from the University of Pittsburgh.[1]

[1] www.lacity.org/council/cd11/cd11bio.htm.

Social Worker in Office: Ciro Rodriguez

Congressman Rodriguez serves on the House
Committee on Appropriations, subcommittee
on Homeland Security and transportation,
Housing and Urban Development, and
related agencies, and legislative branch.
Veterans Affairs Sub-committee on Health,
Disabilities and Memorial Affairs. He also
serves on the House Committee on Veterans'
Affairs in the Subcommittees on Disability
Assistance & Memorial Affairs. Congressman
Rodriguez's leadership is further exemplified
in his involvement with the Congressional
Hispanic Caucus (CHC) where he serves as
the Chair of the Taskforce on Veterans Affairs.

A firm believer in the importance and
power of education, Congressman
Rodriguez began his career in public service as a board member of the Harlandale
Independent School District in 1974. At this time he was working as a social worker
with the Bexar County Department of Mental Health & Mental Retardation, but later
became a trainer for the Intercultural Development Research Association. He served in
this capacity until he decided to launch his legislative career in the Texas State Legislature and began teaching for his alma mater, Our Lady of the Lake University, in 1987.

While in the Texas House of Representatives, Representative Rodriguez drew
from his experience as a social worker and educator to fight to increase Texas high
school graduation rates. As a state representative, Congressman Rodriguez drafted
the landmark Texas law guaranteeing acceptance of the top 10 percent of Texas
high school graduates to any public four-year Texas university. He was also responsible for the development of the "dual-credit" program, which allows high school
students to earn college credit for advanced courses.

Congressman Rodriguez was raised and educated in San Antonio, Texas. He
graduated from Harlandale High School, received his B.A. at St. Mary's University,
and earned his MSW from Our Lady of the Lake University in San Antonio.

http://rodriguez.house.gov/index.php?option=com_content&view=article&id=13&Itemid=2

Social Worker in Office: Earlene Hooper

Earlene Hooper was elected to the New York Assembly
on March 15, 1988 in a special election. Her reelection in November 1988 made Ms. Hooper the only
minority serving in the Legislature from Long Island.
Also, she is the only black woman representing a sub-
urban district in New York State.

Ms. Hooper is a social worker by profession. She
has worked as an administrator in the New York State
Department of Social Services' Division of Children and
Family Services.

An active unionist, Ms. Hooper was a member of the
Executive Board of the Public Employees Federation

(PEF). From 1979 to 1988, she served as shop steward for PEF in her Department of Social Services Office.

A long-time member of the Hempstead Heights Civic Association, Ms. Hooper has provided innovative and effective leadership in an effort to improve the community. As Legislative Chairwoman of the Nassau County Chapter of Jack and Jill of America, she established the DEALS project (Developing and Expanding Adult Life Skills) to help young people make the difficult transition from adolescence to adulthood.

Ms. Hooper is an active member of the National Association for the Advancement of Colored People, the Central Nassau Chapter of the Negro Business and Professional Women's Association, and Delta Sigma Theta Sorority. She also served as Committeewoman for Nassau County.

Ms. Hooper has been involved in the formulation of child care policy on both the state and national levels. Her legislative priorities include securing increased state funding for local school districts, fighting for drug rehabilitation programs and stricter enforcement of drug laws, ensuring safe, affordable housing for all New Yorkers, protecting our environment, and strengthening economic development efforts.

Ms. Hooper serves on the following assembly committees: education; housing; labor; economic development, job creation, commerce and industry. She is a member of the Assembly Task Force on Women's Issues, and the New York State Black and Puerto Rican Legislative Caucus. Additionally, Ms. Hooper was appointed by former speaker Miller to the Permanent Commission on Justice for Children. In January 2001, Ms. Hooper was appointed Chair, Majority Conference by Speaker Sheldon Silver.

She graduated from Norfolk State College with a B.A. in English and received her Master's in Social Work from Adelphi University, Garden City, New York, and Doctor of Humane Letters from Five Towns College, N.Y. She is an adjunct professor at the Adelphi University Graduate School of Social Work.

http://assembly.state.ny.us/mem/?ad=018&sh=bio

Social Worker in Office: Chip Shields

For more than 14 years Chip Shields has been fighting for the people of North and Northeast Portland as an Oregon State Senator, State Representative and as a community leader. From leadership roles in raising the minimum wage and funding our schools, to finding living-wage jobs for hundreds of people through Better People, the Northeast Portland nonprofit job center he started, Chip Shields has delivered results.

Chip has served in the Oregon House and Senate since 2005 where he focuses on living-wage jobs, health care, schools and equality. In the 2009 session, as Co-Chair of the Public Safety Subcommittee of Ways & Means, he protected services for domestic violence survivors, funding for drug and alcohol treatment, and negotiated and passed a bill that invests $1.5 million in pre-apprenticeship training for women and people of color.

Because of his work in the legislature and the community, Chip was recognized with the AFL-CIO Hero of Labor award, the Skanner newspaper Drum

Diversity in Practice

Critical Thinking Question

In what ways do the social worker elected officials profiled in this chapter advance the profession's diversity goals?

Major for Justice award and the Citizen's Crime Commission crime-fighter of the year award.

Chip has a master's of social work from Portland State University.[1]

_____
[1]http://www.leg.state.or.us/shieldsc/

Social Worker in Office: Ross Wilburn

Ross Wilburn has had the honor of being Iowa City's first African American Mayor. He is currently in his third four-year term on the City Council. Prior to being elected to city council, Ross served on the Iowa City Parks & Recreation Commission.

Councilmember Wilburn is employed as the Equity Director of the Iowa City School District. He is an adjunct instructor at the University of Iowa's School of Social Work and is a former director of the school's Quad Cities Graduate Center. A former youth worker at United Action for Youth, he is one of the founders of the Iowa Community Youth Development Training Institute. In addition, he was a trainer for the National Network for Youth and a grant reviewer for the Department of Health and Human Service's Administration on Children, Youth, and Families.

Councilmember Wilburn has a master's degree in Social Work from the University of Iowa. He served in the Iowa Army National Guard for six years and achieved the rank of Staff Sergeant E-6. Ross was recognized as the Distinguished Honor Graduate at the Iowa Army National Guard's Basic Non-Commissioned Officer School.

_____
http://www.icgov.org/default/?id=1116

CAMPAIGN ROLES FOR THE SOCIAL WORK PROFESSION

In addition to the individual policy practitioners who volunteer in and advise campaigns and run for office, the profession as a whole plays an institutional role in political campaigns, primarily through the National Association of Social Workers and the state-level NASW chapters.

NASW's political action committee is called Political Action for Candidate Endorsement (PACE). This federally registered organization endorses and contributes to candidates who support NASW policy issues and mobilizes social workers to vote for PACE-endorsed candidates. While independent of any political party, PACE endorses candidates who will advance NASW policy positions. PACE also serves a political education function, working to train social workers in political advocacy and foster campaign participation among all social workers.

Box 12.6   NASW Endorses Barack Obama for President in 2008

The National Association of Social Workers (NASW) enthusiastically endorses Barack Obama for President in 2008. Mr. Obama holds the ideals of the profession in high regard as evidenced by his support of important legislation such as the Mental Health Parity Act, End Racial Profiling Act, and Healthy Families Act.

Mr. Obama attended Columbia University and moved to Chicago after graduation to become a community organizer in the tradition of Saul Alinksy and in the hometown of legendary social worker Jane Addams. He spent several years working to transform the South Side of Chicago and once noted, "It's as a consequence of working with this organization and this community that I found my calling. There was something more than making money and getting a fancy degree. The measure of my life would be public service."

Barack Obama is an ally to social workers and the clients we serve, including women, children, and people of color. He has vowed to promote equal opportunity and end discrimination, empowering people to make positive changes in their communities and in their lives. He is a strong supporter of civil rights legislation aimed at closing the pay-equity gap, ending racial profiling, and reducing hate crimes across the country. Mr. Obama has promised to make health care affordable for all Americans and has pledged to protect a woman's right to choose.

Barack Obama is an ally to the profession and it is our responsibility to ensure that social work issues stay primary in his campaign. As president, Mr. Obama will be making important appointments that affect the social work profession such as Secretary of Health and Human Services and Director of the National Institutes of Health. These key decisions will have an impact not only on the profession but the entire nation.

There are several ways to ensure that social work plays a prominent role in the next administration. One of those ways is to volunteer with the Obama campaign. You can make phone calls, attend campaign events, or work in campaign offices across the country.

https://www.socialworkers.org/pace/2008election/comparison.asp?back=yes

In July 2008 the NASW endorsed Barack Obama in the 2008 presidential election (see Box 12.6). Examine the social work values used to justify NASW's position in the text of the endorsement (reproduced below).

The NASW state chapters also have formed political action committees, which focus primarily on state-level races (but also may be active in national campaigns). For example, the New Jersey PACE Board of Trustees endorses and contributes to local candidates running for state assembly and senate. In Minnesota, MN-PACE screens candidates such as those to running for governor, St. Paul and Minneapolis mayor, state house and senate, county commissioner, state auditor's School board, and county sheriff to support those whose platforms align with NASW goals. This statement from the MN-PACE Web site explains the members' motivation: "Although some view politics with cynicism, PACE committee members believe that they need to stay active in the system in order to ensure fair and human-centered policy for themselves and the people they serve."[26] In addition to screening, endorsing, and contributing to candidates, state PACE organizations mobilize social workers in their area for GOTV efforts such as staffing phone banks, making literature drops, and door knocking/neighborhood canvassing. Serving on state-level PACE groups is an excellent way to get involved in electoral politics. State PACE groups need local networkers to mobilize local social workers. Local members often interview local and state candidates using standardized interviews established by the NASW-PACE and then present the results to the State PACE committee, which then decides whom to endorse and support financially.

LAWS AND ETHICS OF CAMPAIGNING

Politics can be a hard game. As Susan Lerner of the Common Cause organization observed with respect to her own state of New York, "The warping influence of big money—whether today favoring reform or tomorrow favoring special tax breaks—is still a distortion of our system. Elections should be about the best ideas for getting New York out of its fiscal and ethical gridlock, not who can buy the biggest megaphone."[27]

U.S. history is replete with examples of how powerful, monied interests have determined election outcomes.[28] In the post–World War II era, efforts to ensure honest government and a wider range of perspectives in the public sphere have led to campaign finance reform, lobbying laws, and the promotion of voluntary codes of fair campaigning. For every reform-minded law, though, it seems that there has been a counterbalancing action or set of actions aimed at maintaining a status quo that favors the powerful. For example, redistricting, or the defining of congressional district boundaries, has been used to increase the advantages of incumbency.[29] Another example is the "527" committees discussed earlier in this chapter, which have offered a way for campaigns to benefit from largely unregulated financial support.

Negative campaigning—attack advertisements, untraceable Internet rumor Web sites, and forwarded e-mails that make scurrilous accusations—is another "hard ball" aspect of political campaigning today. Note that there is a distinction between negative campaigning that legitimately focuses on an opponent's record and *ad hominem* attacks that smear a candidate's reputation or family.

Policy practitioners enter the political realm mindful of the "warping influence of big money," and the temptations of going negative in framing the opposition. The social work value of integrity, with its underlying principle that "social workers behave in a trustworthy manner," serves as a guide in helping practitioners through these ethical minefields. Policy practitioners need to know the laws governing their campaign actions, and they strive to carry out the values of the profession while achieving the desired electoral outcomes.

Campaign Finance Reform

The Bipartisan Campaign Reform Act (BCRA) of 2002, otherwise known as the McCain-Feingold Act, was designed to end the use of "soft money" (money raised outside the limits and prohibitions of federal campaign finance law) in federal elections. Provisions include prohibiting national parties from raising or spending nonfederal funds and limiting fundraising by candidates on behalf of party committees, other candidates, and nonprofit organizations.[30]

Table 12.4 provides an overview of limits on campaign finance contributions. (Also see Chapter 5 for information on the Hatch Act, which places some restrictions on political activity for federal, state, and local government employees, and for employees of those nongovernmental agencies that work in connection with programs financed by federal loans or grants.)

Campaign finance laws also operate at the state level. For example, the states of Arizona, Connecticut, Maine, New Mexico, North Carolina, and Vermont have all passed "Clean Election" laws that are designed to minimize the influence of large donors on election outcomes. Typically, a Clean Election law provides public financing of campaigns, provided the candidate demonstrates public support (e.g., as measured by the number of donors who contribute $5). Candidates who abide by Clean Elections guidelines agree that they will not raise additional funds. In some cases, Clean Election candidates receive extra public funds if the opposing candidate has much greater financial resources. While the laws vary to some extent by state, and some have been overturned by state courts, it appears

Table 12.4 2007–2008 Campaign Contribution Limits

	To each candidate or candidate committee per election	To national party committee per calender year	To state, district & local party committee per calender year	To any other political committee per calender year[1]	Special Limits
Individual may give	$2,300*	$28,500*	$10,000 (combined limit)	$5,000	$108,200* overall biennial limit: ▲ $42,700* to all candidates ▲ $65,500* to all PACs and parties[2]
National Party Committee may give	$5,000	No limit	$No limit	$5,000	$39,900* to Senate candidate per campaign[3]
State, District & Local Party Committee may give	$5,000 (combined limit)	No limit	No limit	$5,000 (combined limit)	No limit
PAC (multicandidate)[4] may give	$5,000	$15,000	$5,000 (combined limit)	$5,000	No limit
PAC (not multicandidate) may give	$2,300*	$28,500*	$10,000 (combined limit)	$5,000	No limit
Authorized Campaign Committee may give	$2,000[5]	No limit	No limit	$5,000	No limit

*These contribution limits are increased for inflation in odd-numbered years.

[1] A contribution earmarked for a candidate through a political committee counts against the original contributor's limit for that candidate. In certain circumstances, the contribution may also count against the contributor's limit to the PAC. 11 CFR 110.6. See also 11 CFR 110.1(h). [2] No more than $42,700 of this amount may be contributed to state and local party committees and PACs. [3] This limit is shared by the national committee and the Senate campaign committee. [4] A multicandidate committee is a political committee with more than 50 contributors which has been registered for at least six months and, with the exception of state party committees, has made contributions to five or more candidates for federal office. 11 CFR 100.5(e)(3). [5] A federal candidate's authorized committee(s) may contribute no more than $2,000 per election to another federal candidate's authorized committee(s). 2 U.S.C. 432(e)(3)(B).[1]

[1]www.fec.gov/pages/brochures/contriblimits.shtml (accessed June 30, 2008).

Social Worker in Office: Kyrsten Sinema

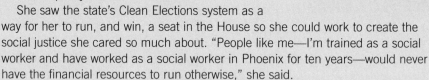

Representative Kyrsten Sinema likes to stay busy. Aside from being a member of the Arizona House of Representatives, she's a college professor and a lawyer. After graduating from college at the age of 18, she began a career in social work as a way to help those in need.

"The goal of social work," she said, "is to create social justice." And that's why she went into politics.

"Over the years as a social worker, I became more and more upset about the injustice in my community. To create systemic social justice, I had to have influence over policy at the state level."

She saw the state's Clean Elections system as a way for her to run, and win, a seat in the House so she could work to create the social justice she cared so much about. "People like me—I'm trained as a social worker and have worked as a social worker in Phoenix for ten years—would never have the financial resources to run otherwise," she said.

With her background in social work, Representative Sinema has made it her priority to work on issues in the legislature that benefit marginalized and oppressed people in her district and across the state. Her opinions on criminal justice, immigration, and lesbian and gay rights issues are heard even louder because she has a seat in the legislature.

"The best thing about running Clean is that when you're in office, no one can pressure you to vote in a certain way. [Recently] I had to vote on a bill to benefit Cox Communications and I was able to vote no on that bill. They tried to stop and see me, but I told them I would vote no."

"I can treat every single person who walks through my door the same because I'm not beholden to special interests."

With Clean Elections, Representative Sinema is accountable only to voters and she knows she has to focus on their needs—or she'll stop getting their $5 contributions. "I know that in two years, I have to get back out to those doors and talk to those same voters and they're going to tell me if they are happy with what I've done or not," she said.

When she's not in the state house, Representative Sinema is an adjunct professor of social work at Arizona State University and practices criminal defense law in the Phoenix community. She serves on the boards of several nonprofit organizations and recently chaired the campaign that defeated the same-sex marriage ban on the Arizona ballot in 2006.

"I am going to use Clean Elections until I run for an office that doesn't have the system," she said. She's in good company. In 2007, more than 200 Clean Elections officials were sworn into office free of special interest influence.[1]

---

[1]Adam Smith, "Profile: Arizona Rep. Kyrsten Sinema." www.publicampaign.org/ (accessed July 20, 2008).

that Clean Election laws are increasing the competitiveness of state house elections, particularly in Arizona and Maine.[31]

Researchers have found that Wisconsin's Clean Election law is less effective than those of Maine and Arizona.[32] From a policy analyst viewpoint, why do you think this is so? (Hint: review the "Special Conditions" row of Table 12.5.)

Table 12.5   Overview of State Clean Election Laws[1]

	Arizona	Maine	Wisconsin	Minnesota	Hawaii
Effective	2000	2000	1978	1976	1996
Qualification	Threshold of 210 $5 contributions. These funds are deposited in public fund program and are not kept by the candidate	Threshold number of $5 qualifying contributions, 50 for House, 150 for Senate. These funds are deposited in the public fund program and are not kept by the candidate	◆ Win primary with at least 6% of total vote for office ◆ Raise threshold amount in $100 contributions ($1,725 for Assembly, $3,450 for Senate)	Threshold amount raised in $50 contributions: $1,500 for House, $3,000 for Senate	Threshold amount raised ($1,500 for House, $2,500 for Senate)
Maximum Grant	◆ Up to spending limit ◆ Matching funds (up to an additional $56,600) provided to participating candidates running against privately financed opponents, and to offset independent against ◆ Independent candidates receive 70% of spending limit	◆ Up to spending limit ◆ Matching funds (up to an additional 200% of original grant) provided to participating candidates running against privately financed opponents and to offset independent expenditures against	◆ $15,525 for Senate (2002) ◆ $7,763 for Assembly (2002)	◆ Amount of direct grants determined by dividing total funds by number of candidates, but may not exceed 50% of spending limit ◆ Small contribution refund program reimburses individuals up to $50 for contribution to participating candidate	◆ Amount of grant limited to 15% of spending limit

Table 12.5   Overview of State Clean Election Laws (Continued)

	Arizona	Maine	Wisconsin	Minnesota	Hawaii
Effective	2000	2000	1978	1976	1996
Spending Limit (contested election)	▲ $28,300 for primary/general in both House and Senate elections ▲ $11,320 for single party dominant districts	▲ $5,406 for primary/general in House ▲ $23,728 for primary/general in Senate	▲ $17,250 for Assembly ▲ $34,500 for Senate ▲ Limits unchanged since 1986	▲ $34,100 for House (2004) ▲ $64,866 for Senate (2002) ▲ Separate spending limits for election and nonelection years	Spending limit fixed as $1.40 x number registered voters in district 2004 range: House: approx. $14,000–$19,000 Senate: approx $23000–$45,000
Special Conditions	▲ Unopposed candidates not eligible for public funds beyond qualifying contributions ▲ Nonparticipating candidates faced additional reporting requirements	▲ Nonparticipating candidates face additional reporting requirements ▲ Participating candidates permitted to raise small amounts	Spending limits apply only if all candidates accept public funds	▲ Spending limits increase by 10% for first time candidates and by 20% for candidates running in competitive primary ▲ Spending limits waived when nonparticipating opponent exceeds threshold expenditures	

Source: Kenneth R Mayer, Timothy Werner, and Amanda Williams, "Do Public Funding Programs Enhance Electoral Competition?" (Paper presented at the Fourth Annual Conference on State Politics and Policy Laboratories of Democracy: Public Policy in the American States, Kent State University, April 30–May 1, 2004; updated March 2005), campfin.polisci. wisc.edu/Wisc%20Camp%20Fin%20Proj%20-%20Public%20Funding%20and%20Competition.pdf (accessed July 25, 2008).

Providing greater access to candidates without the "big" money supporters like social worker and Arizona State Representative Kyrsten Sinema may result in more office holders who are not tied to large corporate interests. With more public financial backing rather than corporate and PAC backing, candidates may have a broader perspective that is focused on the "public good." Bringing this different perspective to the definition of social problems and the detailed policy decisions outlined in Chapter 8 may result in a different political context for policy development, one that is less of a battle among competing private interests and more directed toward finding a consensus about the developing policy for the common good.

Other states such as Texas have created voluntary mechanisms to encourage fair play in campaigns. The Texas Code of Fair Campaign Practices, reproduced in Box 12.7, sets campaign parameters that exclude the use of negative, prejudicial personal attacks, distorted information, intimidation of potential voters, and other unethical practices that work against the public interest.

Note that any of the prohibited behaviors listed in the Texas Code would violate the NASW Code of Ethics for social workers.

Human Rights & Justice

Critical Thinking Question

In your opinion, which violations of the Texas Code of Fair Campaign Practices would cause the most harm to the political system?

Box 12.7   Texas Code of Fair Campaign Practices

There are basic principles of decency, honesty, and fair play that every candidate and political committee in this state has a moral obligation to observe and uphold, in order that, after vigorously contested but fairly conducted campaigns, our citizens may exercise their constitutional rights to a free and untrammeled choice and the will of the people may be fully and clearly expressed on the issues.

THEREFORE:

1. I will conduct the campaign openly and publicly and limit attacks on my opponent to legitimate challenges to my opponent's record and stated positions on issues.

2. I will not use or permit the use of character defamation, whispering campaigns, libel, slander, or scurrilous attacks on any candidate or the candidate's personal or family life.

3. I will not use or permit any appeal to negative prejudice based on race, sex, religion, or national origin.

4. I will not use campaign material of any sort that misrepresents, distorts, or otherwise falsifies the facts, nor will I use malicious or unfounded accusations that aim at creating or exploiting doubts, without justification, as to the personal integrity or patriotism of my opponent.

5. I will not undertake or condone any dishonest or unethical practice that tends to corrupt or undermine our system of free elections or that hampers or prevents the full and free expression of the will of the voters, including any activity aimed at intimidating voters or discouraging them from voting.

6. I will defend and uphold the right of every qualified voter to full and equal participation in the electoral process, and will not engage in any activity aimed at intimidating voters or discouraging them from voting.

7. I will immediately and publicly repudiate methods and tactics that may come from others that I have pledged not to use or condone. I shall take firm action against any subordinate who violates any provision of this code or the laws governing elections.

I, the undersigned, candidate for election to public office in the State of Texas or campaign treasurer of a political committee, hereby voluntarily endorse, subscribe to, and solemnly pledge myself to conduct the campaign in accordance with the above principles and practices.

_____   _____
     Date   Signature
_____

Source: www.ncsl.org/programs/ethics/e_ethicsURLs.htm.

CONCLUSION

This chapter features profiles of several social workers who have served in public office, and the linkages between their social work experience and their priorities as elected officials are easy to discern. The family social worker now serves on the Children and Family Law Committee in the State Assembly. The social services administrator serves on legislative committees for education; housing; labor; economic development, job creation, commerce and industry and on a commission on justice for children. After leading a fight to increase his state's minimum wage, the director of a nonprofit, job placement and counseling program now serves in the state legislature, where he stopped attempts to repeal the voter-approved minimum wage. The social-worker-turned legislator who "made it her priority to work on issues in the legislature that benefit marginalized and oppressed people in her district and across the state"—all show the power of the profession in the political realm. The experience of social and economic inequities did not lead them toward cynicism, but rather toward the resolve that they would address clients' problems at their root.

Log onto **MySocialWorkLab** to access a wealth of case studies, videos, and assessment. (*If you did not receive an access code to* **MySocialWorkLab** *with this text and wish to purchase access online, please visit* www.mysocialworklab.com.)

1. **Review the Health Care Reform SCS.** At the conclusion of the Health Care Reform SCS, Tony d'Amato wins elective office. What role could his participation in the Care4Care campaign have played in his decision to run for office?

2. **Watch the Connecting Core Competency Videos on Human Rights & Justice.** Pay particular attention to the issues raised by homelessness. In the videos, social worker Tom Faxon helps his client seek housing assistance. After reading the Chapter 12 profiles of social workers in elected office, design a campaign platform for Tom Faxon that would address his key issues, were he to run for office.

PRACTICE TEST
The following questions will test your knowledge of the content found within this chapter. For additional assessment, including licensing-exam type questions on applying chapter content to practice, visit **MySocialWorkLab**.

1. Although all campaigns cost money to run, the importance of campaign money increases when:
   a. The economy is experiencing a downswing
   b. The candidate does not have significant personal funds to invest in the campaign
   c. The candidate is running against an incumbent
   d. An incumbent faces multiple challengers

2. Organizations that can accept unlimited contributions from individuals in order to influence federal elections, without explicitly endorsing or opposing any specific candidate are referred to as:
   a. 501K Committees
   b. Push groups
   c. PACs
   d. 527 Committees

3. Identification of message and framing, timing and intensity of outreach, media mix and pacing are all:
   a. Key components of a campaign media plan
   b. Essential elements in campaign fundraising
   c. Elements of the campaign logistics plan
   d. Superficial in nature and handled by lower level campaign staff

4. Social workers can use their involvement in political campaigns as a springboard to elected office. As of 2005 the number of social workers in elected office in the U.S. was:
   a. 1200
   b. 1770
   c. 177
   d. 69

5. The NASW organization that endorses and contributes to candidates who support NASW policy issues, and operates on both national and state levels is called:
   a. LACE
   b. PACE
   c. PAC
   d. N-PACE

6. Some new media that have proven very effective in twenty-first century campaigns in mobilizing voters and donations are:
   a. Laser printed leaflets, text messages, and cell phone "quality" calls
   b. Embedding video in e-mail, and soy ink printed eco campaign materials
   c. Text messages, cell phone video reminders, and laser printed leaflets
   d. Social networking sites like second life, text messages and video embedded in e-mails

7. Ad hominem attacks refer to:
   a. Negative campaign attacks that smear a candidate's reputation or family
   b. Electronic and other non traceable negative campaign attacks
   c. Reactive campaign attacks in response to a negative ad campaigns
   d. A type of negative ad campaign that focuses on an opponent's record

8. The Bipartisan Campaign Reform Act of 2002 had as its objective:
   a. Requiring that candidates invest at least 5% of their own money in their campaign budgets
   b. To end the use of soft money in federal elections
   c. To prohibit fiscal campaign double standards among Republican and Democratic parties
   d. To put a cap on how much money could be raised by any one candidate for a federal election

9. The Clean Election laws that have passed in some states are designed to:
   a. End the use of soft money in state campaigns
   b. To cap the number of large donors that can contribute to a candidate
   c. Maximize transparency of state campaign finances
   d. Minimize the influence of large donors on election outcomes

---

Log onto **MySocialWorkLab** once you have completed the Practice Test above to access additional study tools and assessment.

Answers

Key: 1) c, 2) d, 3) a, 4) c, 5) b, 6) d, 7) a, 8) b, 9) d

13

Evaluating Policy Implementation and Outcomes

CHAPTER OUTLINE

Introduction 347

The Rulemaking Process 347

Rulemaking Case Example 348

A Note About the Budget Process 349

Why Monitoring Implementation and Evaluation are Important 350

Privatizing Eligibility in Indiana: Case Study in Implementation Challenges and Need for Evaluation 351

Types of Evaluation 354

The Context of Policy and Program Evaluation 357

Welfare Reform Policy Evaluation Case Example 358

Evaluation Resources 359

Common Questions for Program/Policy Evaluation 361

Conclusion 364

Chapter Review 365

Practice Test 365

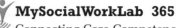 **MySocialWorkLab 365**
Connecting Core Competency videos on Policy Practice
SCS on Housing

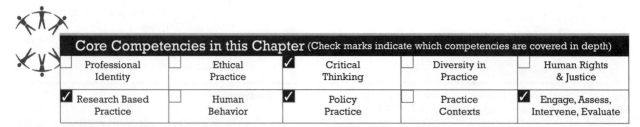

Core Competencies in this Chapter (Check marks indicate which competencies are covered in depth)				
☐ Professional Identity	☐ Ethical Practice	☑ Critical Thinking	☐ Diversity in Practice	☐ Human Rights & Justice
☑ Research Based Practice	☐ Human Behavior	☑ Policy Practice	☐ Practice Contexts	☑ Engage, Assess, Intervene, Evaluate

INTRODUCTION

As previous chapters have indicated, policy practitioners can be very active in policy development, deliberation, and decision-making. Their involvement, though, does not end with the successful passage of a desired policy. After a policy has passed, generally a program must be implemented to enact the policy, whether that is something as comprehensive as universal health insurance for all Americans or a policy as defined as a new eligibility standard for a local food pantry. Either policy will require additional decisions about program specifics to determine how the policy will be enacted so that potential clients receive the intended services. For example, when a local food pantry is inundated with requests for groceries during a recession, the board may decide to make sure its efforts are focused on helping the neediest families. Whereas previously, anyone coming to the pantry was assisted without proof of need or any eligibility standard, the board may decide to use 150 percent of the poverty line as its standard for eligibility. The board may leave the decision about how to implement this policy to the executive director and staff of the agency. Are people just asked their family size and income or are they required to bring in proof of each? What documents will constitute "proof"? Birth certificates for all family members? Last year's income tax form to verify income? Or a current pay stub? How often must such documentation be presented? If the food pantry previously provided food to anyone who came in, keeping only tallies of the number of people served, the agency may need to establish some sort of client record keeping system to document the families' proof of eligibility, leading to additional costs in terms of both staff time and a documentation and record keeping system that was not needed previously. Agency staff may worry that families, without the necessary documents but still in need, may no longer feel welcome and, therefore, not come in. They may also worry that checking documents will result in a less "accepting" atmosphere at the pantry, where all families feel welcome. Their concerns about additional recordkeeping and documentation checking without increases in resources may lead to lower staff morale, sometimes felt by clients as "burnout" and cynicism. Such unintended consequences of the new policy may result in creating barriers to achieving the very goal the board had in mind. All of these questions about the potential impact of a policy point to the importance of monitoring the implementation process and evaluating the results of the policy once it is in place. Social work policy practitioners have a number of roles to play in these processes to make sure that policies are implemented as the policymakers intend or are changed if circumstances suggest the goals are not being met.

This chapter begins by identifying how policy practitioners can influence policy implementation design through the rulemaking process. The major types of policy and program evaluation are discussed with case examples to illustrate some of the challenges in policy evaluation as well as roles for social work practitioners. The chapter ends with some common questions addressed in most policy evaluation efforts, coupled with potential data sources and data collection methods. This chapter is not intended as a comprehensive discussion of policy and program evaluation, but provides an overview of the processes and useful resources at the end.

THE RULEMAKING PROCESS

When federal or state laws are passed, they are generally not specific enough to be implemented without further rulemaking, similar to the case example of the food pantry above. While the legislative branch of government passes the

Generally, the rules are promulgated or published for a period of public comment prior to actual implementation.

law, the executive branch of government creates the rules for implementation. If those two branches are of one mind with regard to the policy, the rules may be clearly aligned with the policy as enacted by the legislative branch. If, however, the two branches of government have different perspectives on the policy as passed, the rules may weaken, strengthen, or otherwise change the policy as enacted. Generally, the rules are promulgated or published for a period of public comment prior to actual implementation. This period of public comment is an important time for policy practitioners to be present at public meetings to testify about possible impacts or outcomes of the proposed rules or submit written comments to the particular office of the executive branch promulgating the rules. The executive branch is under no legal obligation to incorporate suggestions for changes in the rules received during this period of public comment, but frequently suggestions are made that will actually be helpful for policy implementation or that may make the policy more acceptable to the agencies and organizations that will need to be involved in the implementation process. Accommodating some suggestions from the opposition may make a controversial policy more politically palatable to those who have opposed it during the legislative process. Sometimes, the administration is set on how the policy will be implemented and will not be swayed by arguments from those who would like to see modifications and changes. Providing testimony at this stage in the policy process is not that different from the testimony discussed in Chapter 10, but in this case, the practitioner is attempting to influence key policymakers in the executive branch rather than legislators. Given this situation, coalitions of interest groups may be more persuasive than advocates representing single agencies. If practitioners have previously established their credibility and fostered relationships with staff in the executive branch, their input and advice may carry more sway. Advocates may want to mobilize constituent groups of clients and citizens as well to comment and demonstrate their support or opposition to particular proposed rules.

RULEMAKING CASE EXAMPLE

In June of 2006, President Bush issued new rules for Temporary Assistance for Needy Families (TANF), rules designed to further reduce the welfare rolls and move more poor people into jobs. These rules were the result of the federal budget signed by Bush in February of 2006 and represented "the biggest changes in welfare policy since 1996."[1] The rules set "a uniform definition for permissible work activities and require[d] states to verify and document the number of hours worked by welfare recipients."[2] In addition, some noted that the increased focus on process and reporting requirements, such as tracking the daily work activities of welfare recipients, was unusual in a block grant (TANF became a block grant when welfare assistance ceased to be an entitlement program).[3] Previously, states had some flexibility in what activities qualified as meeting work requirements. The new rules reduced the variability across the states with regard to those activities that would count toward the work requirement: "For example, educational homework (unless under formal supervision), arranging for child care, or finding shelter in domestic violence situations could no longer count for job time."[4] Educational programs were limited to no more than two years, thus precluding recipients from receiving support while pursuing four-year college degrees.

In addition, the new rules required that 50 percent of welfare recipients in a state be engaged in work or training activities, in contrast to the 32 percent that were thus engaged in 2004,[5] clearly an effort to further reduce the number of people receiving TANF assistance. Welfare rolls had been reduced by 60 percent from the passage of welfare reform legislation in 1996 to 2004, but the decline had leveled off starting during the recession of 2001,[6] suggesting that the availability of jobs was an important factor in reducing rolls in addition to welfare policy itself. Penalties for states that did not meet the standards were reductions in their state welfare grants by 5 percent the first year and 2 percent additionally for each subsequent year, to a maximum of 21 percent.[7]

In this case of rulemaking, while some advocates protested that these new work requirements could not be achieved, others noted that some states had already met the 50 percent employment requirement. The Republican governor of Georgia reported 69 percent of welfare recipients were working or in training programs with rolls only at 26 percent of levels from 2002.[8] On the other hand, the National Conference of State Legislatures reported that 15 states at the time had work participation rates under 25 percent representing an incredible challenge to meet the requirement in the time mandated.[9] On a Health and Human Services Department-sponsored tour to five cities to discuss the rules and gain input from the states (another good opportunity for policy practitioners to voice their views), Jerry Friedman of the American Public Human Services Association noted,

> The critical question is how we want to define success and whether this represents the very best return on our welfare investment. The agenda that many states hoped to pursue during the second chapter of reform was to address the needs of the working poor by emphasizing job retention, advancement, and income progression. I also believe that TANF reauthorization, as an unintended consequence, could have a chilling effect on the future of other human service block grants. The deal that states originally struck with the federal government was for an expenditure cap in exchange for fewer requirements. A decade later, they are now left with only one-half of that equation.[10]

The comment period in the rulemaking process allows diverse views to be expressed in attempts to influence the final rule that is promulgated. In this case, opposition to the rules had minimal impact and the rules were enacted with few changes.

Sometimes policies are funded, but not at the level to address current need.

A NOTE ABOUT THE BUDGET PROCESS

Few policies and programs can be implemented without funding, funding for staff who will be providing services, funding for computers and software to process applications and generate checks or other benefits, funding for supervision and program management, and so on. Usually, the state or federal budget process is separate from the implementation of specific programs or policies. The budget for the entire state or nation is considered separately from specific policy proposals, though the policy proposal will have a fiscal impact that will be discussed as part of the policy debate. Sometimes federal policies about how states will implement programs provide the states with no additional funding, the "unfunded mandate" that we hear about so often. The 2006 welfare-reform rule discussed above was one such mandate, with the individual daily tracking of client work participation posing an enormous administrative cost to states. Sometimes policies are funded, but not at the level to address current need. Child care vouchers for low-income working families to help reduce their child care costs have historically been under-funded, and, therefore, unable to assist all those families who qualify for assistance. How well a program is funded and whether that funding is adequate to meet the identified need will affect whether or not the program or policy is successful in meeting its goals.

WHY MONITORING IMPLEMENTATION AND EVALUATION ARE IMPORTANT

Research Based Practice

Critical Thinking Question

Sometimes when there are funding challenges with new projects, the evaluation component is eliminated or drastically reduced. What are some essential elements of a cogent argument for the importance of program and policy evaluation?

Once the final rules and procedures for implementation have been issued, the policy or program can be implemented. Much can happen during the implementation process to put the policy or program on a track to being successful or, conversely, undermining the efforts of policymakers. Funding problems have already been touched upon. People implement policies and programs and how those tasked with the implementation go about their work will make a difference in program outcomes. Because program rules usually cannot spell out and clarify all the individual circumstances and variations that may be presented in implementation, there is frequently some professional judgment required in determining eligibility and following through with the delivery of program services. In social work, we frequently talk about the power of the "street-level bureaucrats"[11] in the discretion that they have in policy implementation. In studying TANF implementation in New York, Hagen and Owens-Manley found that

> without clear agency criteria and priorities, accompanied by intensive training of frontline workers, the granting hardship and domestic violence exemptions [of work requirements] is a difficult task for workers to complete and highly dependent on an individual worker's judgment and discretion. Although some administrative discretion on the part of frontline workers may be appropriate, tremendous variability in the granting of exemptions hinders equitable treatment of clients.[12]

In addition to issues of professional discretion, a variety of implementation issues can have an impact on how services are actually provided. Where the offices are located and the hours it is open, the specifics of the application process, the outreach that is provided informing potential program participants about the program or policy, and a variety of other such details can make a tremendous difference in whether the people who could benefit from the program or service ever actually hear about its availability for them and their families and are able to successfully apply for services.

Social workers in community agencies are in an excellent position to monitor new program implementation as they hear about client experiences, either from clients themselves or from other colleagues in other agencies. When policy advocates hear about both early successes and challenges, they can inform policymakers of the effect the new program or service is having on the intended clients. They can also alert policymakers when the program is creating some unintended consequences. The following case example provides a more detailed illustration regarding the importance of policy and program evaluation.

PRIVATIZING ELIGIBILITY IN INDIANA: CASE STUDY IN IMPLEMENTATION CHALLENGES AND NEED FOR EVALUATION

In 2007, Indiana's Family and Social Services Administration (FSSA) entered into a 10-year contract with a consortium of for-profit corporations led by IBM to provide a new document and information management system for state eligibility determination for Food Stamps, TANF, Medicaid and other programs for low-income families. Though IBM employees provided staffing for the call centers and the new Web-based application processes, final eligibility was still determined by state FSSA employees, as required by federal law. This privatization of social welfare services was preceded in the state by contracting out the maintenance and toll collection on toll roads in the northern part of the state to Macquarie Infrastructure Group of Sydney and Cintra Concesiones de Infrastructures de Transporte S.A. of Madrid.[13] The privatization of social services was the result of the belief of the state Republican administration that the private sector would produce greater efficiency, lower costs for the state in achieving desired outcomes, and reduce fraud.

Indiana was not the first state to privatize social welfare services. Nationwide, state child welfare agencies have had a long history of contracting with nonprofit community agencies and for-profit social service organizations for intensive services for needy children, including in-home family preservation services, residential programs, and various specialized therapies. These "privatization" efforts have allowed the state agency to provide highly specialized services in a more flexible way to individual children without directly employing a whole new contingent of specialists and adding to the state payroll. Specialized services could be contracted as needed and then readily discontinued when no longer necessary.

The privatization of welfare eligibility services represents a more wholesale systemic change reflective of a national trend, starting in the 1980s and then accelerating during the Bush administration, when states were looking for ways to save funds by turning over the operation of entire state agency functions to the private for-profit sector and corporations like IBM. Prisons were among the first to undergo a privatization process. A 2001 Monograph of the Bureau of Justice Assistance in the U.S. Department of Justice noted that instead of the anticipated 20 percent cost savings in shifting to privately owned and operated prisons, the prison privatization effort to that time had realized only a 1 percent cost savings.[14] This report also did not support claims of better management or greater safety in private prisons and anticipated a slowing in the growth of private prisons.

In 2005, Texas privatized its antipoverty programs, with disastrous results when low-income families lost Food Stamps and other benefits that they depended upon for their survival. Over 100,000 children lost their health insurance benefits in the first four months. The private companies had promised over $600 million in savings over five years. But when Texas terminated their contracts after less than two years, there had been no savings at all.[15] Other states have experienced similar difficulties with privatizing social welfare services.[16]

Despite publicity about the challenges other states were facing with their privatization efforts, Indiana entered into a 10 year $1.6 billion contract with the IBM consortium with transfer of state staff to the vendor in spring of 2007 and county roll out beginning in October 2007. At the time, some advocates expressed concern that there was no independent evaluation component built into the plan despite the far-reaching nature of the change in the application process and data management system that was anticipated.

Most would have agreed that modernization of access and upgrades of the old computer system (not included in the vendor contract) would have been important new aspects of privatization. Such an investment and conversion process would have been very expensive for the state. But some advocates for vulnerable populations expressed concern about some of the "modernization" aspects of the program.

Besides implementing a new document and information management system, the modernization plan entailed reducing the number of caseworkers working directly with clients applying for benefits and substituting IBM employees responding to inquiries at call centers and to Web-based applications. In addition, applicants could fax documentation materials to the call centers. Providing multiple access points was an important modernization effort to enhance the accessibility of the application process, though some questioned whether the state's most needy citizens had access to these technologies. The roll out of the program was to begin gradually.

There was no provision for an external evaluation of this dramatic change in the way citizens could apply for services. What evaluation is possible is focused on internal data and performance measures, not necessarily on whether people were getting the help they needed. For example, some of the initial feedback at town hall meetings and in data reported out to the public focused on wait times for calls to get picked up instead of whether people were actually getting answers when they called. The other evaluation measures available are the quarterly reports produced by FSSA that include data such as error rates for Food Stamps, TANF benefit amounts and caseloads, TANF work participation rates, call center statistics, and other data across time. These current data raise some interesting evaluation questions when compared to previous years before modernization. They do not answer the question though of why there have been decreases in some caseloads but not others, why sanctions have increased, and why work participation rates have been declining. Additional evaluation strategies for data collection would have to be in place to address more detailed evaluation questions.

Early on, there were problems with the new technology, and the initial roll out was postponed.[17] As implementation began, anecdotes reported increase of long waits on phone lines, difficulty in getting answers to questions, termination of benefits for "failure to comply" when faxes did not go through properly, and other challenges clients faced in using the new technology. Advocates from a variety of social service agencies were among those to bring these concerns to the attention of legislators and others in a position to make changes.[18] As newspaper articles began to appear and town-hall meetings were held in various communities to voice concerns, there were calls for investigation of these process allegations.[19] Efforts to deal with some of these unanticipated difficulties led to an increase in costs.[20]

Even some in Congress became involved. Congresswoman Rosa L. DeLauro issued the following as part of her statement regarding the proposal to suspend Indiana's privatization effort for Food Stamp applications,

> I commend USDA and Under Secretary Nancy Johner for their oversight of the Indiana food stamp privatization process and for taking action to suspend it until the problems are resolved. Many of us in Congress expressed concerns about this contract since it was proposed, and I continue to believe that approving the project was the wrong thing to do.

The Indiana experiment is simply more evidence of what can go wrong when you try to privatize the administration of critical social services. Private contractors ultimately are evaluated by their company shareholders and not by the food stamp recipients they are supposed to serve.

The stories from Indiana about people losing benefits with no ability to appeal, and the difficulty many experienced in navigating the new system moved beyond the anecdotal to become a serious concern. These stories are especially troubling during difficult economic times when working families need food assistance.

Before allowing the state to continue with its roll out, USDA must be completely satisfied that the state is in full compliance with federal law and standards, and that hungry families are not turned away from the food assistance Congress intends them to receive. A similar food stamp privatization experiment in Texas proved disastrous and USDA should consider terminating the Indiana contract if the state's plan is inadequate.[21]

With the postponement of the continuation of the roll out, improvements were made[22] and a new FSSA director assumed responsibility for improving the privatization process.[23] Nevertheless, in the summer of 2009, there was some pressure to cancel the contract if sufficient improvements did not continue. The consortium could provide data about improvements in phone waiting time, but not for some of the questions about what happened to people who just hung up after waiting for a response. The State Budget Committee of the legislature decided to review the privatization plan prior to the 2010 legislative session. In October 2009, the governor canceled the 10-year contract with IBM, saying it "just did not work."[24] FSSA is developing a hybrid model to retain some of the positive aspects of modernization (multiple access points for applications) and restoring some aspects of the previous service delivery model, including more face-to-face contact with caseworkers.

This case provides a good example of how an evaluation of both process and outcomes from the beginning of delivery system change effort might have been helpful. While no eligibility policies were changed, the way that clients accessed the system of assistance was changed dramatically by the privatization process. In fact, several changes happened simultaneously. First, a new document and information management system was implemented. Second, new ways to apply for services were implemented (Web, phone, and fax). And third, much of the staff changed from state employees working in county offices to employees of a private firm. Traditional casework in the local county office was not emphasized as it had been in the past. From an evaluation standpoint, sorting out the effects of these simultaneous but very different changes would have represented a challenge. Had some process or formative evaluation been in place, emergent problems and unforeseen issues might have been addressed before calls for change came from the state legislators and others.

Program evaluation questions that could have been addressed with systematic data gathering include: Was efficiency increased over the previous system? Were costs reduced? Were more people served? Was effectiveness increased in that people were better able to receive needed services? Were there unintended consequences? What happened to people unable to access the application process in a timely fashion? What were both client and worker experiences with and feedback about the operation of the application process? Additional questions such as how does the 2009 rate of participation in the Supplemental Nutrition Assistance Program (SNAP)-formerly the Food Stamp Program-compare to Indiana's rate of 74 percent in 2007,[25] prior to privatization? Instead of simply

Engage Assess Intervene Evaluate

Critical Thinking Question

If you had been hired to complete an evaluation of the Indiana eligibility privatization effort and you used the ethic of care framework (Box 13.3), what evaluation questions would you ask and what measures would you use to evaluate the implementation of this policy change?

In this way, process evaluation can provide a feedback loop to policymakers monitoring implementation processes.

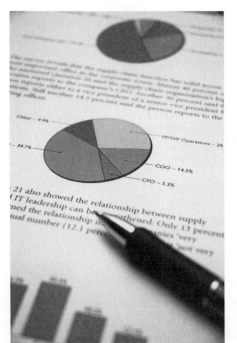

depending on consortium's data about reductions in the length of time clients spent "on hold" waiting for a person or number of days to process applications and the testimony of disgruntled citizens at town hall meetings, the state could have had access to considerably more systematic and reliable data had some pre- and post-measurement data been collected related to specific policy goals. That information would have been helpful in the aftermath of the cancelation of the contract, in planning for the new hybrid model.

In this example, we can see the critical role that evaluation can play in documenting the implementation process. In effective implementation, communication channels between the policymakers and the policy implementers (the street-level bureaucrats) need to be clear, with information flowing in both directions so that modifications in implementation can be made in response to changing conditions on the ground. If the intent of the policy is aligned with the agenda and attitudes of the agency/employees implementing the policy then the implemented policy is more likely to be as the policymakers intend. Those who design and enact the policy are not usually the ones who implement the policy and sometimes there is a disconnect so that something of the original intent is lost in translation, in the implementation process. As noted earlier, having the necessary resources to fully implement a policy is critical to smooth implementation. When the call centers, in the example above, were understaffed, applicants spent too long waiting for a response. Once more staff were added, call wait time was reduced. In this way, process evaluation can provide a feedback loop to policymakers monitoring implementation processes.

TYPES OF EVALUATION

Several types of policy and program evaluation are used to assess program and service delivery effectiveness. Three prominent types of evaluation are (1) process or formative evaluation; (2) summative or outcome evaluation; and (3) cost/benefit evaluation. Formative evaluation is concerned with development, implementation, and service delivery of social welfare programs. Some areas of focus in formative evaluations could include how well the rules, regulations, and procedures developed for the implementation of a policy are working; how unknown factors may contribute to client success or failure in a program, and how knowledge of these factors can improve the development of the program; or how clients and agency personnel experience the process of service delivery and policy implementation. Formative evaluations are generally conducted with the goal of improving policy and program implementation so that policy goals can be achieved. For example, Casper (2004) reported on a formative evaluation on a rent-subsidy program for homeless substance abusers that examined characteristics of those who successfully completed the program versus those who voluntarily dropped out or were involuntarily asked to leave because of noncompliance. They found in their formative evaluation study that those who voluntarily left the program had a past history of living independently but had also recently experienced a job termination. The involuntary leavers were associated with a history of job instability and a low investment in their current job. Based on the discovery of unique characteristics about program leavers, changes in program design were made to improve client retention in the program and achieve greater client success at attaining housing stability and economic self-sufficiency.[26]

Outcome or summative evaluation is concerned with the results that a policy and its programs have been able to accomplish. This type of evaluation may focus on the extent to which policy goals have been attained, the extent to which the social problem has been alleviated, or the number and quality of services provided. For example, the focus of the Child Support Enforcement (CSE) program when it was created as part D of Title IV of the Social Security Act in 1975 was to help states collect child support and establish paternity for children who were AFDC recipients by providing matching funds to states to encourage them to set up Child Support Enforcement Agencies. The federal government aimed to reduce the amount of money it was spending to support needy children, and to shift the responsibility for caring for these children to the absent fathers.[27] Outcome studies on this policy and its subsequent CSE programs looked at how successful states have been in locating absent parents, establishing paternity, getting court orders for child support established, and then examining the actual amount of money states were able to collect from absent fathers; in other words, how well were CSE agencies able to attain the goals set forth in the policy. An examination of reported statistics on the performance of child support agencies helps to assess the outcomes of child support enforcement policy (see Table 13.1). Between 1978 and 2002 child support agencies achieved a twenty-fold increase in child support collections. Nationwide, child support agencies nearly doubled the number of TANF cases for which they were successful in collecting child support; quadrupled the number of child support orders established from absent parents, and saw a 700 percent increase in the number of paternities established.[28] By these quantitative outcome measures, it appears that real successes have been achieved as a result of the CSE policies.

Summative or outcome evaluations can also examine the number of clients served, the extent to which clients' lives have been enhanced or client treatment goals attained, or the level of satisfaction clients feel about the services they received. Outcome evaluation can also examine the impact of a policy on the larger social problem it was designed to address. For example, the 1972 amendment to the Social Security Act that indexed the minimum benefits for retirees to the cost of living is credited with dramatically lowering the poverty level among the elderly. In 1959 (the first year poverty statistics are available on this group) those

Table 13.1 Child Support Program Statistics 1978–2002

Program Measure	1978	2002
Total child support collections (adjusted for inflation)	$1.1 Billion	$20.1 Billion
Average number of TANF cases in which collections were made	458,000	806,000
Number of support obligations established	315,000	1,220,000
Number of paternities established	111,000	697,000
Total administration expenditures	$312 million	$5.2 billion

Source: Committee on Ways and Means, U.S. House of Representatives, "Child Support Enforcement Program," *2004 Green Book* (Washington DC), Section 8, Table 8-1, pg. 6. http://frwebgate.access.gpo. gov/cgi-bin/getdoc.cgi?dbname=108_green_book&docid= f:wm006_08.pdf (accessed July 9, 2008).

65 years and older experienced a poverty rate of 35.2 percent. It steadily declined to around 12 percent by the early 1990s and then slowly declined to an all time low of 9.4 percent in 2006.[29] This policy outcome marks a great success for the Social Security retirement system in its ability to lift older people out of poverty and improve the quality of their lives.

A third type of program and policy evaluation that is commonly used to assess program effectiveness is the cost/benefit evaluation. This type of program evaluation is concerned with the cost of implementing a policy, and delivering the services to the target population, compared to the benefit gained from the policy and its programs. For example, the University of Wisconsin conducted a cost/benefit analysis of the federal School Breakfast Program (SBP) to gain insight as to why Wisconsin has implemented so few SBPs across the state.[30] After assessing the benefits and cost of the SBP in seven rural and urban school districts, researchers were able to identify specific benefits and costs to the program. They discovered that the program offered the benefits of improved nutrition among students; improved academic performance; a reduction in discipline problems; and a decrease in the absenteeism and tardiness. In addition, financial benefits included profitability, job creation, and financial stability in the food services within school districts. Cost of implementing the SBP ranged from $0 to $23,000, depending on whether or not schools already had an onsite food delivery system. Those that did not would be required to acquire space, purchase equipment, and hire staff. Some school districts broke even financially in their SBPs, while others made a profit. Profitability was dependent on high participation rates and charging appropriate prices. Overall, the study found that the SBP provided greater benefits than the School Lunch Program in Wisconsin, and it provided guidelines for successful implementation of SBP in both rural and urban school districts that predicted optimal success. The assessed benefit in terms of child well being, improved school attendance, increased cognitive functioning and academic success, and the likelihood of financial profitability established that the benefits far outweighed the cost of the program.

Policy evaluation studies are guided by specific research evaluation questions which are influenced by the type of evaluation being conducted (see Table 13.2). The actual development of a program evaluation requires knowledge and skill in conducting applied research. These include:

- Developing research questions;
- Selecting and applying appropriate research designs;

Table 13.2   Types of Program Evaluation and Sample Research Questions

Type of Program Evaluation	Sample Research Question
Process or Formative Evaluation	What client characteristics are associated with program completion and program drop out?
Summative or Outcome Evaluation	How successful have the Child Support Enforcement Agencies been in locating and establishing paternity among absent welfare fathers?
Cost/Benefit Evaluation	What are the cost and benefits for school districts electing to implement the federal School Breakfast Program in Wisconsin?

- Selecting or creating data collection instruments and procedures;
- Protecting client rights as research participants;
- Collecting, storing, and safeguarding data;
- Analyzing and interpreting data; and
- Disseminating evaluation outcomes to professionals via appropriate venues such as professional meetings, reports to funders, newsletters, journal publications, and books.

THE CONTEXT OF POLICY AND PROGRAM EVALUATION

Policy and program evaluation always occur within a broader context. As alluded to earlier in the chapter, internal evaluations are sometimes considered politically suspect as biased since they are produced by those implementing the program. External evaluations, on the other hand, depending on the reputation and track record of the external consultants providing the evaluation services, are generally considered more objective in their assessment of program successes and challenges. Many times, however, there is not sufficient funding for an external program evaluation and an agency or program must put a data-collection mechanism in place to provide feedback to staff and policymakers about the status of program processes and outcomes. This political context is particularly important in high stakes policy initiatives that seek to produce significant changes in both the quality of services and their cost.

With recent initiatives related to Evidence-Based Practice (EBT), social work among other professions is emphasizing the evaluation of programs and policies in achieving the desired outcomes for clients. Social workers are also interested in protecting clients from various forms of exploitation in the service delivery process (see the NASW Code of Ethics) and so are committed to process evaluations as well as summative or outcome evaluation. Social work policy practitioners involved in program evaluation are often called upon to assist in program evaluations and to be involved in data collection through client interviews, administering surveys, making observations, and accessing secondary data from client and other agency files. Policy practitioners may recruit clients into an evaluation study, explain the purpose of the study to clients, and clarify clients' rights and roles as study participants. They may also be asked to attend research meetings as a member of the evaluation team or to manage research data to insure confidentiality. Finally, social workers involved in policy evaluation may be invited to present study outcomes at professional meetings or to co-author a journal article with the principal evaluator.

Policy and program evaluation has become a growing industry in recent years as funders of social welfare programs (government and private alike) have demanded evidence of program effectiveness to secure future funding of social service programs. The emergence of evidence-based practice within social work and the human services has also contributed to the mushrooming of the program-evaluation industry. Government agencies and private foundations that fund programs want assurances that the money that taxpayers and private philanthropists spend on social welfare programs is making a difference in people's lives and in the communities they serve.

WELFARE REFORM POLICY EVALUATION CASE EXAMPLE

The welfare reform legislation passed in 1996 (the Personal Responsibility and Work Opportunity Reconciliation Act) was one of the most researched policy changes in the history of United States. Considerable funding was provided to the states and federally for longitudinal and rigorous scientific program evaluation to assess both the process and outcomes of the policy change. Large research and evaluation corporations (Mathematica, Abt Associates, Manpower Demonstration and Research Corporation, and the Urban Institute, among others) secured public and private foundation funding to study how the new welfare rules were implemented and changed the lives of welfare recipients. The Urban Institute even created a research center, "Assessing the New Federalism: An Urban Institute Program to Assess Changing Social Policies" that has recently changed its focus to "low-income working families."[31] Some social work programs were also involved in welfare program evaluation, such as the University of Georgia School of Social Work.[32]

The goals of welfare reform were to increase the number of poor people in the workforce and reduce the old AFDC case loads through eliminating the entitlement that had been in place for many years. What does all this evaluation tell us about the success or failure of this program and policy shift? As welfare reform was implemented in the various states, caseloads declined and more people found work. Many were clearly better off, but not all. Some faired very poorly under the new rules of welfare reform and a work-first approach, particularly those who had disabilities or were caring for family members with disabilities. While the "averages" suggested success, there were still those who were not successful in this new system. They were evicted. If they lost their welfare benefits, they lost access to health care when they lost Medicaid. They were unable to continue in school and meet new work requirements. Their time on welfare was limited. Prior to welfare reform, the average stay on assistance was a little over two years though there was no lifetime limit. Some were on assistance less than two years, but the recipients the public heard about were on for much longer. It is important to remember also that welfare reform occurred during a period of considerable prosperity and economic expansion in this country, when entry-level jobs were available to those coming off the welfare rolls, so they were able to find some financial means of support, even if many of those jobs were temporary, low wage, and without health insurance and other benefits.

So for the first five years, all went according to plan. But then, the economy started to slow down and the families that had been on welfare became working poor families. Some of them lost their jobs. The goal of welfare reform was never to reduce poverty, but some advocates became concerned about rising child-poverty rates and falling employment rates for single mothers starting in 2000.[33] There were few public or community supports for working families so families coming off welfare struggled with access to health care and child care, finding reliable transportation (particularly in rural areas), and creating savings accounts to accumulate assets, in addition to just meeting basic needs for food, clothing, and shelter. Lens (2002) noted that the challenge of keeping a job, particularly a low-wage job where fluctuations in demand might mean fewer hours of work available, was not addressed by the welfare reform efforts in 1996 where the emphasis was on finding a job. She summarized research from many states that noted that close to 20 percent of recipients returned to the rolls within three months and up to a third of recipients were back within one year.[34] Her work raises the question of what the goal or outcome of TANF should be—should we be trying to help families become self-sufficient, i.e. not dependent on any government or community agency programs? Has the policy been focused on the wrong outcome? One New York Times editorial noted: "Ten years into the effort, it's clear that work can help to assuage poverty, as long as the government helps the working poor. When that help is not forthcoming, a low-wage job fails to alleviate poverty, just as cash handouts failed. It's as necessary today for conservatives to back stronger government supports for the working poor as it was 10 years ago for people like President Clinton to get behind work rules for welfare recipients."[35] If government is not going to help and we want the goal to be self-sufficiency, then wages need to be higher or we need to invest in human capital so that those on welfare will have the same chance at self-sufficiency as others. The evaluation question remains: Was TANF successful? It depends on how you define its goals. If success is reducing the number of families receiving assistance and putting more people into low-wage jobs, then we can say TANF was successful. If we have a different goal of self-sufficiency and reduction of poverty, then TANF has fallen short.

> *The evaluation question remains: Was TANF successful? It depends on how you define its goals.*

Just a final note about the time frame used for TANF evaluations. If we just evaluate the number of recipients who become employed, we will have one measure of success. But as Lens points out, we need to look three months and one year after initial employment to determine client status. Are they still employed? At that same job or a different job? Is their economic status better now or worse? What about other measures of success such as their psychological well-being, their health, their children's school achievements, etc.? Are they self-sufficient or still requiring ongoing assistance from a program or agency? As you can see, the question of program evaluation becomes quite complicated very quickly.

EVALUATION RESOURCES

The Federal government has established agencies charged with evaluating its policies. Two such government offices are the U.S. Government Accountability Office (GAO) and Congressional Research Office (CRS). The GAO is considered the "Congressional watchdog," and is charged with improving government performance and accountability, and provides many valuable evaluation reports to the American public (see the Web site www.gao.gov.)[36] The CRS assists Congress in the legislative process and in selecting policy alternatives by analyzing policies and assessing the impact of current and proposed policy alternatives, often bringing to light information that is contrary to established beliefs and assumptions.[37] CRS reports are available through the offices Web site at www.fas.org/sgp/crs/index.html. Other Federal government offices are more focused on the cost/benefit assessment of policies and programs, such as the Office of Management and Budget (OMB) at www.whitehouse.gov/omb/, and the Congressional Budget Office (CBO) at www.cbo.gov/.[38] Box 13.1 provides the summary of a GAO Report on accessibility of mental health services for children in New Orleans post–Katrina, released in August 2009.[39]

The GAO Web site has a searchable (by topic and by agency) database of reports. A search revealed some reports from 2008–09 of interest to social workers in Box 13.2.[40]

Many universities now offer research and program evaluation services to help meet the demands for program evaluators, such as the Center for Child and Family Policy at Duke University in Durham, North Carolina,[41] and the Center for Program Evaluation at the University of Nevada in Reno.[42] Most state- and city-level agencies also have evaluation departments whose sole purpose is to evaluate how well state-level policies and programs are working (see, for example, the Pennsylvania's Department of Public Welfare's Bureau of Program Evaluation at www.dpw.state.pa.us/About/OIM/003670319.htm).

Critical Thinking

Critical Thinking Question
Review the GAO Website for evaluation reports of particular interest to you. After reading one, discuss what you learned about both policy implementation and policy outcomes. What questions about program success were not answered by the report?

Box 13.1   Sample GAO Report Summary

Hurricane Katrina: Barriers to Mental Health Services for Children Persist in Greater New Orleans, Although Federal Grants Are Helping to Address Them

GAO-09-935T August 4, 2009
Full Report (PDF, 11 pages) Accessible Text

Summary

This testimony discusses the protection of children during disaster recovery and to provide highlights of our July 2009 report entitled Hurricane Katrina: Barriers to Mental Health Services for Children Persist in Greater New Orleans, Although Federal Grants Are Helping to Address Them. The greater New Orleans area has yet to fully recover from the effects of Hurricane Katrina, which made landfall on August 29, 2005. One issue of concern in the recovery is the availability of mental health services for children. In our report, we estimated that in 2008 about 187,000 children were living in the greater New Orleans area—which we defined as Jefferson, Orleans, Plaquemines, and St. Bernard parishes. Many children in the greater New Orleans area experienced psychological trauma as a result of Hurricane Katrina and its aftermath, and studies have shown that such trauma can have long-lasting behavioral, psychological, and emotional effects on children. Poor children in this area may also be at additional risk, because studies have also shown that children who grow up in poverty are at risk for the development of mental health disorders. In 2007 the poverty rate for each of the four parishes in the greater New Orleans area was higher than the national average, and in Orleans and St. Bernard parishes, the rate was at least twice the national average. Experts have found increases in the incidence of depression, post-traumatic stress disorder symptoms, risk-taking behavior, and somatic and psychosomatic conditions in children who experienced the effects of Hurricane Katrina. In addition, children in greater New Orleans may continue to experience psychological trauma because of the slow recovery of stable housing and other factors, such as the recurring threat of hurricanes. Data collected by Louisiana State University (LSU) Health Sciences Center researchers indicate that of the area children they screened in January 2008, 30 percent met the threshold for a possible mental health referral. Although this was a decrease from the 49 percent level during the 2005–06 school year screening, the rate of decline was slower than experts had expected. Experts have previously identified barriers both to providing and to obtaining mental health services for children. Barriers to providing services are those that affect the ability of health care organizations to provide services, such as a lack of providers; and barriers to obtaining services are those that affect the ability of families to gain access to services, such as concerns regarding the stigma often associated with mental health services for children. The devastation to the health care system in greater New Orleans caused by Hurricane Katrina may have exacerbated such barriers.

Stakeholder organizations most frequently identified a lack of mental health providers and sustainability of funding as barriers to providing mental health services to children in the greater New Orleans area, and they most frequently identified a lack of transportation, competing family priorities, and concern regarding stigma as barriers to families' obtaining mental health services for children. A range of federal programs are helping to address these barriers, but much of the funding they provide is temporary. Among the 18 stakeholder organizations that participated in our structured interviews, the most frequently identified barrier to providing mental health services was a lack of providers. With regard to families' ability to obtain services for their children, 12 of the 18 organizations identified lack of transportation as a barrier. A range of federal programs address barriers to mental health services for children in the greater New Orleans area by supporting various state and local efforts—including hiring providers, assisting families, and utilizing schools as delivery sites—but much of the funding is temporary. Funding from several HHS programs has been used to transport children to mental health services. Federal programs also provide funding that is used to alleviate conditions that create competing family priorities—including dealing with housing problems, unemployment, and financial concerns—to help families more easily obtain children's mental health services. Louisiana has used federal funds to help support school-based health centers (SBHC), which have emerged as a key approach in the greater New Orleans area to address barriers to obtaining mental health services for children.

Source: Hurricane Katrina: Barriers to Mental Health Services for Children Persist in Greater New Orleans, Although Federal Grants Are Helping to Address Them, U.S. Government Accountability Office, www.gao.gov/products/GAO-09-935T (accessed August 21, 2009).

Box 13.2   Sample GAO Reports of Interest Available at GAO Website

Hurricane Katrina: Federal Grants Have Helped Health Care Organizations Provide Primary Care, but Challenges Remain
GAO-09-588 July 13, 2009

Hospital Emergency Departments: Crowding Continues to Occur, and Some Patients Wait Longer than Recommended Time Frames
GAO-09-347 April 30, 2009

Green Affordable Housing: HUD Has Made Progress in Promoting Green Building, but Expanding Efforts Could Help Reduce Energy Costs and Benefit Tenants
GAO-09-46 October 7, 2008

Social Security Administration: Service Delivery Plan Needed to Address Baby Boom Retirement Challenges
GAO-09-24 January 9, 2009

VA Health Care: Preliminary Findings on VA's Provision of Health Care Services to Women Veterans
GAO-09-899T July 16, 2009

Source: U.S. GAO—Reports and Testimonies Browse by Topic, U.S. Government Accountability Office. www.gao.gov/docsearch/topic.php (accessed August 21, 2009).

As the demand for policy and program evaluation has grown, so has the need for social workers to have working research knowledge not only on how to participate in the evaluation studies as a research assistant, but also on how to interpret and use the data to ensure future funding, to modify programs based on outcomes, and to support new evidence-based program development. Social workers need to be able to incorporate study outcomes into grant requests for funding for current and new social service programs. It is likely that as a social worker working as a direct service worker, a supervisor, administrator, or a policy practitioner, you will be asked to participate in program evaluations as part of your professional responsibilities.

In addition, as policy practitioners, social workers can attend and testify at public hearings that legislative bodies utilize when considering the policy renewals and appropriations at both the state and federal level. In these settings, social workers can present evaluative data from their practice in their agencies that speak to the policy under review, and how it could be enhanced for better client services. Social workers may be able to address the policies that function as barriers to clients accessing services and suggest alternative strategies. Social workers are in a position to evaluate programs against legal and professional standards, as well as from their own perspectives.

COMMON QUESTIONS FOR PROGRAM/ POLICY EVALUATION

Program and policy evaluations typically address questions about both the processes used to implement the program or policy and the outcomes or effects of the policy as enacted. The policy analysis framework in Chapter 9 that uses the ethic of care as its basis lists some of the key questions to consider in each of the areas of caring. Here that framework is somewhat modified and ideas about potential data sources are added.

Using the ethic of care framework to analyze and evaluate policies as they are implemented suggests asking some different questions from some of the outcome evaluations discussed above. Whatever framework is used, that framework and the logically derived questions from it will drive the focus of the evaluation, so selecting a framework that poses the questions that are important for a particular policy becomes a critical part of the evaluation process. For example,

Policy Practice

Critical Thinking Question

For a policy with which you are familiar (perhaps in your internship), how could you use the questions under the "Responsiveness" heading in Box 13.3 Policy Analysis Framework to evaluate the policy and actually collect data from some of the suggested sources?

box 13.3 provides a list of policy evaluation questions that would logically flow from the the ethic of care framework discussed in Chapter 9.

Good policy and program evaluation is not the end of the policy practice process. Rather, it points our way to policy/program enhancements and improvements in addressing both individual needs and community concerns. Sometimes, evaluation reports are generated but are relegated to dusty shelves and fail to inform policymakers of the next steps in the policy development process. Frequently, in the course of policy evaluation, new needs and issues emerge that require some new policy, new program, or new direction. For example, when Lens suggested that initial welfare reform strategies did not reinforce job retention enough (as noted earlier in our discussion of welfare reform), she was suggesting that current policy needed to be changed to incorporate more focus on job retention, in order to meet the goals of the original policy, to help people become attached and stay attached to the labor market so they would no longer be dependent on welfare programs to meet their needs. Evaluation reports typically conclude with a series of recommendations to policymakers to retain certain aspects of programs that are working and modify or change those aspects that could be improved. These recommendations can be the starting points for advocates who are interested in making sure that unmet needs are addressed in a timely fashion. And so the policy practice cycle continues, with evaluation as the natural feedback loop.

Box 13.3   Policy Analysis Framework

Areas of Caring to Assess	Questions to Consider	Possible Data Sources

Attentiveness	1. Who is in need of care?
	2. What are their needs?
	3. What maximal care is desired?
	4. How attentive is the policy to the needs of those in need of care in terms of
	   a. Access to care,
	   b. Affordability of care, and
	   c. Goodness of fit of care provided with care needed?
		1. Service providers
		2. Those in need
		3. Potential clients
		4. Community and family members, those who use services

Responsibility	1. Who is responsible for providing care to those in need? What is the balance of responsibility and is it appropriate? Who is overly responsible? Who is left out of the responsibility of care who could and ethically should be included?	1. Policy guidelines compared to implementation, criteria for appropriate balance, use external standards of care as reference
	2. Who determines who is responsible for providing care to those in need? Who else should be involved in determining who should provide care?	2. Policies and procedures as compared to actual implementation
	3. What are the power relations between those in need of care and those providing care (individual to organizational)?	3. Observations and interviews with relevant parties

Areas of Caring to Assess	Questions to Consider	Possible Data Sources
	4. What forms of power and privilege reside in the caring process? How do they shape the nature and adequacy of care?	4. Documentation of power relationships and interviews with those involved
	5. In what ways does the policy encourage and enhance the collaboration of care across the responsible units?	5. Look at policy in practice and degree of collaboration
Competence	1. How competent are those responsible for providing care in meeting the basic care needs of those in need of care, in terms of best practices and cultural competence?	1. Assessment of preparation of staff for assigned tasks, assessment of cultural competence
	2. Who actually provides the care, and how competent are the informal and formal systems of care in meeting needs of those in need of care? How well do they meet the standards of care of the family, the community, the agency, and the legal system?	2. Documentation of who provides services and comparison to external professional standards of care
	3. Are there resources that caregivers need to more competently do their work that is currently not provided by the policy? What are they?	3. Interviews with those receiving care, those providing care, and those supervising
	4. Who attends to the changing needs of those in need of care?	4. Documentation of how ongoing needs are assessed?
	5. What conflicts, if any, exist between the care givers and the care receivers?	5. Documentation of conflicts and how resolved
Responsiveness	1. How responsive are the care givers to the needs of the care receiver?	1. Observations and interviews with care receiver and family
	2. How do those in need respond to the care that is given?	2. Observations and interviews with care receiver and family
	3. What is the proximity of care giver and care receiver, and how does this support or disrupt the integration of comprehensive care?	3. Description of the system of care and analysis of integration of functions
	4. Are caregivers more responsive to some in need than others? Who is left out or marginalized?	4. Observations and case documentation of services received based on needs
	5. What are the consequences of low responsiveness or unresponsiveness to the needs of those in need of care in terms of access to care and quality of care for the care receiver? The family? The community? Who suffers and in what ways?	5. Case studies
Integration of Care	1. In what ways does the policy provide comprehensive and integrated care for those in need? To what extent does it fragment care?	1. Through analysis of both policy and data about outcomes and processes
	2. In what ways does the policy allow for the integration of cultural practices of care giving?	2. Illustrative examples
	3. How does the policy reflect the values of self-determination; inherent worth and dignity, and empowerment?	3. Use this standard as a framework for policy analysis

(Continued)

Box 13.3   Policy Analysis Framework (*Continued*)

Areas of Caring to Assess	Questions to Consider	Possible Data Sources
	4. How empowering is the policy for the care receivers? For the care providers? For institutions responsible for regulating and monitoring care?	4. Describe the empowering aspects for each group
	5. How does this policy reflect the values of caring, collaboration, inclusion, and interdependence? What social constructions of "otherness" undermine the infusion of these values?	5. Examination of values inherent in policy
	6. In what ways does the policy support those who "care about" those in need, and include them in the caring process?	6. Documentation of how others are included in the process
	7. What challenges to comprehensive and integrated care does the policy present? What gaps in care remain?	7. Interviews with all constituency groups plus policy analysis
	8. What ethical issues does this policy raise in the delivery of care, and in the maintenance or creation of care disparities?	8. Evaluation of policy in context of ethic of care and other ethical codes

Evaluation as feedback loop to identify unmet needs.

Sources: Hugman, R. "Professional Ethics in Social Work: Living with the Legacy." *Australian Social Work,* 56, no. 1 (2003): 5–15; Meahger, G., and N. Parton. Modernising Social Work and the Ethics of Care. *Social Work and Society,* 2, no. 1 (2004): 10–27; Tronto, J. "Care as a Basis for Radical Political Judgments." *Hypatia,* 10, no. 2 (1995): 141–149.; Tronto, J. "An Ethic of Care." *Generations,* 22, no. 3 (1998): 15–21; Tronto, J. "Care Ethics: Moving forward." *Hypatia* 14, no. 1, 113–119. Sevenhuijsen, S. "The Place of Care." *Feminist Theory,* 4, no. 2, (2003): 179–197; "A Place of Care: The Relevance of the Feminist Ethic of Care for Social Policy." *Feminist Theory,* 4, no. 2, 179–197.

CONCLUSION

Policy evaluation is a critical aspect of policy practice. Social workers, with their community and agency-based perspectives, are in an advantageous position to collect information about policy implementation processes "on the street" and to assess the impact of policies on the clients they serve. Systematic data collection, following research protocols, will enable social work policy practitioners to provide important information to policymakers about both the successes and the shortcomings of social welfare policies as implemented. With this information and feedback, policymakers can continue to refine and reconfigure social welfare policies to meet emergent human needs.

Log onto **MySocialWorkLab** to access a wealth of case studies, videos, and assessment. (*If you did not receive an access code to* **MySocialWorkLab** *with this text and wish to purchase access online, please visit* www.mysocialworklab.com.)

1. **Watch the Connecting Core Competency videos on Policy Practice.** After viewing the videos, assume a new policy is initiated in the prison. What criteria would you use to assess whether or not the new

policy was a success or not? Using the ethic of care framework (Box 13.3), what evaluation questions would you ask and what measures would you use.

2. **Review the Housing SCS.** If you were to evaluate the sustainable affordable housing built in the Housing SCS, how would you measure success? What outcomes would you advocate and how would you measure achievement of those outcomes?

PRACTICE TEST
The following questions will test your knowledge of the content found within this chapter. For additional assessment, including licensing-exam type questions on applying chapter content to practice, visit **MySocialWorkLab**.

1. Before implementation of a new policy, the suggested rules or guidelines for implementation are:
   a. Reviewed by a judicial board to make sure all rules are constitutional
   b. Published for a period of time for public comment
   c. Forwarded to a rulemaking committee for final adjustments to the rule framework
   d. Evaluated by a review board to ensure that the suggested rules are practical and affordable

2. Two major factors that dictate how successful a policy is in meeting its goals are:
   a. How well a policy is funded and if that funding is adequate to meet the policy's stated goals
   b. Which politicians backed the policy, and if they will continue to support the policy in the future
   c. The current economy and political climate that provides support for the policy
   d. How many suggestions were offered during the public period for comment on policy rules, and how many suggestions were implemented

3. Professional discretion, office location and hours, application process and outreach services informing potential program participants about a new program are all:
   a. Issues that must be addressed at the time the policy is created and developed
   b. Policy implementation issues that can have an impact on how services are delivered to clients.
   c. Minor details that make little difference in practical policy implementation and service to client groups
   d. Decisions of the program coordinator

4. The three major types of program and policy evaluation are:
   a. Cost/benefit evaluation, development evaluation and analytical evaluation
   b. Service delivery evaluation, process evaluation and outcome evaluation
   c. Process evaluation, summative evaluation, and cost/benefit evaluation
   d. Outcome evaluation ,program assessment evaluation and summative evaluation

5. The development, implementation and service delivery of social welfare programs are the main focal points of:
   a. Developmental evaluation
   b. Summative evaluation
   c. Cost/benefit evaluation
   d. Formative evaluation

6. Summative or outcome evaluation's focus is primarily:
   a. The sum total that the program was able to save compared to similar programs
   b. The extent to which actual outcomes matched projected program outcomes
   c. The results a policy and its programs have be able to achieve
   d. The total number of target groups a program was able to effectively reach

7. The most common type of evaluation to assess program effectiveness is:
   a. Process evaluation
   b. Formative evaluation
   c. Summative evaluation
   d. Cost/benefit evaluation

8. The government agency charged with improving government performance, accountability, and providing evaluation reports to the American public is known as:
   a. The IRS (Internal Revenue Service)
   b. The CRS (Congressional Research Office)
   c. The GAO (Government Accountability Office)
   d. The SOS (Supplemental Organizational Service)

9. When conducting a policy analysis focusing on competence of the policy, one good data source to use is:
   a. Case studies
   b. Policy guidelines
   c. Documentation of power relationships between staff and clients
   d. Comparison of staff training to external professional standards of care

---

Log onto **MySocialWorkLab** once you have completed the Practice Test above to access additional study tools and assessment.

Answers

Key: 1) b, 2) a, 3) b, 4) c, 5) d, 6) c, 7) d, 8) c, 9) d

14

A Vision for Political Empowerment

CHAPTER OUTLINE

Introduction 367

Opportunities 369
A New Era
New Strategies

Challenges 370
Overcoming Cynicism
Countering the Upsurge in Hate Groups
Thinking Globally

Making a Difference in Your Corner of the
World 374

Chapter Review 376

Practice Test 376

MySocialWorkLab 376
Connecting Core Competency videos on
Human Rights and Justice
Housing SCS

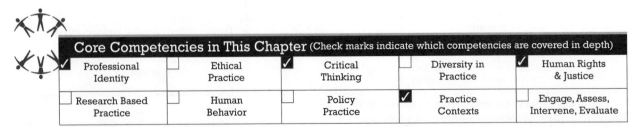

Core Competencies in This Chapter (Check marks indicate which competencies are covered in depth)				
✔ Professional Identity	☐ Ethical Practice	✔ Critical Thinking	☐ Diversity in Practice	✔ Human Rights & Justice
☐ Research Based Practice	☐ Human Behavior	☐ Policy Practice	✔ Practice Contexts	☐ Engage, Assess, Intervene, Evaluate

INTRODUCTION

This is how change happens . . . . It is a relay race, and we're very conscious of that, that our job really is to do our part of the race, and then we pass it on, and then someone picks it up, and it keeps going. And that is how it is. And we can do this, as a planet, with the consciousness that we may not get it, you know, today, but there's always a tomorrow.

ALICE WALKER

In each of the Simulated Case Studies (SCSs) that accompanies this textbook, policy practitioners experience the satisfaction of having a real impact on policy formation, both through their own actions and by empowering others to engage in the political process. In doing so, they live up to the standards set by the National Association of Social Workers (NASW) for social workers' ethical responsibilities to the broader society: "Social workers should engage in social and political action that seeks to ensure that all people have equal access to the resources, employment, services, and opportunities they require to meet their basic human needs and to develop fully. Social workers should be aware of the impact of the political arena on practice and should advocate for changes in policy and legislation to improve social conditions in order to meet basic human needs and promote social justice."[1]

In the access to health care SCS, Pam Baker, a Care4Care member, e-mails the group to celebrate how far they've come in advocating for universal access to health care:

Well folks we are at the beginning of an exciting story. A lot has happened. We acted at one of those "tipping points" of history in Factoria and we will therefore be able to have influence and input as things change.

The big news is that Governor Kneifler has appointed a fact finding policy committee on health care. There will be a statewide series of hearings. We are well represented on the committee, as is Ricardo's group. In an unheard of bipartisan spirit, or maybe just fear on both candidates' parts, they have **both** pledged that no matter who is elected, the work will go forward. Let's hope these aren't empty campaign promises, but I suspect we can hold them to it! Plus, it takes them off the hook to come up with a new plan!

In other words, our work is truly beginning. Thanks to all for getting us here, now let's make the difference.

In the low-income sustainable housing SCS, the successful effort to change local building codes, a revision needed to accommodate green construction techniques, increases access to affordable housing that provides a healthy environment for residents and lower energy costs. In the following e-mail housing authority social worker Annette Taylor thanks her mentor for inspiring her to get involved in policy practice:

Hey mentor, friend, bud, policymeister of the world!!

Your advice was so good way back when which seems like a year ago. You said to face up to policy change needs or nothing would happen. Who would have thought (OH, I KNOW, YOU!!) that getting a few building restrictions changed, i.e., no "energy-generating equipment more than two feet off of the ground" would open the way to our own little mini-green revolution. Getting an ordinance removed (there to protect against unsafe and unsightly generators), made solar panels possible, led the way to new insulation methods, led the way to the Sunstar Terrace housing development, which has shown all the doubters that affordable and green CAN go together!!

So let me say officially "Thanks!" Policy does affect practice.

Your convert,
Annette

In the same SCS, homeowner/activist Serena Honesta, whose effective advocacy was instrumental in getting the housing development approved, also experienced the power of having a public voice:

Annette,

We are thriving in our new housing. The asthma has stopped, the roaches of course are nonexistent, and we are just plain proud to live here. Report cards are great, I'm signing up for some community college courses now that I don't have to be obsessed with my child's health and our living conditions.

To think that we did this together. It was a fateful day when we all met up at that energy meeting at the school. We discovered our separate multi-talents combined into a REAL engine of change. I'm proud to have been a part of this team. Thanks so much to you and Erik, my two heroes. I'll be sending you an attachment of Darrin's latest science poster. A long cry from a few years ago.

Many blessings,
Serena Honesta

In the gay marriage, SCS policy practitioner Julia Cohen gets caught up in the drama of seeing the deciding votes cast against a proposal that would have effectively ended the possibility of laws allowing same sex marriage in the state. She e-mails a colleague that "IT'S AMAZING HERE," and the sense of increasing excitement as the state senators cast their votes is reflected in the rapid-fire exchange of text messages Julia sends to her colleagues.

All of the characters in the SCS experienced first hand the sense of accomplishment that is part of successful policy practice. The social workers in the case studies also live up to the profession's value of social justice, which calls for social workers to strive to ensure "meaningful participation in decision-making for all people."[2]

The purpose of this textbook is to start you on the path to policy practice; to raise your awareness of how policy practice is key to realizing the aims of the social work profession; to offer an introduction to the skills needed by policy practitioners; and to place the policy practitioner in the larger political-economic context in which she or he operates. This book is subtitled "New Strategies for a New Era" because we are at a unique moment in which policy practice is central to the national agenda *and* when social welfare policies must rise to the challenges of a deep global economic downturn and its aftermath. The opportunities and challenges of this new era require new strategies—the use of new technologies to mobilize supporters and engage the general public; a recognition that "insider politics" may give way to greater political inclusiveness; and a commitment to data-driven policies that get the most out of policy resource investments in tight financial times.

We are at a unique moment in which policy practice is central to the national agenda.

OPPORTUNITIES

A New Era

The election of Barack Obama as president, after he ran on a social justice-oriented platform, represented a striking ideological change from the preceding, more hawkish Bush administration. With Democratic control of the House and Senate, the political climate shifted from the Right's "less is more" approach to government to the Left's "together we can achieve great things" philosophy of active government. As noted in Chapter 12, the NASW endorsed Obama because of his platform's alignment with NASW policy goals. Suddenly, issues such as health care reform, public housing, the environment, and civil rights were again on the nation's policy agenda.

The election results galvanized community organizers, who saw Obama as one of their own. Indeed, as Michelle Obama once said, "Barack is not a politician first and foremost. He's a community activist exploring the viability of politics to make change."[3] The shifting political climate led the American Sociological Association to explore the theme of "The New Politics of Community" at its August 2009 meeting, which also featured a mini-symposium on "The Sociological Significance of President Barack Obama" to explore "how the historic election of Barack Obama might signal a new politics of community in action":

> Barack Obama's election is often described as a "defining moment," one marking some sort of fundamental change for American democracy. But what exactly has changed, or might change, and why? This session explores how the election of Barack Obama catalyzes new thinking about the meaning of democracy and change in the United States. Our panelists examine some important factors associated with change, such as new forms of political engagement by youth, new immigrant populations, women, and similar populations; new ways of organizing democratic institutions themselves that reflect a changing, heterogeneous American population; as well as the seeming commitment to community service and similar values thought to be associated with the revitalization of democratic institutions.[4]

The administration's philosophy of government was reflected in the early decision to rename the Office of Public Liaison the Office of Public Engagement to "create and coordinate opportunities for direct dialogue between the Obama administration and the American public, while bringing new voices to the table and ensuring that everyone can participate and inform the work of the president."[5] One of the office's first activities was the publication of a citizen's briefing book[6] that conveyed ordinary citizens' input on policies to the president.

New Strategies

New technologies for reaching out to people, technologies that were used to powerful effect in the presidential campaign, also present an opportunity for policy practice. The "many to many" networked nature of Web 2.0 tools is congruent with a grassroots approach to politics. Masters of this approach, the Obama administration acted quickly upon entering office to keep its grassroots support active and mobilized in support of the president's policy priorities. The primary means of doing so was through the Democratic National Committee

Critical Thinking Question

Are Web 2.0 strategies politically neutral? Reflect on the Tea Party's use of new media.

Box 14.1   Mobilizing Support for Health Care Reform through Organizing for America

President Obama is holding a live strategy meeting on Thursday at 2:30 p.m. Eastern Time for all Organizing for America supporters. I hope you can join us, online or by phone.

The President will update us on the fight to pass real health insurance reform—what's happening in D.C., and what's happening around the country. He'll lay out our strategy and message going forward and answer questions from supporters like you. And we'll unveil the next actions we'll organize together.

This is a critical time in this President's administration, and in the history of our country. I hope you can join us.

Here are the details:

What: Organizing for America National Health Care Forum

When: Thursday, August 20th, 2:30 p.m. Eastern Time

RSVP and submit a question for the President.

——————

Source: Christopher Hass, "Thursday: Strategy Meeting with the President," Organizing for America blog, posted August 18, 2009, http://my.barackobama.com/page/content/hqblog (accessed August 28, 2009).

(DNC)-housed group Organizing for America, the successor to the Obama for America campaign organization.[7] Obama for America was highly successful in generating a 13-million-person e-mail list of supporters. However, the list could not be used by the White House because it was generated as a campaign activity, and so Organizing for America was created to keep the newly developed grassroots alive.[8]

Organizing for America's first big challenge was mobilizing support for the president's health care agenda. Box 14.1 offers an example of an e-mail communication to its list of supporters.[9]

The health care reform agenda faced stiff political opposition, and was further weakened by a lack of active support from the younger voters who had been a strong component of Obama's electoral victory.[10] While polls showed that young people support the idea of health care reform, and are more likely than the national average to be uninsured, those facts were not sufficient, over the spring and summer of 2009, to motivate large numbers of young people to attend town meetings, contact their elected officials, or engage in other forms of activism to advance the cause of health care reform.[11] As of this writing, it remains to be seen whether Organizing for America will succeed in fully capitalizing on the networks of grassroots support that were formed during the presidential campaign. One thing does seem clear, however, and that is that the electrifying presidential campaign of 2008 revealed the potential for a new style of tech-savvy politics grounded in the core skills and values possessed by policy practitioners: community organizing, coalition building, and an abiding belief in the power of average citizens to make change.

CHALLENGES

The economic downturn of 2008 ushered in the worst global recession since the Great Depression of the 1930s. Broadly stated, analysts have identified two macrolevel causes of the downturn: the intertwined failures of (1) government and private sector loan oversight, leading to the subprime mortgage crisis and (2) the increasing complexity of global financial systems and high-risk, "high-unknowns" investment products such as derivatives, leading to widespread overextension of financial firms into investments whose losses they could not cover and the collapse of the international banking system and many local banks throughout the United States.[12] Both triggers caused investors to lose confidence in the market and consumers to lose confidence in the marketplace. Characterized by a shortage of available credit for businesses and individuals, high levels of unemployment, and precipitous drops in gross domestic product (GDP), the economic downturn had a severe impact on states' budgets as outlined in the following excerpt from a Washington Post story (Box 14.2) that focuses on how proposed budget cuts would affect the most needy.

These cuts came at a time of increased demand for social services, putting greater pressure on nonprofits, which also saw a decrease in private philanthropy when wealthy and middle-income contributors reduced their giving. Two-thirds of public charities experienced a decrease in donations in 2008.[13] Giving in the human services sector declined an estimated 12.7 percent in current dollars, to $25.88 billion. In inflation-adjusted dollars, the drop was 15.9 percent.[14] According to the GivingUSA survey,

Practice Contexts

Critical Thinking Question

How, in your opinion, did the economic downturn affect social work policy practice?

- "Compared with 2007, 54 percent of human services charities saw an increase in need for their services in 2008;
- For 2009, 60 percent of the surveyed human services organizations were cutting expenses, including cutting services or staff, due to funding shortages;
- The type of human service agency most likely to be underfunded was youth development/serving children and youth. Of this type of group in the study, 74 percent said they are underfunded or severely underfunded, meaning that current available funding was insufficient to meet current demand; and

---

Box 14.2   The Washington Post Reports that States are Hit Hard by Economic Downturn—Excerpt

BY KEITH B. RICHBURG AND ASHLEY SURDIN

Monday, March 31, 2008

NEW YORK—State budgets have been hit hard by a worsening national economy, including rising costs for energy and health care. In addition, fallout from the subprime mortgage crisis—declining home sales, deflated property values and mounting foreclosures—has caused a slide in states' anticipated tax receipts.

At least half of the nation's states are facing budget shortfalls, some of them severe, and policymakers in most of the states affected are proposing and passing often-painful measures to trim costs and close the gaps. Spending on schools is being slashed, after-school programs are being curtailed and teachers are being notified of potential layoffs. Health-care assistance is being cut for the elderly, the disabled and the poor.

Some analysts worry that the impact is being felt disproportionately by the most needy.

"It's disappointing, the extent they tend to focus their cuts on the most vulnerable," said Iris J. Lav,

deputy director of the Washington-based Center on Budget and Policy Priorities, a liberal think tank that monitors state budget issues. "It does appear to disproportionately affect low-income people."

* * *

A recent 50-state survey by the Associated Press showed that hundreds of thousands of poor children, the disabled and the elderly stand to have their health coverage eliminated as a result of budget cuts, and more than 10 million people would lose access to dental care, specialists and name-brand prescription drugs.

Budget experts said they see a repeat of the pattern that happened during the recession of 2001: States generally cut health services and medical benefits first, because these costs are often rising more rapidly than others, and the savings tend to be immediate.

Source: Keith B. Richburg and Ashley Surdin, "States Are Hit Hard by Economic Downturn," *The Washington Post,* March 31, 2008, www.washingtonpost.com/wp-dyn/content/article/2008/03/30/AR2008033002138_pf.html (accessed August 22, 2009).

▶ Among organizations working to meet people's basic needs (food, shelter, clothing, etc.), more than half (53 percent) said they are underfunded or severely underfunded for 2009."[15]

In such tight financial times, it is imperative that policy solutions draw on the best evidence, be very well executed, and be as cost-effective as possible. Data analysis, policy implementation, and evaluation skills are all the more important when resources are stretched so thin.

In August 2009 economists were beginning to see signs of economic recovery.[16] It is too soon to tell whether the Obama administration's economic stimulus initiatives played a significant role in the upswing, but it is likely that the administration will increase regulatory oversight to help avert future economic disasters.[17] Similarly, it may be time (past time!) for the nation's policy community to develop policies that will help reduce the impact of future economic recessions on the most vulnerable. The nation's social welfare system was constructed during the Great Depression, and from the ethic of care perspective, it is crucial to the future well-being of *all* U.S. citizens to assess whether that "safety net" is appropriate and responsive enough for today's economic woes in the globally interdependent social, economic, and political context of the twenty-first century.

There are constraints on action that make this a challenging goal. As is being seen in the debate over health care reform, party dynamics are complicating the prospects for large-scale change. The Blue Dog Democrats allied with Republicans in voicing concern over the scope and cost of proposed changes; meanwhile, progressive Democrats fought for a public option that was demonized as somehow involving "death panels." In the current economic climate it is very difficult to argue for massive state investments (although that was precisely what Franklin Delano Roosevelt's New Deal did in the 1930s). As expected, the 2010 midterm elections reflected public dissatisfaction with the slow economic recovery and frustration with the gridlock in Congress. With Republican control of the House, Obama will need new strategies to find common ground. Perhaps we too can find the political will and capacity to turn the current crisis into a long-term expansion of care for the most vulnerable.

Beyond the immediate economic situation, there are other current challenges to policy practice for social workers.

Overcoming Cynicism

While there does seem to be an opening to a new, more inclusive way of thinking about politics, we must overcome the cynicism that is easy to acquire in public life—the insider view that restricts our attention to the horse race of who's ahead in the political game. Reading a statement from the Citizen's Briefing Book such as "We are not protecting the youngest and most innocent of our society to the best of our abilities" can serve as a reminder that policy practice is not just for the professional social worker. Our clients have voices and knowledge that must be part of the public debate, and we are charged with facilitating that access.

Countering the Upsurge in Hate Groups

According to the Southern Poverty Law Center's annual survey, the number of hate groups has risen 54 percent since 2000, increasing at a greater pace since the election of the first African American president and also in response to the stresses of a faltering economy.[18] Unfortunately, these groups also use the tools of new technology to spread their message and seek converts. As an ethical responsibility, social workers must stand united to counter hate groups and other groups that fuel anti-immigration and anti–social justice movements. This is work that must be undertaken in the public sphere, so that the profession's human-centered perspective can confront the forces of fear that work against inclusiveness and social justice.

Thinking Globally

The ethic of care perspective stresses our human interconnectedness. This is true not only within U.S. society but also on an international level. Global interdependence leads to policy issues/solutions that need to be understood and enacted at the global or multistate level. This is a task of daunting complexity, but one that has been facilitated by the advent of the Web. New technologies have allowed for real-time collaboration and sharing of knowledge to occur throughout the world, minimizing national boundaries. The Millennium Project (a futures-research think tank) produces an annual *State of the Future* report that is an example of the power of collective global insight. Drawn from the knowledgebase of 2,700 leading scientists, futurists, scholars, and policy advisors, the 2009 report emphasizes that global problems can be addressed:

Global interdependence leads to policy issues/solutions that need to be understood and enacted at the global or multistate level.

> The good news is that the global financial crisis and climate change planning may be helping humanity to move from its often selfish, self-centered adolescence to a more globally responsible adulthood. The G-20 [an organization of industrial and emerging-market countries] is improving international financial regulations, market supervision, and accounting rules, and has brokered massive stimulus packages to prevent the world from falling into even deeper global financial crises. The December 2009 climate-change conference in Copenhagen has focused attention around the world on the practical details of how to address climate change. World leaders in politics, business, academia, NGOs, and international organizations are increasingly cooperating. Many perceive the current economic disaster as an opportunity to invest in the next generation of greener technologies, to rethink economic and development assumptions, and to put the world on course for a better future.[19]

Human Rights & Justice

Critical Thinking Question

What technologies can policy practitioners use to be heard on an international level?

Issues such as climate change, the status of women, infant mortality, and fair trade and sweatshop-free working conditions are global in nature. Policy practice happens at all social levels, from the local community to the transnational United Nations. The challenge of thinking globally is one that policy practitioners should consider as being part of their practice.

MAKING A DIFFERENCE IN YOUR CORNER OF THE WORLD

In writing *Policy Practice for Social Workers: New Strategies for a New Era* it was our hope that the policymaking process would be demystified and that connections to direct practice and the overall goals of the profession would be made clear. Jane Watkins, past president of the National Association of Foster Grandparent Program Directors, offers this advice to those starting out in policy practice: Being a successful policy practitioner is "no great mystery—with lots of hard work and passion, it's easy."[20]

Your policy practice will develop as your skills develop, and as that happens, you will gain confidence in your ability to have an impact on public policy. Table 14.1 outlines some of the core skills introduced in this textbook, along with some policy areas and sample actions you can take to build your policy practice skills. Of course, the possible actions apply to most or all of the issues; the intent is to illustrate how skill-building actions can be applied across the spectrum of the social work policy agenda.

In this unique moment of great potential for democracy and great economic and cultural challenges, there are no guarantees that the world will be a better place in the future. In 15 years time we may see the positive results of a more equitable health care system, real progress made in bringing down the

Table 14.1 Making a Difference in Your Corner of the World

Policy Practice Skill	Policy Area	Skill-Building Action You Can Take
Knowledge of the political system and the overall context of policy practice	Health care reform	Read health care reform coverage in a national newspaper such as the *New York Times* and in your local newspaper every day; browse the National Library of Medicine's collection of course syllabi at http://www.nlm.nih.gov/hmd/collections/digital/syllabi/index.html
Engagement skills—developing and nurturing relationships	Child welfare	Participate in Lobby Day and follow up with a personal note to a legislator.
Oral and written communication skills; knowledge of new technologies	Global poverty	Serve on the communications committee of your campus' global poverty organization (if your campus doesn't have one, start a student organization focused on reducing global poverty). Write a letter to the editor and revamp the organization's Web site to attract more students to the cause; use social networking tools as well. Start a blog on actions students can take to fight poverty.
Assessment skills—problem analysis, weighing proposed policy options	Aging	Take a gerontology course to become more cognizant of issues related to aging and policy options—see the free open courseware class materials for Health Issues for Aging Populations at Johns Hopkins Bloomberg School of Public Health, at http://ocw.jhsph.edu/courses/agingpopulations/
Ethical reflection	Mental Health	Contact the National Alliance on Mental Illness to arrange an In Our Own Voice presentation for social work majors at your university; take time to reflect on your own attitudes toward mental illness (see www.nami.org/template.cfm?section=In_Our_Own_Voice)
Ethical decision-making skills	Immigration	Find mentors who can discuss how they've dealt with difficult situations in their policy practice role of advocating for immigrant populations.

Table 14.1 (Continued)

Policy Practice Skill	Policy Area	Skill-Building Action You Can Take
Data collection and analysis, including library research skills, using data-bases, constructing/ conducting surveys	TANF	Research your own state's TANF rules and regulations; review the evaluative and longitudinal information is posted on the state agency's Web site and suggest your own hypotheses about changes in participation rates, applications, and sanctions that you observe; following appropriate research protocols, conduct your own survey of TANF recipients to determine their recent experiences with TANF rule changes.
Problem solving and negotiating skills	Civil rights	Get involved in campus-based affinity groups such as NOW or the Latino Student Union; volunteer to represent the group in student government.
Networking and collaborating skills	Hunger and homelessness	Join NASW and seek out members working on these issues; volunteer on their projects.
Policy Analysis	Juvenile justice	Apply the Policy Analysis framework used in the text (Chapter 9) to current sentencing policies in your state to determine how they address the ethic of care and the goal of rehabilitation.
Policy evaluation skills	Domestic violence	Apply policy evaluation criteria of adequacy, equity, and equality to a review of your state's domestic violence laws; present results at a social work student organization meeting.
Knowledge of legislative processes	Select an issue of importance in your state legislature	Serve as a legislative intern or get involved with your state's PACE organization. Track a bill through the legislative process and report to classmates. Watch C-SPAN for national issues.
Campaigning skills	Identify issues that are important to you and to other social workers	Find a candidate who supports these issues and volunteer on his or her campaign.

CO_2 levels that cause global warming, and have civil rights be recognized for more sectors of U.S. society and increasingly throughout the world. Or we may see ever-widening economic and health disparities; climate-related famines, water shortages, and conflicts on a global scale; and a rise in intolerance that strains the fabric of civil society. The *State of the Future 2009* identifies the mindset that is needed to "fight against hopeless despair, blind confidence, and ignorant indifference—attitudes that too often have blocked efforts to improve the prospects for humanity. Ridiculing idealism is shortsighted, but idealism without the rigors of pessimism is misleading. We need very hardheaded idealists who can look into the worst and best of humanity and can create and implement strategies of success."[21]

Social work has many allies in the long campaign to "improve the prospects for humanity." Historically, though, the profession has had an impact greater than its actual numbers and economic power, by virtue of the field's deep engagement with issues that are in the domain of public policy. As a policy practitioner you are part of a larger force for good. We urge you to take this opportunity to be that 'hardheaded idealist' who can make change happen in the world.

Professional Identity

Critical Thinking Question

As a citizen of the world and a policy practitioner, how would you assess our current situation? What needs to be done?

Log onto **MySocialWorkLab** to access a wealth of case studies, videos, and assessment. (*If you did not receive an access code to* **MySocialWorkLab** *with this text and wish to purchase access online, please visit* www.mysocialworklab.com.)

1. **Recall all Simulated Case Studies (SCS).** For each, identify a global issue that connects to the issues raised in the case study.

2. What motivated the social worker to commit time and energy to influence policy? What moved these "hardheaded idealists" to action?

PRACTICE TEST The following questions will test your knowledge of the content found within this chapter. For additional assessment, including licensing-exam type questions on applying chapter content to practice, visit **MySocialWorkLab**.

1. In the 2008 presidential election NASW endorsed Barak Obama because:
   a. He promised to oust republicans opposed to social programs
   b. His social justice oriented platform was in alignment with NASW's policy goals
   c. The majority of his supporters were in the social work profession
   d. He promised to support all of NASW's policies and proposals during his term

2. Using cutting-edge technology of Web 2.0 in a grassroots political approach:
   a. Has been commonplace in the national political arena for the last decade
   b. Was how the Republican party gained additional senate seats in the 2008 election
   c. Was a critical tool for mobilizing support used by the Obama campaign
   d. Has been banned in national presidential elections

3. In tough financial times successful policy solutions must:
   a. Draw on the best evidence, be very well executed, and be cost effective
   b. Not cost very much, employ a significant number of people, and be macromanaged
   c. Glean the best evidence, secure several sources of income, and serve a large target population
   d. Be cost-effective, include a long term policy plan, and identify all potential client groups

4. The rise in the number of hate groups in the U.S. since 2000, jumping especially quickly in 2008 and 2009, is primarily attributed to:
   a. An increase in the U.S. population, and the American desire for the troops to return home from the middle east
   b. Response to the war on terror, and an increased number of illegal immigrants
   c. Increased levels of immigration, and a response to prolonged lack of government organization and action
   d. The weakened economy, and the election of Barak Obama, as the U.S.' first African American president

5. The Ethic of Care perspective focuses upon:
   a. Taking care of the elderly in their own family
   b. Supporting efforts to recruit more gerontology doctors and support workers
   c. Human interconnectedness
   d. Acquiring proper paperwork before administering care to the elderly

---

Log onto **MySocialWorkLab** once you have completed the Practice Test above to access additional study tools and assessment.

Answers

Key: 1) b, 2) c, 3) a, 4) d, 5) c

Appendix

POLICY ROLES IN NASW

If your focus in coming into social work practice is on helping people who face a variety of challenges and crises, NASW, your professional association, may seem somewhat remote and distant. You may wonder what would be the point in belonging. And while student membership dues are low, the price of membership sometimes seems expensive to the new social work graduate. NASW serves its members' need for continuing education through its journal *(Social Work)*, national and state newsletters, professional meetings, conferences, and online continuing education conferences. But in addition to its membership services that are directed toward social workers, NASW has a long tradition of advocacy for policies to benefit both the profession and the clients we serve. The support for single-payer health insurance is only one of many issues that are part of NASW's policy agenda.

If you decide to join NASW, you will have opportunities to serve in a variety of policy positions. You may want to be a member of your state's public policy committee. Typically, these committees of NASW members and staff develop the legislative agenda for the state chapter. That agenda will include legislative initiatives that the chapter wants to promote in the upcoming legislative session. It may also include stopping other initiatives that are counter to social work values and ethics and inconsistent with NASW's official policies. In the gay marriage Simulated Case Study that accompanies this book, you can see NASW as part of a coalition of organizations trying to stop efforts to pass a constitutional amendment banning gay marriage in the state. NASW is frequently part of these coalition efforts at the state level. As we discussed in Chapter 11 on Coalition Building, most legislative work is accomplished through the work of many organizations working collaboratively toward a common goal. Once the agenda is set, the Public Policy Committee will be involved in working with both the staff and a lobbyist (if one is employed by the chapter) to mobilize the membership in letter or e-mail writing campaigns and other efforts to influence legislators regarding particular bills or resolutions under consideration. Involvement in your state chapter's Public Policy Committee is a good way to further develop a wide range of policy practice skills including developing relationships with state legislators, framing issues, research and policy analysis, and planning an issue campaign. Being part of a group, you also have the opportunity to observe and learn from others, particularly those more experienced in your state. They can give you advice about how to go about approaching a particular legislator to ascertain his support of a bill. They can also be valuable in determining the appropriateness of a particular tactic or the timing of an activity to maximize its effectiveness.

Many states now have an annual (or biennial, depending on the frequency of the state legislative sessions) Lobby Day, a time that social workers and social work students gather at the state capital for both an opportunity to learn more about particularly salient policy issues that year and an opportunity to meet with state legislators to express their views and positions on pressing social work issues. Influencing State Policy, a national organization that encourages social work students to get involved in state policy practice, attempts to track the number of students who participate in Social Work Lobby Day events. In 2005–2006, Influencing State Policy faculty reported that over 6,000 students visited their state houses while over 8,000 visited in 2004–2005.[1] Students report how empowered they feel upon attending their state's Lobby Day:

> "Walking into the State House and seeing a mass of people coming together to express themselves was something I had never seen before or participated in. It was an empowering feeling. It helped to put everything that's taught in class in perspective."
>
> "I now have a hands-on understanding of the political and legislative process as well as an appreciation of the impact of lobbying by both professionals and ordinary citizens. I can truly say I did not realize the extent of my potential influence on social policymaking. These experiences reified for me the importance of social work's commitment to promoting social justice and to advocating for social reform. I found the entire experience thrilling and empowering."[2]

As both a student and social worker, you can participate in your state's Lobby Day in order to become more actively engaged in the policymaking process. After you have participated at least once, you might want to develop your policy practice skills by volunteering to be on the committee that plans the event in your state. It may be the NASW public policy committee, another committee of NASW, or another group entirely. In Indiana, the home of one of the most successful Lobby Day events, LEAD (Legislative, Education, and Advocacy Development) was first started by a group of social work faculty and social workers in advocacy roles in the state. In its sixth year, it became a standing committee of the state NASW chapter. Some schools and programs do their own Lobby Day rather than participating in a statewide event. Regardless of auspices, such planning committees usually welcome additional volunteers, including students who can help make sure the planned events will be appealing to student participants.

Participating in planning a Lobby Day will help hone your skills in planning an event for maximum effect on both participants and targets of the event, including legislators, media, and other targets. Sometimes that means putting a face on a particular issue by helping legislators learn how particular policies and decisions will affect their constituents. You could do the research on an issue for the PowerPoint presentation. You could create the policy briefs to be distributed at the event. You could make follow-up phone calls to invited legislators to make sure they plan to attend. You could be in charge of creating some effective cheers or chants to use for maximum media impact, with an appearance on the local 6 o'clock news. You could update the Lobby Day Web site with information about the event, directions, agenda, and links to relevant Web sites for further information. You could even be one of the presenters, discussing your practicum agency's policy advocacy efforts on a particular issue. Participation

---

[1]Influencing State Policy, www.statepolicy.org/ (accessed June 18, 2007).

[2]Linda Cummins, "Teaching Policy Practice" (presentation made at the Indiana Association of Social Work Educators, Indianapolis, IN, 2000).

in Lobby Day planning, like being a member of the Public Policy Committee, offers opportunities to develop multiple policy practice skills within the supportive context of a group of other committed social workers.

NASW is a nonprofit organization with a board of directors, both at the national level and at the state level. Both BSW and MSW students have designated board positions, so you could start early in your NASW involvement and run for your student representative position. At the state level, the board is responsible for setting the policy for the state chapter within the guidelines of the policies set by the national board of directors. In the example used earlier, in Indiana, the board of NASW created the LEAD Committee to bring the Lobby Day event under the official umbrella of the NASW chapter office.

One essential board responsibility is hiring and evaluating the executive director of the chapter. Board members are also expected to be active and involved in a number of committees, including finance, public policy, strategic planning, and others. Being on the board allows members to have input into the policymaking discussions of the chapter, including how to allocate its resources, how best to meet the continuing education needs of social workers, and how to pursue its legislative agenda. Working as a board member, social workers use their communication and negotiating skills to work through differences in perspective to arrive at a decision supported by the majority. Sometimes tensions can develop in boards when there are factions supporting different perspectives that are unable to find common ground. Leadership from the executive committee (the officers of the chapter) can help set a positive, collaborative tone to the board that will be of assistance in working through differences. Board members cannot confuse the policymaking and oversight role of the board with the executive power of the chapter director to implement the board policies and supervise the staff. Learning to be an NASW board member can assist social workers in gaining a greater appreciation of the work of their own boards, if they work in nonprofit organizations. In addition, such work can prepare you for service on boards of other social service agencies in your community.

In many states, particularly where concentrations of social workers are some distance from the state capital where the chapter office is typically located, regional NASW committees discuss and decide on more local activities, including continuing education programs and celebrations for March, Social Work Month. While the regional organizations are typically not in policymaking roles, participation in these local groups is sometimes logistically easier than participation in other state wide groups and events. Participation does build your professional network that can be useful and important in mobilizing social workers and others with regard to an issue or a political campaign as discussed in Chapter 12. In addition, regional NASW committees are a good place to begin to develop your collaborative and leadership skills that you will need in policy practice. Particularly if you work as the only social worker in an agency, you will appreciate the professional support from the members of the regional NASW committee.

NASW policies are set by its members at Delegate Assembly, a meeting of 200 elected delegates held once every three years.[3] Both bylaws changes that govern how NASW itself is governed and policy statements are considered at

---

[3]NASW Delegate Assembly, www.socialworkers.org/da/default.asp (accessed June 18, 2007).

Delegate Assembly. The policy statements covering a wide range of social welfare issues are compiled in each new edition of *Social Work Speaks*, a compilation of official NASW policy statements on a wide range of social work issues. Each time Delegate Assembly meets, past policy statements are reviewed and updated, while new policy statements are proposed for consideration. The last Delegate Assembly met in August of 2008 but much of the work of reviewing potential changes was done prior to the actual gathering. Policy statements in the seventh edition that were reviewed included civil liberties and justice, economic policy, family planning and reproductive choice, health care, international policy on human rights, and transgender and gender identity issues, among others.[4] Delegates are elected in statewide elections so they are frequently social workers who have already demonstrated some leadership skills and commitment to the profession. Assembly delegates, like delegates to a political convention, must be well informed on the issues to be able to present compelling arguments in support of their positions on issues they are passionate about. Skills in framing, developing coalitions, and coming to compromise are also essential.

When looking for employment, NASW can be of assistance as well, with postings of available positions. If you are especially interested in policy practice targeted to the NASW priorities, then looking for a position with NASW itself may be in your future. BSWs are sometimes hired for membership services positions to assist the state NASW chapter in a variety of ways, including answering questions about licensing and staffing some of the standing committees. Some chapters hire social workers with strong policy practice skills for legislative liaison positions. These NASW staff members work closely with legislators, legislative study committees, advocacy coalitions and NASW's public policy committees to advance the legislative priorities of the chapter. Comparable positions for social workers with NASW are also available at the national level. NASW national offices are located in Washington, D.C., in order to be close to the political and legislative action, and also to be close to other national professional associations and advocacy groups for ease of collaboration around issues and policies of common concern.

With some experience particularly in leadership and administration, an MSW degree, and a commitment to advancing the profession and its goals of social justice, you could qualify for the executive director position. This person provides leadership to the social workers in the state who volunteer to work on chapter activities, such as the legislative agenda and the state conference. The director also translates the policies and initiatives passed by the board into action, facilitating the action of both chapter staff and volunteers. In addition to the ability to organize, collaborate, and delegate, the director must be skilled in motivating social workers to get involved with their professional association. The director needs to be able to respond to multiple demands for both time and expertise. The director may need to testify at a legislative committee hearing on a bill to provide birth control services to low-income women or be able to work behind the scenes with the psychologist association to get a compromise worked out on a contentious provision of the state licensing law. Developing relationships and building trust with social workers, legislators and other public policy decision makers, the media, and

---

[4]For a look at some of NASW's policy statements, see: National Association of Social Workers, *Social Work Speaks* (Washington DC: NASW Press, 2009).

other policy advocates over time will ensure that NASW and the social work profession will command attention and will likely be significant contributors to local, state, and national social welfare policy formation.

The final policy practice role for direct service social workers related to NASW is serving on the state PACE committee. PACE stands for Political Action Candidate Election. PACE is NASW's political action committee (PAC) and, as such, is a separate organization from NASW itself. Just as there is a national NASW Board and boards for each state chapter, there is a national PACE Committee focused on national elections and PACE committees in each state that focus on state elections. PACE funds come from member-earmarked contributions and fundraising events. Prior to each state and national election, the PACE committees survey candidates on the issues important to NASW members to determine the compatibility of their positions on these issues with those of NASW. If the candidate is an incumbent, the committee will consider his/her voting record on these and related issues. The PACE Committee then decides which candidates to endorse, and which candidates to contribute money to their campaigns. PACE may choose not to endorse any candidate in a particular race. When deciding where to put its limited campaign funds, PACE will contribute to races where it is thought a contribution will make a difference in the outcome of the race. Sometimes, a candidate in a close race who has a realistic possibility of winning will receive funds when another candidate challenging an entrenched incumbent will not. Participating in the PACE committee requires skills of communicating effectively with candidates so they will complete the surveys and then negotiating skills with other committee members when the tough decisions about endorsements and funding must be made. These tasks must be accomplished in a timely way so that endorsed candidates get both the endorsement and funding early in the election process, when it can have the greatest impact on their campaign. To borrow the words that are the origin of the name of Emily's List, another PAC, "**E**arly **M**oney **I**s **L**ike **Y**east, because it helps raise the dough."[5]

---

[5]Emily's List, www.emilyslist.org/ (accessed June 18, 2007).

Notes

Chapter 1

1. E. J. Clark, "From the Director: Advocacy: Profession's Cornerstone," *NASW* (July 2007), 3.
2. U. Bronfenbremmer, *The Ecology of Human Development* (Cambridge, MA: Harvard University Press 1979).
3. Robert D. Putnam, "Bowling Alone: America's Declining Social Capital," *Current,* no. 373 (1995), 3. *Academic Search Premier,* EBSCOhost (accessed June 12, 2007).
4. Everett Ladd, *The Ladd Report* (New York: Free Press 1999). Matthew Reed, "Apathy and Its Discontents: Social Capital and Social Awkwardness in American Life," *New Political Science* 23, no. 3 (2001). *Academic Search Premier,* EBSCOhost (accessed June 5, 2007).
5. Richard Stengel and Ann Blackman, "Bowling Together," *Time,* July 22, 1996. *Academic Search Premier,* EBSCOhost (accessed May 30, 2007).
6. Sean W. Mulvenon, Charles E. Stegman, and Gary Ritter, "Test Anxiety: A Multifaceted Study on the Perceptions of Teachers, Principals, Counselors, Students, and Parents," *International Journal of Testing* 5, no. 1, 37–61.
7. National Association of Social Workers, *Code of Ethics* (Washington, DC: NASW Press, 1996), 1.
8. Ibid.
9. Bruce Jansson, *The Reluctant Welfare State: American Social Welfare Policies—Past, Present, and Future.* 5th ed. (Belmont, CA: Brooks/Cole, 2005) 485.
10. Amanda Barusch, *Foundations of Social Policy: Social Justice, Public Programs, and the Social Work Profession* (Itasca, IL: F.E. Peacock Publishers, 2002) 375.
11. R. Schneider and L. Lester, *Social Work Advocacy: A New Framework for Action* (Belmont, CA: Wadsworth/Thomson Learning, 2001) 65.
12. National Association of Social Workers, *Legal Brief Bank,* www.socialworkers.org/ldf/brief_bank/about.asp (accessed May 5, 2009).
13. J. Figueira-McDonough, "Policy Practice: The Neglected Side of Social Work Intervention," *Social Work,* (1993), 38; D. Iatridis, "Policy Practice," *Encyclopedia of Social Work,* 19th ed. (Washington, DC: NASW Press 1995) 179–188; Bruce Jansson, *Social Policy: From Theory to Policy Practice* (Belmont, CA: Brooks/Cole; K. Dittrich, *Integrating Social Welfare Policy and Social Work Practice* (Pacific Grove, CA: Brooks/Cole 1994); N. Wyers, "Policy-Practice in Social Work: Models and Issues," *Journal of Social Work Education,* 27 (1991), 241–250.
14. Cynthia J. Rocha and Alice K. Johnson, "Teaching Family Policy through a Policy Practice Framework," *Journal of Social Work Education,* 33, no. 3 (1997), 433–444. *Academic Search Premier,* EBSCOhost, http://web.ebscohost.com/ehost/detail?vid=4&hid=3&sid=60317cf4-78f9-48bc-920e79d14ef95551%40sessionmgr9 (accessed March 10, 2007).
15. D. Iatridis, Policy Practice.
16. Harry Specht and Mark Courtney, *Unfaithful Angels: How Social Work Has Abandoned Its Mission* (New York: The Free Press 1994).
17. Sharron Parrott and Sherman Arloc, "TANF at 10: Program Results Are More Mixed Than Often Understood," *Center for Budget and Policy Priorities,* www.cbpp.org/8-17-06tanf.htm (accessed June 26, 2007).
18. R. Greene and R. Knee, "Shaping the Policy Practice Agenda of Social Work in the Field of Aging," *Social Work,* 41, no. 5 (1996), 553–560.
19. Rocha and Johnson, "Teaching Family Policy," 433–444; *Academic Search Premier,* EBSCOhost (accessed March 10, 2007).
20. Katharine Byers and Janet Dickinson, "Educating BSW Students to Influence State Policy," *Influence* 5, no. 2 (2001), 12.
21. "Influencing State Policy," www.statepolicy.org/contest/contest-winners.html#2006 (accessed July 18, 2007).

Chapter 2

1. Jane Adams, *Philanthropy and Social Progress: Seven Essays* (Boston, MA: Thomas Crowell, 1893).
2. Mary E. Richmond, *The Long View: Papers and Addresses by Mary E. Richmond* (Russell Sage Foundation, 1930) 173.
3. Phyllis Day, *A New History of Social Welfare,* 4th ed. (Boston: Allyn & Bacon, 2003) 49.
4. Walter I. Trattner, *From Poor Law to Welfare State: A History of Social Welfare in America,* 5th ed. (New York, NY: The Free Press, 1994) 181.
5. Michael Katz, *In the Shadow of the Poorhouse: A Social History of Welfare in America* (New York: Basic Books, 1986) 159. See also his reference to Allen F. Davis, *Spearheads for Reform: The Social Settlements and the Progressive Movement 1890–1914* (New York: Oxford University Press, 1967) 3–12.
6. Day, *New History,* 245.
7. Walter Trattner, *From Poor Law to Welfare State,* 6th ed. (New York: Free Press, 1999) 92.
8. Michael Katz, *In the Shadow,* 83.

9. Day, *New History,* 234.
10. Day, *New History,* 235; see also her reference to Blanche Coll, *Perspectives in Public Welfare: A History* (Washington, DC: U.S. Government Printing Office, 971) 63.
11. Day, *New History,* 234.
12. Day, *New History,* 235; see also her reference to June Axinn and Herman Levin, *Social Welfare: A History of the American Response to Need,* 2nd ed. (New York: Harper & Row, 1982) 134.
13. Bruce Jansson, *The Reluctant Welfare State: American Social Welfare Policies—Past, Present, and Future,* 5th ed. (Belmont, CA: Brooks/Cole, 2005) 127.
14. Trattner, *Poor Law,* 6th ed., 257.
15. Ibid., 240.
16. Ibid.
17. Ibid., 245.
18. Council on Social Work Education, Overview of Accreditation, www.cswe.org/CSWE/accreditation/ (accessed May 5, 2009).
19. Trattner, *Poor Law* 6th ed., 258.
20. Day, *New History,* 262.
21. Katz, *In the Shadow,* 166.
22. Trattner, *Poor Law,* 6th ed., 185.
23. Howard Jacob Karger and David Stoesz, *American Social Welfare Policy,* 6th ed. (Boston, MA: Allyn & Bacon, 2010) 230.
24. Ibid.
25. Day, *New History,* 298.
26. Philip Popple and P. Nelson Reid, "A Profession for the Poor? A History of Social Work in the United States," in *The Professionalization of Poverty: Social Work and the Poor in the Twentieth Century,* ed. Gary R. Lowe and P. Nelson Reid (New York, NY: Aldine de Gruyter, 1999) 9–28, 19.
27. Trattner, *Poor Law,* 6th ed., 311.
28. Roland L. Guyotte, "Cohen, Wilbur (1913–1987)," *NASW, Encyclopedia of Social Work,* 19th ed. (Washington, DC: NASW Press, 1995) 2579.
29. Elizabeth Hoffman and Danielle Ewen, *Families, Nurturing Young Children: Early Head Start Programs in 2006,* (Washington, DC: Center on Law and Social Policy, 2007) 2–3, 10.
30. Day, *New History,* 339.
31. James Wolk, "Are Social Workers Politically Active?" *Social Work,* 26, no. 4 (1981), 283–288.
32. Harry Specht and Mark E. Courtney, *Unfaithful Angels: How Social Work Has Abandoned Its Mission* (New York, NY: The Free Press, 1994).
33. Gary R. Lowe and P. Nelson Reid, eds., *The Professionalization of Poverty: Social Work and the Poor in the Twentieth Century* (New York, NY: Aldine de Gruyter, 1999).
34. David Stoesz, "Ideological Nostalgia, Intellectual Narcosis," in *The Professionalization of Poverty: Social Work and the Poor in the Twentieth Century,* ed. Gary R. Lowe and P. Nelson Reid (New York, NY: Aldine de Gruyter, 1999) 145.
35. Ibid., 159.
36. Ibid.
37. Steven G. Anderson and Brian M Gryzlak, "Social Work Advocacy in the Post-TANF Environment: Lessons from Early TANF Research Studies," *Social Work,* 47, no. 3 (2002), 303.
38. Cecilia Kleinkauf, "Social Work Lobbies for Social Welfare: An Alaskan Example," *Social Work,* 33, no. 1 (1988), 56–57.
39. James Wolk, *Are Social Workers.*
40. James Wolk, "Political Activity in Social Work: A Theoretical Model of Motivation," *International Social Work,* 39 (1996), 443, http://isw.sagepub .com (accessed May 7, 2009).
41. Robert Fisher, "Political Social Work," *Journal of Social Work Education,* 31, no. 2 (1995), 194–203. *Academic Search Premier,* EBSCO*host* (accessed May 5, 2009).
42. Mimi Abramovitz, "Social Work and Social Reform: An Arena of Struggle," *Social Work,* 43, no. 8, 523–524.
43. NASW Web site, "Social Workers in State and Local Office 2008," www.socialworkers.org/pace/ state.asp (accessed May 3, 2009).
44. "Volunteers for Change," *Hungry for Change: Newsletter of the Hoosier Hills Food Bank* (May 2009) 6.
45. NASW, *Turning Priorities into Action: How the Social Work Profession Will Help,* http://www. socialworkers.org *(accessed May 5, 2009).*

Chapter 3

1. Susan B. Hyatt, "The Obama Victory, Asset-Based Development and the Re-Politicization of Community Organizing," *North American Dialogue,* 11, no. 2 (2008), 17–26. See also Barack Obama, "Who Organizes? Problems and Promise in the Inner City," in *After Alinsky: Community Organizing in Illinois,* ed. Peg Knoepfle (University of Illinois at Springfield, 1990), and Peter Dreier, "Will Obama Inspire a New Generation of Organizers?" *Dissent Magazine,* www. dissentmagazine.org/article/?article=1215 (accessed April 23, 2009).
2. A. Sanner, "Obama Signs Service Bill, Says Volunteers Needed," *Associated Press,* www. google.com/hostednews/ap/article/ ALeqM5jauMTmO8OWPIcS2–jaRx8hgm-XgD97N325G0 (accessed April 21, 2009).
3. Corporation for National and Community Service, "House Sends Landmark National Service Bill to President," www.nationalservice.gov/about/ newsroom/releases_details.asp? (accessed April 21, 2009).
4. Civilian Conservation Corps Legacy, "Civilian Conservation Corps: Preserving America's Natural Resources 1933–1942," www.ccclegacy.org (accessed April 27, 2009).
5. Corporation for National and Community Service, "Edward M. Kennedy Serve America Act of 2009," www.nationalservice.gov/about/serveamerica/ index.asp (accessed April 27, 2009).
6. M. Lang, "Obama Continues JFKs Challenge to Americans to Get INVOLVED," *The Lang Report,* www.thelangreport.com/featured/obama-continues-jfks-challenge-to-americans-to-get-involved (accessed April 27, 2009). See also, Frank Rich

"Ask Not What JFK Can Do for Obama," *New York Times,* www.nytimes.com/2008/02/03/opinion/03rich.html (accessed April 27, 2009).

7. R. B. Leibowitz, "One on One: Regulating the Pursuit of Self," *Jerusalem Post,* www.jpost.com/servlet/Satellite?cid=1233304687464&pagename=JPost/JPArticle/ (accessed April 8, 2009).

8. Bureau of Labor Statistics, "Archived News Releases," www.bls.gov/schedule/archives/all_nr.htm#VOLUN (accessed April 27, 2009). See also Independent Sector, "Giving in Tough Times: The Impact of Personal Economic Concerns on Giving and Volunteering," www.independentsector.org/programs/research/toughtimes.html (accessed April 27, 2009).

9. J. H. Ehrenreich, *The Altruistic Imagination* (Ithaca, NY: Cornell University Press, 1985).

10. Miriam Dinerman, "The 1959 Curriculum Study; Contributions of Werner W. Boehm," in *A Quarter-Century of Social Work Education,* ed. M. Dinerman and L. L. Geismar (Washington, DC: National Association of Social Workers, ABC-CLIO, Council on Social Work Education, 1984).

11. J. H. Adrich, "Political Parties in a Critical Era," *American Politics Quarterly,* 27, no.1 (1999), 9–32.

12. D. J. Siemers, *Ratifying the Republic: AntiFederalists and Federalists in Constitutional Time* (Palo Alto, CA: Stanford University Press, 2002).

13. Information in this section was taken from the following sources: Ralph L. Ketcham, *The Anti-Federalist Papers and the Constitutional Convention Debates: The Clashes and the Compromises That Gave Birth to Our Form of Government* (New York City: Signet Classic, 2003); Herbert J. Storing, *What the Anti-Federalists Were For* (Chicago: University of Chicago Press, 1981); James Madison Center, James Madison University, Harrisonburg, VA, www.jmu.edu/madison/center/main_pages/madison_archives/constit_confed/rights/document/document.htm (accessed August 14, 2007).

14. Information in this section was taken from the following sources: Thomas A. Bailey, David M. Kennedy, and Lizabeth Cohen, *The American Pageant: A History of the Republic,* 12th ed. (Belmont, CA: Wadsworth Publishing, 2001); Copernicus Election Watch (2000), "The Parties," www.edgate.com/elections/inactive/the_parties/ (accessed September 18, 2006).

15. Storing, *Anti-Federalists,* 3.

16. M. R. Hershey, *Party Politics in America,* 12th ed. (New York: Pearson-Longman, 2007) 15.

17. M. Morris, P. Fiornina, Paul E. Peterson, Bertam Johnson, and D. Stephen Voss, *The New American Democracy,* 4th ed. (Boston: Pearson/Longman, 2005).

18. Bailey, Kennedy, and Cohen, *American Pageant.*

19. Election Center 2008 (January 12, 2009), "Full Results by State," www.cnn.com/ELECTION/2008/results/president/allcandidates (accessed May 26, 2009).

20. See the respective Web sites of the Democratic National Committee at www.democrats.org and the Republican National Committee at www.gop.com.

21. Hershey, *Party Politics.*

22. Ibid; and Informationen zur politischen Bildung (1997), 199. Politisches System der USA. *Bonn, BpB.* As summarized by Hartmut Wasser in "Parties, USA" in *D@dalos,* www.dadalos.ort/int/parteien/Grundkurs4/USA/merkmale.htm (accessed September 22, 2006).

23. Bailey, Kennedy, and Cohen, *The American Pageant.*

24. Informationen zur politischen Bildung (Politisches System der USA, *Bonn, BpB.* 1997), 199, as summarized by Hartmut Wasser in "Parties, USA" in *D@dalos,* www.dadalos.ort/int/parteien/Grundkurs4/USA/merkmale.htm (accessed September 22, 2006).

25. Information on the section on third parties was taken from the following sources: Hershey, *Party Politics;* Morris P. Fiorina, Paul E. Peterson, Bertram Johnson, and D. Stephen Voss, *The New American Democracy* 4th ed. (Boston: Pearson-Longman); Michael R. Alvarez and Jonathan Nagler, "Economics, Issues and the Perot Candidacy: Voter Choice in the 1992 Presidential Election," *American Journal of Political Science,* 39, no. 3 (1995), 714–744; and Infoplease (2006), Presidential Election of 2000, Electoral and Popular Vote Summary ©Pearson Education, www.infoplease.com/ipa/A0876793.html (accessed January 31, 2006).

26. Election Center 2008 (January 12, 2009), "Full Results by State," www.cnn.com/ELECTION/2008/results/president/allcandidates (accessed May 26, 2009).

27. Ibid.

28. H. Adrich, "Political Parties in a Critical Era," *American Politics Quarterly,* 27, no. 1 (1999), 9–32.

29. CNN (November 3–5, 2006), "President Bush Overall Job Rating," PollingReports.com, www.pollingreport.com/BushJob.htm (accessed January 31, 2007).

30. Washington Post-ABC News Poll, *The Washington Post,* February 27, 2007 (accessed May 26, 2009), www.washingtonpost.com/wp-srv/politics/polls/postpoll_022607.htm.

31. A. Koppelman, "Was 2008 a Realigning Election?" (April 20, 2009), www.salon.com/politics/war_room/2009/04/20/sabato (accessed May 26, 2009).

32. Gallup, "Gallup Daily: Obama Job Approval" (April 29, 2009), www.gallup.com/poll/113980/Gallup-Daily-Obama-Job-Approval.aspx (accessed May 26, 2009).

33. USNewsclassroom.com, "Political Ideologies," *U.S. News and World Report,* www.usnewsclassroom.com/resources/activities/act010604.html (accessed December 5, 2006).

34. H. J. Karger and D. Stoesz, *American Social Welfare Policy: A Pluralist Approach,* 5th ed. (Boston: Allyn & Bacon, 2006).

35. Ibid.

36. Ibid.

37. Information in this section was taken from the following sources: Hershey, *Party Politics;* USNewsclassroom.com, "Political Ideologies,"

U.S. News and World Report, www.usnewsclassroom. com/resources/activities/act010604.html (accessed December 5, 2006); M. Abramovitz, "Ideological Perspective and Conflicts," in Joel Blau's *The Dynamics of Social Welfare Policy,* (Oxford: Oxford University Press, 2004), 119–173.

38. H. J. Karger and D. Stoesz, *America Social Welfare Policy: A Pluralist Approach,* 5th ed. (Boston: Allyn & Bacon, 2006).

39. Eyal Press, "Even Conservatives Are Wondering: Is Bush One of Us?" (May, 2004), www.thenation .com/doc/20040531/press (accessed March 6, 2007).

40. Bart Barnes, "Barry Goldwater, GOP Hero, Dies," *Washington Post,* May 30, 1998, A01, www. washingtonpost.com/wp—srv/politics/daily/ may98/goldwater30.htm (accessed March 6, 2007); Barry Goldwater, *The Conscience of a Conservative* (New York: Putnam Books, 1960).

41. Abramovitz, "Ideological Perspective and Conflicts," 119–173.

42. Milton Friedman, *Capitalism and Freedom* (Chicago: University of Chicago Press, 1962).

43. Henry J. Kaiser Family Foundation (September 2, 2003), "Bush Executive Order Limits State Dept. Funding for International Groups That Provide Abortion Services; Exempts AIDS-Related Work," *The Body: The Complete HIV/AIDS Resource,* www.thebody.com/content/policy/art11329.html (accessed May 26, 2009). See also Edwin Chen, "Bush Further Limits Funds for Groups Counseling Abortion," *Los Angeles Times, World Section* (August 30, 2003), articles.latimes.com/2003/ aug/30/world/fg-family30 (accessed May 26, 2009).

44. Abramovitz, "Ideological Perspective and Conflicts," 119–173. Tom Barry, "Glossary of the Right-Wing Sectors in U.S. Foreign Policy," *Right Web: The Architecture of Power That's Changing,* December, 2003, rightweb.irc-online.org/charts/ glossary_body.html (accessed March 6, 2007). See also Amy E. Ansell, ed., *Unraveling the Right: The New Conservatism in American Thought and Politics* (Oxford: Western Press, 1998).

45. David Masci, "Religion and Politics," *Congressional Quarterly Researcher,* 14, no. 27 (July 30, 2004).

46. "Empire Builders: Neoconservatives and Their Blueprint for US Power," *Christian Science Monitor,* June, 2005. See also "Condi on Top," *New York Magazine,* March 5, 2007, and Tom Barry, "Glossary of the Right-Wing Sectors in U.S. Foreign Policy," *Right Web: The Architecture of Power That's Changing,* December, 2003, rightweb.irc-online.org/frame-top.html (accessed March 6, 2007).

47. Information in this section was taken from the following sources: D. M. DiNitto, and L. K. Cummins, *Social Welfare: Politics and Public Policy* (Boston: Allyn & Bacon, 1993); W. Safire, *New Political Dictionary* (New York: Random House, 1993).

48. R. Dolgoff and D. Feldstein, *Understanding Social Welfare: A Search for Social Justice,* 7th ed. (Boston: Allyn & Bacon 2007); See also

Abramovitz, "Ideological Perspective and Conflicts," 119–173.

49. Abramovitz, "Ideological Perspective and Conflicts," 119–173.

50. Ibid.

51. Information in this section was taken from the following sources: Edward Epstein, "Pelosi must Corral 3 Dem Factions to Unite on Agenda," *San Francisco Chronicle,* November 17, 2006, www.sfgate.com/cgi-bin/article.cgi?file=/ c/a/2006/11/17/MNG7VMELL71.DTL (accessed March 7, 2007); "What's a Blue Dog?" *BlueDogDems.com,* www.bluedogdems.com/index. html (accessed March 7, 2007); "Blue Dogs Demand Fiscal Accountability in Iraq," *The Blue Dog Coalition,* Press Release, January 19, 2007, www.house.gov/list/speech/ar04_ross/morenews/ 011907iraq.html (accessed March 7, 2007); "What are 'Blue Dog' Democrats? Are They Any Relation to 'Yellow Dog' Democrats? Chelmsford, MA – 11/16/00," *Capitol Questions with Ilona Nickels, C-Spann's Resident Congressional Scholar,* www. c-span.org/questions/weekly55.htm (accessed August 14, 2007).

52. Andy Sher, "Blue Dogs' Seek to Elevate Role," *Chattanooga Times/Free Press,* www.house.gov/ lincolndavis/newsmay32005.htm (accessed August 14, 2007).

53. Christopher Hayes, "Blue Dogs Bark," *The Nation* (February 11, 2009), www.thenation.com/doc/ 20090302/hayes (accessed May 26, 2009).

54. BlueDogDems.com, "National Debt Clock" (June 9, 2010), http://www.house.gov/melancon/BlueDogs/ www.thenation.com/doc/20090302/hayes (accessed May 26, 2009).

55. Information in this section was taken from the following sources: Edward Epstein, "Pelosi Must Corral 3 Dem Factions to Unite on Agenda," *San Francisco Chronicle,* November 17, 2006, www. sfgate.com/cgi-bin/article.cgi?file=/c/a/2006/11/17/ MNG7VMELL71.DTL (accessed March 7, 2007); "The New Democrat Credo," *Democratic Leadership Council,* January 1, 2001, www. ndol.org/ndol_ci.cfm?kaid=86&subid=194& contentid=3775 (accessed March 7, 2007); "The New Democrats' Declaration," *Blueprint Magazine,* Democratic Leadership Council, July 27, 2003, www.ndol.org/ndol_ci.cfm?kaid=86&subid=194&co ntentid=251925 (accessed March 7, 2007); New Democratic Coalition, "New Dems Meet with President Obama" March, 2009, tauscher.house.gov/ ndc/index.php?option=com_content&task= view&id=154&Itemid=61 (accessed May 28, 2009); and Howard J. Karger and David Stoesz, *America Social Welfare Policy: A Pluralist Approach,* 5th ed. (Boston: Allyn & Bacon, 2006) 15–17.

56. Information in this section was taken from the following sources: Edward Epstein, "Pelosi Must Corral 3 Dem Factions to Unite on Agenda" *San Francisco Chronicle,* November 17, 2006 (accessed March 7, 2007); "Progressive Promise: Fairness for All," Congressional Progressive Caucus, October,

2005, http://cpc.lee.house.gov/ (accessed March 7, 2007); Congressional Progressive Caucus, "Caucus Member List" (February 20, 2009), http://cpc.grijalva.house.gov/index.cfm?ContentID=166&ParentID=0&SectionID=4&SectionTree=4&lnk=b&ItemID=164 (accessed May 28, 2009).

Chapter 4

1. M. Albright, Speech made at the Democratic National Convention, July 29, 2004, Boston, MA, www.asksam.com/cgi-bin/as_web6.exe?Command=DocName&File=Conventions&Name=Madeleine%20Albright (accessed June 30, 2009).
2. USDA Marketing Service, "The National Organic Program," *Organic Foods Production Act of 1990: 6501 Purposes*, www.ams.usda.gov/nop/archive/OFPA.html (accessed November 26, 2007).
3. Human Rights Campaign (June 4, 2009), "Statewide Marriage Prohibitions," www.hrc.org/documents/marriage_prohibitions_2009.pdf (accessed June 30, 2009).
4. The Human Rights Campaign, "Marriage and Relationship Recognition, 2009 www.hrc.org/documents/Relationship_Recognition_Laws_Map.pdf (accessed June 30, 2009).
5. Table constructed from information taken from the following sources: Neil Gilbert and Paul Terrell, *Dimensions of Social Welfare Policy,* 6th ed. (Boston: Allyn & Bacon, 2005); and Seumas Miller, "Social Institutions," *The Stanford Encyclopedia of Philosophy* (Stanford University, 2007), http://plato.stanford.edu/entries/social-institutions (accessed January 3, 2008).
6. U.S. Department of Labor, Bureau of Labor Statistics, "Table 1A Consumer Price Index for All Urban Consumers (CPI-U): U.S. City Average, by Expenditure Category and Commodity and Service Group," Archived in 2000, www.bls.gov/cpi/cpid00av.pdf (accessed December 30, 2007).
7. U.S. Department of Labor, Bureau of Labor Statistics, "Table B, Employment Hours, and Earnings from the Current Population Statistic Survey, 1997–2007," http://data.bls.gov/PDQ/servlet/SurveyOutputServlet (accessed December 30, 2007).
8. U.S. Department of Labor, Bureau of Labor Statistics (July 2009), "Labor Force Statistics from the Current Population Survey," http://data.bls.gov/cgi-bin/surveymost (accessed August 29, 2009); and "Employment Situation Summary, August 7, 2009," www.bls.gov/news.release/empsit.nr0.htm (accessed August 29, 2009).
9. U.S. Department of Labor, Bureau of Labor Statistics, (August 2009), "Consumer Price Index—Chained Consumer Price Index," http://data.bls.gov/cgi-bin/surveymost (accessed August 29, 2009).
10. Congressional Budget Office (January 26, 2009), "Cost Estimate: HR 1 American Recovery and Reinvestment Act of 2009," www.cbo.gov/ftpdocs/99xx/doc9968/hr1.pdf (accessed August 29, 2009).
11. Michael Watts (September 1998), "What is a Market Economy?" Joint Council on Economic Education, Washington D.C., http://usinfo.state.gov/products/pubs/market/ (accessed November 26, 2007).
12. Ibid.
13. Information in this paragraph was taken from the following sources: U.S. Census Bureau (2000), "Census 2000 Brief: Overview of Race and Hispanic Origin; Census 2000 Brief: Gender 2000" (Washington DC: Author) www.census.gov/population/www/cen2000/briefs.html (accessed January 3, 2008); This Nation.com (2008), "The United States Congress Quick Facts," www.thisnation.com/congress-facts.html (accessed August 29, 2009).
14. Open Secrets.org (December 2008), "Politician and Elections: Presidential," www.opensecrets.org/pres08/index.php (accessed August 30, 2009).
15. Gallup (2009), "Election Polls: Vote by Groups, 2008," www.opensecrets.org/pres08/index.php (accessed August 30, 2009).
16. Open Secrets.org (December 2008) "Politician and Elections: Presidential," www.opensecrets.org/pres08/index.php (accessed August 30, 2009).
17. Ibid.
18. Diane DiNitto (with Linda Cummins), *Social Welfare: Politics and Public Policy*, 6th ed. (Boston, MA: Allyn & Bacon, 2005).
19. Change.gov, The Office of the President Elect (n.d.), "The Agenda," http://change.gov/agenda (accessed August 30, 2009); see also Organizing for America (n.d.), "Organizing on the Issues," www.barackobama.com/issues/, (accessed August 30, 2009).
20. U.S. Department of State (2009), "*U.S. Department of State Information Related to the American Recovery and Reinvestment Act of 2009,*" www.state.gov/recovery (accessed August 30, 2009).
21. Jeff Mason (August 23, 2009), "New Deficit Projections Pose Risks to Obama's Agenda," Reuters, www.reuters.com/article/politicsNews/idUSTRE57M0WV20090823 (accessed August 30, 2009).
22. Information about Governor Tommy Thompson and the Wisconsin workfare programs was taken from the following sources: John Pawasarat and Lois M. Quinn, "Wisconsin Welfare Employment Experiments: An Evaluation of the WEJT and CWEP Programs," Employment and Training Institute, University of Wisconsin-Milwaukee, September 1993, www.uwm.edu/Dept/ETI/pages/surveys/each/wlss93.htm (accessed January 3, 2008); Governor Tommy Thompson (R-WI) and Dr. William J. Bennett, "The Good News About Welfare Reform: Wisconsin's Success Story," The Heritage Foundation, Lecture #593, March 6, 1997, www.heritage.org/Research/Welfare/HL593.cfm (accessed January 3, 2008); and "Tommy Thompson, Secretary of Health and Human Services (2001–2005)," The White House, www.whitehouse.gov/government/thompson-bio.html, (accessed January 3, 2008).
23. Vikki Valentine, "Q & A: Issue behind the Port Security Uproar," NPR.org, February 24, 2006, www.npr.org/templates/story/story.php?storyId=5228775 (accessed January 4, 2008).

24. Rasmussen Reports (February 24, 2006), "Just Over 17% Favor Dubai Port Deal," www.rasmussenreports.com/public_content/current_events/other_current_events/just_17_favor_dubai_ports_deal (accessed January 4, 2008).

25. NPR.org, (November 6, 2006), "Election 2006 Results," www.npr.org/news/specials/election2006/map (accessed January 4, 2008).

26. Information on supply side economics and Keynesian economics discussed in this section were taken from the following sources: Paul Craig Roberts, "My Time with Supply-Side Economics," *The Independent Review* 7 no. 3 (2003), 393–397; James D. Gwartney, "Supply-Side Economics," *The Concise Encyclopedia of Economics* (Library of Economics and Liberty), http://econlib.org/library/Enc/SupplySideEconomics.html (accessed January 7, 2008); Alan S. Blinder, "Keynesian Economics," *The Concise Encyclopedia of Economics,* Library of Economics and Liberty, (accessed January 7, 2008), http://econlib.org/library/Enc/KeynesianEconomics.html; Kit Sims Taylor, "Chapter 11, The Keynesian Revolution," in *Human Society and the Global Economy,* Online economics textbooks, SUNY-Oswego, Department of Economics, March; Howard Jacob Karger and David Stoesz, *American Social Welfare Policy: A Pluralist Approach,* 5th ed. (Boston, MA: Allyn & Bacon, 2006).

27. Robert Hessen, "Capitalism" in *The Concise Encyclopedia of Economics* (The Library of Economics and Liberty, 2002), paragraph 8, www.econlib.org/library/Enc/Capitalism.html (accessed January 5, 2008).

28. Ibid.

29. Citizens for Tax Justice, "Effects of the First Three Bush Tax Cuts Charted," June 4, 2003, www.ctj.org/pdf/allbushcut.pdf (accessed January 4, 2008).

30. Congressional Budget Office, "Revised Estimate of Cost of Maintaining SCHIP Programs in 2008," (Memorandum from Jeanne DeSa, Eric Rollins, and Robert Stewart, December 14, 2007), http://cbo.gov/ftpdocs/88xx/doc8883/SCHIP-memo12-14-07.pdf (accessed January 6, 2008).

31. Congressional Budget Office "Historical Budget Data: Discretionary Outlays, 1962 to 2006," http://cbo.gov/budget/data/historical.pdf. (accessed January 6, 2008).

32. Congressional Budget Office Testimony: Statement of Peter Orszag (Director), "Estimates of Costs of U.S. Operations in Iraq and Afghanistan and Other Activities Related to the War on Terrorism," Congressional Budget Office: Washington DC (October 24, 2007), http://cbo.gov/ftpdocs/86xx/doc8690/10-24-CostOfWar_Testimony.pdf (accessed January 6, 2008).

33. William Branigin, "Bush Urges Emergency War Funds to Avoid Defense Layoffs," *Washington Post*, November 30, 2007, AO4, www.washingtonpost.com/wpdyn/content/article/2007/11/29/AR2007112901774.html?nav=rss_politics (accessed January 6, 2008).

34. Howard Jacob Karger and David Stoesz, *American Social Welfare Policy: A Pluralist Approach*, 5th ed. (Boston, MA: Allyn & Bacon, 2006) 7.

35. Christina D. Romer, "Business Cycles," *The Concise Encyclopedia of Economics*, ed. David R. Henderson, (Indianapolis: Liberty Fund, Inc., 2002), www.econlib.org/library/Enc/BusinessCycles.html (accessed January 6, 2008).

36. Bureau of Labor Statistics, "Employment Status of the Civilian Noninstitutional Population 1940 to Date," 2009, ftp://ftp.bls.gov/pub/special.requests/lf/aat1.txt (accessed January 6, 2008).

37. Bureau of Labor Statistics, "Employment Situation Summary" (August 7, 2009), www.bls.gov/news.release/empsit.nr0.htm (accessed August 29, 2009).

38. U.S. Department of Agriculture, "The Benefits of the Food Stamp Program," December 23, 2005, www.fns.usda.gov/fsp/outreach/pdfs/bc_benefits.pdf (accessed January 6, 2008).

39. U.S. Department of Agriculture, "The Business Case for Increasing Food Stamp Program Participation," November 16, 2007, www.fns.usda.gov/fsp/outreach/business-case.htm (accessed January 6, 2008).

40. The History of Economic Thought Website, "Monetarist Thought," http://cepa.newschool.edu/het/essays/monetarism/mpolicy.htm (accessed January 7, 2008); Milton Friedman (Biography of), *The Concise Encyclopedia of Economics*, Library of Economics and Liberty, www.econlib.org/library/Enc/bios/Friedman.html (accessed January 7, 2008); see also, Allan H. Meltzer, "Monetarism," *The Concise Encyclopedia of Economics*, Library of Economics and Liberty, www.econlib.org/library/Enc/Monetarism.html (accessed January 7, 2008).

41. Federal Reserve Bank, "Selected Interest Rates" Federal Reserve Statistical Release (August 24, 2009) www.federalreserve.gov/releases/h15/current/h15.htm (accessed August 30, 2009).

42. U.S. Department of State, "U.S. Department of State Information Related to the American Recovery and Reinvestment Act of 2009" (2009) www.state.gov/recovery (accessed August 30, 2009).

43. Robert Hessen, "Capitalism," *The Concise Encyclopedia of Economics* (The Library of Economics and Liberty, 2002, paragraph 8), www.econlib.org/library/Enc/Capitalism.html (accessed January 5, 2008).

44. U.S. Census Bureau, "*Poverty: Percentage of People in Poverty by State Using 2- and 3-Year Averages: 2004 to 2006*," www.census.gov/hhes/www/poverty/poverty06/state.html (accessed January 8, 2008).

45. Center on Budget and Policy Priorities, Robert Greenstein and Zoe Neuberger, "President's Vetoes Could Cause Half a Million Low-Income Pregnant Women, Infants, and Children to be Denied Nutritional Benefits in One of Nations Most Effective Programs," www.cbpp.org/11-27-07fa.htm (accessed January 7, 2008).

46. Bruce H. Webster, Jr. and Alemayehu Bishaw, "Income, Earnings, and Poverty Data from the 2006 American Community Survey" (US Census

Bureau: American Community Survey Reports, August 2007), www.census.gov/prod/2007pubs/acs-08.pdf (accessed January 8, 2008).

47. U.S. Census Bureau, "American Families and Living Arrangements: 2006," Table A2: Family Status and Household Relationship of People 15 Years and Over, by Marital Status, Age, Sex, Race, and Hispanic Origin: 2006, www.census.gov/population/www/socdemo/hh-fam/cps2006.html (accessed January 8, 2008).

Chapter 5

1. L. K. Cummins, J. A. Sevel, and L. Pedrick, *Social Work Skills Demonstrated: Beginning Direct Practice* (Boston: Allyn & Bacon, 2006).
2. A. Slowther, C. Johnston, J. Goodall, and T. Hope, *A Practical Guide for Clinical Ethics Support* (London: Ethox Centre, 2004).
3. J. Rawls, *A Theory of Justice* (Oxford: Oxford University Press, 1972).
4. U.S. Census Bureau, "Preliminary Estimates of Weighted Average Poverty Thresholds for 2008," www.census.gov/hhes/www/poverty/threshld/08prelim.html (accessed March 1, 2009). See also Institute for Research on Poverty, "What Are Poverty Thresholds and Poverty Guidelines?" www.irp.wisc.edu/faqs/faq1.htm (accessed March 1, 2009).
5. Slowther et al., *Clinical Ethics.*
6. Ibid.
7. J. C. Tronto, *Moral Boundaries: A Political Argument for an Ethic of Care* (New York: Routledge, 1993).
8. G. Meagher and N. Parton, "Modernising Social Work and the Ethics of Care," *Social Work & Society,* 2, no. 1 (2004), 10–27.
9. Ibid. and J. C. Tronto, "Care Ethics: Moving Forward," *Hypatia,* 14, no. 1 (1999), 112–149.
10. D. Engster, "Care Ethics and Natural Law Theory: Toward an Institutional Political Theory of Caring," *The Journal of Politics,* 66, no. 1 (2004), 113–135. See also S. M. Keigher, "The Challenge of Caring in a Capitalist World," *Health & Social Work,* 25, no. 2 (2000), 83–86.
11. A. Minahan, "Purpose and Objectives of Social Work Revisited," *Social Work,* 26, no. 1 (1981), 5–6.
12. J. H. Ehrenreich, *The Altruistic Imagination* (Ithaca, NY: Cornell University Press, 1985).
13. K. S. Haynes, and K.A. Holmes, *Invitation to Social Work* (New York: Longman, 1994); F. G. Reamer, "Ethical Standards in Social Work: The NASW Code of Ethics," in National Association of Social Work's *Encyclopedia of Social Work,* 19th ed. (Washington, DC: NASW Press, 1997); and National Association of Social Workers, "Code of Ethics," www.socialworkers.org/pubs/Code/code.asp (accessed July 1, 2009).
14. T. P. Holland, and A. C. Kilpatrick, "Ethical Issues in Social Work: Toward a Grounded Theory of Professional Ethics," *Social Work,* 36, no. 2 (1991), 138–144.
15. C. K. Brill, "Looking at the Social Work Profession through the Eye of the NASW Code of Ethics,"

Research on Social Work Practice, 11, no. 2 (1998), 223–234; see also, F. G. Reamer, "Ethical Standards in Social Work: A Critical Review of the NASW Code of Ethics," In National Association of Social Work's *Encyclopedia of Social Work,* 19th ed. (Washington, DC: NASW Press, 1998).
16. The National Election Studies, "The 2004 NES Panel Study" (Ann Arbor: University of Michigan, Center for Political Studies), www.electionstudies.org.
17. Ibid.
18. NASW (1996).
19. M. J. Hirschfeld and D. Wikler, "An Ethics Perspective on Family Caregiving: Justice and Society's Obligations," *Generations,* Winter (2003–2004), 56–60.

Chapter 6

1. A. Mitchell, "Two Clinton Aides Resign to Protest New Welfare Law," *The New York Times,* September 12, 1996, A1, www.lexisnexis.com/us/lnacademic/results/docview/docview.do?docLinkInd=true&risb=21_T6909198991&format=GNBFI&sort=RELEVANCE&startDocNo=1&resultsUrlKey=29_T6909198994&cisb=22_T6909198993&treeMax=true&treeWidth=0&csi=6742&docNo=21, (accessed from Lexisnexis, June 28, 2009).
2. Peter Edelmann, "The Worst Thing Bill Clinton Has Done," *The Atlantic Online* 279, no. 3 (March 1997), 43 paragraph 2, www.theatlantic.com/issues/97mar/edelman/edelman.htm (accessed June 30, 2009).
3. Ibid, 58.
4. Senator Barbara Mikulski's Web site, "Senator Barbara A. Mikulski," http://mikulski.senate.gov/SenatorMikulski/biography.html (accessed September 25, 2007).
5. Ibid.
6. Project Vote Smart—Public Statements, 2007, http://votesmart.org/speech_detail.php?sc_id=307513&keyword=social&phrase=&contain= (accessed September 25, 2007).
7. Senator Debbie Stabenow's Web site http://stabenow.senate.gov/ (accessed September 25, 2007).
8. NASW—PACE, "Social Workers in State and Local Office," www.socialworkers.org/pace/state.asp (accessed December 7, 2009).
9. Heidi Sfiligoj, "Amicus Briefs are Filed in Cases Significant to Social Workers and Their Clients: NASW Helps Influence Legal Decisions," *NASW News* (June 2009), p. 4.
10. Ibid.
11. NASW Web site, www.socialworkers.org/. (All NASW amicus curiae briefs are available to NASW members under the Legal Defense Fund tab on the NASW Web site).
12. NASW Web site, "NASW Statement on the Nomination of Judge Sonia Sotomayor to the US Supreme Court," *NASW Press Release,* June 12, 2009, www.socialworkers.org/pressroom/2009/061209.asp (accessed June 30, 2009).
13. Grafton H. Hull, "Joining Together: A Faculty-Student Experience in Political Campaigning,"

Journal of Social Work Education, 23, Fall 1987, 37–43.

14. ACT Web site, "We Work to Build Self Advocacy," www.selfadvocacy.org/ (accessed June 30, 2009).

Chapter 7

1. M. Fishman, "News and Non-Events: Making the Visible Invisible," in *Individuals in Mass Media Organizations,* eds. J. S. Ettema and D. C. Whitney (Beverly Hills, CA: Sage, 1982), 219–240.
2. J. W. Tankard, L. Hendrickson, J. Silberman, K. Bliss, and S. Ghanem, "Media Frames: Approaches to Conceptualization and Measurement" (paper presented at the annual meeting of the Association for Education in Journalism and Mass Communication, Chicago, IL, 1991).
3. S. D. Reese, O. H. Gandy, Jr., and A. E. Grant, eds. *Framing Public Life: Perspectives on Media and Our Understanding of the Social World* (Mahwah, NJ: Erlbaum, 2001).
4. D. McQuail, *McQuail's Mass Communication Theory,* 4th ed. (London: Sage, 2000).
5. M. McCombs, and S. I. Ghanem, "The Convergence of Agenda Setting and Framing," in *Framing Public Life: Perspectives on Media and Our Understanding of the Social World*, eds. S. D. Reese, O. H. Gandy, Jr., and A. E. Grant (Mahwah, NJ: Lawrence Erlbaum Associates, 2001) 67–81.
6. Pew Internet & American Life Project, "Latest Trends" (2007), www.pewinternet.org/trends.asp (accessed July 7, 2007).
7. Ibid.
8. Pew Internet & American Life Project, "The Internet's Role in Campaign 2008" (2008), www.pewinternet.org/Reports/2009/6–The-Internets-Role-in-Campaign-2008.aspx?r=1 (accessed April 23, 2008).
9. McCombs, "The Convergence," 67–81.
10. J. Salzman, *Making the News: A Guide for Nonprofits & Activists* (Boulder, CO: Westview Press, 1998).
11. Ibid.
12. American Association of Public Health, "APHA Media Advocacy Manual," www.apha.org/ (accessed July 7, 2007); K. Bonk, H. Griggs, and E. Tynes, *Strategic Communications for Nonprofits* (San Francisco: Jossey-Bass, 1999); and J. Salzman, *Making the News.*
13. J. H. Barkow, L. Cosmides, and J. Tooby, eds., *The Adapted Mind: Evolutionary Psychology and the Generation of Culture* (Oxford: Oxford University Press, 1992).
14. P. Day, *New History of Social Welfare,* 5th ed. (Boston: Allyn & Bacon, 2005); and B. Stadum, "The Dilemma in Saving Children from Child Labor: Reform and Casework at Odds with Families' Needs (1900–1938)," *Child Welfare,* 74, no. 1 (January/February 1995), 33–55.
15. B. Franklin, ed., *Social Policy, the Media, and Misrepresentation* (London, Routledge, 1999); and T. Gitlin, *The Whole World is Watching—Mass Media in the Making and Unmaking of the New Left* (Berkeley, CA: University of California Press, 1980).
16. B. Franklin, ed., *Social Policy, the Media, and Misrepresentation* (London, Routledge, 1999); and W. Van de Donk, B. D. Loader, P. G. Nihon, and D. Rucht, eds., *Cyberprotest: New Media, Citizens and Social Movement* (London: Routledge, 2004).
17. K. Bonk, H. Griggs, and E. Tynes, *Strategic Communications for Nonprofits* (San Francisco: Jossey-Bass, 1999); R. A. Sevier, and R. E. Johnson, *Integrated Marketing Communication* (Washington, DC: CASE Books, 1999); and J. Salzman, *Making the News.*
18. K. Bonk et al., *Strategic Communications.*
19. J. Carver, *Board Members as Fund-Raisers, Advisers, and Lobbyists* (San Francisco: Jossey-Bass, 1997).
20. A. Fine, *Momentum: Igniting Social Change in the Connected Age* (San Francisco: Jossey-Bass, 2006).
21. Ibid., 12–13.
22. J. Barker, "U.S. Politics Gets Wired," *National Post,* January 4, 2008, http://network.nationalpost.com/np/blogs/posted/archive/2008/01/04/u-s-politics-gets-wired.aspx (accessed January 6, 2008).
23. M + R Strategic Services & the Advocacy Institute, "eNonprofit Benchmarks Study: Measuring E-mail Messages, Online Fundraising, and Internet Advocacy Metrics for Nonprofit Organizations" (2006), www.e-benchmarksstudy.com/pubs/eNonprofit_Benchmarks_Study.pdf. (accessed July 7, 2007).
24. B. J. Fogg et al., "How Do People Evaluate a Web Site's Credibility? Results from a Large Study" (Palo Alto, CA: Persuasive Technology Lab, Stanford University, 2002), 23, www.consumer-webwatch.org/pdfs/stanfordPTL.pdf (accessed July 7, 2007).
25. Ibid.
26. Ibid.
27. P. Hirshberg, "Discovery, News and Blogson the New Technorati.com" (2007), http://technorati.com/weblog/2007/12/405.html (accessed December 9, 2007).
28. A. Fine, *Momentum: Igniting Social Change in the Connected Age* (San Francisco: Jossey-Bass, 2006).
29. M. Brown, "Web 2.0 Services: These Objects are Closer Than They Appear" (2006), www.educause.edu/ir/library/pdf/DEC0606.pdf (accessed July 8, 2007).
30. Pew Internet & American Life Project, "Adult and Social Network Web site," www.pewinternet.org/Reports/2009/Adults-and-Social-Network-Websites.aspx (accessed June 30, 2009).
31. Pew Internet & American Life Project, "Social Networking Web sites and Teens: An Overview" (2007), www.pewinternet.org/pdfs/PIP_SNS_Data_Memo_Jan_2007.pdf (accessed December 12, 2007).
32. J. Reisman, A. Gienapp, and S. Stachowiak, "A Guide to Measuring Advocacy and Policy," *Evaluation Exchange,* 8, no. 1 (Spring 2007), www.gse.harvard.edu/hfrp/eval/issue34/bbt3.html (accessed July 7, 2007).
33. Ibid.

Chapter 8

1. Linda K. Cummins and Katharine V. Byers, "Teaching Policy Practice Skills: An Integrated Model" (Introduction adapted from a paper presented by authors, paper presented at the Indiana Association for Social Work Education State Conference, Indianapolis, IN, October 6, 2000).

2. Information contained in Box 8.1 was taken from the following sources: Anthony Center for Women's Leadership, "The History of US Suffrage Movement Timeline 1792 to Present," (Rochester, NY: University of Rochester, 2006), www.rochester.edu/sba/suffragetimeline.html (accessed April 22, 2008); National Women's History Museum (n.d.), "Emma Hart Willard," *The History of Women and Education: Biographies,* www.nwhm.org/exhibits/education/Biographies_Willard.htm (accessed April 22, 2008); R.J. Connors, "Frances Wright: First Female Civic Rhetor in America," *College English,* 62, no. 1 (1999), 30–57; National Women's History Project (n.d.), "Timeline of Legal History of Women in the United States, A Timeline of the Women's Rights Movement 1848–1998," www.legacy98.org/timeline.html (accessed April 22, 2008); "American Women Through Time 1970–2001." (2007), www.mtsu.edu/kmiddlet/history/women/time/wh-recent.html (accessed April 22, 2008); and M. A. Imbornoni, "Women's Rights Movement in the US. Timeline of Key Events in the American Women's Rights Movement" (2007), www.infoplease.com/spot/womenstimeline1.html#WHM-1980 (accessed April 22, 2008).

3. For an overview of several policymaking models see, B. Wharf and B. McKenzie, "Policy Making Models and Their Connection to Practice," in B. Wharf and B. McKenzie, eds., *Connecting Policy to Practice in the Human Services* (Oxford: Oxford University Press, 1998), 22–38.

4. Michael Carley, *Rational Techniques in Policy Analysis* (London: Heinemann Educational, 1980). Books as cited in Wharf and McKenzie, "Policy Making Models," 22–38.

5. Wharf and McKenzie, "Policy Making Models," 22–38.

6. H. A. Simon, "Rationality in Psychology and Economics," *Journal of Business,* 59, no. 4 (1986).

7. T. P. Holland and A. C. Kilpatrick, "Ethical Issues in Social Work: Toward a Grounded Theory of Professional Ethics," *Social Work,* 36, no. 2 (1991), 138–144.

8. U.S. Department Health and Human Services "TANF Families—Through December, 2006" (Washington, DC: Administration of Children and Families, Office of Family Assistance), May 24, 2007, www.acf.hhs.gov/programs/ofa/caseload/2006/tanf_family.htm (accessed April 14, 2008).

9. G. Acs and P. Loprest, "TANF Caseload Composition and Leavers Synthesis Report" (Washington, DC: The Urban Institute, 2007), www.urban.org/UploadedPDF/411553_tanf_caseload.pdf (accessed March 31, 2008).

10. J. Brooks-Gunn and G. J. Duncan, "The Effects of Poverty on Children," *The Future of Children: Children and Poverty,* 7, no. 2 (1997), 55–71. See also, G. J. Duncan and J. Brooks-Gunn, "Family Poverty, Welfare Reform, and Child Development, *Child Development,* 71, no. 1 (2000), 188–196.

11. Wharf and McKenzie, "Policy Making Models," 22–38. See also D. M. DiNitto (with Linda K. Cummins) *Social Welfare: Politics and Public Policy,* 6th ed. (Boston: Allyn & Bacon, 2005) 5.

12. A. Rubinstein, *Modeling Bounded Rationality* (Cambridge, MA: MIT Press, 1998).

13. H. Simon, *Models of Bounded Rationality: Empirically Grounded Economic Reason,* 3 (Cambridge, MA: MIT Press, 1997), 291. See also, *The Concise Encyclopedia of Economics,* "Biography of Herbert Alexander Simon (1916–2001)," www.econlib.org/library/Enc/bios/Simon.html (accessed April 15, 2008).

14. Wharf and McKenzie, "Policy Making Models," 22–38. See also, H. Simon, *Models of Bounded Rationality;* A. Rubinstein, *Modeling Bounded Rationality;* and DiNitto, *Social Welfare: Politics and Public Policy,* 6–10.

15. For a case study on this dynamic, see D. Schorr, "The Politics of Policymaking," *New Leader,* 74, no. 6 (1992), 4.

16. G. Sussman, and B. W. Daynes, "The Impact of Political Ideology on Congressional Support for Presidential Policymaking Authority," *Congress and the Presidency,* 22, no. 2 (1995), 141–154.

17. C. A. Torres, "The Capitalist State and Public Policy Formation: Framework for a Political Sociology of Educatonal Policymaking," *British Journal of Sociology of Education,* 10, no. 1 (1989), 81–102.

18. DiNitto, *Social Welfare,* 6–10.

19. Ibid, 8–10.

20. C. A. Torres, "The Capitalist State," 81–102. See also, G. Sussman, and B. W. Daynes, "The Impact of Political Ideology on Congressional Support for Presidential Policymaking Authority," *Congress and the Presidency,* 22, no. 2 (1995), 141–154.

21. C. E. Lindblom, "The Science of Muddling Through," *Public Administration Review,* 19 (1959), 79–88.

22. Charles E. Lindblom, "Still Muddling, Not Yet Through," *Public Administration Review,* 39, no. 6 (1979), 517–526.

23. Ibid., 520.

24. Wharf and McKenzie, "Policy Making Models," 22–38; DiNitto, *Social Welfare,* 10–13.

25. G. E. Shambaugh, IV and P. J. Weinstein, Jr., *The Art of Policy Making: Tools, Techniques, and Processes in the Modern Executive Branch* (New York: Longman Publishers, 2003).

26. Ibid.

27. U.S. Department of Health and Human Services, *Indicators of Welfare Dependence,* Annual Report to Congress (Washington, DC, 1997), http://aspe.hhs.gov/hsp/indicators97/front.htm#tablist (accessed April 19, 2008).

28. Shambaugh, *The Art of Policy Making.*

29. The stages of policymaking presented in this section were influenced by Neil Gilbert and Paul Terrell, *Dimensions of Social Welfare Policy,* 5th ed. (Boston: Allyn & Bacon, 2002), 273–296.

30. J. Blau (with Mimi Abramovitz), *The Dynamics of Social Welfare Policy* (New York: Oxford Press, 2004).

31. United State Conference of Mayors, "Hunger and Homelessness Survey: A Status Report on Hunger and Homelessness in America's Cities" (December, 2007), www.usmayores.org/uscm/news/press_release/documents/hh_121707.pdf (accessed April 26, 2008).

32. National Coalition for the Homeless, "How Many People Experience Homelessness?" *Fact Sheet,* August 2007, www.nationalhomeless.org/factsheets/How_Many.html (accessed July 6, 2008); United State Conference of Mayors (December, 2007), "Hunger and Homelessness Survey: A Status Report on Hunger and Homelessness in America's Cities," www.usmayores.org/uscm/news/press_release/documents/hh_121707.pdf (accessed April 26, 2008).

33. United State Conference of Mayors (December, 2007), "Hunger and Homelessness Survey: A Status Report on Hunger and Homelessness in America's Cities," www.usmayores.org/uscm/news/press_release/documents/hh_121707.pdf (accessed April 26, 2008); see also Western Regional Advocacy Project (November 14, 2006), "Without Housing: Decades of Federal Housing Cutbacks, Massive Homelessness, and Policy Failures," http://wraphome.org/wh/index.php (accessed April 26, 2008); and the National Coalition for the Homeless "Who is Homeless?" (August 2007), www.national-homeless.org/factsheets/who.html (accessed April 26, 2008).

34. See C. S. North, K. M. Eyrich, D. F. Pollio, and E. L. Spitznagel, "Are Rates of Psychiatric Disorders in the Homeless Population Changing?" *American Journal of Public Health,* 94, no. 1 (2004), 103–108; and N. Jainchill, J. Hawke, and J. Yagelka, "Gender, Psychopathology, and Patterns of Homelessness among Clients in Shelter-Based TCs," *American Journal of Drug and Alcohol Abuse,* 26, no. 4 (2000), 553–567.

35. D. E. Chambers, and K. R. Wedel, *Social Policy and Social Programs: A Method of Practical Public Policy Analysis* (Boston: Allyn & Bacon, 2005).

36. Centers for Disease Control, *Morbidity and Mortality Weekly Report,* 30, 305–308, www.cdc.gov/hiv/resources/other/PDF/MMWR%2025%20Year.pdf (accessed April 30, 2008).

37. "Ryan's Story" (n.d.), www.ryanwhite.com/pages/story.html (accessed June 2, 2008).

38. U. S. Department of Health Resources and Service Administration (n.d.), "The Ryan White HIV AIDS Program," http://hab.hrsa.gov/livinghistory/timeline/1991–1995/1991.html (accessed April 30, 2008). Also from the same Web site, see "The Ryan White Program: Funding," http://hab.hrsa.gov/reports/funding.htm (accessed April 30, 2008).

39. Centers for Disease Control, *Morbidity and Mortality Weekly Report,* 30 (July 3, 1981), 305–308, www.cdc.gov/hiv/resources/other/PDF/MMWR%2025%20Year.pdf (accessed April 30, 2008).

40. Information regarding Medicare Modernization Act of 2003 and the doughnut hole problem was taken from the following sources: National Committee to Preserve Social Security and Medicare, calculations based on data from *The Annual 2006 Report of the Board of Trustees of the Federal Hospital Insurance and Federal Supplementary Medical Insurance Trust Funds* and the U.S. Department of Health and Human Services Centers for Medicare and Medicaid Services, *Fact Sheet: Drug Benefits Enrollment Up, Costs Down from Competition and Beneficiary Choices,* June 8, 2006; and National Committee to Preserve Social Security and Medicare, http://www.ncpssm.org/news/archive/donut_hole_facts/ (accessed July 19, 2010).

41. Kaiser Family Foundation, *Health Insurance Coverage of the Total Population, States (2005–2006), U.S. (2006)* (October 22, 2007), www.statehealthfacts.org/comparebar.jsp?ind=125&cat=3 (accessed June 20, 2008).

42. D. U. Himmelstein, E. Warren, D. Thorne, and S. Woolhandler, "MarketWatch: Illness and Injury as Contributors to Bankruptcy," *Health Affairs: The Policy Journal of the Health Sphere,* February 2, 2005, http://content.healthaffairs.org/cgi/content/full/hlthaff.w5.63/DC1 (accessed June 20, 2008).

43. G. M. Shaw, "The Role of Public Input in State Welfare Policymaking," *Policy Studies Journal,* 28, no. 4 (2000), 707–720.

44. Ibid.

45. These basic questions about policy design and analysis have evolved over time, and it is hard to know who the original creator may have been. The authors have been primarily influenced by the following works: N. Gilbert and P. Terrell, *Dimensions of Social Welfare Policy,* 6th ed. (Boston: Allyn & Bacon, 2005); J. H. Karger and D. Stoesz, *American Social Welfare Policy: A Pluralist Approach,* 5th ed. (Boston: Allyn & Bacon, 2006); R. Dolgoff and D. Feldstein, *Understanding Social Welfare: A Search for Social Justice,* 7th ed. (Boston: Allyn& Bacon, 2007); and, P. R. Popple and L. Leighninger, *The Policy Based Profession,* 3rd ed. (Boston: Allyn & Bacon, 2004).

46. Information in this paragraph relied upon the following sources: D. Longshore, Review of the book *Policy Implementation in the 1980's, Contemporary Sociology,* 18, no. 2 (1989), 251–252; DiNitto, *Social Welfare;* Shambaugh, *The Art of Policy Making.*

47. M. Lundin "When Does Cooperation Improve Public Policy Implementation?" *Policy Studies Journal,* 35, no. 4 (2007), 629–653.

48. B. S. Jansson, *Becoming an Effective Policy Advocate* (Pacific Grove, CA: Brooks/Cole, 2003).

49. See H. Hoynes, "Work, Welfare, and Family Structure: What Have We Learned?" *NBER Working Paper No. 5644* (1996), http://ssrn.com (accessed

July 9, 2008); H. Hoynes, "Does Welfare Play Any Role in Female Headship Decisions?" *Journal of Public Economics,* 65 (1997), 89–117; S. Danzinger, G. Jakubson, S. Schwartz, and E. Smolensky, "Work and Welfare are Determinants of Female Poverty and Household Headship," *The Quarterly Journal of Economics,* 97, no. 3 (1982), 519–534; R. Moffitt, "Welfare Effects on Female Headship with Area Effects," *Journal of Human Resources,* 29, no. 2, (1994), 621–636; R. Moffitt, "The Effect of the U.S. Welfare System on Marital Status," *Journal of Public Economics,* 41, no. 1 (1990) 101–124; and R.D. Plotnick, "Welfare and Out-of-Wedlock Childbearing: Evidence from the 1980s, *Journal of Marriage and the Family,* 52, no. 3 (1990), 735–746.

50. Lectric Law Library's' stacks, *The ACLU's Most Important Supreme Court Victories* (1996), www.lectlaw.com/files/cur59.htm (accessed June 30, 2008).

51. Information on the history and evolution of welfare policy was taken from the following sources: S. W. Blank, and B. B Blum, "A Brief History of Work Expectations for Welfare Mothers," *The Future of Children,* 7, no. 1 (1997), 28–38; U. S. Department of Health and Human Services (n.d.), "A Brief History of AFDC," http://aspe.hhs.gov/hsp/AFDC/baseline/1history.pdf (accessed June 26, 2008) 'Lectric Law Library's' Stacks "The ACLU's Most Important Supreme Court Victories" (1996), www.lectlaw.com/files/cur59.htm (accessed June 30, 2008); DiNitto, *Social Welfare.*

52. Thomas D. Gilovich, "The Hot Hand' and Other Illusions of Everyday Life," *Wilson Quarterly,* 15 no. 2 (1991), 52, *Academic Search Premier,* EBSCO*host,* http://web.ebscohost.com.library.capella.edu/ehost/detail?vid=6&hid=8&sid=5a859860-c2ff-4392-a3c5-b58ec65781d3%40sessionmgr13&bdata=JnNpdGU9ZWhvc3QtbGl2ZSSZzY29wZT1zaXRl#db=aph&AN=9610240111 (accessed July 30, 2008).

Chapter 9

1. See the following empirical studies on risk factors and child abuse: S. Louise Germain, Couture Ethier, and Carl Lacharite, "Risk Factors Associated with the Chronicity of High Potential for Child Abuse and Neglect," *Journal of Family Violence,* 19, no. 1 (2004), 13–24; A. M. Windham, L. Rosenberg, L. Fuddy, E. McFarlane, C. Sia, and A. K. Duggan, "Risk of Mother-reported Child Abuse in the First 3 Years of Life," *Child Abuse and Neglect,* 28, no. 6 (2004), 647–669; J. Harder, "Research Implications for the Prevention of Child Abuse and Neglect," *Families in Society,* 86, no. 4 (2005), 491–501; J. Frederick and C. Goddard, "Exploring the Relationship Between Poverty, Childhood Adversity and Child Abuse from the Perspective of Adulthood," *Child Abuse Review,* 16 (2007), 323–34; J. Taylor, N. Baldwin, and N. Spencer, "Predicting Child Abuse and Neglect: Ethical, Theoretical and Methodological Challenges," *Journal of Clinical Nursing,* 17 (2008), 1193–1200.

2. See J. Kaufman, E. Zigler "Do Abused Children Become Abusive Parents?" *American Journal of Orthopsychiatry,* 57, no. 2 (1987), 186–192; and, J. E. Oliver, "Intergenerational Transmission of Child Abuse: Rates, Research, and Clinical Implications," *The American Journal of Psychiatry,* 150, no. 9 (1993), 1315–1324.

3. Frederick and Goddard, "Exploring the Relationship" (2007), 324.

4. Ibid., 323–334.

5. U. S. Department of Health and Human Services, "Prior HHS Poverty Guidelines and Federal Register References" (Washington DC, January 23, 2008), http://aspe.hhs.gov/POVERTY/figures-fed-reg.shtml (accessed May 5, 2008).

6. Missouri Research and Economic Center (n.d.), "Cost of Living Fourth Quarter, 2007" (Missouri Department of Economic Development), www.missourieconomy.org/indicators/cost_of_living/index.stm (accessed May 12, 2008).

7. USDA, Center for Nutrition, Policy and Promotion, "Official USDA Food Plans: Cost of Food at Home at Four Levels, US average August, 2007" (September, 2007), www.cnpp.usda.gov/Publications/FoodPlans/2007/CostofFoodAug07.pdf (accessed May 12, 2008).

8. Urban Institute (2001), "Child Care is a Major Expense for America's Working Families," www.urban.org/url.cfm?ID=900031&renderforprint=1&CFID=33015803&CFTOKEN=91629257 (accessed May 12, 2008).

9. A. A. Galbraith, S. T. Wong, S. E. Kim, and P. W. Newacheck, "Out of Pocket Financial Burden for Low Income Families with Children: Socioeconomic Disparities and Effects of Insurance," *Health Services Research,* 40, no. 6.1 (2005), 1722–1736.

10. U.S. General Accounting Office, "Earned Income Tax Credit Participation," Letter to the Subcommittee on Oversight of the House of Representatives' Committee on Ways and Means, GAO-02-290R, Washington DC: 2005 (December 14, 2001), www.gao.gov/new.items/d02290r.pdf (accessed July 21, 2008).

11. Data used in this analysis of the federal poverty line standard for a family of four were gathered from the following sources: Galbraith et al., "Out of Pocket Financial Burden" (2005), 1722–1736; Social Security Online, "Social Security and Medicare Tax Rates, Trust Fund Data," (December 2007), www.ssa.gov/OACT/ProgData/taxRates.html (accessed May 12, 2008); Tax Foundation, U.S. Federal individual income tax rates history 1913–2008 (2008, January), www.taxfoundation.org/taxdata/show/151.html (accessed May 12, 2008); USDA, Center for Nutrition, Policy and Promotion "Official USDA Food Plans: Cost of Food at Home at Four Levels, US Average, August, 2007" (September, 2007) www.cnpp.usda.gov/Publications/FoodPlans/2007/CostofFoodAug07.pdf (accessed May 12, 2008); Urban Institute (2001), "Child Care a Major Expense for America's Working Families," www.urban.org/url.cfm?ID= 900031&

renderforprint=1&CFID=33015803&CFTOKEN=
91629257 (accessed May 12, 2008).
12. Wider Opportunities for Women "The Self
Sufficiency Standard" (2008), www.wowonline.
org/ourprograms/fess/sss.asp (accessed August 5,
2008).
13. N. Gilbert and P. Terrell, *Dimensions of Social
Welfare Policy* (Boston: Allyn & Bacon, 2005); D. E.
Chambers, and K. R. Wedel, *Social Policy and
Social Programs: A Method for the Practical Public
Policy Analyst* (Boston: Allyn & Bacon, 2005).
14. H. Holmes and C. R. Sustein, *The Cost of Rights:
Why Liberty Depends on Taxes* (New York: W.W.
Norton, 1999); Gilbert and Terrell, *Dimensions*
(2005); A. M. Okun, *Equality and Efficiency: The
Big Tradeoff* (Washington, DC: The Brookings
Institution, 1975); J. Rawls, *A Theory of Justice*
(Oxford: Oxford University Press, 1972).
15. Interagency Council on Homelessness (March 18,
2004), "Samaritan Initiative Targeted to Ending
Chronic Homelessness" (Washington DC, 2004),
www.ich.gov/library/samaritan.html (accessed
May 8, 2008).
16. U.S. National Archives and Records Administration
(January 27, 2003), "Notice of Funding Availability
(NOFA) for the Collaborative Initiative to Help End
Chronic Homelessness," *Federal Register,* 68, no.
17 (2003), 4019, http://edocket.access.gpo.gov/
2003/pdf/03–1801.pdf (accessed August 7, 2008).
17. U.S. Department of Health and Human Services,
HHS 2008 Poverty Guidelines (January 23, 2008),
http://aspe.hhs.gov/poverty/08Poverty.shtml
(accessed August 31, 2008).
18. C. S. North, K. M. Eyrich, D. F. Pollio, and E. L.
Spitznagel, "Are Rates of Psychiatric Disorders in
the Homeless Population Changing?" *American
Journal of Public Health,* 94, no. 1 (2004), 103–108;
Western Regional Advocacy Project, "Without
Housing: Decades of Federal Housing Cutbacks,
Massive Homelessness, and Policy Failures" (San
Francisco: Western Regional Advocacy Project,
2006), http://wraphome.org/wh/index.php,
(accessed April 26, 2008); United State Conference
of Mayors (December, 2007), "Hunger and
Homelessness Survey: A Status Report on Hunger
and Homelessness in America's Cities," www.
usmayors.org/uscm/news/press_release/documents/
hh_121707.pdf (accessed April 26, 2008). National
Coalition for the Homeless (August, 2007), "How
Many People Experience Homelessness?" (Fact
Sheet) www.nationalhomeless.org/factsheets/
How_Many.html (accessed July 6, 2008); United
State Conference of Mayors, "Hunger and
Homelessness Survey: A Status Report on Hunger
and Homelessness in America's Cities" (December,
2007), www.usmayors.org/uscm/news/press_
release/documents/hh_121707.pdf (accessed April
26, 2008).
19. Gilbert and Terrell, *Dimensions* (2005).
20. H. J. Karger and D. Stoesz, *American Social
Welfare Policy: A Pluralist Approach,* 5th ed.
(Boston: Allyn & Bacon, 2006).
21. P. R. Popple and L. Leighninger, *The Policy-based
Professional: An Introduction to Social Welfare
Policy Analysis for Social Workers,* 2nd ed. (Boston:
Allyn & Bacon, 2001).
22. Chambers and Wedel, *Social Policy* (2005).
23. R. Dolgoff and D. Feldstein, *Understanding Social
Welfare: A Search for Social Justice,* 7th ed.
(Boston: Allyn & Bacon, 2005).
24. S. Sevenhuijsen, *Citizenship and the Ethics of Care*
(New York: Routledge, 1998); S. Sevenhuijsen,
"Caring the the Third Way: The Relationship
Between Obligation, Responsibility and Care in
Third Way Discourse," *Critical Social Policy,* 62
(2000), 5–37; S. Sevenhuijsen, "A Place of Care:
The Relevance of the Feminist Ethic of Care for
Social Policy," *Feminist Theory,* 4, no. 2 (2003),
179–197.
25. J. Tronto, "Care as a Basis for Radical Political
Judgments," *Hypatia,* 10, no. 2 (1995), 141–149; J.
Tronto, "An Ethic of Care," *Generations,* 22, no. 3
(1998), 15–21; J. Tronto, "Care Ethics; Moving
Forward," *Hypatia,* 14, no. 1 (1999), 113–119.
26. G. Meahger and N. Parton, "Modernising Social
Work and the Ethics of Care," *Social Work and
Society,* 2, no. 1 (2004), 10–27.
27. R. Hugman, *Power in Caring Professions* (London:
MacMillan, 1991); R. Hugman, "Professional Ethics
in Social Work: Living with the Legacy,"
Australian Social Work, 56, no. 1 (2003), 5–15.
28. B. Fisher, and J. C. Tronto, "Toward a Feminist
Theory of Caring," in *Circles of Care: Work and
Identity in Women's Lives,* eds. Emily Abel and
Margaret Nelson (Albany: State University of
New York Press, 1990).
29. Ibid., 40.
30. Meahger and Parton, "Modernising Social Work"
(2004), 10–27.
31. Ibid. and J. Tronto, "An Ethic of Care," (1998), 15–21.
32. R. Hugman, "Professional Ethics" (2003), 5–15.
33. J. Tronto, "Care as a Basis" (1995), 141–149;
S. Sevenhuijsen, "A Place of Care," 179–197.
34. J. Tronto, "An Ethic of Care" (1998), 15–21;
J. Tronto, "Care as a Basis," (1995); S.
Sevenhuijsen, "A Place of Care" 179–197.
35. J. Tronto, "Care Ethics" (1999), 113–119.
36. J. Tronto, "Care as a Basis" (1995); J. Tronto, "Care
Ethics" 113–119; S. Sevenhuijsen, "A Place of
Care" 179–197; Meahger and Parton, "Modernising
Social Work" (2004), 10–27.
37. R. Hugman, "Professional Ethics" (2003), 5–15;
J. Tronto, "An Ethic of Care," (1998), 15–21;
S. Sevenhuijsen, "A Place of Care," 179–197.
38. R. Hugman, "Professional Ethics" (2003), 5–15;
S. Sevenhuijsen, "A Place of Care," 179–197.
39. J. Tronto, "An Ethic of Care" (1998), 15–21.

Chapter 10
1. National Urban League, "History of the National
Urban League," www.nul.org/history.html
(accessed April 30, 2008).
2. NASW, "NASW Foundation National
Programs, NASW Social Work Pioneers,"

www.naswfoundation. org/pioneers/g/gustafson. html (accessed May 25, 2008).

3. Afterschool Alliance, www.afterschoolalliance.org/ prog_docs/advoc_chart.pdf (accessed May 15, 2008).

4. Mackinac, "Living Wage Laws Kill Privatization," comment posted on Mackinac Center for Public Policy Web site, www.mackinac.org (accessed July 1, 2008), and Resources for Business, "Living Wage Ordinances," comment posted on U.S. Chamber of Commerce Web site, www.uschamber. com (accessed July 1, 2008).

5. George Lakoff, *Don't Think of an Elephant: Know Your Values and Frame the Debate—The Essential Guide for Progressives* (White River Junction, VT: Chelsea Green Pub. Co., 2004).

6. Indiana Business, "Lawsuit Filed Against FSSA," InsideIndianaBusiness.com, Report, 5–19-08, www.insideindianabusiness.com/newsitem. asp?id=29421 (accessed May 21, 2008).

7. Testimony at Town Hall Meeting, "Family Social Services Administration Privatization," June 25, 2008, Bloomington, Indiana.

8. John Edwards (Former Democratic presidential candidate), "One Democracy Initiative: Returning Washington to Regular People," www.johnedwards. com/issues/govt-reform/ (accessed April 11, 2008).

9. Jonathan Turley, "Case Bringing Scrutiny to a System and a Profession," *The Washington Post*, January 4, 2006, A Section; Jonathan Turley, "109th Congress Just Can't Resist," *USA Today*, October 18, 2006, www.usatoday.com/news/opinion/ editorials/2006–10-18-forum-congress_x.htm?POE= click-refer (accessed August 30, 2009).

10. John Broder, "Amid Scandals, States Overhaul Lobbying Laws," *The New York Times*, January 24, 2006, Section A; Linda Feldmann, "Abramoff Scandal Spurs Lobbying Reform," *Christian Science Monitor*, January 9, 2006, Section USA.

11. James Madison, The Federalist Papers, No. 10 (New York, New American Library, 1961) 77–84.

12. Clive Thomas, ed., *Research Guide to U.S. and International Interest Groups* (Westport, CN: Praeger, 2004), 4.

13. Ibid., 13, 41–47.

14. Ibid., 13.

15. Peter J. Williamson, "Corporatism and Neocorporatist Theory," in *Research Guide to U.S. and International Interest Groups,* Clive Thomas, ed. (Westport, CN: Praeger, 2004), 48–53.

16. Mancur Olson, *The Logic of Collective Action: Public Goods and the Theory of Groups* (Cambridge, MA: Harvard University Press, 1965).

17. Terry M. Moe, "A Calculus of Group Membership," *American Journal of Political Science,* 24 (1980), 593–632 and Terry M. Moe, "Toward a Broader View of Interest Groups," *Journal of Politics,* 43 (1981), 531–43.

18. Jack L. Walker Jr., "The Origins and Maintenance of Interest Groups in America," *American Political Science Review,* 77 (June 1983), 390–406; Frank R. Baumgartner, "The Growth and Diversity of U.S. Associations: 1956–2004: Analyzing Trends Using the Encyclopedia of Associations" (Working paper), March 9, 2005.

19. Frank Baumgartner and Beth Leech, *Basic Interests: The Importance of Groups in Politics and in Political Science* (Princeton, NJ: PUP, 1998).

20. Data from Christopher J. Bosso, "Environment Inc.: Grassroots to Beltways" as noted in Jeffrey M. Berry and Clyde Wilcox. *The Interest Group Society,* 4th ed. (New York: Pearson/Longman, 2007) 24.

21. Federal Election Commission, "Summary of PAC Activity," www.fec.gov/press/press2001/053101 pacfund/pachis00.htm (accessed June 30, 2008).

22. Thomas ed., *Research Guide*, 9.

23. Berry and Wilcox, *The Interest Group Society,* 6–8.

24. Thomas ed., *Research Guide*, 8–9.

25. Barbara Teater, ""Your Agenda Is Our Agenda": State Legislators' Perspective of Interest Group Influence on Political Decision Making," *Journal of Community Practice,* 16, no. 2 (2008), 201–220.

26. R. Friedman, and M. L. O'Leary, "United States: The Children's Health Insurance Program Reauthorization Act of 2009: What It Means for Private Employer Health Plans," Mondaq Web site, www.mondaq.com/article.asp?articleid=79748&login= true&nogo=1 (accessed May 1, 2009).

27. Berry and Wilcox, *The Interest Group Society,* 59.

28. Amy Snow Landa, "AMA Major Force in Federal Lobbying," amednews.com (October 15, 2001), www.ama-assn.org/amednews/2001/10/15/ gvsd1015.htm (accessed April 30, 2008).

29. Opensecrets.org, "Top Spenders," www.opensecrets.org/lobby/top.php?showYear=2007& indexType=s (accessed August 28, 2009).

30. John Hogan, "Election 2004: How Older Voters Could Make a Difference," *AARP Bulletin,* www. aarp.org/bulletin/news/Articles/a2004–10-06-older- voters.html (accessed May 1, 2009).

31. R. L. Hall, and A. V. Deardorff, "Lobbying as Legislative Subsidy," *American Political Science Review,* 100, no. 1 (2006), 69–84.

32. A. Rosenthal, *The Third House: Lobbyists and Lobbying in the States,* 2nd ed. (Washington, DC: CQ Press, 2001), 1.

33. A. J. Nownes, *Total Lobbying: What Lobbyists Want (And How They Try to Get It)* (New York: Cambridge University Press, 2006), 7.

34. B. L. Leech, F. R. Baumgartner, T. M. La Pira, and N. A. Semanko, "Drawing Lobbyists to Washington: Government Activity and the Demand for Advocacy," *Political Research Quarterly,* 58, no. 1 (2005), 19–30; D. Lowery, V. Gray, M. Fellowes, and J. Anderson, "Living in the Moment: Lags, Leads, and the Links Between Legislative Agendas and Interest Advocacy," *Social Science Quarterly,* 85, no. 2 (2004), 463–77.

35. Leech et al., "Drawing Lobbyists to Washington," 2005.

36. J. R. Wright, *Interest Groups and Congress: Lobbying, Contributions and Influence* (Needham Heights, MA: Allyn & Bacon, 1996); R. J. Hrebenar, *Interest Group Politics in America*, 3rd ed. (Armonk, NY: M.E. Sharpe Inc. 1997).
37. Alliance for Justice, "What Is Lobbying?" www.afj.org/assets/resources/nap/lobbying-defs.pdf (accessed May 18, 2008).
38. IRS Manual, "Taxable Expenditures of Private Foundations," www.irs.gov/irm/part7/irm_07–027-019.html (accessed July 12, 2009).
39. Minnesota Council of Nonprofits (List quoted from the Minnesota Council of Nonprofits Nonprofit Lobbying and the Law), www.mncn.org/lobbylaw.htm (accessed May 18, 2008).
40. John Pomeranz, "A Summary of the Laws Governing Lobbying by 501(c)(3) Organizations," The National Council of Nonprofit Associations, www.ncna.org/index.cfm?fuseaction=page.viewPage&PageID=294 (accessed May 18, 2008).
41. The Federal Election Commission has produced a resource Web site on HLOGA provisions at www.fec.gov/info/guidance/hlogabundling.shtml (accessed August 28, 2009); Also see the U.S. Senate, "Lobby Disclosure Act Guidance," www.senate.gov/legislative/resources/pdf/S1guidance.pdf (accessed May 18, 2008).
42. R. Runningen, "Obama Freezes Pay, Toughens Ethics and Lobbying Rules," Bloomberg.com., www.bloomberg.com/apps/news?pid=20601087&sid=azQJo_wu7f64 (accessed May 1, 2009).
43. Kathy Byers, "Influencing State Policy Update," (Spring 2009), e-mail distributed to members via e-mail by Kathy Byers (chair).
44. NASW, "Legislative Agenda for the 111th Congress," www.socialworkers.org/advocacy/images/grmaterials/111th%20Legislative%20Agenda.pdf (accessed July 6, 2009).
45. Adapted from the Legislative Agenda for the 111th Congress, at www.socialworkers.org/advocacy/images/grmaterials/111th%20Legislative%20Agenda.pdf. (accessed July 6, 2009).
46. A. Rosenthal, *The Third House: Lobbyists and Lobbying in the States*, 2nd ed. (Washington, DC: CQ Press, 2001); J. C. Freeman, "Advocacy in Aging Policy: Working the Bills on Capitol Hill(s)," *Generations*, 28, no.1 (2004), 41–47.
47. NASW, "NASW Government Relations Materials," www.socialworkers.org/advocacy/grassroots/toolkit/dosDonts.asp (accessed May 18, 2008).
48. NASW, "Legislative Office Visit Follow-up Report Form," www.socialworkers.org/advocacy/grassroots/toolkit/reportForm.asp (accessed July 6, 2009).
49. R. Allen Hays, *Who Speaks for the Poor? National Interest Groups and Social Policy* (New York, NY: Routledge, 2001).
50. Rickie Solinger, "Forging Fragile Alliances," *Women's Review of Books*, 14, no. 5 (1997), 29, *Academic Search Premier*, EBSCO*host* (accessed December 11, 2007).

Chapter 11

1. "Senate Kills Family Cap Provision," *Human Events*, 51, no. 37, (1995), 22. *Academic Search Premier*, EBSCO*host*, http://web.ebscohost.com/ehost/detail?vid=7&hid=107&sid=c15c4881-cc8a-4405-8ba9-237024600892%40sessionmgr111&bdata=JnNpdGU9ZWhvc3QtbGl2ZQ%3d%3d#db=aph&AN=9510114079 (accessed June 23, 2008).
2. "Right Questions, Wrong Answers." *America*, 7, no. 3 (October 1995), 3–5. *Academic Search Premier*, EBSCO*host*, http://web.ebscohost.com/ehost/pdf?vid=9&hid=107&sid=c15c4881-cc8a-4405-8ba9-237024600892%40sessionmgr111 (accessed June 23, 2008).
3. Patricia Donovan, "The 'Family Cap': A Popular but Unproven Method of Welfare Reform," *Family Planning Perspectives*, 27, no. 4 (July/August 1995), 166–171. *Academic Search Premier*, EBSCO*host*, http://web.ebscohost.com/ehost/detail?vid=16&hid=107&sid=c15c4881-cc8a-4405-8ba9-237024600892%40sessionmgr111&bdata=JnNpdGU9ZWhvc3QtbGl2ZQ%3d%3d#db=aph&AN=9508210906 (accessed June 23, 2008).
4. Susan T. Gooden and E. Douglas Nakeina, "Chapter 17: Ever Present, Sometimes Acknowledged, but Never Addressed: Racial Disparities in U.S. Welfare Policy," in *The Promise of Welfare Reform*, ed. Keith M. Kilty and Elizabeth Segal (Haworth Press: New York, 2006), 207–222.
5. Karl E. Weick, *The Social Psychology of Organizing*, 2nd ed. (Reading, MA: Addison-Wesley, 1979).
6. Seattle Human Service Coalition, http://shscoalition.org/ (accessed July 3, 2008).
7. Darlyne Bailey and Kelly McNally Koney, "Inter-organizational Community-Based Collaboratives: A Strategic Response to Shape the Social Work Agenda," *Social Work*, 41(1996), 602–611.
8. Michael Reisch, "Briefly Stated: Organizational Structure and Client Advocacy: Lessons from the 1980s," *Social Work*, 35, (1990), 73–74.
9. Richard Hoefer, "Making a Difference: Human Service Interest Group Influence on Social Welfare Regulations," *Journal of Sociology & Social Welfare*, 27, no. 3 (2000), 21–38. *Academic Search Premier*, EBSCO*host*, http://web.ebscohost.com/ehost/pdf?vid=22&hid=2&sid=c15c4881-cc8a-4405-8ba9-237024600892%40sessionmgr111 (accessed December 11, 2007).
10. Richard Hoefer, "Altering State Policy: Interest Group Effectiveness among State-Level Advocacy Groups," *Social Work*, 50 (2005), 219–227.
11. Indiana Coalition of Human Services, www.ichson-line.org/ (accessed July 3, 2008).
12. Alan Rosenthal, *The Third House: Lobbyists and Lobbying in the States* (Washington, DC: Congressional Quarterly, 1993), 152.
13. Human Services Coalition of Oregon, *Taking Action for Basic Human Needs*, http://oregonhsco.org/blog/about-hsco.html (accessed August 3, 2009).
14. Indiana Coalition of Human Services, *2007 Public Policy Statement*, Indianapolis, IN. 2007.

15. Coalition of Human Needs, www.chn.org/ (accessed June 23, 2008).

16. CHN Human Needs Report, February 3, 2006, "House Cuts $38.8 Billion from Budget; Slashes Health Care, Student Loans, Child Support and Help for People with Disabilities," www.chn.org (accessed July 7, 2008).

17. "The Older Americans Act is Reauthorized," October 4, 2006, www.chn.org (accessed July 7, 2008).

18. CHN Human Needs Report, "Victory: 13 More Weeks of Unemployment Benefits," July 1, 2008, www.chn.org (accessed July 7, 2008).

19. David Lowery and Holly Brasher, *Organized Interests and American Government* (Boston, MA: McGraw Hill, 2004).

20. Rosenthal, *The Third House,* 150.

21. Grace P. Sutherland Smith, Bruce A. Thyer, Claire Clements, and Nancy P. Kropf, "An Evaluation of Coalition Building Training for Aging and Developmental Disability Service Providers," *Educational Gerontology,* 23, no. 2 (March 1997), 105. *Academic Search Premier,* EBSCO*host* http://web.ebscohost.com/ehost/pdf?vid=32&hid=2&sid=c15c4881-cc8a-4405-8ba9-237024600892%40sessionmgr111 (accessed August 3, 2009).

22. Seattle Human Services Coalition, http://shscoalition.org/ (accessed July 2, 2008).

23. Rosenthal, *The Third House,* 172, note 4.

24. Ibid, note 9.

25. Willard C. Richan, *Lobbying for Social Change,* 2nd ed. (New York, NY: Haworth Press, 1996), 77.

26. Jeff O. Korgen, "Commentary on, 'The Seamless Garment of Life: Organizing in the Roman Catholic Community,'" *Social Policy,* 34, no. 1 (2003), 38–39. *Academic Search Premier,* EBSCO*host,* http://web.ebscohost.com/ehost/pdf?vid=5&hid=2&sid=d436aa73-033f-4d45-88ab-27efb14cd78f%40sessionmgr14 (accessed June 23, 2008).

27. John W. Kingdon, *Agendas, Alternatives, and Public Policies,* 2nd ed. (New York, NY: Longman, 1995), 163.

28. William P. Browne and Delbert J. Ringquist, "Diversity and Professionalism in a Partisan Environment," in *Interest Group Politics in the Midwestern States,* ed. Ronald J. Hrebenar and Clive S. Thomas (Ames, IA: Iowa State University Press, 1993), 138.

29. F. D. Butterfoss, R. M. Goodman, and A. Wandersman, "Community Coalitions for Prevention and Health Promotion," *Health Education Research,* 8, no. 3 (1993), 315–330.

30. Laura M. Downey, Carol L. Ireson, Svetla Slavova, and Genia McKee, "Defining Elements of Success: A Critical Pathway of Coalition Development," *Health Promotion Practice,* 9, no. 2 (2008), 130–139, http://hpp.sagepub.com (accessed July 9, 2008).

31. Rosenthal, *The Third House,* 154.

32. Stephanie Armour, "Foreclosures Skyrocket 65% in April; Housing Downturn Might Last into 2010, Some Experts Say," *USA Today, May 15, 2008 Thursday Section: MONEY, 1B,* Lexis-Nexis Academic, www.lexisnexis.com/us/lnacademic/results/docview/docview.do?docLinkInd=true&risb=21_T7096062337&format=GNBFI&sort=RELEVANCE&startDocNo=1&resultsUrlKey=29_T7096062341&cisb=22_T7096062340&treeMax=true&treeWidth=0&csi=8213&docNo=2 (accessed August 4, 2009).

33. Amanda Smith Barusch, *Foundations of Social Policy: Social Justice in Human Perspective,* 3rd ed. (Belmont, CA: Brooks/Cole, 2009), 87.

34. Bruce Jansson, *Becoming an Effective Policy Advocate: From Policy Practice to Social Justice* (Belmont, CA: Thomson, Brooks/Cole, 2008), 439.

35. Margaret S. Sherraden, Betsy Slosar, and Michael Sherraden, "Innovation in Social Policy: Collaborative Policy Advocacy," *Social Work,* 47, no. 3 (2002), 209–221.

36. Ibid.

37. Michael Sherraden, "Assets and Welfare," *Society,* 29 (November/December 1991), 64–72. *Academic Search Premier,* EBSCO*host,* http://web.ebscohost.com/ehost/pdf?vid=11&hid=2&sid=d436aa73-033f-4d45-88ab-27efb14cd78f%40sessionmgr14 (accessed August 3, 2009).

38. Sherraden, et al., *Innovation in Social Policy,* 2002.

39. Ibid.

40. Ibid.

41. Ibid.

42. Jenny M. Lewis, "Being Around and Knowing the Players: Networks of Influence in Health Policy," *Social Science and Medicine,* 62 (May 2006), 2125–2136, Science Direct. Com www.sciencedirect.com/science?_ob=MImg&_imagekey=B6VBF-4HJS5GP-2-3&_cdi=5925&_user=1105409&_orig=browse&_coverDate=05%2F31%2F2006&_sk=999379990&view=c&wchp=dGLbVtb-zSkWA&md5=bdbe4b57fd615e3c8e08cc6b211458d8&ie=/sdarticle.pdf (accessed December 9, 2009).

43. Bailey and Koney, *Inter-organizational Community-Based Collaboratives* (1996), 605.

44. Sherraden, et al., *Innovation in Social Policy,* 2002.

45. Thomas Wolff, "A Practitioner's Guide to Successful Coalitions," *American Journal of Community Psychology,* 29, no. 2 (2001), 173–191, Springerlink.com www.springerlink.com/content/kr91467244l27788/?p=eef3f2b9131b4ec19d4fc38374af3928&pi= (accessed December 9, 2009).

46. Cynthia Cannon Poindexter, "Promises in the Plague: Passage of the Ryan White Comprehensive AIDS Resources Emergency Act as a Case Study for Legislative Action," *Health & Social Work,* 24 (1999), 35–41.

47. Ibid., 37.

48. Ibid., 37.

49. T. Sheridan, "Changing the System: Don't Mourn—Organize!" in *HIV and Social Work,* ed. D. Aronstein and B. Thompson (New York: Haworth Press, 1998), 541–560 as noted on page 39 of Poindexter, Promises in the Plague (1999).

50. Poindexter, "Promises in the Plague," 40.

51. Sherraden, et al., *Innovation in Social Policy,* 2002.

52. John Bonelli and Louise Simmons, "Coalition Building and Electoral Organizing in the Passage of Anti-Discrimination Laws: The Case of

Connecticut," *Journal of Gay & Lesbian Social Services,* 16 (2004), 35–53. *Academic Search Premier,* EBSCO*host* http://web.ebscohost.com/ehost/pdf?vid=5&hid=107&sid=c15c4881-cc8a-4405-8ba9-237024600892%40sessionmgr111 (accessed April 23, 2008).

53. Ibid., 40.
54. Ibid., 43–44.
55. Ibid., 47.
56. Melanie D. Otis, "One Community's Path to Greater Social Justice: Building on Earlier Successes," *Journal of Gay & Lesbian Social Services,* 16 (2004), 17–33. *Academic Search Premier,* EBSCO*host,* http://web.ebscohost.com/ehost/pdf?vid=4&hid=107&sid=0a43cea7-1d96-4be1-8b44-8f818f306c95%40sessionmgr104 (accessed April 23, 2008).
57. Ibid., 20.
58. Ibid., 24–25.
59. Ibid., 28.
60. Jerold M. Starr, "The Challenges and Rewards of Coalition Building: Pittsburgh's Alliance for Progressive Action," *Contemporary Justice Review,* 2, no. 2 (1999), 197. *Academic Search Premier,* EBSCO*host* (accessed April 23, 2008).
61. Ibid.
62. Kenneth Alan Miller, "There is No Alliance for Progressive Action in Pittsburgh," www.thomas-mertoncenter.org/The_New_People/Sept2004/there_is_no_alliance_for_progres.htm. (accessed July 14, 2009).
63. Terry Mizrahi and Beth B. Rosenthal, "Complexities of Coalition Building: Leaders' Successes, Strategies, Struggles, and Solutions," *Social Work,* 46, no. 1 (January 2001), 63–78.
64. Mary Perry Alexander, Ronda C. Zakocs, Jo Anne L. Earp, and Elizabeth French, "Community Coalition Project Directors: What Makes Them Effective Leaders?" *Journal of Public Health Management and Practice,* 12, no. 2 (2006), 201–209. *Journal of Public Health Management and Practice,* http://journals.lww.com/jphmp/Abstract/2006/03000/Community_Coalition_Project_Directors__What_Makes.14.aspx (accessed December 9, 2009).
65. Maureen E. Metzger, Jeffrey A. Alexander, and Bryan J. Weiner, "The Effects of Leadership and Governance Processes on Member Participation in Community Health Organizations," *Health Education & Behavior,* 32, no. 4 (2005), 455–473, Sage Journals Online http://heb.sagepub.com/cgi/reprint/32/4/455 (accessed December 9, 2009).
66. Ibid., 458.
67. Ibid.
68. Mizrahi and Rosenthal, "Complexities of Coalition Building."

Chapter 12

1. Jessica Anne Ritter, "An Empirical Study Evaluating the Political Participation of Licensed Social Workers in the United States: A Multi-State Study," (Ph.D. dissertation, The University of Texas at Austin, United States–Texas, 2006), 107,

Dissertations & Theses: A&I database (Publication No. AAT 3245329) (accessed July 26, 2008).
2. Ibid.
3. Ibid.
4. Ritter, "An Empirical Study."
5. Daniel M. Shea, *Campaign Craft: The Strategies, Tactics, and Art of Political Campaign Management* (Westport, CN: Praeger, 1996).
6. Gary C. Jacobson, *The Politics of Congressional Elections,* 7th ed. (New York: Pearson Longman, 2009).
7. Ibid.
8. Ibid., 66.
9. Ibid., 67.
10. Campaign Finance Institute, "April Presidential Reports: Small Donations Continue to Fuel Democrats; McCain Has His Best Month; Clinton's Debts Rise to $19.5 Million," www.cfinst.org/pr/prRelease.aspx?ReleaseID=191 (accessed May 15, 2008).
11. opensecrets.org, "What is a PAC," www.opensecrets.org/pacs/pacfaq.php (accessed June 30, 2008). *For more information on the role of PACs in elections, see Chapter 11.*
12. Federal Election Commission, "FEC Issues Semi-Annual Federal PAC Count," www.fec.gov/press/press2006/20060223paccount.html (accessed June 30, 2008).
13. Jeffrey M. Berry and Clyde Wilcox, *The Interest Group Society,* 4th ed. (New York: Pearson/Longman, 2007), 17.
14. Federal Election Commission, "FEC Issues Semi-Annual Federal PAC Count" www.fec.gov/press/press2006/20060223paccount.html (accessed June 30, 2008).
15. Stephen R. Weissman and Kara D. Ryan, "Soft Money in the 2006 Election and the Outlook for 2008: The Changing Nonprofits Landscape" (A Campaign Finance Institute Report) www.pewtrusts.org/uploadedFiles/wwwpewtrustsorg/Reports/Campaign_finance_reform/NP_Softmoney_06-08.pdf (accessed May 15, 2008).
16. Berry and Wilcox, *The Interest Group* Opensecrets.org Web site (accessed 30 April, 2008).
17. Ritter, "An Empirical Study."
18. Ibid.
19. NASW Practice Standards, www.socialworkers.org/diversity/intl/012606.asp (accessed April 30, 2008).
20. M. A. Zimmerman, and S. Warchausky, "Empowerment Theory for Rehabilitation Research: Conceptual Methodological Issues," *Rehabilitation Psychology,* 43 (1998), 5; See also, D. M. Linhorst, *Empowering People with Severe Mental Illness* (Oxford University Press, 2005).
21. NASW Pace, "Vote," www.naswnys.org/members_only/pace_06/voter.htm (accessed July 30, 2008).
22. Ibid.
23. M. Hanrahan, S. Matorin, and D. Borland, "Promoting Competence through Voter Registration," *Social Work,* 31, no. 2 (March–April 1986), 142.

24. NASW, "Demographics of Social Workers in Elected Offices, 2005," www.socialworkers.org/pace/characteristics.asp (accessed July 28, 2008).

25. NASW, "Why Social Workers Should Run for Office," www.socialworkers.org/pace/why_run.asp (accessed June 20, 2008).

26. NASW, "MN-PACE (Political Action for Candidate Endorsement)," www.naswmn.org/displaycommon.cfm?an=6 (accessed July 30, 2008).

27. S. Lerner, "Friday Faceoff: Allowing Millionaires' Expenditures on Election Campaigns is Unfair," *Rochester Democrat and Chronicle* (July 18, 2008). www.democratandchronicle.com/apps/pbcs.dll/article?AID=/20080718/OPINION02/807180348/1039/OPINION (accessed July 30, 2008).

28. A. Gierzynski, *Money Rules: Financing Elections in America* (Boulder, CO: Westview Press, 2000); R. K., Goidel, D. A. Gross, and T. G. Shields, *Money Matters: Consequences of Campaign Finance Reform in U.S. House Election* (Lanham, MD: Rowman & Littlefield, 1999); G. C. Jacobson, *Money in Congressional Elections* (New Haven, CT: Yale University Press, 1980).

29. G. W. Cox and J. N. Katz. *Elbridge Gerry's Salamander: The Electoral Consequences of the Reapportionment Revolution* (Cambridge: Cambridge University Press, 2002); Gary C. Jacobson, *The Politics of Congressional Elections* 7th ed. (New York: Longman, 2009); Richard G. Niemi and Alan I. Abramowitz. "Partisan Redistricting and the 1992 Congressional Redistricting," *The Journal of Politics*, 56 (1994), 811–817.

30. Federal Election Commission, "Campaign Finance Law Quick Reference for Reporters," www.fec.gov/press/bkgnd/bcra_overview.shtml (accessed July 28, 2008).

31. Kenneth R. Mayer, Timothy Werner, and Amanda Williams, "Do Public Funding Programs Enhance Electoral Competition?" (Paper presented at the Fourth Annual Conference on State Politics and Policy Laboratories of Democracy: Public Policy in the American States, Kent State University, April 30–May 1, 2004; updated March 2005), campfin.polisci.wisc.edu/Wisc%20Camp%20Fin%20Proj%20-%20Public%20Funding%20and%20Competition.pdf (accessed July 25, 2008); Thomas Stratman, "Some Talk: Money in Politics. A (Partial) Review of the Literature," *Public Choice* (2005), 124.

32. Mayer et al., 2005.

Chapter 13

1. Robert Pear, "New Rules Force States to Curb Welfare Rolls", *New York Times,* 28 June 2006, http://nytimes.com/2006/06/28/washington/28welfare.html (accessed June 28, 2006).

2. Ibid.

3. Jerry Friedman, *Policy & Practice of Public Human Services,* Director's Memo, September 2006, 3, *Academic Search Premier* EBSCO*host* (accessed August 30, 2009).

4. Phyllis Day, *A New History of Social Welfare,* 6th ed. (Boston: Allyn & Bacon, 2009), 479.

5. Robert Pear, "New Rules Force States to Curb Welfare Rolls".

6. Ibid.

7. Ibid.

8. Ibid.

9. Sheri Steisel and Jack Tweedie, "TANF Rules Tough on States," *State Legislatures,* 32, no. 3, March 1, 2006, page 23, *Academic Search Premier* EBSCO*whost* (accessed August 30, 2009).

10. Jerry Friedman, *Policy & Practice of Public Human Services* Director's Memo.

11. Michael Lipsky, *Street-level Bureaucracy* (New York: Russell Sage Foundation, 1980).

12. Jan Hagen and Judith Owens-Manley, "Issues in Implementing TANF in New York: The Perspective of Frontline Workers," *Social Work,* 47, no. 2 (April 2002), 171–182, *Academic Search Premier* EBSCO*host* (accessed August 30, 2009).

13. Amy Goldstein, "Privatization Backlash in Indiana: Plan to Turn Over Toll Road to Foreign Firms Spawns Political Storm," *Post-Gazette.com, Pittsburgh Post-Gazette,* June 18, 2006, www.post-gazette.com/pg/06169/698927–84.stm#ixzz0Opo21GVm accessed August 21, 2009.

14. James Austin and Garry Coventry, "Emerging Issues on Privatized Prisons," Monograph, Bureau of Justice Assistance, U.S. Department of Justice, NCJ 181249, February 2001, www.ncjrs.gov/pdf-files1/bja/181249.pdf, (accessed August 21, 2009).

15. Celia Hagert, "Learn from Texas Privatization Disaster," *The Journal Gazette,* August 27, 2007, www.journalgazette.net/apps/pbcs.dll/article?AID=/20070827/EDIT05/708270361 (accessed November 9, 2007).

16. Ken Kusmer, "ACS, vying for $1Billion State Contract, had Problems Elsewhere" *Associated Press Financial Wire,* August 21, 2006, Lexis Nexis Academic www.lexisnexis.com/us/lnacademic/results/docview/docview.do?risb=21_T8127130434&treeMax=true&sort=RELEVANCE&docNo=68&format=GNBFULL&startDocNo=51&treeWidth=0&nodeDisplayName=&cisb=22_T812713042&reloadPage=false (accessed December 10, 2009).

17. Ken Kusmer, "AP NewsBreak: FSSA Postpones Rollout of Privatization," *The Associated Press State & Local Wire,* October 19, 2007, Lexis Nexis Academic, www.lexisnexis.com/us/lnacademic/results/docview/docview.do?docLinkInd=true&risb=21_T7238379896&format=GNBFI&sort=RELE-VANCE&startDocNo=1&resultsUrlKey=29_T7238379899&cisb=22_T7238379898&treeMax=true&treeWidth=0&csi=304481&docNo=7 (accessed August 21, 2009).

18. Ken Kusmer, "Critics Call for Daniels, Lawmakers to Investigate Privatization," *The Associated Press State & Local Wire,* March 11, 2008, Lexis Nexis Academic, www.lexisnexis.com/us/lnacademic/results/docview/docview.do?docLinkInd=true&risb=21_T7238608589&format=GNBFI&sort=RELE-VANCE&startDocNo=1&resultsUrlKey=29_T7238608595&cisb=22_T7238608594&treeMax=true&tree

Width=0&csi=304481&docNo=18 (accessed August 1, 2009).

19. "State Sen. Simpson to Host Town Meeting on Family and Social Services Agency Privatization," *US States News,* June 18, 2008, Lexis Nexis Academic, www.lexisnexis.com/us/lnacademic/ results/docview/docview.do?docLinkInd=true&risb =21_T7238533206&format=GNBFI&sort=RELE- VANCE&startDocNo=1&resultsUrlKey=29_T723853 3209&cisb=22_T7238533208&treeMax=true&tree Width=0&csi=296938&docNo=1 (accessed August 21, 2009).

20. Ken Kusmer, "State Welfare Contract Ballooning: Amendments, Additional Work Add $180 million to Fees Paid to IBM," *The Journal Gazette,* August 4, 2009, www.journalgazette.net/apps/pbcs.dll/ article?AID=/20090804/LOCAL/308049971/1002/LO CAL&template=printart, (accessed August 31, 2009); Richard Gootee and Bryan Corbin, "Welfare Rollout Criticized: Bills Would Halt System's Spread," *Courierpress.com,* February 3, 2009, www.courierpress.com/news/2009/aug/04/welfare- woes-the-issue-state-paying-millions-our/ (accessed August 21, 2009).

21. States News Service, DeLauro Statement on Suspension of Indiana's Effort to Privatize Social Services, July 31, 2008, Lexis Nexis Academic, www.lexisnexis.com/us/lnacademic/results/docview/ docview.do?docLinkInd=true&risb=21_T718689921 8&format=GNBFI&sort=RELEVANCE&startDocNo= 1&resultsUrlKey=29_T7186899221&cisb=22_T7186 899220&treeMax=true&treeWidth=0&csi=8058&doc No=3 (accessed August 21, 2009).

22. Ken Kusmer, "Ind. Streamlines Welfare Applications After Gripes," *Associated Press Financial Wire,* April 6, 2009, Lexis Nexis Academic, www.lexisnexis.com/us/lnacademic/ results/docview/docview.do?docLinkInd=true&risb =21_T7238868943&format=GNBFI&sort=RELE- VANCE&startDocNo=1&resultsUrlKey=29_T723886 8946&cisb=22_T7238868945&treeMax=true&treeWi dth=0&csi=288311&docNo=1 (accessed August 31, 2009).

23. "FSSA's Overdue Step," *The Journal Gazette,* 7, February 7, 2009, www.journalgazette.net/apps/ pbcs.dll/article?AID=/20090207/EDIT07/30207998 4 (accessed August 21, 2009).

24. Mary Beth Schneider & Bill Ruthart, "Indiana Axes Welfare Contract with IBM: Governor Cancels $1.34 B IBM Deal, Saying Welfare Plan Was 'Failed Concept,' " Indystar.com, www.indystar.com/apps/ pbcs.dll/article?AID=/20091016NEWS05/910160379/ Ind (accessed October 21, 2009).

25. "USDA: States Fall Short in Administering Food Stamps," *The Herald Times,* November 28, 2009, B12.

26. E.S. Casper, "A Formative Evaluation of a Rent Subsidy Program for Homeless Substance Abusers," *Journal of Social Service Research,* 31, no. 2 (2004), 25–39.

27. Committee on Ways and Means, U.S. House of Representatives, "Child Support Enforcement Program," *2004, Green Book* (Washington DC: Section 8), http://frWebgate.access.gpo.gov/cgi-

bin/getdoc.cgi?dbname=108_green_book&docid= f:wm006_08.pdf (accessed July 9, 2008).

28. Ibid. Section 8, Table 8–1, 6.

29. U.S. Census Bureau, "Historical Poverty Tables: Table 3—Poverty Status by Age, Race and Hispanic Origin, 1959–2006," August, 2007, www.census. gov/hhes/www/poverty/histpov/hstpov3.html, (accessed July 9, 2008).

30. H. Hileren, *School Breakfast Cost/Benefit Analysis: Achieving a Profitable SBP,* (Madison WI: University of Wisconsin, 2007), http://dpi.wi.gov/ fns/pdf/sbp_cost_benefit_analysis.pdf (accessed July 9, 2008).

31. Urban Institute Policy Centers, "Assessing the New Federalism," www.urban.org/center/anf/index.cfm (accessed August 31, 2009).

32. Ed Risler, Larry Nackerud, Christopher Larrison, Rebecca Rdesinski, Alison Glover, and Lea Lane-Crea, *The Georgia Welfare Reform Research Project: The Remaining TANF Recipients, A Research Based Profile*, Report #2. (University of Georgia School of Social Work, 1999).

33. "Editorial: Mission Unaccomplished," *The New York Times/nytimes.com,* August 24, 2006, www.nytimes.com/2006/08/24/opinion/24thu1. html?th=&emc=th&pagewanted=print (accessed August 24, 2006).

34. Vicki Lens, "TANF: What Went Wrong and What to do Next," *Social Work,* 47 (July 2002).

35. "Editorial: Mission Unaccomplished," *The New York Times/nytimes.com,* August 24, 2006, www.nytimes.com/2006/08/24/opinion/24thu1. html?th=&emc=th&pagewanted=print (accessed August 24, 2006).

36. U.S. Government Accountability Office (n.d.), *About GAO,* gao.gov/about/index.html (accessed July 9, 2008)

37. U.S. Congressional Research Services (n.d.), *About CRS,* www.loc.gov/crsinfo/whatscrs.html (accessed July 9, 2008).

38. The idea for this paragraph came from J. H. Karger, and D. Stoesz, *American Social Welfare Policy: A Pluralist Approach*, 5th ed. (Boston: Allyn & Bacon, 2006).

39. U. S. Government Accountability Office, "Hurricane Katrina: Barriers to Mental Health Services for Children Persist in Greater New Orleans, Although Federal Grants Are Helping to Address Them (Summary)" www.gao.gov/ products/ GAO-09–935T (accessed August 21, 2009).

40. U.S. GAO—Reports and Testimonies Browse by Topic, U.S. Government Accountability Office, www.gao.gov/docsearch/topic.php (accessed August 21, 2009).

41. Center for Program Evaluation, "Center for Child and Family Policy (n.d.) www.childandfamily policy.duke.edu/evalsvcs/index.html (accessed July 9, 2008).

42. Center for Program Evaluation (n.d.), Division of Health Sciences, University of Nevada, Reno, http:// hhs.unr.edu/cpe/ (accessed July 9, 2008).

Chapter 14

1. National Association of Social Workers, *Code of Ethics* (Washington, DC: NASW Press, 1996), 27.
2. Ibid., 5.
3. Marc Ambinder, "The Rise of the Alinsky Explanation," *The Atlantic* (August 2009), http://politics.theatlantic.com/2009/08/conservatives_learn_the_rules_for_radicals.php (accessed August 22, 2009).
4. The American Sociological Association, "The Sociological Significance of Barack Obama," www.asanet.org/cs/root/leftnav/meetings/the_sociological_significance_of_president_barack_obama (accessed August 20, 2009).
5. The White House, "About the Office of Public Engagement," www.whitehouse.gov/ope/about/ (accessed August 21, 2009).
6. The White House, "Citizens Briefing Book," www.whitehouse.gov/assets/documents/Citizens_Briefing_Book_Final2.pdf (accessed August 18, 2009).
7. Organizing for America, "About Organizing for America," www.barackobama.com/learn/about_ofa.php (accessed August 28, 2009).
8. Jim Rutenberg and Adam Nagourney, "Melding Obama's Web to a YouTube Presidency," *The New York Times,* January 25, 2009, www.nytimes.com/2009/01/26/us/politics/26grassroots.html?_r=1 (accessed August 22, 2009).
9. Christopher Hass, "Thursday: Strategy Meeting with the President," Organizing for America blog, posted August 18, 2009, http://my.barackobama.com/page/content/hqblog (accessed August 28, 2009).
10. Associated Press, "Young Obama Backers Skip Health Care Fight," *MSNBC,* August 24, 2009, www.msnbc.msn.com/id/32542988/ns/politics-more_politics/ (accessed August 28, 2009).
11. Ibid.
12. Peter Walker, "Is the Worst of the Economic Downturn Over?" *CNN,* May 11, 2009, www.cnn.com/2009/BUSINESS/05/11/execed.economy.

downturn/ (accessed August 22, 2009); Online NewsHour, "U.S. Economic Downturn Worsened at End of 2008," March 26, 2009, www.pbs.org/newshour/updates/business/jan-june09/economy_03–26.html (accessed August 22, 2009); United Nations Conference on Trade and Development, "UNCTAD Officials Say UN Should Be Involved, All Countries' Interests Reflected in Response to Financial Crisis," October 16, 2008, www.unctad.org/Templates/webflyer.asp?docid=10721&intItemID=4697&lang=1 (accessed August 22, 2009).
13. GivingUSA Foundation, "U.S. Charitable Giving Estimated to $307.65 Billion in 2008," June 10, 2009, www.givingusa.org/press_releases/gusa/GivingReaches300billion.pdf (accessed August 22, 2009).
14. Ibid.
15. Ibid.
16. CNN International, "IMF: Nascent Recovery Under Way," August 20, 2009, http://edition.cnn.com/2009/BUSINESS/08/19/imf.recovery.ft.ft/ (accessed August 30, 2009).
17. See, for example, "S.E.C. Audit Urges Changes to Rating Agency Rules," *New York Times,* August 28, 2009, http://dealbook.blogs.nytimes.com/2009/08/28/sec-audit-urges-changes-to-rating-agency-rules/ (accessed August 30, 2009).
18. Mark Potok, "SPLC's Intelligence Report: Hate Group Numbers Rise Again," Southern Poverty Law Center, February 28, 2009, www.splcenter.org/blog/2009/02/28/intelligence-report-hate-group-numbers-rise-again/, (accessed August 28, 2009).
19. Jerome C. Glenn, Theodore J. Gordon, and Elizabeth Florescu, *2009, State of the Future* (Washington, DC: The Millennium Project, 2009). Executive summary available online at www.millennium-project.org/millennium/sof2009.html#print.
20. Jane Watkins (past president, National Association of Foster Grandparent Program Directors), interview, August, 2009.
21. Ibid.

Photo Credits

Chapter 1:
Marc Pokempner/Stone/Getty Images, p. 1; Kevin Horan/Getty Images, p.17

Chapter 2:
Tony Linck/Getty Images/Time Life Pictures, p.26; Grey Villet (Time & Life pictures)/Getty Images, p. 41

Chapter 3:
Jonathan Nourok/Stone/Getty Images, p.49; Brandi Pierce/Dreamstime.com, p.66

Chapter 4:
Brian F Alpert/Hulton Archive/Getty Images, p.76; FPG (Retrofile)/Getty Images, p.99

Chapter 5:
Robyn Mackenzie/Getty Images—IStock Exclusive RF, p.101; Gandee Vasan (photographer's choice)/Getty Images, p.117

Chapter 6:
Jonathan Nourok/Getty Images, Inc./Riser, p.121; Digital Vision (Digital Vision)/Getty Images, p.136

Chapter 7:
Robert E Daemmrich/Stone/Getty Images, p.143; Jpa 1999/istockphoto, p.156

Chapter 8:
Robert E Daemmrich/Stone/Getty Images, p.169; Ojo Images (Workbook Stock)/Getty Images, p.198

Chapter 9:
Yellow Dog Productions/Getty Images, Inc./Riser, p.209; Brent Stirton (Reportage)/Getty Images, p.234

Chapter 10:
David Joyner/Getty Images—IStock Exclusive RF, p. 241; Rubberball/Getty Images, p.262

Chapter 11:
Hisham Ibrahim/Photographer's Choice/Getty Images, p.281; Loren Santow (Stone)/Getty Images, p.306

Chapter 12:
Tetra Images/Getty Images, Inc./Tetra Images Royalty Free, p.318; Tdmartin/Dreamstime.com, p.324

Chapter 13:
Jose Luis Pelaez/Getty Images, Inc., p.346; jingwuming/istockphoto, p.354

Chapter 14:
Ron Sherman/Stone/Getty Images, p.366; Noel Hendrickson (Photographer's Choice RF)/Getty Images, p.373

Index

527 groups, 322, 323

A
Abbott, Edith, 36
Abbott, Grace, 37
Abortion, party platforms on, 58
Abramoff, Jack, 256
Addams, Jane
  at Hull House, 27–29
  Nobel Peace Prize, 37
Adequacy, 213, 217
Adler, Felix, 102
Adobe Acrobat Connect Pro, 302
Advocacy
  definition of, 9
  for policy change, 10
Advocacy publics, 153
Advocacy web sites, 158–160
Advocates, 257
Affordable Green Housing Simulated Case Study, 272, 274
Affordable Health Care Act of 2010, 189–190. *See also* Health care reform
Agenda-setting news flow, 146
Aid to Families with Dependent Children (AFDC)
  coalitions and, 282
  end of, 43
  family cap, 21
  policy evaluation and change, 204–205
  in welfare reform case study, 18
Albright, Madeleine, 77
Alinksy, Saul, 50
Allen, Mike, 66
Alleviative policy interventions, 219–222
Alliance for Progressive Action (APA), 314
American Recovery and Reinvestment Act of 2009, 91, 97
Americans with Disabilities Act of 1990, 311
Amicus curiae brief, 11, 12, 134
Anderson (Saenz) v. Roe, 12
Anspach v. City of Philadelphia, 12
Anti-Federalists, 53–54
Antitrust laws, 94
APA (Alliance for Progressive Action), 314
Aristotle, 104
Assessment skills, 19–20
Attentiveness, 231–232, 234, 237, 362
"Attorney's Fees and the Individuals with Disabilities Education Act Myths and Realities," 253–254

B
Bachelor in Social Work (BSW) programs, 34
Bailey, Darlyne, 284, 310
Bailey, David M., 56
Balz, Dan, 74
Bane, Mary Jo, 129
Barusch, Amanda, 9, 10
BCRA (Bipartisan Campaign Reform Act) of 2002, 338
Berry, Jeffrey M., 259, 260
Bill of Rights, 54, 55
Bipartisan Campaign Reform Act (BCRA) of 2002, 338
Blackman, Ann, 6
Blau, J., 187
Blogs, 160, 161
Blue Dog Democrats, 71–72
Bonelli, John, 312
Bounded rationality, 183
Branding, 300
Brasher, Holly, 287
Browder v. Gayle, 40, 42
Brown, M., 161
Brown v. Board of Education, 39, 42, 135
Browne, William P., 296
Budget analysis of social problems, 212–213
Budget process, 349–350
Burke, Edmund, 210
Bush, George W., 45–46, 65, 95
Business cycles, 95–96
Butterfoss, F. D., 296
Byers, Kathy, 139, 154, 162, 266

C
Campaign finance reform, 338–343
Campaigns, 318–345
  benefits of social worker political participation, 319–320
  campaign organizations, 325
  contribution limits, 339
  instant messaging, 326
  introduction to, 319–320
  launching, 10
  laws and ethics of, 337–343
    campaign finance reform, 338–343
    contribution limits, 339
    state clean election laws, 341–342
  overview of processes, 320–327
    media, 326–327

resources, 321–323
staffing, 323–325
plan components, 321
roles for social work profession, 336–337
social workers as candidates, 331
social workers in
Jason Carnes, 330–331
Karen Persichilli Keogh, 329
social workers' roles, 327–329
Careers in policy practice, 121–142
overview of, 126–127
case study, 122–125
community settings
campaign director or worker on a campaign, 136
direct service practitioners, 140
grass roots organizer of community groups, 140
informal opportunities to be a policy advocate,
140–141
lobbyists, 137
part-time or volunteer policy advocate, 137
policy practitioner/education, 138
professional associations, 141
research/policy analysis positions, 137–138
concept map of, 126
executive settings
advisor/staff to policymaker, 130
appointed executive policymaker, 128–129
direct service worker, 131
elected executive, 127–128
role of agency board in making policy, 130
introduction to, 122
judicial settings
advocate in judge appointment processes, 135–136
amicus curiae briefs, 134–135
consultants in judge education programs, 135
elected judge, 135
expert witness, 134
legislative settings
legislative assistant/constituent services, 133–134
legislative policymaker, 131–133
roles by setting and environmental level, 128
social workers as policymakers
administrators, 179
advocates, 176
community organizers, 178
direct service workers, 175
managers, 179
planners, 178–179
researchers, 176–178
Carnes, Jason, 330–331
Case finding, 189
Casper, E. S., 354
Catholic Charities, 282
Catholic Church, 21
Causal chain, 226
CED (Community economic development), 309

Center for Disease Control, 189
Chambers, D. E., 229
Charity Organization Societies, 29–31
Chicago Bar Association, 30
Chicago Civic Federation, 28
Chicago Women's Club, 30
"Child saving" movement, 27–28
Child labor laws, 32
Children's Bureau, 33
Child support program statistics, 355
Children's Health Insurance Program (SCHIP), 132, 260
Christian Right, 69
Civic and social responsibility, 50–53
Civil rights movement, 39–40, 242–243
Clark, Elizabeth J., 2
Classic conservatives, 68
Clients, involving in advocacy efforts, 278–279
Clinton, Bill, 6
Clinton, Hillary, 65, 74
CMHC (Community mental health centers), 90, 225
Coalition building, 10, 281–317
introduction to, 282–283
agenda for inclusion, 293–296
finding common ground, 294
integrating new members, 295–296
inviting others to attend meetings, 294–295
challenges, 305–308
disagreements, 305–306
fund raising, 308
power sharing, 307
staying organized, 307
characteristics of successful coalitions, 310–315
coalitions vs. networks, 283
committees, 303–304
creation of ongoing networks of influence, 308–309
development of
building the group's expertise, 298–300
critical indicators of development progress, 297–298
engaging participants in action, 302
identity, 300–302
involving members in organizational structure,
303–305
development stages, 296–305
electronic newsletter, 299
formation of, 283–293
defining, 283–287
identifying likely allies, 288
membership pros and cons, 287–288
problems and goals, 288–290
recruitment strategies, 291–293
leadership, importance of, 315
success, 316
Coalition on Human Needs, 285, 286, 299, 301
Cohen, Wilbur, 41
Collaboration, 217, 219
Columbia University Graduate School of Social Work, 34

Common ground, 22
Communication skills, 20
Communication strategies, for policy campaigns, 151–155
Community economic development (CED), 309
Community Mental Health Act of 1963, 90
Community mental health centers (CMHC), 90, 225
Community settings, social work roles in, 136–141
    overview of, 128
    campaign director or worker on a campaign, 136
    direct service practitioners, 140
    grass roots organizer of community groups, 140
    informal opportunities to be a policy advocate,
        140–141
    lobbyists, 137
    part-time or volunteer policy advocate, 137
    policy practitioner/education, 138
    professional associations, 141
    research/policy analysis positions, 137–138
Competence, 232–233, 235, 238, 363
Congress, underrepresentation of women and
        minorities in, 87. *See also* Legislative process
Congressional Research Office (CRS), 359
Consequential perspective, 103, 106–107
Conservative political ideology, 68–70
Consortium for Citizens with Disabilities, 252, 311
Contribution limits, 339
Conyers bill, 16
Corporate welfare, 85
Cost/benefit evaluation, 354, 356
Council on Social Work Education, 34, 42, 44–45
Courtney, Mark E., 42–43
"Creating a Powerhouse Coalition," 290
CRS (Congressional Research Office), 359
Curative policy interventions, 219–222

D
Data collection and analysis, 191–193
Data presentation, countering negative perceptions,
        253–254
Day, Phyllis, 27, 41
Dean, Howard, 57, 63, 156–157
Defensive lobbying, 262–263
DeLauro, Rose L., 352, 353
DeLay, Tom, 256
Democratic Leadership Council (DLC), 74
Democratic National Committee (DNC), 57, 63
Democratic Party
    Great Depression and, 65
    national committee, 57, 63–64
    platforms on prominent issues, 58–63
Democratic-Republican Party, 57
Deontological perspective, 104, 106–107
Devine, Edward T., 31
Diagnostic Related Groups, 43
DiNitto, D. M., 184
Direct lobbying, 264
Direct service workers, 189

Discrimination, 31, 36
Distributive justice, 103, 106–107, 108
DLC (Democratic Leadership Council), 74
DNC (Democratic National Committee), 57, 63
Documentation, 189
Dolgoff, R., 229
Domestic violence, 251
Doughnut hole, 189, 190
Downey, Kristin, 36–37
Downey, Laura M., 296

E
Earned Income Tax Credit (EITC), 6, 123
EBT (Evidence-Based Practice), 357
Economic conservatives, 68–69
Economic forces, role in policy formation, 93–98
Economic theories, 93–98
Economy
    fairness of, 98
    party platforms on, 58–59
    role of and function as social institution, 80, 81–82
Edelman, Peter B., 129
Editorial boards, 147
Education
    first social work school established, 34
    party platforms on, 59–60
Edward M. Kennedy Serve America Act of 2009, 51–52
EESA (Emergency Economic Stabilization Act of
        2008), 248–249
EITC (Earned Income Tax Credit), 6, 123
Election law, 337–343
    campaign finance reform, 338–343
    contribution limits, 339
    state clean election laws, 341–342
Electronic newsletter, 299
E-mail, 157–158, 271, 301
Emergency Economic Stabilization Act of 2008
        (EESA), 248–249
Endorsements, 261–262
Energy, party platforms on, 60
Engagement skills, 19
Environmental levels and settings, 11–16
Equality, 217, 218–219
Equity, 217, 218
Ethic of care
    overview of, 104–105
    components of, 105
    elements of care
        attentiveness, 231–232, 234, 237, 362
        competence, 232–233, 235, 238, 363
        responsibility, 232, 234–235, 237–238, 362–363
    vs. other ethical frameworks, 106–107
    policy analysis for rescinding the lowest bidder rule,
        237–238
    policy analysis framework, 230–239
        overview of, 234–236
        application of model, 236–239

framework, 233–236
  traditional language vs. ethic of care language, 231
values, 219
Ethical dilemmas, steps for resolving, 118
Ethical lobbying, 263–266
Ethics, code of, 8–9, 23, 106–108, 109–111
Ethics in policy practice, 101–120
  introduction to, 102
  application of ethical decision making, 115–119
  boundaries of, 109–115
    overview of, 109
    laws, 113–115
    NASW Code of Ethics, 8–9, 23, 106–108, 109–111
    NASW standards for advocacy and political
      action, 111–112
    societal norms and personal beliefs, 115
  core values/ethical principles, 108
  elements of care
    integration of care, 233, 235–236, 238, 363–364
    responsiveness, 233, 235, 238, 363
  empowering clients in policy arena, 111
  ethical frameworks, 103–108
    comparison of, 106–107
Evaluation of policy implementation and outcomes,
    346–365
  introduction to, 347
  budget process, 349–350
  common questions for, 361–364
  context of, 357
  importance of, 350
  Indiana Family and Social Services Administration
    privatization case study, 255, 351–354
  policy analysis framework, 362–364
  resources, 359–361
  rulemaking case example, 348–349
  rulemaking process, 347–348
  types of, 354–357
  welfare reform policy evaluation case example,
    358–359
Evidence-Based Practice (EBT), 357
Executive settings, social work roles in, 127–131
  overview of, 128
  advisor/staff to policymaker, 130
  appointed executive policymaker, 128–129
  direct service worker, 131
  elected executive, 127–128
  role of agency board in making policy, 130

F
Facebook, 165, 166
Factoria. *See* Health Care Reform Simulated Case Study
Faculty profiles, 138–139
Fairness Ordinance, 313
False dichotomy, 32
Family, role of and function as social institution, 80
Family and Social Service Administration (FSSA),
  255, 351–354

Family cap, 282
Federal Election Campaign Act (FECA), 322
Federal Emergency Management Agency (FEMA), 77
Federal poverty guidelines, 213–216
Federalist No. 10, 257
Federalist Party, 57
Federalists, 53–54
Feldstein, D., 229
FEMA (Federal Emergency Management Agency), 77
Figueroa, Juan, 312
Fine, Alison, 156
Fisher, B., 229
Fishman, M., 145
Flexner, Abraham, 34
Formative evaluation, 354, 356
Fosdick, Harry Emerson, 50
Foster grandparents program case study, 274–277
Fox, Sam, 323
Frederick, John, 212
Freud, Sigmund, 34
Friedman, Jerry, 349
Friedman, Milton, 97
Friendly Visiting Among the Poor (Richmond), 33
"Friendly visitors," 30, 52
"Friends of the court," 134
FSSA (Family and Social Service Administration),
  255, 351–354

G
GAO (Government Accountability Office), 359–361
Gay marriage, 60, 79
Gay Marriage Simulated Case Study, 144, 294, 305,
  307, 368
Generalist practice, 9, 16–17, 21–22
GI Bill of Rights, 38
Gienapp, A., 165
Gilbert, Neil, 228
Goddard, Chris, 212
Goldwater, Barry, 68
GoToMeeting.com, 302
Government Accountability Office (GAO), 359–361
Gramm, Phil, 282
Grassroots lobbying, 264
Great Depression and the New Deal, 35–38, 64–65
Green Party, 64
Greenbaum, Jon, 40
Grigsby, Tamara, 332
Grutter v. Bollinger, 135
Gustafson, Howard, 242

H
Hagen, Jan, 350
Half a Man (Ovington), 35–36
Hamilton, Alexander, 54
Hatch Act, 113–115
Hate groups, 372–373
Head Start, 41

Health care, party platforms on, 60–61
Health care reform, 370. *See also* Affordable Health Care Act of 2010
Health Care Reform Bill. *See* Affordable Health Care Act of 2010
Health Care Reform Simulated Case Study
    case studies of the uninsured, 193
    coalition formation, 288–290, 296, 302, 316
    "Creating a Powerhouse Coalition," 290
    media, 144
    organization, 307
    policy goals, 197
    policymaking models, 189–200
    political empowerment, 367
Hessen, Robert, 94
Highlander Folk School, 40
"Highlights of the Edward M. Kennedy Serve America Act," 51
HIV/AIDS, 187–188, 189
HLOGA (Honest Leadership and Open Government Act of 2007), 263–264
Hoefer, Richard, 284
Homelessness
    initiative to help end, 221–222
    policymaking models, 187
    social problem analysis, 224–228
Honest Leadership and Open Government Act of 2007 (HLOGA), 263–264
"Hoovervilles", 35
Hooper, Earlene, 334–335
Hoosiers for a Commonsense Health Plan, 292
Hopkins, Harry, 36
Horton, Myles, 40
Hospital Survey and Construction Act of 1946, 38
HSCO (Human Services Coalition of Oregon), 285
Hugman, R., 229
Hull House, 27–29
Human Services Coalition of Oregon (HSCO), 285
Humanistic liberals, 70–71
Hutchings, Gail P., 221

I
Iatridis, D., 17
Ideologies. *See* Political ideologies
Illinois Board of Public Charities, 30
Illinois Conference of Charities and Corrections, 30
Immigration, party platforms on, 61
Immigration Acts of 1921 and 1924, 31
In re Gault, 42
Inclusion, 217, 219
Incremental model of policymaking, 180, 184–186
Indiana Coalition for Human Services, 308
Indiana Family and Social Service Administration (FSSA), 255, 351–354
Individuals with Disabilities Education Act, 253–254
Instant messaging, 326
Integration of care, 233, 235–236, 238, 363–364

Interdependence, 218, 219
Interest groups, 256–262. *See also* Lobbying
    endorsements, 261–262
    expertise in areas of specialization, 262
    money and, 261
    political parties and, 260–261
    power, sources of, 261–262
    recent growth of, 258–261
    role of in U.S. political and economic contexts, 259–261
    theoretical approaches to understanding, 257–258
International Workers of the World, 35
Interviews, 150
Iraq War, 62, 65
Issue framing, 251
Issue identification, 250–252

J
Jansson, Bruce, 9, 10, 32
Jefferson, Thomas, 259
Jobless benefits, 36–37
Johnson, Alice K., 17, 23
Judicial settings, social work roles in, 134–136
    overview of, 128
    advocate in judge appointment processes, 135–136
    amicus curiae briefs, 134–135
    consultants in judge education programs, 135
    elected judge, 135
    expert witness, 134
Justice, distributive, 103, 106–107, 108
Juvenile court, development of, 28, 30
Juvenile Court Law of 1899, 30

K
K Street Project, 256
Kaine, Tim, 64
Kansas Healthy Choices program, 202–203
Kant, Immanuel, 104
Kantian ethics, 104, 106–107
Karger, H. J., 229
Katz, Michael, 31, 34
Kelley, Florence, 35
Kennedy, John F., 39, 50, 90
Kennedy v. Louisiana, 134
Kentucky Fairness Alliance, 313–314
Keogh, Karen Persichilli, 329
Kerry, John, 323
Keyes, John Maynard, 95
Keynesian economic theory, 94, 95–97
King, Jr., Dr. Martin Luther, 39
Koney, Kelly McNally, 284, 310
Koppelman, Alex, 66
Korgen, Jeff O., 294

L
Lathrop, Julia, 29, 30, 33
Law, election, 337–343
    campaign finance reform, 338–343

contribution limits, 339
state clean election laws, 341–342
Laws, in ethical policy practice, 113–115
Legislative agenda of NASW, 268
Legislative Education and Advocacy Development
(LEAD), 267
Legislative process, 243–256
advocacy as a bill become law flowchart, 246
advocacy roles in, 249–256
overview of, 250
assess and analyze data, 252–253
conference committee, 255
develop, support, and present proposal, 254
generate a proposal/write a bill, 253–254
identify and frame an issue, 250–252
monitoring rule making and implementation, 255
ongoing monitoring to detect changes in need,
255–256
sign bill or veto, 255
assignment to committee, 244–245, 248
changes in legislation, 248–249
Congressional standing committees, 244–245
gay marriage amendment, 247
passed out of committee, 249
state legislatures, 247
U.S. Congress, 247
Legislative settings, social work roles in, 131–134
overview of, 128
legislative assistant/constituent services, 133–134
legislative policymaker, 131–133
Leighninger, L., 229
Lerner, Susan, 337
Lester, L., 9
Letter to the editor, 147, 148
Letter writing, 271–272
Letters to the editor, 147, 148
Lewis, Jenny M., 310
Liberal political ideology, 70–73
Lindblom, Charles, 184–185
LiveMeeting, 302
Lobbying, 262–277. *See also* Interest groups
case study, 274–277
communication not considered lobbying, 264–265
direct, 264
disclosure form, 275
ethics in, 263–266
grassroots, 264
how to, 269–277
letter writing and e-mails, 271–272
talking points, 269–271
testimony, 271–274, 275–277
involvement of clients in advocacy effort, 278–279
proactive vs. defensive, 262–263
social workers as lobbyists, 266–269
Lobbying Act of 1976, 263
Lobbying activities of NASW, 268–269
Lobbying Disclosure Act of 1995, 265, 269

Lobbyist, 257, 263
Lopez, Richard E., 222
Lowe, Gary R., 43
Lowery, David, 287
Lowest bidder rule, 237–238
Low-income family costs for basic needs, 215
Lynch, Rufus Sylvester, 134

M
Madison, James, 54, 257
Maintenance of Effort (MOE), 123
Making the News (Salzman), 147
Masters in Social Work (MSW) programs, 34
MASW (Missouri Association of Social Workers), 309
McCain, John, 89, 325
McCain-Feingold Act, 338
McGovern, George, 72
Meagher, G., 229
Media
in campaigns, 326–327
policy formation, role in, 92–93
Media and public opinion in policy practice, 143–168
introduction to, 144
communication strategies for policy campaigns,
151–155
advocacy publics, 153
communications process, 155
summary model, 154–155
updating supporters, 154
evaluating advocacy communication, 165–167
new media advocacy, 155–165
advocacy web sites, 158–160
blogs, 160, 161
e-mail, 157–158, 271, 301
e-mail and YouTube advocacy, 164
social networking tools, 165
user-generated advocacy, 162–163
White House and, 166
podcasts, 160–165
understanding the news media, 145–146
agenda-setting news flow, 146
news selection factors, 145
working with news media, 147–151
interviews, 150
meeting with editorial boards, 147
pitching story ideas, 147
press conferences, 147–148
press releases, 147–150
writing letters to the editor, 147, 148
writing opinion-editorial pieces, 147
Median income, 98
Medicare Modernization Act of 2003, 189
Medicare Part D, 190
"Mega" coalition, 285
Mental Health Parity and Addiction Equity Act, 249
Micro practice, 7–8
Mikulski, Barbara, 45, 131–132

Milford Conference, 34
Mill, John Stuart, 103
Millennium Project, 373
Miller, Pam, 266
Minorities, underrepresentation of in Congress, 87
Missouri Association of Social Workers (MASW), 309
MOE (Maintenance of Effort), 123
Moe, Terry M., 258
Monetarism, 97
Money, as source of power, 261
Moral uplift, 30
MySpace, 165, 166

N
NAACP, 35, 40
Nader, Ralph, 64
National Association of Social Workers (NASW)
  amicus curiae briefs, 12, 134
  in civil rights movement, 242
  code of ethics, 8–9, 16, 23, 106–108, 109–111
  establishment of, 38
  ethical responsibilities, 367
  legislative agenda, 268
  lobbying activities, 268–269
  lobbying "dos and don'ts," 269–270
  Obama endorsement, 337
  policy priorities for the Obama administration, 46
  political action committee, 336
  practice standards, 108
  role of, 27
  standards for advocacy and political action, 111–112
  Standards for Social Work Practice with Clients with Substance Use Disorders (SUD), 111–112
National Coalition for the Homeless, 187
National committees of political parties, 57, 63–64
National Council of Nonprofit Associations, 265
National Mental Health Act of 1946, 38
National Organizations Responding to AIDS (NORA), 311
National School Lunch Program of 1946, 38
National service, 50–53
Negative campaigning, 338
Negative perceptions, countering, 253–254
Negotiation skills, 20
Neoconservatives, 69–70
Neocorporatism paradigm for understanding interest groups, 257–258
Networking and collaborating skills, 20
New Deal. *See* Great Depression and the New Deal
New Democrats, 72
New media advocacy, 155–165
  advocate in judge appointment processes, 158–160
  blogs, 160, 161
  e-mail, 157–158, 271, 301
  e-mail and YouTube advocacy, 164
  podcasts, 160–165
  postal and e-mail communications to Congress, 158
  social networking tools, 165
  user-generated advocacy, 162–163
  White House and, 166
New York Charity Organization Society, 34
News media, 147–151
  interviews, 150
  meeting with editorial boards, 147
  pitching story ideas, 147
  press conferences, 147–148
  press releases, 147–150
  writing letters to the editor, 147, 148
  writing opinion-editorial pieces, 147
News selection factors, 145
Newsletters, 116, 299
Ney, Robert, 256
Nobel Peace Prize, 37
No Child Left Behind, 8, 10
Noddings, Nel, 104
NORA (National Organization Responding to AIDS), 311
Norquist, Grover, 256

O
Obama, Barack
  2008 presidential election, 65, 89, 157
  campaign organization, 323–324
  civic and social responsibility, 50, 52
  as community organizer, 369
  election of, 39, 50
  lobbying guidelines, 265
  NASW endorsement, 337
  NASW policy priorities for, 46
  political agenda, 91–92
  use of new media, 46
Olson, Mancur, 258
Op-ed pieces (opinion-editorial), 147
Opensecrets.org, 322
Opinion-editorial pieces, 147
Organization initiator, 139
Organizing for America, 370
Outcome evaluation, 354–355, 356
Ovington, Mary White, 35–36
Owens-Manley, Judith, 350

P
PACE (Political Action for Candidate Election), 45, 336
PACs (Political action committees), 259, 322
Parks, Rosa, 39–40
Parrott, Sharon, 18
Parton, N., 229
Party platforms, 58–63
Patronage, 56
People for Change (PFC), 312
Perkins, Frances, 36–37
Perot, Ross, 64
Personal beliefs, 115

Personal Responsibility and Work Opportunity Reconciliation Act of 1996. *See also* Welfare reform
  evaluation case example, 358–359
  passage of, 91
  rational model of policymaking, 181–182
  resignations resulting from, 129
Person-in-environment perspective, 5–7
Perspective, relevance of, 21–22
PFC (People for Change), 312
Planned Parenthood, 282
Plessy v. Ferguson, 33
Pluralism paradigm for understanding interest groups, 257–258
Podcasts, 160–165
Poindexter, Cynthia Cannon, 311
"Poison pills," 249
Policy, 76–100
  definition of, 77–78
  formation of, 79–98
    overview of forces shaping, 79
    economic forces, 93–98
    political economy, 85–88
    social institutions, 80–85
  social welfare system in a democratic-capitalist political economy, 98–99
Policy analysis, 10
Policy analysis framework, 362–364
Policy examples, by setting and environmental level, 14
Policy interventions, 219–222
Policy making organizations, by environmental level, 13
Policy practice, 1–25
  activities, 10
    advocating for policy change, 10
    building coalitions, 10. *See also* Coalition building
    launching a campaign, 10. *See also* Campaigns
    policy analysis, 10
  introduction to, 2–3
  conceptualizing in action
    generalist practice, 16–17
    interactivity of environmental levels and settings, 15–16
    settings and environmental levels, 11–15
  at the core of social work, 3–8
    experiences of social workers, 3–5
    person-in-environment perspective, 5–7
    policy practice vs. micro practice, 7–8
  definitions of, 8–11
  five principles, 17
  future of, 45–46
  micro practice, relationship to, 7–8
  political forces, 88–93
  politics of. *See* Politics of policy practice
  preparation for roles, 23–24
  recommitment to, 23
  retreat from, 34–35
  social work perspective on, 19–23
    ability to find common ground in disputes, 22
    assessment skills, 19–20
    commitment for the long haul, 21–22
    commitment to and belief in the possibility of change, 21
    communication skills, 20
    engagement skills, 19
    generalist practice perspectives, relevance of, 21–22
    networking and collaborating skills, 20
    passion for social justice and empowerment, 22
    problem solving and negotiating skills, 20
    systems perspective in understanding issues, 22
  stakeholders, 10
  strategic use of power, 17
Policy practice, history of, 26–48
  introduction to, 27
  1970s to the present, 42–45
  future of, 45–46
  Great Depression and the New Deal, 35–38
  historical roots in social work's dual focus, 27–31
    Charity Organization Societies, 29–31
    Jane Addams at Hull House, 28–29
  Progressive Era reforms, 31–33
  retreat from activism, 38
  social reforms of the 1960s, 39–42
  social work's first retreat from policy practice, 34–35
  today's social workers, 45
Policymaking, 169–208
  introduction to, 170–175
  approaches to, 179–186
    incremental model, 180, 184–186
    models of, 180
    political model, 180, 183–184
    rational model, 180–183
  process of, 186–207
    building public support and developing coalitions, 198–200
    data collection and analysis, 191–193
    informing the public and identifying stakeholders, 194–196
    policy evaluation and change, 204–205
    policy evaluations, 206–207
    policy implementation, 201–206
    problem identification and case finding, 189–191
    program design, 201, 202
    selecting policy options and developing policy goals, 196–198
    stages of, 188
  social workers as policymakers, 175–179
    administrators, 179
    advocates, 176
    community organizers, 178
    direct service workers, 175

managers, 179
planners, 178–179
researchers, 176–178
Political action committees (PACs), 259, 322
Political Action for Candidate Election (PACE), 45, 336
Political agendas, 90–92
Political economy, 85–88
Political empowerment, 367
Political empowerment, vision for, 366–376
  introduction to, 367–368
  challenges, 370–373
  countering hate groups, 372–373
  making a difference, 374–375
  new strategies, 369–370
  opportunities, 369–370
  overcoming cynicism, 372
  thinking globally, 373
Political forces, 88–93
Political ideologies, 67–73
  conservative, 68–70
  liberals, 70–73
  spectrum of, 67
Political model of policymaking, 180,
    183–184
Political participation, benefits of, 319–320
Political parties
  definition of, 56
  evolution of, 53–66
    Democratic Party, 57
    Democratic-Republican Party, 57
    Federalist Party, 57
    Federalists and Anti-Federalists, 53–54
    national committees, 57, 63–64
    Republican Party, 57
    Whig Party, 57
  Great Depression and the New Deal, 64–65
  interest groups and, 260–261
  major party platforms, 58–63
  platforms on prominent issues, 58–63
    abortion, 58
    economy, 58–59
    education, 59–60
    energy, 60
    gay marriage, 60
    health care, 60–61
    immigration, 61
    Iraq War and War on Terror, 62
    Social Security, 61
    welfare, 62–63
  political ideologies and, 67–73
    conservative, 68–70
    liberals, 70–73
  throughout history, 57
Politics of policy practice, 49–75
  introduction to, 50
  civic and social responsibility, 50–53

political ideologies and political parties, 67–73
political parties, evolution of, 53–66
Politics/government, role of and function as social
    institution, 80, 82
Popple, P. R., 229
Poverty guidelines, 213–216
Power
  sources of for interest groups, 261–262
  strategic use of, 17
Power sharing, 307
Pragmatic liberals, 70
Presidential election of 2008, 65, 66, 89–90
Press conferences, 147–148
Press releases, 51, 147–150
Preventive policy interventions, 219–222
Primus, Wendell, 129
Privatization, 351–354
Proactive lobbying, 262
Problem analysis, 222–228
  causal chain, 226
  sample of, 226
  steps in, 225
  usefulness of, 225–228
Problem solving skills, 20
Process evaluation, 354, 356
Progressive Democrats, 72–73
Progressive Era, 31–33
Progressive Party, 36, 64
Project Coming Home, 221
Public policy. *See also* Policy
Public policy, types of, 78. *See also* Policy
Putnam, Robert, 5

R
Radio talk show host, 138–139
"Raise Poverty Line to Reflect Economic Reality"
    (Schwarz), 214–215
Rational model of policymaking, 180–183
Rawls, John, 103
Recession of 2008, 370–372
Reform Party, 64
Reid, P. Nelson, 43
Reisman, J., 165
Religion, role of and function as social institution, 80
Republican National Committee (RNC), 64
Republican Party, 56, 57, 58–63, 64–65
Responsibility, 232, 234–235, 237–238, 362–363
Responsiveness, 233, 235, 238, 363
Richburg, Keith B., 371
Richmond, Mary, 27, 32–34, 52
Rickards, Lawrence D., 222
Ringquist, Delbert J., 296
RNC (Republican National Committee), 64
Rocha, Cynthia J., 17, 23
Rodriguez, Ciro, 334
Roe v. Wade, 69, 135

Roosevelt, Franklin, 37
Roosevelt, Theodore, 64
Roper v. Simmons, 11
Rosendahl, Bill, 333
Rosenthal, Alan, 287, 291
Rulemaking case example, 348–349
Rulemaking process, 347–348
Ryan White Care Act, 188, 220, 311

S
Sabato, Larry, 66
Salisbury, Lord, 170
Salzman, Jason, 147
Scarbrough, Gayle, 221
SCHIP (State Children's Health Insurance Program), 132, 260
Schneider, Robert, 9, 44, 139
Schorr, Daniel, 144
Schwarz, John E., 214–215
Schwerner, Michael, 39
Seattle Human Services Coalition (SHSC), 289
Second Life, 327
Self-sufficiency standard, 216–217
"Senator Accused of Siding with Centrists" (Balz), 74
Settings, and environmental levels, 11–16
Settlement house movement, 28–29
Sevenhuijsen, S., 229
Sherman, Arloc, 18
Sherraden, Margaret S., 312
Sherraden, Michael, 312
Shields, Chip, 335–336
SHSC (Seattle Human Services Coalition), 289
Simon, Herbert, 182–183
Sinema, Kyrsten, 340, 343
Slosar, Betsy, 312
Social and civic responsibility, 50–53
Social conservatives, 69
Social Diagnosis (Richmond), 34
Social institutions, role of in policy formation, 80–85
Social networking tools, 165
Social policies, 78
Social problem and policy analysis, 209–240
    introduction to, 210–211
    budget analysis, 212–213
    ethic of care policy analysis framework, 230–239
        overview of, 234–236
        application of model, 236–239
        elements of care, 231–233
        framework, 233–236
    ethic of care values, 219
    policy analysis, 228–229
    policy interventions, 219–222
    problem analysis, 222–228
        causal chain, 226
        sample of, 226
        steps in, 225
        usefulness of, 225–228
    theoretical analysis, 211–212
    value perspectives, 213–219
        overview of, 217–218
        adequacy, 213, 217
        collaboration, 217, 219
        equality, 217, 218–219
        equity, 217, 218
        inclusion, 217, 219
        interdependence, 218, 219
Social reforms of the 1960s, 39–42
Social Security Act of 1935, 35, 36, 37
Social Security, party platforms on, 61
Social values, spectrum of, 229
Social welfare
    overview of policies, programs, and benefits, 83–85
    role of and function as social institution, 80
Social welfare policies, 78
Social welfare system, 98–99
Social Work Lobby Days, 266
Social workers in elected office
    Bill Rosendahl, 333
    Chip Shields, 335–336
    Ciro Rodriguez, 334
    Earlene Hooper, 334–335
    Kyrsten Sinema, 340
    Ross Wilburn, 336
    Tamara Grigsby, 332
Societal norms, 115
"The Sociological Significance of President Barack Obama," 369
Specht, Harry, 42–43
Spoils system, 56
Stabenow, Debbie, 45, 131–132
Stachowiak, S., 165
Stakeholders, 10, 194–196
Starr, Jerold M., 314–315
State Children's Health Insurance Program (SCHIP), 132, 260
State clean election laws, 341–342
State of the Future, 373, 375
"States Are Hit Hard by Economic Downturn" (Richburg/Surdin), 371
Steele, Michael, 64
Stengel, Richard, 6
Stoesz, David, 43, 45, 229
Storing, Herbert J., 54
Story ideas, pitching, 147
"Street-level bureaucrats," 350
Student PIRGs' New Voters Project, 326
"Students Speak Out About Lobby Day," 267
Suer, Kevin, 157
Summative evaluation, 354–355, 356
Supply-side economics, 93–95
Supporters, updating, 154

Surdin, Ashley, 371
Sustainable housing Simulated Case Study, 227–228, 236–239, 367–368
Swift Boat Veterans for Truth, 323
Systems perspective, 22

T
Talking points, 269–271
TANF (Temporary Assistance for Needy Families). *See* Temporary Assistance to Needy Families (TANF)
Tanner, John, 71
T.B. v. L.R.M., 11–12
Teater, Barbara, 260
Temporary Assistance to Needy Families (TANF)
  overview of, 123
  coalitions and, 21, 282
  issue framing, 251
  passage of, 43
  policy evaluation and change, 205, 206–207
  rulemaking case example, 348–349
  welfare reform case study, 18
Terrell, Paul, 228
Testimony, congressional, 271–274, 275–277
Texas code of fair campaign practices, 343
Theoretical analysis of social problems, 211–212
Third parties, 64
Thomas, Clive, 257, 259
Thompson, Tommy, 91
Traditional conservatives, 68
Triangle Shirtwait Company fire, 33
Training School in Applied Philanthropy, 34
Tronto, Joan C., 104, 229
Turning Priorities into Action, 46
Twitter, 166
Typepad.com, 302

U
Unfaithful Angels (Specht and Courtney), 42
Unfunded mandate, 349
Uninsured citizens by state, 192
Unions, 32
User-generated advocacy, 162–163
Utilitarianism, 106–107

V
Value perspectives, 213–219
Violence Against Women Act, 251

"Viral List Building" (Suer), 157
Virtue ethics, 104, 106–107
Vocational Rehabilitation Act of 1954, 38
Volunteers for Change, 46

W
Wald, Lillian, 35
Walker, Alice, 367
War on Poverty programs, 41
War on Terror, party platforms on, 62
Warner, Charles Dudley, 282
"Was 2008 a Realigning Election?" (Koppelman), 66
Watkins, Jane, 374
Web 2.0. *See* New media advocacy
Webconferencing, 302
Wedel, K. R., 229
Weicker, Lowell, 313
Welfare, party platforms on, 62–63
Welfare reform. *See also* Personal Responsibility and Work Opportunity Reconciliation Act of 1996
  case study, 18
  evaluation case example, 358–359
  policymaking models, 185–186
Whig Party, 57
White, Ruth, 138–139
White, Ryan, 187–188, 311
Wider Opportunities for Women (WOW), 216–217
Wilburn, Ross, 336
Wilcox, Clyde, 259, 260
William J. Clinton Foundation, 6
Williamson, Peter J., 258
Window of opportunity, 248–249, 311
Wolff, Thomas, 310
Wolk, James, 42
Wolk, James L., 319
Women, underrepresentation of in Congress, 87
Women's rights movement, 172–175
Women's Trade Union League, 33
World Trade Organization (WTO), 289–290
WOW (Wider Opportunities for Women), 216–217

Y
Young, Whitney, 39, 242
Young, Whitney, Jr., 39
YouTube, 164